D1083458

Science and International Affairs
Melvyn B. Nathanson, General Editor

It Seems I Am a Jew
By Grigori Freiman.
Translated and edited by Melvyn B. Nathanson
Readings in Comparative Criminology
Edited by Louise I. Shelley
Crime and Modernization
By Louise I. Shelley
Up Against Apartheid
By Richard Pollak

TRIDENT

D. Douglas Dalgleish
and
Larry Schweikart

Southern Illinois University Press
Carbondale and Edwardsville

Printed in the United States of America
Edited by H. L. Kirk
Designed by Kathleen Giencke
Production supervised by Kathleen Giencke

Permission to reprint from the following sources is gratefully acknowledged:

The figure from "Heritage of Weakness," by Elmo R. Zumwalt, Jr., and three figures from "The Defense Budget," by Sam Nunn. © 1980 Institute for Contemporary Studies.

Fig. 4-3, by Norman Augustine, in Jacques Gansler, *The Defense Industry* (Cambridge, Mass.: MIT Press, 1980). Reprinted by permission of Norman Augustine and MIT Press.

Library of Congress Cataloging in Publication Data

Dalgleish, D. Douglas.
Trident.
(Science and international affairs series)
Bibliography: p.
Includes index.
1. Trident (Weapons systems) 2. United States.
Navy—Procurement—Case studies. I. Schweikart, Larry.
II. Title. III. Series.
V993.D34 1984 359.8'3 83-16777
ISBN 0-8093-1126-7

To

Elizabeth M. Dalgleish　　Eunice Schweikart Chandler
Christa B. Dalgleish　　Shari R. Schweikart
Our Mothers and Wives

To
Douglas P. Dalgleish
August 24, 1962–December 17, 1983
friend, son, historian

and to
the survival of his generation
under Trident deterrents,
portrayed here to the best of our ability.

Contents

Illustrations

(following p. 120)

Tables

Figures

Preface

Callimachus is credited with a saying that rang in our ears as we completed this book: "*Mega biblion, mega kakon,*" or, loosely, "A big book is a big pain." Many observers have tried to apply similar reasoning to the Trident submarine—"a big boat is a big pain"—and at times they have been right. Still, just as the Tridents are large with reason, so we produced this large volume seeking only to be thorough in this presentation.

As scholars, and not professional military men, we undertook the Trident study as a policy analysis of a major defense program with the goal of showing that a great deal can be learned about defense procurement from outside military circles. In this pursuit we were hardly original, yet at the same time we wanted to challenge the standard news-media approach whereby extremely complex issues are reduced (with mutilationist glee, it seems) to the space allowed in a newspaper column or the two-minute time slot on the evening news.

We have attempted both to present a historical perspective on modern bureaucratic, legislative, and defense contracting processes, using one of the most important weapons of the decade as the mechanism, and to include an analysis of the system's current and future capabilities. We have attempted to place a seemingly narrowly defined weapon—the Trident submarine—in a much broader milieu of other directly related defense programs, such as its bases and its missile programs, and we have also attempted to relate it to an entire spectrum of past and present alternative systems, geopolitical ramifications, operational continua, and technological implications. Our particular intent has been to show how the Trident, like most major weapons systems, affects and is affected by a vast array of military and nonmilitary factors. We have, moreover, relied almost entirely on published sources; our goal has been not to tantalize the reader with this or that piece of quasi-classified information or to rely on "unnamed sources" but, hopefully, to demonstrate the advantages a free society offers to researchers through available documentation. In the very few cases in which a source is anonymously cited, it was at the explicit or implicit request of the source.

However, research in some areas, specifically those involving planning and programming, was necessarily limited. We did not have access to internal Department of Defense material even to the extent Harold Sapolsky did in his study of the Polaris system. Similarly, we had no access to Naval Sea Systems Command materials. Therefore our presentation is naturally slanted toward funding by Congress and away from planning and programming; we have not intentionally ignored that aspect of the Trident project.

Although this book is intended for the informed reader, a list of acronyms was needed despite our original attempts to weed them out. The general reader may decide to ignore the notes, collected at the end of the book. We have chosen to put a great deal of related explanatory information, of appeal to more specialized readers, in the notes, and, for that reason, they are extensive.

We have also sought here to rectify the effects of a decade's worth of semantic overlay, provincial argumentation, and ideological vindictiveness afflicting the Trident system, in essence, in order to rescue it from a sea of journalistic and other muddy thinking. This requires a fresh approach to the view of a defense contractor as somewhat different from other private entrepreneurs. The general public should appreciate the fact that no weapons system or program is ever ideal or perfect, but it can be argued that a strategic weapon system that incorporates a finely blended balance of defensive and offensive capabilities is functionally more cost-effective than one that exaggerates or overemphasizes obtaining one capability (speed or size, for example) at the expense of the other indispensable capabilities—a Soviet tendency.

And while in the same spirit we have attempted in the concluding chapter to rehabilitate profitability in the defense sector, it most emphatically should not be assumed that the authors are recklessly tolerant of waste and mismanagement. We therefore assume that the Internal Revenue Service and the appropriate corporate tax brackets, plus more recently introduced and other forthcoming DoD internal procurement reforms, will routinely deal with "excessive defense contractor profits."

Professional scholars will furthermore recognize that we, in the tradition of Leo Strauss and Eric Voegelin, reject relativistic approaches that might suggest "right" and "wrong" to be unknowable. Indeed, it has been our major point that standard reports about the Trident program have been wrong in both fact and interpretation. We similarly reject historicist separations of "facts" and "values" (all "facts" are equal, and "values" do not play a role in the scholarly process). Rather, the very concept of defense is predicated upon the philosophical assumption that society is of present value, worth preserving for the future, and therefore worth defending now. Especially, then, neo-Marxian and econometric methodologies are both misleading and irrelevant as they are applied to defense policy matters. Consequently we have no hesitation about the use of terms like *good, bad, irresponsible, ill-advised,* or *dysfunctional.* On the contrary, as George Gilder has shown, in the absence of practical application of these terms to economics, the only possible result is experiential and intellectual chaos. Ultimately, the same practical application of these concepts must return in a commonsense way to discussions of national security.

Thus we have pursued four major themes in this work:

1. The problems facing constitutional democratic governments as they try to achieve continuity in, and financial support for, large defense programs. Using Trident as a case study, this question involves a reexamination of the points discussed by Jacques Gansler's *Defense Industry* of trying to employ capitalist competitive processes in what are essentially noncompetitive programs.

2. As hinted earlier, we will challenge the view of most media reports of the Trident program. This aspect of the study will question whether a mere presentation of information in a highly simplistic manner can deal adequately with questions of national defense and complex weapons programs.

3. A third theme is the interrelationship of the Trident in the strategic equation in a broad sense. Its role in affecting NATO plans, for example, will be given attention, as will its impact on the planning and selection of alternate and new U.S. weapons.

4. Finally, our objective has been to repeat the studies of other policy analysts by investigating the political and military considerations affecting weapons selection in a democracy.

Since theme three, presented mostly in Chapters 8 through 11, involves discussions that sometimes deal with oncoming or future systems, some of the material therein naturally is speculative. But the impact of the Trident system is not—the nation overall obtained an excellent fighting machine at a reasonable cost over great obstacles.

Introduction

In Groton, Connecticut, the Electric Boat shipyard was alive with unusual excitement at 4.32 A.M. when Admiral Hyman Rickover—eighty-one-year-old czar of the U.S. Navy's nuclear shipbuilding program—arrived. To the admiral's chagrin, the area was teeming with reporters and news photographers. Rickover had hoped that so early a start would dissuade some of the media representatives who had come to cover the initial sea trial of the *Ohio*, the first Trident submarine—America's biggest, quietest, deadliest ballistic-missile nuclear sub—but the giant undersea craft was news too big not to cover at any hour. The admiral's appearance was mere frosting on the cake, a fact Rickover probably understood, but he nonetheless did not appreciate the presence of the press. Screaming at the photographers from inside his car, Rickover "tried in vain to wave them away" and then, catching sight of Electric Boat's company photographers waiting inside the gates, turned his car around and left. Not until a few minutes later, when the Navy provided a van for him, did Rickover board the *Ohio*, with sailors holding mattresses to screen him from the photographers as he charged up the gangway.

Rival clusters of cheering sailors and jeering antinuclear protesters lined the fences and railings, and several protesters tried to swim or float out to the submarine. Security patrols intercepted them or turned them away. The *Ohio*, already in the water, was guided out of Electric Boat, accompanied by a small flotilla of tugboats, Navy observation ships, and protesters' vessels, as well as an occasional airplane or helicopter.

June 17, 1981: the *Ohio* was finally at sea—almost. Before it reached deep water it had to navigate the Thames River to Long Island Sound.

Then the crew discovered that the billion-dollar boat was missing a part, which someone had inadvertently left ashore. A tug brought the part to the *Ohio* "while Rickover fumed," all under the watchful eyes of television reporters and the surveillance of the ever-present Russian spy trawler *Ekwater*. (Another spy trawler would intercept the *Ohio* when it passed the Juan de Fuca straits in the summer of 1982 en route to its home at Bangor, Washington.[1])

Depending on the source, observers have claimed that the first Trident was four years behind schedule and $700 million over budget. Although the *Ohio* met or exceeded virtually every design expectation during its sea trials, only its cost and delay seemed to interest the members of the press and other media. Only cost, delay—and Rickover.

Acronyms and Abbreviations

No one deplores the use of military acronyms and abbreviations in a book intended for the general public more than the authors of this work. Nevertheless, it seems unavoidable here. The following list has been pared to an absolute minimum, omitting acronyms used sparingly—SURTASS, for example. In any case, the acronym's first appearance in text is always preceded by its complete term or name. Still, for some of the most frequently used acronyms and abbreviations, the authors recommend the following *general* guidelines: An S usually means "submarine," as in SSN (nuclear attack submarine) or SLBM (submarine-launched ballistic missile). An M usually means "missile," an L usually means "launched," and N usually denotes "nuclear." An A preceding an acronym usually refers to a countermeasure ("anti"), as in ABM or antiballistic missile. Using these guidelines, the reader can guess the meaning of the most important terms with a good chance of accuracy.

These acronyms or terms appear most frequently in this book:

ABM	Antiballistic missile
AEGIS	Shipboard-point defense system against missiles utilizing antimissiles and phalanx Gatling guns
ALCM	Air-launched cruise missile
ASAT	Antisatellite (weapon)
ASROC	Antisubmarine rocket (ship launched)
ASW	Antisubmarine warfare
AWACS	Airborne warning and control system
BMD	Ballistic missile defense
CEP	Circular error probability
C^3I	Command, control, communications, and intelligence

DARPA	Defense Advanced Research Projects Agency
DoD	Department of Defense
DSARC	Defense Systems Acquisition and Review Council
ECM	Electronic countermeasures
EDC	European Defense Community
ELF	Extremely low frequency (communication)
EN	Engineering notice
FY	Fiscal year
GFE	Government-furnished equipment
GIUK	Greenland–Iceland–United Kingdom (Gap)
GPS	Global positioning system
ICBM	Intercontinental ballistic missile
LASER	Light amplified simulated emission radiation
LoADS	Low altitude defense (vs. ICBMs)
MAD	Mutual assured destruction; also, magnetic anomaly detection (depending on context)
MaRV	Maneuverable reentry vehicles
MIRV	Multiple independently targeted reentry vehicles
MRV	Multiple reentry vehicles
NATO	North Atlantic Treaty Organization
n.m.	Nautical miles
RV	Reentry vehicle
SAR	Selected Acquisition Request
SLBM	Submarine-launched ballistic missile
SLOC	Sea lines of communication
SOSUS	Sound surveillance system (a hydrophone system under the seas)
SSBN	Nuclear ballistic-missile submarine
SSGN	Nuclear (guided) cruise-missile submarine
SSN	Nuclear attack submarine
TRIAD	The American strategic deterrence system resting on three "legs"—submarine-launched ballistic missiles, land-based intercontinental ballistic missiles, and manned bombers
UHF	Ultra high frequency (communications)
ULMS	Underwater Long-range Missile System (Trident)
VHF	Very high frequency (communications)
V/STOL	Vertical (or) short takeoff and landing (aircraft). Example: British Harrier jet.

1

The Ultimate Weapon?

Development of the American Strategic Submarine and Strategic Planning

> *In the fifteenth century, conscious of their wealth and proud of the new life which their inventions and advances in art and scholarship had ushered in, they became used to looking down upon the other European powers whose social system and intellectual life was still in the shackles of superstition and prejudice. Now, in the sixteenth century, the fate of Italy lay in the hands of those very states which the Italians had believed they had a right to despise. . . . Because the superiority of Italian civilization in the economic and intellectual sphere was manifest, they blamed their neglect of the modern techniques of war [for their defeat].*
>
> —Felix Gilbert, *Machiavelli: The Renaissance of the Art of War*

As vote tallies came in across the country on November 4, 1980, computer terminals printed out projections that would be announced by obviously startled newscasters: Ronald Reagan had been elected president of the United States. The projections had come unusually early, and the mandate from Amercians was surprisingly clear. Reagan rode to victory almost totally on his dual promise to restore the economy and to rebuild American defense to a position of military superiority. Although at first many observers believed the economic proposals were the central issues of the campaign, subsequent polling and analysis revealed that a majority of Americans shared deep concerns about the country's shrinking military and defense capabilities.

For more than a decade, preceding administrations had not merely continued American unilateral weapons reductions but had accelerated the pace. Several proposals—including the B-1 bomber, the neutron warhead, the MX missile, the XM-1 tank, and the cruise missile—had experienced political delays, technological problems, or outright cancellation. Under Jimmy Carter's administration the Navy suffered serious ship cutbacks, to the point that Navy officers testified they had lost their "slim margin of superiority," and Senator Sam Nunn described American's position vis-à-vis the Soviets as "clinging parity." Studies made in the early 1980s placed areas of earlier American military superiority—anti-submarine warfare, high-energy lasers, charged-particle-beam weapons, satellite-borne radars, and extremely low-frequency communications systems—in the "status uncertain" category. Meanwhile, the Soviets continued to outspend the United States by a ratio of three to one on defense.[1]

A serious and heated debate about the American strategic forces (carried, in part, in n. 2) seemed resolved at the time of Carter's election in 1976. By that time America's long-standing defense concept of TRIAD had degenerated into MONAD with the obsolescence of the B-52 bomber force and the increased number and accuracy of Soviet missiles rendering American intercontinental ballistic missiles (ICBMs) vulnerable to a surprise attack or first strike. But if there was tentative agreement over the dangerous inadequacy of American forces, there was also considerable indecision over the method of correction. Carter proposed a mobile MX missile (discussed in chap. 10), but environmental and political opposition stalled the plan and left its fate to his successor. President Reagan's series of strategic defense decisions on October 2, 1981, addressed improvements in two critical areas by ordering one hundred B-1B bombers as a stopgap measure between the B-52 and the so-called Stealth bomber and by starting construction on the MX missile, which was to be temporarily based in hardened shelters until the Townes commission recommended a permanent basing mode in the summer of 1982. But at the time of Reagan's decision only the United States Navy, particularly the strategic submarine force, was undergoing a modernization designed to reestablish its credibility as a deterrent to a Soviet strike. Even the submarine force faced problems, however. The older-model Polaris submarines were showing their age and were scheduled to be replaced in the late 1970s. As a follow-on program, the United States Navy in 1971 had chosen the Trident submarine and missile system. The Navy's need for a successor boat to the Polaris rested on the punctual development, delivery, and error-free sea trials of the new Trident combination. Indeed, for a brief period the entire concept of TRIAD and, with it, America's defense capabilities depended on the new ship.[2]

It is therefore extremely unfortunate the Trident has been error-free in neither construction nor design and has faced what were proclaimed massive cost increases coupled with faulty initial construction and potentially disastrous delays. *U.S. News & World Report* and other magazines celebrated the *Ohio*'s problems in a soap-opera, to-be-continued series of articles. Even journals that could otherwise be considered sympathetic to the defense industry attacked the Trident program, often on the basis of superficial impressions. The June 1979 issue of the *Armed Forces Journal* reported in an article called "A Blunted Trident" that Secretary of Defense Harold Brown was "seeking to end the program after seven submarines" and was "publicly embarrassed by the weakness of the Navy's senior managers" of the program. The article claimed "it is virtually certain . . . 14 Trident SSBNs will never be built," a less capable submarine would replace Trident, and "some other element of the Triad or Navy" would have to be cut to pay for the project. Such supposedly objective reports as the Congressional Research Service's *Issue Brief* on U.S. defense industrial preparedness have contended the Trident project "appears to demonstrate all three categories of symptoms mentioned . . . delay, *severe cost overruns*, and *poor workmanship* [italics added]." Opponents protested the vessels' construction, and "perennial protest singer" Pete Seeger personally appeared in Groton to protest the completion of the *Ohio* on November 2, 1981. Seeger's "comrades-in-arms" one year later assaulted a Trident sub by breaching security at Electric Boat and splashing their own blood on the vessel. Internal disputes have strained the program as well. A bitter, vicious fight over inflation, costs, claims, and counterclaims put the shipbuilder, the Navy, and Congress in a triangular free-for-all from 1976 until 1981. Work stoppages, strikes, and, as one report suggested, "alchoholism, drugs, and sex" have all found their way into the Trident controversy. In the special television news program "20/20" the American Broadcasting Company attributed the sub's problems to "mismanagement" by the Navy, and such renowned naval experts as Norman Polmar have stated "the slow Trident submarine building rate, and the high cost of the *Ohio* class ($1.5 billion per submarine in fiscal year 1980) demand that a new approach be taken to the SSBN program." At one point in the program, the Trident system seemed to be approaching the levels of Teapot Dome and Watergate as the scandals of the century in some eyes.[3]

Many early criticisms of the Trident program were valid, and a few may continue to be. Such a critical contention nevertheless does not mean Trident cannot ultimately play a significant strategic role in the fulfillment of its primary mission. While many early critics of the Trident program now appear justified in some of their original concerns, far more attacks on Trident have proved ill-based in fact, ill-conceived in theory, or simply out of touch with political and military realities. At the same time, the Trident program raises basic questions about weapons procurement and development, the appropriations process, interaction of the public and private sectors, differing perceptions of American security and, most significantly, about overall directions in American defense strategy and the provision of real capabilities to follow them. The procurement process in particular fosters the least noble traits among legislators, contractors, and military actors, many of whom have viewed the Trident in particular from their own perspectives. Slicing of the budgetary pie has historically involved tenacious fighting in the representative process. Therefore the statistical methods of reporting "cost overruns" will be examined in subsequent chapters, as will the implications and considerations upon which reports of "cost overruns," "soaring costs," or contractor and "managerial incompetence" are based.

What is Trident, then—boon or boondoggle? Indispensable strategic element or undesirable nuclear redundancy? A prime example of American weapons technology or the epitome of military and bureaucratic waste? Another point of division between America and its European allies or a potential unifying element? Obsolete monument to outdated military theories or the embodiment of tomorrow's strategic doctrines?

Although the answers will not always reflect a simplistic boondoggle approach, some problems clearly have been as understated as others have been overemphasized. The difficulties with the submarine itself are merely symptomatic of the procurement system as a whole and pose deep questions about the government–contractor relationship. They also reveal interesting aspects of the role of innovation in the American defense industry, since few, if any, new weapons systems really constitute absolutely innovative systems and since they usually incorporate very high percentages of previous technological and fiscal commitments. The Trident submarine may still prove the most persistently effective and fiscally efficient American weapons program since the Jeep (a point admittedly difficult to confirm, since Trident's true efficiency as a weapon of deterrence ultimately relies upon its not being used). Ironically, and a point possibly only now coming to be appreciated, the Trident hull may have many civilian or other military uses other than those the Navy originally intended. Should future engineering plans eventually fulfill these promises, the Trident could be one of the first weapons systems to incorporate truly "space-age" technologies—technologies eventually able to render nuclear weapons as obsolete as the spear and catapult. The Trident may herald the "revolutionary" while representing the "obsolete," technologically bridging different eras of strategic doctrine and corresponding capability.

Whether or not these prospective developments will actually endow Tridents with proportionally greater strategic capabilities than they now possess remains a matter of reasonable speculation. Some observers already argue for wider submarine use in defense planning: *New York Times* military correspondent Drew Middleton once even labeled the submarine the "Ultimate Weapon." Middleton's contention that submarines, not bombers, put Japan out of business in World War II and that improper use of the submarine by the Germans was all that rescued Britain in World War I are persuasive but do not render a balanced appraisal of other theaters or weapons of war. Nevertheless, the concept of "ultimacy" is perpetually intriguing. In the case of the 1982 Falklands War, for example, British deployment of nuclear-powered attack submarines dominated the strategic capabilities of both sides. Therefore, is the submarine—or can it be—the ultimate weapon? If so, in the military context, are American submarines capable of avoiding or sustaining attacks from Soviet antisubmarine-warfare ships and planes? Do strategic submarines carry the firepower necessary to deter Soviet moves even without land-based ICBMs and manned bombers? If not, what complementary systems must be integrated for use with a submarine force to offset possibly deficient capabilities? Finally, assuming hypothetically that the submarine is the ultimate weapon, whose strategic submarine best fits the bill? Answers to none of these questions are simple, and a more complete understanding of this complexity requires an examination of the historical role of the submarine in American naval operations and strategy.[4]

Middleton holds that the inability of the British to recognize the value of the submarine cost them dearly in two world wars. America accepted the submarine as a weapon of war more than did the British in World War II, although it remained an erratic and faltering commitment, evidenced by such tragic omissions as the prewar construction and testing of a consistently reliable attack torpedo and appropriate detonator. Once these problems became evident, however, the U.S. Navy took effective corrective action. Similarly, in terms of the development of the strategic submarine, if the Russians led the way in the direction of the missile-firing submarine, U.S. reaction was timely, effective, and innovative, so the United States has never trailed qualitatively since.

American submarines were not deployed in large numbers until World War II, and then primarily in the Pacific to prey upon Japanese commerce and shipping. The queens of the seas, the aircraft carriers, made all the headlines. Senior officers, "convinced by their [World War

II] experience of the superiority of the carrier as *the* naval weapon, began to dominate naval thought and, more important, commands." For a short period following the war their arguments seemed logical: the long-range aircraft was the only potential weapon available to foreign enemies (after 1949 these aircraft could drop atomic bombs), making air bases vulnerable to counterattacks. But carriers, unlike air bases, had mobility. Even better, the admirals argued, the carrier could perform a variety of missions, including invasion support, bombing, and sea control.[5]

Hyman George Rickover played an important role in transforming the pro-carrier naval proclivity. Visiting Oak Ridge in 1946, Rickover learned of the potential of nuclear fission as a method of ship propulsion. As early as 1939 the Navy had funded a nuclear-propulsion program, and in 1944 a four-man committee studied the potential for using nuclear-powered vessels in the post-war period, marking the real birth of nuclear power in the U.S. Navy. Excluded from the original group of officers selected to design and develop the forthcoming nuclear navy, Rickover eventually succeeded in using his unique position as a concurrent member of an armed service and a civilian agency, the Navy and the Atomic Energy Commission, to stimulate the development of a nuclear submarine. Several obstacles stood in Rickover's path, yet he proceeded doggedly until the keel of the first nuclear-powered submarine, the *Nautilus*, was laid in 1952. Launched in 1954, the *Nautilus* represented a breakthrough in both technology and operational concepts. Like earlier submarines appearing after 1944, the *Nautilus* could travel faster beneath the surface than above, did not require frequent surfacing to recharge batteries, and could remain submerged for sixty days. In addition, the *Nautilus* became the first submarine to reach the North Pole.[6]

Any "carrier admirals" theretofore unimpressed by the *Nautilus* soon learned of its capabilities. Two other classes of nuclear submarine—the *Seawolf* and the *Skate* classes—followed, with the *Skate* earning the distinction of being the first submarine to cross the Atlantic submerged without using snorkel tubes and the first submarine to surface at the North Pole. As the ultimate insult to "carrier admirals," during exercises in the Mediterranean the high-speed, teardrop-hulled *Skipjack* "sank" every aircraft carrier in the maneuvers. The final shadow of doubt over the submarine's capabilities disappeared after the first Polaris ballistic missile was fired from a submerged position in 1960. From that point on, cities and airfields became as much targets for the submarine as traditionally merchant vessels and naval surface ships had been.[7]

Advances in design and strategy greeted each succeeding class of American submarine. Two separate types of submarine now emerged: the attack submarine, which carried torpedoes and generally was designed to threaten ships, other submarines, and shipping, and the strategic submarine, which carried nuclear missiles. During the early 1960s through 1975 thirty-seven *Sturgeon*-class attack submarines joined the fleet and forty-one ballistic-missile subs were added. Comprising the ballistic-missile submarine fleet were the *George Washington* class (5), a modified and extended attack vessel; the *Ethan Allen* class (5), the first designed from the keel up as a ballistic-missile boat; the *Lafayette* class (31), of which the final twelve form the *Benjamin Franklin* class, basically identical but with quieter machinery.[8]

Acceptance by navy strategists also depended on proving that undersea missile technology could keep up with submarine hull, fin, and power-plant design. The earliest attempts to mate submarines and missiles involved mounting a Regulus cruise missile to the deck of the sub. This proved workable but with a number of attendant handicaps, including reduced underwater speed, high hydrodynamic turbulence, and all the difficulties associated with surface firing. Designers consequently began work on missile and firing-tube compatibility to allow a submarine to fire from beneath the surface, cluminating with the successful firing of a Polaris missile from the submerged *George Washington* on July 20, 1960. Polaris missiles (Models A-1, A-2, and A-3, with ranges of 1200 n.m., 1500 n.m., and 2500 n.m. respectively) soon gave way to Poseidon missiles (Model C-3, with minimal range of 2500 n.m.) (See fig. 2-4). Each of the ballistic-missile submarines carried sixteen missiles, whatever their type. Besides improvements in specific missile designs, dealt with in a later chapter, Poseidon missiles were MIRVed—that is, fitted with as many as fourteen multiple independently targeted warheads (reentry vehicles, or RVs), although normal deployment was ten, to get more range. Theoretically, each of the warheads could strike a different target, but their range on separating from their "bus" vehicle is limited. With the introduction of the 2500-n.m. Polaris A-3, ranges for the entire fleet varied only slightly, even with the introduction of the Poseidon missile, but Poseidon provided more punch with ten to fourteen RVs compared to only three for the Polaris A-3, with each of the former having greater accuracy.[9]

By the early 1970s several new weapons systems, some already in development and construction, were promised by the Nixon administration in order to gain ratification of the Strategic Arms Limitation Treaty (SALT I) by the United States Senate. America's defense policy, called TRIAD by 1970, had already begun to exhibit some cracks in a once-sound foundation. Until 1970 a somewhat nebulous strategic-weapons posture, including intermediate-range ballistic missiles of the Jupiter and Thor varieties, carrier aircraft capable of releasing nuclear bombs, and the 280-mm self-propelled atomic cannon, supplemented the Strategic Air Command's long-range bombers, ICBMs, and submarines. Gradually the TRIAD concept emerged. TRIAD relies on three "legs" of defense, each with a strength and weakness. Theoretically, each leg is not only independently survivable but is also interdependent with the other two. The missile leg is protected by its deep and hardened silos, intended to enhance the capability of the missiles to withstand all but a direct hit. In a retaliatory attack the ICBMs could be launched under warning of attack as a so-called first-strike force or could ride out the opening attack in diminished numbers for a retaliatory, or second, strike. The purposes of the second strike also include clearing out air defenses for subsequent penetrations by the slower bombers. Manned bombers, theoretically, should pick up other surviving fixed targets or destroy targets not obliterated in the introductory missile attack. Submarine missiles constitute another set of second-strike capabilities.

For the TRIAD system to be credible, however, some portion of each leg must survive a surprise attack in order to assure the destruction of such so-called hard targets as enemy missile silos and such soft targets as population centers. The leg that supported the United States throughout the 1950s was the manned bomber. Several types saw service—the B-36, B-47, B-52, B-58—but only some of the latest versions of the B-52 now remain active. Bombers are comparatively slow but have the advantage of human redirection in flight to accommodate changing target compositions. An additional leg of TRIAD then took over much of the primary deterrent duties during the 1960s: the ICBM. Early Atlas and Titan missiles were succeeded by Minuteman missiles in the mid-1960s, with a mixture of follow-on Minuteman IIs and IIIs still retained in service, as were some improved Titans until very recently. While missiles obviously outstrip bombers in speed, they cannot be recalled once fired, although midflight destruction is possible in some cases, and their stationary emplacement makes them more easily destroyed by Soviet missiles fired in a surprise attack if the United States decides to weather the first strike. Until recently ICBM warheads also lacked any selective direction to various dispersed targets otherwise within the blast area of a multiple-warhead load. The evolving capability to hit such scattered targets more or less precisely is called MIRV (Multiple Independently targeted Reentry Vehicles). At one time, the hardened emplacements contributed to the ICBM's protection, but recently the Soviets have increased both the accuracy and payload of their missiles to the point of beginning to "strangle" any single ICBM silo by a progressively narrowing zone of target focus, called circular error probable, or CEP. TRIAD's third leg, the nuclear submarine, can escape a first strike, thanks to its diving ability and relative difficulty of location by enemies. However, communication with subs is poor, and until recently, since submarine-launched ballistic missiles (SLBMs) suffer from poorer accuracy and less payload capacity than ICBMs, they have been primarily assigned to a role as a soft-target weapon.[10]

Due to the interdependence of each leg of TRIAD, any development that jeopardizes any constituent element of TRIAD generates problems for TRIAD strategy as a whole. The Carter administration's cancellation of the B-1 bomber (with Congress' blessing) merely underscored the concern some have voiced unsuccessfully over the past fifteen years that contemporary replacement systems required exceedingly longer lead times—time from design to actual deployment. Following the B-1 cancellation, TRIAD's bomber leg has had to be completely reevaluated: even later-model B-52s are simply obsolete as penetrating bombers, and they are increasingly being assigned a so-called standoff role with cruise missiles. Still, Americans were told they retained a strategic edge over Russia. Editorials reassured Americans that "the second leg of the TRIAD, the atomic submarine, retains its offensive potency" and that submarines could carry the burden. According to one official, "What's holy about three legs? Why not two? Another suggested reliance on an "augmented dyad" of ICBMs and submarines.[11]

Additional pressure was shifted onto the Trident program as two other problems gained public notice. First, the Russian ICBM buildup of the late 1960s through the mid-1970s met with almost no American response and with little media attention. Behind this ICBM buildup also was a tremendous Soviet growth in overall military spending. Not counting retirement pay, Soviet defense spending from 1955 to 1975 was increased by more than 3 percent of the total gross national product (in 1977 rubles):

Year	**Percent**
1955	11.0
1960	8.5
1965	9.5
1967	10.5
1970	12.5
1975	13.5–14.5

From 1970 to 1975, Soviet defense expenditures increased by 10 billion rubles, and funds for research and development grew by 2 billion, according to Central Intelligence Agency estimates (fig. 1-1) that substantially understated the real trends. Tactically, both European and American defense experts hoped to offset Soviet tank and manpower advantages through technology, including precision-guided munitions, new man-launched antitank rockets, and suggestions to utilize neutron warheads or other tactical nuclear weapons. During this period the motto for armed forces in Europe became "Fight Outnumbered and Win!"[12]

Strategically, Secretary of Defense Robert McNamara in this period developed a policy known as MAD—mutual assured destruction. The McNamara policy proposed that as long as one of the major powers retained sufficient retaliatory punch to destroy the civilian population and industry of the other, neither side would dare initiate a nuclear war. To do so, McNamara held, would sentence the population of the aggressor as well as the defender to certain death. Sheer numbers of weapons therefore mattered little; what counted was the surviving response capability. Few Americans appreciate the logical but infrequently stated assumption of that plan: the defender (presumably the

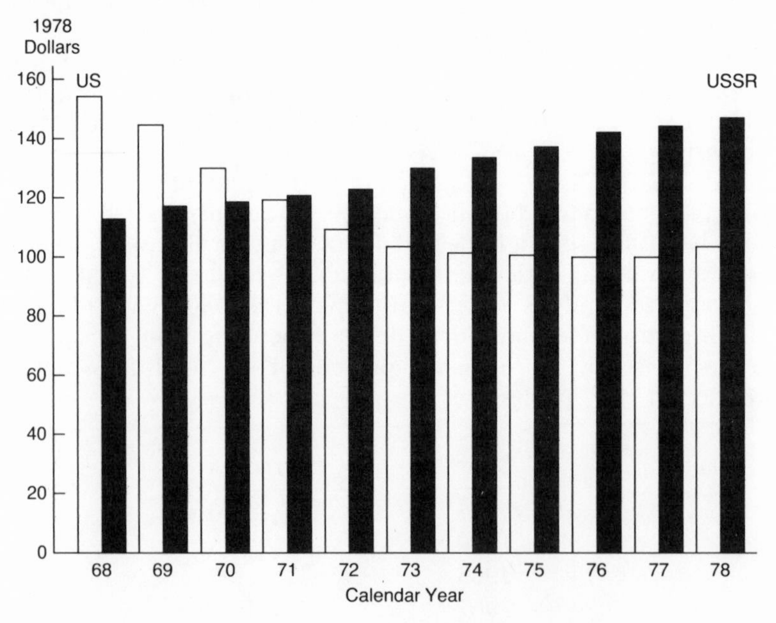

Source: W. Scott Thompson, *National Security in the 1980s*, p. 377.

Fig. 1-1. Total U.S. and Soviet defense activities: net assessment.

United States) would not employ a launch-under-attack policy. As the MAD scenario has it, even though highly reliable evidence exists that an attack has been prepared and launched, American missiles will be commanded to stay in their silos and ride out a first strike. The span of time necessary to qualify a retaliatory strike as second is a rather vacuous concept, since orders launching a U.S. retaliatory strike could be given beginning with satellite confirmation of multiple ICBM silo firings and ending any time after the destructive impact of Soviet RVs. General proponents of this strategy point to recent "scrambles" caused by radar picking up Canadian geese which, they argue, could have triggered a launching. Clearly the personality of a particular American president, combined with Soviet perceptions of his probable responses, plays a significant role in potential uses of a launch-under-attack doctrine. Although launch under attack remains an unpopular option, recent congressional hearings and executive directives indicate that the MAD counterbalance option is progressively being displaced by surgically more precise counterforce targeting options. MAD nevertheless continues to assert some residual influence on this country's basic strategy.[13]

At face value, MAD might appear a viable plan. But even if America's defenses could guarantee a retaliatory strike of sufficient magnitude to deter any Russian thoughts of a first strike, another problem has now appeared. Russia's overwhelming superiority of nuclear weapons has allowed Soviet planners to develop an alternative to MAD that will be referred to here as a surgical nuclear preemptory strike (SNPS). Soviet strategists, despite certain of their other technological disadvantages, are becoming able to target all 1053 Minuteman and Titan sites in the United States with *two* RVs each to assure their destruction. With each passing day they can probably extend their ability to do so further simply by adding reentry vehicles and more missiles, since at some point quantity can usually overcome quality. Soviet literature has also indicated that the Soviets believe they could eliminate the entire American ICBM force with a loss of American life of the magnitude of less than 1 percent. According to SNPS, the remaining American bombers and sub-based missiles, lacking a hard-target capability, would have only Soviet cities as retaliatory targets. United States submarine payloads are not yet sufficiently accurate to knock out Soviet missile silos, some of which can be refitted with new missiles and refired. In this scenario, an American president would have to face surrender or exchange strikes on population centers with a country having an antiballistic missile system, superior air defense, and superior civil defense. The Soviets, of course, would be aware of their advantage, having already evacuated their cities, and would offer peace terms with the alternative of destruction of American cities. A discussion of the SNPS theory appears in note 14, but response to this scenario from American neutralists and antimilitarists has traditionally been that the scenario is unrealistic because "no one can win a nuclear war." Unfortunately, what is at issue is whether Soviet strategists (and, more important, Soviet leaders) *believe* they can win or, at least, gain a significant global advantage through a nuclear war. Thus, not only have the Soviets *not* accepted the MAD theory and not only do they daily prepare their own strategic defense *and* offense, but these developments have also occurred largely with American acquiescence.[14]

In light of the strategic planning on both sides, no weapon can upset the balance as much as the nuclear submarine. According to President Carter in 1979, "Just one of our relatively invulnerable Poseidon submarines . . . carries enough warheads to destroy every large and medium-sized city in the Soviet Union." Even with the older and noisier Polaris submarines on patrol, the Soviets had great difficulty detecting them in the 1960s. That edge continues: as of 1981, the strategic submarine force's subs had carried out more than 2000 patrols without successful Soviet long-term contact, according to some sources. The Trident program was expected not only to preserve the Polaris/Poseidon deterrent but also to improve upon it. While Trident was still in the development stage Rear Admiral Albert Kelln predicted that its high survivability, high system effectiveness, and flexibility would make it "the most survivable and cost effective sea-based system we could build." Kelln added that Trident is a major new strategic initiative that will "extend the sea-based deterrent survivability we currently enjoy into the 21st century." Although many consider the aircraft carrier the central asset of the modern navy, projections for the twenty-first century (including the latter half of the twentieth) note that "greater emphasis on strategic nuclear sea-based systems will occur." In a statement to the House Armed Services Committee in 1972, former Secretary of Defense Melvin Laird concluded the ULMS program, as Trident was then called, "is the most appropriate alternative [for new strategic initiatives], since the at-sea portion of our sea-based strategic forces has the best long-term prospect for high pre-launch survivability." Eight years later, during the Trident construction program, William J. Perry, Undersecretary of Defense for Research and Engineering, echoed Laird's statement: the "SLBM force continues to be the TRIAD element in whose survivability we have the greatest confidence."[15]

Strategic planning, however, requires more than simply adding new weapons systems helter-skelter or loading up those the nation has with more warheads. Two major areas must be considered when evaluating weapons systems (especially one as large and costly as the Trident): What objectives does the enemy wish to achieve and what objectives does the United States wish to achieve? The Soviet navy has different goals in its planning, and up to this point Soviet sea control has been concerned with denying the United States various sea lanes or with disrupting reinforcement efforts of European NATO from North America. American sea power, conversely, must aim for protection of sea lanes, invasion support, and quick reinforcement. Each side's submarine forces likewise are expected to perform different tasks. While the Soviets can concentrate on attack subs as well as cruise missile subs, to comply with the MAD doctrine the United States must first maintain its strategic ballistic-missile fleet while somewhat relegating attack submarines to a lower strategic priority.[16]

Decline in Numbers of Vessels Built

An ominous trend has developed in overall U.S. shipbuilding. While the Soviets have accelerated their naval and maritime programs to a pulse-pounding pace, American ship production has dropped in numbers from the presidential requests to the actual congressionally authorized ships and dropped again from those authorized to those actually appropriated, thus affecting the real numbers of ships built (see table 1). Typically, 110 to 140 of those vessels are submarines.[17]

Table 1
U.S. Navy Shipbuilding, 1970–1979

Fiscal Year	President's Budget	Authorized and Funded	Actually Built
1970	16	14	10
1971	14	15	15
1972	19	16	15
1973	20	10	8
1974	14	14	14
1975	30	22	22
1976	23	15	15
1977	16	15	15
1978	22	18	18
1979	15	13	13
Ten-year average	18.9	15.2	14.5
Nominal size of the Navy	570	465	435

The Trident System in Historical Perspective

The emphasis placed on the submarine and, eventually, on the Trident surprisingly had its start in the mid-1960s when social reform, political upheaval, and opposition to the Vietnam War forced rearrangement of several defense budget systems. Many considered the submarine a cheap alternative to comprehensive renovation of the entire strategic

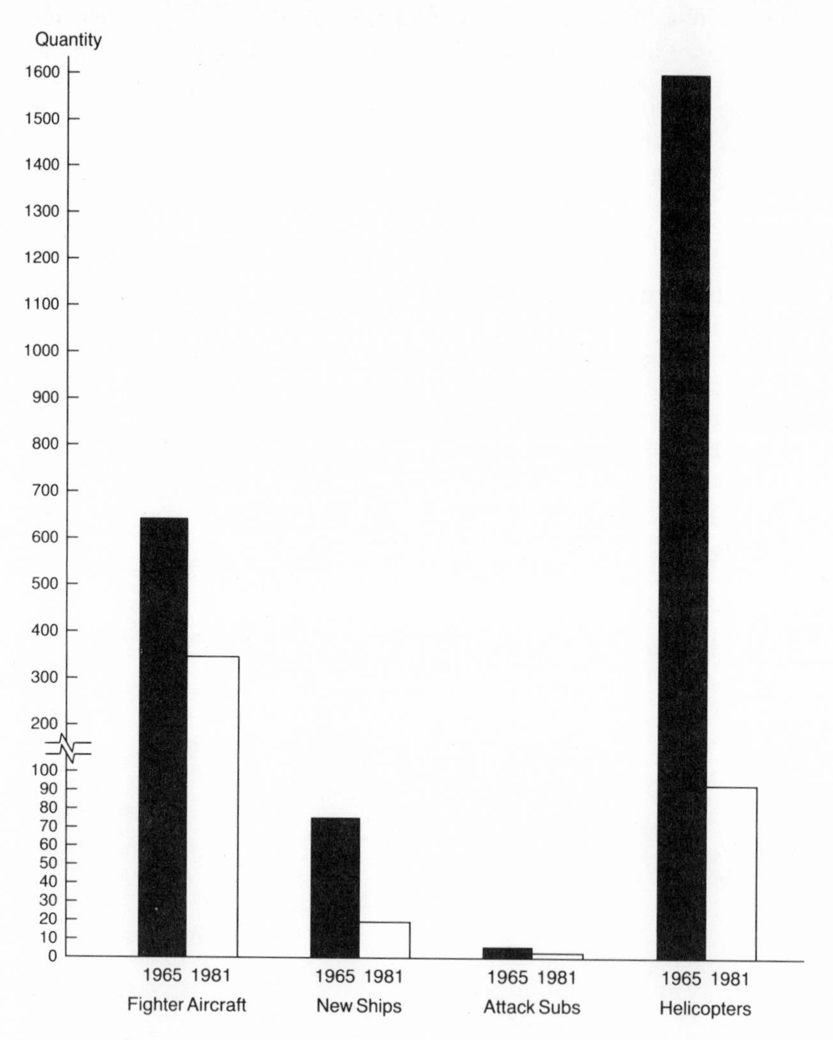

Source: W. Scott Thompson, *National Security in the 1980s*, p. 381.
Fig. 1-2. Procurement: 1964 and 1981.

system previously promised to key military leaders and congressional defense advocates in return for their support of SALT I. Consequently, on February 1, 1968, Chief of Naval Operations Admiral Thomas Moorer issued an Advanced Development Objective for an undersea long-range missile system (ULMS) designed to be a follow-on to the Polaris and Poseidon subs. Although Chief of Naval Operations Admiral Elmo Zumwalt explained to the Senate Appropriations Committee that the Navy had conceived of the Trident program "the day we first began to build the Polaris boat," the true impetus for Trident did not come until the 1966–1967 Pentagon STRAT-X study, thus leaving an eventual gap between the actual commissioning of the last *Benjamin Franklin* SSBN boat in 1967 and whatever would become the commissioning date for the first Trident. Under Defense Secretary Robert S. McNamara, STRAT-X was designed to evaluate and measure more than 125 various weapons concepts. As a result of rising concerns over the vulnerability of the land-based systems to a first strike, the Department of Defense approved further research on the Navy's proposal for a long-range missile submarine. Following Moorer's 1968 Advanced Development Objective, ULMS gained support from varied (and somewhat unexpected) sources, including groups traditionally dedicated to cutting military spending.[18]

The genesis of the Trident funding program will be examined in detail in chapters 3 and 4, but appropriations for its research occurred in one form or another between 1969 and 1972, with the program reaching concrete development in 1973.[19]

No part of Trident funding has come easily, as will be seen, and no spending for it has been inconsequential. Even so, most cost estimates for the Trident sub have not included the cost of the missiles, reactors, or the many related installations ultimately necessary for the boat's final deployment. Cost estimate overruns, a repeated topic of public attention, threatened for a time to take a back seat to problems in construction, ranging from ill-fitting hatches to pipes without connections. An unsuspecting auditor for the government by chance turned up welds that failed to meet specifications; indeed, it appeared there might be up to 35,000 such faulty welds. Other investigators found steel used of a quality below Navy specifications. Even commonplace construction problems have been sensationalized. In October 1976, for example, columnist Jack Anderson reported the first Tridents were developing cracks in more than a hundred places.[20]

Throughout the controversy the Navy has charged that these problems were the result of poor workmanship by Electric Boat, while the shipbuilder claimed most of the problems arose because of changes submitted by the Navy. If the Navy's charges are valid, some of these flaws could really affect the sub's survival and capabilities. If not, the Navy has succeeded only in airing its dirty laundry in public. Both the Navy and Electric Boat until recently besieged each other with charges and countercharges, all under the eyes of befuddled congressmen who have paid for the Tridents and quite understandably have expected them to be delivered in whatever is a reasonable period of time. To exacerbate matters, Admiral Rickover decided to engage in a personal war with Electric Boat and two other shipbuilders over the nature of the procurement process. Rickover charged that the traditional profit motive had expired because shipbuilders found it more profitable to file claims suits against the government. As this battle droned on, Electric Boat Company retaliated by threatening the government with work stoppages, culminating ultimately with the Secretary of the Navy foolishly suggesting the United States would hire foreign shipbuilders to build Tridents.[21]

Why have there been so many problems with the Trident? Are these problems typical of all new weapons systems, and if so, why? Is the Pentagon relying too heavily on the Trident, or too little? Is the "throw weight" dilemma insoluble, or can the Trident II missile perform in a manner to redress the problem? Are there other options that can be examined and employed, even within the Trident system itself? Is the strategy upon which the Trident has been developed correct; if so, could it be improved? Can the procurement process by rescued, and if so, how could it be reformed? What has been Rickover's role? Are claims to be forever a part of Navy contracts? What are the Russian responses to Trident, both offensively and defensively, and what is their possibility of success? What are the implications for NATO of Trident deployment? How will the Trident affect the deployment and production of other competing weapons systems? Will laser-beam weapons and other new technology alter the Trident's role, and if so, how? What are the diplomatic and ecological ramifications of Trident deployment, in terms of both the sub and the base?

These questions serve as the springboard for corresponding chapters, but first another must be answered: What exactly are the Trident submarine and missile and what are they expected to do? With a specific image of Trident before the mind's eye, it is the authors' intention that no one can ever again consider the Trident project a typical defense program.

2

The Look of Leviathan:

A Description of Trident

Canst thou draw out leviathan . . . ? None is so fierce that dare stir him up. . . . I will not conceal his parts, nor his power, nor his comely proportion. . . . When he raiseth up himself, the mighty are afraid.
Job 41:1–15

Writers of fiction from Jules Verne to Herman Melville have offered their audiences a variety of exotic monsters from the ocean depths. The great white whale Moby Dick, giant squids, mechanical devices such as Captain Nemo's *Nautilus*—all elicited fear, horror, and awe from wide-eyed readers for more than a hundred years. In most cases the authors combined mammoth size with deadly beauty, as in Melville's whale or Verne's submarine, and in this respect Trident would have fulfilled these authors' requirements for a powerful, graceful, dangerous sea monster. For sheer technological beauty and deadly grace, no underwater vessel in the world compares with a Trident, including the squatty Soviet counterpart, the 25,000-to-30,000-ton *Typhoon*. But despite its similarities even to fictional sea beasts, a Trident stalks its prey not with the purposeful fury of a Moby Dick or the hunger-driven madness of a killer shark but with a controlled destructive potency and survivability unmatched by any Leviathan, dead or living. Fortunately, also in contrast to true aquatic killers, a Trident's life's aim is ultimately accomplished only if it never has to do more than stalk its prey. So viewed, the Trident could best be likened to the lionfish: armed, deadly, but not aggressive unless provoked.

Even so experienced a seafarer as Melville's Ishmael would feel awe when gazing at a Trident. From its symmetrically round and blunt bow to the conical tip of its single screw the *Ohio* stretches 560 feet. It has a displacement of 16,600 tons standard when surfaced and 18,750 submerged. The *Ohio* is a "traditional design" vessel—meaning, among many other things, that unlike the Soviet *Typhoon*, the *Ohio*'s missile tubes are located behind the sail area, its diving planes are not located forward, and it has what is by now regarded as a conventional feature, a "sail" (erroneously spoken of as a conning tower). The pressure hull begins approximately 35 feet from the tip of the bow. At the end of the superstructure, about 160 feet from the stern, the Trident hull progressively reduces in diameter to the point of the screw. From this point forward the pressure hull attains a 42-foot diameter, maintained well forward of the sail area, until it tapers to a bulbous shape forward of the forward ballast tank. The external shape of the outer hull is therefore perfectly symmetrical except in the superstructure area covering the missile magazine, where the side-by-side nesting of twelve pairs of two tubes each necessitates some flattening of the superstructure, under which the tubes stand some 2.5 feet "proud" (vertically free) of the pressure hull. This hull diameter was chosen to make allowance for the deployment of the 44-foot-long Trident II missile, sometime in 1989.[1]

Again unlike the new Soviet *Typhoon* design, the *Ohio*'s sail bears the traditional two diving planes. Each plane is approximately 16 feet long horizontally and 12 feet wide and is tapered from leading to trailing edge in an airfoil chord to facilitate diving and ascent. These controllable diving planes are located about 15 feet up on the sail, somewhat below the submarine's identification number. During dives or ascents they are inclined to help direct the submarine down or up, in conjunction with the stern elevators, whose degree of incidence can be independently varied or fully coordinated as a particular maneuver requires. The sail itself towers approximately 25 feet above the hull, not counting the extensible height of its various periscopes and radio antennae when raised. Viewed bow on, the sail is nearly 9 feet thick, also expanding in a chord shape near the midline from a round bow shape to a sharp trailing upright edge viewed stern on from the deck of the missile magazine. The sail extends some 30 feet from bow to stern along the longitudinal axis of the ship. It has a very slight molded top shape to match the streamlining of the sail's vertical chord.

The sail features radio antenna masts, attack periscopes, a large navigational satellite receiver, electronic countermeasures mast, search radar, identification beacons, snorkel induction masts, other radio antennae, buoy-launching ports, and other similar but classified equipment. Extensible equipment is housed in hydrodynamically clean sleeves, appropriately camouflaged with a mottled gray-and-blue scheme, which are raised out of the sail to clear the unit being employed above the surface, so that the finest feather is generated to the surface observer's eye and so that the sail itself can be kept submerged at a lower level than otherwise would be possible, thereby diminishing the prospects of the sail's own turbulence being spotted directly at the surface level. For tests, the *Ohio* also uses a removable telemetry mast located behind the sail to track and measure missiles on launch. Other standard features contained in the sail include the traditional command cockpit with portable steering and diving controls and command communications, navigational lights, an escape trunk, and a small external access hatch. When all extensible equipment is retracted, the top of the sail is perfectly clean and smooth. For observation purposes the sail also contains a port located at its head, above the line of the sail, so that visual observation of the surface can be made from inside the sail in heavy seas. Immediately below is an opaque aperture out of which operate such sonar and acoustic equipment as the WLR-9 acoustic intercept receiver, employed to detect active search sonars and acoustic-homing torpedoes; the WLR-8(V)5 receiver, used to detect enemy fire-control signals and to monitor radio communication frequencies.[2]

At various times the Navy has tried putting television cameras in the periscopes to allow a quicker circular survey of the surface. The officer can tape the reconnaissance and study it when the periscope is retracted. However, according to one officer, the cameras failed easily, and the Navy has apparently abandoned the idea. At this time the *Ohio* is not thought to incorporate this type of system, although it may utilize cameras in other modes.[3]

As it true of other submarines, the superstructure of the *Ohio* passively admits water to fill up the open volume of space throughout that part of the hull where the launching tubes extend vertically above the pressure hull. Thus the superstructure functions as a somewhat flat fairing over the missile section. Rather than employing numerous open venting ports with their associated effects of increased friction and hydrodynamic disturbance, as is Soviet design practice, the superstructure is vented port and starboard by a single open seam beginning slightly forward of the sail and extending horizontally around and somewhat abaft the missile section to a point of attachment to the pressure hull's after section. Somewhat abaft the twin rows of twelve missile-tube hatches, the hull gradually tapers toward the stern to the point of the screw. Each diameter change is smooth and as moderate as possible to permit even hydrodynamic flow.

The stern of the *Ohio* provides solid visual evidence that it is a unique vessel. Here a single 26-foot-diameter screw (approximately) caps an internally housed drive shaft. Slightly forward of the screw, viewed stern on, the hull sports two horizontal control fins starboard and port, capped by stationary vertical stabilizing fins, and a split rudder positioned directly along the ship's axis. The vertical fins are 20 feet high and 20 feet wide, while the horizontal stabilizing fins extend 20 feet outboard to port and starboard and are 34 feet deep at the point of attachment to the hull, tapering to 20 feet at the point where the vertical fins are attached. The horizontal planes are built similar to the elevators on an aircraft with the after fin controllable, operating variably in synchronization with the diving planes on the sail. Attached to each of the two vertical planes is a nozzlelike housing that permits extension of the tow-assisted sonar arrays (TACTAS). The stern cross section, viewed from astern, appears in figure 2-1. Some dimensions such as missile sizes and hull diameters, are precise; others such as stabilizer sizes, are approximate.

When Navy and Department of Defense planners first considered a vessel to replace the Polaris boats, they established a number of design objectives. Many involved achieving cost effectiveness through variations of launcher units and hull lengths; others concerned minimizing the turnaround time for maintenance and overall ease of refitting and resupplying the ship as built. Several design objectives, however, applied directly to technology used in the hull. For example, besides incorporating a unique strategic submarine design for adding more and larger missiles combined with a more powerful reactor, the design was intended to provide greater survivability, thoroughgoing sleekness, maximum demagnetization, maximum internal airborne noise dampening, turbulence reduction, hull strength, and maximum equipment retraction (the anchors, for example, are stowed within the ballast tanks). The hull was also designed to allow maximum room for such future components as new sonar, weapons systems, or control systems while simultaneously providing the greatest possible resistance to external concussion. Another significant objective was to facilitate equipment repair and maintenance. The hull contains three 6-foot-diameter access hatches—one fore and two aft (one of the after hatches allows access to the reactor section and another allows access to the turbine and drive, while the hatch forward of the sail allows access to the command and control area). Each hatch has separate seals at two levels, permitting complete removal, derricking, and replacement of any component at any of four deck levels. Besides being sized to the hatch diameter, components were designed in such a way that they could be easily removed sequentially, making it unnecessary to employ the earlier technique of cutting out whole sections of the hull to effect repairs of inaccessible equipment. Any module can be replaced in twelve to eighteen hours.[4]

The only original basic design objective not met with the Trident design was a target-acquisition-reduction paint to baffle active sonar

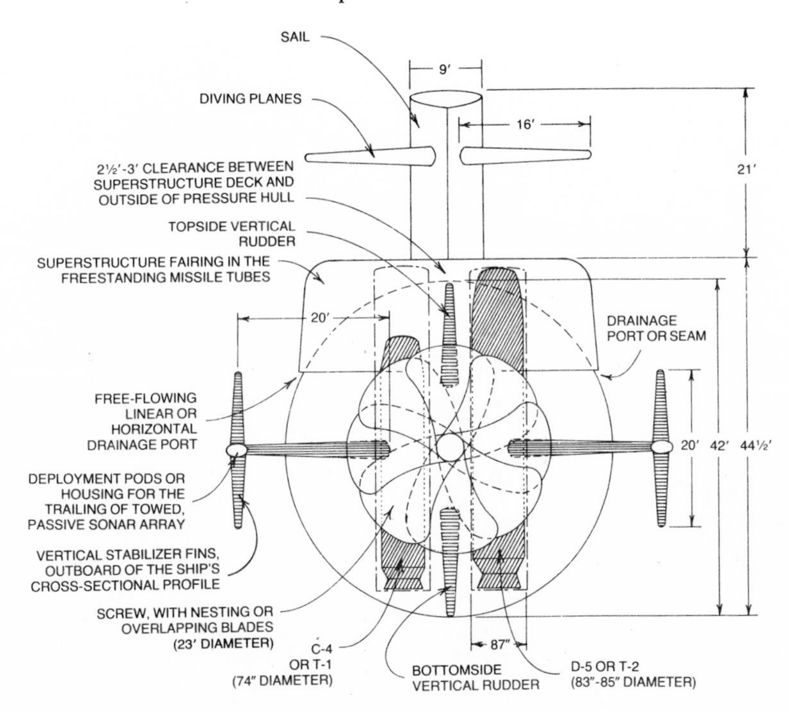

Fig. 2-1. *Ohio* stern-on cross-section.

directed at the Trident by attack vessels. This objective has now been attained, or soon will be, so that any Trident unit not painted with it at the time of its virgin voyage may be so treated at its first major overhaul; subsequent ships will possess this highly advanced anechoic skin as original issue.

The new Trident hull shape, sleeker than that of the *Poseidon* boats, represents a small part of the submarine's unique features. For instance, 139 pressure hull cylinders, each reinforced internally with a round I-beam rib, form 41 primary hull cylinders, each welded together in sequence to yield a completed hull. Each I beam, while variable as to flange width and even standing height, is forged into a ring providing the inner skeletal support of the submarine. The outer carbon steel plate measures somewhat less than 5 inches in thickness, leaving the interior diameter of the submarine roughly 40 feet over most of its useful length, the shaft housing unit being the principal exception because of its cone shape. Exterior attachments, such as hawse eyes, are noticeably absent, thereby reducing to a minimum external hydrodynamic hull turbulence and sonar eccentric definition phenomena. Missile tube hatches, when closed, lie flush with the surface of the superstructure, likewise enhancing speed and quietness. The bow section features a reinforced fiberglass dome that facilitates passive sonar detection and also provides bow fairing. Behind the sonar bow cap, as major hull components, comes the forward ballast tank, with an access trunk connecting the sonar section with the pressure hull, followed by the forward compartment (with facilities for command, communication, living, cooking, recreation, fire control, information control, and so on), the missile compartment, the reactor compartment, turbine room, and main ballast area.

Only a dull black epoxy paint shows when the vessel is surfaced, although beneath the water line Tridents are painted with a rust-red primer over approximately the bottom two-thirds of the hull to a height of about 36.5 feet. The submarine's number in white paint toward the top of the sail, displacement scale numbers on the forward and stern hull sides and on the topside rudder plane, and white Xs and Os on the access hatches mark the principal exceptions to the surface black and rust-red hull motif. The compounds in the hull paint may also help, together with degaussing, to reduce magnetic detection.

Other than the stern section, the Trident hulls, while large, appear quite ordinary, but closer examination reveals a number of interesting features. In the bow section, across the top of the hull to the sail, are six power-supply ports in three twin sets ready to receive shore-based power lines while the submarine resides at dockside, and aft of the missile compartment there are five such ports. These furnish energy to run the life-support systems so that maintenance crews can shut down the reactor for inspection or repair. Located in the lower hull in the command and control section are four torpedo tubes, slightly angled outward at 5 degrees, designed to fire the Mk-48 advanced-capability torpedo. As in other submarines, the tubes can eject a variety of items. They are also capable of firing Harpoon missiles (although it is not certain that fire controls for monitoring Harpoons are on board). Four other launching tubes are located port and starboard, below and abaft the sail, flush with the hull but facing forward at an angle. These tubes, among other functions, eject the mobile submarine simulators (Mk-70 MOSS), deployed to confuse attacking subs. Emitting sonar signatures highly similar to those of the Trident itself, these simulators decoy enemy submarines away from the real vessel. Angled slightly forward, the MOSS tubes constitute an infinitesimal drag in the otherwise excellent hydrodynamics of the Trident, an observation to which the only other exceptions would be the set of four handrails located portside above the waterline just abaft the MOSS ports, and the handrail affixed to the sail with which to ascend from the deck of the superstructure to the horizontal surfaces of the diving planes.[5]

The active defense measures such as the Mk-48 torpedoes, it is argued, of course cost the Trident added passive defenses to some extent. Alternatively, it can be argued that the emphasis on active defensive systems has deprived the boat of more offensive capability such as additional ballistic-missile launching tubes. The torpedoes, fire control, reloads, and specialized crews occupy space and add weight while detracting from other capacities, such as speed and maneuverability. But few submariners would feel comfortable relying on evasive capability alone for their survival, so the Trident is a true fighting ship.[6]

No piece of defensive equipment is more important to a ballistic-missile submarine than its sonar. The Trident has a special sonar roughly comparable to the BQQ-5 found in the *Los Angeles* class, the BQQ-6 (a designation of "submarine multipurpose or special sonar," series 6). A digital system integrates conformal hull- and bow-mounted sonar arrays with the towed array deployed from the housings mounted on the vertical planes at the stern. The BQQ-6 on the Trident is a fully integrated system but lacks active sonar capability, meaning it does not bounce out and back detective sonar impulses or "pings." To achieve a detection at 10,000 yards, an active sonar unit requires half a million watts of power. Passive sonar uses hydrophones to pick up sea noises, from which submarine sounds are differentiated by the operators. While less accurate than active sonar, passive arrays need only half a watt of power for a 10,000-yard detection. To achieve much higher accuracy with a SUBROC antisubmarine rocket, for example, a submarine needs an active sonar array to fix the range, direction, nature, and speed of its intended target, but with an increased risk of counterattack. But the essence of Trident's defense exclusively depends upon highly sophisticated techniques of passive localization. If necessary, in the future a Trident could avail itself of its TACTAS astern to detect enemy ASW aircraft in conjunction with a new submarine-launched antiaircraft missile, the SIAM, although the SIAM is not yet deployed. Since BQQ-6 resembles the BQQ-5 sonar used in the *Los Angeles* class very closely, Trident sonars probably have a WLR-9 acoustic intercept receiver to detect not only active sonars but acoustic homing torpedoes as well. Tridents contain the WLR-8(V)5 electronic warfare countermeasure set, the Mk-98 digital computer missile fire-control system, and the Mk-118 torpedo fire-control system.[7]

Computers integrate all bow, conformal, and towed sonars on the Trident, directing the listening hydrophones and identifying the approach direction of separate threats. Each listening beam utilizes a different frequency. The operators switch back and forth on "channels" much like those on a television set, each channel representing a direction. Although computer processors handle the acoustic signals initially, crew members must interpret, correlate, and classify the signals individually. Because of the computer systems used with the BQQ-6, the Trident sonar crew is far smaller than that used with preceding systems, requiring no more than four watchstanders.[8]

Throughout the hull are distributed a variety of different sensors to test water salinity, pressure, flow, and temperature; to identify biological phenomena such as plankton; to clock water speed; to take hydrostatic soundings, and to identify other ocean readings. Admiral J. C. Metzel has indicated that the purpose of gathering data through the hull sensors is to allow the sub commander a choice of patrol areas. Tridents, Metzel suggested, might patrol in "prevailing seasonal storms" or in an area of "high biological noise" as well as hide in areas of high salinity or in thermal layers. These factors can severely reduce detection by space satellite as well as by air- and seaborne ASW units. The water current readings permit the sub to maintain itself against a current so that, by running at the same speed as the current, it can remain virtually motionless, somewhat like World War I and II maneuvers of diesel subs, which however would lurk literally motionless on the ocean floor in relatively shallow waters.[9]

The screw is the last exterior item of interest on the hull. The Trident—unlike the Soviet *Typhoon,* which has a compound drive train—has a single unit capable of switching between a high-speed and a low-speed set of turbines and reduction gears for its single shaft and screw to obtain maximum performance with a minimum of noise. This feature alone holds several implications. First, while individual components may be complex, the drive train as a whole possesses the simplicity and reliability of a single system. In other words, with only one reactor, one propeller shaft, and one screw, the Trident has 50 percent fewer main drive and power units to malfunction than does a Soviet *Typhoon.* Second, a single screw generates far less turbulence than two since there is only one source of turbulence, rather than two, and there is also no compound interaction of two sources of turbulence. Of course, a third implication—and disadvantage—is that, should any main power, turbine, shaft, or drive unit break down, there is no major alternate back-up system (although this is not exactly true, in an auxiliary sense, in the case of the Trident, as will be explained).

A Trident's propulsion system employs a very remarkable and highly advanced screw design. Since there is only one screw, it does perform with exceptional efficiency, generating substantially less total turbulence as measured by duration, violence, acoustics, volume, or underwater "feather." Consequently, in the screw alone the Trident achieves several design objectives: great speed, less turbulence, and reduced acoustically detectable water displacement.

Perfectly concentric reconvergence of water because of the hull configuration also contributes to the screw's efficiency since the water displaced at the bow by the intrusion of the hull mass becomes reconstituted in its mass by its convergent flow at the screw's location. A shorter trail of turbulence also reduces the "blind" zone behind the screw in which attack subs might seek to screen themselves from a towed-array sonar. Placement of the split rudder and stabilizing and diving planes forward of the screw also enhances the performance of their functions because they occur in nonturbulent leading rather than trailing water. Furthermore, because of the highly efficient screw design, the shaft can move at fewer revolutions per minute to achieve greater speed with less turbulence. Even in battle situations, where high speed for evasion must be generated, the shaft and screw deliver the greater speed with relatively less turbulence than earlier designs could. Overall, therefore, this particular design makes the Trident a far more efficient submarine in its overall combination of speed, quietness, reliability, and diminished turbulence than any other submarine in existence, any contemporary Soviet submarine from *Typhoon* to *Alpha* to *Oscar* to *Delta III* included. A priority in security, therefore, is to make sure that Soviet intelligence in no fashion manages to obtain the screw's actual design.

Toward the stern of the vessel, aft of the reactor room, are several auxiliary machinery facilities and climate-control functions, water purification, and an extensive onboard repair capability. Between these compartments and the reactor room lies the turbine room. There the steam turbine converts the raw energy expelled by the heated water from the reactor into steam to turn the shaft.

A 90,000-horsepower nuclear-fueled GE S8G reactor plant, generating enough electricity "for a city of perhaps 50,000," provides the thrust for the massive submarine. Originally the Navy hoped to have an entirely new reactor for the Trident, but there is little in Navy publications or congressional testimony to indicate the reactor currently in use in the *Ohio* is a totally new design. P. Takis Veliotis, the general manager at Electric Boat, has indicated the opposite, implying that Rickover has continued to rely upon older reactor designs (which Veliotis calls "coffeepots"), while the Soviets in the interim may have developed increasingly more powerful reactors such as that used aboard the *Alpha*.[10] The reactor, in any case, definitely has Rickover's mark on it. The Soviets may have improved designs, but this is not certain. How much of the *Alpha*'s speed is attributable to the energy capability of its reactor, how much is due to its reduced weight, and how much is due to its unsafe operation because of its weight and inadequate shielding cannot be determined. At any rate, the *Ohio* boasts the most efficient reactor currently available to the Navy, with four times the power of the Poseidon reactors and at least twice the power of the 688s. Its expected core life is nine years, and its more than 60,000 shaft horsepower can propel the submarine substantially over the Navy's avowed rating of +25 knots, in the neighborhood assuredly of 40 knots or more (see chap. 8).* A Trident's nuclear capacity saves it an estimated seven million barrels of oil in its lifetime. Too, advances in radioactive shielding, in terms of more protection for less weight, have led to substantial savings in weight and cost. Despite Soviet advances in titanium, the USSR substantially trails the United States in the fabrication of lightweight shielding. The so-called free-circulating cooling system for the reactor, running off water convection currents, diverts from direct propulsion less power for cooling purposes, thereby also saving further power and reducing airborne noise caused by the operation of the circulating pumps.[11]

Should the reactor develop difficulties (as it did on its sea trials when the crew left a part at Electric Boat), a diesel engine can lock onto the shaft to generate an emergency speed of 5 knots. However, if both the reactor system and propeller shaft malfunction, a third system takes over. This back-up system drives two emergency screws, located inside the rear ballast tanks, that can push the vessel through the water at an emergency speed of just under 5 knots. This ultimate emergency system is affectionately called "bring-it-home" capability by U.S. Navy personnel. The geared turbines themselves were supplied by General Electric, and the main power train was provisionally assembled and tested at West Milton, Massachusetts, along with the reduction gear.[12]

Another related element in utilizing a larger and more powerful reactor is a method of controlling engine-room heat. At Rickover's insistence, the Navy installed a 40-ton air-conditioning system for each Trident, compared with 15-ton air conditioners on many other submarines (the Navy recommendation until Admiral Rickover succeeded in overriding it). These air conditioners ensure that the crew will enjoy an improved degree of comfort, an important factor in the Trident's increased on-station time, as well as regulate climate levels throughout the ship to protect hardware and software equipment from deterioration caused by dampness, irregular temperature, and salty air.

The missile tube section, nicknamed Sherwood Forest, houses twenty-four missile tubes that resemble giant incubators. Each is equipped

*The authors wish to make it clear that this is an extrapolation from published sources cited in the notes and not U.S. Navy information.

with a Westinghouse missile launcher inside. Although the 32.5-ton missiles will be examined independently later in this chapter, each Trident I (C-4) missile stands 34.1 feet in height, including thrust nozzle, and is 74 inches in diameter. Therefore, not only are they shorter than the 42-foot diameter of the pressure hull, but each missile's diameter is smaller than its tube (87 inches) by 13 inches, as each tube was designed originally with the 83- to 85-inch-diameter Trident II (D-5) in mind. To keep the undersized Trident I missiles from movement or shock inside the tubes, liner pads embrace the missile tightly and aid it in achieving a straight launch. These elastomeric liner pads bonded to the inside of the launch tubes form horizontal rows and vertical columns to protect the missile, absorb "horizontal shock impulses during storage, and to stabilize the trajectory of the missile during launch."[13]

During launch a gas/steam generator system ignites a small fixed rocket with an exhaust directed through cooling water to the base of the launch tube, allowing the steam pressure to expel the missile from the tube. To permit firing, the outer hatch is opened in the superstructure, unmasking a launch tube closure. This is a "rigid dome-shaped shell structure" approximately 0.25 feet thick made of an asbestos phenolic material that extends spherically over the end of the launch tube and measures 79.5 inches in diameter and 28 inches in shell-shaped height. When the missile firing commences, it is shattered first "into regular rings and then into segments by a network of linear-shaped explosive charges mounted on the underside of the shell. . . ." To insulate the missile from excessive temperature variation, and to absorb blast effects from the explosive charges, "a low-density, open-cell urethane foam material is bonded to the underside of the shell with honeycomb crushable energy-absorbing material shaped to the form of the C-4 nose so pressure is uniform on the nose fairing." After the gas has forced the missile out of the launcher and the missile has cleared the surface, the first-stage solid-propellant boost motor ignites, shortly after which the drag-reducing aerodynamic spike telescopes into position from its stowed position in the nose. The aerospike, made by Unidynamics, increases the range of the blunt-nosed missile by 300 nautical miles. This operation requires a moderate draft of water over the hull to protect the boat; unlike early Polaris in tests, a Trident I cannot be dry-launched without the possibility of inflicting some damage to the vessel.[14]

Theoretically, upon losing 65,000 (or 73,000; see n. 14) pounds on one or the other side, assuming surface firing, the vessel would tend to yaw violently upward on the side liberated of the missile weight. However, when a Trident I missile is actually launched, the vessel is backflooded with water immediately, resulting in a slightly heavier ship, since the Trident I missile occupies only 34.1 feet of the tube, with the unoccupied volume filled with static air, abruptly filled with a volume of water equal to the space previously taken up by the missile and its air envelope. The crew must therefore increase total bouyancy. The Trident II, at ± 114,000 pounds (57 tons), on the other hand,will-constitute more missile weight in the tube in combination with a reduced volume of air in its envelope, so a relative reduction in buoyancy will be necessary to keep the vessel in trim.[15]

Launch sequence in the event of an optimum, or "ripple," fire would take on a precise format. (For a more detailed discussion of firing and targeting, see chap. 12.) The tubes, numbered 1 through 24, appear as below, with the first four firings shown thus (. . . . .) and the last four thus (——):

Firing Number	Tube Number		Firing Number
1	··················> 1	2 <··················	3
5	3	4	7
9	5	6	11
13	7	8	15
17	9	10	19
21	————> 11	12 <————	23
24	————> 13	14 <————	22
20	15	16	18
16	17	18	14
12	19	20	10
8	21	22	6
4	··················> 23	24 <··················	2

magazine

In the firing sequence, missile 1 would be followed by missile 24, not 2. This sequence allows the vessel to maintain its balance and ballast from bow to stern and port to starboard, as it is never more than the appropriate weight of one tube temporarily out of trim. In an analogous situation aboard the SSBN 643, *George Bancroft*, each Poseidon missile took approximately 56.6 seconds to be fired, for a total firing sequence of less than fifteen minutes for its magazine of sixteen missiles. This total elapsed time conforms very closely to French experience in firing their *L'Inflexible*-class magazine of sixteen M-4 SLBMs. Calculating total elapsed firing time for the Trident magazine would analogously provide a time set of slightly less than twenty-three minutes for its twenty-four Trident I missiles. However, due to highly improved and more instantaneously effective fire-control equipment aboard the *Ohio* class, some authorities speculate the total sequence is even less than fifteen minutes—indeed, probably less than six minutes—while it will probably be more than six for the Trident II. Future improvements, to become operative with the next set of ten Trident boats, indicate total firing time will be reduced still further. Following a missile firing and reballasting, the hatch is closed so that a sub can fire one or two sets of missiles and then dive deeper, or move on to hamper space or surface detection, and then erratically (as to timing or location) approach the surface and fire another one or two sets, until in this fashion the entire magazine would be expended.[16]

Working in conjunction with the missile system, the Trident's strategic weapons system includes the Mk-98 FCS fire-control system, navigational equipment, and a command control center. When launching a missile, the Mk-98 FCS system must know two positions: the ship's fix and the target's. On a Trident, the two Mk-2, MOD 7 Ship's Inertial Navigation Systems (SINS) provide the first position. A complex system "of gyroscopes, accelerometers, and computers . . . relate movement and speed of the ship in all directions to true north . . . give a continuous report" of these crucial data. Basically the Trident's system is the same as the Poseidon's, with the addition of an electrostatically supplied gyro monitor, additional cooling, better noise reduction, and reengineering of the sonar system and WSC-3 satellite communications receiver. Of course, NAVSTAR global positioning satellites (discussed in chap. 9) will greatly enhance navigational capability. A UYK-7 computer processes data for the entire weapons complex, while a Mk-118 digital fire control system (adapted from the Mk-117s on the *Los Angeles*-class subs) with a Mk-92 attack control console directs the defensive weapons. As in all submarines, each system takes up as little space as possible, with seats at the control console fitted to moving rails, allowing them to slide under the consoles when unmanned. Firing controls for the missiles remain covered and locked to avoid accidental release.[17]

Anyone inside the command center is surrounded by dials, knobs, pipes, lights, controls, and computers. Most of the "desk jobs" such as sonar, fire controls, sensors, and navigation stations have built-in chairs. The periscope tubes bisect the room, with fire controls on one side and navigational controls on the other. In this general area, computers linked to NAVSAT process data used in navigation and targeting. A separate, integrated radio room features RCA equipment to handle messages automatically. All aspects of shipboard control, weapons, and communication are fully integrated with sonar and internal radio systems.[18]

Although Trident has more interior living and equipment space than any previous U.S. strategic submarine, conditions will still appear cramped to any landlubber. However, to submariners used to really cramped undersea conditions, the Trident has an abundance of room. Part of the reason for extra room is the planned equipment growth space built into the vessel, but the Navy has also incorporated greater room to make living conditions at sea more comfortable. A Trident carries a 157-man crew of 15 officers and 142 sailors (see chap. 12). Crew size has varied greatly over the planning period. One 1975 report put the crew size at 14 officers and 136 enlisted men, "although one officer billet, for a doctor, may be changed to an additional hospital corpsman, one especially trained for independent duty." Unlike other submariners' quarters, which resemble smaller versions of Pullman sleeping-car berths, Tridents have dormitory units, each of which accommodates nine men. Each area has, in addition to the individually curtained bunk areas, large locker spaces under each bunk and hang-up space for the crew's dress uniforms. These units also contain small booths which function as desks, giving the sailor some measure of privacy where he can write letters, listen to a tape recorder, or read. Officers are assigned "roomy" separate simulated-wood–paneled staterooms. Each stateroom has a pair of collapsible chairs, a foldout table, a built-in clock, and desk space. Naturally, special commissioned officer wardroom, petty officer lounges, and various enlisted men's facilities are available. The vessel contains such entertainment facilities as videotape players for the television on board, a 1000-book library, a free jukebox, a study area, a gym with body-building equipment, a Ping-Pong table, an ice-cream machine, a built-in hi-fi system with tapes, hobby kits, painting material, and textbooks and other academic paraphernalia sufficient for a college-credit program. *All Hands*, a U.S. Navy magazine, suggests that the Trident's living spaces exceed those of the Polaris/Poseidon subs in virtually every respect. Possibly the area with the most room improvement has been the mess. By comparison, an attack submarine's entire mess area would fit inside a Trident's galley, where chefs in their red kerchiefs and tall hats serve hot meals. Once again, the Navy's concern for crew comfort over the extended time (seventy days) spent at sea led it to incorporate better food preparation, dining space, and dining atmosphere in the deck interior of the four-level Tridents.[19]

Below decks is the compartment for storage batteries, which provide start-up power for either the diesel engine or the reactor to furnish a continuous flow of electricity at all times, with regulated recharge taking place from reactor-powered dynamos.

Quietness played a major role in inducing the Navy to provide more room on board. Smaller equipment, especially smaller pumps and air compressors, make less noise and are more easily baffled or silenced than larger components. All mounts are duplicated to ensure an additional degree of noise muffling. While the Navy has used the quietest systems now available, sound-muffling improvement for component parts continues, so it may be possible soon to replace the smaller compressors, for example, with larger systems without any increase in the noise level. Therefore the vessel can accommodate growth in nearly all of the subsystems. To offset the prospective increase in weight of new equipment, Trident currently carries lead ballast so that it will not suffer from increased displacement as new equipment is added later.[20]

Although a new generation of software is rapidly becoming available, the first ten Tridents contain the current generation of computer software. As newer software becomes available, the Navy will be able progressively to upgrade future Tridents, resulting in extensive savings of weight and space. This prophesies a dual factor of growth. First, new components will be more fully automated, integrated, and dependable, thus reducing maintenance time. Shorter turnarounds at base will reduce manpower needs, both at the base and on board the ship. Second, due to the smaller size and weight of the components, the vessel itself will weigh less and contain more space. Crews can be reduced, meaning that the Navy can either increase pay for submarine crews, spend less on recruitment, or both. Operationally, the number of human errors will decrease. In short, a very hefty margin for growth of all derivations has been consciously built into the sub's design, a feature that boldly anticipates most, if not all, future technological and subcomponent changes with margin to spare. Little, if any, of this elasticity of response could have been provided by "smaller" Tridents, so often recommended by certain schools of critical thought (discussed in chap. 4 and 10) who tend to confuse "costliness" with "effectiveness" to the point of diminishing returns for the latter.

The missiles also reflect concern for potential growth. With the same height and the same diameter as the Poseidon C-3 missile, the Trident C-4 missile fits into the older Poseidon-era submarines of the *Lafayette* and *Franklin* classes (see fig. 2-2). While it weighs the same (65,000 pounds) or a little more (73,000 pounds) than the Poseidon C-3, it has a range of 4000 n.m., a 1500-n.m range gain. Navy researchers, in fact, extracted a little more range from the Trident I missile than originally

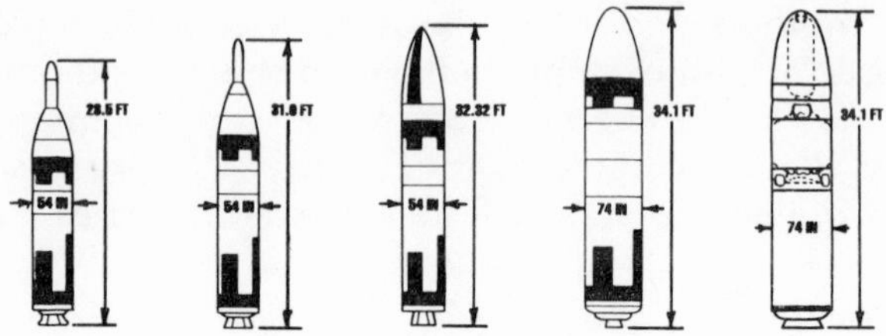

0) **Options**	**Polaris A-1**	**Polaris A-2**	**Polaris A-3**	**Poseidon C-3**	**Trident (T-I) C-4** Reference (Standard)
1) **Year**	1960	1962	1964	1971	1979
2) **Range**	1,200-1,500 NM	1,500-1,800 NM	2,500-2,800 NM	2,500-3,200 NM	4,000 NM
3) **Weight**	28,000 lbs	30,000 lbs	35,000 lbs	65,000-73,000 lbs	65,000 lbs
4) **Propulsion**	2-stage solid fuel	♦♦♦	♦♦ (1st stg. composite)	♦♦♦	3-stage solid fuel
5) **Powered Stages**	2	♦♦♦	♦♦♦	♦♦♦	3
6) **Motor Case Materials**	Glass Fiber Both Stages	♦♦♦	♦♦♦	♦♦♦	Keflar fiber
7) **Nozzles**	4, each stage	♦♦♦	♦♦♦	1, each stg. Single movable nozzle actuated by a gas generator	♦♦♦
8) **Controls**	?	?	1st stage, rotating. 2nd stage, fluid injection	♦♦♦	♦♦♦
9) **Launch Method**	Gas steam generator for all classes, except SSBN-608, which employed air ejection				
10) **Guidance**	Inertial	♦♦♦	♦♦♦	♦♦♦	Inertial, with stellar update
11) **Warhead**	1 RV of 1 MT (?)	♦♦♦	1 RV of 1 MT (?) or 3 MRV of 200 KT	14 MIRV warheads of 50 KT out to 2,500 NM or 10 of 50 KT to 3,200 NM	8 MK-4 MIRV vehicles of 100 KT, up to 24 MIRVs of lower KT force
12) **Platform**	SSBN-598 "George Washington" (5), and SSBN-608 "Ethan Allen" (5)	SSBN-608 "Ethan Allen" (5), and SSBN-616 "Lafayette" (first 8 vessels of this class only)	SSBN-598 "George Washington" (5), SSBN-608 "Ethan Allen" (5), SSBN-616 "Lafayette" class (19), and SSBN-640 "Benjamin Franklin" class (12)	SSBN-616 "Lafayette" class (19) and SSBN-640 "Benjamin Franklin" class (12)	On 12 vessels of SSBN-616 and 640 classes, as a retrofit, and all SSBN-726 until D-5(T-II) update
13) **CEP**	± 2,400 meters (?)	♦♦♦	± 1,200 meters (?)	± 900 meters (?)	± 300 meters (?)
14) **Other Options**					T-I and T-II can also be equipped with MK-500 Evader (maneuverable) MIRVs, called MARV

♦ Denotes a characteristic identical to preceding entry at left.

Sources

Pretty, Ronald T., Editor. *Jane's Weapons Systems: 1977.* New York. Franklin Watts, Inc., 872 pp. 1976.

Moore, John E. *Jane's Fighting Ships: 1977–78.* New York: Franklin Watts, Inc., 829 pp. 1977

Moore, John E. *Jane's Fighting Ships: 1980–81.* New York: Franklin Watts, Inc., 780 pp. 1980.

Polmar, Norman. *The Ships and Aircraft of the U.S. Fleet.* XI Edition. Annapolis: Naval Institute Press. 350 pp. 1978.

Fig. 2-2. Fleet ballistic missile system evolution and Trident missile options.

33
Description of Trident

Trident I C-4 U (Improved Accuracy)

Trident I Long C-4 TFS (Terminal Fix Source)

(Development options not deployed because of D-5 program acceleration.)

Trident II D-5 Reference (Standard)

Trident II CD D-5 (Clear Deck D-5)

Trident II D-5 TFS (D-5 Terminal Fix Source)

Aerospike
Nose Fairing
Third Stage Motor
Equipment Section
Adapter Section
Second Stage Motor
Interstage Section
First Stage Motor

34.1 FT | 44 FT | 44 FT | 44 FT | 44 FT

74 IN | 74 IN | 83 IN | 83 IN | 83 IN

	Trident I C-4 U	Trident I Long C-4 TFS	Trident II D-5	Trident II CD D-5	Trident II D-5 TFS
1) **Year**	?	?	1989	1989(?)	1989(?)
2) **Range**	♦♦♦ *	♦♦♦	6,000+ NM	♦♦♦	♦♦♦
3) **Weight**	♦♦♦	♦♦♦	126,000-130,000 lbs	♦♦♦	♦♦♦
4) **Propulsion**	♦♦♦	♦♦♦	♦♦♦	♦♦♦	♦♦♦
5) **Powered Stages**	♦♦♦	♦♦♦	♦♦♦	♦♦♦	♦♦♦
6) **Motor Case Materials**	♦♦♦	♦♦♦	Not determined	♦♦♦	♦♦♦
7) **Nozzles**	♦♦♦	♦♦♦	Not determined	♦♦♦	♦♦♦
8) **Controls**	♦♦♦	♦♦♦	Not determined	♦♦♦	♦♦♦
9) **Launch Method**					
10) **Guidance**	♦♦♦	TFS	Inertial, with stellar update	♦♦♦	TFS
11) **Warhead**	♦♦♦	♦♦♦	14 MIRV of 150 KT each, or 7 MIRV, with MARV of 300 KT each	♦♦♦(?)	♦♦♦(?)
12) **Platform**	♦♦♦	♦♦♦	SSBN-726 exclusively	♦♦♦	♦♦♦
13) **CEP**	?	?	± 122 meters	♦♦♦(?)	± 30 meters
14) **Other Options**	♦♦♦	♦♦♦	♦♦♦	♦♦♦	♦♦♦

Polmar, Norman. *The Ships and Aircraft of the U.S. Fleet.* XII Edition. Annapolis: Naval Institute Press. 421 pp. 1981.

Couhat, Jean Labayle. *Combat Fleets of the World: 1982–83: Their Ships, Aircraft and Armament.* Annapolis: Naval Institute Press. 873 pp. 1982.

Trident Project Management Office missile chart, and *FBM Facts: Polaris, Poseidon, Trident.* Washington, D.C.: Strategic Systems Project Office. 19 pp. 1978.

planned because the final model weighs 5000 to 6000 pounds less than test models. Greater range over the Poseidon missile was achieved by advances in propulsion, microelectronics, and weight-saving materials. A C-4 missile contains three stages and a maneuvering equipment section, but the Navy has urged Lockheed to keep external changes to a minimum. Unlike the Poseidon missile, each of the three-stage boosters utilizes "a high-energy, high density cross linked double-base propellant" and each has a boost rocket motor with advanced case materials, a single lightweight, movable thrust nozzle, and a thrust vector control system of an improved lightweight gas-hydraulic design. Each missile at present has the Mk-5 guidance system, which has both all-inertial and stellar-inertial capabilities, thus increasing its accuracy over the added range.[21]

Trident I missiles currently can carry either seven or eight Mk-4 reentry vehicles (RV), each with a W-76 warhead having a yield of 100 kilotons (kt). These RVs, when fitted with stellar inertial units, have an advertised circular error probability (CEP) of 1300 feet or less, even at extended ranges. The Trident I missile has a single-shot kill probability against a Soviet ICBM silo of 12 percent (against 7 percent for a Poseidon missile). Without the stellar inertial units the circular error probability would increase approximately to 1500 feet. Ultimately, with Trident II, combinations of propellents, warheads, and guidance systems are expected to yield a hard-target kill capability at ranges of 6000 n.m. or more with a CEP possibly of only 30 meters. Moreover, some vehicles may house only dummy warheads designed to appear on radar as real warheads. If, as many current analysts of Soviet defense systems believe, the Russians have advanced antiballistic-missile systems, these dummies would siphon off a number of such defensive weapons. Both the Trident I and the Trident II permit combination of real and dummy warheads. A single Trident with twenty-four missiles could have a total combination of 192 warheads and dummies. Assuming there are 200 high-value targets in the Soviet Union, a single Trident vessel is availed of 38,400 combinations (24 missiles × 8 RVs × 200 targets) of warhead/target options, roughly figured (a further discussion of targeting appears in chap. 12).[22]

In 1981 President Reagan ordered increased research and development on the Trident II (D-5) missile. This larger and heavier missile (83 to 84 inches in diameter and 114,000 to 126,000 pounds) could be equipped with eight to ten Mk-12A reentry vehicles used on the Minuteman III ICBM. The Navy would rename its new reentry vehicle the Mk5. With each reentry vehicle carrying a W-87 warhead (or dummy), the missile could pack a total yield per warhead of 475 kt, although Navy officials have argued for a warhead with a total yield of between 300 and 335 kt. Fourteen reentry vehicles of the 150-kt range could be substituted, according to one report. Once again, accuracy improvements could further lower the CEP to 750 feet. Besides the extra size and power of the Trident II engines, payloads can be reduced to accommodate greater range. In an additional discovery impacting on range, the Navy has recently found a stabilizer with combustible qualities, with the effect of increasing range for the same weight of propellent. When the new stabilizer/fuel combination finally reaches the required safety and dependability to allow the Navy to use it on either the Trident I or Trident II, the range of each may increase yet further. Currently, the Aerojet Strategic Propulsion Company is experimenting with nitroglycerine as a fuel, which, the company's vice-president of fleet ballistic-missile programs explained, "exceeds the energy content of some of the current missile systems."[23]

More missile implementation options have previously existed than just the Trident II (see fig. 2-2). For example, the Navy once suggested an elongated version of the C-4, extending the missile by 8 to 9 feet. By extending the body to carry more propellant, the C-4 thus might have achieved a range comparable to the D-5, with similar accuracy but with fewer RVs. Yet another option was a "flat deck" missile in which the third-stage rocket motor would be removed to make room for more reentry vehicles, probably ten Mk-12A RVs, at some sacrifice in range. If the Navy develops any of these options, it must also keep in mind

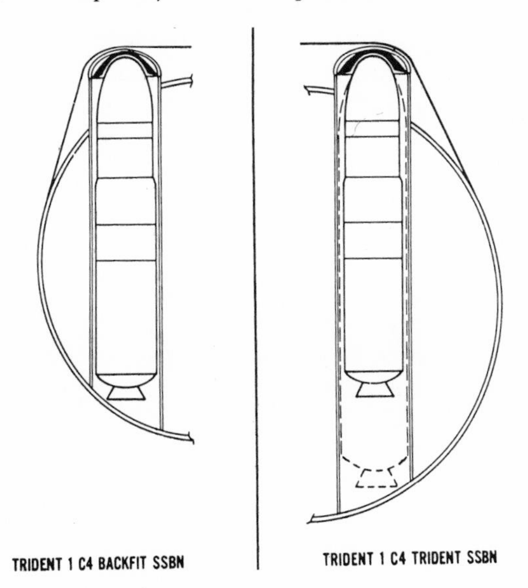

Fig. 2-3. Trident growth potential.

apparent attempts by the Department of Defense to maintain commonality between booster stages of the Trident II and the Air Force's MX missile, to the degree that awaiting full specification of the MX does not result in a totally unacceptable delay in the crucially needed Trident II. Achieving commonality, though, has become increasingly difficult, as the Air Force now looks more favorably on the 92-inch-diameter, 50-to-60-foot-long version of MX. Only the 83–85-inch-diameter missile fits the Navy's requirements for launch from Trident tubes (see fig. 2-3).[24]

Whatever option the Navy ultimately chooses, it must continue to institute improved precision guidance of its RVs to achieve a counterforce capability (the ability to knock out enemy missile silos by combining accuracy with throw weight). For several years the Defense Department has worked on an advanced ballistic reentry vehicle program (ABRES) and will soon "develop options for advanced maneuvering re-entry vehicles [AMARV] with preprogrammed evasion capability against Soviet ICBMs." When combined with precision guidance, the Navy's MaRV, the Mk-500 Evader, could provide a maximum combination of punch, evasion capabilities, and accuracy. Most sources agree evasion capabilities reduce accuracy and, therefore, for some time reciprocal concessions to one or other of these two qualities will be necessary. In the long term, however, the combination of increased range, accuracy, and evasive capabilities of the Trident missiles can only act as a multiplier on the capabilities of the submarine. Whereas the increased operating area promised by the 6000-n.m. range of the Trident II will further contribute to the submarine's ability to avoid detection, this advantage is less important than the greater accuracy and payload. Conceivably, other improvements in missile control subcomponent and firing systems could further economize on the numbers of crew members needed in the future, further reducing operational costs while at sea.[25]

Thus, with the Trident's combination of speed, quietness, firepower, survivability, at-sea capability, living conditions, and overall technology, no submarine ever built compares with it. Gains made by the Soviets in the area of speed consign the Soviet subs to dysfunctional complexity, cramped living spaces, frequent breakdowns, systems redundancy, and excessively noisy boats. Operational at-sea reliability remains the only unanswered question about Trident, and it is a question only time and repeated deployment can answer. If the Trident's reliability matches its awesome power, the odds will be even greater that no enemy will dare test the destructive capability of this Leviathan.

At the time of its conception, however, this giant seemed anemic, and no one could visualize what it would look like when it grew up. Soon, at least one characteristic became evident: the monster had an appetite for greenbacks like a whale for plankton. Feeding it required repeated and precarious trips to Capitol Hill.

3

Trident's Budgetary Birth:

Planning, Programming, and Funding, 1968–1974

"To preserve is easier than to acquire. . . ."
Clauswitz, *On War*

Media coverage of Trident's funding battles has concentrated on the problem of cost overruns, occasionally to the exclusion of all else. As noted in chapter 1, virtually every report on the system incorporated phraseology of this nature: "The USS *Ohio* should have logged two years with the Navy's Pacific Fleet. Instead, the state-of-the-art leviathan sits, 40 percent over the original budget and still not quite finished, in its builder's dock" or "TRIDENT BUDGET TO RUN FURTHER IN THE RED." Nevertheless, appropriations for the Trident system have come forth steadily, perhaps because, until Reagan announced his new strategic modernization package, the Trident program gradually had become the only one of three strategic force modernizations (bomber, submarine, and missile) proposed in the early 1970s actually in production. So-called Trident cost overruns admittedly have occurred and will continue to occur, as much a consequence of inflation as the *Ohio*'s delay. Much of the serious legislative, bureaucratic, and military infighting on the Trident, as with any weapons system, went on in closed-door or classified sessions. A substantial record nonetheless remains. The history of the Trident's funding goes well beyond battles in Congress over allocations. It ultimately has involved a whole series of actors, including the Congress, the President, the Defense Department, the Navy, and Electric Boat Company, with bit parts played by labor unions, environmental groups, disarmament activists, and offstage roles played by retired admirals and even former secretaries of defense. The medieval alchemists' goal of transforming lead into gold has in a sense been reversed: the modern struggle is turning money into a credible strategic deterrent made of electronics and steel.[1]

Put in the context of other weapons systems, the Trident has differed significantly in many crucial aspects of its development. The TFX fighter, now familiar as the F-111 fighter-bomber, was perhaps the first case of weapons-procurement "reform." Secretary of Defense Robert S. McNamara introduced to the Department of Defense the new concept of systems analysis, whereby individual weapons programs were supposed to be considered in the context of their operation defined by the program goal (such as sea control or strategic deterrance) rather than on the particular needs of a service branch. With the TFX, McNamara's analysts asked how effective the proposed fighter would be in its support and air-control roles. After pitting nine airframe builders and three engine manufacturers against each other in competition, the Air Force and the Defense Department settled on two prototypes and, following head-to-head competition, gave the contract to General Dynamics rather than McDonnell Douglas Aircraft. By the time the production contract was awarded, the plane's cost had increased 200 percent more than predicted at the outset of the application of systems analysis, demonstrating that (among other points) competitive prototype building does not necessarily guarantee lower cost.[2]

Nor are the above problems unique to American weapons procurement programs. Ingemar Dörfer showed in his study of the Swedish Viggen fighter acquisition that the degree of weapons systems urgency represents one element central to a program's cost and reliability. Along with the studies of the TFX and other related works, Dörfer has highlighted some of the problems facing defense planners. Need for the system constitutes the single most important factor in obtaining a weapon, but availability of competing firms willing to bid for the contracts also remains a significant element.[3]

Harold Sapolsky's study of the Polaris system depicted a military and government program that achieved most of the results in terms of cost and reliability the taxpayer ideally pictures in a healthy procurement process. The Polaris system was touted as cost-effective, it ran ahead of schedule in many cases, and people associated with it were not only dedicated but also "extraordinarily skillful in the art of bureaucratic politics." A similar conclusion is presented in James Baar's and William Howard's book *Polaris!*, where each minor program defeat or potential technological disaster seemingly was overcome by a dedicated (and brilliant, of course) young government scientist or a battle-toughened, experienced naval officer. When no way could be devised, for example, to test the Polaris gas compressor ejecting the rocket from its launch tube, an innovative engineer, bedecked in a white frock, suggested using sandbags of weight equal to the then-unavailable missile. It worked, naturally. Baar and Howard's dramatization is important because the favorable experience they described with the Polaris system led many Americans to view that program as not only typical but also perhaps as the standard by which other defense projects should be judged. Sapolsky's thesis and conclusions—that the Polaris system was remarkably cost-efficient and on the whole was a well-run program—were in an undoubtedly more scholarly treatment than *Polaris!*, yet it also supported this impression. Unfortunately, Polaris is inappropriate as a criterion for the Trident system.[4]

While those most directly involved with the Polaris system were a smaller, more cohesive, homogeneous group, their administration was less affected by turnover. Conversely, the Trident system has seen the inauguration of five presidents of the United States, four secretaries of defense installed, five chiefs of naval operations (CNOs) appointed, and five general managers of the Electric Boat shipyard—yet at no time has any single person been in complete control of the entire Trident program. Whereas Rear Admiral James D. Murry was acting (in 1981) as the Trident program director, the development of the nuclear reactors until recently remained within Rickover's jurisdiction, while the Bangor base falls under the command of Admiral James Williams, 1981 Commander, Naval Base, Seattle. Murray, as Trident System Project Manager, has "overall responsibility for the development and acquisition of the TRIDENT system," but several other key technical managers play various roles. Among those with influential posts outside the Trident project are Director—Strategic Systems Projects (of the Strategic Weapons System Division); Project Manager, TRIDENT Ship Acquisition Project (from Submarine Systems); Project Manager, Special Communications Project (External Communications); and Officer in Charge of Construction. The job of Chief of Naval Material is to coordinate and synthesize all the various activities of all the offices. Despite this pattern of managerial complexity, the Trident program has exhibited substantial direction through the activities of its advocates even though they have displayed less unity of voice than the Polaris group. In fact, the concentration of power in the Polaris project, especially in the hands of Rickover and William Rayborn, while indispensable to getting it off the ground, set precedents for the "Lone Ranger" activities of Rickover that often damaged the Trident program.[5]

Extraneous factors outside the navy's control have also contributed to the impression that the Trident is consistently over budget and behind schedule. The most significant of these factors, inflation, affected every aspect of each step in the construction process. Polaris development, for example, occurred at a period when annual inflation never exceeded 10 percent. Moreover, the Polaris development issued out of a widespread national concern over growing Soviet power in all areas: technology, science, ideology, and geographic expansionism. In this period Americans were inclined to be swayed by visions of the first Russian atomic explosion, the Sputnik launch, the Chinese revolutionary conversion, the Korean War, and of a shoe-banging Khrushchev promising to bury them. These incidents unmistakably compelled Americans to respond to the need for advanced military technology. In contrast, Americans of the Trident era, at least until the late 1970s, lived through a period of the military's unpopularity born out of the Vietnam War, manifested a paranoia of the Machiavellian "military-industrial complex," and attended countless lectures by scholars intellectualizing about vague (and imaginary) Soviet desires for peace. In addition, Polaris was a new system, whereas Trident ran into the "we already-have-one" syndrome. Because of these inverted influences, many of those who had supported the Polaris system in 1958 displayed apathy or outright opposition to the Trident in 1972. Although unmeasurable, these factors, in conjunction with inflation and overriding strategic considerations, created the milieu in which the Trident prototype appeared.

In 1966 Secretary of Defense Robert McNamara ordered a strategic study known as STRAT-X, (for strategic study, experimental). Based on a previous study done by the Institute of Defense Analysis earlier that year called PEN-X (for "penetration of enemy missiles, experimental"), the deliberately nebulous title was concocted to prevent bias in the study toward any land-, sea-, or air-based system. Positing the likelihood that the Russians would deploy extremely powerful and highly accurate ICBMs as well as an effective antiballistic-missile system in the 1970s, McNamara's study requested appropriate countermeasures. The STRAT-X study group was headed by General Maxwell Taylor. Although it included executives from several major defense contractors and independent corporations, the majority of the panel members were military men. Rear Admirals George H. Miller and Levering Smith, the Navy contingent on the STRAT-X panel, "representing both the [Naval Operations] staff and the 'hardware' side of the Navy" participated, but Naval Reactors Branch, which furnished the nuclear power plants for all nuclear-powered Navy vessels, did not.[6]

STRAT-X investigated and reviewed over 125 different missile-basing systems for the purpose of finding the most efficient and survivable option, the only prerequisite being that the candidate system had to be unique in comparison with previous or existing platforms. Going into the study, the Air Force had lobbied for a replacement for the

Minuteman ICBM, and it appeared initially as though the Air Force missile might be chosen, but the requirement for new ideas worked in the Navy's favor. Barred from submitting an improved Poseidon, it proposed a different submarine concept called ULMS (Underwater Long-range Missile System). After examining these and other alternatives that ranged from the sublime to the ridiculous, such as missile-firing submersibles, ICBMs carried on trucks, surface ships or barges, new bombers, seabed platforms (perhaps located in Hudson Bay) with fixed SLBMs, and submarines stationed in the Great Lakes, the STRAT-X panel concluded in 1968 that the Navy's ULMS represented the least costly and most survivable alternative. Miller claimed the panel envisioned a "rather austere" ship with little speed and, consequently, a small nuclear power plant.

Norman Polmar and Thomas Allen, in their biography of Rickover, support the view that "ULMS was to incorporate very-long-range missiles into submarines of rather conservative design, based on existing submarine technology. . . . The proposed submarine would not necessarily be deep-diving . . . and would carry more than sixteen missiles." According to Polmar and Allen, at least one ULMS proposal featured missiles carried horizontally outside the submarine's hull, a concept that "died rapidly as a result of arguments . . . that a shorter-range missile . . . could be developed more rapidly and be fitted into the existing Polaris–Poseidon submarines." In fact, the external-missile concept had reached the rigor-mortis stage long before. Moreover, as will be discussed in Chapter 10, carrying missiles externally creates a host of serious problems, not the least of which is the chance of minor collisions erupting into full-blown disasters (there have been at least fourteen *reported* collisions involving nuclear submarines since 1962, five of which involved ballistic-missile submarines). Nevertheless, the "austere" ship design supposedly specified a 440-foot-long submarine displacing 8200 tons submerged, "about the size of a later Polaris–Poseidon submarine but with more and longer-range missiles." It is important to differentiate between the STRAT-X panel's assignment—to investigate radical new missile platforms—and the Navy's job, which was to flesh out the concept after it was accepted. Even though the Navy proposed the idea, its designers probably never intended to cram 50 percent more missiles, fire controls, and accessories into a hull "about the size of a Polaris–Poseidon." The addition of the missiles alone would have extended the sub by nearly 20 feet, and even the missile concept lacked clarity at the time. Since the D-5 (Trident II) missile appeared as a concept in 1972, and since the STRAT-X panel "urged a *brand new, 6,000-mile missile*" (italics added), it must be assumed the Navy planned for such a substantially larger missile when examining design possibilities in 1970 and 1971.[7]

Complicating the planning process, Vice Admiral Hyman Rickover, through his position in the Naval Reactors Branch, had control over the size and type of the nuclear power plant to propel the submarine. Although the sub itself would be designed separately by Navy Strategic Systems, an office in Naval Material (PMS-396), and the missile by Navy Strategic Systems, under the direction of Levering Smith, the power plant used would be one of the most important factors that determined the final design. Indeed, Polmar and Allen place the blame for the Trident's size on Rickover, for his insistance in the early design stages that the ULMS have the S8G reactor capable of developing at least 60,000 horsepower. Because Rickover held both a civilian position in the Atomic Energy Commission on the one hand and on the other the Navy position of Assistant Chief of Nuclear Propulsion in the Navy Bureau of Ships, Admiral Elmo Zumwalt, who became Chief of Naval Operations in July 1970, felt it necessary to gain Rickover's support for the ULMS. Whether Zumwalt actually opposed the reactor size suggested by Rickover, as Polmar and Allen imply, remains unproved. What Zumwalt did consider was that the reactor might increase the sub's cost, thereby taking money from other shipbuilding programs. When Zumwalt told *The Washington Post* that "it was a very close choice," he referred to the choice of more surface ships or an effective ballistic-missile submarine. He needed Rickover's support "because you couldn't get Congressional support without it." It was "clear that we badly needed to get the Trident missile to sea. The only way we could do it was buy Adm. Rickover's reactors. . . . I considered the Russians a bigger problem than Rickover."[8]

Few elements of the ULMS development caused as much controversy as the size of the submarine. The question remains: Did Rickover determine the vessel's size with his demand for the S8G reactor? Only insofar as he calculated the size of the reactor necessary to propel such a displacement as could carry twenty-four D-5 missiles. Certainly not in terms of hull diameter. Even early designs for 6000-mile missiles (later known as the D-5, or Trident II) recognized that such a missile would approach 60 tons in weight and 42 feet in length by 7 feet in diameter. Therefore, consideration of the possible deployment of the longer-range missile accounted for a minimum of 28 feet of additional length, allowing for no space between missile tubes. Admiral Issac Kidd, Jr., former Chief of Navy Material, summarized the situation: "The missile sized the submarine." If so, the Navy's decision proved fortuitous in light of studies conducted in 1977 that found a hull diameter of approximately 40 to 42 feet projects the least detectable sonar image of all reasonable submarine hull diameters.[9]

The reactor concept, like the submarine concept, reflected Rickover's concerns with many performance factors other than speed. He saw an opportunity to make the submarine quieter by using a larger power plant running at a lower level of strain, since the speed level, not the reactor size, produces the noise. In short, the ULMS concept, ill-defined at the outset, simply met STRAT-X guidelines of providing for a new missile platform. Defensive capabilities, quietness, and expanded crew comfort for its longer patrols all were added along the way and were not part of the STRAT-X directives, nor were they intended to be. Rickover may have forced a reactor on the Navy, but he did not force upon the Navy a submarine with all the capabilities of an undersea fighting ship. Virtually *all* design options were concerned with mating the missile, rather than the reactor, to the hull.

Early Funding of ULMS

During this period of design uncertainty, funding for missile development and other submarine blueprint work came from the general Navy research and development (R&D) appropriations, which totaled $21.1 million in FY 1968 and $24 million in FY 1969.* These R&D outlays occurred during a five-year drop in R&D relative to procurement appropriations (see fig. 3-1). Half the Navy's 1968 R&D money went for ship and missile research, and out of this ULMS received $0.6 million in 1968 and $5.9 million in 1969, a modest start for what subsequently became a prodigious program. However, another $110 million went to ULMS research under the Atomic Energy Commission budget line, for reactor R&D.[10]

While research steadily proceeded, there was little urgency about ULMS until February 1, 1968, when Admiral Thomas R. Moorer, then Chief of Naval Operations, issued an Advanced Development Objective emblazoned with a 1-A importance classification. Shortly thereafter, in May, the Department of Defense (DoD) formally recommended a program to develop a replacement for the Polaris and received $5 million to initiate a study covering the general system requirements. On October 4, 1969, the CNO established the ULMS to help centralize the project. ULMS fell under the domain of the Special Projects Office (SPO), which had pushed the Polaris through. Levering Smith had headed Special Projects since 1965. The office, created

*The dollar amounts are given as that year's dollars for the year of the official statement—e.g., $21 million is given in 1968 dollars. This will be the procedure followed throughout unless otherwise specified.

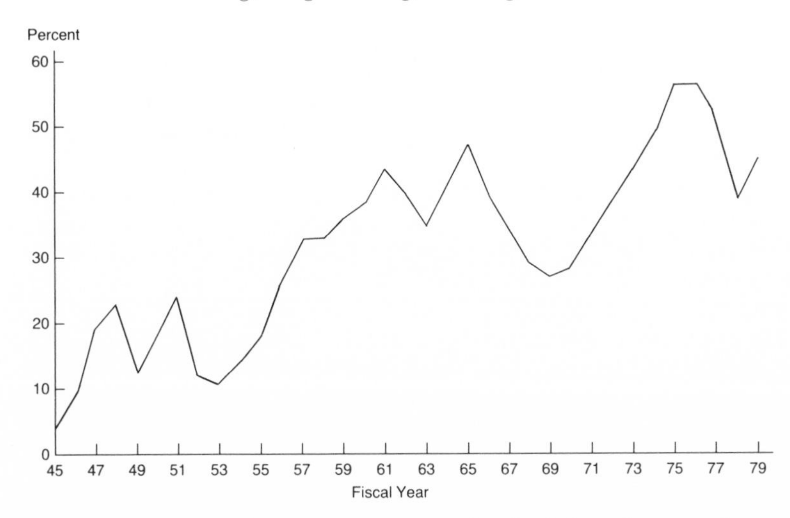

Fig. 3-1. Ratio of R&D outlays to procurement outlays for defense (in terms of constant 1976 dollars). Source: Gansler, *Defense Industry*, p. 102.

in 1955 to centralize management of the fleet ballistic missile system, was designed expressly to handle radical new projects. Hence attack submarines such as the *Los Angeles* class that were built later, which did not represent radical new systems, did not have a project office or fall under SPO. Placing ULMS under Special Projects gave it several advantages already available, thanks to the Polaris programs. First, it gained organizational autonomy "to obtain the resources and authority to control independently the design, construction, and maintenance" of the proposed force. Pursuing the dual purpose of keeping a broad base of support, inside and outside the Navy, and seeking "to prevent the rest of the Navy and the rest of the government from interfering," the ULMS again followed in the footsteps of Polaris. But there were important differences, even though Special Projects was in charge of both. Unlike Polaris, which Sapolsky showed "was always operated on a wartime basis,"ULMS was not. And where the Polaris program managed to co-opt or absorb administrative positions into its organization that could have posed threats to the stability of leadership in the program, ULMS—especially where Rickover was concerned—was not quite as successful.[11]

By 1970, ULMS also began to attract attention from liberal lobbies supporting it as an opportunity to force the abandonment of several other systems, including the B-1 bomber and the hotly debated anti-ballistic missile (ABM) system. A report submitted by the Members of Congress for Peace through Law (MCPL) recommended continued work on the ULMS, calling the ULMS "the epitome of the blue-water option at a time when the probable obsolescence of fixed-base [silos] has become clear." It concluded that "ULMS is cost effective" when viewed as a successor to land-based missiles. Then, to demonstrate its commitment to arms reduction, the MCPL called for overall defense cuts of $5 billion. Another organization dedicated to defense cuts, the National Urban Coalition, proposed in its 1970 *Counterbudget* reductions overall cuts in defense spending but expanded funding for ULMS. It was the MCPL support, however, that gave ULMS the "kiss of life."[12]

Moorer's development objective had already received funds. From fiscal 1969 to 1972 Congress appropriated $165 million for ULMS research, not including the previously authorized $6.5 million received. Significantly, other research objectives such as sonar and torpedo improvements received separate funding, considerably more than $165 million actually found its way into research associated with components used in, or with, the ULMS during that period. For example, the AEC absorbed the specific costs of developing the ULMS reactor ($1.9 million in 1971), although some initial start-up funds were earlier provided in the $110 million allocated the AEC in 1968 and in sums thereafter. In the same fiscal year ULMS received $.6 million for R&D and another $5.9 million in 1969. Throughout 1970 the ULMS staff prepared a development-concept paper to present to the Armed Services Committees of both houses of Congress. During the paper preparation lull, Congress' interest waned and ULMS funding was cut from $20 million to $10 million, with the surviving $10 million going into hull design research and new missile studies in 1970. Responding to the cut, Senator Russell Schweiker chided the Senate Armed Services Committee for lacking "a sense of priority" in its failure to maintain ULMS funding. Consequently, the program received $43.7 million in fiscal year 1971 for R&D, and from January to June of 1971 Moorer's group requested funding of $111.3 million for FY 1972, receiving instead $104.8 million.[13]

By 1971 the Pentagon had to decide on the missile and its contractor. The STRAT-X panel had recommended a large new missile with a range of 6000 miles, a feature that contributed heavily to the size of the proposed ULMS sub. Secretary of Defense Melvin Laird and his deputy David Packard realized a transition missile, capable of fitting into existing Polaris/Poseidon subs, was needed instead. Although retrofitting might delay actual deployment of the ULMS submarines, they ordered the transition missile, the C-4 (later called the Trident I), from Lockheed Missile and Space, the Navy's exclusive missile supplier. Some observers felt that Lockheed, struggling financially at the time, had thus received a huge noncompetitive award, but, looked at from another viewpoint, the secretary acted in a cost-effective manner in the sense that his decision extended the life of the *Lafayette* group of Poseidon subs in a substantial and timely way.

Although his decision did not interrupt research and development on the longer-range missile, two cost disadvantages accompanied the decision, offsetting whatever competitive gains might have been realized by opening the bidding to companies other than Lockheed. First, by postponing production of the longer missile, inflation would relentlessly take its toll. Second, by having a smaller transition missile, a certain minor specific cost of installing cradles in the larger missile tubes in the ULMS would accrue. In the circumstances of the day, Laird apparently felt the technology in place at Lockheed would allow it to funnel both missiles into production sooner than if a different company were introduced into the weapons-acquisition process. All missile-size studies were officially completed that spring, but Lockheed had actually bluffed about the availability of the missile, acting on an optimistic assumption about the progress of its missile division. Ironically, the company nevertheless beat its deadline and, since the missile was delivered on time, Lockheed did not have to atone for its earlier miscalculation. Meanwhile, with missile-studies data completed, the ULMS group presented its concept paper to Secretary of Defense Melvin Laird, who ordered the practical development of the ULMS to proceed in that summer. Consequently, in July an additional $20 million was released for continued ULMS work.[14]

During the pivotal year of 1971, five basic ULMS options were considered, refined, and developed, in anticipation of a September decision on subsystem elaborations. Although Elmo Zumwalt, who was then CNO, and Rickover had disagreed as to the design of the ULMS, concern about the SALT Interim agreement (soon to expire) led Zumwalt to abandon his opposition and present with him a united front to the nation's lawmakers. Five basic options appeared feasible as a starting point to present the program, but they would first be tested on the Department of Defense, for Laird would have to be firmly supportive of the project before Congress.

Option number one—do nothing, cancel the program—was hardly taken seriously but was included in deference to congressional sensitivities. Time still remained to scrap the program totally without excessive research losses. As it turned out, the ULMS had support in both houses and needed only the proper presentation to win approval. More important, ULMS had Rickover's support, something an alternative program might lack.[15]

The second option was an extended-range Poseidon, continuing concurrently with ULMS submarine research. This, however, was unattractive. The aging Polaris force had undergone an extensive facelift by having many vessels refitted with Poseidon C-3 missiles beginning in 1967 (again, see fig. 2-4). Besides, as tests would show, new propulsion units needed to increase the missile range from the C-3 to the C-4 would preclude their use in the Polaris boats because of tube- and hull-diameter restrictions, the C-4 being 20 inches wider in diameter. Another disadvantage to refitting the Poseidons was cost: the forty-first Poseidon refit cost $100 million and the price would soon escalate even higher. Given the additional increasing maintenance costs, a ULMS would soon prove more cost-effective than a refitted Poseidon.

A third option consisted of adopting only the ULMS submarine as a follow-on program to the Polaris/Poseidon submarines. Once again, however, there were disadvantages. The ULMS with missile was projected to be deployed only one year later than the Poseidon/ULMS missile duo.

Option four combined the ULMS and an extended-range Poseidon. This still carried the disadvantage of the Poseidon sub's age. The final option involved deploying the extended-range Poseidon, followed by the ULMS in the distant future. Again, the age deficiencies were present.

As the Department of Defense neared a decision for the budget by the middle of September, it leaned toward the third option. However, no matter which option DoD chose, accelerated production rates could not deliver any submarine in time to replace the Polaris boats going off line in the late 1970s. No one liked the idea of tinkering with a hull design—especially in submarines—but perhaps a slight modification in the Poseidon rocket tubes could accommodate a missile with some extended range and greater payload. By refitting the ULMS missile in the older submarines, the Navy could provide an adequate deterrent during the crucial period in the late 1970s and early 1980s when the earliest of the Polaris subs would meet retirement for reasons of inadequately ranged missiles, increased operational vulnerability to Soviet ASW, reactor fuel depletion, and expiring hull life. Such an option was formulated as Development Concept Paper 3b 10c, which meant that the missile could be developed first and installed in the Poseidon subs before the ULMS sub was finished. Although no official announcement heralded the occasion, this was the option chosen by Laird and Packard. On October 28 an additional $81.3 million was released out of FY 1972 funds for option 3b, as it was called, including long-range materials purchases for the ULMS-1 (today known as the *Ohio*). An urgent request to accelerate the program by two years accompanied the releasing of the funds.[16]

Prior to the final DoD decision, Laird had also advised the naval group presenting the concept paper to commence engine development of the ULMS missile with a target deployment date of 1977. Unaware of Lockheed's earlier overoptimistic projection, Congress targeted 50 percent of the FY 1972 ULMS funding for missile development. Missile-propulsion projects drew the lion's share of the funds, since they represented the "greatest challenge to the ULMS-1 missile," according to Admiral Levering Smith, whom the Navy had charged with early research and development.[17]

During the development period, Smith played an important role in the entire missile and hull selection. Exactly how much influence he had over either, however, remains a matter of considerable conjecture. Polmar and Allen see Smith's office as "primarily responsible for the [ULMS] having twenty-four missiles" and report some participants in the ULMS program thought the delays that plagued the submarine's construction in the late 1970s "could be traced to the fact that Rickover and Levering Smith had 'captured' the [ULMS]." Partly due to the pressure of awarding a design contract by August 1972, generated by Zumwalt's and Laird's concern for the expiration of the interim arms treaty, "delays" that would appear in the future were already built in. No one party is really responsible for any form of delay except that excessive speed without a finished design eventually creates some increased costs. Nevertheless, from his position as head of the Special Projects Office Smith had control of much of the initial research, and, if the ULMS had a single father, Smith was he, and might therefore be considered the "Red" Rayborn of the Trident program.[18]

By November 1971 the ULMS group had completed its own study of subsystem design options for the secretary and the Office of the Secretary of Defense, based on deterrence needs and maintenance and rennovation costs. The ULMS group concluded the ULMS was the "only attractive option" for the Navy to pursue, and it could put the Navy in the pivotal position of being the nation's prime deterrent force. Had the Secretary given an unfavorable response, it would have meant the Navy would have to find a way to extend the life of the entire Polaris/Poseidon fleet while watching the Air Force push its new programs for updated and new ICBMs and bombers. But Navy anxiety proved groundless. Increased Soviet arms buildups, continued negotiations involving antiballistic missile limitations, and the financial drain caused by the Vietnam war all pointed to the adoption of a cost-effective system, which ULMS seemed to be. Moreover, the Navy continuously suggested that accelerating the program would not cause undue difficulties. The Navy hoped to press ahead on the platform while continuing to develop its final design, conscious of making practical progress without making haste. Funding orders came on December 23, 1971, when Secretary Laird issued Progress Budget Decision 317, opening up the previously mentioned $104.8 million for ULMS construction to be available in FY 1972. Laird not only approved the program, he also urged the Navy to accelerate it and to complete the rest of the system for deployment in 1978. For this purpose he requested $942 million from Congress, some of it targeted to start production. As Admiral Robert Kaufman happily reported, the ULMS had "brickbat priority," a term developed in the 1950s meaning that, by personal presidential order, the effort had first claim on all scarce materials.[19]

The very fact that no final design existed underscored the STRAT-X purpose: to investigate and recommend launch-platform alternatives only. Thus, new planning problems arose immediately. No one in the STRAT-X group had been instructed to analyze all of the eventualities involved in mating a new missile to a new submarine (as demanded by the study's guidelines), nor had anyone been ordered to consider the advantages presented by increasing the size of the sub. Instead, since the Navy was given the job of transforming a platform concept into an actual weapons system, through the programming process, some of the advantages, including technological breakthroughs, became apparent only after the hull size had been established.

As ULMS finally moved toward actual production it began to gather opposition. Just after the January 4, 1972, announcement of Progress Budget Decision 324, which allocated an additional $35 million from FY 1972 funds to ULMS, Senator William Proxmire challenged the rate of development. In a letter to Hyman Rickover, Proxmire asked "Why are we rushing into ULMS at such a fast pace[?]" Referring to the Navy's policy of testing a weapon, or at least a prototype, before purchase, Proxmire wondered "Where is the 'fly before you buy'?" He predicted the ULMS ultimately would cost $30 billion and warned the Navy and Congress were "moving toward another procurement disaster." Admiral Harvey Lyon defended the acceleration: "If we waited another 5 years . . . [of course] we could have better technology in certain areas." But, he continued, fifteen years worth of previous technology was available at that moment for ULMS. Proxmire's criticisms, although the first of many, had little impact in 1972. In a letter from the Senate Armed Services Committee on February 25, 1972, the committee approved Laird's acceleration of the Trident program to "permit deployment of the first ULMS submarine in 1978, at least 2–3 years earlier than would have been the case in the regular program," in attempting to meet the "continuing Soviet strategic offensive force buildup."[20]

In recommending a construction rate of 1–3–3–3, Laird cited four reasons for requesting $942 million for the program in 1972. First, since ULMS was already underway as a major development program, it did not "involve disruption of ongoing programs which already have high priority, such as Poseidon conversions and constructions of nuclear attack submarines." Second, ULMS offered "the best technical program currently available to provide future sea-based strategic force capability." It made the greatest use of new propulsion quieting technology and was "capable of carrying a larger ballistic missile [that] provides flexibility for increased range . . . or alternatively a capability to carry . . . advanced penetration payloads at less range." Third, Laird argued, deployment of ULMS, with a capability to carry a larger number of missiles, meant "a given nuclear payload [may be] deployed with fewer boats and crews." Finally, the ULMS missile development program would provide the option to retrofit the shorter-range ULMS I missile into Poseidon submarines.

At another hearing, Admirals Rickover, Smith, and Lyon said the decision to accelerate was not based on "any single additional or recent threat but on an assessment . . . of analysis" of Soviet strategic improvements overall. Actually, Laird's budget represented a $3.2 million cut from the original Navy request of $945.2 million, but the admirals warned, even with acceleration, "we could not have the ULMS at sea in any significant numbers until 1980." Even so, the proposed 1–3–3–3 rate would deliver more capability, in both survivability and numbers of warheads, than it would replace.[21]

Following Laird's testimony, the Senate Armed Services Committee approved the acceleration of the Trident program on February 25, 1972, to "permit deployment of the first ULMS submarine in 1978, at least 2–3 years earlier than would have been the case in the regular program," in attempting to meet the "continuing Soviet strategic offensive buildup." Although Congress believed it was radically accelerating the pace of ULMS construction, even the official Navy spokesmen could hardly know how overly optimistic its proposed building rate really was.[22]

An initial Senate vote in April 1972 rejected the $942 million when it was learned the Navy had not completed the design studies. While the Senate was voting, negotiators representing the United States and the USSR hammered out a Strategic Arms Limitation Treaty, known as SALT I. President Richard Nixon signed the SALT treaty in May 1972, but, in order to obtain ratification of the treaty, Nixon and the treaty's chief architect, Henry Kissinger, found it necessary to gain the support of the Joint Chiefs of Staff. Admiral Thomas H. Moorer, chairman of the Joint Chiefs, balked at the idea of supporting the treaty for many reasons, including the fact that the treaty counted all B-52 bombers—even those consigned to the Davis–Monthan scrapyard—while not counting the Backfire bomber or Russian MRBMs. He reluctantly agreed only after receiving assurances from both Congress and the White House that a strategic modernization package would receive funding. Among the specific bargaining chips Moorer demanded were the B-1 bomber, the MX missile, and funding for an accelerated ULMS program. The Nixon administration, while complying with the ULMS portion of the Moorer deal, gave the other elements of modernization only minimal support. In the case of ULMS, the administration resubmitted its 1972 request, slightly trimmed to $903 million, but Congress raised the figure back to the original $942 million. Most of the $942 million went toward adapting the Polaris/Poseidon submarines to the C-4 (later called the Trident I) missile, per Laird's 1971 decision. Only $110 million actually was specified for the new submarine, with about $803 million going toward the conversion program and some $30 million allocated to missile development and related items. The Navy's ULMS study proposed the C-4 missile be "compatible with Poseidon SSBNs" and have a new guidance system and advanced "penetration ability," combined with a range of about 4000 n.m., compared to the Poseidon missile's 2500-n.m. range. Lockheed received the new missile contracts, based on the company's rosy projections of its previous experience with both the Polaris and the Poseidon missiles. The reentry body of the C-4 greatly resembled its prototype, an extended Poseidon C-3, except "souped up with a third stage rocket." Other contractors involved in the rocket production included AEC (Sandia), which was to supply the reentry body design, while Raytheon and MIT/Draper handled guidance development. Research and development under standing contracts from 1971 continued, including a launcher development contract with Westinghouse, fire control development contracts with General Electric, and missile-fire control studies with a host of companies: Challenger Research, Kamen Nuclear, and Sperry. According to Admiral Elmo Zumwalt, missile development during 1972 proceeded to an "urgent basis."[22]

Funding not devoted to missile support was immediately siphoned off into hull design, quieting studies, sonar improvements, and propulsion (although, as has been pointed out, there is no way of tracing the Atomic Energy Commission funds actually diverted to ULMS reactor research). Among the contractors and government laboratories involved in development of the early ULMS subsystems, Bolt, Beramek & Newman worked on acoustics and sonar, as did Hamilton Standard, Honeywell, IBM, MPL, NURDC, Tetra Tech, and Washington Associates. Research in hull structure was contracted to Ehrenpreis, Pearl Harbor, and Portsmouth NSY. All these contractors were on the payroll for ULMS as of FY 1973, as were dozens of materials development concerns, integrated-circuit designers, support facility construction companies, electric plant designers, and a host of training, research and analysis, and other general subsystem firms. Advance procurement funds had purchased the steel, engine room parts, construction spares, and other subsystems. Nevertheless, no part of boat construction actually had started prior to 1972.

Several technical objectives had been established for the FY 1972 funding. Among these, selection of a propellant system, establishment of a missile staging ratio, and definition of the missile system all drew on the missile allocations. A follow-up to the transition missile, the D-5 missile (Trident II) was also in the early stages of research. Part of the early controversy about the sub—that is, designing the submarine to include the option of the D-5 missile—led to new design considerations. While the D-5 would have a range of 6000 n.m., its substantially larger diameter and greater weight mandated a submarine design of imposing proportions. Consequently, the rough-draft ULMS boat design revealed a submarine of 18,000 tons displacement and a length 25 percent greater than the length of the Polaris/Poseidon boats. To make efficient use of the hull/reactor combination the Navy, through a series of tests, settled on a magazine numbering twenty-four missiles. This number worried some senators, as they hoped a reduction in the number of missiles carried might also act to bring down costs. Admiral George Miller accused the Navy and the Department of Defense of selecting an "arbitrary" number of twenty-four "just to make the expensive sub look more cost effective." One report noted senators were "angered" by the Pentagon's tactic of withholding key data about the flexibility of the number of missiles. The Navy, claims the report, used a "supremely opportune moment" to reassure Senator Henry Jackson of Washington, a key defense committee member and an important figure in the ratification of the SALT I treaty, that the number of tubes could be reduced as late as the fall of 1973.[23]

The submarine's size had in fact already been partly determined by the size of the long-range missile, as well as by a number of other considerations. Given the size of the vessel, studies showed twenty-four was the optimum number of missiles to achieve cost effectiveness from the hull. Determination of the size of the missile magazine was not "arbitrary" but rather faced the basic fact that the long-range missile was to be bigger than the Poseidon missile, and, if it were to be carried vertically, a bigger hull would be needed. Some suggested carrying the missiles at an angle; however, such a posture would not only pose launching complications but would also extend the length of the boat due to the combination of the triangular dead space at the base of the first missile set and over the back of the last set. Consequently, when all factors are examined in context, blaming Rickover's reactor for the boat's size and blaming the boat's size for the need to carry more missiles to "look more cost effective" are convenient but flawed arguments, which can become self-fulfilling. Furthermore, why should the Navy *not* strive for more cost effectiveness?

Debate over Size and Design

Early submarine designs spurred questions about the boat's size and vulnerability. With its twenty-four missiles, rather than the sixteen carried by a Polaris–Poseidon sub, concern over its survivability grew. The Navy conducted more than 120 parametric studies from 1970 to 1973, pitting the ULMS against then-current and future ASW threats. As the Department of Defense reported, the ULMS "provides the capability to adjust to any possible Soviet ASW breakthroughs." Nevertheless, opposition to ULMS continued to grow. In an article in *The Economist* Dr. Morton Halpern wrote: "There is at present no sign of any Soviet technological breakthrough in the direction of being able to find and destroy the Polaris/Poseidon [fleet]. . . . A new fleet designed to be immune to an unknown threat would probably be wrong for its purpose." Some designers went overboard trying to squeeze more cost-effectiveness out of the submarine by making it larger. One proposal suggested stretching it to hold even more missiles, but Rear Admiral Robert Kaufman dismissed further hull extension as technically impractical. Commenting to a Senate subcommittee, he said; "I think we would all be throwing up our hands if you told us to build a submarine with 50 to 100 missile tubes in it." Certain disadvantages of weight would accompany each added missile, with any number past twenty-four posing such great weight increases that the power plant would begin to lose effectiveness. Kaufman's comments highly suggest that Admiral Rickover was probably already working with fairly firm design expectations about missile magazine weight and corresponding total displacement when designing his reactor, if his power plant were to maintain its speed "effectiveness."[24]

Psychologically, the design of the submarine intimidated some observers, particularly those inclined toward disarmament. The C-4s were to be MIRVed—equipped with several independently targetable reentry vehicles (RVs) in each missile—and the thought of a Gargantua loose beneath the seas with twenty-four missiles, each containing several warheads, and in the worst case under the control of a maniacal Admiral Strangelove, seemed the antithesis of the good will present in the SALT and ABM talks. New Hampshire Democratic Senator Thomas McIntyre noted in March 1972 that the ULMS "promises to be one of the major and most controversial issues to be considered by the Congress," not because a follow-on to the Polaris was necessary but because of the size of the system and the fiscal commitments in 1973. Moreover, the hull size began to elicit questions about the potential speed and quietness of the submarine. The Navy countered these arguments by producing the conclusions of the 1971 missile studies, all of which supported the trade-off of hull diameter for extended missile range. Consequently the ULMS FY 1973 goals included development of "detailed acoustic quieting designs and criteria for ship and hull substructure designs," complete development of "improved submarine structural design analysis procedures," and initial detailed designs of the sub. In short, the Navy planned to overcome the additional size by making the sub quieter, less "visible" on sonar, and faster.[25]

Considerable disagreement still exists over Rickover's claim to make the vessel "very quiet so as to make the ship difficult to detect" while simultaneously maintaining "a high speed capability." Norman Polmar and Thomas Allen call this a "tragic flaw" in Rickover's logic. "At slow speeds," they note, "a submarine can be quiet. . . . But as speed increases, the submarine gets noisier." Although admitting noise-abatement equipment on the internal machinery can quiet much of the noise, Polmar and Allen contend that at "high speeds there is also noise generated by the submarine's propeller turning and the movement of the submarine through the water." Any speed gained for the purpose of evasion results in offsetting noise generation, they argue. In the case of the ULMS, the Navy attended to these criticisms as it designed the boat. By incorporating the single screw mounted on a shaft exiting at the apex of the teardrop design, a concept standard in all U.S. Navy subs since the *Skate* (the dual-engined *Triton* was the sole exception), the ULMS sub gained the various quieting *and* speed advantages described in chapter 2. Careful attention was paid to reducing noise outside the hull caused by the sub's movement through the water, including increased efforts at keeping the hull "clean" of free-flowing limber ports and free of exterior mountings, hawse-holes, blemishes, deck railings, or protrusions of any sort that might generate water turbulence. But the greatest gains were planned to deal with dampening airborne interior noise, where the Navy R&D experts incorporated two sets of quieting systems. Each system serves a different function: one quiets the sub at slow speeds, and at high speeds a second system takes over. The ULMS was designed to make relatively little more noise at high speeds than at low. Yet another factor justified a larger sub. Numerous defensive weapons and evasive devices were installed, a feature impossible on a smaller sub. Rickover probably foresaw these additions. If not, his idiosyncratic demands nevertheless certainly fit the needs of the later design like a glove, making him lucky rather than insightful.[26]

Refitting older subs with the newer missiles brought little opposition, but creation of a new and bigger submarine resulted in a stern test for the ULMS during the FY 1973 vote taken in 1972. The Navy asked for research, development, testing, and evaluation (RDT&E) funds of $520.4 million, military construction money for the shipyards of $27.3 million, training funds of $23.5 million, $13 million in weapons system appropriations, and funds for lead-time submarine items of $361 million. After Laird trimmed $3.2 million the Department of Defense presented the $977 million package to Congress, which represented accelerated funds of $508.4 million—including the $35 million advanced in 1972, which needed to be covered. In the Senate, the Armed Services Ad Hoc Research and Development Subcommittee voted to drop the $508.4 million of accelerated funds, in essence returning the ULMS to its original schedule. Apparently, when Secretary Laird's acceleration order of December 23, 1971, finally manifested itself in the budget, many of the early ULMS supporters abandoned ship. When the full Armed Services Committee voted on cutting these accelerated funds, a cliffhanging eight-to-eight tie ensued, broken by the chairman, John Stennis of Mississippi, in favor of keeping the accelerated production funds. Stennis acted after receiving a telephone call from President Richard Nixon at the eleventh hour. Undaunted by the full committee vote, Senator Lloyd Bentsen (Democrat of Texas), a member of the ad hoc committee concerned over cost increases caused by the absence of a completed design, launched an attack on the floor to get the full Senate to restore the cuts. Arguing that the tie vote amounted to a "hung jury," Bentsen found the lack of typical and traditional enthusiastic support among the members of the Armed Services Committee "a little unusual." The committee, he believed, had "serious misgivings, as reflected by the 8–8 vote." A rollcall vote on July 27, 1972, produced a 47–39 rejection of Bentsen's cuts, but only after a long debate. However, only $852.9 million actually was appropriated in FY 1973, representing an actual cut of $124 million from Laird's original request effectively for $977.1 million. This in turn represented a cut of $127.2 from the Navy's original request.* Bentsen denied accusations that he obstructed ULMS funding. "I am not opposed to the [ULMS]," he maintained, "but I do not believe that it is either good planning, good sense or good economics to rush into the system with so many questions unanswered." Since the design contract was still being negotiated as of July 1972, Bentsen's point was valid. Concerns over costs remained.[27]

Liberals who had supported the earlier funding had abandoned ULMS by mid-1972. Most voted in favor of the Bentsen cuts. In a 180-degree reversal of their earlier proposals, both the MCPL and *Counterbudget* groups recommended rejection of the ULMS program. One MCPL report urged cuts of all but $330 million in research money and suggested those funds be used to accommodate the C-4 missile to the Poseidon subs. Only $50 million was recommended for continued research on the submarine component. Dr. Herbert Scoville, Jr., representing the Federation of American Scientists, contended there was "absolutely no requirement to replace [Polaris/Poseidon] by a new system." The ULMS, he argued, was "dangerously premature . . . also strategically unnecessary and wasteful. [It was] being justified on political grounds. . . ." He and others questioned the Defense Department's warnings about advances in Soviet ASW. Therefore, the ULMS, he concluded, "is a solution in search of a problem." Viewpoints of this type not only allow for little elasticity in program response to future threats but also ignore the fact that a hiatus in SSBN design and construction had already been entered, and if the ULMS building began immediately in 1972, SSBN force levels would still drop vis-à-vis the retiring of the oldest Polaris boats. This line of thinking, as Admiral Issac Kidd warns, ensures "block obsolescence."[28]

Others who criticized the program feared a new submarine would fuel the arms race. Senator William B. Saxbe of Ohio contended that "accelerating the [ULMS] submarine could prove a negative factor in

***The FY 1973 funding is as follows** (*in millions*):

Navy original request, including $35 million advanced in 1972	$980.3
Laird reduction	– 3.2
Laird request	$977.1
Attempted Senate cut	– 508.4
	$468.7
Restored by full Senate	+ 508.4
	$977.1
Final cut by Congress	– 124.2
Final FY 1973 funding	$852.9

the development of our new-found relations with Russia." Senator Edward Kennedy added "I believe that going forward with an advanced weapons system at a stepped-up pace clearly flouts the spirit of the SALT accord and threatens the . . . success of subsequent SALT discussions. . . ." Kennedy viewed the ULMS as an "ante in the middle of the table." William Proxmire, representing the MCPL, placed in the *Congressional Record* further critical testimony showing a purported U.S. advantage in submarine firepower and survivability, while another MCPL posture statement concluded "an accelerated new submarine construction program now could jeopardize SALT negotiations."[29]

Additional arguments held that the Soviet ASW capability could not possibly threaten the American ballistic-missile submarine force. The MPCL report of April 10, 1972, warned "There is a danger . . . that any new submarines we build today could be rendered obsolete in much the same way as the submarines we now have." George W. Rathjens of MIT argued that the Soviets could not possibly destroy the whole submarine missile force, and "thus, commitment to production of [ULMS] at this time is grossly premature." Senator J. W. Fulbright added that one Poseidon submarine could destroy 160 Soviet cities and that the Soviets were far behind in ASW. Rickover testified to the contrary earlier, but he said his testimony had received "derision" by the "pseudo-intellectuals in Congress." Yet the opposition line of arguments contradicted the very evidence other opponents had used against the submarine's proposed size, namely that Soviet advances in ASW would threaten the ULMS![30]

Finally, other (possibly the most effective) arguments were posed by Stuart Symington, Jack Ruina, and Rathjens, who attacked the projected cost of the ULMS. The submarine, according to Rathjens and Ruina, "will cost so much that research for other weapons programs will be slighted. . . . One cannot help but suspect that a factor in the decision to postpone the development of the C-4 [missile] for a year might have been concern that the early availability of the new missile would have undercut the case of a new submarine." Rathjens also compared the submarine to the canceled B-70 bomber: "If we jump the gun and commit ourselves to a new vehicle with no clear idea of what the threat may be, we could have a fleet of underwater B-70s . . . on our hands—at over a billion dollars a copy." Proposing a solution that reverberated in the halls of Congress for the following eight years, Ruina suggested, if a new sub is needed, "go in the opposite direction" from the ULMS with smaller subs purchased in greater numbers. Rickover's standard and effective response to this argument consisted of an offer to build a fleet of wooden sailing ships, which, he sarcastically jabbed, would allow the United States to greatly outnumber the enemy! Symington reiterated Proxmire's argument that adoption of the ULMS violated the fly-before-buy concept. "Fly before buy," a favorite catch phrase of so-called defense reformers (defense-budget "trimmers"), is a completely inappropriate procurement method for capital ships and strategic submarines in most cases. Yet this viewpoint has lingered for years, as if ULMS opponents actually intended to build a prototype SSBN and test-drive it as casually as one does a new car before submitting their block order. In fact, the Navy has never built a radical prototype ballistic-missile submarine de novo, and to consider building one under the conditions of urgency facing the ballistic-missile submarine force in the 1970s would have been irresponsible.[31]

Vice Admiral Philip Beshany effectively refuted most of these arguments in a 1972 hearing. He pointed out that refitting older vessels can only go so far, with Poseidons having no room for new sonars or power plants. The older engines would only grow noisier, making the subs more vulnerable to detection, while their maintenance costs were growing so great in relative terms that operational cost alone dictated a replacement. Further, he argued, during "the peak of our SSBN building program we delivered 12 ships in a single year," but the industrial base had deteriorated since then. The Navy therefore hoped to avoid making any "block replacements" because the capacity of the shipbuilders might be unable to handle a surge of that nature. Viewed from the perspective of 1983, his remark has turned out to be highly prescient, since there is only one yard actually capable of producing the Trident. As to critics who saw the ULMS as a destabilizing influence on the "arms race," Beshany argued just the opposite: "It becomes so monstrous a system to counter, requiring so much effort on [the Soviets'] part, that it in fact becomes a stabilizing influence and they don't try to counter it." At least in terms of the appearance of the *Alpha* attack submarine in 1973 and the *Typhoon* SSBN in 1980, Beshany appears not so prescient; the USSR has embarked on nine new submarine construction programs in the last few years, excluding the aforementioned subs, completely without any shipbuilding "provocation" by the United States. This trend demonstrates that weapons programs are as frequently tailored for the fulfillment of uniquely defined national defense requirements as they are mirror images of an adversary's program, meaning that use of the term *arms races* often serves short-term partisan political interest.[32]

In May 1972 the Navy renamed the ULMS program. Originally, the "early edge in the Navy's namestakes" was for the name Perseus, after the Greek god with a helmet of invisibility who decapitated the serpenttressed Medusa. But the image of Perseus, as he is normally pictured holding Medusa's head aloft, repulsed many of the Navy's public relations experts. Further, abbreviated versions of the name—such as Percy—offended some Navy swashbucklers as too feminine even for ships. Consequently, the program kept with an aquatic, deity-related motif and adopted the name Trident (after the Greek god Poseidon's three-pronged spear). According to an official Navy publication, the name Trident is particularly "fitting" because the program was composed of three parts: submarine, missile, and base. The C-4 missile became the Trident I, and the planned D-5 was redesignated the Trident II missile.[33]

Not until 1976 did the first Trident submarine, the *Ohio*, receive its name. Naming the new sub after a state broke tradition, as the Navy previously had named ballistic-missile submarines only after famous Americans or patriotically *sympatico* foreign personalities. Early SSBNs thus bore the names *George Washington, Ethan Allen, Patrick Henry, Will Rogers*, and *Simón Bolívar*. Since ballistic-missile subs came to replace battleships as the Navy's capital ships, the Ford administration introduced the practice of naming the new Trident subs for states. To follow the *Ohio*, the Navy named the next Trident, the *Michigan*, after Ford's home state, and the third, the *Georgia*, after Carter's home state. As the construction progressed throughout the 1970s, the Navy was building submarines faster than the nation elected presidents, so two nonpolitical names followed: the *Florida* and the *Rhode Island*. Currently the Navy is bringing some of its battleships out of mothballs, so that an unlikely "name conflict" could occur at some future date if more than forty-six Tridents are ever built to compete with the names of the four battleships.[34]

Newly named and despite the criticism, the Trident program moved toward production with the contracts let out to subcontractors. Missile subcontractors covered the full range of electronics companies, small motors plants, metallurgical laboratories, and pyrotechnics specialists. Motorola, RCA, and T.I. worked on microelectronics devices, Rocketdyne prepared the small motors, Union Carbide made the nose caps, and Ensign-Bickford together with Exploration Technologies supplied pyrotechnics materials. For the submarine itself, all of the early subcontractors (as well as some new ones) commenced production. For example, National Forge began producing the main propulsion shafts, HY80 hull machinery components such as the dive plane and rudderstock forgings, and columns for mounting various secondary systems. Uncle Sam provided many large items under SARs (Selected Acquisition Requests), but since no specific budget outlays appear for these classified items, no budgetary figures include them. Hence a final absolute cost of a single item may be impossible to establish if it incorporates any part supplied by an SAR. Insofar as SARs shroud the entire military budget, the assumption that "it will all even out" does indeed eventually come to be fulfilled at the bottom line of the total defense budget (although government-supplied steel for a submarine would account for a far higher percentage of that item's total cost than material for, say, a jeep or a tent). Preservation of secrecy demands this technique, but it also provides a useful method of avoiding the publication of a much higher total unit cost for technologically intensive weapons systems. In other words, when a Navy witness tells an armed services committee that the total cost of X program is Y dollars—and he is telling the truth as far as he knows it—several million more may be buried in SARs. While some may find this technique evasive or devious, the fact is that Congress would have difficulty approving funds for any piece of equipment larger than, say, a machine gun if the entire cost were known. The process greatly resembles buying a new car. Although the sticker price explains what accessories come with the car, the customer soon learns that the whitewalls cost extra, the dealer adds taxes later, and the ever-present license fees are not included. To use a Trident-related example, the FY 1973 budget included a deleted amount of money to start construction on a land-based prototype of the ULMS nuclear reactor. This bill, however, went to the Atomic Energy Commission, which provides all reactor research, development, and prototypes, rather than to the Navy's Trident account. Specifically, Rickover, as chief of the Naval Reactors Branch of the AEC, handled the reactor's development, all under the AEC, not the Navy, budget. For the taxpayer, the result is the same, but the Navy can shelter a major cost in this manner.[35]

Similarly unnoticed in the fiscal year 1973 budget fights, small allocations appeared for military construction at Point Mugu, California. The Navy received $665,000 to begin construction of a small tracking base there. It was correctly not cited as officially being part of the Trident program, although it would later be regarded as a facility from which Trident missile tracking services were leased. Similarly, Cape Canaveral would come to support Trident work, although the public views it as an Air Force facility. Russell Warren Howe, however, in his book on weapons programs, reported over 465 workers at Cape Canaveral were "directly related" to the Trident program.[36]

Leased services from such facilities with mixed responsibilities complicate the determination of an absolutely reliable final cost figure for the Trident program, since a breakout of Trident-related costs is inherently impossible. To illustrate, how precisely can the man-hour costs be determined for the amount of time a missile-firing programmer at Point Mugu spends on scheduling Trident firings against the time he spends on scheduling other firings? Is he paid basically for being a firing programmer or is he paid for being a part-time Trident firing programmer?

The converse of the Point Mugu cost accounting problem was the construction of a submarine base at Bangor, from the outset avowedly an integral Trident facility. As such, it drew considerably more attention than the auxiliary facilities of Point Mugu and Cape Canaveral. On February 16, 1973, Secretary of the Navy John Warner announced plans to deploy the Trident in the Pacific, using as the home base an old torpedo station near Bangor, Washington. Some considered this a surprise choice; Senators Strom Thurmond and Ernest Hollings, both of South Carolina, had lobbied heavily for a base in their home state. Charleston, already the site of a large Polaris submarine base, seemed a natural site. Navy studies conducted of "virtually every potential site on both coasts, on the Gulf of Mexico, and even some places outside the continental U.S." concluded Bangor was the best location, however. Preparations commenced for filing an environmental impact statement; but, since the Bangor area was experiencing serious layoffs in the aerospace industry, the Navy anticipated little local opposition. Navy estimates revealed the new base would provide permanent employment for 3000 military and 3000 civilian personnel, earning estimated gross salaries of $7.5 million a month. Critics of the site selection charged Senator Henry Jackson of Washington, later reported as "stridently" in favor of the Trident sub and an initial opponent of the interim SALT agreement, had earned the base through his staunch prodefense record; the base allegedly was payment for Jackson's approval of the SALT agreement. Aides denied those charges, however, saying flatly "Scoop Jackson never asked for this base." While Jackson did not publicly lobby for it (prompting an aide to add "You can't say the same about the South Carolina delegation") it is highly unlikely Jackson's home state received the base without some effort on his part.[37]

Meanwhile, groups such as the MCPL did not abandon their attempts to "knock out funds for Trident acceleration," despite the apparent Trident victories of 1972. Representatives Les Aspin and James Abourezk drew the MCPL assignment to study the Trident request. In March 1973 MCPL announced it would oppose "a very substantial amount" of the FY 1972 Trident budget. Senator Joseph S. Clark, chairman of the Coalition on National Priorities, an organization ideologically sympathetic to MCPL, stated flatly that the "ULMS . . . should be terminated." He suggested scrapping two-thirds of the

TRIAD, keeping only the Polaris/Poseidon force. But, he added, "the ULMS . . . should not be funded since the Polaris and Poseidon submarines are vulnerable [*sic*] to Russian attack and wholly adequate as a deterrent." Any problems of growing vulnerability Polaris/Poseidon subs were experiencing could be corrected by backfitting, he added. But, as Trident Program Coordinator John Nicholson later testified, the SSBNs had deficiencies exceeding correction by backfitting, such as increasingly obsolete power plants and sonars. Nevertheless, MCPL and similar groups mounted another anti-Trident movement in mid-1973.[38]

Some evidence exists that some other legislators supporting the Trident looked at it as an alternative to the proposed antiballistic-missile system, which the defense community hotly debated during the Trident's early funding controversy. One of the major purposes of the ABM was to protect a set of ICBM silos, another was to defend one other soft target such as Washington, D.C. But if the Trident could offer a safer "version" of the ICBM, and ABM, then it presented an opportunity to slash the military budget by opting for the strategically "cleaner" Trident program instead of the more complicated ABM/ advanced ICBM concept. The major complication with this theory of trading the Trident for other systems involved the previously discussed bargains made by the Nixon administration to gain SALT ratification supported by the Joint Chiefs and key pro-defense congressmen. Those legislators who at this time supported the Trident at the expense of the ABM, however, had a consistent record of otherwise opposing defense expenditures. It is therefore unlikely the Navy really counted on their help in the future.[39]

In drawing up the FY 1974 budget, the Department of Defense planned to ask for $1,712 million. Besides the $285 million to be paid to Electric Boat on the initial contract, $302 million more was requested for materials procurement for items other than the hull itself, for a total of $587 million. Additionally, $658 million for R&D—still necessary in the early years of the program—and $182 million for military construction work on the Trident refit complex and support facilities was requested. The FY 1974 request also included $281 million for advance procurement of the second sum, as well as $5 million for "technical support of the missile facilities." Combining the FY 1973 funds of $194 million with the FY 1974 $587 million, the total program cost now hovered near $781 million for the first sub alone.[40]

Critics marshaled their forces and apparently had won a crucial committee vote on August 1, 1973, when the Senate Armed Services

Committee trimmed Trident funds by $885 million from a Navy request of $1.5 billion. In perhaps one of the most crucial votes in the entire legislative history of the Trident program, Senator Barry Goldwater, absent on voting day, announced that Senator Strom Thurmond had miscast his proxy vote. Although Goldwater had voted two years in a row against Trident acceleration, Admiral Rickover in a special presentation to the Arizona senator had managed to change his mind. On August 3 a crucial vote of forty-nine to forty-seven restored the $885 million by a fateful hairline margin. Earlier, the House had approved the full Navy request of $1.5 billion for the program, so the Trident was not a subject of discussion at the conference committee meetings. Congress, apparently in a prodefense mood, had increased the final authorization for the DoD as a whole, with the $500 million difference between the House and Senate being the subject of the conference committee. Moreover, the Senate committee approval left Trident opponents with few options. Beaten on the committee funding, they sought in September to delay the program on the floor by two years through an amendment offered by Thomas McIntyre of New Hampshire and supported by Peter Dominici, a Republican from Colorado. A "rare closed-door session," in which a "strange triumvirate"—Elmo Zumwalt, Rickover, and Secretary of the Navy Warner—presented classified information detailing threats posed by new Soviet ASW breakthroughs, resulted in the amendment's defeat. An intense floor fight ensued, mainly directed at the votes of eighteen "undecided" senators, highlighted by "two weeks of intense lobbying" by the administration (one of the few times any administration actively aided the program) and particularly by Zumwalt. The Zumwalt blitz antagonized some of its audience. According to one staff member, Zumwalt conveyed "the idea that a vote against Trident is a vote for the Russians. I didn't like that." Additionally, in answer to a question from Senator Stennis as to which was more important, a nuclear carrier or the Trident, Zumwalt "inferred to put the carriers first." Zumwalt's efforts nevertheless apparently succeeded. One final attempt to cut the funds also appeared to fail when Senator Jackson of Washington explained that cutting the money "will not save it . . . we are going to pay at least $1 billion more if we delay the program." However, the House Appropriations Committee had a surprise up its sleeve, and on December 1 it cut $253.9 million from the House bill of $1.5 billion, although $13.9 million of the cuts were restored. On December 13 the Senate agreed to the reduction, which only affected long-range procurement for Trident subs 5, 6, and 7. However, the Senate Appropriations Committee, concerned about a possible delay in the first Trident, told the DoD to seek a supplemental funding bill if the $240 million cut would delay the first sub.*[41]

The Contract Controversy

Trident opponents in the legislature had expended themselves without much success, but as the decision date for the first submarine contract neared, new problems arose: (1) What Navy contractor had the capabilities to constuct the new system? (2) How should the contracts be written—on cost-plus-incentive or fixed-price bases? Contracting the massive sub proved the single most controversial step in the entire program. Straight incentive contracts were ruled out, probably because the Navy already knew what Gansler reported in his book: namely, that defense firms do not see the small differences represented by incentive fees as being sufficiently profitable. To contractors, the key element is large serial production. Traditionally, therefore, the Navy has used cost-plus-incentive contracts for lead vessels of a line involving radical designs. Lead vessels, at least for major classes, often cost substantially more than anticipated, so this method provides fairer and more realistic contracts for both the Navy and the builders, a conclusion to which the Navy came when Admiral Isaac Kidd, Jr., was Chief of Navy Material. With respect to the application of the cost-plus-incentive policy in the construction of nuclear-powered submarines, however, the historical record is substantially different in many cases. For example, before the Trident contract, the 617 (*Lafayette* class SSBN), the 637 (*Sturgeon* SSN), the 640 (*Benjamin Franklin* SSBN), the 671 (*Narwal,* one-of-a-kind experimental vessel dedicated to the exploration of noise-abatement technology), the 685 (*Lipscomb* SSN, dedicated to research on an electrical drive in contrast to the geared turbine system), and the 688 (*Los Angeles* SSN) were all built without a cost-plus-incentive contract. In many ways, if fairly stable economic conditions prevail (low interest rates, low inflation, and low unemployment), this

*Action taken on the FY 1974 Trident was as follows:
Navy requested $1.5 billion.
House approved $1.5 billion, July 31, 1973.
Senate Armed Services Committee removed $885 million, September 1, 1973.
Senate Armed Services Committee restored $885 million, September 3, 1973.
Conferees approved $1.5 billion, October 20, 1973.
House Appropriations Committee removed $240 million, December 1, 1973.
Senate Appropriations Committee agreed with House to remove $240 million, December 13, 1973.
Final Navy appropriation $1.260 billion.

type of contract (cost plus profit, but no extra incentive), even for lead vessels, is not peculiarly unfair to the contractor if allowance is made for the subsequent submission of legitimate claims based on added costs resulting from engineering changes and if the contractor enjoys some real prospect of a serial order upon completion of the prototype. Since the transfer of technology from one to the next submarine design is usually about 60 to 70 percent, the risk of an overrun on a related follow-on design normally should be minimal. In fact, because the profit is tied to costs, the manufacturer has a greater incentive to raise his costs in the cost-plus contract. However, for the 688 *Los Angeles* class and the 726 *Ohio* class (Trident), nothing at all like it had been attempted in the nuclear period except perhaps the *Nautilus* itself, so the cost-plus advantages outweighed the disadvantages. Since an incomparably greater range of factors was being advanced technologically (hull size, sonar sophistication, quieting, weapon size, propulsion, etc.), each factor compounded the normally minimal cost factor of the other. To regard the *Ohio* as being directly related to its immediate predecessor is to argue that a supertanker is nothing more than a descendant of a World War II fleet oiler.[42]

Under a fixed-price contract, while the builder estimates a price and must meet it, he is given some latitude in "ceilings" included in the contract. In the case of the Trident, then, one Navy group "was bent on sustaining the impression that the cost could be nailed down in advance, in just the amount . . . that Congress had already budgeted." This group insisted that the contract be of a fixed-price type. The second group favored the cost-plus-incentive contract on the grounds that no one could predict the ultimate "prototype" cost because less than 15 percent of the design engineering was completed at the time. Subsequent controversy about "cost overruns" directly confirmed the position advocated by the second group. Nevertheless, the fixed-price faction won—largely due to Rickover's influence and involvement, according to some sources.[43]

The deputy chief for contracts in Navy Sea Systems Command had overall responsibility for issuing the Trident contracts. At the time the contract for the first Trident was to be drawn up, Rear Admiral Kenneth Woodfin, who served as the deputy chief for contracts, met with "great pressure" to use fixed price. Capitol Hill, assured the Trident was "bread and butter ship building" by Rickover, supported the fixed-price arrangement. Fearing reductions in other areas of the shipbuilding budget, the winning Navy faction also wanted a fixed-price type. Some Navy brass, led by Admiral Kidd, expressed reservations. Kidd steadfastly maintained "a cost-type contract is the responsible and proper instrument to build a first-of-class ship. The lead Trident is no exception."[44]

Rickover had his reasons for preferring a fixed-price contract. Whether or not he actually believed the Trident was not radically different from its predecessors, as one article reports, or whether he testified insincerely will remain a mystery. But his paranoia about shipbuilders inflating their costs led him to advocate fixed pricing as a necessary discipline on the construction process.[45]

When the Navy asked two major shipbuilders to submit bids to build the *Ohio* on a fixed-price basis, both refused. Newport News Shipbuilding and Drydock Company of Virginia submitted a counteroffer to build the ship on a cost-plus-incentive basis but could not deliver it until 1981, more than three years later than the Navy's advanced date. In the light of the subsequent adverse publicity about the *Ohio* being overly priced and overdue, the Newport News schedule for a 1981 delivery appears a most reasoned and experienced conclusion, and therefore much of the brouhaha over Electric Boat's "poor performance" seems artificially inflated and motivated. Electric Boat Company of Groton, Connecticut, a division of General Dynamics, also refused to build the *Ohio* on a fixed-price basis because of the "inherent cost uncertainties," but submitted instead a cost-plus bid. Navy Sea Systems Command told Electric Boat to resubmit its bid in the proper fixed-price form. Electric Boat officials still hesitated but agreed to negotiate further with the Navy. To set up the contract each side formulated its own costs from experience and from estimates based on man-hours needed to build a particular part of the submarine. When the completed estimates for each side were submitted in March, 1974 (see table 2), Electric Boat set its price for total hull construction at $308.9 million, which allowed for a profit of 14.2 percent. The Navy estimated the costs at $244.7 million.[46]

Not all Navy planners agreed with the proposed cost projections. P.

Table 2
Electric Boat and U.S. Navy Estimates
to Build the *Ohio*, March, 1974
(*in millions of dollars*)

	Electric Boat	**Navy**
Material	64.6	53.3
Labor	98.6	68.7
Overhead	74.4	53.2

W. Peterson, a Navy financial specialist who prepared an internal paper on the Trident's cost, stated a "more realistic target price" would have allowed an additional $34.9 million for unexpected costs and $31.1 million for profit. He criticized the Navy figures as being $66 million short of full funding.[47]

The differences in the cost estimates pushed the company and the Navy apart, and negotiations threatened to alienate the two parties further. Admiral Kidd dispatched a memo to Vice Admiral Robert Gooding on March 18, 1974, expressing concern the "budget figures [were] driving the price of the ship contract," budgets were dictating the use of "an inappropriate type of contract," and the Defense Department had set an "unreasonable delivery date of December, 1977."[48]

Returning to another sixty-day-long negotiating period, Electric Boat and the Navy produced a "marvelously inventive rubber document." Gooding described it as a fixed-price contract with "rather liberal provisions." Rear Admiral Woodfin called the contract "in *reality* a 'cost-type with a ceiling.'" The contract set a target cost and a ceiling price; the target cost was ideally the low-ball expectation, while the ceiling price was the high-ball price. As actual costs began to exceed the target price under the terms of the contract, the formula for determining the Navy's costs changed. For the *Ohio*'s hull the target cost was $253 million, with an incentive clause of $32.4 million if this price was met. Excessive costs beyond those stated in the target price fell under provisions known as share costs, whereby the Navy agreed to pay 95 percent of the first $26.6 million of the costs beyond the target cost. As costs escalated above the target figure the contractor would be given progressively less of the $32.4 million bonus. Counsel for Electric Boat, William Gorvine, characterized this provision as a way of writing into the contract the target figure "we really believed in." This made the real target price $279.6 million but allowed the Navy to stay within its "official" budget of $253 million.[49]

Other provisions followed. Of the next layer of costs from $279.6 million to $385.4 million incurred by the contractor, the Navy pledged to pay 85 percent (152 percent of the target cost). Electric Boat thereafter would become fully liable for all costs beyond that point, although the Navy would pay 100 percent of cost overruns attributable to inflation, without regard for date of delivery or fault of late delivery. Finally, Electric Boat promised, "in a touch of pure showbiz," to make its "best efforts" to deliver the *Ohio* by December, 1977, and "guaranteed" to deliver the sub by April 1979, although neither the promise nor the guarantee was binding on Electric Boat. Obligations were not confused at this point with aspirations. Neither of the final provisions had penalties for late delivery. No one had specified the number of subs to be built, but Electric Boat wanted exclusive options for any follow-on vessels. Clearly, the massive retooling and shipyard construction necessary to build a single Trident would leave the company with huge capital investments (and losses) if no other contracts followed. Congress had not funded any further construction, so the Navy gave Electric Boat prices it would pay the shipbuilder if the contracts came through. The Navy set the price for its proposed four Trident hulls at $1.2 billion.[50]

Gordon W. Rule, civilian head of the Navy's Procurement Control and Clearance Division, opposed the contract at every turn. Rule's office reviewed all Navy business contracts prior to release. In the *Ohio*'s contract Rule found a "built-in overrun" and charged the Navy with a "flagrant and unforgiveable example of . . . knowingly insisting upon the wrong kind of contract." He refused to clear the document.[51]

Rule's rejection sent the contract to Deputy Defense Secretary Bill Clements, who gave it to his aide, Vice Admiral Eli T. Reich, for analysis. Reich informed Clements that the fixed-price type of contract ran counter to Navy policy for lead ships. However, since the project manager (Levering Smith) and the contract officer (Kenneth Woodfin) seemed "sanguine that the contract can be brought in successfully under the [fixed-price incentive] arrangement," Reich agreed. He and Clements did "not share [Levering and Woodfin's] extreme optimism," but Reich asked Clements to personally receive "a concurrence" by Electric Boat's top management that it was satisfied with the contract. Clements received that concurrence, and the contract was signed on July 25, 1974.[52]

Representative Les Aspin heard of Rule's rejection of the contract and immediately launched an investigation. Aspin, a perennial Navy critic and member of the House Armed Services Committee, wrote Charles Bennett, a Florida Democrat and head of the Seapower Subcommittee of the House, asking Bennett to see if the contract was headed for a "major screw-up." Bennett disliked the role of overseer, but he asked the General Accounting Office for an advisory opinion. He also asked Rule for his opinion, which Rule delivered in the form of a nineteen-page response "so blistering that Admiral Kidd forwarded it only with some anguish." Kidd added his own cover letter defending the contract and saying Rule had "transgressed the bounds of propriety." The hybrid contract could be presented to advocates of a fixed-price contract as being such since a target figure seems to serve as a base figure, and, alternatively, it could be presented to advocates of the cost-plus-incentive contract, since two threshholds of cost overruns are included. Therefore, Kidd's endorsement of the contract was not necessarily inconsistent with his previous position. Rule's letter repeated his earlier objections, accused the Navy of "caving in" to Rickover, and alleged the contract was actually a four-ship contract with the three follow-up ships representing a quid pro quo for Electric Boat's acceptance of the fixed-price arrangement. He further charged the price limitations "were meant to guarantee that Newport News would never invest the $50 million needed to get started" as a Trident competitor (he underestimated this cost by a factor of 10). Rickover, Rule wrote, "must no longer dictate to the Navy the type of contract."[53]

The General Accounting Office report was not completed until Feburary 1975, long after some lead items for the follow-on ships had been purchased. It reached many conclusions similar to Rule's. Uncertainties in design, in meeting performance goals, in completing the facilities, and in obtaining necessary material and labor dictated against a fixed-price contract. Therefore, the report stated, such a contract "does *not* seem appropriate." The report questioned how the Navy could project "realistic" or "valid" costs with only 15 percent of the drawings complete; there was no way of determining whether the target costs were underestimated or overestimated. Trident was, the report continued, erroneously labeled "competitive procurement," with the first contract effectively excluding Newport News as a competitor. Even the Navy's insistence on the delivery date of the option ships by December 1980 excluded Newport News from competition since the latter yard had realistically foreseen a delivery date for the lead boat of no sooner than May 1981. Finally, the report concluded, commitments for the option ship prices were made "too early."[54]

Armed with the report, three GAO officials met with Bennett on Feburary 12, 1975. Bennett, buoyed by an echelon of naval officers involved in the Trident contracting who "had close ties with Rickover," engaged in a heated and "agitated" cross-examination of the GAO officials. When the GAO delegation listed the contract's faults, Bennet accused them of "supplying ammunition to the country's enemies." Bennett contacted the comptroller general and head of the GAO, Elmer Staats, urging Staats to summarize the opinion of the agency in a sentence rather than submit a report that could "only confuse and mislead." Staats responded by writing "We do not believe the Navy's choice of a contract was wrong." The report only proposed some "minor" criticisms, he concluded.[55]

Rule, hearing of the report, blasted Bennett. The congressman, Rule charged in a six-page letter, had attempted a "cover-up" and had done a "disservice" to the country. He accused Bennett of helping "to perpetuate the horrible track record we have of buying ships in recent years." Bennett "browbeat" Staats into watering down the report, while Rule labeled as "misleading" and inaccurate" news releases headlining

"GAO Finds Trident Contract Charges Generally Unfounded." Bennett had tried to bury the GAO's "unlaundered" findings, according to Rule.[56]

In the debate over the contracts, two points must be kept in mind. First, at the starting line *no one* wanted the Trident contract, at least on the Navy's terms. Electric Boat refused it just as Newport News had. Yet Electric Boat exhibited enough competitive interest to submit counteroffers and to negotiate further. A contract can hardly be called noncompetitive if the other half of the competition throws up its hands and says, in essence, "OK, it's yours." Nor can Electric Boat be blamed for negotiating the most advantageous deal possible for a contract the company had only reluctantly pursued. With only 15 percent of the designs ready, the company's management would have been considered incompetent if it accepted any contract failing to protect the company. Perhaps a cost-plus-incentive could have offered the proper protections. However, given the risk and capital investment needed for the Trident, Electric Boat acted properly to cover its interests.

Second, expectations of competition in a program like the Trident must confront reality. No company in the industrialized world would, with any sensitivities to its stockholders, invest $450 million—not $50 million as the *Washington Post* claimed—just to build a prototype vessel with no guarantee of serial production. While a true entrepreneur might argue such a capital investment would virtually guarantee the company further contracts because it could eventually supply the product at a lower unit cost, the risk of a $450-million investment in today's industrial circles demands some sort of official guaranty or "lock-in." Conversely, critics are foolish to argue the Navy should have opened up the bidding for follow-on subs in the program. Once the construction equipment has been built, the yards renovated, and the workforce hired, the Navy would court disaster to induce another builder to assume the same set of risks. Of course, no other yard would do so with the knowledge that the Navy's "loyalty" to a particular program is fleeting, especially considering the size and cost of the project and the number of units to be procured. While criticism of the contracting and procurement process is demanded by the initial blunders in the history of the Trident contract process, once let, subsequent criticism is misplaced if directed at the lack of competition.

Rather, as at least one of the instigators behind the adoption of the Trident contract, Rickover should receive a large portion of the blame for ramming it through the Navy and Congress. He would later rather hypocritically charge Electric Boat with filing "omnibus claims" when the company tried to collect on the inflation clauses specifically included in the contract to rectify its weaknesses. Still, most of those involved in the early phase of the Trident contract shared William Gorvine's view on why the Navy insisted on a fixed-price type of contract: "My more-than-belief is that it was Admiral Rickover." The Navy never reprimanded the admiral for misrepresenting the Trident as a bigger Polaris, probably because it would be difficult to prove intent. But the role played by the "father of the nuclear navy," if overestimated in the controversy over the Trident's size, has been understated in the contract turmoil.[57]

Both Congress and the GAO must share the blame as well. Each had its opportunity to challenge the contract, although the first Trident was in the incipient stages of construction by the time either Congress or the GAO had enough information to act. But a central element, discussed at the beginning of this chapter—need or urgency of building a weapon system—cannot be discounted here. As is shown in Chapter 6, attempts to force contractors to "toe the line" in various projects sometimes amount to cutting off the country's nose to spite its face. The grim predictions by Rule and others about the "cost overruns" due to the contract may at some future date fill the speeches of Pentagon reformers. During the course of the negotiations for the lead Trident, however, the central question remains why the Navy could not furnish sufficient incentive to entice both Electric Boat and Newport News to bid, using a cost-plus arrangement. The answer is the dilemma of procurement—making the figures show "cost effectiveness" at each and every stage of funding, regardless of the necessity or performance of the final product.

Even as the contract situation was being resolved, Electric Boat encountered other pressing problems. Another series of Rickover's boats, the SSN-688 *Los Angeles* class attack submarines, were to be built at its yard after Newport News turned out the lead vessel. Both yards would then share the construction of other 688s. Electric Boat received contracts for this class in 1972, causing many officials and congressmen to express concern over whether the burden of the program would swamp Electric Boat, even with an expanded work force.[58]

A staff member asked Admiral Harvey Lyon if he thought, "with a present level of 200, that taking on a program approaching a billion dollars [if it was] practical to build up a staff adequate to accommodate . . . a 10-fold increase in program level?" Lyon did not think it impractical. The staffer then asked Admiral Philip Beshany if he could recall any previous program where "a 10-fold increase in dollars . . . was effectively applied to any major weapons system?" Beshany quickly replied "The Polaris system." Beshany then submitted some charts to prove his point, the first showing $18.4 million for Polaris in FY 1956 and $138.2 million in FY 1957. Comparable illustrations followed—

Poseidon development ($43.8 million in FY 1956, $295.8 in FY 1957) and Polaris shipbuilding and conversion ($52 million for FY 1960, $1.004 million in FY 1961). Admiral Levering Smith compared the Trident and Polaris manpower requirements. At its peak, the Polaris/Poseidon program employed 3000 workers at Electric Boat alone, not counting the workforce employed to produce propulsion plants already in production or employed in such other yards involved in the total program as Mare Island Naval Shipyard, Portsmouth Navy Shipyard, and Newport News. Smith estimated those plants required another 500 employees. For the Trident, Smith thought 2700 might be needed to start, with an additional 200 Poseidon workers transferred over as the Poseidon program slowed and the Trident system accelerated. Ultimately, as Admiral Lyon added, 4000 to 6000 workers could be employed on the Trident. According to Lyon, "the ship portion [of Trident] looks like 1,300, 000 man-days of effort over 4 years." Missile workers comprised another 100 employees; in-house laboratory researchers added another 200.[59]

On July 25, 1974, when the "infamous" contract for the Trident left the Navy for the offices of Electric Boat Company, the shipbuilder's offices were abuzz. For the $285 million the Navy paid, Electric Boat began building the submarine and refitting the yard to handle an entire line of Tridents. Revolutionary new equipment to weld and measure the hull plate sections was ordered for future installation. To fulfill the contracts, Electric Boat hired thousands of new workers, mostly untrained, and then put them through a crash course in welding and submarine construction. General Electric contracted to supply Rickover's big reactor, and Lockheed neared completion of the first C-4 missiles for testing (the same missiles not off the drawing board when Lockheed submitted in its bid). In relation to Lockheed's contract, Laird issued an order to backfit the Poseidon submarines with the Trident I (C-4) missile as soon as it became available in 1977. The Navy force had been MIRVing the Poseidon missiles since 1967, scheduled for completion just in time to beat the Trident backfitting planned to begin in 1977. Electric Boat also placed a purchase order with FMC Corporation (Northern Ordnance Division) in August 1974 for "the manufacture of a prototype shipset (consisting of 24 missile tubes) and a test vehicle." Electric Boat's experience with previous nuclear submarine programs described in chapter 5 and its ability to reduce redundancy and waste in the backfit designs made it the logical choice for the backfitting assignment as well. Contracts for the second and third Trident boats followed on February 28, 1975, very soon after Representative Bennett and the GAO officials had their discussion.[60]

Force Levels and Building Rates

Few programs at the outset are dedicated merely to the production of a prototype. While some weapons-system programs face expiration after a prototype conclusively proves ineffective or abortive, initially a program proceeds by definition upon the assumption several copies of perhaps a further modified version of the original will be made. Serial production underlies the concept of cost effectiveness—over a series of units the development costs of the lead item will be reduced pro rata until its originally conspicuous cost eventually will be diluted by the entire program. Therefore establishing the number of Tridents provisionally programmed is important in attempting to calculate a cost per Trident copy. According to a 1981 statement by Electric Boat, the target cost of a seven-vessel program would be $1.793 billion, or $256 million per hull copy, whereas, it will be recalled, the option price of the first four hulls was $300 million per hull copy (see table 3).

This lower per-unit hull cost, a net per-unit cost reduction of $44 million, however, was predicated on the assumption of a building rate of three ships every two years. According to the earliest reports on scheduling, the original rate was 1–2–1–2–1. However, Rear Admiral Albert Kelln pointed out that in 1974 the program had been stretched from an original rate of "1–2–2–2–2–1" to the 1–2–1–2–1–2–1 rate, thereby adding three ships to the so-called original rate and changing the reported production schedule, indicating also the Navy planned a force of ten at a very early date.[61]

Table 3
Trident Program*

Current Program Cost vs. Original Contract (000)	
Original target cost for seven ships	$1,793,000†
Change orders (engineering and actual)	65,976
Subtotal	$1,858,976
Authorized escalation (for inflation)	1,010,757
Total contract value	$2,961,565
Overrun/(Underrun)	$ 91,832
Percent Overrun/(Underrun)	3.2
Current ceiling (marginal restraints)	$3,723,978
Underrun to Ceiling	$ (762,413)

*Source: Electric Boat Co., June, 1981.

†1972 constant dollars.

Without much fanfare, this program of ten ships implicitly became the accepted total squadron. Not being totally forthcoming at this point about the real Trident force level the Navy planned would also hereafter contribute further to confusing the relative per-unit cost reductions as a result of an extended (7→10) serial production and would equally contribute to avoidable per-unit offsetting increases occasioned by untimely requests for lead items for follow-on ships after the seventh vessel. Thus, when queried in 1974 about the eventual ten-ship force and whether it would be sufficient to replace the Polaris force, Rickover evaded a discussion of optimal squadron size by saying it would be "premature." When asked if a force of even ten would be inadequate, Rickover answered only that the advance funding for 1978 was directed beyond ten. By 1977, however, Admiral Kelln admitted eventually, to replace the total number of launchers provided by the Polaris boats, a force of some "27 or 29" Tridents would be needed. He then referred to the 1975 basing study of East Coast submarine sites, the selected one of which would probably be the home of a second squadron of ten boats, for a minimal force of twenty. Kelln qualified his statement by adding "I am trying to differentiate between a shipbuilding program and a basing program," an esoteric difference that presumably somehow accommodated the seven- to nine-boat discrepancy seeking a budgetary port. Further confusing the planned force size was the fact that Electric Boat only had "guarantees" on four vessels.[62]

Expansion in the program over seven would in any case further churn the entire deliberative process upon which funding assumptions were based. An expanded program should mean extra units would cost proportionately less, with each subsequent unit drawing on increasingly more standardized parts and more experienced installation techniques. In addition, these two factors in interaction should also contribute to reduced per-unit cost because of the correspondingly heightened skills of the supervisory force. In the case of the Trident this has been particularly true, for much of Electric Boat's original cost estimate included an intensive training program to teach workers to use new equipment and techniques in the construction of a novel design. Alternately, extra units do not necessarily equate with a lower cost per unit, especially in military equipment requiring purchasing of lead items and materials as much as five years in advance if assumptions about eventual purchase prices are adversely modified by the intervening years of inflation. Estimates of materials needed to build seven Tridents were made in terms of 1972–1973 economic assumptions. Then, adding three more ships to the schedule necessitated new purchases of long-lead items several years farther out than the 1972–1973 assumptions, further compounding the effects of inflation for years that turned out to be economic mutants. So, while some per-unit costs may be decreased by expanding a program, others actually may increase. Even so, certain other program restrictions apply when compensating for anticipated adverse economic trends. For example, it would have been impractical or perhaps even impossible to double the original building rate in order to achieve a 50 percent reduction in anticipated inflation.[63]

At issue, then, is the question of how many Tridents the Navy intended to build in 1972. If a ten-ship force was the goal from the outset instead of a seven-ship force, were enough long-lead items ordered in 1972 when the figure bandied about was still four vessels? If they were not, how many more long-lead items would the Navy have needed to order to defray the future effects of accumulated inflation by the time these items were delivered? The answers significantly affect Electric Boat's refutation of charges made by Vice Admiral Earl B. Fowler of Naval Sea Systems Command in 1981.[64] Fowler's charges are dealt with in chapter 6, but it is important to note that Electric Boat omitted in its 1981 defense an analysis of the accumulated economic effect to 1980/1981 of these bewildering Navy force predictions. Some Navy authorities probably knew all along what force they wanted and needed, with ten subs being a minimal force necessity, but they politically opted for a "stretch-out" approach from seven in order to make the program appear annually more budgetarily palpable to legislators. (The public tends to think in one-year spans of time; representatives think in two-year spans, and senators think in six-year spans.) The resulting increase in cost of this approach can only be estimated, but as the tenth Trident's advance procurements were denied authorization until FY 1982, ten years of intervening inflation must be taken into account. Using a conservative annual inflation index of 8.85 percent per year, procurement savings on the three additional ships (less missiles and reactors) would have amounted to $912 million had they been incorporated in the original purchase.[65]

The rate of inflation itself became a source of friction between Navy witnesses and congressmen at appropriations hearings. Generally the Navy used an inflation rate of 7.95 percent. The Department of Defense, however, reported actual rates (see table 4). Total defense-related inflation for the period 1973–1976 varied between 37.7 and 36.3 percent, depending upon whether the figures used were those marked Outlays or Total Obligational Authority. Either category dwarfs the 23.85 percent that results from the annual 7.95 percent Pentagon figure, a difference of 14 percent. Yet in committee hearings in 1974, Admiral Metzel stood fast in his opinion that 7.95 percent was a realistic rate. Congressmen William Dickenson of Alabama chal-

Table 4
DoD Adjusted Inflation Rates
(in percentage)

Fiscal Year	Consumer Price Index	Wholesale Price Index	GNP Deflator	Inflation on Defense Budget: Outlays	Inflation on Defense Budget: TOA
1973–74	9.0	16.1	8.1	9.4	11.0
1974–75	11.9	18.3	11.3	14.4	13.3
1975–76	9.5	4.7	9.0	9.9	8.4
Compound Total 1973–76	33.5	43.8	31.2	37.7	36.3

lenged it. Questioning Admiral John Nicholson, Dickenson tried to pin down the admiral on what he believed was a realistic inflation rate. When Nicholson equivocated, Dickenson exploded, "I would be glad to discuss this inflation mess anytime you want. I have been harping on it for 4 years." The Navy, Dickenson charged, has "used unrealistic inflation factors ever since I have been on this committee . . . knowing that they are not right and knowing that they are wrong or misleading."[66]

Following Dickenson's outburst, the Navy brought more comprehensive inflation figures to the next session of 1974 hearings. Metzel produced a chart showing projections "as to the additional cost at escalation [inflation], 6 percent, 8 percent, 10 percent, and 12 percent." Dickenson thanked Metzel for complying with his request. But while the Navy admitted that by weighing (i.e., compounding) inflation rates, inflation actually "comes out to 13.5%," Metzel concluded the session by restating his position: 7.95 percent was a realistic rate.[67]

Admiral Metzel appears to have stood analytically on somewhat safe economic grounds with his 7.95 percent figure, at least for the time he spoke. He probably based his predictions on the previously even effects upon the consumer price index of four factors: (1) escalation in costs of advanced acquisitions of materials such as steel, (2) escalation of overhead costs such as energy or electricity, (3) escalation of direct labor costs, calculably moderated by the control of three-year rather than one-year contracts, and (4) by variations in the workload according to changes in vessels contracted out, where labor reductions would tend to increase labor costs by extending the completion of work, and where increases of labor would tend to have converse effects. Nevertheless,

Metzel's economic crystal ball failed him: he underestimated inflation for the forthcoming period by 14 percent. Even after Dickenson compelled him to construct a more realistic compound figure of 13.5 percent, Metzel continued to stand by his predictions.

By combining a massive inflation rate with the "on-again, off-again" additional three submarines, an inflation "tax" of probably over $912 million was added to the cost of the first ten ships. Pentagon indecision over a seven- and ten-ship program is illustrated in the Department of Defense annual reports for FY 1974 and FY 1975. According to the FY 1975 DoD report, "after starting the first TRIDENT [*sic*] submarine in FY 1974, we now propose to build the nine remaining TRIDENT submarines *discussed here last year* at a rate of two a year (instead of *three* a year) beginning in 1975 [emphasis added]." The 1974 report, it will be recalled, *made no mention of ten ships*! Instead, it stated the FY 1974 funds included $281 million in advance procurement funds "*for additional* TRIDENT ships." Furthermore, the only reference to a building rate of *three* per year came from Rear Admiral John Nicholson, Director of Strategic Submarines and Trident Program Coordinator. He said in a 1974 hearing there was to be a three-per-year rate after the initial Trident was constructed. Perhaps he was instead referring to the rate mentioned by Admiral Metzel to a committee: "the Trident building rate presented to the Congress [as of January 1975] envisioned the procurement of *three submarines every two years* . . . with a planned force level of ten submarines [emphasis added]." Although Admiral Fowler's 1981 statement could have made some justifiable adjustments for delays, he nevertheless noted "the Navy initially planned a Trident procurement rate of . . . *a little over one per year* [emphasis added]." This wholly inconsistent and disingenuous ex post facto presentation of the Navy's "original" building schedule can only be matched in these qualities by the Navy's corresponding statements about flotilla force levels. It is difficult to differentiate here between Navy program strategy, honest adaptive modifications of programs necessitated by changes in objective circumstances, and simple personal and historical confusion. Yet the Navy, by failing to avoid compounding confusions, missed an opportunity to develop a reputation for consistent institutional reliability and to inspire unqualified public trust.[68]

Evidence supplied by Electric Boat reveals that the original projection was for seven—not ten—ships. Realistic building estimates at no time projected more than two submarines in a year; this rate eventually slipped to three every two years. Compelled to anticipate Polaris/Poseidon block obsolescence, the DoD had enough information to project that the force level would be at least ten, and the Navy knew absolutely that the force level it wanted was ten, while somewhat secretly hoping it would be more. The only remaining question is whether a substantial number of SARs and advance materials procurements were made under the auspices of other funding, thus to account for the $912 million that would have been added by inflation as a consequence of not purchasing those items in 1972. The classified nature of the SARs prohibits a final judgment in this matter.

It might appear that the Navy must assume substantial responsibility for a variety of vital confusions. Security reasons do not seem sufficient to explain the obscurity surrounding force levels. Tridents are far too big to hide during the construction process, even in the early stages of modular construction, while the Soviets are committed to building as many of a particular weapons system as they deem requisite regardless of what the United States builds in a comparable category. In this case, a clear statement of the number of subs to be built under the first program would have alleviated much of the congressional confusion from 1973 to 1976 and abated much congressional and public suspicion of the program and of the Navy as well. Moreover, a more accurate prediction in 1973–1974 of force levels, costs, and inflation would measurably have preempted the grounds on which later "cost overrun" critics laid their case. More significantly, since the proper advance procurements for the additional three subs were not made in 1972, the Navy must take some responsibility for the $912 million additional cost. Finally, a clearer concept of the force level could have made the early contracts to Electric Boat less risky and possibly have enticed Newport News into entering the competitive process.

From the standpoint of Washington politics, however, the Navy is blameless. Naval representatives were involved all along in playing the appropriations game—a game inherently wasteful, unpredictable, and fateful from the viewpoint of interservice rivalry, and highly competitive. In this respect, naval planners achieved as much as could be expected—indeed, more—during a period when newspaper headlines heralded the demise of a president and mass antimilitary protests. Clearly, Navy brass knew they should not ask for the moon. Instead, they carefully targeted funds, pulling the program along, vote by vote, until it became a reality. It was achieved despite the efforts of a fairly dedicated and active opposition, in spite of Rickover's contract meddling, in the absence of any significant personal involvement from either President Nixon or President Ford, and achieved, so the record seems, even without the active support of congressional hawks, who in some cases atypically voted outrightly against the program. The Navy nevertheless also suffered some losses during this phase—its prestige dipped after the contract information leaked out—and the confusion over the size of the vessel and the number to be built caused some Navy supporters on Capitol Hill understandably to shake their heads in bewilderment. But even if the Navy's original intention to build ten ships was not cushioned by numerous advance procurements and SARs and even if this did result in exposing the entire ten-boat program to the avoidable $912 million inflation, compared with the current controversy over the MX missile, the Trident program represented a substantial success for both the Navy and the nation as a whole. Naturally, competition for funds came not only from other service branches: the Navy had to balance the Trident within the context of its other needs and mission priorities. Senator Stennis' question to Elmo Zumwalt—whether he would rather have the Trident or an aircraft carrier—reflected the complex and very real questions of resource allocation facing the Navy in its own budget requests. Although performance in an armed conflict would prove the only conclusive measure of whether the Navy chose correctly, it appears, in 1983 at least, that the Navy's other shipbuilding programs have not suffered for the Trident's sake.[69]

Yet 1974 was just the beginning of the battle of the budget. Despite the original contract squabble that year, the Trident program elicited growing enthusiasm and sustained little damage in congressional budget struggles. However, much enthusiasm turned sour as production problems appeared and as the shadow of Rickover's hybrid contract spread. Trident was a good deal farther from going to sea than anyone imagined.

4
Adolescence and Maturity:
Planning, Programming, and Budgeting the Trident, 1974–1982

Safety from external danger should be . . . the most powerful director of national conduct.
—Alexander Hamilton,
The Federalist

All elements of the Trident program—sub, missile, base, and even the related retrofitting of the Poseidon boats—had begun to take shape by 1974. New inflation and funding battles heated up, fueled by fights on related but not integral parts of the system. Yet some observers already were seeking alternatives to the Trident, particularly a smaller sub that some touted as having the same capabilities. Congressmen who had fought to see the Trident program accelerated instead found it delayed, and they demanded to know why. Trident's troubles coincided with new administration attempts to combat inflation by trimming budgets, a move the Navy felt as deeply as other departments. The Trident program was not untouched by the new fiscal constraints. As a result some delays had to be ordered by the administration itself—delays that in turn contributed to the inflationary growth in the program.

One of the first areas of the program to receive attention was the construction of the Bangor base. A final environmental impact statement was filed on August 5, 1974. In planning the base the Navy had attempted to preserve not only the natural environment but the human environment as well, by requesting $7 million to assist communities in alleviating the impact of the Bangor base construction. Because the base probably would bring an additional 27,000 to 30,000 people into the area (separate from the actual base personnel or military personnel in many cases), the Navy hoped to offset the drain on some of the public services offered by the town of Bangor. Among the various programs the Navy contributed $5 million to Kitsap County collection and treatment sewage plant, later increased by $1.4 million because of delay and inflation. Despite the Navy's efforts, three environmental groups and two private citizens filed a lawsuit entitled *Concerned About Trident (CAT)* v. *Schlesinger* on August 5, 1974, claiming the Navy had failed to comply with the Environmental Protection Act. After several appeals, a Washington, D.C., federal district court upheld the decision of a Washington state court that had dismissed the suit in favor of the Navy. However, the federal district judge ordered the Navy to file an environmental impact statement supplement within 120 days.[1]

A total of seventeen programs was under contract at the base, including a "new turning basin," a "new pier facility to satisfy the greater explosive safety distances of the Trident missiles" (the fuel, not the warheads), and general administrative buildings. Part of the funding went toward construction of ammunition-processing facilities at Indian Island Annex near Bangor. The Navy increased the Indian Island funding by $27 million because it could also be used for non-Trident-related weaponry and ammunition. Overall, by 1974 the Navy happily reported Bangor construction to be "6 months ahead of schedule."[2]

For FY 1976 the Navy requested $140 million to be used in Trident facilities construction, not including Point Mugu or general nuclear weapons security. Actual authorization exceeded the Navy's request by $46.5 million. In this funding the diversity of Trident spending was apparent. Weapons security accounted for an additional $6.5 million. Some of the $7 million allocated for community relief was directed to the Department of Housing and Urban Development. More than $92,000 sent to HUD was to be used to relieve potential local tax burdens caused by the base, although some of this sum would be targeted for job counseling. Most local governmental agencies had already promised to try to match federal money spent in the area. Admiral Metzel estimated the total requirement to establish the Bangor base harmoniously in the community to be $202.8 million: local agencies, $83 million; other governmental agencies (whose budgets would be increased apart from the Navy's needs), $80 million; and the Department of Defense, $39.8 million.[3]

Two test facilities occasionally received funds under the Trident program, Point Mugu and Cape Canaveral. Both were involved in testing Trident missiles and used on a special "rental" basis described in chapter 7. They warrant consideration when trying to determine the program's costs.[4]

Not all construction projects required allocations from Congress. Some complexes were to be built at Bangor only through savings in total costs reduced at other projects. These additions represented only low-priority buildings not usually named in hearings.[5]

Base construction presented one set of funding questions related to the submarine; research and development offered another. The Director of Research and Engineering to deal with the Trident program was Dr. Malcolm R. Currie, an inventor, laser expert, and engineer who "personified the Pentagon's new preoccupation with electronics." After presiding over the early Trident research, development, testing, and evaluation (RDT&E), in 1974 he reported RDT&E "has peaked and will continue to decline as submarine production proceeds." For FY 1975–1976 he requested $95.3 million for the Trident missile system and also asked for $35 million for MaRV development (warheads having independently maneuverable reentry flights). While this latter program was principally directed toward an eventual mating with the Trident missile, the funding was charged strictly to the Research and Engineering Office of DoD. In general, because the Navy seldom builds actual prototypes, Navy R&D has the great advantage of defraying prototype costs, which instead are funded under production. Numerous other submarine-related programs continued outside the Trident system's track development. Project SANGUINE, developed by GTE-Sylvania, had for years carried out research on a massive underground extra-low-frequency (ELF) transmitting system to maintain emergency communications with subs operating at increased depths. This program particularly affected the Trident, with its exceptional diving abilities. Even the similar concept of navigation information transmitted from satellites instead of underground senders obtained $3.6 million. Named NAVSTAR, this project proposed to send navigational information as well as commands to deep-diving submarines, land vehicles, and aircraft, and obviously had broader applications than just for Trident, although the new subs would be prime beneficiaries. Currie also submitted a request for initiating "SSBN subsystem development" because the demands on related areas of submarine research had taxed the general program and he felt, with the new 688-class attack subs joining the Trident in production, there was a need for housing together the separate elements of the ongoing submarine research program on a comprehensive basis.[6]

Rising Costs and Trident Alternatives

When all aspects of the program are accounted for as of 1974 (less the R&D costs, Point Mugu, weapons security, and various other "related but unrelated items") the projected price tag totaled $12,431.1 million. The FY 1975 request included

> a total of $2,043 million—$107 million for continued component development of the submarine, $927 million to complete the funding for the second and third TRIDENT submarines, $240 million for advanced procurement for two TRIDENT submarines per year in FY 1976 and FY 1977, $662 million for the continued development and minor procurement related to the Trident I missile, and $107 million in military construction funds to continue work on the TRIDENT Refit Facility at Bangor, Washington. [This was only the refit section for the Polaris subs.]

Another $25 million was included in the FY 1974 supplemental budget "to protect the option for the procurement of two Trident submarines in FY 1975." Currie's SSBN-X gained a $16-million spot in the budget, with the funds going toward "commencement of a conceptual and feasibility design effort."[7]

In Currie's testimony appeared the first indications of research on an alternate, smaller Trident. Currie nevertheless still defended the Trident's size on technological grounds. He explained that its larger components could run at a lower speed, thereby generating less noise. The power plant was quieter than previous models, and the hull was sized in anticipation of the Trident II missile. Despite its satisfaction with the Trident system overall, the R&D office therefore continued to look (on a contingency basis) at the feasibility of a smaller SSBN with many of the Trident's capabilities. A so-called SSBN-X—a Trident derivative—designed with a different type of reactor emerged as an alternative to the Trident program. It was to be "a 640 class [submarine]" with a hull cost only 65 to 70 percent of that of Trident. The S5G reactor came from the SSN-671 *Narwhal* (a single submarine class) and featured natural convection currents to circulate reactor coolant rather than pumps. But its lack of room for growth precluded its use as a Trident II missile carrier. Although the concept SSBN-X was brought up in the FY 1975 request, it was curiously not mentioned in the FY 1976 R&D budget request.[8]

Still, congressmen hardly had to look around to see that costs were rising. In questioning Currie during the 1974 hearings on the FY 1975 request, William Dickenson pointed out that the Trident budget so far was off by $3 billion. He stated that, if Currie or the Department of Defense "missed the $3 billion by underestimating with inflation, then somebody made a boo boo." Currie nevertheless maintained that, although "we have gone over [budget] $3 billion since . . . last spring," the program "is now adequately funded and exceptionally well managed."[9]

In 1976 Admiral Albert Kelln drew some tough Congressional interrogation, too, requiring him to account for the increased Trident costs. Changes in development, scheduling, and inflation since December 1973 had by 1976 accounted for almost $6 billion, of which, Kelln explained, $922 million was due to the schedule change alone (see fig. 4-1). Two stretchouts had necessitated this change: one, from a building rate of 1–2–2–2–2–1 to 1–2–1–2–1–2–1; and a second, from a rate of 1–2–1–2–1–2–1 to 1–2–1–1–2–1–2. The first stretchout was the most expensive, adding $603 million. Besides the rate changes, an additional $1.4 billion represented funds for the eleventh submarine and forty-eight missiles, while estimated inflation for 1976 was expected to account for $787 million. Kelln explained that real stretchout costs actually constituted only $224.9 million, but related effects on other shipbuilding, workforce reassignment, and related inflation ate up the remainder. When the House panel asked why the stretchouts were necessary, Kelln cited "fiscal constraint reasons." Said Kelln, the "Navy was trying to do all the things that had to be done within allowed funds."[10]

Trident Missile Development and Related Programs

Considerable attention to the Trident missile's development and related programs accompanied the growing concern with costs. The

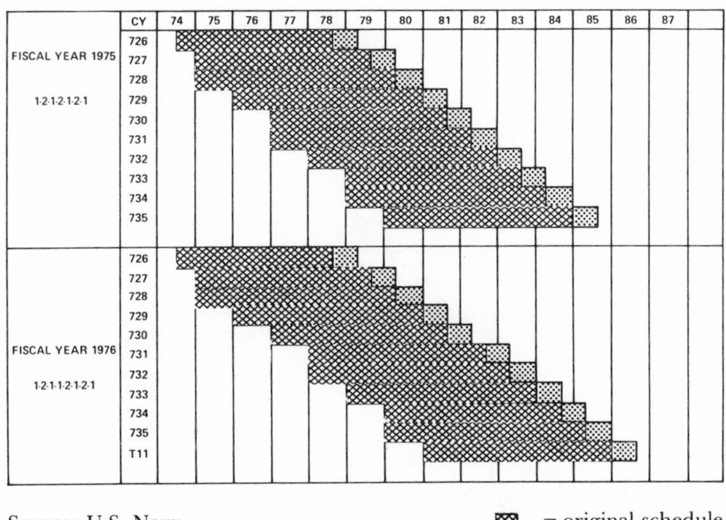

Source: U.S. Navy.

Fig. 4-1. Trident submarine building rate.

= original schedule

= stretchout schedule

Department of Defense announced, in the Annual Report for FY 1975, that the Trident I missile was to be ready by "the fourth quarter of 1978 . . . which coincides with the [deployment] of the first Trident submarine." Also planned for the missile was its mating to the Mk-500 MaRV warhead. This maneuverable warhead, called the Evader, was designed "to help it evade an ABM interceptor, rather than to increase its accuracy." It did not present the same range possibilities the 6000-n.m. Trident II would, but Trident I with Evader could more assuredly penetrate its target.[11]

In addition to the advances in penetration and accuracy, the Trident I missile program captured a great deal of attention because of the backfitting of the Poseidon subs, which approached somewhat sooner than did the launching of the *Ohio*. Scheduled to begin "in the third quarter of FY 1979," the backfitting promised a temporary extension of the Poseidon lines long enough to deploy a suitable number of missiles at sea eventually in Tridents. Ten Polaris submarines deployed between 1959 and 1963 would soon face out-and-out retirement; thirty-one Poseidon submarines would nevertheless remain in service. Initially, the Carter administration planned to backfit twelve of the Poseidon subs. These converted boats profited by the Mk-500 testing. When married to a Trident I missile, a backfitted Poseidon carried nearly as sophisticated deterrent hardware as a Trident boat but of course did not possess the same platform survivability features, range, or total magazine strength.[12]

Apparently the Poseidon conversions arrived in the nick of time. In 1974 the Navy began to experience some failures with Poseidon missiles during testing. According to the Department of Defense, "the deficiencies encountered in the POSEIDON . . . tests are typical of those experienced in other new weapons systems. . . . None of them is related to the basic design of the POSEIDON missile, which . . . is entirely sound." Consequently, a corrections program was instituted at a cost of $126 million; $23 million went for changing missiles already in production, including, in part, $38 million for testing small parts, $24 million to replace detonating fuses with newer designs, $18 million for improving gimbal assemblies, $10 million for modifying firing units, and $2 million for replacing hoses. All of the Poseidon subs were to have improved Poseidon missiles, including the twenty already deployed. An "improved Poseidon retrofitting" commenced, due to end in 1977 with all thirty-one Poseidon submarines carrying the modified missile. Thus the Trident retrofitting program followed on the heels of the broader Poseidon retrofitting program. Fortunately for crew morale, none of the Tridents would be retrofitted into Poseidons that had just been retrofitted.[13]

At the 1974 House Hearings on Research and Development, Malcolm Currie estimated that the cost of the Trident backfit program would total $2.54 billion. Each sub also required $6.6 million for missile installation. Furthermore, Currie's budget included $35 million for Evader development, which was at least partially directed at the Trident program, $735.1 million for the Trident I missile, and $83.8 million in general Trident-related research funds. Several programs funded by Currie's budget held more than a passing interest for Trident supporters. One item—referred to as the "fleet ballistic missile program"—covered a myriad of submarine- (hence Trident-) related projects but was not the same budget line as SSBN subsystem development. In a total request of $65.8 million, $14.8 million was for sonar improvement and submarine survivability research, the technological spinoffs of which profited Trident.[14]

The heavy emphasis on R&D for the Trident I missile and Evader warhead was beginning to pay off by 1975. Admiral Kelln reported "the C-4 [Trident I] status today was [*sic*] 2 years further along toward deployment than the A-3 [Poseidon missile]" was at its equivalent stage of development. In 1977 the Evader completed successful testing, while the Navy received the even happier news that the Poseidon missile tests proved that "the deficiencies encountered in [1973] were minor in nature and could be successfully corrected." But, by late 1975 the Department of Defense planned only to retrofit ten submarines, not twelve. Nevertheless, for the first time since its creation during Strat-X, the basic Trident components of missile, warhead, ship, base, and retrofitting seemed to be jelling.[15]

Newer aspects of the Trident also began to take shape. In the FY 1976–1977 Department of Defense Annual Report, defense officials announced an option to deploy a higher-throw-weight missile in the late 1980s. Early funding for this higher-throw-weight missile, the Trident II, proceeded at a "moderate pace." Although $3 million from the FY 1976 budget and a request for $10 million in the FY 1977 budget seemed inconsequential at the time, the Trident II missile has subsequently emerged as one of the long-range keys to a more cost-effective Trident system overall. Another new branch of the Trident sapling, SSBN Subsystem Technology, continued to contribute to the entire program. Eventually, work on submarine antiaircraft defense, submarine shock protection, and sonar improvements evolved from the SSBN Subsystem Technology Division. This element of the program acquired $2 million in the FY 1976 budget, while the Secretary of Defense submitted a request for $4 million in FY 1977. By 1982 Trident-related defense programs totaled thirteen.[16]

Costs Increase

Progress seemed evident in all areas of the programs, but inflation relentlessly pushed prices higher. Included in the Department of Defense Annual Report in FY 1975–1976, an appendix illustrated the impact of inflation on materials and labor for the most recent twelve months available: steel, 41 percent; aluminum, 43 percent; copper wire, 33 percent; aircraft industry labor earnings, 5 percent; shipbuilding labor earnings, 6 percent. Because of "the financial strain" on the Defense Department, primarily due to inflation, and in order "to relax the pressure on the shipbuilder," the DoD "again slowed the TRIDENT submarine construction schedule from a two-a-year to an alternating 1–2–1–2 a year rate." As has been shown, the two-a-year rate never reached the production line, if it was ever taken seriously. The rate of 1–2–1–2 consistently had been the Navy's true goal. Perhaps the Department of Defense believed, in the early funding stages, that the illusion of an accelerated building rate would increase the congressional ante. Or perhaps the unrealistic rate was set to create a built-in scapegoat of Electric Boat if anything went wrong. Whatever the reason, it is unlikely the Navy or the Department of Defense ever realistically expected a rate of two subs per year every year, and certainly never realistically expected Nicholson's rate of three per year. The first contract, it will be recalled, was for only one, regardless of which rate is used, and two were to follow the subsequent year. Hereafter the record is muddled, but little evidence exists to support an official expectation of two Tridents per year.[17]

Another problem was the nagging gadfly of inflation. Reductions in numbers of suppliers—industrywide, nationally, and internationally—gradually caused the lead times for procuring strategic materials and parts to slip (see table 5). When inflation is figured into these delays, both the price and the delivery rates are adversely affected.[18]

Funding requests for FY 1976 greatly resembled those of FY 1975: a total of $2,142 million to be divided among research and development ($817 million), procurement ($1,130 million), and military construction ($195 million). Of the research money, $84 million was appropriated for the submarine and $733 million for the missile. Procurement funds were divided among advance procurement for the fifth, sixth, and seventh subs ($43 million) and Trident I missile production ($237 million), and $290 million was to cover the cost increase of ships funded in fiscal year 1975 and prior years "as a result of abnormal inflation," with a further $560 million tagged for completion of the fourth ship. By this time the consequential funding battles essentially had been won and the question asked was less frequently "How much?"

Table 5
Extension of Lead Times for Procuring Strategic Materials and Parts
(in weeks)

Item	December, 1975	August, 1979
Aluminum sheets, plates	12–16	68–73
Bearings	16–20	46–55
Castings	30–32	46–62
Cobalt, molysteel bar	12–18	44–50
Electrical connectors	16–24	47
Fasteners	6–8	39–54
Aluminum, large forgings	48–50	78–89
Titanium	50–55	99–105
Hinges	50–52	72–90*
Hydraulic fittings	36–38	80–84*
Titanium sheets	12–18	76–77

*April, 1979, data.

than "How many?" Although the due date of the first Trident, the *Ohio*, fluctuated, April, 1979, generally now appeared as the target date for delivery.[19]

Trident came to life while the SSBN-X option shuttled back and forth between enthusiasm and apathy. The Trident Program Coordinator, Rear Admiral John Nicholson, spoke in February, 1976, of a smaller, sixteen-tube SSBN with Trident technology. A month later, however, John Walsh, the Deputy Director for the Department of Defense's Strategic Space Systems, told a Senate subcommittee that in 1976 ideas for a smaller, cheaper Trident remained impractical. Because the development of a completely different submarine takes so long—the "womb to boom" time, as former Secretary of State Alexander Haig called it—any "new" submarine would have to use many Trident features. If asked to design a cheaper submarine, Walsh admitted, "we couldn't really do it. We could design a different submarine but it would just be a different Trident because we would use the same technology." Walsh questioned charges that all future Tridents would be increasingly over budget, noting the "first ship always costs considerably more, at least twice as much as follow-on ships."[20]

Just when it appeared that the Trident program had cleared the legislative hurdle, another obstacle materialized from an unexpected quarter. On July 1, 1975, ten thousand workers of the Metal Trades Council at Electric Boat walked out on strike, not to return until

December 1. During the intervening five months component work continued, but submarine construction itself ground to a halt. Not surprisingly, when P. Takis Veliotis took over as Electric Boat's general manager in 1977 he immediately entered into negotiations for a new three-year metalworkers' contract.[21]

Trident Opposition, Fiscal Year 1976

Opponents of the Trident seemed to be either resigned to the fact a program as far along as the Trident was unlikely to be canceled or were disposed toward shifting their opposition to other programs such as the B-1 bomber, where chances of success measurably increased. Some, like Richard Garwin, continued to fight Trident tooth and nail. In the hearings on the FY 1976 budget, Garwin called the Trident and other proposed systems "entirely premature and in any case [it is] unjustified to build the Trident submarine," which, he claimed, "snuck into full scale development." Funding for the Trident, he added, "ought to be terminated with either the second or third ship." Garwin, who erroneously claimed the B-1 bomber and Trident had not been put in competition with other alternative programs, said "continued expenditures on these programs will indeed buy us 'the shadow rather than the substance of first-class military power.'" Garwin concluded by arguing "in no way has a showing been made that we need an expansion of the SLBM force." Sidney Drell echoed Garwin's comments, calling the Trident "a very elegant 'cadillac of the sea.'" He renewed the arguments heard between 1972 and 1974 that "we may be diminishing the overall survivability level of our SLBM force [by putting] 'more eggs in each basket.'" Both agreed Trident construction should be limited to only one submarine a year. Henry Niles, chairman of Business Executives for New National Priorities, went one step further, saying the United States should defer all Trident work. He maintained that the existing missile subs "are invulnerable to destruction." The Trident, he continued, "will be the most expensive weapon system in history and each submarine will carry enough nuclear weapons to destroy any country in the world." Others, like Joseph Addabbo, dug in to oppose Trident subsystem development. Still, the mood of the country was gradually shifting in favor of greater defense spending. The country was also easing out from the burden of spending related to the Vietnam War. The Congress appropriated $1.3 billion for the war in 1975, the last outlay of that magnitude.[22]

One bastion of opposition was the House Armed Services Committee—which, although generally responsive to Pentagon requests, had a vocal and active minority led by Les Aspin of Wisconsin and Patricia

Schroeder of Colorado. In addition, Melvin Price of Illinois became chairman on February 15, 1975, bringing with him a somewhat ambiguous defense record. The committee was dominated by Democrats, including Price, Aspin, and Schroeder, and Price's appointment was not viewed as a significant change in committee direction. The membership remained "basically pro-military" (to such an extent that Schroeder complained "this committee's idea of what's horrible with the Navy is that it's not going to get a new nuclear aircraft carrier"), but committee sources commented on the Pentagon's "non-responsiveness" and lamented the "too often inaccurate" cost estimates. William Dickenson of Alabama, who had repeatedly skirmished with Navy witnesses on earlier occasions, explained that committee members often lacked the expertise needed to question military witnesses accurately. "You have to be pretty smart to know what the question is that will get you the answer you are seeking," he admitted, adding, "I don't think for a minute that the services knock themselves out trying to help you ask the right questions, unless they are anxious to have you ask that question." In the FY 1976 recommendation the committee allowed the Trident program $1.75 billion while cutting other defense programs. Aspin labeled these cuts "phony" and a week later another Democrat, Robert Leggett of California, tried to delete $559.9 million from the actual Trident construction funds, delaying the funding until a later date, on the grounds that Electric Boat was overburdened and could not begin work until 1977. Leggett assured the House that this was "not the perennial Trident amendment" to end the program. In one of the first indications of his position on Trident, Chairman Price opposed Leggett's amendment because it would have increased the costs another $225 million.[23]

Trident opponents had already shifted their attention to deleting funds from Trident I improvements, Mk-500 Evader testing, and Trident II research. Critics of the Trident I improvements spurred rumors that the volatility of the missile's fuel corroded the engine parts, decreasing missile life to five years, a point Admiral Levering Smith denied. The new Evader warheads brought a particularly vocal response from Trident opposition all through Congress. Senator Thomas McIntyre predicted the Evaders would put us in a "hair trigger period" of national defense. Arming the subs in this manner, he said, was "drastic" and "dangerous." Representative Jonathan Bingham chimed in, calling the MaRV a "whole new stage of the arms race" and a "nightmare." Similarly they dismissed any funding of the Trident II missile as "premature." The attempt to limit MaRV testing met defeat in the House but, surprisingly, the same measure passed the Senate. Hubert Humphrey of Minnesota led the opposition to MaRV testing to a 43–41 victory, although two months later conferees "reluctantly" dropped the ban. On August 2, 1975, the conferees provided $602.6 million for fiscal year 1976 for the fourth Trident. This figure represented a cut of $10 million from the administration's own request but retained the bulk of the actual construction funds. The House committee deleted $48.6 million in Trident II missile funds in October, but a month later the entire House restored $38.6 million.[24]

By 1976, both defense spending and opposition to it had increased (figure 4-2). The election led both candidates, Gerald Ford and Jimmy Carter, to promise increased attention to the defense budget. Senator Jacob Javits of New York criticized President Ford's defense plan, suggesting during the campaign that it was "a retreat from federal responsibility for . . . the unemployed." House majority leader Thomas "Tip" O'Neill denounced the budget priorities as "100 percent wrong." Yet it was unclear that a new administration would follow different policies; for, as Senator Strom Thurmond noted, the Congress had a hand in increasing the federal deficit from $52 billion to over $70 billion at the expense of defense. The Congressional Budget Office, he added, "has taken on a definite 'anti-defense' cast," with "a clear majority of the members of the Congressional Budget Committees [historically voting] more favorably for social than military programs." Representative Joseph Addabbo charged that the Department of Defense was "seriously overfunded," especially with some weapons such as the Trident being produced prematurely when they still required research. Another representative, John Seiberling of Ohio, said "The real question never answered is whether we spend our money on the right things. Clearly we do not." Even some prodefense spokesmen agreed: James Hessman of *Sea Power* magazine called the FY 1977 budget "schizophrenic" because it was "dollar rich" and "ship poor." Despite the spending increases, Hessman complained, "the Navy takes it on the chin" because the national defense strategy called for a minimum of thirty-five ships per year and the budget requested funds for only sixteen. But on January 26, 1976, Defense Secretary Donald Rumsfeld revised the five-year shipbuilding plan further downward, thus cutting the program hopes of the Navy to make up in future budgets the damaging deficiencies. Yet the Trident had outsailed widespread opposition; instead, the B-1 bomber caught congressional flak. Some legislators continued to oppose what they considered "fat" in the defense budget, but little enthusiasm was generated over these issues, termed by the lawmakers "Aspin and Proxmire issues." Overall support for defense spending began to grow (figs. 4-2 and 4-3), although Navy spending began to dip below requests in 1975 and 1976. For the first time since 1967 the House recommended an actual

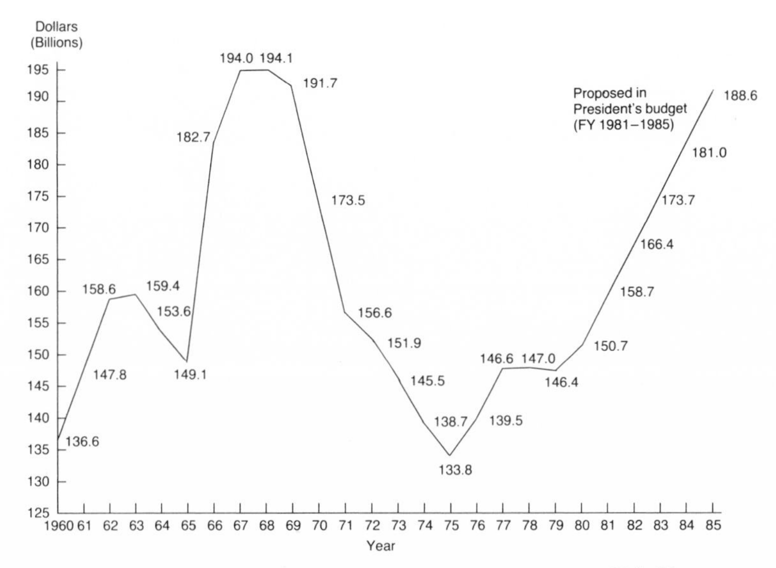

Source: W. Scott Thompson, ed. *National Security in the 1980s*, pp.385–86.

*Total Obligational Authority.

Fig. 4-2. Department of Defense total budget (TOA*) 1960–1985 (FY 1981 constant dollars).

increase (of $699 million) over the Department of Defense total department request, and Ford's suggested budget represented "the first real growth in national defense spending" after "eight years of decline."[25]

President Gerald Ford faced an ever-growing division within his own party on defense issues as the various state primaries commenced. To deflect criticism from challenger Ronald Reagan in this area, Ford announced an intensive new shipbuilding program. Trident submarines, usually considered separately from general shipbuilding appropriations because they fall within the category of strategic forces, not directly Navy Forces, would not normally have been affected by Ford's program. But Ford's plan had ramifications for the Trident in research and development and numerous other programs associated with, but not necessarily under the heading of, Trident appropriations. The FY 1976 funds matched the administration's request: one Trident at $791.5 million plus eighty missiles at $349.8 million, totaling 1,141.3 million. Originally the House had passed funds for two Tridents (a $1,520.3-million total), but the Senate reduced the number back to one, reasoning that Electric Boat's personnel hardly could work any faster.[26]

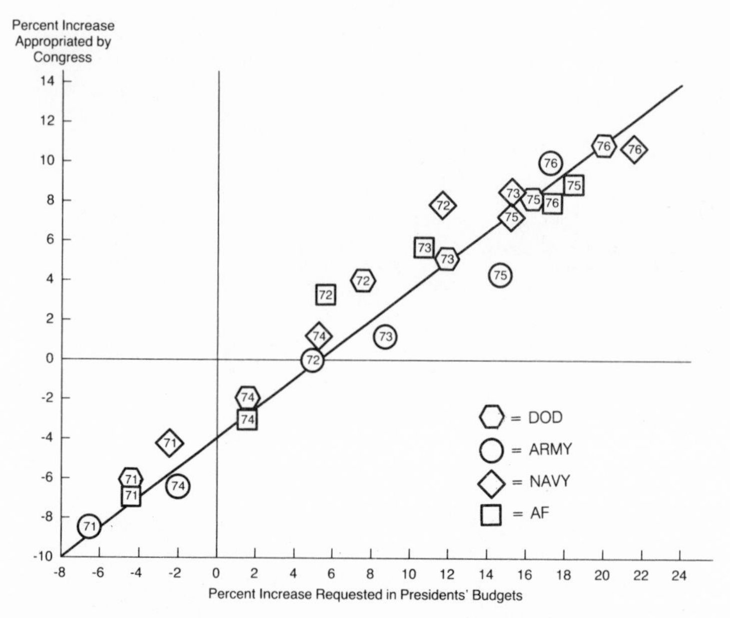

Source: Former Undersecretary of the Army, Norman Augustine.

Fig. 4-3. Percent increases for defense appropriated by Congress and requested in presidents' budgets, 1971–1976.

Joseph Addabbo made yet another 1976 attempt to cut Trident-related funds by offering an amendment to cut $600 million from the $888 million requested for production of the Trident I missile. Eventually $115 million was removed, but only because the start of procurement was delayed by the delays in the submarine schedule.[27]

In fact, delays already had appeared. Admiral J. C. Metzel testified before the House Armed Services Committee in 1977 that the first Trident date had slipped four months, based on an estimate by Electric Boat. Either the Navy demonstrated great gullibility here or the contractor great optimism, for the program had already lost five months due to the metalworkers' strike. Evidence supplied by the General Accounting Office showed delays caused by a host of problems. Of 9220 drawings due by 1977, more than a thousand remained incomplete. Material equipment items had slipped in delivery from two to fifteen months. Productivity at the shipyard dropped, thanks to a declining proportion of skilled personnel; it eroded from 62 percent in January, 1976, to 55 percent in June, 1976, and to 49 percent in 1977.[28]

Electric Boat had on its hands troubles caused partially by the Navy, partially by inflation, and partially by its own workforce. The "hidden tax" was eating the company's profits—it also affected three other yards in the same way—and in December 1976 the four yards filed a $1.8 billion lawsuit against the Navy, of which Electric Boat's portion came to $840 million, to recover money lost due to the effects of unforeseen inflation from the time the contracts had originally been signed until 1976. Electric Boat claimed its losses on the 688 Los Angeles-class submarines would amount to $843 million without a settlement. The Pentagon, however, proposed a countersettlement of $500 to $700 million, contending only 21 percent ($378 million) of Electric Boat's claims were related to inflation. On June 10 William C. Clements, the deputy defense secretary, announced a breakdown in talks with the yards. Many naval officers were unenthusiastic over any type of settlement, fearing it would undermine their authority to enforce other ship-procurement contracts. As the dispute dragged on, officials of both the Ford and the Carter administrations became increasingly disenchanted with the Navy, indirectly blaming it for its inability to end the dispute. Reports also began to leak out that the Trident was already behind schedule and over budget. The Navy announced in November 1977 that the first Trident would not be delivered until early 1981, a year behind schedule and $400 million more than originally planned. Navy spokesmen refused to place the blame on Electric Boat, but no reason was given for the overruns and delays, making it appear Electric Boat's fault.[29]

The Navy's Response to Opposition

Although the Trident's problems had aroused considerable interest, it was also during 1976 that the Senate Armed Services Committee on Research and Development learned of the positive features of the submarine through a Navy "briefing blitz." One recurring problem in all submarine construction has been replacement of malfunctioning parts after construction or correcting errors inside the sub during construction. The Trident's modular construction solved most of the latter problems. In the March, 1976 hearing the committee was informed that, to ease replacing machinery inside the sub, three 6-foot-diameter logistic trunks were installed in each hull, representing only one of the extensive improvements in the Trident design over previous hull designs. Although minor improvements such as the hatch insignificantly increased the Trident's cost, the savings in maintenance time would increase the time the ship could spend at sea. These advantages became apparent when, one year later, the same Senate subcommittee heard testimony on a per-vessel comparison of the at-sea rates and missile availability of the Trident and the Poseidon, although it should be noted the Poseidon figures were actual, while the Trident statistics were estimates (see table 6). The numerous small but costly innovations in submarine, hull, and missile design finally yielded more visible results for the committee members to see. They learned that the Trident not only would stay at sea longer but would also require less maintenance time while in port. Furthermore, as Admiral Kelln and Rear Admiral Don Harvey explained, the Tridents could be pressed into emergency service even during repairs. The crews "maintain its readiness consistent with repair work" by only deranging "certain equipment at certain intervals in a certain sequence so that the ship can be buttoned up and sent back to sea if needed."[30]

Table 6
At-Sea Rates and Missile Availability of
the Poseidon and the Trident

	Poseidon	**Trident**	
Patrol length (days)	68	70	
Off-patrol period (days)	32	25	
Overhaul (months)	16	12	
Time between overhauls (months)	6	9	
Life cycle-at-sea availability	55%	66%	(21% compound increase of time at sea)
Weapon at-sea availability	72%	78%	
Missile tubes available	16	24	(63% similarly compound increase in weapon at-sea availability)
At sea per sub	11.52%	18.72%	
Weapon at-sea (%)	55	66	
Missile tubes	16	24	
Missile at-sea availability	8.73	15.90	(82% compound increase, including the fact that the longer-range Trident I comes on station closer to home port than does Poseidon)

Funding the Bangor Base and Related Facilities

Discussions about maintenance and repairs, coupled with the slowly approaching deployment date of the *Ohio*, directed a great deal of congressional attention to Bangor base construction. Although the bases and other facilities are discussed in chapter 7 it is important to view their funding in the context of the budgetary pressures and successes of the program as a whole. Again some of the research and development funds exhibited dual applications. For example, a process utilizing magnetics and electromagnetics, called the "linear chair" program (and sometimes referred to as degaussing), is an important defensive procedure for all submarines, including Trident. In FY 1978, $3.9 million in R&D money was requested for linear chair. Most of the funds for Bangor, however, went directly toward constructing typical military-base buildings—cafeterias, service stations, and barracks. Bangor's plans included tennis courts, cafeterias, and hobby shops. There also were several other unique features to the Bangor base. The submarine "pens" actually more or less resembled wharves. This submarine service area was to be delta-shaped to handle two Tridents at once, with a third in drydock, possibly one in the explosive-handling wharf, and even one or two at the marginal wharf; it was also required because of "environmental considerations" and "explosive safety quantity distance areas." Admiral Marschall testified that "the Trident program, with congressional support, is proceeding [in Bangor] without any major setbacks." By the end of FY 1978 he anticipated having "between 800 and 900 military on duty at the Bangor sub base, and more than half will be accompanied by dependents." At the time of Marschall's testimony the base population had reached over 2000. Some estimates showed 5400 personnel housed there by 1985.[31]

Base-related facilities continued to comprise a substantial amount of Bangor funds, with the Brownsville sewage-treatment plant getting $7.3 million, an increase of $900,000 since the 1976 hearings. Support missile test facilities in Cape Canaveral had begun Trident expansion in 1974 and, by the 1977 hearings, were "essentially complete." This facility incorporated a $30-million wharf turning basin for the larger submarine, also completed by 1977. Through refinements in estimates the Navy actually reduced its request for the construction program by $300,000 in FY 1977. Nevertheless, in a program review the base construction program (Bangor, Indian Island, the Keyport, Washington, training facility, and Cape Canaveral missile testing facilities) ran $129,328,000, plus $8 million for the Bangor community in FY 1977. Not included was Point Mugu, which performed some Trident-related functions. As of 1976, the base construction program had totaled $727 million.[32]

Another base-related problem became apparent to the Navy by 1977. Due to an agreement with the government of Spain, the United States scheduled its nuclear weapons for removal in 1979 from the American base at Rota, Spain. This redeployment would require either an Atlantic Trident base in its own right or would force Bangor-based Tridents to journey around South America for Atlantic deployment since the Panama Canal Treaty prohibits strategic missiles in transit. Now, for the first time, word of a submarine base at Kings Bay, Georgia, began to circulate, although at first it was discussed only as a Poseidon relocation facility. Sparking accusations of pork-barrel politics, for two other Georgia bases—Fort Benning and Fort Stewart—had just received appropriations for expansion, the House Appropriations Committee allowed $19.5 million for advance procurement of base construction materials. More than one observer noted the base announcements occurred as a new president entered office: Jimmy Carter from Plains, Georgia.[33]

Carter's election meant Ford's budget might be substantially revised, and when he entered office the size of the defense budget was the topic of numerous media speculations. *The Christian Science Monitor* announced in February, 1977, "Military's 'Wish List' for new weapons up by $18.5 billion"; the *Wall Street Journal* noted "Pentagon Weapons-Cost Estimate Rises $18.5 Billion in Biggest Spurt Since 1970"; and the *Denver Post* headlined "U.S. Weapons Bill Soars." Carter therefore began to consider various defense cuts, to be made in conjunction with the upcoming SALT II talks. "Serious opposition" to the cuts, much of it by influential elements of the Democratic-controlled Congress, pressured him to abandon any plans for cutting the defense budget in 1977. But the opposition was scattered—neither military nor civilian leaders, for example, could decide on whether the Soviet civil defense system actually existed—and a public disagreement over Soviet particle-beam-weapons development (see chap. 9) between the Joint Chiefs of Staff and Major General George Keegan, former intelligence chief of staff for the U.S. Air Force, split opposing groups even further. Ultimately a compromise weapons bill with funds for a nuclear-powered carrier, which Carter opposed, emerged and was passed, but the B-1 bomber was canceled, leaving just four prototypes. With the B-1 cancellation, the Pentagon's weapons estimate fell by $19 billion, although increased costs in the Trident reabsorbed $671.1 million of those funds. In July 1977, Carter ordered the Minuteman III production line shut down so, despite the increased defense spending, two of the three TRIAD legs were adversely affected in the first year of the Carter presidency and continued to deteriorate thereafter. In January 1978, after meeting with NATO defense ministers, Carter promised to increase defense spending, despite his campaign promise to cut military funds by $5 to $7 billion. The budget nevertheless remained fairly constant in real dollars.[34]

With the FY 1978 Department of Defense appropriations request the multidimensional scope of the Trident program had fully flowered, with funds requested for ABRES, the Poseidon backfit with Trident I missiles, Trident submarine construction, base construction, and the distantly related Poseidon modifications to correct missile problems. Defense Department officials requested funds for two Trident submarines in FY 1978 (costing $1,778 million) and another in FY 1979. Contracts for these two boats (numbers 6 and 7) went to General Dynamics on Feburary 28, 1978. Officials rendered a positive decision on production of the Trident I missile on January 17, 1977, following three successful test flights. Therefore, a request in the FY 1978 budget of $1.1 billion for ninety-six missiles was included. Admiral R. H. Wertheim assured the Senate Subcommittee on Research and Development the Trident I was "in better shape than any of those predecessors [the Polaris/Poseidon missiles]." Evader warheads continued to improve in consistency and reliability, so Defense and Navy officials directed more research and development funds toward other areas of submarine protection. Renewed concern arose over submarine communication, particularly at increased depths. Almost unnoticed in the 1977–1978 budget was a continuing request for fourteen naval aircraft "starts" under the R&D section. Code-named Tacamo (for Take Charge and Move Out), these aircraft carried very low frequency (VLF) transmitters for contacting submerged submarines. Research officials established a target date of 1982 for completion of the fourteen aircraft. Tacamos have been the primary means of emergency communication with submarines since the late 1960s (see chap. 9). These aircraft maintain constant patrols—at least one is aloft at all times—so they can transmit orders to submarines should the land-based communications centers be destroyed in war.[35]

Two other Trident-related projects, at first under the R&D budget and later under other budget lines, continued to be the subjects of intense legislative wranglings. Perhaps the most daring communications project in history, the Seafarer, had to fight funding and environmental battles for its existence. Seafarer, previously called SANGUINE, was a proposal for a massive underground radio antenna bed able to feed extremely low frequency (ELF) signals to deep-diving subs. The 1978 battle over Seafarer heralded one of the "longest running defense fights in decades." More than $23.7 million was requested under the R&D budget, most of which survived a House-attempted cut. By 1979, however, fears that the Seafarer, which was then planned for installation under Lake Michigan, would destroy the environment led to emasculation of the funding for ELF research with a cut of $13.5 million. The final communications project, code-named NAVSTAR, represented an attempt to combine an intelligence satellite with a communications satellite. Once again, the Senate in 1977 stepped in to restore many of the House-induced cuts for NAVSTAR. Since it appears less of a threat to the environment than Seafarer, NAVSTAR consistently has met less opposition in Congress. The fact that the Seafarer, Tacamo, NAVSTAR, and other projects complementary to the Trident vessel now in the R&D stage commanded the center of attention in 1977 underscored the routine nature of Trident funding bills among the vast majority of the legislators. Congressional approval with little quibbling of all funds requested for the eighth Trident in the series further emphasized this standing.[36]

A sudden reversal in the Navy's dispute with Newport News in March 1978 directed Congress' attention to the claims problem. Less than two weeks later all three of the major shipbuilders were again pressing their claims. The Navy made a specific offer to General Dynamics of $544 million to settle its contract claims, an offer General Dynamics refused on March 14. Electric Boat threatened to halt all work on 688-class attack submarines, calling the move a "last resort," although it said work would continue uninterrupted on the Tridents. General Dynamics claimed the Navy had "materially breached" the contracts because the original contracts did not sufficiently allow for inflation, and as a result Electric Boat was experiencing a massive cash-flow drain. The Navy claimed the costs were the result of "incompetent management," and Rickover accused the shipbuilder of a "consistent pattern of misrepresentation." Electric Boat responded by maintaining that it had spent $370 million since 1974 for wages and materials that "rightfully should have been paid by the Navy." Failure to solve the problem would result in the shipbuilder laying off 8000 workers, company officials said. In fact, according to William Bennett, vice president of Electric Boat in charge of Quonset Point, the company was losing $15 million a month until Veliotis took over in 1977. Congress, caught in the middle, expressed concern the 688 problems would spill over to Trident. Defense officials conceded that the problems in the attack subs were "contributing to delay in the deployment of Trident ballistic-missile submarines" but pressured the shipbuilder into extending the deadline by two months, to June 12, 1978, thanks to an announcement by the Navy on April 6 of a provisional increase of $66.5 million in the contract price of *Los Angeles* subs, with an immediate payment of $24.8 million sent to General Dynamics for its "cash flow" problems. Despite the extension, General Dynamics warned that it "cannot afford" to continue absorbing losses caused by changes resulting from inflation.[37]

Admiral Hyman Rickover suggested that General Dynamics had submitted outrageous claims "to avoid reporting to its stockholders potential losses amounting to hundreds of millions of dollars." Indeed, General Dynamics reported a yearly profit of 3.8 percent ($103.4 million) that year, counting the pending claims, but the company had not paid a dividend since 1970. Litton Ingalls had been charged by a federal grand jury with filing a false $30-million submarine claim in 1977, but General Dynamics executives denied any incidence of fraud in the attack-submarine claims. Rickover, following his retirement, blasted the Justice Department for its inability to successfully prosecute the shipbuilders. David Lewis, chairman of General Dynamics, blamed the problems on Navy changes, which he said "flood in at a rate of 200 or 300 a week." For this reason, he explained, the company took 7.1 million man hours to build the first attack sub when it had planned on 3.8 million. Vice Admiral C. R. Bryan charged that Electric Boat's productivity was "disappointing" and that Electric Boat had expanded the workforce too rapidly to ensure productivity. A former labor relations manager for the shipyard, Stanley Eno, supported Bryan's contention, saying the "growing pains were unbelievable" because the firm hired "women, minorities, and hard-core unemployed." "Drugs, alcoholism, sex and discrimination incidents became a way of life," Eno added, and "unrest, fights and problems [occurred] as people tried to learn shipbuilding trades." A machinist union official also testified that workers were "constantly demeaned, harassed, misdirected and blamed as a smoke-screen for management to cover their [*sic*] accounting manipulations with the Navy." Eno said "workers, supervisors and others [were] trying to look busy for eight hours a day either because of lack of materials or lack of direction by management."[38]

On June 12 the Navy and General Dynamics reached a settlement after "hundreds of hours of negotiations." General Dynamics agreed to take a $359-million loss on the attack subs, although its after-tax loss would be only $157 million. The alternative, a General Dynamics spokesman said, was "a long court suit." Consequently, although record earnings had been forecast that year, the loss absorbed by the company would put it in the red for 1978 while the Navy consented to pay $484 million over the $1.8 billion original contract price, including a $300 million lump-sum payment immediately, to aid the struggling firm. General Dynamics' loss translated to an after-tax loss of $187 million. While the *Wall Street Journal* called the settlement a major victory for the Navy, Chairman David Lewis of General Dynamics termed it "painful." Navy Secretary W. Graham Claytor said it was "rough justice" for both sides, and beamed that the settlement "is the most important thing from the standpoint of the Navy we've accomplished since we've been in office." One key factor in achieving the settlement occurred when the Navy hired an accounting firm to check the company's estimate of losses. The firm verified General Dynamics' claim of $843 million in losses, and the settlement provided for $125 million to be subtracted from that figure (as the Navy had already agreed it owed General Dynamics the $125 million and had started payment). Although both Litton and Newport News still had similar claims pending, the General Dynamics settlement "broke the ice," and Litton settled on June 21. Senator William Proxmire called the settlements a "bailout" despite the findings of the independent audit.[39]

Partially because of the fear the shipbuilding problems might spill over to the Trident as well as because the Tridents already were behind the original 1974 accelerated "best honest effort" schedule, legislators renewed their infatuation with an adumbrated version of the Trident. On August 5, 1978, a House committee added $3 million for continued research on a less-expensive sub to follow the Trident and, on January 27, 1979, the Senate Armed Services Committee increased to $10 million the original request for this purpose. Continued funding of the SSBN-X seemed to ignore the technical testimony of the previous four years. When the Senate Subcommittee on Research and Development had reviewed the SSBN-X concept in 1974 it found "there was relatively little cost gain to be realized by reducing the hull length of the submarine." Nevertheless, the 1977 ERDA request included $30 million for the development of a new power plant "potentially applicable" to a future smaller submarine design. The size of the power plant presented only one of a number of problems involved in scaling down a Trident, since the major problem remained the Trident II missile's 44-foot height and 83-inch diameter and since no resizing could overcome that problem without changing the straight, vertical missile tubes. Some authorities have suggested a slanted-tube concept, discussed earlier, but it in turn reduces the number of missiles each sub can carry, because slanting displaces more usable space, in turn requiring more subs. Moreover, a submarine loses some sonar-evasive capability when hull diameter falls below 37 feet, with the optimum being 42 to 43.5 feet.[40]

This particular research and development hearing further confused the issue of the planned Trident force level when Navy witnesses R. H. Wertheim, A. L. Kelln, and Don Harvey made reference to a five-year process eventually netting thirteen Trident subs. Research, indeed, already was underway for numbers 14 through 16, and the March 14, 1977, *Wall Street Journal* headlined the Navy's intent "to Purchase 16

Tridents Instead of 13 as Stated Earlier." As noted in the preceding chapter, estimates among supposedly informed Navy officials about force levels ranged from ten to twenty-nine, indicating that a great deal of confusion on this subject continued to plague the Navy even as late as 1978, and to a lesser degree on up to 1982.[41]

The research and development by now had invested the Trident with numerous innovations. For example, more than $6 million was set aside in the R&D budget for anechoic coating, which improved the subs' ability to evade sonar "stealthily." The Tridents also would come equipped with an XBT, or external buoyant thermometer (thermocline). This device "floats to the surface then plummets down for several thousands of feet [sending] telemetry back to the submarine." In addition to these devices or processes already developed, numerous other research programs continued under the FY 1978 budget. Just under $1 million was allocated for Mobile Submarine Simulators (MOSS), small submarines ejected from special tubes penetrating the Trident's hull. Emitting noises and projecting a sonar "signature" virtually identical to the Trident's, they decoy enemy torpedoes or missiles away from the actual vessel. Sonar processing equipment received $11.8 million, sub-quieting got $13.2 million, and a mysterious $1.6 million was allocated for research on an "ingenious little device," perhaps some supersecret version of confounding sonar searching with a dischargeable version of the octopus' "ink." General Trident research totaled over $68 million, with another $5 million used in research for the Trident II missile. While the latter item received funds in FY 1978, each following year would bring a growing debate about its deployment.[42]

Two advantages accompanied the potential deployment of the Trident II missile: increased range and/or a bigger payload. The extent of increased range gained with the new missile would vary (fully loaded, the Trident II has a range of 6000 n.m.), but the versatility of using smaller payloads could increase the range more (some suggest 6200 n.m.), thereby improving the potential for South Pacific deployment. The Navy's claim that the Trident submarine with Trident I missiles "can essentially be in missile range from Charleston or Bangor" was technically correct, but Trident II will definitely make the sub a legitimate threat to most parts of Russia from those areas. Trident II's capability to destroy hardened silos—its increased payload and 6000-pound throw-weight—evoked the most resistance. The Trident II can carry up to fourteen MIRVs, each with a "clout 1200 times that of Hiroshima" and an accuracy around 300 yards (advertised) with perhaps a better accuracy ("less than 100 feet"). Both the arms-limitations groups and the budget cutters viewed this missile as either provocative or unnecessary, even though no specific warhead was as yet selected. Although FY 1979 funds for another submarine were approved, the $40.6 million for the Trident II missile was deleted by the Senate Armed Services Committee because there was "no clear statement of need" and because it would rival (a rather absent rivalry in retrospect) the MX missile under development by the Air Force.[43]

Opponents to any sort of submarine-launched ballistic missile incorporating either a greater payload or improved accuracy argued that a "hard target kill capability has profound implications for U.S. strategic policy." The Congressional Research Service *Trident Issue Brief* of 1981 summarizes the opposition arguments:

> We gain nothing by threatening [Soviet] forces, as we will not launch a strategic attack first.
>
> A counterforce capability is useless for a retaliatory strike, which would hit only empty silos or malfunctioning missiles.
>
> To acquire a hard target capability . . . might cause the Soviets . . . to launch their ICBMs on warning of attack, in which case computer malfunction or human error could lead to nuclear war.
>
> Hard target capability is very costly, yet the Soviets could offset it cheaply by launching ICBMs on warning of attack.
>
> Trident II would be particularly threatening to the Soviets. Since they could be launched from waters near the U.S.S.R., the Soviets would have less warning than they would for an attack by ICBMs.
>
> The U.S.S.R. is more threatened by hard target kill capability than the U.S. because about 75% of Soviet strategic warheads are ICBMs, vs. about 25% for the U.S.

Along with the debate over the Trident II missile came suggestions for strategic alternatives to MAD. None of these options included the Trident II to any great extent, and planning continued for its development.[44]

However, Defense Department officials emphasized cost-cutting in the Trident missiles in any way possible. Secretary of Defense Harold Brown suggested in a letter to Melvin Price "a less expensive 'stretched' [the long C-4 with terminal fixed source] Trident I with improved accuracy [Trident I C4U] and increased maximum payload range" or the alternate larger Trident II "that maximizes SLBM payload to a level permitted by the size of the Trident submarine launch tube." An optional greater range would be possible with fewer reentry vehicles (see fig. 2-4). Brown pointed out that a Trident I "stretch-out" would cost $1–1.5 billion, and with improved accuracy might reach $4 billion (causing Congressman Dickenson to wonder "Why wouldn't it be best to go forward with, say, the Trident II missile [instead of the $75 billion dollar MX missile]?"). Budgetary restraints in Trident II development encouraged DoD officials to seek greater commonality between the Trident and MX missiles. Consequently, both a two-stage version and a three-stage version of the same basic missile were planned, according to the FY 1980 Department of Defense Annual Report. Commonality in missile design, it noted, "could save one to two billion dollars in development costs on the Trident II missile."[45]

Trident I testing continued to prove fruitful for use in both the Tridents and in retrofitted Poseidons. With fourteen successes in seventeen launches, Trident I continued to draw justifiable praise as "better than POLARIS and POSEIDON at comparable phases of their development." Shipboard tests from the *Francis Scott Key* were scheduled for the spring of 1979.[46]

Even so, Trident I funding actually dropped in the FY 1979 budget compared to the previous year ($1.2 billion compared to $1.5 billion), a development some interpreted as the first step in a number of Navy cuts. According to James Canan's *War in Space,* Harold Brown wanted the defense budget redirected toward a land-oriented European force, which left the admirals "flying force 10 storm signals." Worse, a struggle broke out between Brown, director Edward Jayne of the Office of Management and Budget, Carter, and Congress. As a result, noted Canan, the final budget contained much of what nobody wanted and little of what anyone wanted. Canan also reported that Navy Secretary W. Graham Claytor "was especially assertive" in opposing Carter's use of Jayne in his position at OMB to look over the shoulders of the services, and Claytor did not trust Brown's promise to "maintain a two-ocean Navy." Relations between the Navy and the administration grew so strained over "the treatment the Navy was taking" in the budget that former CNO Thomas Moorer and former Navy Secretary G. William Middendorf urged the CNO at that time, Admiral James L. Holloway, to resign in protest. On top of all this, Claytor and Jayne developed mutual animosities during this budget process. Eventually Carter vetoed the original defense bill that included a nuclear carrier, because of the continued slippage in delivery dates at the shipyards, and also because Congress had dissected and rebuilt the budget to suit itself. The House sustained the veto, 206 to 191, at which point Senator Stennis agreed to "take out the . . . carrier and sew it back up," but only after Carter promised to include a conventional oil-powered carrier in the next budget, and only after Brown sold the congressmen on the advantages of having numerous aircraft contractors across the country, which would stand to gain by passing the bill, happy at election time. The Navy lost one Trident, an Aegis cruiser, a conventional cruiser, a conventional destroyer, and a carrier all in the same fiscal year.[47]

More than the practical successes of any of the various aspects of the program, it was increasingly the growing Soviet strategic threat that induced more cooperation on Trident budgetary matters. While it does not hurt the Secretary of Defense to announce that a program is ahead of schedule in some areas, the Defense Department is more likely to get a favorable congressional response when the secretary reports, as Secretary Harold Brown did in 1979, "I believe that a Soviet surprise attack in which our forces would 'ride out' the attack poses a severe test." Nor is it surprising that the new concern with Soviet military growth was evidenced by an especially long annual report in which the strategic forces of each side were examined with unusually careful attention. Part of the FY 1980 report resembled those of previous years, calling for funding of one Trident at $1,478.9 million (of which $287 million was cost growth), as well as $824.1 million for Trident I missiles (no specific number given) and $40.6 million for Trident II missile development. An underlying theme of survivability for all three legs of the TRIAD is nevertheless emphasized in this report. To underscore the abilities of each leg, and their vulnerabilities, Brown included a table of strategic force characteristics (see table 7).[48]

Some of the SLBM characteristics would not necessarily be attributable to the Trident. For example, the development of the Trident II

Table 7
Current Strategic Force Characteristics

	ICBM	**SLBM**	**Bomber/ALCM**
Secure and reliable C[3] [command, communication, and control]	yes	?†	?
Flexibility/responsiveness	yes	?†	no
Assured penetration	yes	yes	?
Prompt counterforce capabilities	yes	?†	no
Sovereign basing	yes	no	yes
Enduring survivability	*	yes	?
Survives without tactical warning	*	yes	no

*May be "yes" with Multiple Protective Structures (MPS) and some other survivable basing modes.

†Would require new programs and/or changes to SSBN operational practices.

would constitute a formidable counterforce capability, and Trident boats will be fully based in the United States.

The FY 1979 budget made no mention of an SSBN-X option, and Admiral Kelln had stated flatly in 1978 the "Navy is . . . not considering any other platform but the Trident as a replacement for our current SSBN's." However, the FY 1980 report noted that alternative submarine designs already were under way. Three goals of the program included (1) designing a less expensive submarine than the Trident, (2) bringing "competition into the SSBN acquisition process," and (3) providing "an option for an expanded SSBN shipbuilding program should the need arise." Once again, however, two immediate problems blocked any new, cheaper version of the Trident: reactor size and missile size. The third goal was reasonable but, as there is only one yard with the trained personnel (to say nothing of the physical and capital facilities) to build ballistic-missile submarines, the second goal had to be something of a pipe dream.[49]

Carter's defense reversals led his opponents to charge him with hypocrisy by 1980. Under the stated goal of improving the military in numbers and quality, he had reversed his own position on the neutron bomb, rejected the Navy's request for another aircraft carrier, and killed the B-1 bomber. Obviously, by this time recollections of the original "compact" between the Joint Chiefs of Staff and the Nixon administration preliminary to the ratification of Salt I had dimmed to the point of historical irrelevance. Representative Pete Domenici of New Mexico called Carter's performance "the most cynical sequence of actions in his four-year term." Fortunately for Trident supporters, however, Carter generally left their program intact. Advance procurement for the program, as well as the substantial opposition Carter had encountered on the other military issues (especially the carrier) and the strong shipbuilding lobby for predominantly Democratic states reduced the chances of any further Navy cuts. Both houses of Congress, uneasy over the Soviet invasion of Afghanistan, exhibited a greater propensity to grant the Pentagon its budget requests. The Carter administration even proposed a 4.6 percent growth in real terms from the FY 1980 budget. Increasingly, more congressmen began to question the types of weapons being purchased, and the disagreements transcended party lines. Although the Trident escaped mention, a sharp debate among Republicans over defense issues broke out in November 1980, with Ronald Reagan urging resumption of production of the B-1. Whatever role Carter played in the Trident program usually came in the form of statements by Secretary of Defense Harold Brown, although Brown's role is somewhat enigmatic. Brown, for example, supposedly fought tooth and nail for greater defense funding and, at least according to James Canan, recognized the seriousness of the Soviet threat from the outset. Nevertheless, Brown, as Secretary of Defense, had presided over a massive shift in strategic power in favor of the Soviets. Whether he extracted the maximum concessions from Carter and Congress, as Canan suggested, or he was myopic, as the editorials of *Aviation Week* claimed (see chap. 9) remains to be settled. As far as the Trident was concerned, Brown, although supporting the submarine construction program in general, registered his opposition to $36.4 million in funding for the Trident II missile, arguing that comparable improvements could be achieved with the Trident I. Eventually, however, Congress directed the Pentagon to transfer $33 million from other projects to the Trident II missile development.[50]

Hereafter, discussion of alternative designs turned from the question of necessity for a Trident-type submarine toward the capabilities of such a vessel. This "capabilities" argument flowed over into the debate on attack submarines. Should the United States build more submarines less capable in speed, diving ability, or noise abatement? Or should the country hold out for the "extra 10 percent" of performance that comes with new technology? Both sides of the argument found sympathetic ears in Congress in the 1970s, although the "high technology" proponents seemed to triumph at that time. "This committee will not approve a slower, less capable submarine," Paul S. Trible, a Republican member of the House Seapower Subcommittee, stated flatly. In line with his comment, the committee called for increasing the building rate of the considerably more sophisticated *Los Angeles* class. But the confusion concerning eventual direction of the SSBN program was apparent when both the Senate and the House voted increases in funding for a larger version of the Trident. Just the opposite of the SSBN-X, this Trident included more midsections holding even more missiles. Supporters of a larger boat argued that it would save money because fewer ships could carry as many missiles as more of the regularly sized Tridents. Neither the elongated Trident nor the SSBN-X received balloon-bursting receptions; rather, a commonsense Congress in December 1980 voted funds for the ninth Trident submarine, almost matching the administration's request. Moreover, the conference report added $28.1 million for a longer-range missile, an indication of growing support for Trident II in preference to manipulating the size of the Trident hull.[51]

So far the *Ohio* had still not put to sea, returning to Groton for further work following the first sea trials in 1980. By now it was behind schedule by a least a year, although some observers cynically predicted it would not go to sea until 1982 at the earliest. Following the 1975 metal trades strike at Electric Boat, an eight-month draftsmen's union strike hit the company in September 1979. The management had just relaxed following a successful renegotiation of the metal trades contract in July. Together the two strikes accounted for over a year's worth of Trident delays. Electric Boat's contract claims fight threatened to delay it further, thereby eliciting a somewhat negative congressional response. According to one report, both armed services committees favored delaying the tenth Trident for a year. Actually, pushing funds back one fiscal year could delay actual delivery by as little as a month or two. Both committees followed through by delaying exercise of the option for the tenth contract on May 9, 1981, although they later added $110 million for parts procurement for the following two Tridents ($75 million of that paid for the FY 1982 work, which would have been done anyway). The *Ohio*'s delays had initiated another controversy. Vice Admiral Earl B. Folwer, in a statement that deliberately or otherwise became public, accused Electric Boat of shoddy workmanship, poorly sealed welds, use of below-grade steel, and numerous other indiscretions and examples of poor construction. Fowler's charges (dealt with in depth in chap. 6) renewed the high technology-versus-low technology debate and even further clouded the program alternatives. But when the same problem caused staff member Larry Smith to ask Admiral J. C. Metzel in 1977, "Is there any noticeable effect on either the pace or cost of the Trident submarine construction program [caused by welding problems]?" Metzel responded that to his knowledge "there [had] been no effect on either the cost or on the schedule."[52]

Debate over Trident's cost effectiveness soon dragged the 688 *Los Angeles* class into the discussion since it was also made by Electric Boat. Appearance of the extremely quick *Alpha* (or *Alfa*) stirred up a new round of debates over optimum size, speed, and defensive characteristics. Congressional staff member Anthony Battista asked William Perry, Undersecretary of Defense for Research and Engineering, "Where are we going in the submarine world[?]" While the *Alpha* is faster than the 688s, the Research and Development Office had proposed "a follow on to our 688 class boats [called] the Fat Albert [Fleet Attack, or FA], which is a slower submarine than the 688." Perry explained that "the Soviets have elected to go for a hot rod," but he expressed doubt they were fully committed to the *Alpha* program. "It may simply be an experimental program," he noted, or it may simply have been a "technological imperative." Whatever their reason for building the *Alpha*, the Russians "have been very, very slow, untypically slow, in going into production with this submarine." Some sources, such as the *Daily Telegraph* in Britain, reported the Soviets having four

Alpha's at sea as early as 1979. "West Outclassed by Latest Soviet Submarines," the *Telegraph* proclaimed, but Perry—and naval authorities in general—seemed at least somewhat unconcerned. Perry told the subcommittee: "We have . . . developed technologies which, if deployed in large quantities, could put a large portion of the Soviet SLBM force at risk. We don't believe the Soviets are capable of exploiting these ASW technologies in the near term and, in any event, such a deployment would be very expensive and observable (so we would have many years' warning)."[53]

Perry, of course, because of his position as Secretary of Defense for Research and Development as well as his personal qualifications as a doctor of mathematics and his expertise in the technologies of surveillance, was well acquainted with highly secret advances in ASW technology on both the American and Soviet sides. Coupled with the *Alpha*'s noisy operational mode, the United States' expanded-range ASW weapon under development as of 1980, would *favor* a slow but quiet American sub over a fast but noisy sub. "We will maintain [our] lead by continuing our emphasis on quieting . . . [and] acoustic processing," Perry noted. "We intend to continue converting our advantage in computers and signal processing technology into a growing advantage in submarine detection, so that our submarines will be able to detect Soviet submarines (and take appropriate action) long before the Soviet submarine is aware of our presence."[54]

Hyman Rickover, always an advocate for higher performance, also opposed the Fat Albert. When the FY 1982 budget finally dropped all Fat Albert funding, Representative Samuel Stratton of New York said "I was happy to see . . . that Fat Albert has expired," to which Rickover responded "I share your happiness. But I am also saddened that we put people at the head of the Navy who have such backward ideas as building slower, less-capable ships."[55]

During a debate in the House Seapower Subcommittee, some critics suggested converting the *Los Angeles* boats into SSBNs to replace the Trident. But such a move would fundamentally alter the actual purpose and design of the vessel. The Trident/*Los Angeles* controversy increased following Fowler's charges leveled at Electric Boat in the early spring of 1981. Electric Boat had fallen behind schedule on both the Trident and the attack submarines, causing Secretary of the Navy John Lehman, Jr., to negotiate contracts for three other future attack subs with Tenneco's Newport News shipyards in Virginia. Having counted on the future contracts, P. Takis Veliotis, the general manager of Electric Boat, predicted 3000 workers would have to be laid off at Groton if the contracts went elsewhere. While the Navy legitimately and effectively could threaten to give Newport News the three attack submarine contracts, threats to take the Trident contracts to other domestic or, as one source reported, "foreign builders" were hollow. Only Electric Boat had the physical facilities and experience to handle the Tridents, to ignore the issue of the program's security vulnerabilities if built abroad.[56]

By 1983, ten Tridents had been authorized and long-lead funding allocated for three others. Two Tridents are currently (1983) at sea, the *Michigan* and the *Ohio*, and the *Florida* was launched in November, 1981. Although the originally scheduled number 9 had been canceled, Congress appropriated $1,645 million in FY 1982 for it, bringing the number actually under construction (as of 1983) to eight, with three more currently authorized and a budget request in for two more. According to *Trident Issue Brief*, the Navy projects fifteen to be authorized through FY 1986, although twenty-four "might be built by 1997"[57] (see table 8).

Missile funds for both procurement of the Trident I and research and development of the Trident II increased with inflation. For the Trident I, procurement funding in FY 1980 was $765.5 million, with

Table 8
1983 Trident Construction Status

Hull	Fiscal Year Authorized	Delivery Date Estimated by:		Pct. Complete (Jan., 1981)
		Contractor	Navy	
1. SSBN 726 (*Ohio*)	1974	June, 1981	Dec., 1981	95*
2. SSBN 727 (*Michigan*)	1975	Nov., 1981	Dec., 1982	84
3. SSBN 728 (*Florida*)	1975	July, 1982	Sep., 1983	69
4. SSBN 729 (*Georgia*)	1976	Mar., 1983	May, 1984	52
5. SSBN 730 (*Rhode Island*)	1977	Nov., 1983	Jan., 1985	35
6. SSBN 731 (*Alabama*)	1978	July, 1984	Sep., 1985	25
7. SSBN 732	1978	Mar., 1985	May, 1986	14
8. SSBN 733	1980	May, 1986	Jan., 1987	N/A†
9. SSBN 734	1981	—	Sep., 1987	N/A‡
10. SSBN 735	1983	—	—	

*The *Ohio* underwent sea trials in June 1981. Electric Boat did estimate the *Ohio* would be ready for delivery in October, 1981, and this date was, indeed, met.

†The Navy executed the contract for this submarine in January, 1981.

‡On April 1, 1981, the Navy let its option to have Electric Boat build this submarine expire. The contract for SSBN 734 was later renegotiated and signed on January 7, 1982.

planned or proposed funding for future years reading: 1981, $837.9 million; 1982, $933.6 million; and 1983, $932.1 million. Trident II funds reflected an even more dramatic rise: FY 1980, $25.6 million; 1981, $97.6 million; 1982, $242.9 million; and 1983, $354 million.

Trident missile development narrowly escaped a potential problem, though, in June, 1980, when the voters of Santa Cruz County rejected convincingly a measure aimed at forcing Lockheed to stop Trident program work. Although supporters of the measure lost, they attempted to shut down the company's headquarters the following day. This demonstration failed when five persons trying to deface the buildings were arrested. The Trident missile program and other associated Trident programs continued to grow, despite the threatened interruption. Backfitting of the Poseidons received $4.3 million, and under that funding the twelfth (and, under the Carter program, final) Poseidon submarine would be equipped with Trident I missiles.

The Carter administration requested an additional $5.7 million for military construction not related to the Trident bases. For those bases, $211 million was programmed by the Navy ($36 million in FY 1981 and $175 million in FY 1982), but the Carter administration eventually reduced the FY 1982 funding to $123.9 million. The selection of Kings Bay, Georgia, as the East Coast site prompted the administration to send much of the money there. Bangor neared completion, scheduled for full operation on July 1, 1981, so the new base received a substantial share of the funds. For FY 1982, Carter recommended $98 million for funding of Kings Bay, with the rest to go to Bangor. One positive aspect of the Trident's ship delays has been that neither Bangor nor Kings Bay construction has required acceleration.[58]

Reagan's election sparked anticipations that he would increase the defense budget in real dollars. The Reagan administration announced increases in the budget, especially in the shipbuilding plan, with an eventual goal of a 600-ship Navy, and originally hoped to accelerate Trident construction to three per year through 1985, a perhaps still unrealistic goal but one better within reach than when it was suggested in 1974 by the Navy, due to the experience factor at the shipyard. Reagan also planned to accelerate development of the Trident II missile. By February, 1981, work on both the *Los Angeles* class and the Tridents had increased. Electric Boat promised that the *Ohio* would be delivered within the year. Reagan may have foreseen no problems with the Trident; Congress saw things differently. In May the House Armed Services Committee deleted the $960.8 million for another Trident (by the original numbering system, it would have been the eleventh). The committee cited the problems at Electric Boat to justify its decision. However, the panel left $330.7 million worth of advance fundings for future Trident long-lead purchases. Despite Reagan's promise to boost the defense budget, at least one analyst warned that the strategic mess was "too big for dollars alone to cure." Benjamin Schemmer reminded the country, in an article for the *Armed Forces Journal,* "there are not enough dollars in *any* foreseeable American defense budget . . . to bridge the chasm that now exists between U.S. and Soviet military capabilities." The proposed short-term fixes "add up to 'band aid' first aid on a patient nearing terminal illness."[59]

Besides overall generalized criticism, a media blitz charged that the defense increases represented "quick fixes." A favorite phrase among critics was that Reagan was "throwing money at" problems. Senator Gary Hart of Colorado complained, "We are just going to spend more everywhere," while, on the opposite side of the debate, Secretary of Defense Caspar Weinberger, once known as "Cap the Knife" for his budget cuts in previous administrations, now gained the new nickname "Cap the Shovel." Both the *Los Angeles Times* and the *New York Times* editorialized against a larger defense budget. *Time* magazine ran a cover-story feature on the defense budget called "How to Spend a Trillion." The trillion-dollar figure in particular elicited a response bordering on stark terror among some anti-Pentagon groups. *Atlantic Monthly, Newsweek, Time, Fortune,* and even *Playboy* featured major defense-related stories in early 1981, each stressing the "money won't buy performance" approach. James Fallows, whose *Atlantic Monthly* article ("America's High-Tech Weaponry") was followed by a book (*National Defense*), criticized the nearly exclusive tendency to procure progressively more sophisticated pieces of machinery. He charged that "a wonder-weapon mentality" dominates military thinking with a priority to "keep dollars moving." J. R. Seesholtz provides an effective critique of the Fallows approach, concluding that "technology is not the 'culprit' in system effectiveness, cost, and complexity," and while "the right answer may not be obvious . . . blaming technology is the wrong answer."[60]

Lawrence J. Korb anticipated much of the trillion-dollar antagonism in an article for the March 1980 issue of the *Naval War College Review* entitled "The FY 1981–85 Defense Program: Is a Trillion Dollars Enough?" In a conclusion quite similar to a statement by Caspar Weinberger in *Newsweek* ("We have not, as we thought, saved money by reducing military spending in the last decade; we have merely postponed spending"), Korb calls the 1961–1975 period the "Lost Decades for Defense." Korb points out Carter's (and now Reagan's) "trillion dollar 5-year defense program, as large as it is, addresses only a few of the [weaknesses]" suggested in the article, and "in real terms or constant dollars the FY 1981 defense budget will not be very much above the level of FY 1964." Moreover, "when the higher costs of personnel and operations are factored in, the new program will not match the purchasing power of the FY 1961–65 program." In a rough comparison with Soviet levels of defense spending, William Perry noted, in 1980, "during the last decade . . . the Soviet Union invested in aggregate $240 billion more than the United States in defense," including research, development, and procurement. Perry gave the House Research and Development Subcommittee "a sample of what $240 billion . . . might buy." He included in his subjective list 1000 F-16 fighters, 1000 F-18s, 10,000 XM-1 tanks, 20 Aegis cruisers, 50 attack submarines, the entire M-X missile force, the entire Trident force (subs, missiles, bases, and all), plus an extra $70 billion for research and development.[61]

These issues presented Reagan with a set of hard choices immediately upon taking office: Should he use a "quick fix" to solve especially the Minuteman II (but Minuteman III's growing) vulnerability problem or adopt a long-range solution? Build the B-1 bomber; a variant, the Stealth bomber; or a combination of any or all? Produce the Trident II missile? Continue building large aircraft carriers or go with smaller, cheaper ships? Come up with a smaller version of the Trident and *Los Angeles* subs or continue with the programs as they are? Albert Wohlstetter presented a thorough and convincing argument in the January 22 *Los Angeles Times*, noting that Reagan's budget would "address a perilous imbalance." However, he admitted that Reagan would not really be able to effect serious changes until FY 1983, when he would no longer be confined to tinkering with limits already budgetarily in place from the Carter administration. In the fall of 1981 the Reagan administration announced its new strategic program to close the "window of vulnerability." The program included a decision to build 100 MX missiles, temporarily deploying them in existing Titan II silos; replace all Minuteman II missiles with Minuteman IIIs; build 100 B-1B bombers; continue R&D on the Stealth bomber; and develop the Trident II (D-5) missile for a target deployment date of 1989. Reagan also proposed to double the Pentagon budget by FY 1986 by further adding a nuclear carrier, escalating other production rates, and bringing at least two battleships and a conventional carrier out of mothballs as interim measures to beef up the forces. Senator John Tower perspicaciously noted that, even if the budget requests by the President were "eye-popping," actual military spending would not rise much because outlays usually trail authority.[62]

As a consequence of this shift in policy, the Navy and the Air Force immediately found themselves in direct competition for funds. A study ordered by the Senate Armed Services Committee concluded that a navy of up to 800 ships might be necessary to national security, a conclusion that seemed to convey to the Navy the edge in the money race. Moreover, the Air Force's MX missile continued to encounter environmental, regional, and even church opposition to its missile-basing proposal. Both branches were tempered by European commitments and questions about how much of their own defense the Europeans were willing to fund. The NATO countries had promised Carter they would elevate their defense budgets by a 3-percent net real increase, but they simultaneously pressured Reagan to begin new arms talks (START) with the Soviets (Brezhnev accordingly swung from wild denunciations of Reagan to passionate and transparently hokey pleas for peace). Whatever the European outcome, so far as it might affect Army (and to a lesser extend Air Force) budgetary needs, the Navy would nevertheless have to make some adjustments.[63]

Consequently, the 1981 defense budget actually grew by 5.1 percent while Reagan succeeded in cutting back $36.6 billion from growth in the rest of the budget. Criticism that the big defense buildup would be inflationary prompted Weinberger to maintain that increases would not spur inflation. Much of the anxiety over inflation centered on the administration's supply-side tax cuts, instituted in conjunction with the defense buildup. But the two are not incompatible, as Arthur Laffer pointed out in an editorial in the *Los Angeles Times*, nor are defense expenditures worse than other public spending, as supply-side theorist George Gilder made clear in *Wealth and Poverty*. According to the principles of the supply-side cuts, when the government chooses to spend a billion dollars—"to build a submarine" is Gilder's coincidental example—"what chiefly matters is not the extraction of resources . . . but the *impact on the incentives and creativity of business and workers*" (emphasis added). As discussed in chapter 12, the potential uses of the hull make the creativity factor invested in Trident quite valuable although—as with all other advances in technology—initially unmeasurable. The same can be said for the revolutionary construction process. Moreover, as most liberal economists will ultimately admit under pressure, there *is* a multiplier difference in money spent in the defense industry (which employs consumers who tend to purchase from industries that utilize high investment—hence high growth—levels) as opposed to some entitlements (which, as Gilder showed, have essentially *non*productive results, and, as even he failed to point out, in the case of some welfare payments can disappear from the economy entirely through purchases of illegal goods or services). Finally, defense spending is inflationary to a greater degree when the economy is at full productivity, which is not now (1983) the case of the U.S. economy.[64]

Another part of Reagan's plan was to continue Carter's insistence that the NATO allies and Japan increase their share of the defense burden, allowing the United States to "ease up." NATO countries reaffirmed their commitment to increase defense spending in the stipulated amount, but only after U.S. intelligence presented the ministers in Brussels with a "grim" report. Nevertheless, most of the Reagan administration's decisions about major strategic systems remain in place, definitely valuable first steps have been taken toward rebuilding a respectable strategic posture.

Reagan and Weinberger, profiting from Carter's projected increased FY 1981 spending, intended to sustain their momentum in the FY 1982 budget. Carter's original projection had called for one Trident sub, procured at a cost of $1,329.7 million; but, after some revisions, Congress appropriated $1,995.5 million, of which $1,434.5 million was directed toward procurement and R&D on the submarine and Trident I missile.[65]

Just as the administration inherited a military imbalance not of its own making, it also became the fortuitous beneficiary of good publicity, for which it could take little credit, when on June 18, 1981, the *Ohio* finally sailed off on its sea trials with Admiral Rickover aboard. Launched on April 7, 1979, in ceremonies attended by Senator John Glenn of Ohio, the submarine had gone to sea after two years of anticipation. Waiting for the *Ohio* off Long Island, a Soviet spy trawler lurked, posing as a fishing ship. It intended to use its electronic "fishing" equipment to monitor the Trident's test run. The sendoff had included not only a number of applauding and cheering sailors, but fifty antinuclear demonstrators as well, two of whom "dove into the chilly water and swam to the shipyard" in an attempt to block the boat's maiden voyage, claiming it was "important" to show that "this unspeakable madness did not go on without protest." Although a minor turbine malfunction stranded the submarine at sea until a crew arrived with a part that had mistakenly been left ashore, the *Ohio* completed the sea trials on June 20, 1981. Vice Admiral N. R. Thunman, Deputy Chief of Naval Operations for Submarine Warfare, told the House Armed Services Committee's Seapower Subcommittee that the *Ohio* "exceeded its performance design specifications in such significant areas as *speed and quietness* [italics added]. Sometime after its trials it "flawlessly launched" a Trident I test missile that "flew perfectly over 4000 nautical miles." During the launching, the U.S. Navy "embargoed" the launch time to try and keep Soviet visitors away, but the Russian trawler attended the launch anyway, since notice of the time had been published along with the launch coordinates in local mariner's digests, alerting all civilian ships to stay clear. Despite the presence of the Soviets and protestors, the *Ohio* continued through the trials uneventfully; and, after its return on June 20, Electric Boat workers attended to the final details of the ship in preparation for its November 11 commissioning. Long in arriving, the *Ohio* could not escape controversy even at its departure for sea trials. Yet as a product of unrealistic expectations, the Trident had finally shaken its growing pains and was ready to leave its awkward adolescent stage.[66]

As an adult, the Trident also had found a friend and protector. For FY 1983, the Reagan administration requested two Trident submarines (a total of $2,820 million). Trident I missile funds of $779 million ($36.2 million in R&D and $742.8 million for missiles), base construction funds of $188.3 million, and support funds totaling $568.5 million make a FY 1983 Trident budget of $4,355.8 million. In addition, the administration requested $366.7 million for R&D on the Trident II missile. All told, the supportive Senate passed a FY 1983 defense bill $8 billion higher than the administration requested, although the House eventually trimmed the entire package. Indeed, throughout the 1982 budget debate some House liberals and "fiscal conservatives" joined forces in attacking the defense budget as too large, and the White House and Senate have virtually dragged a kicking and screaming House of Representatives along regarding defense appropriations. In light of attacks such as these, charges that the Trident is constantly "over budget" and that it is not "cost effective" make the program all the more vulnerable to congressional vacillation.

Yet another debate over "cost effectiveness" appears to be on the horizon—deployment of the Trident II missile. Originally, with the Reagan strategic forces decision announcement, Trident II was expected to see operational status by 1989. In 1982, however, Secretary of Defense Caspar Weinberger and the Navy studied methods to accelerate Trident II introduction. After examining the design goals and added cost of accelerated introduction, Weinberger decided on June 1, 1982, to retain the original schedule but also to rephase the method of introducing the Trident II. Under the original program, the Navy planned to backfit the Trident II into submarines constructed for the C-4 Trident I missile. The first hull built "from the keel up as a D-5 configured ship" would have been the thirteenth Trident. Weinberger altered that schedule by introducing the D-5 into hull 9, saving $680 million in Trident I procurement costs but also delaying SSBNs 734, 735, 736, 737, and 738 by one year in their delivery dates. Thus, more "delays" are built into the system, possibly adding in more "cost overruns" into the eventual costs of Tridents 9 to 13. Yet these boats will "come off the line" armed with the Trident II. How is cost effectiveness determined when these factors are taken into account?[67]

Whether the Trident program has really proved cost-effective and thereby deserves its spot in the budget or whether it has contributed to unwise defense spending will be dealt with in this book's conclusion. As of May 3, 1982, the program cost was estimated by the Defense Department at $28.5 billion, with another $11 billion in funds needed for the fiscal years 1984–1987, for a total of $39.5 billion. However, once Trident II funds and Poseidon retrofitting are included, the estimate jumps to $51.3 billion. Compared with the 1974 estimated program acquisition costs of $12.4 billion, this may seem a substantial escalation. It must be kept in mind that many, if not most, of the figures and cost estimates used by Congress—and hence by the media—emanate from the Congressional Budget Office (CBO), which has been less than accurate in predicting and measuring a number of economic indicators and trends. For example, as George Gilder pointed out in *Wealth and Poverty*, the CBO envisaged California's 1978 Proposition 13 property tax cut as depressing the state's economy, reducing employment, and cutting tax revenues in the state. Supply-side economist Arthur Laffer had predicted just the opposite: personal income and state tax revenues both would rise, and employment would increase. Laffer was right and the CBO staggeringly wrong. Thus CBO's figures are not to be entirely relied upon in the case of Trident cost overruns.[68]

Still, for the purpose of further illuminating the cost-overrun concepts, the following discussion has used Congressional Research Service data, along with some others that may contain a great deal of CBO computations.

Of the current program cost, $17,374.6 million was allocated through FY 1982, with $3,363.7 million budgeted for FY 1983. From FY 1984 through 1987, estimated expenditures are $7,578.8 million, and $181.3 million from then until program completion. According to the *Trident Issue Brief*, "the ultimate cost . . . will depend . . . on the number of Trident SSBNs procured. . . . A 21-ship Trident program could cost more than $37 billion, and a 28-ship program could exceed $50 billion." In FY 1981 dollars, a single Trident, excluding only missiles, fuel, and a proportional base cost, averages $1.226 billion. According to the Defense Department's SAR summary of December 31, 1981, however, through the last quarter of 1981 that period's program costs actually decreased by $1,832.6 million, due mainly to fewer purchases of Trident I missiles in anticipation of the Trident II. The Navy had lost $900 million on the adverse effects of scheduling during that period but had saved over $1.5 billion in its "tougher" cost estimate, perhaps suggesting that the influence of Weinberger and Frank Carlucci (assistant secretary of defense) may finally be taking hold.[69]

Electric Boat, however, has a different view of the program's "cost overruns." According to a statement furnished by Electric Boat, the original target cost was $1,793 million in 1972. (This estimate is for the original seven ships.) The Navy added $65.976 million in order changes, making the subtotal nearly $1,859 million. Furthermore, the Navy also has permitted an inflation authorization of $1,010 million, thus bringing the total contract value of the first seven ships to $2,869 million. The latter figure represents a *target more than a budget*, for the Navy also maintains a ceiling of $3,723.9 million. As of the official completion date for building the *Ohio* (February 28, 1981), the program cost was $2,961.5 million, allowing Electric Boat an "underrun to ceiling" of $762,413,000. The losses brought about by the claims struggle with the Navy, however, still caused General Dynamics, the parent company, to lose money: it had to report a 10 percent drop in profits for the fourth quarter of 1980.[70]

Juggling figures in this manner suggests neither that the Trident has not been unexpectedly costly nor that Electric Boat necessarily is totally right in its claims. It does, however, attack the problem of determining exactly what a "budget," a "ceiling," or a "cost overrun" is. Economists scarcely agree on a definition of inflation; so it also is with terms such as "cost overrun." Is it a cost overrun when, in beginning a totally new program, utilizing components never before made, with untried construction techniques, the original "estimate" is exceeded? How can anyone, expert analyst or otherwise, estimate the man hours involved in fitting together two completely new elements using a totally new method, with brand-new equipment? The result is a strict guess, and perhaps the true wonder of such guesses is that they are as close as they are. American consumers who deal with customized items know the risks and costs of designing or developing new equipment. Furthermore, how exactly are costs such as labor strikes to be figured in? While obviously it represents a program cost, it simply cannot be "budgeted." Lawsuits, such as those involving the Bangor base, are yet another unforeseen but costly element. Finally, per-unit costs decrease with each succeeding unit as long as new technology is not added in as it becomes available. Although Trident technology represents the most advanced available in most regards, it still does not employ a titanium hull. Should officials later decide (technology and the budget providing) the Trident should accommodate a titanium hull, a new budgetary problem would arise. Would it then be appropriate to integrate a corresponding cost "increase" in the total Trident "cost"? Clearly, a number of elements bear consideration before a program is indicted for "cost overruns."

Laws passed with civilian welfare in mind also have affected shipbuilding costs. One industry expert noted that before World War II "the book of specifications for an entire ship could be carried around in a man's hand. Today, there are several books the size of an unabridged dictionary with thousands of related specs for specific items of material or machinery." The plethora of specifications grew so involved that "a few years ago . . . a major machinery supplier refused to take another Navy order becaue the 1,250 applicable specs were so confusing and contradictory that compliance with the contract was impossible."[71]

A project "ripe for buck passing," the first Trident inaugurated itself with "botched" welds requiring restoration at $2.6 million and an improperly designed turbine that cracked, costing $3 million. Yet, in comparison to other programs launched at approximately the same time, the Trident still appears to be the cheapest at this point in its evolution. If the MX missile ever sees deployment in its racetrack shelters, it would cost at least $75 billion. Although the B-1B bomber has now received its order for production, some estimates now put the cost of producing the force of 100 B-1s at $24 billion. What that last B-1B will actually cost when the production run is complete (and, if the history of such programs is any indication, it will fold up at less than the now-cited hundred copies!) is an open question. Other considerations render conclusive comparisons even more useless: the Trident, because of its speed, size, capacity, and ease of repair, stays on station more and uses little fuel (since it is nuclear-powered). Most significantly, the Trident is an undetectable and workable threat of lethal dimensions, really cruising the ocean depths now and soon in growing numbers. While cruise missiles, the MX, and the B-1 are in differing degrees still largely paper weapons (a significant number of cruise missiles are just being deployed as of 1983), the *Ohio* already dives and patrols. Questions of cost overruns must be met with a question of greater importance: How much is America's only modernized strategic element worth, as a guarantor of national survival for the intermediate future, at least, until other strategic acts finally succeed in updating their respective scripts?[72]

Vice Admiral Hyman Rickover visiting the USS *Nautilus*, the world's first nuclear submarine

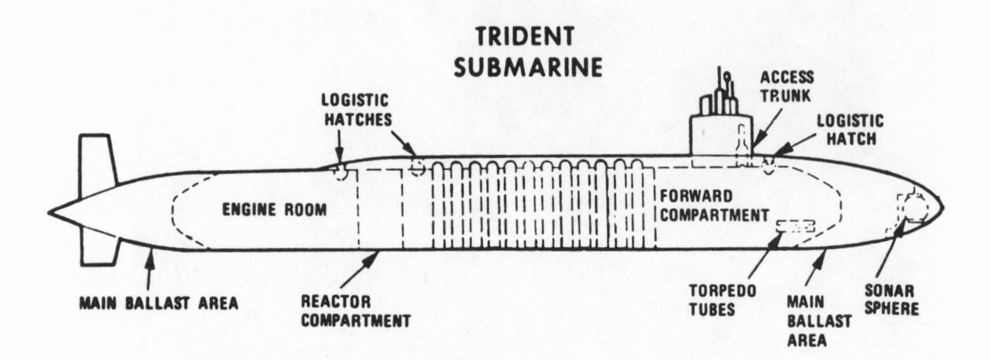

Sketch of the USS *Ohio*

USS *Ohio* at sea

Control room of USS *Ohio*

USS *Michigan*

MK-48 torpedo in the USS *Ohio*

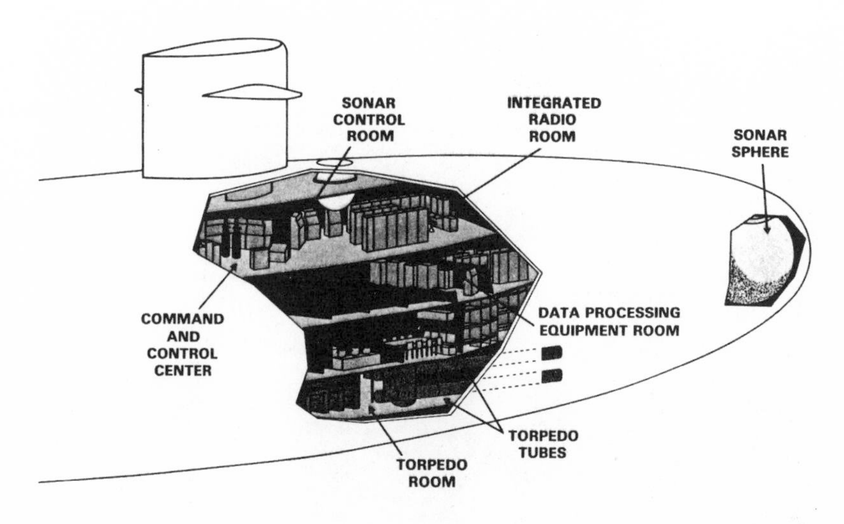

Diagram of the Trident Tactical System

USSR *Typhoon*, the world's largest ballistic-missile submarine

Trident missile tubes looking forward

Trident I missile in launch

Mess of the USS *Ohio*

Rear Admiral Levering Smith, 1973, Director, Special Projects Office (later called SSPO), 1965–1977

Admiral Elmo Zumwalt, 1973, Chief of Naval Operations from July 1970, to June, 1974

Rear Admiral Albert Kelln (probably 1976), Director, Strategic Submarine Division and Trident Program Coordinator

Vice Admiral Earl Fowler, 1974, Chief, Naval Sea Systems Command, 1981–present

P. Takis Veliotis, General Manager of Electric Boat Company and Vice-President, Marine Division, General Dynamics, 1977–1982

Secretary of the Navy John Lehman, January, 1981–present

Submarine Base, Bangor, Washington

Delta Refit Pier at Bangor

Magnetic Silencing Facility located on Hood Canal, Bangor, used to remove a submarine's magnetic signature

Soviet Hormone KA-25 antisubmarine helicopter

Soviet TU-95 "Bear D" bomber

USSR *Alpha*, the fastest and deepest-diving Soviet submarine

USSR Delta III submarine, mainstay of the Soviet ballistic-missile submarine fleet

U.S. P-3C Orion antisubmarine aircraft

LAMPS MK-III ship/air weapons system operates off the guided missile USS *McInerny* FFG-8

A Tomahawk missile launch sequence

5

A Hanger Strap Here, a Continuous Weld There:

The Trident Construction Process

Find a way or make one.

—Robert E. Peary,
The North Pole

From the Trident's stormy budgetary history to its base construction, to say nothing of the submarine's design, every aspect of the total program has been unusual. Not surprisingly, the Trident's construction process also combines new machinery and innovative building techniques to form a submarine construction process unmatched in the free world. In most instances even Soviet advances in construction techniques, such as the large-scale employment of titanium for pressure-hull construction, cannot parallel the overall level of technological skill evident in the Trident construction processes at Electric Boat Company at Groton, Connecticut. Probably more astounding is the fact that Electric Boat (EB) has recently accelerated its production to try to regain earlier scheduling goals while at the same time (in 1981) the company delivered six attack submarines and one Trident (*Ohio*); prepared a second Trident, the *Michigan* (SSBN-727), for contract delivery in September 1982; and delivered two additional attack subs in June and December 1982 as well. This schedule means for the 1981–1982 block of time Electric Boat delivered at least two Tridents and ten attack boats for commissioning and there are four "wet" Tridents (*Ohio, Michigan, Florida,* and *Georgia*) as of the end of the year.

Founded in 1899, Electric Boat completed work on "America's first effective submarine," the 54-foot *Holland* (SS-1), recalled today with great affection by retired Chief Engineer O. B. Nelson for the fact that, in its basic teardrop shape (unelongated and undisrupted by a missile section) and with its single screw, it closely anticipated many Trident features of configuration in a simplistic but predictive way. The company opened a subsidiary to build diesel submarine engines at Groton,

Connecticut, in 1911, although for the first thirteen years at Groton the company only designed submarines. In 1924, EB established a building yard in Groton to work on another submarine for the U.S. Navy, the *Cuttlefish*. Completed in 1931, the *Cuttlefish* represented advances in American submarine design and construction. Sections of it were welded rather than riveted, "and thereafter all submarines were completely welded." At its peak level of submarine production in World War II, Electric Boat launched a new submarine every two weeks.[1]

The company's role as America's premier submarine contractor was enhanced on September 30, 1954, when the nuclear-powered USS *Nautilus* was commissioned at Groton before further glorifying herself and EB by remaining submerged on her shakedown voyage from New London, Connecticut, to San Juan, Puerto Rico, covering 1300 nautical miles at an average speed of 16 knots (18.4 mph). The sub again made news when it "passed under the Geographic North Pole on August 3, 1958, and then transited the polar ice pack from Pearl Harbor to Portland, England." Since those events Electric Boat has remained in the forefront of U.S. submarine builders, a position reaffirmed when Electric Boat (see Chapter 3) submitted a successful bid to design and build the first four Trident submarines, displacing Newport News Shipbuilding, which had unsuccessfully submitted a bid to build Trident on a cost-plus-fixed-formula profit basis and did not compete on the fixed-price-plus-incentive basis on which the contract was finally based.[2]

Because of the volume of submarine business—both attack and strategic vessels—and the size of the proposed Trident, Electric Boat set out to rebuild one entire section of the Groton yard and to move a significant portion of the operation to Quonset Point, Rhode Island, site of an old naval air station and onetime home of the famous Seabees. Construction began in 1973 on the Groton renovation, officially called the Land Level Submarine Construction Facility (LLSCF) at Groton. The complex covers eight acres and, on completion in 1976, had cost $140 million. P. Takis Veliotis, Electric Boat's general manager, in a 1977 reference to the company's initial outlay for modernization, asked sarcastically "Where's the Navy's capital modernization commitment?" In fact, combined with the $120-million investment in the Automated Submarine Frame and Cylinder Manufacturing Facility at Quonset Point, together with less specifically assignable investments, Electric Boat's initial commitment totaled at least a third of a billion dollars of private investment and "in today's environment would cost at least $800 million and require more than five years" of equivalent construction time. When subsequent subsidiary investments are included, the original investment figure probably is closer to $450 million.[3]

The Land Level Facility at Groton, Connecticut

Sprawled over the three acres under cover (inboard) and the five acres outside (outboard) at the Land Level Facility are several significant facilities. Most of the assembly work occurs in Building 260, a 126,360-square-foot enclosed construction area containing five giant bays and thirteen separate stations (work areas). The Land Level Facility allows workers to construct two or more classes of submarines in modular assembly processes simultaneously. Outside the building stands a 242,000-square-foot platform to erect the hull and outfit the vessel, as well as a pontoon graving dock (617 feet long by 96.5 feet wide) for launching and drydocking submarines. There are two piers for working on submarines while they are in the water: the North Pier (653 feet long by 170 feet wide), used for work on both strategic and attack-class vessels, and the South Pier (598 feet long by 99 feet wide), which can service both classes and to which the *Ohio* was moored just prior to her June 1981 sea trials. A series of cranes also dots the facility's landscape, including a 337-ton portal crane, two 280-ton bridge cranes, four 25-ton bridge cranes, and a 100-ton hammerhead crane. In addition, a separate facility devoted to the construction of attack submarines is not included in the features noted above and is situated north or upstream of Building 260.[4]

The frame and cylinder facility features dimensions of 615 feet wide by 459 feet long by 125 feet high, including three clear-height interior bays 205 feet wide by 459 feet long by 85 feet high, the equivalent in floor area of 6.2 football fields. The foundations and slabs contain 32,300 cubic yards of concrete, enough to lay a sidewalk thirty miles long. Such massive foundations are necessary (indeed, they are supported by deep-level pilings sunk 16 feet or more into solid rock) not only to support the colossal weight of the rigid jigs and cylinder- and frame-making fixtures but also to ensure that the fine tolerances repeatedly expected of them are not jeopardized by even the most undetectable of ground movements leaving only weather-caused thermal variations of metallic dimensions with which to contend. The facility uses as much power as a city of ten thousand people, while the amount of wiring installed could wire all the homes in the same-size city.[5]

Quonset Point Facility, Rhode Island

Quonset Point officially opened its doors on November 23, 1973, and started "limited steel fabrication on Feb. 4, 1974, with a workforce of 20 employees." By 1979 it had received most of its modern equipment and a workforce of more than four thousand were employed as of 1982. All thirty-three welding machines and fixtures were in place by

December 1980, including ten hull-frame fabrication fixtures, eight hull-shell fabrication fixtures, twelve hull-cylinder assembly units, and three hull-cylinder pairing fixtures. This facility can be simultaneously engaged in constructing 27- to 35-foot cylinders for the *Los Angeles* 688 attack class and 33- to 42-foot cylinders for the *Ohio* class. In short, the automated facility can handle the two primary sub classes today, while Newport News cannot even handle its 688 class contracts with such a facility, although a contract offer by EB at the behest of R. B. Barton to that effect was unsuccessfully proffered. Consequently Newport News makes some of its own shells and frames and orders others built by Vickers in Canada. Besides the 18.5 acres of land owned by General Dynamics, the Quonset Point facility stretches across 160 acres of the former Quonset Point Naval Air Station land, now leased from the Rhode Island Port Authority. Work performed in these buildings includes steel processing (cutting, shaping, and forming), electrical, sheet metal, structural and pipe-component fitting, including construction of subcomponent assemblies ranging from tiny dowels to large tank and deck assemblies. Like the Groton works, Quonset Point has several large cranes and a motorized ground transporter. Although each of the six radio-controlled bridge cranes has less individual lifting capacity (15 tons) than those at Groton, they can be interlocked to lift 30 tons. Electric Boat acquired the frame and cylinder fixture units from Vivoy Engineering of Switzerland, a company with which General Manager Veliotis had worked in conjunction with his earlier pioneering interest in constructing the vast dome-shaped natural gas storage cells for the LNG-class commercial tanker. Whereas the construction of an automated submarine frame-and-cylinder facility is easier than the construction of the LNG domes, no manufacturer in the United States was able to supply these fixtures. Credit for this audacious innovation is exclusively deserved by Veliotis, according to William Bennett, in charge of the Quonset facility.[6]

At the beginning of the construction process for a Trident, orders go out for long-lead items such as the reactor, communication equipment, sonar, steel, and missile tubes. Electric Boat initiates its construction program at the Automated Submarine Frame and Cylinder Manufacturing Facility, where the sophisticated Swiss-produced fixtures fabricate the basic units of the submarine hull. First, HY-80 low-alloy steel ingots are heated, quenched, and tempered into billets and are then forged into steel plates of variable thickness, with hull pressure shells being more than 4 inches thick as a minimum, graduating upward in accordance with load and pressure requirements. Under temperatures varying from 1750 to 2100 degrees, grain size is altered until the final version of the plate is able to withstand minimum loads of 50,000 to

60,000 pounds per square inch, "yield" loads of 80,000 pounds, or "break" loads of 100,000 psi. Second, under the control of an automated processing center, fabrication begins in a numerically controlled process with plate preheating and microprecise cutting procedures. In a four-stage process, hull shells are shaped evenly under jig pressure and dimensional control into perfectly welded units; hull frames are shaped from an I-beam shape into perfectly sized and welded reinforcing ribs or frames; shells and frames are welded into the basic units of the pressure hull; and, finally, cylinder assemblies, ranging in number from two to four and 24 inches to 14 feet in axis length, are completed in still another phase of precise welding.[7]

The cylinder frame stock varies from 12 to 24 inches in vertical height cross-sectionally and exhibits narrower or wider flanges, according to use and bearing strength needed. Bow and stern hull components have external rather than internal frames in some cases. On a spherical basis, a hull frame of 12 inches can reduce the useful inside diameter of the pressure hull by as much as 24 inches, but, since the hull is not double, much equipment can be handily installed between sets of hull frames.[8]

The cost effectiveness of the automated facility definitely deserves separate treatment. To build one frame in accordance with earlier techniques would take somewhere between five and seven weeks of grunting, groaning, pounding, and shoving, while it now takes the same number of days and will eventually require only three days. Framing work that once required about a thousand tradesmen to perform now takes 150 and may take even fewer in a couple of years of more confident experience. At the outset of the use of the facility's jigs and fixtures the productivity-cost curve "overflew" the trend with older techniques until trades skills, and especially supervisory personnel, could be thoroughly trained—a temporary but natural aberration that contributed to some cost "overruns" on the *Ohio* and precipitated trepidation among Navy supervisory personnel. However, within seven months the system was working so well that shell-frame-cylinder assembly costs had already been reduced by 70 percent over former techniques. With the introduction of a scanning system and an increase in the accountability of floor supervisors, who are retrained every two years, the entire facility was within budget about fifteen months after start-up. Conceivably, by the end of 1983 a further one-third reduction in time expended on this phase of construction may be possible, meaning that hull-cylinder turning that once consumed twenty-four hours of work by many workers can now be done in two hours and with fewer than one-sixth of the old force.[9] While the cost of the hull's fabrication is only about 15 percent of the total cost of the submarine, at the point of optimum operation of the automated frame and cylinder facility, an additional 20-percent cost reduction per hull seems eventually possible—assuming no inflation, of course, in a year (1982) when inflation in June seemed headed below 13 percent per annum. Finally, aside from cost-effective considerations, these new procedures of pressure hull construction generate many other cost-effective and qualitative advantages cumulatively throughout the entire building process. Cylinder shells do not need to be built with 3- to 4-inch extra outside margins to assure hull fitting at the point of cylinder pairing. By the old technique they were proportionately torched away to effect final fitting. Now, subsequent installations of equipment installed in cylinder pairings no longer need be individualized per pairing and from vessel to vessel. Sizing, angle confrontation, structural strength, welding consistency, and engineering presumptions can proceed on the basis of consistency, reliability, and technical confidence on a serial basis for as many Tridents *and* 688-class attack boats as may be built. The whole automated process is estimated to shorten the process of hull erection per vessel by one and one-half years.

The automated welding process equally deserves individual attention. EB welders take at least nine weeks of training, at which point they are only 50 percent effective even at EB's automated facility. Two more years are probably necessary for a welder to become fully effective, keeping in mind that practically all welding is automatic, whether hull cylinders or subcomponents are involved. Inasmuch as the question of defective welding received so much public and congressional attention in 1981 (see chap. 6), the practical side must be examined aside from the individual factor. First, even automated welding must transpire under circumstances, hardly humanly controllable, in which outside influences such as weather conditions, variations in the quality of welding wire, or the technical competence of one welder versus another all constitute causes of "defects." A reasonable figure for "defective" welds (since perfection is inherently unattainable) is 7 percent; EB is operating overall at less than 7 percent, with some shop units operating at less than 4 percent at Quonset Point.

At this point, the issue of a "defective weld" must be confronted (see chap. 6 for a full discussion of the program effects this issue raised with the lead ship, the *Ohio*). All welding performed by Electric Boat on Tridents and on 688s, with the possible exception of very minor spot welding and repairs, is automated, regardless of whether it is performed in or out of the huge automated jigs and fixtures on hull units, and all welding seams are exposed to radiographic examination where pressure hull welds are involved or to magnetic particle inspection for all other purposes. When either of these two inspection techniques discloses a "defect," the location of the defect is marked and its kind and severity are determined by "shooting" the bad weld with a sound machine. Slugs, porosity, severe lacunae, and cosmetic blemishes are turned up in this manner and their location determined. Superficial defects can be repaired from the outside of the weld itself, regardless of whether it is located on the external or internal side of a cylinder. Severe defects are arced or dug out, rewelded, and reinspected, and the process is repeated if necessary until inspection is completed. Cylinder shell welds, it should be noted, are not two separate seams of welding connecting one +4-inch HY-80 steel plate with another but are rather a continuous and complete seam the very same thickness as the plates being married, as the following cross-sectional diagram shows:

real seam

popularly imagined seam, with plates butted together and externally seam welded

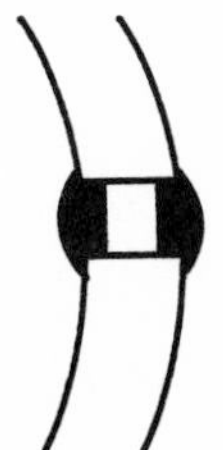

popularly imagined seam, with plates welded together in separate seams inside and outside

Since the hull diameter is 42 feet, each cylinder seam weld is 131.95 feet (pi × 42) in circumference. Inspection by radiographic means occurs on a 16-inch basis, with a 2-inch overlap top and bottom, for a total of 132 inspections. If a defect is discovered in five differently positioned locations, since a "defect" is identical with the length of the inspected area, it would mean 5/132 (4 percent) of the seam's circumference was "defective" from a report standpoint. Actually, the five specific defects together might really attain a total length of only 2 inches, in which case the defects only comprise 2 inches of 1583.4 inches, or less than 0.126 percent of the total rim.[10]

Besides the serial production of hull units, utilizing its other eight main buildings and 2 million square feet of plant space, Quonset Point also performs an increasing proportion of the interior fitting out of the constituent hull units. Building 1 conducts major outfitting, for example, while Building 17 fabricates fore and aft hull cones and executes light outfitting. Sheet metal work, piping, and installation are vital functions performed here. With some 36,000 final pipe details to be performed per boat, some 60 percent is performed by full automation, with whole sections of piping now arriving as total fixtures, thus bypassing the necessity to build up units successively inside the hull. Because of microexact plate cutting, savings as high as 30 percent in manpower time are obtained over previous techniques in the fabrication of some tanks. The Quonset Point facility now performs about 20 to 25 percent of the total work done on a Trident, of which 10 percent consists of man hours dedicated to the erection of the hull, with 75 to 80 percent being man hours necessary for equipping the hull's interior and with the remainder in man hours comprising ancillary operations such as the placing of covering structures, inventorying, and so on. If the Quonset Point facility were equipped with a rail transfer system, larger cranes of 1200- or 2000-ton capacity, and larger barges than those now used to transfer fused units of three hull-cylinder pairs on the six-and-a-half-hour, 50-mile trip to the Groton docks, fused units of six pairings weighing as much as 2000 tons could be transported to Groton. Thus the entire ship could be built at Groton in four or five sections. The Groton Land Lock facility, in turn, would require upgrading of its own docking facilities in order to land such outsized sections, including replacing the 337-ton capacity of the Groton cantilever crane with a capacity equivalent to that needed at Quonset Point. In this sense, Groton is ultimately the limitation determining the total Trident construction rate and capacity, but since more outfitting is coming to Quonset Point anyway, even more relief to Groton could be generated here if a radically higher production rate were desired.[11]

When Trident sections arrive at the land-level facility, the dockside portal crane lifts them into bay 2, which, like the other bays, is enclosed to ease climatic conditions. Here, to the extent that it has not already been accomplished at Quonset Point, begins or concludes the process of outfitting the interior of the hull's subcomponent lengths and further fusing them. The outfitting process is called end-loading. The process employed in the construction of earlier submarine classes was to build up the pressure hull plate by plate and then at various points in the hull cut holes sized according to the equipment to be dropped through for interior installation. The sequence was to work from the outside of the hull commencing with core areas and working back by construction strata to the inward most-accessible strata, a process defined *more* by construction *logic* than by actual physical *location*. Not only did this entail working in cramped and inconvenient conditions, with work at closer or more remote points held up until installation elsewhere was completed because of the problems of blockage and obstruction, but, if an error was made, frequently all the intervening work had to be undone back to the core position, the error rectified, and the installation repeated back to the point at which the error was detected. Not only did this delay construction and increase costs, it also increased the potential for another round of different errors in the remedial process. End-loading, on the other hand, means that access for installation is available from opposite points as well as at any level, simultaneously, so that work can proceed at several deck levels more or less concurrently, with a clearer perception of the sequences of the process and with little or no congestion occurring at different points because of a necessity to consider forward and aft sequences of installations at remote points in the hull. In the overall process of moving hull-cylinder sections in their natural sequence, if a logjam is created by one particular cylinder not progressing per plan, two 280-ton overhead-bridge cranes inside the covered facility can lift one section from its assigned location, overfly the offending 300-ton cylinder, thereby effecting a bypass, and deposit it at an advanced spot in the line so that work can continue until the offending unit is straightened out and flown back into its natural sequence. Speed, simplicity, roominess, convenience, perspective, flow, and virginity of installation all characterize end-loading.[12]

Inside the Land Level Facility Electric Boat employs an innovative construction process by which the hull sections are assembled as modules sequentially from bow sternward, essentially. Hull sections rest on electrically powered transfer cars with hydraulic jacks to stabilize huge strongbacks at static positions. The transfer cars move along a series of rail tracks laid out in a grid, over which a hull section can be turned, directed, and moved in any direction. Consequently, the hull sections can go to the work areas in the other bays to be matched to their appropriate outfitting equipment—not the other way around—and the workers at each station can do a specific type of work on several different sections without leaving their station. Thirteen stations inside the facility operate in serial or repetitive production style. For example, the missile compartment station erects and loads the compartments into the cylinders in their assigned area on a repeat basis. Tradesmen, such as machinists, welders, electricians and pipefitters, perform tasks at a stationary location in this concept, and, more important, material flows through the facility in a steady and orderly fashion.[13]

When all stations have completed work on a particular hull subsection, it is moved along into another bay area for joining with other related equivalents. Major structural components such as piping, tanks, bulkheads, wiring, and cabling are further installed as appropriate. At the final assembly area each section is moved into its proper place to be joined with the other sections until the sonar dome is finally fitted. The majority of the deck packages—sail, missile cape section or superstructure, and so on—are installed next. The diving planes are installed on the sail and the major electronics and sonar equipment, as well as periscopes, antennas, and navigation lights are next fitted out in the sail.[14]

During this joining process, another unusual aspect of the construction process reveals itself. As each joined section is completed the transfer cars move the entire assembly line forward, with the finished section moving out the door of the facility and onto the outboard erection platform, one of Electric Boat's four docks. Gradually the Trident hull emerges from the facility. Unfinished areas such as the sail, the bow, and access hatches are kept covered to facilitate work regardless of external climatic conditions and to provide close at hand the necessary construction equipment and supplies which otherwise would be located overboard at dockside level. Certain security functions are provided by these structures as well. A shroud covers the screw during the presence of uncleared visitors, for example. In the case of the sail, a small cabin encloses the entire top area so that crews can work on the sail itself without being subject to interruptions by climate and weather disturbances. Although the hull by this time is essentially complete, the giant sonar dome made of permeable material is kept in its protective cradle on the side of the dock until close to the final stages of construction. When the hull has been completely joined, the inspectors conduct final checks, welds are polished smooth so that the hull has no protrusions, and final painting takes place.[15]

Throughout the period of forward movement onto the dock by one Trident, new sections of its sister ship file into line behind and to starboard of it to permit the joining of the next submarine. While one submarine is on the dock, therefore, a second is in the joining stage and a third in the sectional loading stage. A fourth prospective hull would also be under construction at Quonset Point, with subcomponents in the incipient stages of assembly. Once a submarine goes into the water for final fitting and testing, the next submarine resting fully on the dock is moved to the graving dock position and the process continues, with yet another sub poking its bow out of the facility as sections are added to its hull.[16]

Launching the Ohio

Once completed, a Trident defies traditional "launching down the ways" because of its size. It must be moved from its position in front of the exit to the port side of the dock onto a pontoon setting inside a 37-million-gallon graving dock, where the ninety-three transfer cars are removed. This leaves the Trident sitting on its thirty-one strongbacks on the pontoon. The dock is then superflooded to float the pontoon clear of the dock, and one mobile side of the graving dock retracts. To lower the pontoon with the vessel still on it, the dock director then pumps down the water in the graving dock until the pontoon grounds itself on blocks. Workers open flood ports in the pontoon, and the dock is reflooded. The submarine floats free from the flooded pontoon and can be towed out after the launching ceremonies.[17]

Before launching, however, the submarine undergoes numerous preparations in the dock. Crews check the ballast tanks, operate all valves, flooding and ballasting equipment, and controls, and test the drive train and all underwater power. All electrical circuits and sonar also must be checked in the water. Flaws in construction obviously can be corrected far more easily in the graving dock than at sea.

In the case of the *Ohio*, trade work ended on March 15, 1981. Noise surveys and preparations for dock trials took up most of April and May. Dock trials commenced on June 6 and 7, followed by the *Ohio*'s first and second sea trials from June 7 to June 21. At that point Electric Boat put the *Ohio* in drydock for another short examination, followed by two more sea trials. In such sea trials the Navy makes the vessel go through virtually all of the maneuvers it would have to perform on operational duty. Four months later, on October 28, Electric Boat officially delivered the *Ohio* to the Navy.[18]

While conducting sea trials the *Ohio* carried no missiles. Rickover took part in the trials, being officially in charge of testing the reactor, turbines, drive shaft, screw, throttle controls, and so on. A minor engine malfunction slowed the sea trials but crews on board the *Ohio* corrected the problem and the sub successfully completed its trials.[19]

Construction Complications

With the official delivery of the *Ohio*, all involved breathed a sigh of relief. Certainly most of the problems in designing and building a completely new submarine with totally new technology and an innovative construction process appeared solved as expected, along with a host of unexpected complications. According to one analyst, the major difficulty was that "the prime contractor had but one customer, and the customer was too impatient." Many of the Trident's construction problems can be traced to the 688 program, which had drifted behind schedule at Newport News (where the SSN 688 prototype was built).

Electric Boat's sudden expansion of the Groton workforce from eleven thousand people in 1972 to twenty-nine thousand in 1977 resulted in a dilution of the "experienced first line supervision . . . accompanied by a tremendous reduction in the proportion of skilled trades personnel." Other troubles quickly mounted:

- The office of the Chief of Naval Operations delivered approval of the vessel's characteristics ten months late.
- The Long Lead Materials Contract, including orders for hull steel, was awarded eighteen months late.
- The Marine Draftsmen's Association, as noted in an earlier chapter, went on strike.
- The Navy decided to build a prototype power plant on land, an event not in the original schedule, so its construction had to precede the actual construction of the ship's plant.
- Missile fire control and navigation equipment arrived thirty-three months late.

All of the effects of an expanded but poorly trained workforce compounded the delays, while Congress and the Navy pressed for earlier delivery.[20]

In 1977, P. Takis Veliotis assumed the managerial mantle from Gordon MacDonald. Veliotis acted quickly and decisively. He discharged 3500 employees and retrained the supervisors. His training solutions included setting up special programs in conjunction with the University of Hartford. Further steps taken to correct the situation included reducing overhead and support functions (at a savings of $126 million through 1981), undertaking an inventory of the plant and materials, implementing computerized management and control systems, and a review of the unrealistic schedules and budgets. Veliotis also recognized the importance of avoiding future strikes, and, after the Metal Trades Council at Electric Boat elected Thomas Kiddy its president, Veliotis opened negotiations on a new contract. The two reached an agreement in June 1979, the first time in twenty years Electric Boat had reached a settlement without first experiencing a strike.[21]

Delays and "cost overruns" in the 688 program had already had an impact on Trident costs and schedules. Because both vessels were built at the same yard, congressmen reasoned that claims filed by General Dynamics for initial cost disparities in the 688 class reflected a trend on the part of General Dynamics to "build now, claim later." In short, the claims settlement set forth in Public Law 85-804 (which resulted in the Navy and Electric Boat splitting the cost of the claim, each assuming

$359 million) led the Navy and Congress to expect the worst from Electric Boat.

Matters deteriorated rapidly when, in 1979, Electric Boat reported (reluctantly, in the Navy's view) that inspectors had indentified a number of serious construction problems in the Trident program. These included inadequate welds, use of noncomforming carbon steel, peeling paint, and a variety of ill-fitting pipes, accessories, and attachments. Prior to those reports Veliotis apparently had gotten the program under control and had reestablished credibility with the Navy and Congress. His credibility seemed to plummet following these revelations.[22]

Attack-submarine delivery showed a delay of only one and one-half months each as a result of the steel problem. However, Veliotis maintained that the fifty pounds of nonconforming steel removed from the *Ohio* had no real delay effect whatsoever. (Both Vice Admiral Earl Fowler's allegations and Veliotis' defense appear in chapter 6; the concern here is to establish the impact of the various problems on the *Ohio*'s construction.) Electric Boat provided no estimate of delay caused by the rewelding or the repainting. However, the turbine repair necessitated by the non-balanced government-furnished turbine rotor accounted for a delay of forty-two days. Defective government-furnished control valves caused a further delay of 124 days.[23]

Despite these problems, the modular construction process continued to prove itself throughout 1979 and 1980, as more than two dozen key events in the construction process took place virtually on schedule. Among these construction milestones, the main seawater system's strength and tightness were successfully tested, torpedo gear was successfully installed, the diesel engine experienced its first run, the ship's service turbine generator was run, penultimate installation trades were completed, and the sub underwent dock trials. Only five of thirty-two key events occurred more than one month behind schedule.[24]

The vast majority of the construction delays came as a result of Navy design changes. While no one would question the sensibility of making design changes on the lead vessel before unwanted features could creep into the program, the official tendency to blame Electric Boat for at least those delays caused by Navy changes is unwarranted (see table 9). When combined with the draftsmen's strike (ninety days) and the eight months Veliotis claimed were used up in negotiations over waivers on Navy changes and blueprint alterations, two years of delay in the Trident program are more reasonably explained than certain Trident critics are willing to concede. Considering the failure to order the

Table 9
Delays Caused by Navy Design Changes Since 1979
(in days)

Changed Item	Delay
Air conditioning piping and steam flow instrumentation	21
Spray nozzle modification	7
Deck modifications	14
Bulkhead penetrations	35
Stowages and cleaning and painting*	92
Trim and drain, system priming	96
Steering and dive linkage, defective hydraulic valve	28
Total	405

*The Navy claims this is not a change but is standard finishing procedure on all vessels.

long-lead items early enough and accounting for the fire control equipment delays, the truly amazing fact is that the *Ohio* (and, indeed, the whole program) was not farther behind than it was.[25]

"Much about the Trident is revolutionary," observed Gerard Burke; Veliotis has emphasized "a Trident is not just a bigger *Poseidon*, it is a technological marvel—the most sophisticated submarine ever built." Burke and Veliotis are correct. The fact that two Tridents will be operational and a third commissioned by the end of 1983, with at least six others under construction testifies to the industrial capacity of Groton and Quonset Point. The revolutionary construction process, briefly outlined here, contributed heavily to the successful launching of the *Ohio*, and its viability will be even more apparent as the intermediate stages of the total building program are now entered in the next two to three years.[26]

6

Claim-as-you-go?:

Trident and Quality Control

> *The decision may be either a battle, or a series of great combats—but it may also consist of the results of mere relations.*
>
> Clauswitz, *On War*

Throughout the Trident's funding battles the question of claims filed against the Navy played an increasingly major role. President Carter vetoed the fiscal year 1980 defense budget primarily because of the controversy over the then-unsettled claims filed by the three largest shipbuilders, reasoning that uncertainty over future costs posed by the claims made budgets meaningless. The 97th Congress voted to delay funding of the ninth Trident because Electric Boat drifted farther behind in production and yet seemingly surged farther ahead in pressing its claims. More than one Navy source felt that the claims settlements not only fed the appetites of greedy defense-oriented industrialists but also threatened the entire procurement process. Admiral Rickover's warning to the House Appropriations Committee that the "standard profit incentives are not working with large shipbuilders" reached sympathetic legislators who had already heard Admiral Earl Fowler blast the workmanship of Electric Boat and seen the Secretary of the Navy award the contracts for three attack submarines to Newport News without allowing Electric Boat Company to submit bids on them. The Navy, pledged Secretary John Lehman, would not pay for defective workmanship.[1]

Simmering since the first stages of construction and its concomitant contract revisions, the nagging problem of faulty workmanship on the Tridents and the 688 *Los Angeles*-class subs became a matter of public record when Vice Admiral Earl Fowler testified before the Seapower Subcommittee of the House Armed Services Committee on March 12, 1981. Rather than actually exposing previously unpublicized errors in construction and workmanship of which the Navy, Electric Boat, and Congress already were aware, directing public attention to a matter the Navy should have handled more discreetly, Fowler leveled charges that Electric Boat had employed substandard (no pun intended!) steel in the submarines, had performed deficient welding, and had applied unstable paint compounds. In the ensuing melee, both the Navy and Electric Boat sought to salvage their own prestige, triggering volleys of charges and countercharges from all parties involved. Personal antagonism developed between Rickover and the manager of Electric Boat, P. Takis Veliotis, resulting in exchanges of professional insults between the two men, each of whom viewed the Trident program with some personalized exclusivity.[2]

From the Trident program's inception, several forces tugged it in conflicting directions. The controversy over claims involved three major conceptual areas. First, Electric Boat embarked on a program of recovering losses for defective workmanship, errors in construction, and replacement of subspecification steel as mandated by the navy, confined to its 688 class of attack submarines in its first round of claims. Included in this group of claims were costs resulting from deficient welds (the infamous "10,000 places") and defective painting. Tied to these claims but contractually different, a second group of claims on items involving design modifications by the Navy not the responsibility of Electric Boat added even higher prices. Occasionally claims overlapped: each side, for example, accused the other of responsibility for the painting defects. Rickover and others have also charged Electric Boat and other major shipbuilders with employing a tactic that consists of filing what may be termed open-ended claims—claims that have no expiration date. This type of claim allows a shipbuilder to make a change ordered by the Navy at one date and then later file a claim for all subsequent losses under that particular change, whether the subsequent costs were related to the change or not. The Navy, meanwhile, wanted its submarines and expected them customized. Yet the Navy had no wish overtly to antagonize its only Trident shipbuilder. Therefore it intended to cajole, coerce, entice, or otherwise stimulate Electric Boat into producing Tridents and other submarines on schedule, near planned cost, and in complete conformity with Navy design. This goal required the matter to be kept sub rosa, since public examination of the matter could force either the Navy and/or Electric Boat directly to bear the blame for the costs and faulty workmanship.[3]

Congress placed additional pressures on the deteriorating buyer-contractor relationship by expecting one side or the other to assume full responsibility. After all, legislators reasoned, multimillions of dollars had been unhesitatingly allocated for these submarines, for which they received in turn only a series of gigantic claim suits. Capitol Hill had a right to know who was responsible for the mess. But congressional exposure put the Navy in the awkward position of defending Electric Boat in public while simultaneously chastising it in private. For its part, the shipbuilder could not howl too loudly back at the Navy over the substandard skill levels of its inadequately trained shipyard force.

Tensions of this order, of course, can easily derail the most vital of such programs. Other factors, however, exposed the Trident program in particular to an even greater share of public scrutiny. Rickover's personal involvement attracted media attention that aided in forcing all of the major participants into corners, pushing the Navy into the position of defending its entire procurement policy, and especially the Trident program. Rickover also encouraged congressional investigations of the entire procurement process, which in turn made Congress put the Navy, shipbuilders in general, and Electric Boat in particular on the spot. Finally, Electric Boat counterattacked by pressing a full range of claims, an action that eventually led to ill-advised threats by the Secretary of the Navy to suggest constructing submarines in foreign countries. And for an added pinch of controversy, Rickover resurrected an old threat of delegating some ship construction to government shipyards.[4]

At the heart of the controversy involving Trident construction delays was the question of quality control and responsibility. Did Electric Boat make errors in construction unjustified by the novelty of the undertaking? Electric Boat officials admitted that the company was responsible for some faulty construction. When it was awarded the first Trident contract on July 25, 1974, Electric Boat was confronted with an unprecedented manpower need for highly skilled shipbuilding crafts. Fowler's charges unsympathetically implied negligence bordering on the criminal. The use of substandard steel in hull plating, for example, can mean life or death in the case of submersibles operating under the stress of crush pressures. Although in theory all parties agreed that quality control truly requires an effort by all parties involved—the Navy, the shipbuilder, and even Congress—the methods by which the government sought to attain its goal seemed heavy-handed and demonstrated an unfortunate lack of experience manifested by diplomatic immaturity on the part of Secretary of the Navy John Lehman in his initial response to these problems.

Several elements have combined to make the relationships among the major participants highly volatile. First, Electric Boat pressed a number of claims against the Navy throughout the 1970s, as did other shipbuilders. This led the Navy to adopt an adversary attitude toward the shipbuilding community. Second, while the Navy and Electric Boat should more or less equally share the blame for the poor work, defective parts, and overall shoddy quality control in many places, the tendency has been for each to exculpate itself unilaterally. The Navy definitely supplied some defective materials and did not sufficiently inspect the submarines for quality workmanship. Electric Boat was also responsible for substandard welding, together with incomplete welding inspection records, and for very limited use of improper-grade steel. Design changes, another source of friction, eventually prompted the actual claims. These design changes amounted to more than 35,000 blueprint alterations, many of which arrived after the appropriate point in construction, according to Electric Boat officials. The major claims suit filed by all of the major shipbuilders and discussed in chapter 4 resulted in a settlement whereby Electric Boat ended up absorbing a $350-million loss, prompting Admiral Rickover to charge that Electric Boat had originally underbid deliberately in the expectation of later filing compensatory claims. These allegations made him a hero to Congress but earned him the unqualified enmity of Electric Boat.[5]

Standard Procurement Practices vs. the Case of the Trident

Before examining Rickover's criticisms, the typical procurement and bidding process must be understood. In some cases, the respective military service interested in acquiring a new weapon may choose to have manufacturers engage in a competition of building prototypes before the contract for serial production is let. Such was the case with the TFX fighter plane, the air-launched cruise missile, and the Army's DIVAD gun system. In this type of procurement, however, the weapon will generally justify its development cost on account of the greater numbers of copies thereafter procured and because the total development cost for the prototype represents a relatively small investment in terms of the overall value of the contract. A company's investment in this kind of prototype, that is, will eventually be more than justified as greater production numbers progressively reduce per-unit costs and as per-unit profits increase proportionately. With a 1972 projected cost for the first Trident of about $750 million and with a force level undetermined as of 1972, the Trident, however, would otherwise normally have fallen under the more typical procurement policy of shipbuilding involving large-scale unprecedented classes, which is competitive bidding on the basis of cost plus profit.[6]

Traditionally, all contractors interested in bidding on a weapon will thoroughly price out the costs of the weapon, then add any anticipated changes (usually a formula can produce some estimate) and a reasonable profit. At one time, three major shipbuilders had yards capable of building submarines, but Ingalls Shipbuilding, a subsidiary of Litton Industries, has since withdrawn from sub construction. Of the two remaining yards, Electric Boat (of General Dynamics) and Newport News (of Tenneco), only Electric Boat submitted bids on the Trident. Newport News competed with Electric Boat for the 688-class attack submarines, receiving the contract for the first vessel, but a pattern developed afterward in which Electric Boat usually underbid its competitors. Up to that point no deviation from normal procurement procedure existed. Claims, however, changed this.

A puzzling situation developed: Newport News, even throughout the bidding of the 1970s, proved at this point a more efficient shipbuilder than Electric Boat. Its attack subs were launched nearer schedule and with fewer defects than the attack subs from Electric Boat. Despite that record, Electric Boat received contracts for twenty subs, compared to the thirteen contracts awarded to Newport News. Rickover viewed this discrepancy in performance as due to deliberate underbidding by Electric Boat while entertaining the intention eventually to recover the differential through claims to be asserted later. To allow for this suspicion by denying Electric Boat a 688 contract eventually would, however, put the Navy in the position of being an omniscient judge of shipbuilders' profitability before the accounting proof of the fact. Nevertheless, in his suggestions to Congress Rickover had urged that authorizing agency heads direct contract awards to other than the low bidder when "the agency head determines the contractor has bid unrealistically low" or when the head determines that an award to other than the lowest bidder is likely to result in lower cost to the Navy. Besides charges of "conflict of interest," which would be directed at any official who gave a contract to other than a low bidder, what are the criteria for determining an "unrealistically low bid" and for the "likelihood" of resulting lower costs?[7]

Insurance has further altered the traditional government-shipbuilder role by providing what Rickover believed to be a cause for the shipbuilder to become complacent about the cost of shoddy construction. Defense acquisition regulations allow shipbuilders to purchase insurance coverage for defective workmanship. This insurance is intended to protect the shipbuilder against such faulty construction as is the unintentional result of incompetence, overly difficult tasks, unplanned failure, or accident. Under these regulations, "insurance premiums are acceptable as allowable costs under Government contracts" only if the contractor is making a good-faith effort to meet performance, time, and quality requirements. Secretary Lehman argued that "to the extent the Contractor's risk are covered by insurance, there is a reduced likelihood that the Contractor will submit claims against the Government to recover additional costs attributable to such risks." While this is perhaps a valid enough point, the cost of the premiums needs to be compared with the cost of the claims. In either case the taxpayer bears the cost. Furthermore, Rickover has argued that another element of distortion is injected into the process by shipbuilders' retention of staffs of claims lawyers who "have developed lucrative practices helping shipbuilders . . . prepare and prosecute contract claims." Lehman acknowledged before Congress that, while the Navy had accepted the concept of risk insurance with the attendant pressure of prospective litigation (Electric Boat is insured with Lloyds of London), the point of defective workmanship "is not a black and white issue." What constitutes defective workmanship, he noted, and "what constitutes normal cost of doing business, is clearly an arguable matter."[8]

Despite the important roles of workmanship defects, bidding procedures, and insurance claims in the government-contractor relationship, the "bottom-line" results, so to speak, peculiarly affect the shipbuilder, who has a quarterly responsibility to report a profit to stockholders and to maintain in the marketplace a reputation for corporate viability. For example, contractors will naturally reckon into their balance sheet pending claims as unqualified receivables from the government. This treatment of claims at one level allows the corporate conglomerate at another level to construct a perhaps artificially more favorable corporate profit picture in its yearly statement than the ultimate disposition of the claims might support. In 1977 General Dynamics recorded corporate profits of $103 million, a balance statement that, however, included an $840-million claim against the government through Electric Boat on the 688 program (which suggests that General Dynamics suffered losses in other areas as well). Predictably, with the disclosure of a profit, General Dynamics stock rose, even though the Electric Boat claim had not really been settled. Electric Boat's "cost overruns" prompted the Justice Department to conduct a "very active" criminal investigation of the company involving both the matters of claims and "cost overruns" since the settlement.[9]

Caught in the middle between Congress and his only Trident builder, Secretary of the Navy John Lehman reluctantly had to acknowledge Electric Boat's various shortcomings. But the Congress, fresh off the 688-class claims controversy, wanted unadulterated answers as to who was responsible for the "cost overruns" and delays in the Trident program. Apparently selected as the bearer of bad tidings, Vice Admiral Earl Fowler in a diplomatically rather unsophisticated fashion, or in deliberate posturing, confirmed by his statements the worst fears of Congress about both the 688 and the Trident programs in his testimony before the House Seapower Subcommittee in March 1981.

Vice Admiral Fowler's Charges

According to Fowler's testimony, both the Trident and the 688 designs specified use of a grade of weldable mild carbon steel (equivalent to industry specification ASTM-A36) for some "nonpressure hull applications including some where a lesser strength steel could be used." An Electric Boat employee discovered in November 1978 that some steel bar stock did not match the color code designating its grade. Fowler said this meant that it "may not be strong enough for its specific end use." Electric Boat initiated an audit and reported in May 1979 that five sizes of steel bar stock were in inventory even though they fell below specifications for assigned applications. Fowler revealed that by July additional investigations showed that the problem encompassed other sizes of bars "which could have been installed in as many as . . . 126,000 locations in SSBN Trident Class submarines." Eventually fifteen grades of nonconforming steel were discovered and impounded.[10]

To test the impounded steel, Electric Boat subjected the lowest-quality grade to "worst case" testing, assuming that and if those grades passed that test, grades with higher specifications could be used anywhere. "This testing," claimed Fowler, "indicated that the strength of some grades fell below that of the required steel." Fowler declined to give a precise estimate of the duration of the delay on submarine delivery caused by the steel problems.[11]

Fowler then addressed the welding problem. In December 1979 a quality-assurance auditor from the office of the Supervisor of Shipbuilding discovered some deficient welds on the *Los Angeles*-class submarines. Electric Boat delegated two inspectors to check all submarines then under construction and to review the welding records. They found numerous records missing or incomplete. By February 1980 Electric Boat had recognized the need for a reinspection of its own with two new inspectors, but the Navy found their conclusions unsatisfactory. In one sampling of structural drawings, 37 percent were not retrievable, indicating to the Navy that Electric Boat had not made the proper inspections or at least had not retained the proper records. Another review by Electric Boat revealed the magnitude of the problem. Out of 36,149 welds in the *Ohio* submitted to magnetic particle inspection, 9693 (26.3 percent) lacked inspection records. Of those that had records, 2772 (33 percent) needed repair of variable severity, ranging from cosmetic to internal-structure, although none involved the hull. Trident subs 726 and 728 were delayed because of the welding problem, but inexplicably 727 does not seem to have been afflicted by these problems. The attack sub *Bremerton* (SSN 698), which was on sea trials when the problem first appeared, was immediately recalled to port.[12]

Several other problems elicited Fowler's criticism, including material identification, improper paint, and defective painting. In December 1976 a threaded plug on one of the attack submarines (SSN 694) fell out of a piping system, resulting in 400 gallons of water flooding the engine room. The plug had corroded because it was made of steel instead of nickel-copper alloy, and workers had installed it because of its incorrect identification. The Navy found "enough deficiencies . . . to warrant continuance of [this] inspection program." Evidence of defective or improper painting also appeared inside the *Ohio* in December 1980. Subsequent Navy inspection showed that 25 percent of the surface area inside the ballast tanks required repainting.[13]

Fowler ended his testimony by noting that "basic procedural elements of a quality system existed . . . [but] there was not adequate implementation and execution of those elements." Although the "latest Trident submarine contract with Electric Boat incorporates this revised Quality Program Plan," he concluded that "if the actions . . . eventually agreed to by Electric Boat had been taken immediately upon the first indication of problems . . . I believe that the full scope of these problems and, therefore, their eventual correction, would have occurred in a more timely fashion."[14]

As Electric Boat would point out at length, Fowler admitted that much of the government-furnished equipment (GFE) arrived at Groton with defects. Turbines furnished by General Electric had developed cracks in the rotors, a defect discovered in September 1979. Two months passed before Electric Boat received new turbines, presumably Navy-certified, which were found to be out of balance upon installation, thereby generating unacceptably high levels of airbone noise and vibration. The turbine generator rotors had to be rebalanced, a process that took another three weeks. Another incident of Navy-supplied and -certified equipment involved the propulsion screw. Because of the unique design of the single crew, the blades must be perfectly balanced. When it arrived with imbalanced blades it posed severe off-center torque on the shaft when tested.[15]

Mishaps such as these the Navy attributed to the Trident's unique nature, although some equipment failures can perhaps be attributed to shipping damage and to other less easily identified causes. Admiral

Thomas Hayward explained that the Trident's difficulties "are not dissimilar from those of the first ship of any new class. Some of them are created by failures of the Navy to anticipate problems or plan properly." Other problems arose from "changes we wanted to make as designs unfolded and things weren't working precisely as we wished them." But, Hayward admitted, "some of them are due to Government furnished equipment that did not turn out right."[16]

Also regarding the matter of contract changes, two points bear emphasizing. First, not all contract changes entail actual physical modifications of the vessel; sometimes a worker discovers blueprint errors as simple as misspellings requiring literary corrections. On other occasions, either prior to or after provisional installation, a worker may make a physical change of a minor nature in the vessel—for example, moving a bolt over one inch to accommodate ease of removal—that necessitates a blueprint alteration of advantage in future applications. Since the shipbuilder must record and perform these blueprint changes, in the Trident's case the Navy sent lists of alterations to Electric Boat, communicated by an engineering notice, or EN. Second, the Navy may decide to upgrade technology in the course of shipbuilding—for example, adding new equipment to the radio room, as in the case of the *Ohio*—with which the shipbuilder by contract must comply. The latter changes are legitimate claims items. No shipbuilder can be expected progressively to customize U.S. Navy vessels at its own expense. Indeed, the majority of the blueprint changes fall short of imposing any additional labor or expense for the shipbuilder.[17]

In his testimony Fowler maintained that the Navy sent only 25,000 Trident revisions to Electric Boat out of 10,600 original drawings, for an average of 2.4 revisions per drawing. Fowler compared this average to other classes of ships (see table 10). Fowler repeated Rickover's

Table 10
Trident Revisions Relative to Other Classes of Ships

Class	Revisions per Drawing
SSN 637	5
FFG 7, LHA, and DD 963	4 to 7
SSBN 616 Class (Follow-Shipbuilder)	6
SSN 688	5.2
SSBN 726	2.4*

*Based on 25,000 drawing revisions identified as of February, 1981.

observation that not all drawing revisions require actual physical work by the contractor. During 1980, he stated, about 40 percent of ENs issued required no work by the shipbuilder.[18]

Fowler concluded by saying that "the quality assurance problems at Electric Boat significantly delayed both the SSN 688 and Trident programs." Of the total delay, "repairs to Government-furnished equipment and changes originating with the design contractor contributed to a lesser extent." Consequently, Fowler produced a chart for the Trident delivery schedule (see table 11).

Following Fowler's testimony, Navy Secretary Lehman suggested publicly that the Navy might have to drop the Trident program after the seventh submarine because of the delays in production schedules. He made his statements in an announcement in which he also awarded a $1 billion contract to Newport News Shipbuilding for the construction of three 688 attack subs without offering Electric Boat an opportunity to submit a bid on the subs, expressing his concern about Electric Boat's ability to meet its schedules. Lehman threatened that the Navy would consider canceling the Trident or gearing up government yards as an alternative to continuing the Trident production at Electric Boat. Electric Boat reacted immediately. David Lewis, chairman of Electric Boat's parent company, General Dynamics, called the Navy's criticisms "very unfair and uninformed." The company blamed Navy design changes and flawed parts furnished by the government for the problems, and later a "bitter" company spokesman said the Navy had "cast aside" fairness.[20]

Table 11
Trident Delivery Schedule

Ship	Original Contractor Delivery Date	EB Estimate Feb., 1978	EB Estimate* Aug., 1980	Navy Estimate
726	4/30/79	11/80	6/81	12/81
727	4/30/80	11/81	11/81	9/82
728	12/30/80	7/82	7/82	9/83
729	8/31/81	3/83	3/83	5/84
730	4/30/82	11/83	11/83	1/85
731	12/31/82	7/84	7/84	9/85
732	8/31/83	3/85	3/85	5/86
733	5/31/86			1/87

*Electric Boat advised the Navy in October, 1980, that these dates were under review.

What was Fowler's point in presenting this series of broad and in some cases erroneous or overstated accusations? Was he acting as Lehman's agent? Lehman, it might be noted, a very young Secretary of the Navy, could scarcely admit the Navy's own responsibility for the problems involving the 688s and the Trident if he wished to press forward with the Navy's request for a 600-ship fleet. The fiscal year 1983 Navy budget perhaps attests the skill with which Lehman manipulated these dramatic acts of shadowboxing after his initial ill-advised attempts to threaten the shipbuilders.

Electric Boat's Response

One week later, P. Takis Veliotis, executive vice president–marine for General Dynamics and general manager of Electric Boat, testified before the same House committee that had heard Fowler. He expressed his concern about both the timing and substance of the criticisms. Veliotis pointed out that the Secretary of the Navy had precipitously awarded three SSN 688 contracts to Newport News before Veliotis could respond to Fowler's charges, and he had reason to believe that the Newport News bid was higher than the bid submitted by Electric Boat. Veliotis emphasized that the hearings represented Electric Boat's first opportunity to present its side of the story. But, like Fowler's testimony, Veliotis' appearance masked the more substantive objectives, including Electric Boat's attempt to retain the three 688 contracts and the ninth Trident contract as well as to satisfactorily conclude the ongoing claims negotiations with the Navy.[21]

A primary cause of the problems experienced by Electric Boat prior to the management change in October, 1977, that brought Veliotis in as general manager was the "unrealistic scheduling." Veliotis stressed that during 1977 the company had established new schedules and subsequently had delivered three attack submarines ahead of schedule at $6.8 million under the revised budget (see fig. 6-1). The general manager believed at that time that the Trident program was on or ahead of schedule as well. The problems detailed in 1981 by Fowler, Veliotis emphasized, were primarily problems encountered in 1979 and were not necessarily contemporary problems. Veliotis said the House should "keep in mind" several questions as he responded to Fowler's testimony: Who discovered the problem—and how? How extensive did the problem really turn out to be? What is the current status—is the problem still with us or behind us? Have adequate measures been taken to prevent recurrence—and by whom?[22]

He proceeded thereupon to refute Fowler's criticisms. Electric Boat, not the Navy, had discovered the nonconforming carbon steel, he

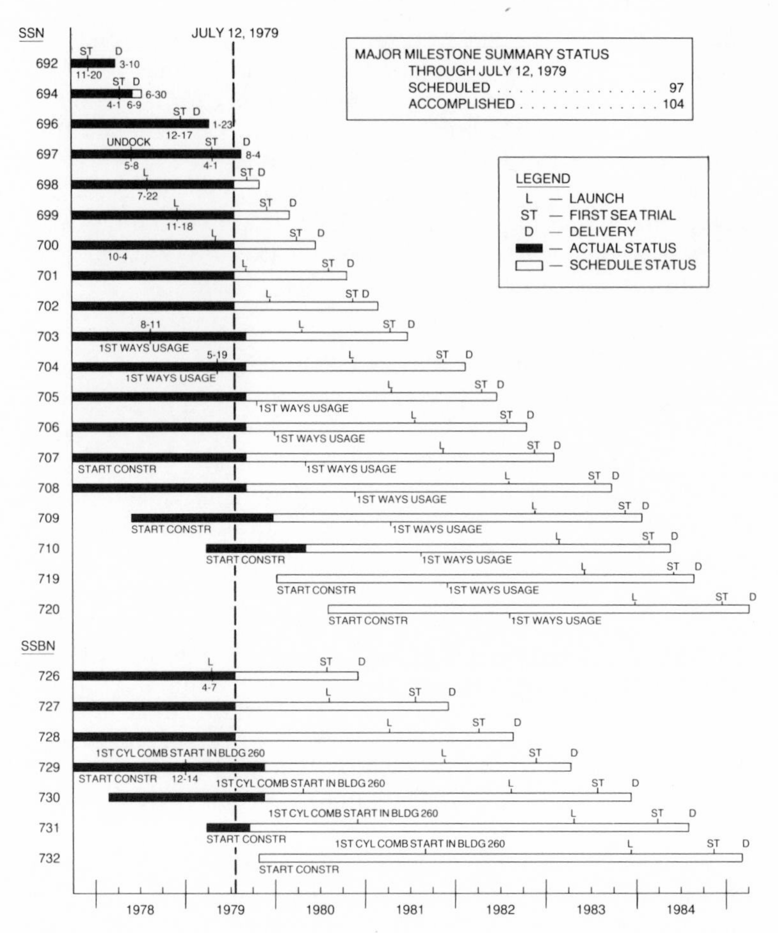

Source: U.S. Congress, House, Hearings, statement of P. Takis Veliotis.

Fig. 6-1. New construction milestone summary.

emphasized. Although the nonconforming steel did not meet all of the requirements of the specifications, Veliotis stated, “it does not necessarily mean the steel was unfit for its various uses.” Furthermore, “none of this material was, or could be, used in pressure hull or SUBSAFE applications” such as structures, piping, and systems either exposed to submergence pressure or essential for the safety of the ship.” It was applied only on pipe and electrical hangers, small foundations, mounting spools, and shims. Veliotis, on discovery of the misapplication, himself had ordered the impoundment of all potentially nonconforming steel in stock, established new certification requirements "over and above Navy requirements," hired the American Bureau of Shipping to inspect and certify compliance, and increased shipyard testing. In addition, Electric Boat had implemented a thorough engineering analysis to identify all possible shipboard applications. Admiral Fowler's description, Veliotis said, was "basically correct, including the fact that there were 126,000 locations on a Trident submarine where this non-conforming steel could possibly have been installed." But Fowler's description, he added, must have left the House members "with great concern over the frightening possibility that the *Ohio* was riddled with bad steel."[23]

Fowler failed to tell the committee that "only 41 pieces of steel weighing 50 pounds ended up being replaced" out of 23.6 million pounds of steel purchased for the *Ohio*. Admitting that Electric Boat had a problem with nonconforming steel, Veliotis reminded the committee that "*we* discovered it, *we* addressed it, and *we* solved it." Steel problems ultimately caused the *Indianapolis* and *Bremerton* attack subs to fall behind schedule by one and one-half months net, as Electric Boat had prepared them for delivery up to two months early. "No delay effect whatever" occurred to the Trident ship delivery. To further put the nonconforming steel in perspective, 30 percent of the carbon steel bar in the Navy's own supply system was nonconforming, compared to 12 percent at Electric Boat.[24]

Next Veliotis dealt with Fowler's criticisms of Electric Boat's welding. Veliotis maintained that both the Supervisor of Shipbuilding and Electric Boat discovered the welding problems together, in addition to finding some welding records missing. Once again, the problem areas "did not affect the submarine's pressure envelope." Rather, they centered around "secondary structural welds . . . such as pipe hangers, and deck support systems." Electric Boat's investigation showed that the weld problem dated from 1975 and was related to the rapid manpower buildup between 1972 and 1977. Fowler's data, however, "presented the situation . . . in the worst possible light" and may have left the committee "with the distinct impression that these submarines could be loaded with dangerously defective welds." Veliotis assured the committee that he considered the welding problem a "*serious problem*." Still, "a weld is a weld without regard to whether it is one inch or ten feet in length, and a defect is any defect ranging from a cosmetic imperfection to a complete absence of weld metal," thereby unavoidably injecting a judgment factor into the process. At Electric Boat, "this judgment factor becomes ultra-conservative when a full-scale reinspection and investigation are going on." In the *Ohio*, there were "117,400 welds that require magnetic particle inspection, not 36,149 as you were told." Of this number, 2772 welds needed replacement for a total portion of 2.4 percent.[25]

To gain a more meaningful measure of the welding program, Veliotis suggested the committee should "not be distracted by the *number* of welds." Instead it should measure the length of welds. On the *Ohio*, of the over 65 miles of welding requiring magnetic particle inspection, Electric Boat repaired or replaced 18,700 inches (0.5 percent) of these welds, and "in the judgment of [Electric Boat's] welding engineers, over 50 percent of these involved minor cosmetic defects only and were satisfactory for the intended service." Not only did Electric Boat take action to solve the problem, but "we kept looking until we were satisfied that there were no further deficiencies." Among the various steps taken to improve the quality of workmanship, Electric Boat increased audit activity to verify work completion, modified work instructions to require a foreman's signature certifying completion of tests, developed a computerized system to account for all shipboard structural welds, and instituted a comprehensive training and retraining program for the workforce. Veliotis concluded that "[the welding] problem is behind us."[26]

As for the painting problem, he explained that the paint used on the *Ohio* consisted of a type of epoxy paint that needed warm temperatures to "cure properly." When Electric Boat officials discovered "some deterioration of the paint system in the *Ohio* primarily caused . . . by the fact that the epoxy paint had been initially applied during the winter" they identified less than 5 percent (not 25 percent as Fowler had claimed) of the paint as actually in the process of deterioration. Repainting, if performed in a normal cycle at Navy insistence, would have occurred in December, January, and February, cold winter months that Electric Boat officials believed would exacerbate the paint deterioration. Working with experts from the International Paint Company, Electric Boat found an alternate paint system applicable in cold weather to protect the boat until the vessel's first postdelivery drydocking, scheduled to occur in warmer months when the originally specified epoxy could be properly applied. The Navy denied the request, forcing Electric Boat to apply the epoxy paint in winter, which prompted Veliotis to warn: "I will not be surprised, and you should not be either, if at some later date deterioration is again found to have occurred."[27]

Unfortunately, he continued, the Navy regarded these problems as exclusively the responsibility of Electric Boat rather than as joint problems. Veliotis expressed his displeasure at the way the problems came to light. The quality assurance program at Electric Boat was installed in

1969, with the Navy reviewing and auditing the program in 1971, 1973, 1974, 1977, and 1979, and it has been under continuous supervision ever since. At each date the Navy approved the program as meeting quality assurance standards. Nevertheless, on October 27, 1980, Electric Boat submitted a "quality modernization and upgrade program" on its own initiative that included implementation of a computer system for accountability of shipboard welds, upgrading of all documentation data, an expanded training program, and closer monitoring of material suppliers.[28]

Next Veliotis addressed the problem of GFEs. In the *Ohio*, Electric Boat rebalanced the ship's service turbine generators, a job the workers had to perform "within the crowded engine room compartment." The Navy next directed Electric Boat to replace the main turbine rotors, after the main propulsion plant had been installed, hooked up, steam cleaned, tested, and operated. This direction "entailed the ripout of a large amount of completed work to secure access to the turbines." Workers tore out "hundreds of piping joints and foundations, as well as a number of lockers and electrical components and associated cabling" (see figs. 6–2, 6–3, and 6–4). The impact of this reinstallation disrupted ten major ship systems and "interrupted testing and operations across the entire ship."[29]

In 1979 the Navy submitted over 8000 notices of defects in government-furnished materials. Electric Boat workers dedicated 750,000 man hours to correcting GFE deficiencies. Veliotis counted over 676 of these deficiency notices sent to the shipyard in the first two months of 1981 alone, a rate of 2856 for all of 1981 involving approximately 195,000 man hours (see fig. 6–5).[30]

Drawing revisions flooded in at a greater rate than the deficiency notices. Veliotis made clear he did not blame the Navy for revisions, which were "inherent in the very nature of a new ship design." Rather, he criticized instead the Navy's "refusal to give proper recognition to the effect on delivery" of these revisions. During replacement of the turbine rotors, Electric Boat received a new directive to modify the

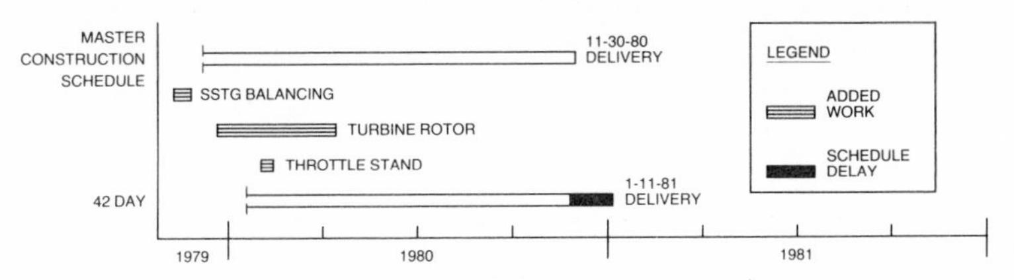

Source: U.S. Congress, House, Hearings, statement of P. Takis Veliotis.
Fig. 6-2. SSBN 726 delay analysis: 1-11-81.

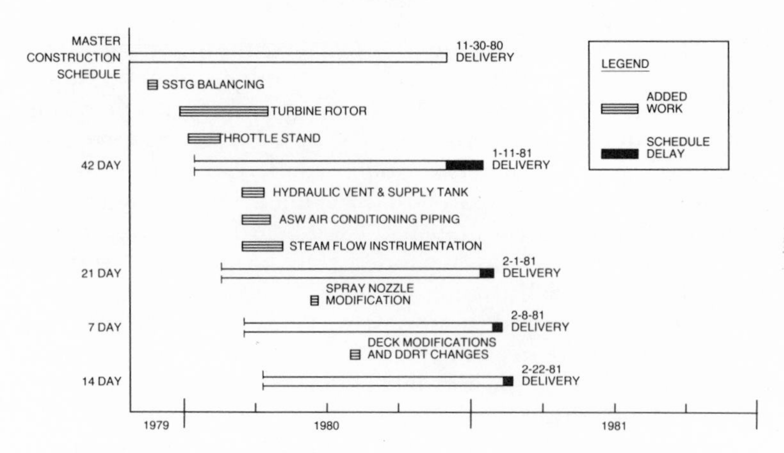

Source: U.S. Congress, House, Hearings, statement of P. Takis Veliotis.
Fig. 6-3. SSBN 726 delay analysis: 2-22-81.

throttle-stand foundation. Other changes similarly delayed delivery, including reworking the air-conditioning pipes and numerous changes in the engine-room decks. Workers completed the torching and welding inside the crowded compartment, thereby unavoidably disturbing and delaying other work in a cumulative fashion. Later, officials found that the "trim and drain system—as designed—did not function as required," forcing another delay. In still another case, Veliotis said the

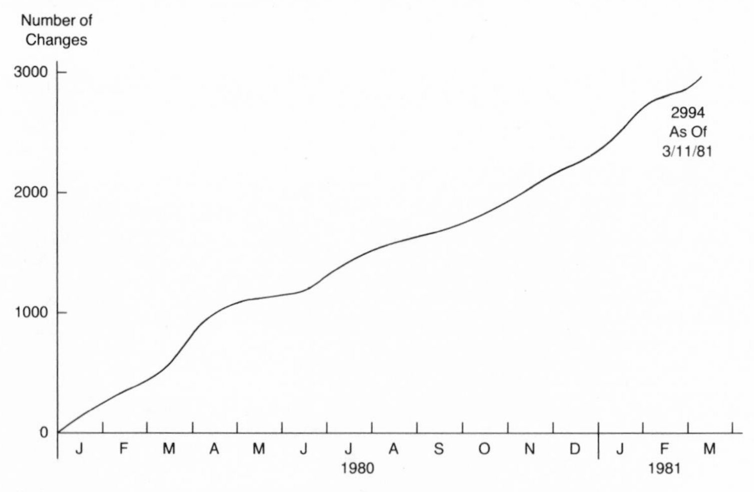

Source: U.S. Congress, House, Hearings, statement of P. Takis Veliotis.
Fig. 6-4. Trident design changes requiring shipyard work (cumulative).

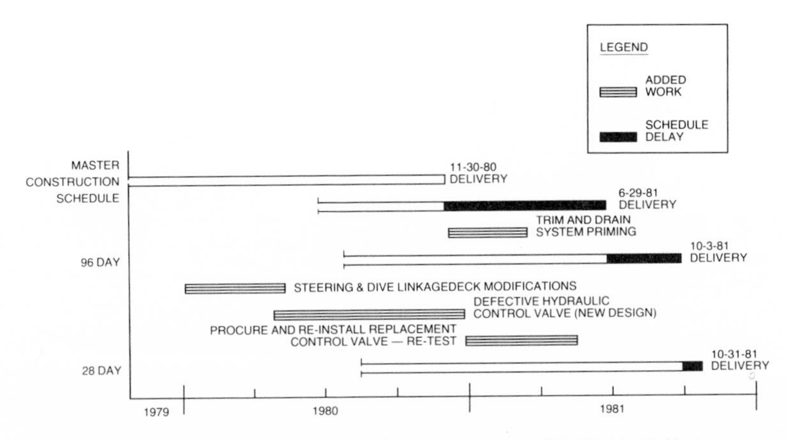

Source: U.S. Congress, House, Hearings, statement of P. Takis Veliotis.
Fig. 6-5. SSBN 726 delay analysis: 10-31-81.

Navy repeatedly used a "high-risk" complex valve that eventually malfunctioned, for which a new, less complex design was substituted. The number of these structural revisions, said Veliotis, created less of a practical burden in terms of man hours directly involved than did their out-of-phase sequence. Even as late as January 1980, when the *Ohio* was entering its final construction phase, Electric Boat continued to receive over 2900 revisions that "required the performance of physical work in the shipyard—not just paper changes." More than twenty changes a day arrived at Electric Boat's offices.[31]

The prospective delay facing the *Ohio* prompted a February 20, 1980, Electric Boat request for the Supervisor of Shipbuilding to review the changes with regard to their impact on the schedule and to announce a corresponding schedule readjustment. He refused, notifying Electric Boat that it was to perform all changes "*notwithstanding cost and schedule impact.*" After adopting an interim procedure that "proved to be a disaster," the Navy agreed on October 9 to Electric Boat's original review recommendation. Eight months had elapsed since the first Electric Boat request for schedule modification (see fig. 6–6), during which time Navy brass and Electric Boat officials met on a daily basis.[32]

Problems nevertheless continued to mount. The Supervisor of Shipbuilding refused to authorize revisions in block form, insisting that each design revision be considered apart from its effect on the schedule. As a result, the number of revisions submitted by the Trident office outdistanced those authorized by the Supervisor of Shipbuilding, attaining by November 1980 a progressively unbreachable dis-

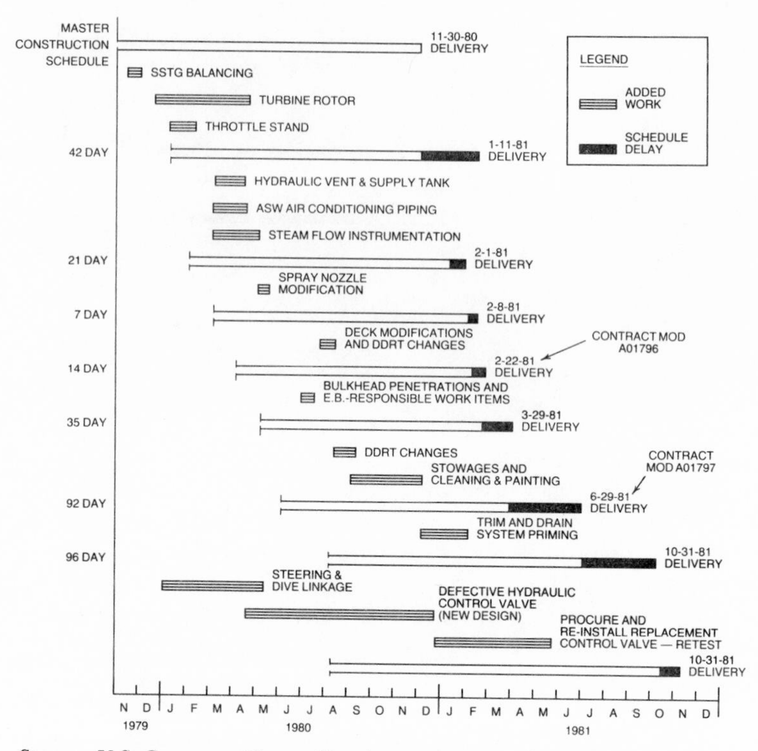

Source: U.S. Congress, House, Hearings, statement of P. Takis Veliotis.
Fig. 6-6. Cumulative delays to SSBN 726.

crepancy. Electric Boat argued that each separate change could not be considered "in a vacuum," for a delay in one area meant potential delays throughout construction. It was, Veliotis claimed, "equivalent to saying that one could never be killed in an avalanche because no individual snowflake could possibly hurt you." The Navy, he charged, "preoccupied with avoiding 'huge omnibus claims,'" had lost sight of its primary construction goal of delivering the subs at the earliest possible date and at lowest cost. Moreover, the Navy insisted Electric Boat make modifications but submit a statement with the completed work order saying no delays in delivery would result. In a letter that "infuriated the Navy," Veliotis refused, and Secretary of the Navy Hidalgo intervened personally. Soon thereafter, Veliotis testified in November 1980, followed by a meeting with Fowler wherein the two men broke the logjam, a move due in part to the Navy's realization that Veliotis was an effective political infighter and that he was justifiably critical of this disfunctional procedure. Apparently, Veliotis said in a

1981 interview with the authors, the Navy was willing to compromise much earlier, but his sources indicated the logjam "all boiled down to one admiral, and nobody was in a position to argue or overrule him." When asked by the authors if Rickover was the admiral in question, Veliotis replied, "That's what our Navy sources told us." At any rate, since the meeting with Fowler, "work resulting from design changes and drawing revisions [was] authorized by the navy in a timely manner," although the delay stemming from the authorization discrepancy was irrecoverable.[33]

Veliotis also defended the Trident schedule. "Everywhere we turn," he told the House committee, "we hear that the lead Trident submarine, *Ohio*, is two and a half years late and that it is all Electric Boat's fault. This is simply not correct. . . ." Whereas Electric Boat had planned to have the *Ohio* ready for April 1979, contract modifications unavoidably extended this to November 30, 1980. Other contract modifications further stretched the delivery date to no earlier than October 1981. Many of the delays Veliotis attributed to Navy modifications, but he refused to blame the Navy. Delays accompanied "every recent class of both surface ships and submarines" (see fig. 6–7). Comparable "late" delivery dates for various classes included: LHA-1,

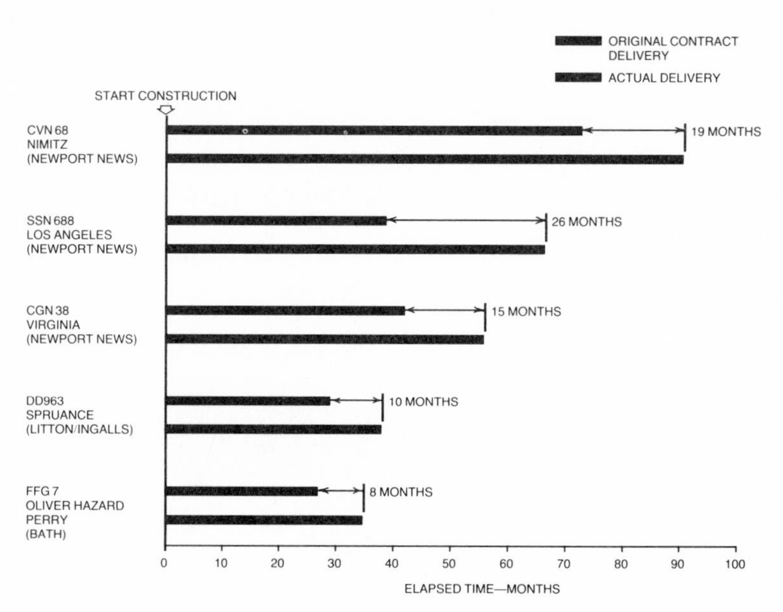

Source: U.S. Congress, House, Hearings, statement of P. Takis Veliotis.
Fig. 6-7. Representative U.S. Navy lead ship delivery delays.

38 months; SSN688, 26 months; CVN-68, 19 months; CGN-38, 15 months; DD-963, 10 months; FFG-7, 8 months. Modifications of delivery dates, when caused by change orders, government-responsible causes, and other contract-allowable circumstances, do not constitute real "lateness." Especially the *Ohio*, as the lead vessel in its class and because of its complex construction, simply had needed disproportionately more changes than previous submarines. While Electric Boat officials had thought the *Ohio* was ahead of schedule in late 1979, the problems discussed in this chapter threw the entire schedule into confusion. Keeping the Navy abreast of each new projected delivery date during this period proved impossible, and the effects of the problems on the schedule can be seen in figures 6–2 through 6–6. The situation eventually stabilized sufficiently for Electric Boat to set a new schedule when the yard finally completed all trade work on March 15, 1981. At this point the *Ohio* was physically completed, with only painting, cleaning, and the finishing touches remaining. Electric Boat then set the *Ohio*'s delivery date for October 31, 1981, with the *Michigan* (SSBN 727) to follow a year later and the *Florida* (SSBN 728) ten months thereafter.[34]

As for Trident's costs, Veliotis felt that "the false impression has been conveyed to the American people that the Triden program is a financial disaster" principally due to Electric Boat's faulty performance. At the time of his testimony, Electric Boat's Trident contracts covered seven ships. Therefore, the proper way to evaluate the company's cost performance should be over the entire schedule (see fig. 6–8), using the initial target costs along with change orders and escalation added to the base cost, dividing this modified cost figure by the contracted number of vessels to attain a true unit cost. Thus, computed out of a program completion total of $2.9 billion, Electric Boat's cost growth to initial estimates totaled only 3 percent, running $750 million *under* the publicized ceiling price. In fact, this performance allowed the Navy to transfer $69.5 million out of the FY80 Trident request, specifically through "demonstrated reductions in the overhead rate at Electric Boat."[35]

Pentagon Reaction

So ended Veliotis' testimony before the House. He had demonstrated directly to the Navy and indirectly to Rickover that he would defend Electric Boat before Congress in a far more effective manner than had his predecessors. However, five days later the Pentagon attempted to regain the offensive by announcing that it was looking for additional foreign or domestic shipyards to construct Trident submarines. Secre-

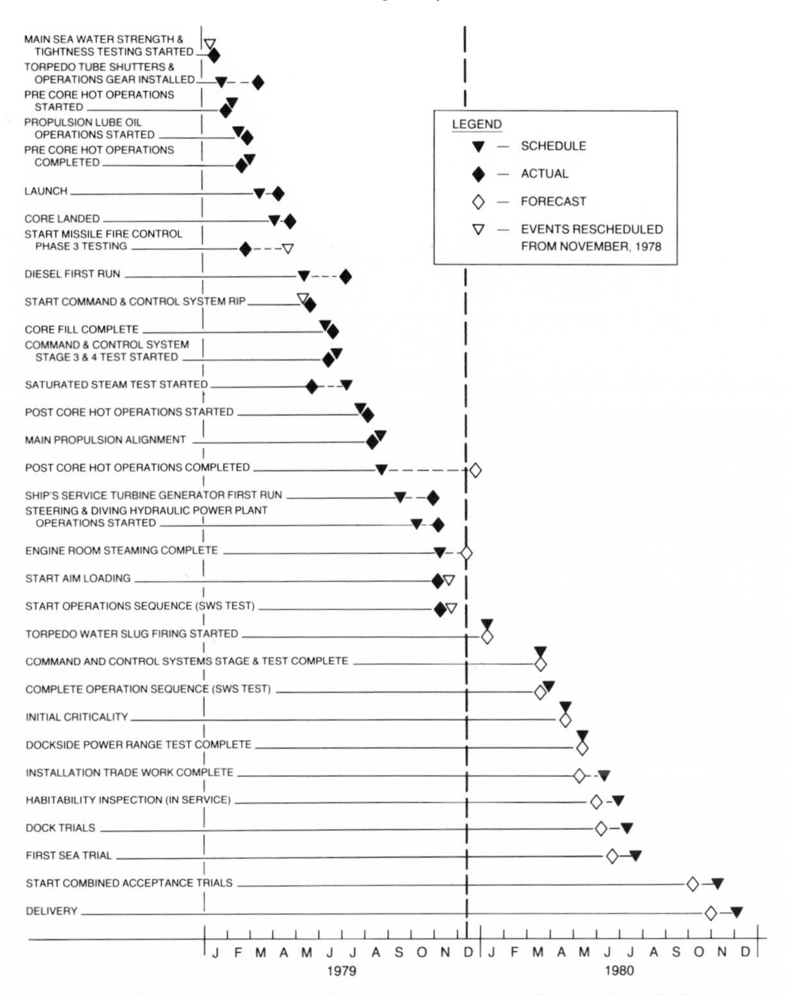

Source: U.S. Congress, House, Hearings, statement of P. Takis Veliotis.
Fig. 6-8. SSBN 726 key event analysis, as of December, 1979.

tary of Defense Caspar Weinberger remarked that he did not "rule out procurement from any source, including overseas sources," a suggestion repeated by Lehman, to which Veliotis retorted that he "could save [Lehman] a consultant's fee and tell him where he could get good delivery on the Trident—from the Soviet Union." Even Rickover later admitted that "the people of this country would not stand for us building atomic submarines in a foreign country." Besides being a self-evidently ridiculous threat from the standpoint of compromising national security for a strategic weapons system, it should further be noted that Lehman's and Weinberger's threats also ignored the value of the learning cycle already banked with the *Ohio*'s construction. It also failed to take into account the fact that no other foreign or domestic shipyard possessed the unique Quonset Point frame and cylinder facility or the Groton land level construction facility, with their corresponding capital investments.[36]

Lehman nevertheless continued the Pentagon's sharp criticism of Electric Boat's handling of the Trident program. On April 2, 1981, the Navy further penalized Electric Boat by dropping the pending option for the ninth Trident sub, reasoning that Electric Boat had already drifted behind schedule and the stimulus of dropping the option might prompt the company to take "a more compliant stand on the Navy's demands." In a statement before the defense subcommittee of the Senate Appropriations Committee a short time later, Veliotis again responded. To keep a consistent and strong work force, Electric Boat needed to receive both 688 and Trident contracts on a predictable basis. However, Veliotis stated, "instead of moving steadily along on an even grade, we have been on a roller coaster" of contract awards. An oscillating rate in the volume of government work had forced Electric Boat to watch its workforce of skilled trades drop from 9000 to 4000. A typical Electric Boat shipwright with the proper skills cost $17,000 after training, Veliotis explained. When EB was compelled to drop such a worker because of the erratic pattern of the contract award process, a worker must be hired and trained anew. In this connection, Veliotis continued, Electric Boat must "hire three people to end up with one," whereafter each new worker retained takes six to nine months to achieve full productivity. Thus, he reasoned, the Navy's decision to award three 688 contracts to Newport News without allowing Electric Boat to submit a bid "does not make very good sense" and could trigger another fluctuation in the workforce, labeled "minilayoffs" by Electric Boat management. These fluctuations were unnecessary, Veliotis maintained, for by 1981 Electric Boat had the capacity to build three attack submarines and two Tridents per year. Since the damage had already been done, Veliotis urged the Navy immediately to award the ninth Trident contract and another 688 contract. Further, the Navy should reconsider its plans to defer the tenth Trident. The country had "seriously under-utilized" Electric Boat's facilities, and the way to correct the problem was for the Navy to award Electric Boat more contracts overall and on a more consistent basis.[37]

Maintenance of the industrial base posed a serious problem for the Navy should the "boom and bust" style of awarding contracts continue. Veliotis' testimony was not lost on Southern senators in particular, who realized that Litton-Ingalls of Pascagoula, Mississippi, for example, had ceased to build submarines, while the Newport News shipyard in Virginia could (and would) build only attack submarines. Moreover, the award found Newport News facing a substantial shortage of trained workers, leaving the shipbuilder in much the same situation as Electric Boat had been when it received the contracts for the Tridents. It will be recalled that Electric Boat's sudden manpower buildup resulted in many of the problems leading to the claims. Conversely, the award to Newport News meant Electric Boat would have to lay off a large portion of its attack-submarine workforce because, without the additional three contracts, two-thirds of the attack-sub workers would not have sufficient oncoming work to keep them busy in 1982 and not all of them could be redirected to the Tridents. In retrospect, the sudden contract award to Newport News seems ill advised.

Rickover's Countercharges

Soon after Veliotis concluded his case before the House and Senate, Admiral Hyman Rickover delivered a new broadside, mostly composed of the same charges Fowler had lodged previously. Rickover has constantly been at temperamental and philosophical odds with all major shipbuilders providing service to the Navy. As one author explained, Rickover "insists that it is [the shipyards'] patriotic duty to build Navy ships and submarines and build them perfectly, profit or no." Moreover, Rickover, like the proverbial elephant, never forgets. He reminded a House committee that in 1972 the Navy overpaid Electric Boat by $28 million, and Electric Boat had managed to keep the case out of court for four years. His recollection at this point in time of the claims controversy with the shipbuilders in the mid-1970s simply rekindled fires apparently quenched by the Veliotis-Fowler negotiations. Rickover had warned the Chief of Naval Operations in 1978 that "unless special precautions are taken, [Electric Boat] might very well attempt, several years from now, to recover all or a portion of the $359 million [loss] they are presently agreeing to absorb by claiming events subsequent to the June 9, 1978 claims [settlement] caused increased cost at the shipyard." His warning, which appeared in one of a series of memos from Rickover, resulted in a meeting with then-Undersecretary of the Navy Edward Hidalgo and Graham Claytor, the assistant secretary, on August 21, 1978, in an attempt to contain Rickover. During an intermission in their meeting, Rickover "bluntly" told the two secretaries that the office of the Secretary of the Navy was primarily responsible "for the mess we have in shipbuilding today." Upon receipt of several other memos from Rickover dated December 10, 11,

12, and 13, Hidalgo told a *Washington Star* reporter that Rickover was "trying to hamper the construction of the Trident submarines" and "trying to create ill will between the Navy and the shipbuilder."[38]

Rickover has constantly described Electric Boat's executives as "absentee management," knowing full well that Veliotis, as head of General Dynamics' Marine Division, had several shipyards to oversee, including shipyards at Quincy, Massachusetts, and its facility at Quonset Point, Rhode Island. In reference to the competition between Newport News and Electric Boat, in which Newport News demonstrated greater efficiency than Electric Boat even though Electric Boat received more contracts, Rickover maintained that both companies were run by absentee management. "Apparently," he added, "Electric Boat's absentee management is worse." At this point it should be noted that even in Veliotis' subordinate role as general manager at Electric Boat Company, his position per se required extensive time to resolve problems of public relations, political conflicts, and legislative misinformation whose compound effect nevertheless always affects shipbuilding efficiency (directly). Perhaps Rickover's reference to Electric Boat's "absentee management" was a revelation of his subconscious awareness that, for the first time in his recent career, Rickover sensed the manager of a shipyard seriously rivaled him in political skills at the highest level. The admiral made it a point to note that Veliotis, in his position as executive vice president of the Marine Division of General Dynamics, managed the yards at Quincy, Massachusetts, and Charleston, South Carolina, which build liquified natural gas tankers. Rickover carefully omitted his usual appeal to Congress to further develop the U.S. shipping industry, of which the LNG tankers play a significant role. Indeed, because of Veliotis' adventurous willingness to involve new technology, especially in the construction of outsized LNG tankers with their revolutionary pressure domes, Veliotis knew he was working on tested grounds in pushing for the advanced welding and sizing technology based on the same Swiss engineering capabilities so well extolled by the Navy in its increasingly frequent visits to the Quonset Point facility. Nor did Rickover mention that the Quonset Point Facility makes components for both the Tridents and the 688s, with which Electric Boat cut shipbuilding costs across the board for both classes.[39]

Rickover disagreed with Electric Boat's claim that drawing revisions had caused increased prices and delay. Electric Boat, he alleged, knew large numbers of drawing revisions accompanied any contract and were "inherent to the shipbuilding process." Historically, he said, this had always been so; generally, contractors roughly estimated these revision costs and included them in the original bid. Rickover contended that revisions estimated in this rough manner "would not have priced [the *Ohio*] 1 cent" higher.[40]

In testimony before the House, Rickover, judged and admired by many congressmen as one of the few Pentagon employees dedicated to acting as a watchdog over taxpayers' money, provided some specific examples of Electric Boat's "unreasonable" claims regarding contract revisions. In one case Navy drawings omitted a piece of wire rope used to close a hatch cover from the sub's interior. Although Rickover maintained that two sailors could go aboard the vessel and complete the installation in two hours (possibly an accurate claim, barring union opposition), Electric Boat estimated the wire rope replacement would take two weeks and cost $2 million! Citing a 1978 incident, Rickover recalled a drawing revision (to correct an Electric Boat error) requiring the drilling of a single 1.5-inch hole in a steel shield box in each of seven ships. This revision involved no other rework or rewiring. Electric Boat, however, viewed this as a contract change and submitted a cost estimate of $1000 per ship to drill the holes.[41]

According to Rickover, the "fly in the buttermilk" of open-ended contracts such as those given to Electric Boat is that the shipbuilder can make later claims on costs unrelated to the original design or system. For example, in the *Ohio* the shipbuilder had to fit numerous stowage compartments on the vessel during the final stages of construction. Installation of these compartments must wait until the necessary primary machinery has been installed and then be fitted into proper remaining areas. When the time for their installation approaches, the Navy submits pertinent drawings to the shipbuilder. Electric Boat anticipated that these change items would measurably delay ship delivery. But instead of substantiating the delay and pricing it out in advance so that the government could routinely pay for it, Electric Boat has held the contracts open in order to claim other costs associated with the delay at a later date. To cure this malady of delayed claims in the final stages of construction, Rickover has suggested a statute of limitations for such claims.[42]

On March 4, 1980, Rickover reported to the Secretary of the Navy that Electric Boat had developed a new justification either for final delays or cost overruns: it had assigned only enough workers to perform "basic contract work" on the vessel so that any secondary changes would create an overload reducible only by overtime pay. Electric Boat, on the contrary, has consistently had trouble getting enough skilled labor, a point the Navy does not dispute. Rickover's charge failed adequately to consider labor problems affecting the industry in general. Rickover nevertheless pressed on in his testimony, charging that

Electric Boat's goal was to "force Newport News out of business." A General Dynamics spokesman responded by saying "We have no comment to make on what has become Adm. Rickover's annual presentation of arbitrary, biased, and inaccurate charges against the American shipbuilding industry in general and Electric Boat in particular."[43]

Veliotis, in a 1981 interview with the authors, contended that Rickover had instigated the 1978 Justice Department investigation of Electric Boat. Besides costing both the government and the shipbuilder "hundreds of thousands of dollars" on the case, "it put tremendous pressure on the company." Rickover "had the ability to make your life very difficult."[44]

Did Fowler and Rickover testify on their own initiative? Rickover, probably. But it is entirely plausible, as has been intimated above, that the youthful new Secretary of the Navy, John Lehman, "suggested" that Fowler make his criticisms public to quickly establish the image of his superior as a tough-minded administrator not easily intimidated by the contractors. Instead, the inexperienced Lehman ironically found himself in the position of defending *both* the Navy and Electric Boat in front of Congress.

Lehman Seeks a Solution

Testifying before the House Appropriations Committee in March 1981, Lehman admitted that Electric Boat had failed to meet Navy specifications in the welding problems. He did not raise the subject of the fixed-price contract, whereby a system of "cost overruns" was built into the program, which had been approved by previous secretaries of the Navy. Nor could he advertise the Trident as a new system with the latest technology and maintain the illusion that the Trident, as implied in the acceptance of the fixed-price contract, represented a submarine of common or routine design. Finally, he did not bring up the topic of Rickover's increasingly public pronouncements, in which the crusty admiral had dragged a private contractual matter into the public forum, obliging Veliotis to respond. But Lehman had apparently decided to first settle the claims and construction problems with Electric Boat and to deal with Rickover thereafter. Thus Lehman adopted a conciliatory tone in his statement, noting that as a result of the subsequent Navy directive Electric Boat made "a massive effort" to correct the welds. He also assumed some of the blame unto the Navy: "We in the Navy have a responsibility to insure that the contractor meets the quality control required of it. 6,000 [*sic*] missing welds should have been noticed by more than just that lady [inspector]." There was, he added, "a dual responsibility in quality control."[45]

Lehman acted both publicly and privately to resolve the problems. Publicly, he appointed a blue ribbon panel—a special committee—composed of three members of his own appointment and three selected by Electric Boat. On March 17 Lehman suggested the panel concept to David S. Lewis, Chairman of the Board of General Dynamics Corporation, and Lewis agreed. Congress was not particularly pleased. Representative John Murtha of Pennsylvania, pointing out that Electric Boat already was "behind" by three years, reprimanded Lehman, saying "I cannot believe, Mr. Secretary, that you are saying it is going to take until December of next year [the deadline for the committee's final recommendations] to decide there is something wrong in that shipyard." Other congressmen further expressed their irritation at Electric Boat's claims in front of Lehman. Joseph Addabbo, the committee chairman, related that "members of this committee visiting the shipyard . . . are told that right now all [Electric Boat is] interested in, is adding up all the claims against the Navy. They are not interested in getting ships out." Addabbo was particularly peeved by Veliotis' printed presentation for the claims: "I have one of the finest presentations by any public witnesses. . . . It is even printed on the finest paper. I wonder who is paying for it. Even [Veliotis'] biographical sketch is done on prime paper." But what "really concerned" Addabbo was "the fancy use of language. . . . Mr. Veliotis, on page 19, goes into great length on discussion of shipbuilder's risk insurance." Quoting from Veliotis' statement, Addabbo selected a section in which Veliotis said Electric Boat had no claims against the Navy "as we all understand the term 'claim.'" There were, he qualified, "insurance reimbursement requests being prepared to recover under the builders risk insurance provisions of our Navy shipbuilding contracts the cost consequences of faulty workmanship performed by Electric Boat employees." Therefore, Addabbo sarcastically concluded, "I stand corrected. Not claims, he is going to ask you to reimburse him for faulty workmanship performed, by his own admission, [by] Electric Boat employees." Addabbo found this "an outrageous position."[46]

The chairman of the House Subcommittee on Procurement, Melvin Price, reported that "it has become increasingly difficult to deal with Electric Boat in day-to-day matters. The company appears to be maneuvering to submit claims on some other basis in the event it is not successful with the insurance claims." But not every lawmaker wanted Veliotis' scalp, however. Senator Christopher Dodd (Democrat of Connecticut) thought "the Navy relied on inadequate and inaccurate information to support its criticism of the Electric Boat Company." David Lewis of General Dynamics reiterated that Secretary Lehman had not even heard Electric Boat's side of the story before Veliotis testified.[47]

Privately, Navy negotiators continued their behind-the-scenes meetings with Electric Boat. It can be reasonably assumed that often the posturing by Fowler, Lehman, Veliotis, and General Dynamics officials were smoke screens for the more substantive private discussions. Perhaps, in reaction to such impatience as expressed by Representative Murtha, and in reaction perhaps to a joint appreciation of the desirability quickly to compose their differences, the blue ribbon panel's recommendation was presented to Lehman on April 20, 1981, roughly eight months ahead of schedule. The Navy appointees to the committee consisted of James Goodrich, Special Consultant to the Secretary of the Navy; Vice Admiral John Williams, Deputy Chief of Naval Operations for Submarine Warfare; and Hugh O'Neill, another Special Consultant to the Secretary of the Navy. Electric Boat's representatives included William Gorvine, General Counsel of Electric Boat; L. Emmett Holt, the Assistant General Manager for Public Affairs of Electric Boat; and Electric Boat's Director of Planning, Norman Victor. Rickover did not hesitate later to make the obvious point that "½ [of] the members of the special committee were Electric Boat employees." On March 31, 1981, Lehman had instructed the committee to investigate four questions: (1) Are the problems of the past (welding, paint, etc.) resolved so that "they will not cause further significant delays"? (2) Can Electric Boat achieve its expected delivery dates? (3) Does Electric Boat have the capability to deliver one and one-half Tridents and three 688s per year? (4) What overall recommendations could the committee offer to assure future progress of the program? To arrive at its conclusions, the committee reviewed data and reports supplied by both the Navy and Electric Boat, conferred with personnel, and inspected Tridents and SSNs under construction.[48]

Report of the Blue Ribbon Panel

Six problem areas were identified by the committee: quality control, nonconforming steel, structural welding, defective painting, defects in GFEs, and design revisions. In the case of the first three problems, the committee reported that actions taken already had satisfactorily redressed the problems. Although the application of the epoxy paint might "show deterioration," the committee did not expect it materially to affect scheduled delivery dates. No other GFEs had manifested deficiencies, so only the design revisions remained an obstacle to fulfillment of the schedule. "Some level of minor problems" that might later appear would not disrupt the schedule, but any major design revisions, of course, would. Therefore the delivery date for the *Ohio* (SSBN 726) was "achievable" but did "not contain additional time for contingencies." If the Navy encountered no other major design problems, it could take timely delivery of the *Ohio* following sea trials. Whereas the *Michigan* (SSBN 727) date was also "achievable," it included "some additional time for contingencies." The committee also concluded that "on a conservative basis," with Electric Boat's trade workforce of 16,000, the shipbuilder could "sustain an annual delivery rate of one Trident and three SSNs per year." Addition of another 1000 trade workers would permit Electric Boat a further increase of this rate to one and a half Tridents per year. Finally, the committee recommended that Lehman request the Chief of Naval Material routinely to provide an additional monthly report assessing progress at Groton under all of the identified headings. David Lewis said the company was pleased with the findings of the committee, although "it hardly compensates for the loss of business that rightfully should have been awarded to Electric Boat."[49]

Report of the General Accounting Office

Following the conflicting testimony by Veliotis and Fowler, Representatives Charles Bennett and Joseph Addabbo requested the General Accounting Office (GAO) to provide a comparative analysis of the testimony, specifically, a side-by-side comparison of Fowler's and Veliotis' testimony. After that, the GAO should provide a more detailed report. On May 4, the "side-by-side" was presented and Bennett set a date of February 1, 1982, for presentation of the final written report. The first report, dated May 5, 1981, not only had a side-by-side comparison of the Fowler and Veliotis statements but included "amplified facts" the GAO deemed important as well. Among the numerous comparisons, Veliotis' statement that the first of the Tridents "was on track to delivery in November 1980" (pp. 4, 5, 29) is contrasted with the "amplified facts" that "two key critical path evolutions" were delinquent and that already there had been a "three-to-four month slip." On the subject of the SSN 688 budget (p. 4), which Veliotis claimed was delivered $6.8 million under budget, the Navy countered by noting that the budget referred to only reflected Electric Boat's portion of the claims settlement. Whereas Electric Boat had claimed that the nonconforming steel was used only in secondary applications (p. 6), the Navy found 536 applications identified by Electric Boat as critical where the nonconforming steel appeared. In several other statements by Veliotis the GAO's statement offered either clarification or outright contradiction. For example, concerning the timeliness of response by Electric Boat in correcting the nonconforming steel, Veliotis in his testimony claimed that Electric Boat "moved quickly to determine the full extent of the problem and to correct it" (p. 6). The GAO offered a different interpretation by citing a series of letters beginning in November 1978 making reference to the steel problem. Although Electric Boat forwarded a "comprehensive status report" to the Navy on June 12, 1979, ten days later the Navy advised Electric Boat that "co-mingled carbon steel was still being used."[50]

Other serious differences exist between the March report issued by Veliotis and the GAO's May report, especially regarding steel quality and defective welds. Veliotis' claim that "30 percent of carbon steel bar stock in naval shipyards . . . were nonconforming" (p. 8) was countered by the Navy's statement that the sample size was "very limited" and a more thorough sampling "produced a rejection rate of 14.7 percent." This rate included specimens that "exceeded specifications" as well as those below grade. In the Electric Boat statement the number of total welds requiring inspection—put by the Navy at 36,149 and by Electric Boat at 117,400 (p. 9)—was originally submitted to the Navy in a "Final Report" of February 17, 1981, with the lower figure quoted by the Navy. Electric Boat's statement "erroneously adds to the population" of the welds, according to the GAO, thus resulting in a lower percentage of welds requiring rectification to the total number of welds. Separate repair of that 50 percent of the welds that involved "minor cosmetic defects" (p. 10) was "an Electric Boat decision to expedite correction and/or more cost effective than the administrative process of obtaining waivers" (a complicated process whereby the Navy accepts changes in original specifications). Replying to Electric Boat's contention that the Navy applied stricter standards to Electric Boat than to other shipbuilders, specifically Newport News, the GAO responded emphatically that "double standards do not exist," meaning that different standards were not being applied to Electric Boat versus those applied to Newport News.[51]

The GAO's analysis of the paint defects also established serious discrepancies between the Electric Boat and Navy statements on this subject (p. 11). When the Navy received Electric Boat's original waiver request on December 12, 1980, the request did not contain any discussion of the application of epoxy paint in cold weather or details of corrective actions. It stated only that "final painting . . . prior to delivery would be an extraordinary burden on the paint department." Electric Boat's figure of 5 percent actual paint deterioration, while accurate, was erroneously compared to the Navy's estimate that 25 percent "of the total surface area of [the ballast] tanks would have to be *reworked* to assure adequate preservation." Another response from Electric Boat, received by the Navy on December 19, failed a second time to address the application of epoxy paint in cold weather. Moreover, the GAO report noted, "epoxy paint is regularly applied in cold weather at other shipyards (Portsmouth Naval Shipyard)," and Electric Boat's own delivery schedule for sea trials for the *Ohio* (June 1981) would have necessitated its application in winter regardless, traditionally six months after delivery.[52]

GAO's investigation of Electric Boat's claim that government-furnished equipment exhibited "hundreds of continuing problems" (pp. 12–13), eventually requiring Electric Boat to "spend over 750,000 manhours correcting [these] deficiencies," assumed a disingenious form. Rather than deny the specific problems—the turbine, the screw, and the like—the GAO argued "Electric Boat is under contract and is paid by the Navy to both inspect and repair all incoming government furnished equipment." Since Electric Boat during 1979–1980 constructed twenty ships for the Navy, the 8000 reports of defects in the GFEs turned in by Electric Boat averaged only 200 reports per ship year. Similarly, as to the 750,000 man hours, when "viewed over the two year period and the number of ships under construction, the average manhours per ship is not significant," still a rather ludicrous claim even if viewed as constituting "a mere" 37,500 man hours each for twenty ships! Neither the GAO nor the Navy statement provides any evidence of improvement in the quality of GFEs over the progression of the twenty ships; it omits any comparison of possible disproportions in the need for corrective manpower between larger and smaller vessels, cheaper or more expensive vessels, or complex or more simple vessels; finally, it lacks correlation to the critical nature of the equipment involved—that is, why cracks in turbine blades should not be as seriously condemned as a failure by Electric Boat to properly weld a component involving the pressure envelope.[53]

Defects in the drive train were not discussed in the GAO report, which seemed meticulously to avoid mentioning deficiencies in governmental agencies outside the Navy. However, the GAO specifically refuted the allegations about the hydraulic vent and control valve. In response to Electric Boat's recommendation for design changes in the hydraulic vent and supply tank, the Navy had correctly noted that the "hydraulic system supports nearly every system in the ship," without which "the ship could lose hydraulic power during critical maneuvers." As to Electric Boat's assertion that the hydraulic control valve failed to work properly due to its extreme sophistication, the Navy had replied it had designed the valves along lines comparable to those used in the 688 class, problems arising therewith only through scaling the design from small to larger, a process that of necessity "carries an element of risk." Even so, the Navy had not tested the valve under operationally realistic conditions, and the valve eventually failed at sea. The Navy then corrected the valve problem and, in disagreement with Electric Boat's statement that attempts to redesign the valves "were unsuccessful, and we had no choice but to proceed with valves of a less complex design" (p. 16), asserted that the "Trident is not going to sea with valves of another design." Because Electric Boat had assumed the valves would need replacement and retesting, it advised the Navy of the probable occurrence of a delay, but the Navy responded that the valves did not require repair or retesting.[54]

A challenge to Veliotis' interpretation of the events that occurred after February 1980, when the situation demanded numerous meetings to review designs, was also included in the report. Several meetings were held, according to the report, but the negotiators for each side disagreed over procedures to be used in future meetings and over reviewing criteria. Electric Boat wanted the Navy to consider the *Ohio* as a prototype ship for delivery purposes, thereby allowing the completion of some nonessential systems to occur after the first sea trials. In short "anything which did not meet the specifications but which did not result in an inability to operate would be deferred or deleted" for the moment. Electric Boat also argued it was "absurd" to provide adjusted schedules that would be "obsolete almost as soon as they were put to paper." These schedules, from the Navy's perspective, "are required . . . to schedule [its] support of Electric Boat" and aid in planning personnel training and logistics. Finally, the GAO questioned Electric Boat's claim that all trade work on the *Ohio* was completed on March 15, 1981 (p. 31): a memorandum from Electric Boat to the Navy dated March 14 contained "25 pages of steel trades, piping trades, and installation trades" remaining to be completed after March 15, 1981.[55]

Meanwhile, Rickover continued to warn that Electric Boat planned new rounds of insurance claims, based on what he viewed as the shipbuilder's victory in 1978. Attempting to derail claims before they were even tracked, the Navy inserted various disclaimers in new contracts. However, all of the shipbuilders feared that the inclusion of these disclaimers would allow the Navy to demand that all errors in workmanship be paid for by the shipbuilder, so the companies recoiled from these contracts. Newport News refused to accept its contract in 1981, and, while Electric Boat agreed to sign its contract, it "insisted on including in the provisions a loophole which would allow Electric Boat to submit claims at any time merely by alleging that an act under another contract gave rise to the claim." This contractual strategy constitutes what is popularly known as cross-contract claims. Ultimately Congress and the Navy sought to improve the contractual situation. When negotiations for FY 1980 and FY 1981 Tridents occurred, NAVSEA (Naval Sea Systems Command) demanded contracts containing provisions updating the previous contracts with the disclaimers inserted. However, Electric Boat insisted upon having its own loophole with its counterdisclaimers. Hidalgo interceded, overruled NAVSEA, and awarded Electric Boat its preferred contract variation.[56]

A Compromise is Reached

Lehman, in an apparent effort to extricate himself from the consequences of his earlier ill-considered adversary relationship, moved toward finding an effective strategy for dealing with Electric Boat. On September 14, 1981, he entered into negotiations with the company for the ninth Trident contract, but warned Electric Boat negotiators that they would have to endure its postponement until the current claims, possibly totaling over $100 million by company estimate, were settled in a fair and mutually beneficial way. Lehman also said "de minimus" terms for a tenth Trident contract include earlier deadlines for establishing costs, a requirement that the contractor pay 50 percent of all cost overruns, and a prohibition for claims on contractor-caused defects. In a final warning Lehman reminded Electric Boat that, while "they [*sic*] have a monopoly at the present time," the company was "competing against what it would cost [the Navy] to produce [the submarines] in government yards." Two days later, Electric Boat accepted the Navy's terms in order to bid on the ninth Trident. The company also agreed to deliver all seven Tridents earlier than scheduled. Lehman, in return, adopted a more conciliatory attitude and praised the shipyard for making "sufficient progress" in correcting its workmanship problems to qualify for reconsideration of current claims. Electric Boat's progress, he noted, "has been real and measurable and has warranted the improvement in relations." Electric Boat projected delivery of the *Ohio* and six 688-class submarines by the end of the year, for a total of seven. "That's a remarkable record," Lehman concluded. Lehman's miraculous attitudinal transformation from earlier in the year to September invokes substantial astonishment and leaves several unanswered questions: (1) Were the tensions between the Navy and Electric Boat generated in the spring of 1981 due perhaps principally to the Secretary's initial insecurity in his new office? (2) Were they due to the Secretary's as yet incomplete reading of himself into the earlier historical record of problems at Electric Boat? (3) Were they due to congressional pressure on Lehman so critical of Electric Boat that the Navy and Lehman feared the fate of the Trident program if "the mess" was not cleaned up? (4) Were they due to a failure by Electric Boat to manage better the projection of a newer image of the Trident program in the wake of Veliotis' growing success in unsnarling the problems affecting the *Ohio* and the program in general? (5) Did the ongoing GAO study intimidate Electric Boat so that the shipyard transferred workers from projects, scheduled for delivery in the future, to the *Ohio* and the six *Los Angeles* subs due in 1981, as the report would later claim? (6) Did the GAO report intimidate the Navy, which also became the subject of its investigation? Whatever the answers may be to these questions, a thoughtful observer of the events of these months in 1981 is likely to conclude that a political rather than a shipbuilding miracle involving both parties took place.[57]

Why did Electric Boat suddenly compromise? Clearly, Lehman's hollow threat to reopen government yards had little to do with it, since Electric Boat exclusively had a $450-million capital investment in Trident-related shipbuilding equipment estimated in 1981 to have a replacement value of $800 million. The company, of course, would have to build a whole series of Tridents actually to make an eventual profit. Each Trident departing Groton allowed Electric Boat to recapture some of this huge initial investment and to reduce production costs through improved-quality trades work on an enhanced learning curve. Moreover, the behind-the-scenes private negotiations finally bore fruit, only coincidentally with Lehman's exhortations, leading the *Armed Forces Journal* to speculate that the Navy's media blasts at General Dynamics and Electric Boat were political moves "designed to show that the Reagan administration could be as tenacious in scrutinizing defense programs as it is in trimming social and economic programs." Most likely, however, the ongoing GAO study probably prompted Electric Boat to directs its managerial and organizational attention to getting the *Ohio* and the six *Los Angeles* boats into the Navy's hands in 1981 to relieve some of the pressure, possibly even at the expense of future schedules.[58]

As the Navy and Electric Boat made up, events exacerbated the mutual dislike shared by Veliotis and Rickover. Rickover delighted in discussing Electric Boat's "absentee management" and when testifying before Congress used his opportunity to blast Electric Boat and Veliotis, saying they were involved in "ruthless money-making schemes." "They don't care if they manufacture horse turds or ships," he said, adding "I wouldn't give those so-and-sos any more contracts until the [claims and quality] problems are resolved." The admiral's tendency to personalize problems and policies may have incited some publicly undisclosed resentment at Rickover for his immaturity of style. Veliotis, for example, ridiculed Rickover's supposedly advanced reactor designs, calling them "coffeepots," and said Rickover was less interested in what the system did operationally than he was in the installation of his reactor units. Rickover frequently interfered in the operation of the yard, to the chagrin of many general managers, Veliotis recalled, and maintained a number of bureau "spies" at all the shipyards. The admiral's experience with Veliotis differed greatly from his previous satrapic inspections at Electric Boat. The first time Rickover charged into Veliotis' office, shouting and pounding on the manager's desk, Veliotis responded by telling him to "go to hell. I am running the shipyard, not you." Following the completion of work on the *Ohio*, Rickover insisted on personally being on board during its sea trials. Upon the sub's return, Veliotis sent a letter to Admiral Thomas Hayward, the Chief of Naval Operations, asking for an investigation of two incidents that had occurred a month earlier. Although Veliotis did not specifically accuse Rickover of anything, his letter implied that the eighty-one-year-old Rickover "failed to give timely orders" when functionally commanding the *La Jolla* and the *Jacksonville* attack submarines on test runs. According to Veliotis, Rickover started to plunge the *La Jolla* dangerously astern while testing a "quick stop" maneuver in which the submerged vessel running at top speed is supposed to be brought to a dead stop by the full reversal of its power train. During this maneuver, reverse power must be terminated as soon as the ship's forward motion has ended; otherwise the reverse pull of the screw will threaten the ship with total loss of control because the screw is propelling the conical shape of the hull astern rather than pushing the full diameter of the hull forward. In both cases, Veliotis said, Rickover had failed to give that timely order. Hayward denied the charges in a response Veliotis termed "very bland." The response did not "recognize the fact that the ship did in fact go out of control."[59]

The entire affair took another strange turn when the *Wall Street Journal* published a misleading report that Veliotis would "step down as general manager of [General Dynamics'] Electric Boat division." Described as a "peace gesture" by General Dynamics to the Navy, Veliotis' resignation supposedly represented a victory for the Navy (and Rickover). In fact, however, Veliotis had assumed the job at Groton *only* until the first Trident submarine had been delivered, with the previously announced declaration that he would resume more general responsibilities after the delivery. His replacement at the yard, Fritz Tovar, indicated just the opposite of the *Wall Street Journal*'s implication that Veliotis had failed; it instead revealed the fruition of Veliotis' project. This conclusion is further reinforced by Veliotis' June 1982 statement of resignation as the general manager of the marine division of General Dynamics, a resignation visibly unexpected by Quincy and Groton, personally justified by the demands of "family business" in Greece. Veliotis also had other problems that required his attention. In

1983, a civil suit alleged that he, his wife, and another General Dynamics executive had accepted $4.5 million in bribes relating to construction of liquid natural gas tankers at the Quincy, Mass., shipyard. The suit alleged that Veliotis and James Gilliland took kickbacks of 10 percent from Frigitemp Corporation and that Veliotis and his wife transferred the money to their Swiss bank account. Particulars of the suit place the alleged misdeeds well before Veliotis took over the Groton yard and the Trident project, and the suit was instigated by a bankruptcy trustee for Frigitemp's assignees, who has dutifully tried to recover as much as possible for his clients. Still, if the allegations are true, a shadow of doubt will be cast over all Veliotis' work, whether related to the incident or not.[60]

Rickover's role in the entire process probably has been his last hurrah. On November 10, 1981, Lehman recommended the replacement of the "near legendary" naval officer, ending Rickover's career. His retirement had been a pending and thorny problem for many secretaries of the Navy. According to Rickover biographer Norman Polmar, the admiral had become "a major burden on the Navy" by 1981, and his constant interference grew "more frightening." Undoubtedly, Lehman happily took advantage of the tenuous nature of Rickover's position—his service required constant duty extensions—although Lehman could have discharged the admiral on grounds of age alone. Lehman, in contrast to his predecessors, because of his incomparable mastery of naval matters, evidenced by his previous public roles, research, publications, and personal interest, perhaps felt more than qualified to "deep six" the Rickover problem. Nonsubmarine admirals have regarded Rickover as "a self-serving satiate," and one must question a system of organization that allows an individual to wield so much power and to become virtually indispensable, although not irreplaceable. Even admirers conceded that by 1981 Rickover should step aside. As one supporter reasoned, "He's done a super job . . . but I'd prefer not to wait until he makes a mistake to retire him." Norman Polmar and Thomas Allen emphasize that point in their biography of the admiral, which has as its final chapter title an apt description of Rickover: "the unaccountable man."[61]

Leaving aside the personal antagonism between Veliotis and Rickover, who should bear the responsibility for the Trident's problems? A synthesized but objective set of answers about the proper ascription of responsibility is called for at this point—with the possibilities logically being by issue: (1) Electric Boat exclusively or partly; (2) the Navy exclusively or partly; (3) both parties jointly in varying degrees; (4) neither party but, instead extraneous and unaccounted causes.

One clear problem area developed when Electric Boat expanded its work force by 18,000 over a five-year period to handle the submarine construction. Often these workers lacked basic technical skills, and most lacked more generalized shipbuilding skills. Consequently, the unrealistic scheduling affected construction from the outset. In this regard Jacques Gansler, an expert on the defense industry, estimated that a new worker is only 50 percent efficient in his first two years, another point not considered when the Trident is said to be "behind schedule." Also, shipyards have tended to face a massive turnover rate (75 percent annually) in their workforce. Since, as a rule, the shipbuilding workforce is not either regionally or nationally mobile, according to this statistic, the location of replacements for workers who abandon their jobs for local employment is peculiarly difficult for this class of worker. Given the 50-percent efficiency rate, therefore, Electric Boat's personnel clearly could not attain any degree of higher proficiency, even in the first three or four years. Whereas responsibility for this problem of slowly improving proficiency can somewhat legitimately be laid by the Navy before the front door of Electric Boat, it is an industrywide malaise, further compounded to some extent by the inflexibility of certain organized union prescriptions.[62]

Although confusion about the matter remains, it appears Electric Boat itself, not the Navy, first discovered and attempted to correct the problem of below-grade steel. The difference in dates cited by the Navy in its correspondence with Electric Boat upon which the Navy's case rests perhaps can be fairly attributed to a normal lag between the date on which Electric Boat discovered the problem and the date on which it reported it in 1976 and 1977. Originally, out of a necessity to resolve labor disputes and other difficulties, Electric Boat effected an organizational rearrangement by which P. Takis Veliotis took over the yard in October 1977. The new manager made an avowedly honest and dedicated attempt to improve these relationships and to place the whole Trident program on a reassuring and effective basis for its entire future. He and other Electric Boat officials embarked on a massive retraining and upgrading effort based on a special training program with the University of Hartford. Veliotis took other steps, detailed in earlier chapters, to put both the Trident and the 688 programs on track, including the conduct of a "comprehensive wall-to-wall inventory" that closed the plant for a week and the favorable settlement of labor-related concerns at the yard. Including other savings programs undertaken by Veliotis, he claims to have saved $126 million a year on behalf of both programs through 1981. With these changes, Electric Boat officials believed they had both programs running ahead of schedule until the steel and welding problems referred to disappointed these predictions.[63]

Resolution of the problem of deficient welding is extremely difficult. A truly objective determination of this problem would require an external audit by independent authority, an undertaking impossible in this work. However, it can nevertheless be deduced that the extent of the actual problem lies somewhere between Electric Boat's claim that the welds were cosmetic and were repaired only because it was easier to correct them than to get waivers and the Navy's disputation that the inadequate welds posed a threat to the safety and operation of the ship. In some cases the possibility may have existed that the safety of the ship was jeopardized, although the Navy statement of May 5, 1981, did not argue this case. Furthermore, the Navy refutation of Veliotis' statements did not challenge the phrase stating that "structural welding is satisfactory for proper conduct of Fast Cruise and Sea Trials." In other words, while the Navy may have argued correctly that Electric Boat had not comprehensively corrected all welds under suspicion, it could have simultaneously chastised Electric Boat for falling behind schedule if Electric Boat took the time to correct those welds. The crux of the problem is to determine how many welds were substandard to what specific extent. A vertical blemish of 2 inches in a welding seam on the exterior face of a hull cylinder can be far more dangerous than a substandard 3-foot weld involving a lightly stressed deck. To determine how many potentially dangerous welds existed in the SSN 698, the crucial piece of evidence here, which neither side has volunteered, is the record of the *percentage of defective welds repaired before the SSN 698 went on sea trials.* With this statistic available, an assumption could be made about the comparable ratio of welding defects for the other subs, including the *Ohio,* thereby indicating how many welds were in fact "cosmetic" and how many were possibly "crucial." Beyond extremely reasonable care in welding and in the inspection and correction process, the only really valid test of a crucially deficient weld would be its actual failure under stress conditions—in all likelihood a terminal test.[64]

Electric Boat conducted its own ongoing investigation, but the Navy wanted an expanded investigation. In that sense, both sides were arguing an empirical basis in which it was agreed that some welds were deficient. Yet the Navy's advocation of an expanded investigation does not ipso facto argue that Electric Boat's deficiencies were more extensive than further evidence might reveal.

The Navy's assertion that other yards apply epoxy paint in the winter avoids the question. Is the Trident's paint the same as applied to all other subs? Some sources indicate otherwise—it may be a special

Teflon-type paint that facilitates noise reduction and the ease of movement through the water. If so, why could not the Navy and Electric Boat agree upon a technically more suitable time to paint the vessel? Apparently the GAO did not pursue this question.[65]

In the case of substandard or inoperable GFEs, the Navy again apparently evaded the question. Just as Electric Boat had tried to minimize the impact of the poor welds by presenting data on weld lengths, so the Navy tried to deny problems with GFEs by arguing that the number of repairs to them was insignificant, and the GAO report left this unchallenged. Of course, if only five pieces of GFE out of a complete suite in five ships fail, the percentage of failure per ship is insignificant if the function, complexity, or cost of the flawed item is ignored. However, if those items are reactors, screws, or turbines, the functional impact, as well as the resulting replacement cost and corresponding installation turnaround, can be devastating. Navy (and GAO) officials did not deny in their statements that major GFE items required replacement. However, their replacement occurred at the most inopportune time possible for the construction of the vessels and necessitated massive ripouts of other components. In its own defense, the Navy correctly replied that ultimately it was Electric Boat's contractual obligation to inspect and repair all GFEs, yet a prior responsibility for GFE quality control still rests with the Navy. No amount of finger-pointing can shift the responsibility for GFE quality control completely *from* the government. Between the GFE problems and those involving steel and welding, better than 75 percent of the increased real cost and unscheduled delay of the *Ohio* can be explained. Since Electric Boat has assumed responsibility for the latter problems and the Navy has quietly shouldered the burden of the former, a fair evaluation of responsibility for the problems involving the Trident program would justify blaming Electric Boat and the Navy equally, even though the Navy enjoys a perhaps undeserved better public image because it has *not* reported on its *own* failures with the *same* specificity, aggressiveness, and completeness it leveled at Electric Boat, although the GAO investigation examined both Navy and Electric Boat quality controls with equal vigor.[66]

This evaluation cannot assess the impact of contract revisions or their effects. Rickover's claim that some revisions involve only changing the spelling on a blueprint, while accurate as far as it goes, ignores those numerous changes that fundamentally alter items already installed, revisions that involve costly and time-consuming work. Without having blueprints of the exact revisions made, an evaluation of responsibility in this area must remain undetermined. The cost and consequence of the blueprint- or contract-revision process probably justifies a separate study—which no party, including the GAO, has furnished (Veliotis or Fowler, for example). Therefore, judgment about it also is impossible here.

New Allegations in the GAO Report

W. H. Sheley, the director of Mission Analysis and Systems Acquisition Division of the GAO, sent a draft of the final GAO report to the Secretary of Defense on January 19, 1982, entitled "Cost Growth and Delivery Delays in Submarine Construction at Electric Boat Are Likely to Continue." The Secretary sent a copy to Richard DeLauer, Undersecretary for Research and Engineering, for comment. The basic points of the report included these:

- In achieving the deliveries of six SSN-688 attack subs and the *Ohio* in 1981, "Electric Boat concentrated its labor force on these submarines at the expense of the remaining submarines still under construction," and the shipbuilder "must make up lost progress on follow-on boats . . . to meet future delivery dates."
- Unless the shipbuilder took immediate action to reverse "unfavorable human resources and productivity trends," some delivery dates "may not be met."
- Both Electric Boat and the Supervisor of Shipbuilding left "room for improvement" in quality control.
- Electric Boat was "not effectively implementing" its inspection procedures.
- Approximately 48 percent of the reviews to determine if paint was properly applied were not performed at Groton, and 62 percent not performed at Quonset Point.
- Inspectors signed off incomplete welds.
- Forty-four percent of the inspectors did not properly mark good welds, which would have allowed other trade work to proceed.
- Actions taken at both Electric Boat and in the office of the Supervisor of Shipbuilding "have not corrected the weaknesses which existed in the past."
- Cost growth in the Trident program was "virtually ensured in each contract negotiated before Oct. 1981."
- Electric Boat used anticipated savings from machinery and facilities improvements "that were overly optimistic," and labor-hour budget estimates were low.

The report chastised the Supervisor of Shipbuilding for not enforcing quality control and recommended close surveillance. Although it admitted that the Veliotis and Fowler testimonies "clouded the issues," the GAO report did not account for its own omission of such problems as the flawed government-furnished equipment or Navy design changes.[67]

Electric Boat's Response

Electric Boat was invited to respond to the report before it became public, and on February 24, 1982, A. M. Barton, Assistant General Manager, Planning and Control, of Electric Boat, submitted a three-page letter to Sheley. Barton noted Electric Boat's strong objection to the contents of the GAO draft because it misrepresented the positive steps taken by both Electric Boat and the Navy over the past two years. It incorrectly implied a continuation of the previous problems long since resolved, and the report's very title was more of a headline than an audit report's title. Furthermore, he argued, any objective report would include the 1981 accomplishments to give a balanced picture of the situation. Barton then ticked off the company's 1981 accomplishments:

- The welding, steel, and paint issues were resolved.
- The *Ohio* was delivered.
- Electric Boat met its commitment to deliver six SSN 688s and one Trident.
- The insurance reimbursement issue was resolved.
- The Navy awarded Electric Boat another SSN 688 contract.
- A contract for the ninth Trident and options for two more were executed by the Navy.

The cost growth cited by the GAO was related to the 688 bid estimates of the early 1970s and had little relation to current operations at Electric Boat, he argued. No account of the labor strikes and trade imbalances, which initially delayed the programs, was included, nor did the GAO mention in detail the Quonset Point facility, which would achieve future savings.[68]

Finally, but most significantly, Barton stressed the GAO's tendency to question out-year delivery schedules when near-term delivery dates were consistently being met. The GAO's term "may miss delivery dates" ignored the recent historical record. Electric Boat recommended the draft be withdrawn and no report at all issued.[69]

GAO declined to include the attachments provided by Barton because they were "too voluminous." While a more advanced stage of the draft went to DeLauer along with the defense submitted by Electric Boat, the GAO stated Barton's comments "did not change the thrust of our draft."[70]

A draft with Barton's arguments (summarized) then went to Undersecretary DeLauer. James Wade, Jr., responded to the GAO for DeLauer and disagreed that both the Navy and Electric Boat continued to have quality-assurance-related problems. Rather, both programs were satisfactory and met contractual requirements. Wade pointed out, as had Barton to a lesser degree, that target costs should not be used to measure cost growth. Although the DoD agreed that Electric Boat might miss some future delivery dates, the report failed to recognize the past year's achievements and threatened the improved working relationship developed between the Navy and Electric Boat. As had Barton, Wade recommended against publication of the report.[71]

In an April 19 memo to Charles Bennett and his counterpart on the Subcommittee on Defense, Joseph Addabbo, the GAO stated its plans to hold the report for thirty more days before release. Bennett, upon receipt of the report, while complimenting the GAO on "a substantial effort," nevertheless was disappointed the GAO did not respond to his chief concern—whether Electric Boat could continue to produce Tridents and 688s in a timely, cost-effective manner. He somewhat criticized the GAO for spending a year on the project without coming to a conclusion on that point. Bennett also expressed concern about the GAO's habit of measuring cost growth from target costs. Unsatisfied, Bennett wrote Secretary Lehman on April 28 with a number of specific questions about the report.[72]

Navy Assessment of the GAO Report

Lehman, in a highly detailed four-page response, repeated DeLauer's contention that submarines built at Electric Boat were safe and reliable. An audit by Naval Sea Systems Command in 1981 had shown the quality-assurance program overall to be adequate, with discrepancies such as those mentioned by the GAO the result of optimistic implementation at earlier dates. He called charges that the Navy had improperly entered into contracts for the 688s "unfounded." The Navy's evaluation of some 688 estimates concluded those estimates were low, but because Electric Boat could still make a profit under the existing contract, the contract was not renegotiated. Overall, the cost-growth portion of the report was "wrong." Only inflation could change the next few submarine cost estimates. Finally, Lehman cut the ground from under much of the GAO report when he revealed that Electric Boat planned to add 940 trade personnel by July 1982 and thus should be able to meet all of its schedules. Lehman's letter apparently satisfied both Addabbo and Bennett, for the matter seems subsequently to have faded into the congressional background.[73]

During the period the report was under review from the various agencies and the contractor, Vice Admiral Fowler again testified before a House subcommittee. He discussed important contract modifications made in August 1981 "which established new delivery dates" for the *Ohio* class. These modifications also released the Navy from claims made prior to July 28, 1981, including those related to the *Los Angeles* subs, and revised the cost estimates for those ships. Included in the price estimates were the ninth Trident and options for two others. He stated that the *Michigan* and the *Florida* would be on time, although he, like the GAO at the same time, expressed doubt as to whether future Tridents would be delivered on time, and contract revisions made on March 5, 1982, recognized a "potential delay" of up to four weeks on the *Georgia* (SSBN 729) and the *Rhode Island* (SSBN 730). "Increased manpower," Fowler argued, was not the sole answer (as if to anticipate Lehman's June letter): productivity, costs, manning, and the ability to perform to plan were "interrelated" and represented "fundamental issues with which the General Dynamics management must come to grips." However, he conceded, the shipbuilder could yet "meet or exceed" its current delivery dates. The *Ohio,* he added, performed as well as or better than predicted by design studies.[74]

Fowler also reported the final decision of the Contracting Officer, issued on October 16, 1981, which found "that insurance coverage provided by the Navy does not apply in the situation as presented by Electric Boat [regarding its own defective welding]." Five days later the shipbuilder withdrew its claim regarding the welds. On August 22, 1981, modifications bringing the *Ohio*-class contracts "essentially up-to-date" were executed, and since then "the business relationship with Electric Boat has been improved substantially." The Navy was in "the best business condition with Electric Boat . . . we have been in since the day we signed the first [contract]."[75]

Based on a chart of *Ohio* class delivery dates, included in Fowler's statement, Electric Boat consistently improved its delivery dates. From Fowler's chart, three important trends are noticeable: (1) since the initial *Ohio* delay there has been virtually no added delay to the subsequent vessels, indicating that the delay was a one-time proposition; (2) Electric Boat has gained considerable time on its March, 1981, schedule—four months, in the *Rhode Island*'s case—but at least three months on all others except the *Ohio*; and (3) beginning with SSBN 733, delays overall should be negligible, to the extent that Electric Boat could actually begin "making up time." The program could be likened to an automobile journey in which a flat tire delays departure, but once on the highway a little extra speed can regain some of the "lost" time. Similarly, when an auto gets a flat tire on a narrow road, it holds up all traffic behind it, but, once repaired, it facilitates the movement of that column of traffic. By 1982, the Trident program seems to have survived a buffeting during the stormy claims controversy, and while it now appears headed for calmer seas, some important policy questions, illustrated by the *Ohio*'s late delivery, still remain.[76]

Evaluating the Charges

Beyond the implications discussed in this chapter of the roles of civilian and Navy personnel (including Rickover); the specific GFE, welding, steel, and labor problems and their resulting delays and costs; and the claims dispute as they pertained to the *Ohio*, the question of the viability and rationality of the procurement process itself must be raised, along with the question of why the Navy eventually took its case to a public forum. Were the expectations about the 688 and the *Ohio* classes too high and unrealistic on the part of the Navy, Congress, Electric Boat, the press, and the American public, in a joint undertaking perhaps more radical and unprecedented than previous experience, especially with the Polaris/Poseidon program, warranted, when problems with separate programs never overlapped?

Any delay in delivery means increased cost, no matter what weapons system is involved. However, defense contractors hardly stand alone in the tendency to set unachievable schedules. In one case, the Navy itself has scheduled delivery of a ship eighteen months earlier than the contractor predicted was possible. Slippage in schedules to some extent and with certain types of ships not subject to serial construction affects all yards, not just Electric Boat. Average slippage for all vessels under Navy contract since 1970 has grown from fifteen to eighteen months, largely caused by the previously mentioned endemic inability to retain trained labor. This in turn creates a backlog of other delays. Even Rickover has admitted that "the Republic will not suffer if there is some slight delay in awarding contracts." On the contrary, however, some of the Reagan administration's cost-cutting proposals include purchases of items ahead of schedule to reduce inflationary costs and minimize interest costs on borrowed capital for inventory purchases cumulatively weighty in unduly stretched-out acquisitions programs.[77]

Equally distressing in the procurement process is the threatening deterioration of the defense base, exemplified for Electric Boat by its trials and tribulations with the *Ohio* and 688 classes. Overall, American defense industry currently operates almost at capacity. It is "hard-pressed to meet even the present, relatively modest, procurement goals of the military services" and it "is old and inefficient" to boot. Almost twice the amount of capital equipment dedicated to weapons systems production exceeds the national twenty-year average age of non-defense industrial equipment. Innumerable subcontractors have left defense at an alarming rate. Consequently, lead times have grown enormously for both subcontracted and finished weapons. The Air Force has estimated that a decision to mobilize for war now would yield the first McDonnell Douglas F-15 no sooner than thirty-nine months later.[78]

Delays in these areas translate into even higher costs when long-range procurement is considered. In the case of the F-14 fighter, 83 percent of the dollars spent go to materials with lead times in excess of two years. Fighter costs are increasing at such a rapid rate that *The Economist* commented wryly, if the Carter administration's 3 percent annual increase in defense spending had continued unaltered, in 100 years it would take the entire U.S. defense budget to buy one fighter plane.[79]

Further intensifying the distortions of rising costs and greater delay is the fact that the United States increasingly must obtain most of its strategic materials from foreign nations, thus increasing costs, transport delays, and market vulnerability. For example, the United States imports almost all of its manganese from the Republic of South Africa. American dependence upon other foreign mineral sources is very extensive in many cases and even increasing in a few cases (see table 12). Consequently, price and delivery schedules will only increase as dependence on sole foreign suppliers grows and as those sources become more economically and politically unreliable, a condition selectively enhanced by Soviet machinations. Thus the United States is vulnerable to "supply disruptions" and "price hikes" for a dozen

Table 12
U.S. Mineral Imports
(in percentage)

Mineral	1965	1975	1985 (est.)	2000 (est.)
Bauxite/alumina	83	85	86	81
Chromium	92	90	92	89
Cobalt	93	98	98	97
Copper	22	13	13	18
Manganese	93	98	98	100
Nickel	73	70	67	67
Platinum group	91	84	81	80
Tin	75	71	67	66
Tungsten	53	50	57	70

Source: Amos A. Jordan and Robert A. Kilmarx, *Strategic Mineral Dependence: The Stockpile Dilemma* (Washington, D.C.: Center for Strategic and International Studies, 1979), p. 18.

strategic and critical materials, the General Accounting Office reported in June 1982.[80]

Because any assessment of responsibility for the Trident program's stretched-out delivery schedule and increased "cost overruns" must consider even more factors than have been so far cited here, reports simply placing blame at the doorstep of either the Navy or Electric Boat fail to come to grips with the complexity of the real procurement process, for which the proposed availability of a duplicate Trident-building facility (government-owned, as Rickover suggested, or otherwise) is an inadequate building recommendation. The magnitude, scope, and exclusivity of the Trident program dictates against such simple-minded reforms. Not only would security risks expand, but a strategic dependence of such a magnitude as to make American reliance on Middle Eastern oil pale by comparison would develop. Such schemes for contracting out crucial strategic programs fly in the face of the dicta to the contrary enunciated by Adam Smith and Alexander Hamilton, heretofore held patriotically sacred. Rickover has suggested reopening government shipyards for the purpose of building attack submarines as yet another alternative, but union opposition alone might prevent such a move, and the overall cost for the renovation of many such facilities, *long neglected*, might also repulse many congressmen earlier responsible for defense cuts obtained by unglamorously ignoring shipyard obsolescence. A better solution, although not without costs of its own, would be to encourage those yards that have produced submarines in the past, such as Litton-Ingalls Shipyards, to reopen attack-submarine facilities. Some of Electric Boat's attack subs then could be shifted to the Pascagoula yard so that Electric Boat could direct its workforce toward fulfilling its unshared capacity by turning out three Tridents every two years, assuming that Congress would refrain from erratically altering the building schedule, at least for an intermediate period of time.[81]

It is also time to dispel, as Gansler does, two myths about the defense industry currently in vogue. One is that defense industries operate in a free market, when more appropriately defense contractors perform in a "unique environment," sometimes subject to competition, sometimes not. "The alternate myth," Gansler explains, quoting Lester Thurow and R. L. Heilbroner, is that the Department of Defense is the "largest planned economy outside the Soviet Union." Instead, Gansler finds in government acquisitions a number of "micropolicies continually being made without consideration of their overall impact." In Trident's case, this became clear as one design change was piled atop another. Defense contractors, unlike true private market sellers, face a demand constantly shaped, adulterated, and modified by a third party—Congress—which often acts in an erratic, unstable manner. The net effect is that the seller does not deal with an economically rational source of demand, but rather with a politically sensitized demand.[82]

The success of the Polaris program left its enduring mark on the Navy procurement process in many still-persistent ways. Polaris is constantly referred to, at least in much of the available public literature, in reverent, almost sacred tones. The Poseidon program inherited much of this aura. Yet Robert Kaufman has reported cost omissions in the Poseidon program, and it may be that Polaris' admittedly fine program record nevertheless nostalgically looks even better twenty years later, especially because the Trident program is so out of scale, in comparison, as to be inherently incomparable. The group of innovators within the Navy who developed Polaris operated within a relatively closed circle under a fairly uniform organizational arrangement and under a different political and social agenda. Unlike, for example, the career of Rear Admiral Levering Smith, who served as director of strategic systems projects uninterruptedly from February 16, 1965, to November 14, 1975 (over a decade), in the Trident program no single officer has been exclusively in charge for any length of time much beyond a normal duty tour. No incoming officer, whatever his personal skills, can bring to the job the necessary Trident-related experience his predecessor had developed. The Navy's policy of *rotating* officers every four years works very well in professional *line* functions and in combat-related professional specialization, but *fewer* are the rewards for skills, mastery, and diplomacy peculiar to the process of weapons *procurement* and quality *control.* So argued, Navy officialdom should more often make exceptions in the case of long-term programs like the Trident, with reasonably timed replacements occurring after appropriate familiarization with the peculiarities of the procurement process. Virgins, so to speak, in the procurement process should be introduced at the supportive level with an absolute minimum of lateral assignment at the top level. As Rickover himself proves, the Navy can suffer if it goes too far in the opposite direction. But terms of six to eight years might prove optimal.[83]

Beyond officer turnover, the Trident's development experienced numerous problems unassociated with the Polaris program because the former is an entirely new system from hull to missile to reactor. Virtually every element of the Trident system in toto incorporated brand-new technology. But, more important, this technology suffered from the effects of national urgency (unlike Polaris), high inflation (also unlike Polaris), a shrinking arena of contractors and subcontractors (again, unlike Polaris), and an increasingly smaller shipbuilding workforce afflicted by economic immobility and extended training periods. Said one member of the Special Projects Team that developed Polaris, "Much of what we did is contrary to [1980] government regulations, including considerable administrative freedom." When deficiencies such as those mentioned are added the imprint of flawed GFEs, poor quality-control procedures by both the shipbuilder and the Navy, and miserable relations that developed in the wake of negotiations over the insurance claims, a sensible comparison of the Trident with the Polaris/Poseidon program is a faulty undertaking.[84]

7

Not Your Basic Bases:

Bangor, Kings Bay, and Support Facilities

He calms the storm and stills the waves. What a blessing is that stillness, as he brings them safely into harbor!

Psalm 107:29–30

From the moment in February 1968 that legislators and the Chief of Naval Operations began to consider the ULMS as a reality, they knew existing bases were inadequate to handle the planned submarines. Size alone dictated larger berths, drydocks, and supply wharves. Coupled with the hull size, the heavier Trident rocket presented problems for conventional loading facilities. The well-established tradition of manning the vessels with alternating crews would require greater attention in the case of the Trident to crew comfort, training, and supplies at the base because of the larger crew forces entailed. Merely refurbishing an existing base would have been difficult and costly enough. Developing an entirely new submarine center, in an undeveloped location, taxed the imagination. There was far more to the construction than simply moving trees, clearing brush, and building dormitories. Local residents wanted assurances that communities would not have to cope with a naval population explosion with local resources only. Environmental groups expressed concern about the placement of new nuclear weapons nearby and the potential destruction of the ecology. Washington state authorities less fearfully saw an opportunity to fill state coffers with streams of federal largesse. Nevertheless, throughout the construction process each problem was solved, deadlines were met, and the project was contained generally within its budget. The facilities represented not only the newest submarine docks, wharves, and armaments buildings but were also hailed by critics as architecturally and aesthetically excellent. Local citizens benefited by the additional jobs brought by industry and by federal impact assistance. As construction progressed, however, it became clear a single base was not sufficient for all of the Trident system's needs. Even after three support bases (Point Mugu, Cape Canaveral, and Indian Island Annex) evolved, the program lacked an Atlantic counterpart of Bangor. Spain's request for the United States to withdraw ballistic-missile submarines from Rota effective after 1979 completed the Trident basing puzzle. Soon thereafter, on January 26, 1978, the Navy announced that Kings Bay, Georgia, had finally been chosen as the East Coast Trident location.

Initially, some critics of the Bangor site selection expressed concern that, since the Trident's entrance or exit from the base would be through the Straits of San Juan de Fuca, enemy minelayers could easily disrupt Trident operations. Others countered that Navy deployment security for submarines egressing from or entering port constituted adequate protection against such underwater dangers. The Juan de Fuca Straits, within U.S. territorial waters, rather quickly change from a channel depth of around 80 feet before passing Port Angeles to a depth of some 125 feet at Clallam Bay, reaching some 170 feet off Cape Alva in the Juan de Fuca Canyon. A thorough check of the main channel for mines or obstacles is routinely conducted, followed by either a small surface craft or an attack sub clearing the way for the "boomer," usually guided to navigable water by a tugboat. Moreover, the Navy undertook a thorough three-year study of eighty-eight potential continental and foreign sites which concluded, on February 16, 1973, that Bangor presented the best alternative. One major factor in the decision to base Tridents in the Pacific was the distance between the base and the Soviet Union. This long attack reach would compel the Soviet navy to undertake an outdistance ASW deployment before it would be able even to attempt "trailing" Trident and, conversely, the Soviet ASW posture off the Pacific coast of North America would be relatively much easier to counteract. The Soviets have mitigated this disadvantage somewhat by acquiring the North Vietnamese harbor facilities at Cam Ranh Bay, but ocean expanse and deployment distance still continue to complicate Soviet ASW activities severely. Other advantages also weighted the basing decision in favor of a continental U.S. base. Transit times to patrol areas are practically eliminated, thereby substantially expanding the effective patrol time. Logistics for U.S. bases have demonstrated great savings by freeing money and time ordinarily needed to transfer crews and material overseas. Finally, security is always easier in the zone of the interior than on foreign soil.[1]

The Bangor base was officially established as a Naval Ammunition Depot (Bangor Annex) in 1944. It served as a shipment, storage, and depot area for ammunition and explosives. According to one authority, some of the original buildings "are still standing, including the ammunition loading center, in addition to apple orchards and a 1944 chicken coop." Consolidated with the Naval Torpedo Station at Keyport, the Bangor Annex adopted the name of the U.S. Naval Ordnance Depot Puget Sound (Keyport). By 1952, however, the facilities returned to separate independent status, with Bangor receiving the title Naval Ammunition Depot Bangor. Commencing with its establishment on September 1, 1963, as an IBM assembly, checkout, and outloading facility in a development status, it has serviced Polaris/Poseidon class SSBNs ever since.[2]

With four major base functions in mind—crew training, ship refit, missile support, and base support—the major contractor, Westinghouse, began construction at Bangor in 1974, utilizing over $118 million authorized in fiscal year 1974. Typically, wharf-construction and harbor-dredging activities comprised most of the early work. Other projects started that year included clearing roads, erecting security fences and gates, clearing a space for the general support areas, and installing the various utility lines, poles, and pipes. A training facility represented one of the most important construction starts that year, as crews needed substantial training on the new equipment before they could actually man the submarines. Consequently, the Navy scheduled it to commence operations less than a year after the initial concrete foundation settled. The missile checkout building, the launch complex, and the guidance telemetry building also received completion dates of 1975. In one case, a warehouse scheduled for a 1976 unveiling was finished in 1975 as well. Navy construction officials issued orders for several other starts, although workers did not actually undertake any work on them until the following year. Those facilities scheduled for construction beginning in 1975 included the explosive handling wharf 1, refit pier 1, utilities site improvements, and a lifting-device proofing facility.[3]

Throughout the early phases of planning and building the Bangor base, the Navy had gone to great lengths to lighten the impact of the program on the towns and counties in the Bangor area. Federal assistance to moderate the distress precipitated by the insertion of a military base is fairly common. After the construction of some of the basic buildings, federal authorities directed their attention to the town and county governments to determine what assistance those levels of government might need to cushion the Trident base's social impact. 1971–1972 census estimates of the local citizenry in the rural, wooded areas of Kitsap County (along with parts of Mason and Jefferson counties) ranged from 86,000 to 90,000. As part of the Puget Sound region, it nevertheless did not enjoy the metropolitan development of the Seattle, Tacoma, or Everett areas. An undiversified extractive economy and a small industrial tax base, resulting from reliance on the federal government's Puget Sound Naval Shipyard in Bremerton as the primary industrial employer, made the area particularly vulnerable to the effects of such rapid growth the Trident base now threatened. The influx of military personnel forced prices up in an area that historically had enjoyed lower prices than the rest of the state. To absorb better the impact of the Trident base community, both the Secretary of Defense and the Secretary of the Navy promised local officials that the federal government would help defray the costs of expanding community facilities. Senators Warren Magnusen and Henry Jackson requested economic assistance, which the Department of Defense provided. To facilitate the movement of these funds, the department created a Trident coordinating office in 1974 with the understanding among various Washington agencies that "impacts resulting from the Trident base would be assigned a high priority for Federal funding." In the case of schools, the amounts allocated proved inadequate; Congress passed a supplemental law, "patterned after . . . the Safeguard ABM system in Montana. . . ." In his comments before the House Appropriations Committee in 1977, Representative Norman O. Dicks emphasized that "the Trident community impact assistance program works."[74]

Federal agencies processed fund requests by determining if a specific project met eligibility requirements and if the corresponding funds were available. If funds were not available but the project was Trident-related, the grant application next went to the Office of Economic Adjustment or the Department of Defense. This involved process, of course, produced numerous delays—sometimes up to twelve months—but was "necessary to assure that only Trident-related projects [were] funded." Moreover, the amount of available funds varied according to the ratio of military to civilian employees stationed on the base. Nevertheless, Dicks summarized the attitude of the area residents by saying "The Trident impact area has welcomed the Trident base because of a long-standing relationship with the Navy: not because of any misconceptions about an economic boom." An impact study showed that only six hundred jobs would be filled from the existing labor pool, which included all of metropolitan Seattle and its population of over a million. The six hundred jobs represented "less than 15 percent of the total number of unemployed in Kitsap County." Dicks noted that the study showed "the military does not pay its own way" and that federal assistance was "absolutely essential." The projects submitted for aid included libraries and parks, which in Kitsap County "are considered frills." However, Dicks underscored the "exhaustive and critical" reviewing process for the applications.[5]

Before projects acquired funds under the Trident-related legislation, the Trident community assistance program put the burden on local people to draw assistance from existing federal programs. For example, schools received money through SAFA (School Assistance for Federally Affected Areas) or HUD (Housing and Urban Development). Home assistance came from FHA (Federal Housing Authority) and the Veterans Administration, while Health, Education, and Welfare concentrated on relieving the "unfair and excessive financial burden" on the local communities. Other agencies involved included the Economic Development Administration, the Department of the Interior, the Department of Transportation, and the County Services Administration.[6]

Kitsap County grew by 28,000 between 1974 and 1976, at an annual rate of 2.5 percent, for a total of about 114,000. This growth was due almost totally to the Trident base (with 15,000 more in normal growth), causing many of the funds to go toward housing and transportation relief. Rents, because of the program, went "sky high," according to Representative Dicks, forcing HUD to create over three hundred units of subsidized housing. Bangor's distance from major commercial centers demanded the establishment of a better transportation system. The submarine base borders the Hood Canal area of Puget Sound; to drive to the small town of Silverdale takes about ten minutes. Bremerton and East Bremerton add another ten minutes to the drive. To facilitate commuter traffic from the Bremerton area, over $1.5 million was allocated for improving the Bucklin Hill road and another $1.3 million went to build state route 303 from the Clear Creek interchange to Poulsbo.[7]

Besides expressing concern for the integrity of the social fabric of their community, many local residents opposed the base on grounds that it would disrupt the surrounding ecology. Soon after work on Bangor commenced, three environmental groups and two property owners, known as CAT (Concerned About Trident), filed a lawsuit in the United States District Court for the District of Columbia, charging the Navy with having ignored or violated various sections of the National Environmental Policy Act. The group also challenged "as arbitrary the determinations (i) to develop the Trident system, (ii) to proceed with it on an accelerated basis, (iii) to operate Trident from a 'dedicated' base, and (iv) to construct that base at Bangor." On May 5, 1975, the first trial ended, with the complaint dismissed on August 22. An appeal initiated on September 22 resulted in the ruling that construction should continue but also required the Navy to submit a supplemental environmental impact statement by February 10, 1977. Few legislators from the Washington federal delegation believed the ecology had been seriously disrupted up to this point. For example, Representative Sikes asked Dicks "How in the world do you ever get a contractor to leave that many trees?" Dicks replied "They work at it," whereupon the representative congratulated Dicks on "preserving it as well as you have." Even the refit piers and the causeways in the delta were designed to "minimize any adverse environmental impacts." Contractors agreed to meet "natural preservation clauses" in their contracts that set "sharply defined limits to the number of trees [they] will be allowed to cut down" in the course of construction. Before contractors exceed their "tree limit," they must first obtain the Navy's approval. Stationed on base at the outset of construction, a resident forest ranger and game warden continue to protect wildlife and supervise landscaping. Consequently, deer can be found inhabiting undeveloped portions of the base and ducks swimming in the ponds. Upon completion, contractors will have cut down only 10 percent of the original woods to make room for buildings. The system of roads ensures that no part of the forest will be farther than a quarter of a mile from a road, to facilitate fire control. Because of such precautions, the CAT lawsuit, like others to follow, met with little success.[8]

In 1975 designers submitted plans for the off-crew administration building, a service station, and tennis courts. During 1976 they started designs on the drydock, the explosive-handling wharf 2, the service pier and port control office, the mess, and exchange complex, missile motor magazines, and an alarm-control-center system. Most of the projects designed during 1975 or 1976 met a 1977 deadline for design completion. Work on them commenced between 1977 and 1979. Congress authorized $379 million in construction funds for the period 1975–1977; by February 1977 the Navy had spent $215.7 million. By 1976 the engineers had added to those 1974 projects already completed a guidance telemetry building, an engineering services building, a warehouse, the first missile assembly building, a strategic weapons supply warehouse, a technical services building, a weapons evaluation center, and a fire station. Other complexes added, through the availability of fresh funds or through additions to plans, included a dining facility for enlisted personnel and a Marine Corps administration and berthing facility. A small-ordnance magazine and flammable-storage building beat their construction deadlines by approximately six months, thereby saving money.[9]

Some of the projects cost less than anticipated (see table 13). Nevertheless, some items increased drastically, like the missile checkout building ($235,000 to $2,158,000) and the lifting device proofing facility (originally without any estimate, which became $467,000). Besides

Table 13
Projects Costing Less Than Estimated
(in thousands of dollars)

Project	Estimated Cost	Revised Request
Refit pier 1	25,000	14,793
Explosive handling wharf 1	23,500	21,295
Warehouse	411	294
Launch complex 25	1,193	962
Guidance telemetry building	235	218

these major increases and several minor ones, no money had been budgeted for land acquisition, which eventually cost $5.1 million. Consequently, after many of the projects funded in fiscal year 1974 had been built, the Navy needed an extra $105,000 (still a modest sum when dealing with projects of this magnitude) to complete the 1974 starts.[10]

Part of the increased cost of land acquisition resulted from the base itself. Builders immediately moved in upon hearing of the base, causing an inflation in land values. The local citizenry quickly prepared a thorough land management plan to protect the community. Their best efforts failed to contain the costs of housing, however; in 1973 a low-priced house built in the area cost $25,000, but within four years the same house had increased by $10,000. An injection of 432 housing units from HUD during that four-span had a negligible effect. In fiscal year 1978 HUD directed that another 125 units be placed in the area. Nevertheless, housing purchase prices in the area ranged from $34,000 to $50,000 by 1977.[11] Transportation problems added to the spiraling housing costs. Off-base military and civilian personnel needed major access roads to reach the base. Representative Norman Dicks of Washington, in a letter to Gunn McKay, the chairman of the Subcommittee on Military Construction, supported the recommendations of the Military Traffic Management Command for a four-lane access highway from the Bremerton area. Quite naturally, property values nearest the base and along the proposed routes of the access road increased.[12]

Part of the Navy's budgeting had fluctuated because of a law enacted by the state of Washington on July 1, 1975. The state statute levied a 5 percent tax on all material and equipment installed by a private contractor under any federal construction contract in the state as well as on any government-furnished material and equipment installed by private contractors. The Army joined the Navy in filing suit on February 13, 1976, to test the validity of the tax, challenging it on the grounds that the taxes unconstitutionally discriminated against the United States. The tax was so adjudged on November 3, 1977. Washington state was ordered to pay back to contractors $1.3 million taken in taxes. The Navy had emerged victorious in a second court battle.[13]

Another kind of battle was being fought over the standard of living in the Bangor region. More than seven thousand people had migrated into the Bremerton area during 1977, and all but a thousand of them had some business or work associated with the Trident base program. The increased population was sure to strain all existing facilities, including juvenile, criminal justice, and medical facilities. Navy sources estimated that the Trident-related caseload represented 66 percent of the total anticipated growth in the juvenile justice system, due simply to the increase in the number of young people in the area. Therefore, beginning in 1977, the local youth home was expanded in both beds and offices, with an interim care facility started in 1978. In each case, the Navy paid its two-thirds share only. Since youth treatment also spread to other systems—the court system, Kitsap County Homes, and Community Resources Consolidated (a diagnostic and treatment center)—the Navy figures matched their costs as well.[14]

The Department of Defense poured money into several other items in addition to allocating $179.324 million to HUD. Among the specific items funded were the state route 3 interchange, the criminal justice system, a water resources survey, and school construction. During 1976–1977 grant proposals flooded in. Kitsap County requested sewers, the cities of Port Townsend and Bremerton wanted water improvements, and the state game and fish department demanded a study of the impact of the base on wildlife. These requests piled atop more typical calls for school assistance, fire protection, and park projects. Trident funds designated for community support also bolstered local police and highway patrol agencies. The funds allowed the highway patrol to hire nine more officers and provided patrol cars for five patrolmen. New prosecutors were added to handle the projected increase in criminal cases. Program funds also upgraded fire protection by creating headquarters for new volunteer districts and purchasing new fire equipment. Step by step the Navy came to find itself invidiously involved in a host of activities unrelated to mainline activities like "driving ships," to the extent that "no rainwater is allowed to run directly from any facility on the base to the fjord." Instead, it "is collected and pumped through filtration systems to ensure it is free of oil and other contaminants."[15]

Oppositon by Environmental Groups

Despite the Navy's attempts to preserve the environment so far as was reasonably possible, Bangor construction continued to evoke opposition from environmental groups, exemplified by a new lawsuit filed in 1976. The Hood Canal Environmental Council charged that the construction of the Delta waterfront was improper and did "not address possible design and location alternatives." It also contended that the Navy had violated the water pollution legislation. A district court judge denied an injunction, and the hearings were postponed. Eventually the case died for lack of prosecution. However, by 1978 other problems had arisen over the placement of facilities inside the base. Then Assistant Secretary of the Navy Edward Hidalgo told a Senate subcommittee about "expressions of concern by certain owners of property immediately adjacent to the proposed site of the [$7 million service] pier. These people oppose the initial pier siting along the southern boundary of the base and prefer a site more distant from the Navy property line." As a result, he concluded, "the Navy has commenced a restudy of the siting of this facility and we undoubtedly will have to move it north." Yet another environmental suit related to the Trident was filed on November 1, 1977. *Loren Bergh et al.* vs. *Harold Brown et al.* challenged the environmental impact statement submitted on the Indian Island missile and ammunition center. Since the suit was not instituted until seventeen months after the final environmental impact statement for Indian Island was filed, the Navy expected little trouble. Nevertheless, even though the base was functionally completed by 1980, environmentalists continue to oppose it. Indeed, local groups planned a "March to Moscow" across Alaska, the Aleutians, and Siberia. That did not take place as scheduled, although they have also announced a "March to Jerusalem," but organizers in all seriousness have not yet decided whether they want to take Soviet dissident Jews with them as they leave Russia. In this regard the United States stands uniquely alone in the world when it comes to considering environmental questions as a part of military operations (one can hardly imagine Soviet Premier Andropov hesitating to build a base because it might endanger the local yak population).[16]

Bangor Nears Completion

Lawsuits and environmental protests had little, if any, success in slowing construction at Bangor. By 1977 all facilities needed for maintenance on the submarines themselves had either neared completion or were well underway. All the other submarine-related facilities had been started. Of all the numerous buildings, recreational areas, military facilities, and civilian annexes, the two that drew the most attention were the Delta Refit Pier and the Explosive-handling Wharf (Figs. 7-1 and 7-2). The Refit Pier is in the form of a modified A, with each of the 700-foot legs assigned to servicing a Trident sub apiece. A 58,000-square-foot support building sits in the middle of the Delta Pier, with the entire facility placed on pilings to protect salmon fingerling migrations back and forth in the Hood Canal, connected to the shore by trestles to facilitate vehicular traffic. Located along the connecting wharf at the base of the Delta Pier, in the water, is the 90-by-700-foot drydock. At 63 feet, it is the deepest drydock the Navy has, with a concrete floor 16 feet thick. Three Tridents can be serviced simultaneously at the pier, and eventually the entire facility can support all ten Tridents expected to be assigned to Submarine Squadron 17. Potential environmental hazards caused by locating the drydock next to the land, as is traditionally done, forced Trident base designers to move the delta 400 feet away from shore so Tridents can directly approach the tie-up berths without a channel having to be dredged. A second highly unusual military facility is the fourteen-and-a-half-story Explosive–handling Wharf. Several factors dictated that the Navy build a unique wharf for the Trident: its size, the size of the missiles,

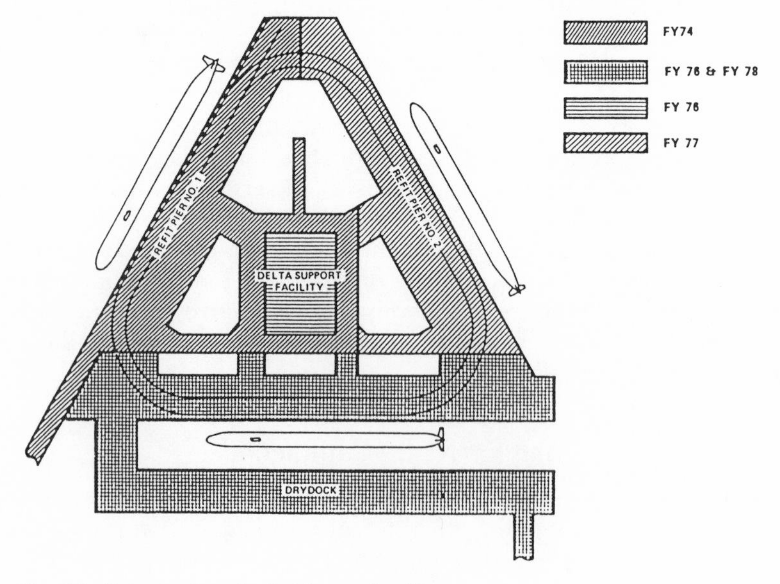

Fig. 7-1. Delta projects by fiscal year funding.

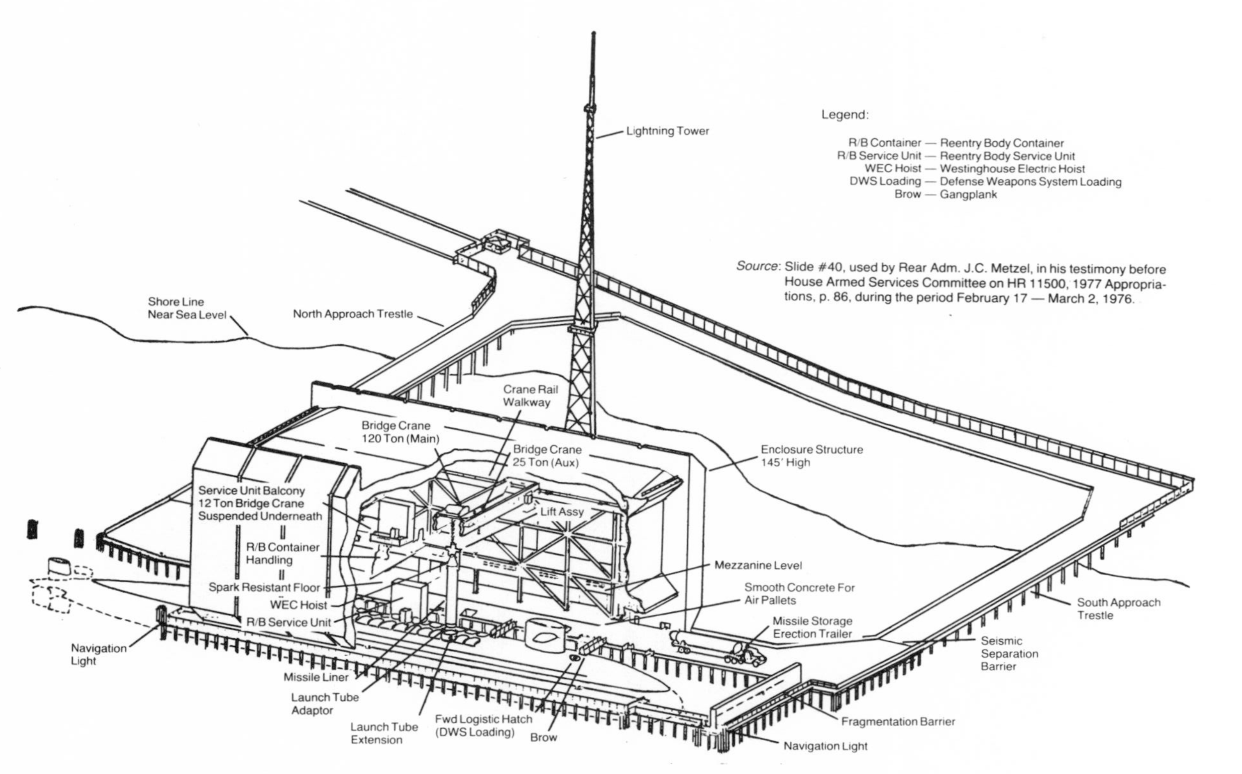

Fig. 7-2. Cutaway view of Bangor base Explosive-handling Wharf, procedures, equipment.

the necessity under SALT I to permit observations of the bow and stern during missile transfer, and the number of missiles carried by each sub. Accordingly, the Navy needed a very large wharf with effective cranes and winches capable of moving a considerable distance, hoisting more than 32 tons and repeating the process twenty-four times without strain. Weather also required the facility to be covered. The architectural design, indeed, won the Civil Engineering Achievement Award from the Tacoma chapter of the American Society of Civil Engineers in 1977. Begun in February, 1975, the massive steel-frame superstructure was in place by 1976. It houses a 120-ton bridge crane traveling along 80 feet above the wharf deck. Covered to protect workers and equipment from the elements, the finished superstructure sits on a wharf that stretches 325 feet and is 250 feet wide. In its completed form, the $2.4-billion wharf resembles a monstrous tunnel with pert, trimmed, angled lines. A gigantic *E H 1* identifies it for the few visitors who may see it and for any lost sailors. Those two facilities not only make the Trident base at Bangor the most modern naval base in the world, they also mark it as a symbol of America's ingenuity and concern for its aesthetic and environmental standards.[17]

In 1978 the Navy requested a second explosive-handling wharf. Admiral Marschall told a House committee he applauded putting the wharf in the program as opposed to waiting, when the activity of the area might tempt contractors to delay more than necessary. According to Marschall, "we are really swinging along the waterfront now." Further, the second wharf would eventually give the base the capability to avoid schedule conflicts between Tridents.[18]

Not every aspect of Bangor construction, however, has run on schedule or under budget. Admiral Marschall reported in 1978 that the Navy needed an additional $8 million for a radiographic inspection building. Unexpectedly, the Navy found that "we are going to have to do more testing than we thought" on missile motors. One building was already planned, but the number of missiles, combined with a longer-than-anticipated test time, led to an overload. The Navy had already learned in working with Poseidon missiles that propellant defects affected the missile motors. Consequently, the Navy embarked on a meticulous X-ray process for all missiles, and that in turn prompted the Navy to request an additional building.[19]

Other unusual features of the ballistic-missile submarine program made the base unique. Two different crews for each Trident will be available: one actually aboard the boat at sea for a seventy-day cruise and the other ashore. Assuming a ten-boat squadron, as is now the case, twenty crews will be assigned to Bangor. Known as the Blue crew and the Gold crew, each unit will have its separate identity, with separate administrative offices. Crews from all of the Trident boats fit into a training cycle at the Trident training facility (TriTraFac), from which seven of the ten total crews ashore actually will be in training at any given time; two will be in the "administrative mode" and one on leave. At this facility, training includes simulation of onboard submarine conditions as well as provides advanced refresher training for experienced officers and enlisted men. Currently, this facility is the largest building on the base and is made of oxidized steel covered with solar-reflective glass to guarantee a "maintenance-free exterior." At a later date, training space for the Trident I missile can be converted to equipment designed to train men on the Trident II missile. By 1981 the Navy had trained 1602 Trident crew members and anticipated a doubling of that number by 1985. Again, assuming twenty crews for ten boats at a billeting level per vessel of fifteen officers and 142 enlisted personnel, Trident crews will constitute about 3140 of the 4800 military (3800 civilians) based here.[20]

Officials believe turnaround time to be a crucial factor in the Trident's credibility as a deterrrent. Trident crews, under the Trident Integrated Logistics Support Plan, can expect to step ashore at Bangor, refuel and restock, and get back to sea within twenty-five days. In dire necessity, the sub has the ability to stay out longer—"literally stuffed with cans of staples and food"—with some submarines at sea for as long as ninety days. Philosophically, Admiral Kelln explained, the goal is to keep the maximum number of boats deployed operationally and to be able to deploy the outfitted boats quickly. "We do not buy missiles for reload," he admitted, because "one could not envision those bases [Bangor and Kings Bay] . . . not to be available other than in some sort of nuclear exchange, at which time we don't believe [we] would consider coming back to them or needing to resupply to any degree." Trident maintenance plans call for reducing the complete overhauls to only once every ten years.[21]

A typical shore support cycle, provided by the personnel of either the Bangor or Kings Bay support facility, begins with the submarine checking into the Trident Refit Facility (TriRefFac). This facility consists of refit berths, drydocks, support shops, resupply areas, and the Delta Refit Pier, which houses a "supply of operable replacement parts, ready to be installed in the submarines" so that vessels can return to sea while the original parts undergo repair. After the submarine's missiles are removed for inspection it proceeds through the rest of the refit cycle, including resupply. This process usually accounts for eighteen of the twenty-five days in the total cycle. In the remaining week, onboard checking of modular replacements and of all repairs is conducted and the boat leaves for duty, provided no last-minute obstacles are encountered. Missile repairs take place at the Strategic Weapons Facility Pacific (SWFPac), which includes the missile-handling pier, stowage magazines, and missile production and assembly facilities. When all refit work is completed missiles are reloaded, with the sub proceeding in the last phase to the degaussing facility.[22] It is important to note that even with the Trident I missile a Trident sub in port could be assigned to some enemy targets from Bangor, making it equivalent to an ICBM. When the Trident II is available the same options will exist from Kings Bay.

Unlike other elements of the Trident program, base construction did hum along on schedule. Admiral Donald Iselin reported in 1978 that "only 10 percent of the on-base military construction at Bangor remains to be authorized and appropriated." Although final touches would dangle until 1984, the base could have received Tridents as early as 1980, with the first group of sailors and officers manning the Trident training facility on duty by September 1977.[23]

The Navy also expressed considerable concern over living conditions for the base personnel. In addition to housing, base facilities include a chapel, food service, shopping, a bank, education, medical and dental care, and a credit union. Navy officials encourage families of Bangor personnel to establish permanent residence on the base. This goal "has a practical basis: in addition to minimizing travel expenses, this allows the men to live in an atmosphere of family stability," an important factor in the retention of volunteers. Conceivably, a man could spend his "entire 20-year tour [of duty] right on the base (except for the time he would spend at sea in one of the submarines)." Bachelor officer and enlisted quarters are also under construction, and a recreation complex features an indoor pool, athletic facilities, hobby shops, and a movie theater. Natural features also attract base personnel, with hunting, fishing, skiing, camping, and hiking activities enhanced by the mountainous and forested areas of the Pacific Northwest.[24]

Arrival of the Ohio

As the Navy prepared Kings Bay for Poseidon support, it continued preparing Bangor to receive submarines, following a revised schedule for submarine arrivals. Anticipating the *Ohio*'s arrival in late 1982, the Navy expected the *Michigan* by mid-1983, the *Florida* in late 1984, followed by the *Georgia* and the *Rhode Island* in 1985. Four others are scheduled to sail to Bangor by 1987. If preparations for the *Ohio* are any indication, each boat will receive a less-than-patriotic welcome at Bangor. Opponents of the "arms race" and of nuclear power in general have scheduled prayer vigils and did attempt to impede the *Ohio* with a blockade of small boats bearing such names as the *Pacific Peacemaker* and the *Lizard of Woz*. Among the protestors, Jim Douglass, a thrice-jailed trespasser who commutes from Canada to oppose the Trident, contended the Trident missiles are "first-strike" weapons. Archbishop Raymond Hunthausen of the Roman Catholic archdiocese of Seattle has echoed Douglass' sentiments, calling Bangor the "Auschwitz of Puget Sound." The Coast Guard has the responsibility of securing the Straits of Juan de Fuca, and it closed off that stretch of Hood Canal when the *Ohio* arrived, limiting viewing to "military personnel and the cameras of Soviet spy satellites." Nevertheless, base security forces will have to continue to be alert to the tactics of protesters like the Reverend Jon Nelson, who has twice served time in jail for "snipping the wires of Bangor" to protest at closer range. Although the *Ohio*'s arrival time was not advertised by the Navy, the National Lawyers Guild and the American Civil Liberties Union planned to challenge the "security zone" concept in court. Indeed, a determination of the exact arrival time of the *Ohio*, if the departure episode at Groton was any indication of the "security" involved, did not turn out to be too difficult. Nevertheless, in the long run the positive effects of the Bangor base alone on the Bremerton economy will probably cause the protests to be all but ineffective so far as the majority of the local residents are concerned. Its continuous operation as a base ensures the economy of a constant influx of federal dollars.[25]

Kings Bay Becomes a Trident Base

Scarcely had ink dried on the last contracts for Bangor than the Senate considered the new problem of removing the Rota squadron of Poseidon submarines. On January 26, 1978, the Navy announced Kings Bay, Georgia, would be the substitute base for the Rota squadron. Workers feverishly commenced preparations to have the base ready to receive submarines by July 1, 1979. Congress concurrently allocated nearly $63 million during fiscal years 1978 and 1979 to prepare the base, of which over $15 million was paid for dredging operations alone. To provide for future expansion, to preempt potential property lawsuits, and to acquire needed acreage for the Poseidon fleet, the Navy acquired 3121 adjoining acres of real estate. Still, Kings Bay at first invited selection merely as a Poseidon base capable of retrofitting the Trident I missile into the Poseidon submarines, indeed only after numerous options were examined at length. Admiral Kelln listed some of the factors the Navy considered:

Squadron size:

1. Single squadron with a tender refit facility
2. Single squadron with a shore refit facility
3. Double squadron with a tender refit facility
4. Double squadron with a shore refit facility

And under those basic options he added eleven suboptions:

1. Costs
2. Schedule and availability
3. Explosive safety and limits
4. Operations and logistics
5. Environmental impact
6. Growth potential
7. Location to highways, airports, railroads, and labor markets
8. Shelter in harbor
9. Distance to 100-fathom curve and to open ocean
10. Traffic level on route to sea
11. Weather

Officials considered four other candidate sites besides Kings Bay, including Charleston, Mosquito Lagoon in Florida, Cheatham Annex in Virginia, and Narragansett Bay. Subsequently it became clearer the Navy had probably had Trident in mind all along when choosing the desirability factors. At the same time, a separate Navy study sought to determine if Kings Bay also presented the most logical Trident site.[26]

When asked in 1978 if Kings Bay figured in the Navy's plans as the new Atlantic Trident base, as was rumored, Admiral Kelln replied consistently that the Navy had initiated a study and would await its results. It is hard to imagine, however, naval officials undertaking a detailed investigation of Poseidon bases only to inaugurate a second allegedly unrelated study a few years later. A Trident's size serves automatically to limit the number of qualified sites. Admirals naturally shudder at the thought of navigating a Trident through a very narrow river channel or in the company of heavy merchant shipping. So, the Navy's denial to the contrary, the Navy very probably used the results of the Poseidon relocation study as a foundation for the permanent disposition of Atlantic-based Tridents. Furthermore, it is illogical and unconvincing to survey and finally select a base to handle Trident I missiles in a backfit program and not utilize those facilities for a Trident submarine. An official announcement of the selection of Kings Bay was issued on January 26, 1978, followed on May 24, 1979, by the naming of Kings Bay as the Atlantic Trident base.[27]

All told, sixty East Coast locations selected by the director of the Trident Atlantic base study appeared to have suitable logistic, geographic, environmental, and safety qualifications. Pared down to a list of five candidates, the list was then studied by a steering group of ten members. Using a secret ballot, so that "there was not external influence that would affect the deliberations," the members voted unanimously for Kings Bay. Several factors contributed to the favorable vote. First, study officials ran cost estimates of the Trident I backfit program at each of the five sites. For a refit facility ashore for one Poseidon squadron, Kings Bay placed exactly in the middle of the five sites—with a tender for refit it rates slightly higher for one and much lower for two squadrons. Kings Bay therefore had demonstrated an important quality: potential for physical growth, including the associated prospect of additional savings. Environmental factors also played a role in the decision. Dredging, a fairly routine procedure at Charleston, would be complicated at Mosquito Lagoon. Planners design bases to leave suitable room between housing facilities and the explosive-handling docks at the waterfronts (roughly 6500 acres for one squadron, with another 1000 for a second). A drydock usually means that adequate safety distances exist. Without a drydock buffered by appropriate space, Navy procedures stipulate crews have to remove all missiles each time a vessel enters the base for refitting. This safety factor forced the Navy to calculate the amount of additional land needed for each base, a cost consideration that by itself tended to eliminate Charleston and Narragansett Bay. But Kings Bay and Mosquito Lagoon both sparkled on this point, as Kings Bay needed little land for expansion and Mosquito Lagoon needed none. The unanimous vote by the steering committee reflected the predominance of Kings Bay's cumulative advantages.[28]

Originally a U.S. Army ammunition storage depot, the Kings Bay base lies just north of the Georgia–Florida border, yet is a part of the Jacksonville metropolitan region. It is "sandy, flat, and riddled with salt marshes and inland wetlands." Immediately south of the base is the small, rural fishing community of St. Marys, Georgia. To the east is Cumberland Sound, with the St. Marys entrance channel south of the sound. The base itself covers 16,168 acres and had forty older buildings built by the Army, including a usable 2000-foot wharf. On the wharf the Army had placed a transit shed, with the entire area joined by rail sidings. Overall, the selection of an ammunition storage facility in a thinly populated region, with plenty of wharf space and railroad facilities, made Kings Bay a wise selection.[29]

The location presented some drawbacks. Poor soil conditions near the waterfront area resulted in the need for a layer of six to eight feet of dredge soil to provide stable footing for construction slabs. This layer took one year to settle. Large quantities of dredge soil were also needed to raise the building elevations above the hundred-year floodplains.

Kings Bay continued as strictly a Poseidon squadron base through 1981, but the initial stages of building roads, dredging, and blasting all gradually changed the Kings Bay landscape. Unlike Bangor, Kings Bay required a massive dredging operation. Since Polaris subs would be using the base during dredging, those operations also took longer than usual. Dredging eventually involved removing over 20.5 million cubic yards to deepen the entrance channels to 44–47 feet. By 1981 Kings Bay contained a drydock, two refit berths, a service craft mooring facility, and the always necessary explosive-handling wharf. An industrial refit center is located in the middle of the base, along with the magazines, industrial facilities, and support buildings. Farther from the waterfront lie the utility plants and public works support core, including the dispensary, dental clinic, Navy exchange and commissary, housing, and the unfinished recreational facility. When the Trident II missile is deployed it will require separate assembly, handling, and production facilities that will approximately double the number of buildings. For Kings Bay, the peak program years will occur over 1984–1986, with construction employment reaching 1000 workers. The Navy made it clear new Tridents would not immediately be sent to Kings Bay as they are commissioned. Instead, the Navy prefers to fill out Bangor with a complete force of ten boats before assigning any at Kings Bay.[30]

Population increases resulting from the establishment of the Poseidon/Trident support base have meant an influx of 4500 military and civilian employees and dependents into rural Camden County, with its 12,200 inhabitants. The county was "unprepared" to accommodate even the first 2000 Navy workers who arrived in 1979 to lay the ground work for refurbishing the support facility. When the Trident program hits its peak in 1987 the remote Georgia countryside will have to accommodate 27,000 new residents, although only 8000 will be directly employed on the bases. Real estate agents sold property at booming rates, even putting rental houses on the market, to no avail. When the submarine tender *Simon Lake* docked with its 1500 sailors, the crew remained on board because of the acute housing shortage, a situation in stark contrast to that of 1976, when local newspapers did not carry classified advertisements for homes. Real estate classified advertisements filled four pages of the newspapers by 1979.[31]

More so than with the Bangor base, "uncertainty and speculation" drove up land prices near St. Marys and other southeast Georgia towns. Hesitation over announcing the selection of an East Coast base may actually have increased expenses for the Navy at Kings Bay. The absence of facilities and affordable housing caused unhappiness among sailors and their families, although by the time the first Tridents arrive most of the problems should be solved.[32]

Kings Bay will not be required as a Trident base until sometime after 1988, although some reports have its operational date as 1990 or 1992. Admiral Kelln indicated that both Bangor and Kings Bay have the capability of handling ten ships (although he refused to limit the shipbuilding program to twenty total Tridents). Planning for the eventual Trident basing at Kings Bay, four facility models were drawn up, each with different sets of requirements specifying especially safety standards for the storage of missile propellants, with a different number of buildings and alternate capacity to handle varying numbers of submariness and tenders. The T-1 Model, for example, included various missile-production facilities, industrial support works, and defensive weapons posts. Each model assumed the Navy's planned use of the existing old Army buildings: the administration building, the engineering shop, and the railroad facilities. The Navy made a concerted effort also to make sure each "model" was compatible with large numbers of Tridents. Navy officials estimated, if the Kings Bay facilities resembled those at Bangor, the cost "would approximate $1.3 billion spread over several programming years for facilities directly on the base," while by comparison the total estimated cost of Bangor was $703 million.[33]

Besides housing shortages, one of the chief differences between Kings Bay and Bangor is that the Georgia base will not require a delta facility because the existing wharf is already 2000 feet long, against the 1400-foot combined length of the two wharves at the Bangor Delta Refit Pier. Kings Bay had the further advantage of incorporating a large waterfront warehouse built by the Blue Star Shipping Company, which had leased the land from the Army. A central point of difference in the two bases is that, while the Navy had built Bangor as a Trident base from the beginning, Kings Bay was planned first as a Poseidon relocation base. Although every planning precaution was taken to anticipate an easy conversion of Kings Bay from a Poseidon to a Trident base, the Navy hedged its bet for the conversion so that a refusal by Congress would have meant that only 3 percent of the conversion budget had been consumed.[34]

In 1981 Admiral William Zobel of Naval Facilities Engineering Command laid out the building plan for base construction at Bangor and Kings Bay before a House subcommittee (see table 14). Defense officials adopted a different design strategy for Kings Bay than for Bangor. To achieve cost reductions, Kings Bay involved fewer and larger design packages than Bangor. This program, Zobel explained,

Table 14
Base Construction Figures for Bangor/Kings Bay
(in millions of dollars to nearest million)

	Fiscal Years 1974–81	Fiscal Year 1982/1983	Cost to Complete	Total Estimated Cost
Facilities	554.6 / —	23.1 / 65.1	22.1 / 1,115.1	599.8 / 1,220.2
Community impact assistance	55.5 / —	— / —	— / —	55.5 / —
Defense access roads	22.0 / —	— / 12.0	— / 5.3	22.0 / 17.3
Subtotal	632.1 / —	23.1 / 77.1	22.1 / 1,160.4	677.3 / 1,237.5
Family housing	26.4 / —	— / 12.7	— / —	26.4 / 1,250.2
Total	658.5 / —	23.1 / 89.8	22.1 / 1,160.4	703.7 / 1,250.2

was "structured over a 9-year period for several reasons. We need to provide an orderly progression of projects to meet operational requirements as they come up." For example, in 1982 the Navy planned two major projects: dredging and road building. Eventually Kings Bay, with a completion date of 1992, would employ eight thousand civilian and military workers with total annual salaries of over $110 million.[35]

Overall, both programs, Bangor and Kings Bay, represented two of the more orderly and steady aspects of the entire Trident project. Their construction schedules fell behind only moderately; their costs, although occasionally leaping when a completely unexpected factor arose, generally remained low compared to other Trident expenditures, and Bangor was ready to receive submarines on its planned date.

Inflation affected base construction costs in the same way it affected the cost of the submarines. In 1978, a comparison of the then-current dollar with a 1969 dollar showed the 1978 dollar to buy about 45¢ worth of construction material. Nine percent of that inflation occurred from October 1977 to January 1978. Such inflation concerned Navy construction officials. Perry Fliakas, the Deputy Assistant Secretary of Defense for Installations and Housing, noted: "In historical perspective . . . construction costs rose at less than the national average in the late 1960's and through the 1970's." He speculated that the excessive inflation might be a "technical adjustment." Nevertheless, he maintained, the Navy's predictions of cost growth—9 percent over four years—were "slightly pessimistic."[36]

Related Trident Facilities

Construction costs and inflation could at least be discussed in congressional hearings as part of the Trident budget. In other areas of construction, though, Trident-related work had been conducted for several years before the actual purpose and extent of that work became clear. Cape Canaveral, for instance, had had more than a hundred Trident-related engineers and scientists inconspicously working there since the early 1970s. Point Mugu operated as a missile test range for several years before its name also became linked to Trident missile testing. Indian Island was the only exception, as Navy witnesses discussed it openly as an ammunition, torpedo, and missile-storage annex. Point Mugu and Cape Canaveral operate apart from any single program, with both facilities in essence "leasing" their equipment to the service needing them at any given time.[37]

Other than for testing, Cape Canaveral had only a minimal role in the Trident program. Its use did require the Navy to dredge and clear a turning basin capable of accommodating a Trident submarine before ballistic-missile launches and tests could be conducted. The test center, of course, already of necessity had the capability to load and unload missiles. Point Mugu, a base located between Oxnard and northern Los Angeles, acts strictly as a missile tracking range for a variety of missiles from all service branches. In all probability, the center also has command and control capabilities, either through its own controls or through NAVSTAR. As far as can be determined, Point Mugu has no actual wharf or basin facilities. It was nonetheless involved in the testing of Trident missiles, and funds from Trident-related programs were allocated for Point Mugu. Some of these funds came directly from the Navy's Trident budget, but often the rental of the facilities of Point Mugu came from the contractor's funds. Indian Island annex, identified as a Trident project from the beginning, provided the Navy a separate explosives-basing facility. Environmentalists used it as the basis of a new lawsuit when the courts indicated Bangor was environmentally sound through decisions rendered in the *CAT* vs. *Schlesinger* and the *Hood Canal* judgments. Indian Island, however, provided the environmentalists with no more judicial euphoria than did Bangor.

Overall, construction of the bases generated fewer problems than the submarine program encountered, largely because building facilities, no matter how unique in design or mission, involves an experience factor unavailable to those who worked on the *Ohio*. Funds also "flowed" more easily for base construction than occurred in other areas of the Trident program since the construction of facilities provokes less local opposition from the site chosen because of the clearly perceptible economic stimulus that comes in its wake. From a "pork barrel" standpoint, only the Gulf Coast seems somehow to have missed the Trident "boat." Occasionally, support facilities were hidden in the budgets, reinforcing the position proposed in chapters 3 and 4 that the submarine itself represents only a part of the entire Trident expenditure. Whereas actual base construction did run somewhat behind, it never lagged to the extent of the delays the entire shipbuilding program experienced. Legislators therefore simply had fewer reservations about voting construction funds on a consistent basis. Generally, legislative opposition to the Trident itself remained mute when it came to voting on naval facilities, perhaps in resignation, feeling the battle already had been lost on the larger issues. Groups of citizens opposing the bases on legal or environmental grounds had minimal success, largely due to the placating effect of federal assistance funds. Lacking specific legislative or executive mandates, Navy engineers on their own initiative designed aesthetically pleasing structures and provided for environmental protection whenever possible. Selecting sites from hundreds of candidate locations, the Navy suceeded in establishing two bases virtually free of the threat of any external interference in any situation short of a general war, each with numerous features promoting protection against terrorist attacks and sabotage and enhancing safety, thus ensuring that Tridents based at those facilities would stand a significantly greater chance of accomplishing their mission than if the same boats used other bases. The needs of a new and unique submarine had inspired the creation of new and unique bases.

8

Bearing Down:

Soviet ASW Capability and Trident Operational Survivability

Possible combats are on account of their results to be looked upon as real ones.

—Clauswitz, *On War*

Trident's strengths and weaknesses have doubtless already been catalogued in great detail by Soviet naval strategists and intelligence personnel. Their examination probably would have proceeded along two major paths. First, they would be interested in Trident's individual offensive capabilities and overall contribution as a new class of ballistic-missile submarine to the seaborne deterrent force, specifically, and the modification of the TRIAD system as a whole. Here are included two general areas of concern for Soviet defensive strategists: the operational range, sea endurance, speed, detectability, ASW vulnerability, communications, diving depth, and magazine strength of the submarine; the flight range, trajectory, reentry vehicle numbers, accuracy, penetration ability, megatonnage, and payload of the missile. Soviet antisubmarine warfare tactics obviously must be geared to the enemy's operational evasive and defensive capabilities, both for individual vessels and for flotilla action. Trident may in fact therefore "dictate" the types of ASW vessels and weapons the Soviets construct and deploy in the future. Trident's nuclear payload will concern the Soviet civilian defense planners who must assess Trident's "soft" threat to cities and will concern military personnel who must protect "hard" targets such as air bases, ground forces, missile silos, C^3I facilities, and SSBN harbor refuges. Second, Soviet naval authorities must consider novel and highly secret forms of operational interaction between and among Tridents themselves and other fleet units, and thus they cannot contemplate successful ASW action simply against a single Trident acting alone with its systems limitations specifically. Other vessels may provide protection, for such forms of operational interaction will compound the Trident's individual survivability and will require Soviet rethinking of ASW selective destruction. It must be pointed out here that while many sources agree on the techniques and practices of ASW as employed by both the U.S. and the USSR, the classified nature of ASW makes the following discussion necessarily speculative, especially when it comes to systems now in research and development. Still, a reasonable conjecture and assessment can be made.

Soviet ASW Doctrine

To appreciate Trident's current and potential impact on Soviet military doctrine, a review of Soviet naval doctrine as it has developed under Admiral of the Soviet Fleet and "father of the Soviet Navy" Sergei Gorshkov is useful. According to Gorshkov, "the dominant role has been assumed by operations of the fleet against the shore" (Gorshkov uses "operations against the shore" in both an offensive and defensive sense). Although there is some disagreement about the exact order of priorities in Soviet naval doctrine, there seems to be no argument that strategic offense and antisubmarine warfare head the list. A 1962 Russian study on military strategy called the Sokolovsky Study listed the primary missions of the Soviet Navy in order of importance as (1) destruction of carrier-based forces, (2) defeat of Polaris subs, and (3) disruption of support of enemy ground troops during landings. Mention of offensive Soviet sub-launched ballistic missiles was omitted, probably because the capacity was not then available. (Limits in the availability of Soviet conventional submarine capability perhaps also explain the omission at this point of the mission later adopted to destroy Western sea lanes of communication [SLOC].) Since 1962, as Russian SSBNs came into the fleet, the "strategic offensive" became a central part of Soviet naval doctrine. Certainly, Russian concerns about devastation of the homeland are understandable, based upon the Russian historical experience with invasions by Teutonic knights, Swedes, Poles, French, British, Sardinians, Turks, and—most recently—the Germans twice. An underlying theme of all Soviet military doctrine, therefore, is that such devastation cannot be endured again. Whereas historical experience suggests defense of the homeland to be the primary mission, defense against SSBNs nevertheless probably remains second on Gorshkov's priority list due to the repeated emphasis on the "offensive." This emphasis holds to the old football adage that the best defense is a good offense and knowledge that, in the event of a nuclear war, surprise and the ability to launch the first strike are of prime importance. Interestingly, the concept of the offensive fits hand in hand with the current force structure of the

Soviet navy. According to Soviet doctrine, the offensive alone is capable of conferring victory and, by its nature, the SSBN is best able to bombard enemy cities and military installations with minimal warning to the enemy. It is, in other words, the perfect offensive weapon. Given this emphasis on the SSBN force, offensive naval operations have clearly been selected as the very top priority, but ASW remains a close second, along with anticarrier and anti-SLOC operations. In the period immediately following World War II, prior to the development of missile-launching submarines, the aircraft carrier posed the greatest threat to the Russian homeland. Consequently, large numbers of fast surface craft and attack submarines were produced in an effort to challenge the American carriers before they could launch attack bombers. These ships, the *Kynda* class, for example, relied on land-based air cover for their own protection and threatened the carriers with primitive but inexpensive cruise missiles. A new and more serious threat appeared in 1960 when the first U.S. ballistic-missile submarine, the *George Washington*, went to sea with its sixteen Polaris missiles. Forty-one U.S. ballistic-missile submarines were completed from 1960 to 1967. Gorshkov correctly realized that this expanding SSBN force now constitued his primary worry, so anticarrier activities took a back seat to ASW. New classes of ASW subsurface and surface ships were subsequently developed, spearheaded by the *November* class of SSN which appeared between 1958 and 1963 and, in 1967, by the *Moskva* and *Leningrad* helicopter cruisers. By the early 1970s, then, the submarine had come to dominate Soviet strategic planning both offensively and defensively.[1]

Doctrinally, the Russians have shown inconsistency in their early approach to ASW against American ballistic-missile subs. In January, 1963, U. A. Alafuzov wrote, in *Morskoi Sbornik,* that sinking the U.S. subs was "not as easy" as previously thought. Four months later, Captain V. P. Rogov countered that notion by claiming Polaris subs had a low percentage of successful launches, were vulnerable in their bases, had difficulties in communication and control and had missiles that were inaccurate due to navigation errors and positioning. Because these statements and others like them lacked any specific data, American intelligence dismissed them as "too general to be convincing." Most observers believe the Soviets' approach to ASW also differs from that of the United States. While employing a "layered" defense consisting of aircraft, sensors, and ships deployed according to range, the Soviets might regard their own ballistic-missile submarines as the best form of ASW.[2]

Several more specific questions involving Soviet responses to the Trident now deserve consideration. For example, what exactly are the capabilities of Soviet ASW forces? Are they sufficient to guarantee the

Soviet homeland relative safety from Trident missiles? What Trident defensive qualities were unavailable to previous American and/or Allied strategic subs? How much Soviet naval effort overall is directed to ASW and how swiftly and massively could it be increased or decreased upon the outbreak of hostilities? Assuming that Soviet SSBN submarines have multiple capabilities, as do our own, what are their offensive versus their defensive roles, and how do they differ from Trident's strategic role? In evaluating Soviet ASW forces, it is important to bear in mind auxiliary roles in which these forces might be employed. Do these roles detract from the primary ASW mission and, if so, by how much? Since Soviet surface ships are built with diverse capabilities, what tactical and command disadvantages does this multiple assignment impose? Finally, an investigation of Russian ASW capabilities and Soviet submarines may reveal several characteristics, capabilities, or qualities similar to American surface and subsurface ASW methods. Which of these do the Soviets emphasize the most, and are they consciously imitative by design or are they due persistently to laggard technology on the part of the Soviets? The answers to these questions will provide some measurement of Trident's survivability and its true value.[3]

Antisubmarine warfare remains one of the most esoteric, frustrating, and unglamorous areas of naval combat, with good reason. Submarines operate in virtually dimensionless volumes of space, frequently with (in the case of the Artic) a protective solid icy covering and with several other natural shielding qualities of its medium—water temperature, sea life, shelfbound drilling, salinity, biological noise, routine maritime traffic, weather disruption, ocean currents, seabed geography, and other forms of sensory confusion. Soviet ASW efforts, notes naval expert Norman Polmar, "are considerable and continuing." But, "although they have expended considerable resources in recent years on anti-submarine warfare, including an intensive ASW research and development program . . . the Soviets have [not] resolved the problem of locating a large number of submarines on the high seas with a degree of probability." Submarines also continue to be the "silent service." As one observer stated, "in all the military, there is no topic more whisper whetting than what's going on in ASW." The four major components of ASW, therefore—search, location, identification, and destruction—will be dealt with separately.[4]

Soviet ASW Capabilities

Search and location duties are assigned to three elements of the Soviet Navy—naval air force (about 1200 aircraft), submarine reconnaissance, and surface craft—and to one element of Soviet space capability, satellites. Of the airplanes whose primary or secondary mission is ASW reconnaissance, the workhorses are the Mail flying boat and the May long-range reconnaissance plane. Ninety Mails and fifty Mays are in service currently, with the out-of-production May having superior range (4500 miles to 2500 miles) and speed (400 mph to 379 mph). Both carry a MAD (Magnetic Anomaly Detection) radar boom designed for picking up metal-induced magnetic flow irregularities in the water. Soviet ASW reconnaissance helicopters include the Hormone, the Hound, and the Haze. Both the Hormone and the Hound carry sonor buoys, a dipping sonar, and MAD. The Haze probably carries buoys and dipping sonar but not MAD, and, like the Hound, is a land-based helicopter. The Haze, however, cannot operate from *Kiev* or *Moskva* class cruisers. The range of the three helicopters varies greatly, with the Hormone capable of 400 miles while the Hound is able to reach only 155 miles. The range of the Haze is unknown, although its speed of 160 mph is superior; it is substantially the largest of the three, so it is probable this class is restricted to under 200 miles. This range limitation, coupled with the fact that the Haze is a land-based craft, greatly restricts any location activities either it or the other types of helicopter might provide. Worse for the Soviets, although it is growing, the Russian Pacific fleet, which will draw primary ASW duty against the Bangor-based Tridents, is the weakest of the four Soviet fleets in numbers of aircraft. As of 1977, only 105 total ASW aircraft were allocated to the Pacific Soviet naval air force. Out of the 105 total, only ten were maritime reconnaissance planes and only fifteen were ASW helicopters (although the deployment of an additional *Kiev*-type ship could change these figures rapidly). No classification breakdown is available, but not all of the helicopters apparently were of the Hormone variety, meaning that Soviet location activities outside the 200-mile zone would have to be borne by ten planes and perhaps a half-dozen helicopters. If the standard maxim of maintenance is that at least one-third of all available mechanical equipment will be undergoing repair or servicing at all times, the Soviets would have had a 1977 capability of only seven planes and four helicopters to cover their own immediate Pacific territorial rim. Whereas these ASW forces were then hardly adequate to cover the Sea of Japan and the Sea of Okhotsk internally, they certainly were not sufficient to cover a significant external belt beyond the Kurile-Kamchatka line or over the Bering Sea. In any case, Trident deployment in these areas is unlikely. Even since 1977, with the addition of perhaps as many as sixty-five helicopters, many deployed on Soviet ASW carriers, the situation has not radically improved, even with the availability to the Red Navy of the Cam Ranh Bay naval facilities.[5]

Perhaps Soviet naval advisers realized how thinly spread these ASW forces were when reconnaissance versions of the Tu-16 Badger and Tu-20 Bear bombers were designed. Variations of both have appeared, including Badger D, E, F, H, J, and K versions, all carrying assorted radar and capable of 600 mph, with a range of 4000 miles. Bear model F (Tu-142) is somewhat slower (550mph) and is turbo-prop driven but has formidable range (over 8000 miles). Another converted bomber, the Blinder C, has been assigned to the Navy. Its limited range (1300 miles) is greatly exceeded by its speed of over 900 mph. Approximately sixty of these are in use with the Navy.

Despite the bomber alleviation of the ASW range problem in the Pacific, the Soviets apparently continue to relegate their Pacific fleet to last place in the allocation of naval aircraft. The northern fleet outnumbers the Pacific in helicopters and reconnaissance planes five to one. Once again, even giving the Soviets the benefit of the doubt and assuming that *all* of their Pacific planes were available 100 percent of the time and that all of them were Bears, Badgers, or Blinders rather than short-legged ASW helicopters, it is far-fetched to believe this total force could be effective in locating a substantial majority of U.S. attack and strategic submarines hiding in the more remote, vaster, deeper Pacific waters (including the Indian Ocean).[6]

ASW surface craft are also valuable in searching for and locating enemy submarines. For this purpose the Soviets have specifically developed a new class of ship, the *Moskva*, which entered service in 1967. Together with her sister ship *Leningrad*, in service in 1968, the *Moskva* represented the first step by the Soviets toward carrier construction. Each of these vessels has a bow and forward section resembling a cruiser and a flat aft helicopter deck. Eighteen Hormone helicopters can be carried by each ship, thereby greatly increasing the range of ASW operations. These vessels can make 30 knots for 2500 miles with their steam turbines or 7000 miles at 15 knots. The Soviets refer to these as "antisubmarine" cruisers (BPK), although in American terminology they are light helicopter carriers. More recently several ships of a new Soviet design have appeared, including the *Kiev*, in service in 1975, followed by the *Minsk* in 1978. The *Kharkov* and the *Novorossiysk* are now making their appearance, with more probably to follow. *Kiev*'s "construction and employment is that of a true aircraft carrier," but one designed for VTOL (vertical takeoff and landing) or STOL (short takeoff and landing) aircraft only. Usually aboard are twenty-five Hormones as well as ten VTOL planes, with force mixtures varying. Nevertheless, as significant as these additions are to the Soviets' sea-roving ASW capabilities, they are but a few ships with limited capabilities compared to U.S. fleet carriers with some eighty-five to ninety aircraft aboard, and, if the standard Soviet strategy of deploying a disproportionate number of ships in the Atlantic area is observed, most of these ships will end up in the Atlantic, with the remainder assigned to the Mediterranean. Currently, the *Minsk* is assigned to the Pacific fleet. Both classes of ship appear designed to move the Russian ASW perimeter out to beyond the maximum range of the Polaris missile (2500 nm for A-3). Presumably, this "far zone defense will increase again when the large Soviet carrier is introduced."[7]

In addition to the deployment of one or more helicopter carriers in the Pacific, there is a standard deployment of over ninety surface craft there. Of these ninety, roughly sixty are coastal patrol boats, such as the *Krupny* and the *SQ-1* classes. While these are quite capable of ASW tactics, their range is quite limited (by their small size rather than fuel consumption); in the Pacific they must be assigned to coastal patrol and defense, thanks to a fleet of similar ships manned by the forces of the People's Republic of China of constant threat to the southeastern maritime flank of Russia. Of the remaining ships assigned to the Pacific fleet, six are cruisers and the rest are destroyers. However, even if one assumes that all of the cruisers are advanced *Kresta* models, which they are not, only ten ASW helicopters would be available to this fleet. In other words, Soviet antisubmarine forces are not greatly improved by the types of surface ships deployed in the Pacific. Further, some of these ships may be assigned to either offensive or defensive mining operations. Therefore, not even all active surface ships could be counted on for ASW services. As with all Soviet vessels, firepower and speed are placed at a premium, leaving them with few reloads, limited fuel, and poor living conditions. Surface ships and search aircraft must also rely on favorable weather conditions. Submarine captains know how to hide in storms that make surface work impossible but leave the depths relatively untouched, thereby almost sadistically compounding problems of surface-level habitability further. The technical level of contemporary Soviet ASW capability in towed array, sonobuoys, MAD gear, and the like is extremely difficult to determine for anyone outside U.S. Naval Intelligence and operations.[8]

Compounding the ASW problem facing the Soviets is the vast size of the Pacific. Inclusion of the Indian Ocean as the responsibility of the Pacific fleet means the Soviets must cover an additional area 6000 miles *across*, in addition to the Pacific's 10,000 miles of north–south axis and 9000 miles of east–west axis. Current Poseidon subs not armed with Trident I work in a 3,000,000-square-mile area. Trident I extends this range to 14,500,000 square miles. The longer-range Trident II submarines will have 42,500,000 square miles, with future booster and fuel advances probably expanding this figure. Fortunately for the

Soviets, neither Trident I or II can reach targets in the deepest interior of the USSR at the maximum distance from the Soviet Pacific coastline. Range on the Trident I missile is approximately 4600 miles, but very few significant military targets are located on or near Russia's maritime coast, a limitation requiring Trident to be short of maximum range in firing near Russia's Pacific coast or from the Persian Gulf if targets in western Russia are to be accurately hit. In other words, the Pacific deployment of the Trident works in its favor for cruising survivability but somewhat against it for strike capability. In this respect, two factors would massively frustrate Soviet ASW efforts: increasing range on the Trident I missile and subsequent deployment of the Trident II; a mix of Atlantic–Pacific–Indian Ocean deployment of Trident with a complementary Arctic–Atlantic deployment of Poseidon. Currently it appears that both concepts have gained the support of the President and the Navy, as evidenced by Reagan's October 1981 strategic directive and by construction of a new Trident base at King's Bay, Georgia. Because of the range added to the Soviet search problem, Michael MccGwire argues that deployment of the Trident will force the Soviets to deploy their ASW forces even farther forward. Perhaps it will, but the increased availability of Tridents will put more RVs on patrol than ever before, placing a strain on Soviet ASW that even forward deployment will not solve.[9]

The ASW weapon least hindered by distance and weather is the attack submarine employed in antisubmarine roles. For this purpose the Soviets have designed several classes of submarines: *November, Echo,* and *Victor* nuclear-powered boats as well as diesel-powered subs such as the *Bravo, Foxtrot, Golf, Romeo, Zulu, Quebec, Whiskey,* and *Tango.* About 158 diesel submarines, which the Soviets turn out "like Mexican fritters," now exist in addition to at least forty nuclear-powered boats. There are also four specially designed radar picket submarines with limited search capabilities. All of these classes of submarine include passive Feniks and active/passive Hercules sonar for submarine detection; many contain a special "Snoop Tray," "Snoop Slab," or "Snoop Plate" surface-search ASW radar. Soviet attack subs probably rely more on general search directions signaled from satellites than on their own sonar or radar. Furthermore, actually tracking a Trident for any extended period of time by submarine would require a Soviet attack sub capable of the same speeds and depths as Tridents. Of these attack sub classes, in terms of submerged speed the *Victors* are the fastest (28–32 knots), followed by *Novembers* at 30 knots, the *Echoes* (25–28 knots), and the relatively slow *Foxtrots, Quebecs, Tangos,* and other diesel subs at speeds ranging from 12 to 17 knots. In order to mass-produce attack subs, the Soviets have sacrificed several qualities: roominess and crew comfort, extensive reloads of torpedoes or missiles, quietness, adequate radiation shielding around their reactors, and, in some cases, even range. None of these classes appear to match the estimated top speed of the Trident as publicized by the German periodical *Stern* in its May 3, 1979, edition—approximately 40 knots (the official Navy figure is "25 + knots"). A very few are probably capable of matching Trident's diving capabilities, conservatively estimated by one authority to be 300 meters, or about 1000 feet, but given its hull frame structure and steel cylinder strength made of I-beam reinforced steel, an estimate of more than 2000 feet seems very reasonable, although Soviet subs that could approximate these depths are very unlikely at all to be older models and, even if they could briefly, they definitely could not maintain an appropriate combination of depth and speed long enough to trail a Trident continuously. In any case, "American ASW forces are in a position to initiate the appropriate countermeasures designed to prevent Soviet boats from successfully initiating trailing operations."[10]

One ominous exception to this observation is the *Alpha* (or *Alfa*). An attack submarine designed for ASW, *Alpha* can more or less match Trident's speed. Some defense sources say that *Alpha* can exceed 45 knots; ABC News reported it could do closer to 50! Such speeds alone make it a formidable foe for Tridents, but apparently it may be able to dive to below 3000 feet as well and, because of the strength and nonmagnetic nature of its titanium hull, effectively evade airborne MAD detection. However, worse from an American standpoint, it presently can almost "outrun" Mk-48 torpedoes fired at it from astern, a capability making it now nearly invulnerable to Trident's defensive suite and to Trident's protective shadow, the *Los Angeles*-class attack sub, thereby compelling the Navy already to upgrade its Mk-48 torpedo program for the benefit of both classes. Further, its speed makes the *Alpha* itself a perfect tracking sub, since it would be difficult for a Trident to escape by sheer acceleration alone. However, the *Alpha* is not an "ultimate weapon" either in terms of its own capabilities or Trident's defensive responses. The Soviets obviously have grave concerns about *Alpha*'s range, durability, and speed over extended periods—confirmed by the Soviet practice of towing the *Alpha* to the start of its patrol. Norman Polmar reported that the *Alpha* has taken ten years since its launching to reach operational status because of "technical problems—probably with the advanced propulsion plant," which resulted in the lead vessel being scrapped. Hence it is unlikely that an *Alpha* can maintain 40 knots or more for more than very brief spurts; relatively speaking, it is quite noisy, as are other Soviet subs—exhibiting, for example, under the sail a number of free-flowing limber ports that are hydrodynamically disturbing. Even so, the Trident is hardly helpless. Its own bow sonar is integrated into the BQQ-6 suite along with its passive conformal and towed-array sonar. A noisy *Alpha* unavoidably will advertise its position very quickly to the Trident's integrated and sophisticated sonars. Even "one on one" with this new series of attack sub in a trailing position, a Trident can fire its defensive Mk-48 torpedoes from any of its four forward tubes. Navigating about and homed in by its own active-passive or acoustic system or with a wire guidance system, the deadly fish would be at least initially blanketed by Trident's screw turbulence. The unfortunate *Alpha* would, in essence, cruise right into Trident's torpedoes, whose maximum speed is at least 40 knots and whose range is between 31 and 40 miles, thus placing the *Alpha* in a zone of severe disadvantage with the range of its SS-N-15 SUBROC-like ASW weapon at about 25 miles. These disadvantages for the *Alpha* in attacking a Trident operate with even greater effect so far as closing speeds and weapon ranges are concerned in a bow-on attack position since the Trident can use its Mk-118 torpedo Fire Control System to fire its Mk-48 as fire protection and then evade the *Alpha* through the operation of its sonar. For all of its speed, unless the *Alpha* is equipped with SUBROC-like missiles capable of withstanding hull-crush pressures at its maximum diving levels, its range of attack weapons is highly limited in variety (SS-N-15s only), range (6- to 15-mile disadvantage), and sophistication (superior Trident passive sonar and electronic countermeasure capabilities).[11]

Less than half a dozen prototype *Alphas* exist now, with the Soviets currently turning out no more than one per year, but they could double that rate on a crash program. (One report lists the Soviets as having five at this time, but Norman Polmar puts the number closer to ten.) Through 1988, this building rate would exceed the proposed Trident delivery schedule, meaning that the Soviets could gain an advantage on a "one-to-one" basis in the next decade. But considering the limitations imposed on Soviet search and location procedure—range, speed, and inability of satellites to maintain constant subsurface contact—a virtual fleet of *Alphas* presents no immediate danger to the Trident squadron even with fairly consistent tracking success. In this regard, Michael MccGwire suggests that deployment of the Trident will force the Soviets into as much trailing as they can manage. Moreover, if the *Alpha* was really designed with the Trident in mind, several theoretical problems arise: Are American SSBN designs now dictating Soviet construction responses? Can the *Alpha* be effective as a Trident-reactive design when the Soviets originally could not really conceive of the Trident's entire operational capabilities? Lieutenant Victor Blenko's testimony about the Soviet MiG-25 Foxbat's development as an anti-B-70 weapon analogously points to an affirmative answer to the first question. A program too consistently oriented toward reactive response exposes itself to the danger of developing a counterweapon for a system that may never move beyond the prototype stage (the B-70 or possibly the MX, for example). The limited attack capability of the *Alpha*, as analyzed here, suggests a negative answer to the second question: To match the Trident's defensive capability with a corresponding offensive capability, the *Alpha* appears to need a complete redesign, if not a wholly new replacement, when its 4250-ton (submerged) hull capacity is viewed for its potential to incorporate radical systems upgrading. A Russian commitment to try to match American Trident technology with an advanced post-Alpha attack mode deserves further observation of future *Alpha* modifications and of possible successor systems. As any auto mechanic specializing in high-performance cars knows, drive-train improvement must take place evenly throughout a machine. For example, impetuously adding a supercharger to the engine may increase its power to the point that the standard clutch turns to dust the first time it is tested. So the *Alpha*'s superiority over earlier Soviet attack subs in speed and depth may have been obtained at the expense of neglecting a fully synthesized design with corresponding radical capabilities and reliability all around. While the *Alpha* may be the Soviet version of a "quick fix" to the Trident, it does not seem to be a replete answer in its own right or a vessel with a sustainable level of maintenance-free reliability. Time will tell on this point.[12]

Trident Defensive Tactics

Egressing from port exposes Trident to detection from three sources: satellites, intelligence trawlers, and trailing subs. Trident's evasion of satellite search assumes three forms: (1) cruising levels below those at which satellite detection can be confirmed by wake or thermal, infrared, electromagnetic, or visual means; (2) cruising in such a way as to operate in ocean areas not surveyed by geosynchronous satellites "spotting" more probable areas of Trident deployment; (3) cruising evasively to escape surface area surveillance by orbiting satellites, whose inspection is discontinous but predictable. Some congressmen have expressed concern about the vulnerability of Tridents to trailing as they exit from Kings Bay, Georgia, but Admiral Kelln explained there was "no real problem" in egressing from Kings Bay. Various surface ships, subs, and aircraft "run interference" for the submarine. On the surface, a frigate can accomplish a "blocking" or screening maneuver easily, keeping a trawler at an acceptable distance. Why not, indeed, occasionally have the U.S. Coast Guard haul over a Soviet "intelligence-fishing" trawler in hot pursuit of suspected drug smugglers? Below the water, this can be accomplished by an attack sub that follows a scissors movement in and out of the Trident wake. Trailing subs pick up the numerous confusing noises and lose the Trident's trail rather easily. On the other hand, the Soviet sub itself thereby exposes itself to detection by American attack sonar, thus potentially making the hunter the hunted. Because Tridents electronically and navigationally target most Soviet bases immediately upon leaving port, the Soviet ASW problem grows infinitely more difficult. There is no zone of operational immunity for the Trident, compared with Polaris/Poseidon, and screening or distraction tactics can be routinely implemented. As one naval witness quipped, "It's a lot easier for us to go out with our [land-based] aircraft and drop noisemakers [off our coast] than it is for [the Russians] to [drop] sonobuoys." Beyond port, a Trident drops out of sight of Soviet satellites by diving; it currently otherwise remains immune to enemy satellite detection except when it approaches the surface to launch missiles. The Trident can probably launch with as little overhead depth as 100 feet, but at this depth once again it becomes visible to Soviet satellites as though it were actually surfaced. Besides satellite detection of the Trident hull itself, space and sonar-based sensor systems can also pick up the signatures generated in terms of wake effects by such submarine communications and detection equipment as towed buoys, trailing wires, and TACTAS. A satellite transmission picked up by the Soviet command center nearest the specific theater—in this case the Pacific—in a real combat situation would next set in motion airborne and fleet ASW units to localize and track the threat further. Given general search-area coordinates by the satellite, long-range reconnaissance planes equipped with MAD then would appear over the general Trident location, thereafter followed by sonar-dipping helicopters, culminating with Trident's possible dispatch by airborne, surface, or, theoretically, by undersea conventional or nuclear weapons. Technology developed in the 1980s even provides a defense against the airborne threat, however. Called the SIAM (self-initiated antiaircraft missile), this weapon uses a towed array sonar to detect approaching airplanes or ASW helicopters and, when fired, hovers for a split-second while its radar homes in on the target before striking. Thus the attack scenarios discussed here can only experience success if the SIAM does not first eliminate the airborne threat and the Mk-48s do not eliminate the surface and submarine threats. Especially in those instances where time and distance militate against the timely arrival of airborne and surface combatants, a Soviet attack sub would be the only real option. Although Tridents do not have SIAM aboard now, the capability for subsequent installation has already been provided.[13]

Even so, in the best of circumstances, a Trident's destruction by any combination of ASW forces is by no means assured. A complex array of factors is involved in any specific attack action, analytically requiring the positing of several variable circumstances: (1) the presence or absence of either sea or air support for a single Trident; (2) the shorter or longer subsurface exposure of the Trident during its firing of one, a few, or a whole magazine of missiles; (3) the presence or absence at the time of Trident detection of an *Alpha* or another equivalently capable vessel; and so on. For example, in a case where two attack subs were available, both could be sent in, with the oldest first in order to harass the Trident, slow it down, and otherwise draw fire. However, except for the *Alpha* none of the other Soviet attack subs can match the Trident's speed, and therefore the best these vessels could do is hope to catch it diving and fire torpedoes at the approximate point while maintaining a probably gradually dissipating sonar contact with it. A Trident is possessed of several options in such situations: it can dive at full speed to outrun enemy torpedoes; it can release its MOSS (Mobile Submarine Simulator) decoys, which divert torpedoes, enemy subs, or both; it can assume an advantageous operational depth and then outrun its pursuers; it can baffle follow-up efforts at relocation by sensing and exploiting ASW-confounding oceanographic conditions. Even when apparently hemmed in by two or more ships, submarines, or a combination, a Trident can outrun most combatants before they can launch their ASW weapons. For the SS-N-14 ASW rocket used by the Soviets on their major cruisers to be effective, the attacking vessel must launch within a range of 25 miles. Shorter-legged Soviet ASW rockets such as the FRAS-1 have a maximum range of 16 miles, and they diminish in range by class from that point on. Soviet ASW rockets face depth as well as range limitations. Since the larger Russian ASW missiles carry nuclear warheads, a Trident would have to be well out of their range to survive an area impact, although the Trident for this purpose is highly shock-resistant. Optimum countermeasures to such a nuclear missile attack would be to dive to a minimally immune depth of between 100 and 200 feet and "hit the throttle." A Trident commander on a solo mission probably would dive and/or release MOSS decoys to thwart an enemy attack sub, perhaps firing his Mk-48 torpedoes for good measure. The enemy commander would consequently confront the simultaneous responsibilities of differentiating between the real Trident and the MOSS ghosts, protecting his vessel against torpedo attack, and trying to continue to track the Trident. Meanwhile, the

Trident commander can hide out of the sonar range of surface aircraft while varying his speed to outrun the search pattern completely or sneak unobtrusively away from it. At that point the Soviet surface commander would be forced to make a decision: to fire his SS-N-14 randomly at a predicted likely spot, hoping the Trident would be in the general area, or to continue the search. Although the blast area of the new SS-N-14s is unknown, the older SS-N-11s had an underwater blast diameter of 3.5 miles. Three problems are involved with a random launching of a nuclear-tipped SS-N-14, the greatest of which is potential destruction of friendly attack subs in the same area. Second, the SS-N-14 cannot be reloaded, and Soviet vessels carry few, if any, reloads; to expend one on a dialectical version of "a wing and a prayer" entails some measure of disfunctional desperation. Finally, a nuclear underwater blast has several undesirable ramifications, including temporary interruption of all sonar activities and shock reverberations sometimes more damaging in its effects on surface ships farther from the blast than on those nearer the blast point. American nuclear-tipped ASROCs, carried on most ASW surface craft, have a much shorter range, causing some experts to believe the launching ship could escape the reverberation shock by actually being closer than a similar Soviet ship would. In other words, a nuclear ASW attack risks losing the Trident vainly in a swirling maelstrom (the boat could be well out of range in about eleven minutes after detection at 40 knots and in about an hour and a half at 5 knots cruising speed) while at the same time endangering many of the attacking surface forces and some of the submarines should they be in the general area.[14]

This scenario might appear to make Trident's escape far too easy. In fact, slower Soviet attack subs, distracted by decoys sending off different depth images and warding off Trident's defensive torpedoes, would need to attack in groups of two, three, or more to heighten their prospects of success against this fighting ship. Soviet abilities to assign attack subs even in this manner must be based on the presumption that *the Trident has been precisely located*, a somewhat grandiose assumption. Compensating for the duration involved in a full firing of the entire magazine, Trident can fire, suggestively, from one to four missiles and then dive deeper before any enemy vessels can vector in with any precision. Repeating this undulating maneuver, a Trident has a much higher prospect of survival in delivering its entire payload. Anticipatory group attack by Soviet ASW forces, in contrast to the opportunistic targeting just discussed, is next to impossible. Since satellites are useful in picking up a submarine moving at depths of less than 300 feet, most SSBNs prefer to cruise very slowly at lower depths, safely within their tolerances. Cruising at speeds no more than 5 knots generates minimal noise, biological displacement, and other traceable evidence. Therefore cruising ASW surface craft, ASW helicopters, and ASW aircraft are at a maximum disadvantage in detecting any SSBN operating in this mode. Other equally baffling modes can be employed in certain circumstances, such as cruising "upstream," so to speak, against an underwater current probably of different salinity and/or temperature than its surrounding strata so that nearly no local motion takes place, or cruising below the protective profile of certain underwater geological formations. Arctic deployments constitute even greater problems for Soviet ASW in terms of ice flows as natural shields against many techniques of detection employed in open waters and in terms of the much more severe weather conditions providing a protective mantle. The use of dipping gear through ice holes is nevertheless a rather ineffectual location technique. Icebergs project stalactites downward into the water, in all shapes and sizes, as deep as 1000 feet. Drop-through dipping equipment is unlikely to function effectively if SSBN sonar equipment (such as BQS-15, 18, 11, or 20 components) is used to take advantage of these inverted valley floors and dead spots. Routine deployment of the Trident in Arctic waters does not appear likely in the near future and will be even less likely when it is deployed with the Trident II. However, complementary to its deployment now in the Pacific and later in the Atlantic, the Poseidon class can be assigned a more significant and expanding role in the Arctic, thus numerically and technologically straining Soviet ASW capabilities to the utmost.[15]

Trident cannot be viewed apart from interaction with other U.S. fleet units and those of its allies. Since certain surface ships possess their own ASW capability against Soviet attack submarines, a combat tactic can be imagined by which a Trident might effect an ambush of a Soviet SSN by evasively leading it in a high-speed chase into the attack zone of a *Los Angeles* submarine or within the range of an ASW-equipped surface vessel for a knockout. Air cover provided by American or Allied bases also makes many Soviet SSBN pursuit missions untenable. American SSBNs in general, and Tridents in particular, of course represent a highly secure second strike force. In this role, should Soviet ASW capacity (especially its SSN variation) substantially improve in the future, Tridents might see operational deployment off the southern coast of Australia, for example, in the South Australian Abyssal Plain—under the protective umbrella of the Royal Australian Air Force and Navy. The Australian government could previously declare and enforce a national security zone in that sector upon the approach of war. Tridents would militarily and politically thereby have multidimensionally protected seas from which to deploy on second-strike missions. Similar protective roles can be envisaged for Diego

Garcia, the Philippines, South Africa, and so on. While obviously the Trident I missile poses virtually no threat to the Soviet Union from the Abyssal Plain and the Trident II only minimally more, the value of these protected zones lies more in their use as "delousing" stations to remove Russian trailing subs. The Diego Garcia zone, however, provides a substantially improved launching area. The ramifications of "protected zones," whether formally declared or operationally created, present Western SSBN strategists incredible options. They could operationally condition Soviet ASW behavior to accept prewar patterns of deployment (such as the Abyssal Plain) until wartime, at which point radical shifts to highly secret and unused alternatives in Trident deployment could occur with bewildering results. Such a plan clearly could drain numerous ASW units—especially those with maximum range—away from the actual launch point. Furthermore, those Tridents working alternatively in protective unison with American surface craft, air cover, or both, would enjoy a mobile "safety bubble" with a diameter as large as a combat fleet can secure with its wide-ranging assets. Any Soviet attempt to break this bubble of quadruple dimensions would not only result in guaranteed losses at the hands of the fleet's defensive weapons but conversely would not necessarily guarantee success of the primary-mission elimination of Trident. As always, SSBNs could slip away at depths beyond Soviet detection capabilities during the course of battle or immediately afterward. The operational genius involved in developing peacetime active and static patterns of conditioning Soviet ASW against Trident consists of the potential for wartime Trident commanders to effect befuddling switches from active decoy "behavior bubbles" to vacuous modes and from formerly innocent behavior bubbles to rather deadly ones.[16]

For their part, Soviet ASW capabilities improved greatly when the *Kiev* and *Minsk*, and, to a lesser extent, the *Moskva* and *Leningrad* were added to the fleet. While the latter ships improved their ASW reconnaissance more than their antisubmarine destructive capability, the *Kiev* does carry ten VTOL Yakolev (Yak) Foragers, which, however, have more limited ASW capability than Hormones. These airplanes suffer from limited range (120-mile operational radius) and frequently languish below decks with mechanical breakdowns. Reports of Yak difficulties, combined with recent revelations concerning Soviet technology in the construction of the MiG-25 Foxbat, raise several questions about the reliability of Russian aircraft in general and about shipboard aircraft in particular. If, for example, all Soviet planes, including the VTOL Yak, face the weight constraints of the Foxbat, carrier decks will take a beating. Further, the range estimates would have to be lowered greatly for follow-on series of aircraft. (The Foxbat used fuel at such a gluttonous rate that its effective range was 186 miles; in other words, it has an outboard range of no more than 93 miles before it had to return to base!)[17]

Finally in this investigation of Soviet ASW capability there remain several variables to ponder. Not all Soviet attack submarines would necessarily be assigned to ASW duty. In the *Okean 75* exercises, Western analysts spotted Soviet attack subs engaged in practice actions against surface shipping. Furthermore, *Okean 75* was unique because of the "increased priority" the Soviets seemingly assigned to sea denial and anti-SLOC missions. Accordingly, overtaxed Soviet commanders especially responsible for ASW missions will naturally tend to expect assistance from other branches of the armed services. Clearly, the Red Air Force (with 900 aircraft available in the Far East) can therefore expect in some situations to be summoned to the aid of the ASW mission. The number of planes and helicopters that might be cross-assigned in this fashion probably would depend greatly on the extent of their combat responsibilities in other theaters. Considering especially the range of the Trident II when eventually deployed, though, this multimission capability of Soviet air forces is highly constricted. Soviet ASW strategists face a more significant problem than simply one of obtaining air backup, however, in that they can no more assume their ASW forces will get to the open seas than they can assume their conventional attack vessels will. America's allies, such as Denmark, Norway, West Germany, Japan, Turkey, and Greece, all contribute defense capability to accentuate the Russian problems of egressing from its major choke points (the Kattegat for the Baltic, the Dardanelles for the Black Sea, the Korean Strait and the Kuriles for the Sea of Okhotsk and the Sea of Japan, and the GIUK barrier for the Barents Sea), which peculiarly affect the Soviet navy. A significant portion of Soviet ASW ships can assuredly be expected to fall victim to air strikes, mines, torpedoes, or surface-to-surface rockets *before they actually get to SSBN "hunting grounds."* Conceivably, in fact, given the high percentage of Soviet vessels in port at all times (in peacetime the Soviets deploy only 10 to 15 percent of their submarine fleet), including especially those directed at the U.S. strategic submarine fleet, whole components may be targeted for elimination at the very outset of war. Furthermore, the Soviets would suffer an extremely severe blow should any of their four helicopter cruisers be dispatched before getting into ASW action. In this light, the four-fleet geographic division of the Soviet navy presents even more staggering mobility problems. Assume that the *Kiev*, on duty in the Mediterranean, should try to reach the South Pacific from the Mediterranean for ASW activities. In trying to get through the Suez Canal it might face attack from Israel, possibly also from Saudi Arabia, NATO forces assigned to the Sixth Fleet, and perhaps even from Egyptian attacks. If the *Kiev* commander chose to exit through the Straits of Gibraltar, he would find himself once again exposed to NATO forces in such combinations, with Spanish admission to NATO now a fact, as British–Spanish, Spanish–U.S., or French–Spanish. If the *Kiev* should alter its deployment in the North Atlantic, heading for the Pacific, it would have to round the Horn of Africa, thereby exposing itself to the possibility of South African interception. In the unlikely event that any or all of these barriers fail, the *Kiev* could next be intercepted by ships and/or planes from Diego Garcia, to ignore throughout all such scenarios the continuous threat of Allied attack subs—all *before* it has launched a single aircraft for ASW work.[18]

Without a stunning new ASW breakthrough, an unlikely prospect since ASW progress occurs incrementally, to emphasize a point, the answer to the question "Are Soviet ASW forces capable of guaranteeing Russia relative security from Trident?" is "Absolutely *not*!" Whereas their capabilities admittedly are good, their effort expanding, their numbers growing, Trident's special abilities, *even acting independently of the fleet,* make it more than a match. Working in conjunction with the U.S. fleet as well as with the entire armed forces of our allies, the Trident can be made virtually invulnerable to all but extensive nuclear reponses in the form of open-ocean barrage and luck. If the Soviets could generally locate the Tridents and attacked with several MIRVed ICBMs per submarine, their chances of destroying the Tridents would improve—but not by much. According to the Office of Technology Assessment's 1981 report on alternative MX missile basing modes, "for conceptual purposes, an approximate rule of thumb would be 20,000 to 25,000 nuclear weapons are required to barrage a million square miles of deep ocean operating area." At the minimum, therefore, given Trident I's 14.5-million square miles of deployment, the Soviets would require at least 290,000 warheads for destruction of any submarines in the area, and for Trident II's 42.5 million miles the Russians would need 850,000 RVs, or roughly *fifty times the total inventory of all the nuclear weapons in existence in the world today*! The absurdity of the barrage strategy lies in the fact that, even if utilized in a highly selective fashion, it would leave the Soviets with no warheads for any other purpose and would be economically insane, environmentally suicidal, strategically ludicrous, and statistically ineffective against its intended target.[19]

Several undesirable side effects accompany even limited tactical nuclear attacks on submarines, as has been mentioned. In the case of the SS–N–12 cruise missile, for example, reduced sonar capabilities for subsequent attacks and increased uncertainty on the part of the launching unit would occur. Missing a Trident with such a weapon also means not only that the Trident would escape but also that the attacker will be committed for some time to the attack area to affirm his "kill" or to search further. The use of a nuclear warhead also requires full assurance no friendly vessels will suffer from the blast unless a calculated sacrifice is unavoidable. This disadvantageous tradeoff is not likely to assure a Soviet naval officer a promotion or the Order of Lenin in the absence of evidence a Trident was really destroyed. Finally, while there exists a happy medium between depth pressure destructively intensified by such a blast and the converse protection the water offers at particular depths, the reflective shock blasts alone of a nuclear missile will not destroy a Trident in most circumstances. According to *The Effects of Nuclear Weapons*, published by the Department of Energy, "in deep water [bottom] reflections are not significant," so, unless a Trident is in a shallow undersea valley, a nuclear shock wave would also fail to knock out the sub. An alert commander would correspondingly place his Trident in the most depth-optimal protection zone possible (100–200 feet) so a "near hit" on the surface would be subcritical. Although a Russian FRAS-1, SS-N-14, SS-N-15, or SS-N-16 would counter that strategy, range limitations hamper those weapons. Finally, the Deputy Chief of Naval Operations for Submarine Warfare would hardly employ an unmodified disposition of either Atlantic or Pacific Trident squadrons in such a fashion that it could be destroyed in any single blow.[20]

Sabotage and Espionage Vulnerabilities

Another threat to the Trident of a different order would be to try to render those Tridents (and Poseidons) inoperable before leaving port. Using spies, saboteurs, and commandos, attempts to destroy the Tridents in port certainly would occur even though countermeasures have been prepared. For security against frogmen and divers, hulls are checked for weapons like limpet mines by divers throughout maintenance overhauls. Tight security maintained on docks and on board the subs during maintenance overhaul enhances the protection offered the boats. The magnitude of this threat is substantial and often ignored. A perhaps suicidal onboard sabotage of the *Ohio*, for example, effected by a deep-cover Soviet penetration mission among the crew would have had the serious, perhaps disastrous effect in the course of the *Ohio*'s sea trials of placing the entire Trident class under investigative and suspensory action. Nonsuicidal variations are also conceivable, involving the exploitation of shipyard personnel, the imitation and substitution of nonfunctional physical components for explosive purposes, the totally veiled sabotage of an innocent but crucial structural componenet at the point of its manufacture by a subcontractor, posttrial remotely activated or timed destructive devices, or a diabolic misuse of a marijuana-smuggling ring to bring aboard enough "packaged" explosive or corrosive stuff "to last" a Trident's seventy-day tour. The 1982 suspended trial of two men before a Fresno federal court for stealing from the China Lake Naval Weapons Center a Sidewinder radar receiver in 1979 illustrates that Navy security at even maximum-security installations is not impenetrable. There was also the 1978 episode in which two gunmen robbed the nuclear submarine tender AS-37, *Dixon*, stationed in San Diego of $200,000, while earlier in October three men were arrested for plotting to recruit a twelve-man crew to steal, for an unspecified "resale," the nuclear-powered Sturgeon-class attack submarine SSN-674, *Trepang*, from its base at New London, Connecticut. A more successful heist occurred in July 1982 when a U.S. soldier for unknown reasons stole an M-60 tank from an army base and "ran amok" in Mannheim, Germany, before he plunged the vehicle into a river. Similarly, the ill-fated West German Air Force's version of the Lockheed F-104 Starfighter fighter-bomber remains under the suspicion that it "may have been sabotaged by Communist agents when its construction was originally modified to meet German requirements." In May 1983, a canvas bag full of NATO documents mysteriously turned up on a London street. Among the documents was a table giving details of submarine operation areas, speeds, depths, and other information. Nor have Trident submarines specifically escaped security breaches. On July 5, 1982, nine antinuclear protestors defaced a Trident submarine by spray-painting *USS Auschwitz* on the hull; they then proceeded to damage two sonar devices and to beat on the missile hatches with hammers. The protestors were mistakenly identified as shipyard workers and were not challenged at all as they "boarded the submarine from a boat they guided through the Thames River" to the Electric Boat shipyard. This rather astounding security breach might have gone completely unchallenged except that the criminals advertised their handiwork to a passing Navy worker, who only called police *after* seeing the defaced sub. One shudders to imagine the damage that could have been wreaked upon the whole Trident program (minus the two vessels already commissioned) if the protestors had been third-party terrorists who left behind on the grounds of the facility a tactical nuclear mine. The crucial point here is that Soviet intelligence has exhibited a continuous capability to conduct "dirty tricks" operations against free-world military technology and equipment, and, given the Trident's disproportionately incomparable strategic significance, action of this sort doubtless is receiving extensive Soviet attention. A "dirty tricks" budget for Department V ("Dark Core") of the Committee for State Security (KGB) and the Chief Intelligence Directorate of the Soviet General Staff (GRU) of, say, the equivalent of $30,000,000 for use against a $1.5 billion submarine is not out of proportion. Having permanent safer ports for Tridents thus prompted American defense officials to make a virtue of necessity in the rebasing of the SSBN squadron from Rota, Spain, to Kings Bay, Georgia.[21]

James Bond scenarios, with their newspaper headlines, often produce highly publicized but short-lived internal security crackdowns accompanied by a similar brief legislative uproar, usually in the form of a congressional committee investigation. More serious a threat to the Trident program in particular is the constant, seemingly unstoppable, flow of high-technology parts and information into Warsaw Pact nations that promises to resurface in ASW equipment. Former Central Intelligence Agency officer William Kampiles, arrested for the 1978 sale of a KH-11 (Keyhole) satellite manual to a Soviet agent in Greece, joined a number of other government personnel and private corporate officers facing trials for espionage. At the time of Kampiles' arrest no fewer than six major espionage trials involving high-technology sales to the USSR or its allies were under way around the world, from Switzerland and West Germany to Miami, Florida. Besides NATO secrets, the accused agents had sold satellite data and semiconductor components and had attempted to sell Tomahawk cruise-missle components and LAMPs antisubmarine secret data. Efforts to plug the leaks have failed (in 1980 a husband-wife team of agents, using a California optical company for a front, shipped high-technology "killer" laser-beam mirrors to the Soviets) and as early as 1979 the flood of material and information rolling into the Soviet bloc grew to such a level that the Russians flauntingly published a series of articles and books detailing "matters regarded highly secret" to the NATO alliance, as if to taunt Allied intelligence and security organizations. Of the more critical information published, the details of convoy defense against submarines and the location of submarine interception lanes directly damage the secrecy surrounding submarine tactics. However, the Trident itself became the object of a direct security breach in open publications when articles revealing the details of the Trident's sonar underwater detection systems appeared in print.[22]

"Technological promiscuity" has only increased since the "killer laser" scandal. In 1981 an Air Force missile officer "divulged enough information to Kremlin diplomats [about Titan ICBMs] to require changing targets, codes and security" for the missiles. At roughly the same time the Titan secrets made their illicit passage to the Kremlin, a former Hughes Aircraft Company engineer gave a Polish agent "more than 20 'highly classified reports' on advanced future U.S. weapons systems or their components.' " In addition to information on the "quiet radar" system designed for the Stealth bomber and "look-down/shoot-down" radar secrets (for use against low-flying cruise missiles), various Patriot and Hawk missile secrets and tank radar system information were also compromised. Again, Trident secrets were involved, with information on other sonar systems passed along as well. Attempts by the Reagan administration to stem the flow of unclassified technology to the Soviet Union, including computer technology and fibre-optics as well as capital itself, have received little support from American corporations, and European allies have cooperated even less in this regard. Acquisition of this technology allows Soviet planners to divert R&D money otherwise directed to solving these problems into other ventures, negating one of the few military advantages left to the United States. Undersecretary of State James L. Buckley supported this conclusion in 1982, saying the United States has learned it was a mistake to believe high-technology sales would alter Soviet behavior. They have, for example, embarked on a program of building nine new classes of submarine. Secretary of Defense Caspar Weinberger noted in May 1982 that the Soviet "strategic weapons program has benefitted substantially from the acquisition of western technology" and added that "the striking similarities between the U.S. Minuteman (missile) silo and the Soviet SS-13 silo very likely resulted from acquisition of U.S. documents." Thus the Trident appears to be at least as vulnerable to the "technology-security leak" as any other U.S. defense program. The Navy hardly needs to be reminded military security procedures all too often "secrete" at their level "nonsecrets" of a post or prior level. Ruthlessly effective security at the level of the subcontractor and the general contractor, together with counterintelligence and positive counterintelligence especially, are the surest ways to protect "real" secrets on an ongoing basis. In this regard there is a direct relationship between the Trident as a quality strategic weapon and the personnel quality of the Office of Naval Intelligence. Consequently, the damage level perhaps done here in the post-Watergate era deserves closer evaluation.[23]

Trident Compared to Other Ballistic-Missile Subs

Once these dangers are cleared, Tridents would move to their patrol lanes or firing positions, where their at-sea combat features would be employed. Several of these features have already been discussed, many of them novel and not to be found on Polaris/Poseidon submarines, including the fact that Trident has been specifically configured to confound ocean-area search. New defensive capabilities include MOSS (acoustic decoy minisubs); salinity, pressure, and other hydrodynamically related sensors in the hull; and, of course, its speed and diving abilities. Offensively, the Trident I missile features new computer targeting and control, while the sub itself will soon be served by an advanced form of extremely low frequency (ELF) communications. Its unique single-shaft multiblade variable screw further differentiates Trident relatively from its predecessors. Although performance improvements in sonar remain classified, where their installation requires unusual space it can be assumed they are particular to the Trident system. Several advanced antisonar programs benefit both the Trident and other subs, including the application of anechoic coating on the hull and electromagnetic degaussing. Yet certain technologies omitted from the Trident construction prevent it from attaining technological superiority *in all areas* over its Soviet counterparts. The newer Soviet *Alpha* attack sub and the newer *Typhoon* strategic sub display titanium hulls (although the *Typhoon*'s size appears to exact an extremely heavy toll on titanium stockpiles). This feature allows them to cruise faster, dive deeper, at least, and to foil MAD detection to the extent its outer hull is not directly magnetic. However, even the newest Soviet titanium-hulled boats remain comparatively noisy, leaving the Trident system overall the most advanced in the world.[24]

United States ASW Capability

In placing the Trident in a tactical and strategic perspective, therefore, Soviet submarines must be examined in the same manner so as to determine how much of their force could be directed at offensive ASW (sinking the Tridents) as opposed to defensive ASW (protecting their own SSBNs from U.S. attack subs and other U.S. ASW craft). Admiral Gorshkov's edict concerning operations "against the shore" awards the Soviet SSBN force the highest priority in funding and technology. Not surprisingly, then, two new Soviet classes have appeared in the last fifteen years (compared to one for the United States in the last twenty years). The *Delta I*, successor to the *Yankee* class, first appearing in 1973, followed by the *Delta II*, first reported in 1973, and by *Delta III*, first laid down in 1974, are somewhat comparable by mission to the Trident, while the gargantuan *Typhoon*, a 25,000-ton titan (according to *Jane's* Capt. John Moore) exceeds the Trident in tonnage by about 50 percent. Both Soviet classes feature nuclear power plants, but the *Typhoon* is distinctive apparently in having a 15-foot separation between the outer casing and the pressure hull to dampen the effects of a warhead explosion. Note should be made of the fact that the inclusion of this protective blast envelope around the pressure hull discloses at least two interesting insights into Soviet operational rationale: (1) the *Typhoon* implicitly is operationally noisy enough to require an acquatic "life-jacket," so to speak, against repeated concussive underwater explosions, including weapons in the atomic range; and (2) the need for this envelope is so great that the added dead tonnage is an acceptable burden on the power plant despite the decreased speed, greater strain, and increased fuel cost it unavoidably entails. So seen, the Trident's design manifests a more optimistic operational and tactical judgment about its survivability. The *Typhoon* carries twenty solid-fuel SS-NX-20 missiles with a range variously estimated between 4000 and 4200+ miles. The *Delta II* has undergone two structural changes—it was elongated from the *Delta I* by 54 feet and the *Delta III* from the *Delta II* by some 9 feet more, to accommodate the SS-N-18 liquid-fueled missile. Soviet subs are also equipped to carry mines or torpedoes, eighteen in the latter case. Unlike the *Typhoon* with its SS-NX-20 missiles, *Delta I* and *Delta II* carry SS-N-8 missiles with a range of 4000 miles, and *Delta III* carries SS-N-18 missiles of the same range. Some older classes of SSBNs continue to operate in the Soviet navy, including the *Yankee*, introduced in 1967, which should remain operational for several more years. *Yankee*s utilize the SS-N-6 liquid-fueled missile capable of a range of 1300–1600 miles, a feature requiring a *Yankee* to leave protected home waters some distance before it can fire. No information is available on electronics, sensors, diving rates, or launch-cycle times for the *Typhoon*. In all cases, though, only about 11 percent of Soviet subs are at sea at any given time, compared to at least 60 percent for American submarine forces.[25]

Once again, Soviet geography offers both advantages and disadvantages as far as submarine strategy is concerned. The majority of the *Delta*s, and, when they become operational, the *Typhoon*s as well, would probably be deployed, at least in part, in the Barents Sea along the Kola Pensinsula, within the protection of Soviet air cover. American attack subs would be placed in an extremely vulnerable position attempting to disrupt launches from that area, for, although satellites monitor surface movement and detect imminent launches, no surface craft or attack submarine is capable of attacking the *Delta*s in the Barents Sea without long-range standoff weapons such as the Harpoon missile adapted to an antisubmarine role or the Tomahawk cruise missile now being backfitted into U.S. 688 subs. *Los Angeles*-class employment in the latter role seems likely to occur from the depths of the Norwegian or Greenland seas or from the Arctic Ocean. On the other hand, it needs to be noted that the Barents Sea itself is bounded by Novaya Zemlya to the east and Franz Joseph Land and Spitzbergen to the north and is a marginally useful launching area, especially in ice-free seasons, because of the shallow depth of the primary exit out of the White Sea (a choke point within a choke point) and because of the area's overall shallowness, ranging roughly from about 100 feet in some areas to 500 feet, except on the southwestern perimeter axis between Narvik in Norway and Spitzbergen. This whole area seems subject to the disruption of submarine operations by the use of nuclear mines, for example, such as the submarine-laid or aircraft-dropped CAPTOR mine, to generate the Van Dorn effect. The whole area of the White Sea, including the Severodvinsk submarine yard, is vulnerable to NATO-theater weapons like the Pershing II, not to mention Trident missiles themselves. Moreover, up to 89 percent of the Soviet submarine fleet sits in port somewhere in the USSR, often without shelter and open to missile attack.

Most discussions of American ASW against Soviet submarines express concern primarily for preventing the Soviet attack submarine force from interrupting American and Canadian SLOC to Europe, virtually to the exclusion of all other ASW concerns. For example, little analysis of American ASW against Soviet SSBNs has appeared in public anywhere until recently, giving the impression, *doctrinally* at least, that the United States has written off this offensive threat as either impossible or too costly to counter. Indeed, as one observer notes, "there are powerful arguments supporting the belief that 'strategic' ASW should be rejected as a 'destabilizing' strategic defense objective." Further, as Thomas Burns contends in *The Secret War for the Ocean Depths*, "by the time a major ASW effort could be mounted [in the event of a future conflict], the SLBN force would long since have fired its missiles." Burns notes: "while the Russians plan for nuclear war at sea, the United States still appears to be concentrating its ASW program in the traditional areas: keeping the sea lanes open . . . and protecting the surface fleet." Current strategy in ASW, then, appears to conform to the Mutual Assured Destruction theory to a tee. However, in view of the current critical qualifications now arising about ICBM warfare with respect to MAD and the transition being affected in SLBMs from countervalue to counterforce (the Trident II), a corresponding transition in *actual* U.S. Navy strategic ASW practice may also be occurring. The evidence of this change is that "American nuclear attack submarines . . . [have occasionally slipped] . . . in and out of the Barents Sea and even in and out of Soviet ports without being discovered," despite the fact that "the Soviets have installed a hydroplane barrier stretching from the Kola Peninsula to Spitzbergen." These accomplishments suggest that our attack subs have a capability to counter the Soviet SOSUS system undetected or that they have bypassed this barrier by entering the Barents Sea between North East Land in the Svalbard Archipelago and Franz Joseph Land or, less likely, between the latter and Komsomlets Island of the North Land Archipelago to the east. The "silent service," in any case, is less likely to disclose a change of its operational attitude than the other services.[26]

A change appears to be in the wind in regard to this curious omission of U.S. anti-SSBN strategy. As described earlier, Soviet SSBNs can no longer presume to be able to fire their entire payloads even if they attempt to do so. Satellites will reveal their position, at least toward the terminal stages of their launch ascent, because of the associated infrared, biological, thermal hydrodynamic, and even overtly visual evidence. Detecting a *Delta* in this posture in Russian home waters is one thing, but destroying it is a different matter altogether. Any American trailing attack subs (assuming the United States had assigned an attack sub to trail every Soviet SSBN) would be an instant target itself for Soviet ASW. Since the Russians presumably would know more or less precisely when they planned to strike, they could begin the trailer-destruction phase of their own ASW immediately prior to their launch sequence. If this phase of undersea warfare follows a first-strike ICBM exchange, sufficient warning will be available to put U.S. attack submarines on an active alert; however, if conflict opens without such introductory strategic combat, more SSNs may be lost before Navy command can react informatively. The American command structure would experience tremendous strain: How long should the individual American submarine commander wait before attacking? How much verification would he require? *How many minutes?* Because of the extremely high numbers of weapons required to perform an open-ocean barrage, most authors ignore the option of the anti-SSBN nuclear strike. Indeed, as explained earlier in this chapter, from the Soviet viewpoint such a barrage would be useless against Tridents. But the reverse may not be true of Barents Sea deployment of Soviet ballistic-missile subs, especially in case all Barents Sea units launch simultaneously rather than in a staggered fashion, in which event a multiple semisurface exposure will take place, fulfilling the utility of a restricted open-ocean barrage, compounded, again, by the Van Dorn effect off the Barents Sea's shallow floor. A duplication of this in the Pacific case seems less likely because of range and differences in water depths. Although Soviet surface craft and planes can provide protection from U.S. attack submarines or U.S. airborne ASW platforms, these defenses are helpless against nuclear strikes, whether ICBM or SLBM. Moreover, as Russian SSBNs will be bottled up in their home ports in disproportionate numbers because of maintenance problems and the like, their vulnerability to both kinds of nuclear attack is extremely high. If, on the other hand, Soviet strategists manage to place a number of *Deltas* in the 800-foot-deep White Sea exit trench or in the shallower trenches off Novaya Zemlya, more RVs would be needed to knock them out. Satellites can generate rather precise images of these Soviet deployments for U.S. targeting, and with a nuclear weapon such images are accurate enough. Norman Polmar points out that the new Tomahawk cruise missile in its *tactical* variation, launched from *Los Angeles* attack subs, with its 1000-pound conventional payload and its 350+-mile range, could be especially devastating in this role. Of course, weapons of this type designed especially for ASW already exist, albeit with much shorter range. The United States has had SUBROC and ASROC combination rocket-torpedoes loaded with nuclear charges in its inventory for many years, although they are scheduled to be phased out in the late 1980s. A tactical nuclear surface-to-surface follow-on weapon was canceled in 1973, and for a time it appeared these tactical nuclear ASW weapons were being phased out in favor of torpedoes with conventional warheads. But in 1980 the Department of Defense approved a new "ASW standoff weapon," presumably with nuclear capability, which appears to be a Harpoon and Mk-46 torpedo hybrid. Except for this new combination, current standoff weapons have limited range and require the launching platform (either a cruiser, destroyer, or aircraft) to be in close proximity to its target—a highly vulnerable spot. Britain likewise has deployed similar nuclear depth bombs in its long-range sub-hunter aircraft, the Nimrod, as well as aboard three helicopter classes, but such delivery contains the dangers that a Soviet SSBN would have plenty of time to launch all of its missiles. Despite such stirrings, Western strategists, at least on the basis of unclassified material, overall seem rather disposed to pursuing a strategy, perhaps too pessimistically, guaranteeing home-protected Soviet SSBNs a basically rather undisturbed launch cycle, although, operationally speaking, alternatives to it exist. As naval expert Michael MccGwire points out, there are "no insuperable reasons why an intercontinental ballistic missile . . . should not be used against high value naval targets." If the United States decides to utilize the Tomahawk in any type of anti-SSBN activity, the launching platform now exists, as already mentioned. *Los Angeles* subs will be originally outfitted with vertical launch systems for the Tomahawk beginning with SSN 709, with the possibility of retrofitting all this class from SSN 688 to 708, while the entire attack fleet of all classes can be equipped with the forthcoming standoff weapon because it is tube-fired.[27]

An additional advantage gained with the relatively close grouping of Soviet SSBNs by the Barents Sea basing is time. Missiles launched directly from the Soviet Union appear on U.S. radar tracking screens within ten to fifteen minutes and almost instantly if SLBN launches are under the watch of geosynchronous satellite reconnaissance vehicles stationed 32,300 miles from earth. Initially, surprise works to the advantage of the launching platform in that it stands a greater chance of delivering its missiles. As discussed in chapter 1, however, this strategy risks an American retaliation in which the United States might launch under attack. While apparently possessing a launching advantage in home ports secure from U.S. SSN attacks, the Barents Sea–White Sea deployment creates a nuclear card game of very high stakes, one even the most brash Soviet strategists might not risk. A massive Poseidon, Trident, and/or Tomahawk retaliation could make the White Sea a nuclear graveyard.[28]

The Soviets nevertheless have other options. By sending *Delta*s under the polar ice cap they can avoid satellite detection and thereby reduce warning time by firing from small holes, fissures, and polyna in the ice pack. Or they can cruise in the deep trenches off the Atlantic, for example, in the Amazon Cone–Puerto Rico Trench line, the Pacific in the Peru–Chile Trench, near Cuba in the Cayman Trench, and in the Sohm Abyssal off the U.S. continental shelf. In the latter case a SLBM RV could reach Washington, D.C., in five to ten minutes and targets like Omaha in the central United States from ten to fifteen minutes. From some of these areas American ICBM bases would not even have enough warning time to launch under attack. Fortunately for the United States, Soviet subs greatly increase their chances of detection and invite trailing when they leave home waters. In the forefront of submarine surveillance programs to deal with these more dangerous deployments are satellites and the SOSUS systems. SOSUS, the Sound Surveillance System, on the ocean floors, and particularly operation CAESAR, which is a system of bottom-mounted hydrophones, "has put the United States into a commanding position in the field of ASW." Developed by Bell Telephone Laboratories in the 1950s, CAESAR was a "sophisticated system which would lay thousands of miles of complex underwater cables and hydrophone assemblies, first at key points along the Atlantic and Pacific coasts, later in other parts of the world." In the 1960s the East Coast CAESAR system became operational, followed by expanded CAESAR systems in shallow areas around Japan and Great Britain. Currently, no Soviet submarine can leave for the open seas at any point without presumably crossing a SOSUS/CAESAR location. (There are certain trenches near the North Sea—the north entrance to the Biscay Abyssal Plain, for example—which can protect a submarine, but most likely in the preliminary stages of prospective hostilities those would be mined or guarded by American submarines.) SOSUS lines have detected submarines up to 10,000 miles away, with more routine detection and identification possible at 3000 miles, concluding with an ability to determine the positions of Soviet submarines in some areas of the ocean to within 50 nautical miles. Indeed, according to a 1977 article in *Ocean Science News*, quoting from *Morskoy Sbornik*, U.S. Naval SOSUS picked up the sound of the crushing of the hull of the *Scorpion* on May 21, 1968, so clearly and accurately that the position of the watery implosion was fixed at a point about 450 miles southwest of the Azores. Subsequent air-sea search confirmed this fixing. Since the *Morskoy Sbornik* contained "a lot of hitherto secret information, including a description of U.S. undersea surveillance systems . . . the article seems to be the result of first-class [Soviet] naval intelligence." (The *Ocean Science News* apparently did not know *how* the Soviet intelligence was obtained but hopefully ONI does!) If the Soviets so desire, they could put the majority of their SSBNs near American shores with the probability that at least a very few would escape detection by SOSUS. As a *possibility* only, the question also arises as to whether some sort of a SOSUS detection line (or a Mexican ASW operational equivalent) exists between San Lucas on the tip of the peninsula of Baja California and Puerto Vallarta on the Mexican mainland, with which to detect a Soviet SSBN sneaking northward up the Gulf of California in its 100-fathom-plus waters for a SLBM "rabbit punch" of San Diego, Tuscon, and Denver. If some equivalent exists, being under the command of Mexican naval authorities, an additional question arises: What is the degree of cooperation established between United States and Mexican naval authorities with respect not only to this specific SSBN threat but with respect to other Soviet variations conducted along the Pacific coast of Baja especially and in the depths of the Gulf of Mexico and of Bahia de Campeche. Other outstanding issues aside, unlike Canada—with whom NATO ties of cooperation exist for these purposes—the Mexican government is not a NATO partner of the United States. However, the prior knowledge of many SSBNs being at sea near our shores issues a warning in itself, contributory to inciting increased U.S. ASW defense measures. Subs unable to avoid detection probably would be trailed by American attack subs, leaving those particular subs' chances of delivering any more than a missile apiece extremely dim. Weaknesses in the SOSUS system include the necessity of installing hydrophone cables in areas that are politically, technically, and geographically favorable. Such a system could not be installed in the

Peru–Chile Trench for geographic reasons or in the waters off Vietnam for political reasons. Consequently, the Navy has examined mobile systems to supplement SOSUS wherever it is located and to replace it where geography or politics prohibit its deployment. Latest interest focuses on towed sensor systems (SURTASS), suspended underwater anchored sensor systems (SASS), and rapidly deployed surveillance systems (RDSS). The former system is towed by surface ships, while RDSS is an air-droppable hydrophone array "somewhat akin to a giant sonobuoy system." Variation on RDSS include a dirigible-towed sensor system (MATASS) and a civilian-operated small towing ship called T-AGOS. Naval planners anticipate the purchase of twelve T-AGOS vessels and hope to have the first operational by 1984. The airship-towed system is still under evaluation. Experiments as exotic as air gun arrays are also being evaluated. Other ASW measures currently include backfitting twelve *Knox*-class ships with the advanced SQR-18 TACTAS (Tactical Towed Array Sonar). Eventually all forty-six ships will be backfitted. And even before encountering these sonar and surveillance systems, a Soviet sub comes under observation by American intelligence agents inside the USSR. This intelligence is so effective that Admiral Don Harvey, who was in charge of Naval intelligence, said his superiors expected him to tell them when a Russian sub "cast off the last line."[29]

Western ASW forces have had plenty of experience in practice against the Soviets. Crazy Ivan, the name given to any Soviet sub commander trying to exit the Danish straits, consistently puts Western forces through the full spectrum of evasive maneuvers and detection. Only those with access to classified materials know the success rate of tracking Crazy Ivan. Still, as early as 1978 *U.S. News & World Report*, followed by the 1981 article in *Scientific American*, reported substantial American advances in ASW.[30]

These systems and procedures not only hold significant implications for Soviet submarines but also provide an overall strategic framework in which the Trident should be considered. Any Soviet sub, regardless of its assignment, must first consider its own survivability, beginning with its initial detection. A "head count" of Soviet subs at sea, in comparison with their home ports of assignment, available first by satellite, becomes readily more apparent subsequently by search quadrants with SOSUS and SURTASS, giving the Trident commander a significant advantage as often as the informational integration of the recorded data is passed to him. Trident commanders, furnished the coordinates of SOSUS lines or MATASS or RDSS arrays, can cruise in those protected areas, forcing any Soviet hunter sub in the area unwillingly to reveal its location first to these systems' monitoring commands and, then, from them to Tridents. Other options bear investigation as well. T-AGOS vessels could accompany Tridents, or, if this practice is detected by the Soviets but secretly discontinued in a way not to precipitate Soviet behavioral modification, T-AGOS ships would make effective ASW operational decoys, serving to occupy valuable enemy ships and time ineffectually. Any off-station activity by the enemy for any reason unrelated to an anti-Trident mission works to a Trident's advantage. A Trident's singular goal in a conflict remains unqualified survival for whatever time it requires to fire its missiles, whether or not it itself thereafter survives and/or returns to an obliterated home port.

Soviet attack subs face two additional restrictions limiting their role as anti-Trident weapons: Western ASW and the Soviets' own strategic doctrinal requirement of sea denial. Both factors act to reduce the availability of boats for concentrated anti-Trident activity. The West has some control over the first factor, while the second necessitates Soviet judgment about priority assignments. Indeed, with respect to the latter policy area, according to Joel S. Wit, perhaps in recognition of their limited resources to conduct strategic ASW warfare in the post-Polaris era, "a large fraction of the Soviet ASW investment is probably made with the goal of improving tactical ASW capabilities designed to provide better protection for new Soviet SSBNs operating near the USSR." So observed, Trident's operational range increase over Polaris and less so over Poseidon apparently has effected a modestly revoluntionary change in Soviet ASW policy. The development of Trident II in 1989 should further reinforce this tendency, of course.[31]

Western antisubmarine warfare directed against attack subs begins the instant a conflict erupts. Indications are, for example, that Denmark would not await NATO's orders to mine the Kattegat and Skagerrak straits, sealing off the Baltic, if Soviet amphibious forces can first be prevented from paralyzing Danish action. Turkey might react the same way by mining the Dardenelles. Recently, mining as a primary form of ASW has aroused new interest. Said Rear Admiral Roy Hoffmann:

> Offensive mining . . . could restrict the full strategic attack capability of the Soviet navy. Ballistic missile-carrying submarines not deployed would be trapped at their bases until safe channels were swept for them. The missiles carried aboard Yankee class nuclear submarines would not be capable of destroying continental U.S. targets. Even the Delta class nuclear submarines . . . would be stripped of their principal advantage of secretly plying the ocean depths and would be vulnerable to air or missile attack.

Moreover, as Commander Jeremy Taylor notes, "mines have profound psychological and political impact. The danger of mines is invariably deemed to be vastly greater than the mines really present." No mining proponent fails to mention the fact that "more Japanese ships were sunk by mines than by any other means of naval warfare." Although Smith contends mines cannot be applied "with such expertness and perfection of timing as to bottle up in port the remainder of either side's ballistic missile submarines [not yet deployed]," the conceivable threat of mines brings into play "that seemingly most dreaded word in the whole vocabulary of strategic warfare: *destabilization*." Finally, mines are difficult to counter. The Soviet's force of 248 ocean minesweepers, with their 108 coastal, shallow-water, and miscellaneous minesweepers, would still be "hard pressed to counter a large coordinated U.S. mining attack." More than the United States, the Soviet Union is quite susceptible to mining in restricted channels and shallow waters. Only a single deep trench parallels the western shore of England, running between the Orkneys and the Faeroe Islands to the open water of the Atlantic. This underwater trench is a prime candidate for a minefield, together with minor fields between the Faeroes and Iceland and in the very narrow trench between Iceland and Greenland. Hoffmann points out the irony of mining as an ASW activity: "The nuclear weapons and propulsion plants that make modern ships and submarines such awesome machines of war may increase their vulnerability to offensive mines in home waters." Any hit in a coastal area could cause a radioactive contamination of nearby populations. Such a concern for the safety of the nearby populations could cause an "unusually high confidence level of sweep efforts" before ships could transit the area. Therefore, "once we have the advertised mines [in service] we can in most instances drop concrete blocks or old bathtubs and still get the desired psychological and political effect."[32]

Currently, the M65 Quickstrike provides the Navy's shallow-water and river mine capability; a rocket-propelled mine, the Continental Shelf mine, or IWD, has been designed for medium depths; and the Captor mine/torpedo (a tethered acoustic- or sonar-activated torpedo-type mine) draws the deepwater assignments. Submarines can launch their own mines, with a new mine called the SLMM in development, as well as the Captor and Mk-57, but this loading is at the expense of torpedoes. Captor has one quality that most mines lack: mobility. It is therefore probably the greatest mine threat technically to the Soviet submarine force in existence, if available in sufficient numbers. Unfortunately, mine warfare still is largely ignored and greatly undervalued as a fleet component for use in conjuction with the Trident—that is, as a "first line of defense" for the Tridents. Requirements for large numbers of mines—perhaps as many as 100,000—also temper some enthusiasm for their use as weapons and constitute a rather "unromantic" commitment from a budgetary viewpoint. The Soviets do not flinch at intensive mine deployments. Rear Admiral Don Harvey notes the Soviets have a "mind-bogglingly high" number of mines. Perhaps in reaction to this Soviet commitment, beginning in 1978 the Captor mine program received extensive funding, with the only other substantial jump in mine-related funds being $140.7 million for construction of a mine countermeasures ship in 1980. Otherwise, mines have indeed been "weapons that wait" for funds. Minelaying should be an integral part of both our anti-SSBN warfare and Trident-protective ASW strategy used in conjunction with SOSUS and trench-lurking attack submarines.[33]

Active Measures Against Soviet ASW Forces

SOSUS lines and the threat of mining illustrate two less active forms of ASW and represent only the outer fringe of a potential ASW network. Both Soviet subs hunting Tridents and Soviet SSBNs, once clear of minefields and their presence at sea announced by the SOSUS system, next face aerial and surface ASW efforts by the United States and Allied nations. Recent indications are that Germany plans to assist England and Norway in North Sea ASW operations with its fleet of eleven destroyers, nine frigates, with four type-122 available in 1982 and at least three others building, five Thetis corvettes, and twenty-four submarines. Once again, deepwater trenches in this area are scarce, thus choking off a path to the open seas for Soviet Baltic subs egressing and Arctic subs seeking Baltic admission. Great Britain's new "through-deck cruisers," basically V/STOL and helicopter carriers, form the modest core of a fleet, further fitted out with fifteen nuclear attack subs, two cruisers, more than thirteen guided-missile destroyers, and more than fifty frigates, designed with ASW in mind. Viewed in terms of ocean-bed topography, Soviet subs would favor sailing farther west through the GIUK Gap rather than risk entrapment in the shallow North Sea area. Naturally, major American ASW efforts will be directed against the GIUK Gap area to whatever extent other NATO naval forces are unable to perform the coverage. Canada militarily and Iceland geographically also lend assistance in patrolling these waters, although Canada's contributions have slipped during the administration of Pierre Trudeau. Aircraft and surface vessels share in watching the gap, with eighteen new Canadian CP-140 Aurora aircraft introduced in 1980, extensively modified from the U.S. Navy's P-3C Orions and supplementing American carrier- or land-based S-3 Vikings and Orions. The Aurora carries MAD, while the Orions' A-NEW Univac ASQ-114 ASW information-integration system combines "the endurance of the P-3C and the automated technology of the S-3." It has launching chutes for dropping 36 active and passive sonobuoys, with racks for 120 reserve sonobuoys, and it can combine torpedoes and depth charges. The Canadian ASW role is extremely crucial defensively against Soviet SSBN and offensively against SSN deployment in the Davis Strait and Baffin Bay areas between Greenland and Baffin Island, in the Arctic in general, and along the Pacific Coast between Bangor and the panhandle of Alaska. Orions have comprised the long-range land-based ASW aircraft in the American forces for several years. Dropping their sonobuoys, the Orions can extend the range of ASW units to well beyond the horizon. An updated version of the Orion promises even greater range, payload capacity, extended ASW abilities, and over-the-horizon targeting capabilities for American Harpoon missile-carrying surface ships. The modernized MAD carried by these planes doubles the range of the previous detectors. Orions themselves are even being backfitted with Harpoons as well as with new nonacoustic sensors. Some observers have suggested using Tomahawks on P-3s. Either weapon gives the P-3 the capability of damaging any subs on the surface or near it. Vikings are ship-based reconnaissance planes featuring a 2300-nm patrol range and an on-station operating time of several hours. Vikings, like the Orions, can carry their own torpedoes, mines, or bombs. They, like the Orions, have undergone improvement programs, with the latest designed to incorporate new computers, sonobuoy receivers, and chaff-countermeasure systems.[34]

Within a more limited range, ship-based helicopters can join in the submarine hunt. The SH-3 Sea King remains the workhorse of the ASW forces, and it has demonstrated an ability to determine submarine range with a high level of accuracy, to use a dipping sonar, and to conduct an attack based on its own real-time contacts rather than upon those based on board a ship-linked computer. Although no specific replacement has appeared in the Navy's plans, preeminent among new helicopter systems is the LAMPs (light airborne multipurpose system), including the updated LAMPs III. Originally, the LAMPs system used the Sikorsky SH-3 helicopter aboard antisubmarine destroyers, frigates, or cruisers, specially equipped with shipboard-to-aircraft computer links. The ship and helicopter work in unison as follows: helicopter-dropped sonobuoys feed back to the helicopter readings that are picked up automatically and analyzed by shipboard computers, with the information fed back to the helicopter. Newer LAMPs III helicopters are Sikorsky SH-60Bs (Seahawks) with a range of 100 n.m.—a 30 percent improvement over the SH-3—but they still maintain shipboard data links. Many LAMP ships can carry two helicopters, using them simultaneously or in relays. Each LAMPs sonobuoy mission resembles airplane sonobuoy missions where the sonobuoys are dropped in a pattern, with each new drop computed on the basis of previous detection indications, a process of progressively narrowing the search quadrant. With a LAMPs system, however, a ship is brought nearer to the action. Helicopters are fitted with ASW torpedoes and immediately following enemy submarine location can engage in their own attack, or the ship can use its ASROCs if within range. One naval analyst suggested tactically concentrating on using the LAMPs helicopter's speed to enable it to simply hit an opposing sub with an initial torpedo, slowing it down, and allowing the ship to make the "kill." In this manner, even the Mk-46 Advanced Lightweight Torpedo could prove a deadly "sub-killer" in that the explosive warhead of the submarine-fired and much heavier Mk-48 would not always be required to register the crippling blow.[35]

Should an enemy submarine escape (S-3 and P-3 patrol) aircraft, ASW helicopters, and LAMP ships, more traditional ASW vessels take over the search. These include any surface ship relying on its own sonar, as opposed to sonar data provided by sonabuoys from LAMPs helicopters. Among these ships, the *Spruance*-class destroyers, the *Ticonderoga-*, *Truxton-*, and *Belnap*-class frigates, and the *Virginia*-class cruisers display the most current ASW capabilities. These classes incorporate sonar mounted in the bow or hull and can carry helicopters (the *Virginia* class is currently undergoing modification that may cause it to be assigned non-ASW roles). A shipboard towed-array sonar usually is available as well. More traditional cruisers and destroyers without hull-mounted sonar, nevertheless, also represent potent ASW surface ships. These either tow their own sonar or receive targeting information from aircraft. Among these types of ships are the *Cleveland* class and the *Coontz* class. Experimental fast surface ships such as hydrofoils and air-cushion ships (sometimes called surface-effect ships) have found several vocal advocates among current naval theorists. Although impractical for bad-weather seagoing operations, these craft could provide excellent coastal ASW defense, but only after identification and location of the submarine by other sources. Their speed, combined with relatively heavy armaments, could make them formidable ASW attack vessels in shallow waters. Currently, however, they are being examined in an anti-surface-craft capacity. Finally, the Coast Guard has requested a more active ASW role and, consequently, has also challenged the Navy to help it by increasing its Coast Guard ASW funds. The *Bear*-class medium-endurance cutter and the *Hamilton*-class high-endurance cutter are the only Coast Guard ship classes having ASW capability, although other classes have had their ASW capability removed. Still, in comparison to the newer classes of ASW ships entering service with the Navy, even the best Coast Guard vessels are of limited capability in ASW operations.[36]

Once a U.S. surface craft locates a submarine, it can unleash a variety of weapons. Shipboard antisubmarine devices usually include torpedoes—either the short-range and lighter Mk-46 or the longer-range and heavier Mk-48—and, in the case of some of our allies, a mortar bomb-type depth charge. The Mk-46 and proposed Mk-XX standoff weapon can also be fired from ASROC launchers, extending their firing range by 25 to 30 miles. Current modifications of the Mk-46 give it improved acoustic guidance and countermeasure resistance features under the program code-named NEARTIP (near-term improvement program). Some analysts continue to express concern over the speed of these torpedoes. Newer *Alpha* class subs may be able to "outrun" a Mk-48 fired from either a trailing ship or dropped by an aircraft, given enough distance, speed, and warning. Worse, most modifications, even those adopted in the NEARTIP program, grew out of plans laid *prior to* the operational appearance of the *Alpha*, so these torpedoes possibly may still be underpowered. Fortunately, attacks on enemy subs can be focused from a variety of directions and with a variety of platforms, such as the P-3 Orion, which can drop a Mk-46 torpedo virtually on top of a submarine, thereby nullifying its speed advantage. As previously mentioned, ASROC comprises another major antisubmarine weapon. As a ship-launched missile it follows a ballistic-missile trajectory to a predetermined point, where the rocket component is jettisoned and either a torpedo or a depth charge drops into the water. If the ASROC is torpedo-armed, the torpedo homing mechanism and motor activate as the weapon hits the water. An ASROC armed with a depth charge sinks to a predetermined depth before detonation. Its Mk-17 depth bomb carries a nuclear charge. Of course, many ships feature standard torpedo mounts lacking the range but certainly not the accuracy of an ASROC. All other American ASW weapons consist of torpedoes. British ships also utilize a Mk-10 "Limbo" mortar system in addition to torpedoes. These mortars, usually mounted in sets of three, launch mortar bombs which can explode at various depths in a pattern; loading is automatic, and thus these weapons surpass traditional depth charges in rate of fire. Range restrictions (2000 meters), however, render the ASW mortar a short-range weapon. A similar short-range rocket launcher, the Hedgehog, appeared long ago aboard American ships; it has a similarly limited range, although it is being modified currently (under the designation Mousetrap).[37]

Another submarine represents a still more potent ASW weapon. According to Senator Robert Taft, Jr., the attack submarine "is perhaps the best anti-submarine weapon in our current force. . . ." Because American subs, especially the 688 class, are so quiet, they can conduct ASW procedures virtually in enemy waters with a high degree of success. The cost of these new attack subs, approximately $855 million for a FY 1983 order, may preclude purchase of enough of them to do the job thoroughly, prompting numerous calls for less expensive diesel subs.[38]

Weapons, capabilities, speeds—all of these factors tend to overindividualize one's perspective of conflict, suggesting that each vessel alone would draw its own target to hunt and presumably fight to the death. But the integration of all of the extensive ASW techniques and platforms under discussion with the Trident system must take into account both Soviet deployment and Soviet mission priority. For example, the *Kiev* will be of little use against a Pacific-based Trident if bottled up in the Mediterranean. Therefore, Soviet/American ASW missions must be examined with two questions in mind: First, what types of Soviet ships are deployed in what areas, and what is the prevailing American/NATO deployment response?; second, which missions must Soviet ships, particularly ASW vessels and attack subs, perform prior to their ASW assignment, and how much do these detract from other missions (such as tracking a Trident)?

Implications of ASW for NATO and Neutral Navies

Russia deploys a four-and-a-half ocean navy, with the Northern and Mediterranean fleets the largest and the Black Sea and Indian Ocean fleets playing second fiddle. In between ranks the Pacific fleet. Intelligence places the *Kiev, Leningrad,* and *Moskva* all in either the Northern group or the Mediterranean fleet, although recent reports suggest one of the *Kiev*-type ships is to be based in the Pacific. Apparently, then, the Soviets plan to use these ships as anti*attack* submarine forces against screening submarines in order better to facilitate Russian surface, aerial, and subsurface attacks on U.S. carriers. Some U.S. naval experts express optimism over a surface battle in the Mediterranean. Not only would Soviet ships have to contend with unpredictable combinations of NATO navies as might be supplied by Greece, Turkey, Italy, France, and Spain, but they would also face air attacks emanating from scores of land-based airfields. Simultaneously, they might have to fend off such potentially unfriendly and locally dangerous naval and air forces as those of Saudi Arabia, Israel, and possibly Egypt, perhaps compounded by the politically unpredictable naval behavior of such "proxy," "client," and "unaligned" states as Libya, Albania, and, especially, Yugoslavia. Quick diplomatic and military moves by the U.S.

could secure, mine, or close off the Dardanelles, the Suez Canal, Gibraltar, Alexandria, the Sicilian Straits, and the Aegean Sea. Meanwhile, unless the Soviet Union successfully invaded and secured Yugoslavia, its own air cover would become far less useful. Even Backfire-B bombers would find their range and options greatly taxed if operating from the southern reaches of the USSR. Conversely, as long as an American carrier remained afloat, Russian land and sea targets would be constantly threatened. Furthermore, *any* substantial contribution by the Greeks, Spanish, Turks, Italians, or Israelis could tie up Warsaw Pact forces in the Mediterranean and still place great pressure on Black Sea naval forces. How long would it require, for example, for a Soviet force to sweep mines from the Dardanelles and from the Aegean under repeated air and sea attacks? Would the Soviets be able to withdraw enough support ships from their attacks on American carriers to protect their minesweepers? The overall resulting strain on Soviet forces probably would force many of their attack submarines to fall back from strategic ASW assignments to participate in antiship defensive activities.[39]

Likewise, neutralist nations (Sweden and Finland) or ideologically torn governments (Iraq and Iran) might find themselves suddenly faced with the immediate choice of supporting the Soviets to the extent of allowing Soviet occupation and invasion, or resisting. In Sweden's case, with its substantial air force and coastal navy, the Soviets could not afford to ignore the possibility the Swedes might choose war when threatened with invasion. Other nations could pose similar thorny problems for the Soviets, and their loss of only one or two major ships to a nonaligned country could prove critical in the battles for control of the choke points.[40]

An even greater decision faces seaborne Soviet sub commanders whose communication links have been severed: whether to begin hunting U.S. SSBNs or commence antishipping missions. The degree to which there exists a missions priority list and the degree to which the individual submarine commander is empowered to fulfill or depart from it on his own authority is simply one of many unknowns. Every day a Russian attack sub spends at sea merely attempting to track even an older Poseidon boat means supplies bound for Europe from the United States advance one day closer. Those Soviet attack submarines "loosely" based in Cuba in wartime would be forced to commence operations only when well beyond the range of U.S. land-based air power. Cuban-based Soviet subs would be more or less geographically committed to shipping attacks on U.S. sea-lane traffic utilizing the Florida Straits or the Yucatan Channel rather than to anti-SSBN attacks. Division of labor among NATO forces could allow American

SLOC protection forces to shift their focus southward to cover both the Gulf and the Middle Atlantic threats. Canadians and the British have the capability to guard the northern shipping lanes across most of the Atlantic, leaving Portuguese and Spanish (Portugal's seventeen frigates and three *Daphne* submarines and Spain's twelve submarines, twelve destroyers, ten frigates, and two corvettes merit serious attention as ASW forces) ASW forces to link with American southern groups to cut off these attacks from Cuban-based subs. Clearly, no impenetrable NATO protective curtain could exist, but, once again, time favors the Allies in a war of attrition at sea. Few Soviet vessels carry either enough reloads or enough supplies to fight this kind of war. With the Mediterranean closed, the Cuban threat quarantined, with other American coasts defended by fairly modern forces such as Mexico's six destroyers and eighteen corvettes (albeit smaller forces in other cases), and with the Soviet Angolan base sure to come under air strikes and commando raids from South Africa, Soviet "superiority" in individual ship firepower will diminish daily in importance.[41]

Yet another aspect of the antishipping/anti-SSBN dilemma facing the Soviets will be greatly compounded by the addition of Trident: Polaris/Poseidon (British-American) subs might be withheld or redirected as European-theater fire-support vessels. Whereas Admiral Kelln testified in 1977 that no submarines "are dedicated to a theater mission," other reports suggest at least three Poseidon boats are assigned to NATO at all times for possible theater use. Whichever report is correct, some consideration has been given in any case to this role in the past and should be again. Not only would a Soviet commander have to decide to direct his attack sub's efforts at U.S. ballistic-missile submarines (including the necessity of surviving long enough to locate, track, and attack an American SSBN), he would also have to consider the possiblity that such a theater-targeted sub he has attempted to locate *may not even be targeted for any action against the Soviet homeland*! Soviet confusions of priority, like "General Winter" in 1812, can be a formidable ally.[42]

Trident's ability to survive Soviet antisubmarine-warfare techniques depends on several factors, including its own abilities individually against the Soviet attack sub, the provision of fleet support to it, the success of American ASW efforts against Soviet attack subs, and Trident's deployment modes, including the creation of cover of various sorts by allies. The United States clearly cannot approximate the Soviets' submarine production rate. Therefore the Navy has elected to produce quality-intensive submarines capable of escaping even large numbers of ASW ships and at the same time to develop ASW ships of its own combining multiple missions with deadly accurate search-and-kill capabilities, such as LAMPs. At some point, of course, numbers will win. One authority warns that any Soviet technological progress proportionately puts the Russians at an even greater advantage. Jaques Gansler, in *The Defense Industry*, in this regard cites Lanchester's law—overall military effectiveness is proportional to the unit effectiveness $\times$ units^2. Thus, as both sides grow more equal technologically, Russia's superiority actually increases disproportionately. Gansler notes how Germany in World War II emphasized qualitative superiority over the Allies' quantitative edge, in a losing cause. But the vast expanse of the oceans acts to dilute Lanchester's law. Submarines, whose main advantage is secrecy, stealth, and purpose, differ greatly from weapons which rely on firepower or fighting capability alone.[43] Other factors also affect the number of Soviet vessels available to be directed against Tridents at a given time: Soviet fleet deployment at the outbreak of war, success of Allied mining operations, success of Allied sonar lines, involvement of some friendly non-NATO powers (Israel, South Africa, Saudi Arabia, Egypt, and various South American countries), Soviet fleet priorities and ship availability for varied missions, and possible theater use of non-Trident SSBNs. Finally, certain natural advantages lie with the Western Allies in the event of any war with Russia. Besides being constantly split into separate fleet units with the corresponding complexities of combination, command, and coordination, the Soviet fleet is always under the handicap of being bottled up geographically. To traverse narrow straits in wartime makes a fleet the target of land and air forces as well as the enemy fleet. From a Soviet viewpoint, its fleet operations can be affected by sabotage and other unconventional operations, such as a U.S.-directed terrorist action sinking a vessel in the narrows of the Bosporus or, once again, blocking the Suez in the same way. While it is beyond the scope of this work to discuss land forces as they relate to control of choke points, nevertheless it is also a factor both the United States and the Soviets must ponder in the formulation of their contingency plans.

Moreover, for Soviet sea-based forces, time is a luxury they cannot afford. While the United States would grow stronger daily in its resupply and reinforcement effort for Europe, lightly supplied Soviet sea forces, cut off from most bases, would find themselves increasingly deprived of missile reloads, torpedoes, and even basic provisions. Time may indeed become the Soviets' worst enemy, especially as Trident II's extended range will soon make the Soviet SSBN hunt an even more arduous long-term proposition.

The Soviets' own ballistic-missile submarines are not invulnerable and should be aggressively and confidently attacked by U.S. ASW forces. It is not realistic to assume the United States could knock out many—if any—of them before some, at least, managed to fire a set or more of missiles. Nevertheless, Trident's at-sea success ultimately depends not only on surviving attacks by employing its own defensive weapons but also depends on pinning down as many types of Soviet forces as can be diverted to other activities unrelated to ASW. The more ships assigned to base protection, minesweeping, channel protection, and theater-weapons strikes, the better the situation for Trident. If American strategists do not doctrinally and operationally treat the Soviet SSBN danger in a "MAD" fashion, if all branches of the Navy, especially the mining arm, are also enthusiastically included in the *known* U.S. naval planning, and if *Los Angeles* subs with their Tomahawks are incorporated into the planning mix as well, no more than five Tridents at sea will virtually represent a sword of Damocles over the Soviet Union—a sword capable of repeated and very terminal slashes. In short, Trident as an exclusive individual threat is not nearly as intimidating strategically as Trident viewed within a panoply of threats.

Finally, since the Trident system per se must constantly be evaluated in a multidimensional setting of total force interaction, it is crucial that its objective survivability be constantly updated in very careful official pronouncements untainted by hysterical expectations of theoretical Soviet ASW "breakthroughs" (neither the Dialectic nor God appears to be on anybody's side in these matters!) or by "overexaggerated assessments of sea-based vulnerability" concocted by one or another vested interest competing with Trident to preserve (the B-1 bomber) or reassert (the MX) its profile in the TRIAD of strategic forces. An independent case for some of these systems *on their own merits* can be made (and is, in chap. 10). Provincially inspired mispronouncements on systems survivability may confuse the Soviets as to actual versus imaginary Trident threats, but the deterrence effect of Trident (and of the whole U.S. SSBN force in general) is depreciated rather than enhanced. The medieval stricture that factional controversy within a fortress should be contained in the face of the besiegers by the limits of a *Burgfrieden* should equally apply to the manner in which debates are conducted within the Pentagon over the systemic directions of the TRIAD. Where honest argument and real institutional forces are involved, technological progress in military affairs from the crossbow to the H-bomb will permanently disqualify only irrelevant, hysterical and radical commitments. The development of the "hybrid" cruise missile, in its different versions, proves that occasionally each service branch can get strategically "refreshed."[44]

9

Buck Rogers Meets Captain Nemo:

Technological Advances and Trident

And they heard a great voice from heaven saying unto them, Come up hither. And they ascended up to heaven in a cloud; and their enemies beheld them.
Revelation 11:12

Within the next two decades a variety of new weapons technologies will join the Trident in service, including laser and particle-beam weapons, cruise missiles, antiballistic-missile (ABM) systems, sea-launched anti-aircraft missiles, long-range ASW standoff weapons, the NAVSTAR (satellites) Global Positioning System, satellite-based laser communications, and the Seafarer extremely low frequency (ELF) communication system. These will complement existing space reconnaissance and communications systems, whose strategic importance continues to grow, enhanced by other technological advances. None of these was specifically developed with Trident in mind, yet it is likely, with the exception of U.S. attack submarines, that no other single weapons program will benefit so much from as many of the new technologies soon available as will Trident. Submarine strategy and tactics will require rapid doctrinal and practical revisions to accommodate even the two technologies becoming most immediately available in the next few years—the cruise missile and NAVSTAR. These tactics, and strategy in general, must also undergo a broader reassessment to better take advantage of the strategic interrelationship of space and the oceans. While few experts agree on the threats posed by Soviet space-related activities in 1982, fewer still doubt the Soviet's goals as they pertain to space, and virtually no one doubts they are advancing toward those goals at a steady pace. Should the United States employ a "worst case" approach and apply alleged Soviet threats to SLBM strategy, communication, reconnaissance, and submarine location, Trident missiles and communication satellites may be very much affected by Soviet space, antisatellite (ASAT), laser-beam, and particle-beam weapons developments. Thus, if only for the hypothetical purposes of assessing potential threats, it will be assumed here that Soviet technological pursuits in these areas are serious, progressively threatening, and relevant to the survival of seaborne deterrence in at least three ways:

1. The capability of these scientific developments in general to threaten the vital C^3I systems (Command, Communications, Control, and Intelligence) from which the submarine must obtain most, if not all, of its information about meteorological conditions, navigational fixes, war progress reports, target changes, and, of course, critical firing orders.
2. The capability of these technologies to threaten the SLBM during its vulnerable ascent stage and the vulnerability of the reentry vehicles vis-à-vis ABM capabilities, at least in the endoatmospheric stage of their descent.
3. The capability of the SSBN itself to avoid space-based detection and location equipment, which is becoming intensively threatening, especially during the vulnerable subsurface launch phase.*

Impact of the Cruise Missile on Trident

While it is difficult to determine which of the above Soviet threats to Trident is most immediate, U.S. technological advances have presented American naval strategists an improved version of a weapon long available to American armed services, the cruise missile. Hence, before analyzing the somewhat more removed current and future space threats, an examination of the cruise missile as it affects Trident may provide a measure of reality before discussion moves to the more theoretical, futuristic, and surrealistic realm of warfare in the galaxies.

Cruise missiles will affect Trident both strategically, in the definition and goals of its mission, and tactically, in the capabilities added to Trident's fighting potential or to auxiliary and integrated forces. While the cruise missile is not new and its use with submarines has been a subject of experimentation since the 1950s, only recently have technological advances made it an attractive, practical weapon for use on submarines. Germany used crude versions of cruise missiles in the form of the V-1 "buzz bomb," which required a catapult to get it airborne at its 450-mile-per-hour speed. The United States developed

*To reiterate the caveat of the previous chapter, much of this analysis, while relying on published sources, is nevertheless somewhat conjectural, especially as it applies to systems now under R&D.

its own cruise missiles, first the short-lived Loon, followed by the Air Force's Matador, which was a 39-foot-long pilotless jet airplane. Improved versions of the Matador, called the Mace A and Mace B, were deployed with Air Force squadrons in Europe and Okinawa. At the same time the Air Force deployed the Mace, the Navy experimented with its own cruise missile, the Regulus. Both surface ships and submarines could launch the Regulus, but, in the case of a submarine, the vessel had to surface before the crew could remove the Regulus' watertight hanger and prepare the missile for launching. The Regulus 2 missile made its first 1000-mile test run in 1957, remaining in service until 1960, when the Polaris made it obsolete as a strategic weapon. Remote-control capacity allowed the Navy to keep versions of the Regulus in operation as drone targets for some time. Although the United States continued to experiment with cruise missiles, long-range cruise missiles were phased out. The Soviets, however, continued to modernize and refine cruise-missile technology, offering a stunning demonstration of their advances in 1967, when a Soviet-supplied Egyptian missile sank the Israeli destroyer *Elath*. This incident prompted the United States to resume its cruise-missile program, eventually producing the Harpoon (now in service) and the Scad, or subsonic cruise armed decoy, which was terminated in 1973 before any missiles were actually produced.[1]

Among the Soviet cruise missiles, the SS-N-12 poses the greatest threat to the U.S. surface fleet and mainland. Its 300-n.m. range means a "Soviet submarine launching an SS-N-12 from the 100 fathom line could bring under fire a large part of this country." It is perhaps because the Soviets know only too well the capabilities of their own cruise missiles they have expressed such vocal opposition to the introduction of the Tomahawk by the United States.[2]

The Harpoon has proved a formidable antiship weapon (in 95 percent of its test launches it scored hits and its reliability is extraordinary) but its 60–80-mile range makes it unsuitable for long-range tactical or strategic operations. Technological advances in a number of areas have allowed U.S. defense planners to contemplate using cruise missiles in expanded roles, including deploying them as strategic weapons with nuclear warheads. In 1977 a series of developmental flights by a submarine-launched antiship cruise-missile version of the Tomahawk, followed by sub-launched land attack, ship-launched antiship, ship-launched attack, and ground-launched versions, demonstrated the feasibility of using the weapon in a variety of missions. Each utilizes a common aft section (not shared by the Air Force's air-launched cruise missile, ALCM), with different fore sections. The land-attack missile is capable of carrying either the W-80 nuclear warhead or conventional warheads, while the anti-ship version carries conventional modified Bullpup missile warheads of 1000 pounds with Harpoon guidance systems. Tomahawk's estimated range for the anti-ship missile is 300–500 n.m. and for the land-attack missile 1500+ n.m., which means that any vessel carrying Tomahawks must operate in forward areas, but its high accuracy makes it valuable nonetheless.[3]

Because of their range and accuracy, cruise missiles make formidable tactical weapons, as demonstrated by the sinking of the British destroyer *Sheffield* in the Falklands conflict of 1982. Yet they are not superweapons. Long-range surveillance AN/SPS-52C radar allows ships to defend themselves against cruise missiles, and the Soviets are developing similar radars. In 1977 the USSR tested high-frequency radio and radar beams designed to disrupt cruise missiles and low-flying aircraft by jamming the homing capability of the incoming missile and aircraft radar, although the exact nature of the defensive system remains the subject of controversy, with some authorities believing it to be an identification system rather than a jamming system. Electronic countermeasures (ECM), one of the more successful methods of attacking a cruise missile, involve such secrecy as to their deployment and effectiveness that little information exists to allow evaluation of the use of ECM. Once alerted to the presence of Exocet missiles in the Falklands, for example, British vessels exercised greater care and, as best as can now be determined, lost only one other ship to cruise missiles (although they did suffer losses from bombs and other types of weapons). In Lebanon, Israeli jets racked up an astounding kill ratio (against Russian-supplied Syrian MiG fighters—at last reports, 86 to zero!), utilizing the E2-C Hawkeye and its combination jamming and targeting systems in a definitive demonstration of ECM effectiveness. Still, American cruise missiles probably have counter-ECM capabilities, and, overall, they are on a different technological plane than the Argentine Exocets or the Israeli ECM warfare sets. Moreover, U.S. cruise-missile technology improves daily, with the Joint Cruise Missiles Project Office studying ways of using subsonic engines to improve reliability and increase range, with production of the new engines estimated for 1985. Perhaps a 2500-mile cruise missile is not far away.

Speculatively speaking, Trident submarines could utilize Tomahawks directly by carrying them individually for firing from torpedo tubes, from launchers in the forward ballast tank, or in a vertical launcher insert in lieu of one or more Trident missiles. Currently either seems a remote possibility, especially as long as the Trident submarines coming on line scarcely replace in numbers the Polaris/Poseidon subs being retired. But in the not-too-distant future the Navy will have the option of trade-offs involving cruise missiles placed on submarines. For example, a Trident could carry at least 192 Tomahawks housed in superimposed vertical Westinghouse rotary launchers contained as sets in each existing Trident missile tube. Since this estimate originally assumed Poseidon boats would be retrofitted, it is a low estimate due to the smaller-sized missile tubes on this class. Conceivably, a Trident could carry 64 to 112 more Tomahawks than a Poseidon. Furthermore, the problem that would face the Polaris/Poseidon subs converted to carry Tomahawks is still the same one that originally induced the Navy to build the Trident: the Polaris/Poseidon subs are nearing the end of their service lives. Of course, the Navy's plan to put cruise missiles on older submarines must weigh a third alternative: installation on the *Los Angeles*-class boats. Plans have appeared to place twelve vertical-launch tubes in the 688's forward ballast tanks behind the bow sonar. Some of the same difficult political and military choices would accompany this deployment as well, however. At present the U.S. attack submarine force is barely sufficient in numbers to carry out its primary mission of hunting other submarines. Removing even three submarines from the force for use only as cruise-missile subs would be a serious loss. However, deployment of Tomahawks aboard surface ships might better fill the breech. Plans for installing Tomahawk individual launchers aboard cruisers and battleships would make the battleships in particular, with their thick armor and massive 16-inch guns, power-projection vessels of a unique kind. Some reports have suggested the eventual installation of vertical box launchers for Tomahawks on the battlewagons, accompanied by the conversion of the aft deck to a V-TOL Harrier deck, further enhancing the ships' survivability by adding to their Aegis air-defense systems. Apparently the Reagan administration intends to make full use of the Tomahawk at sea; a presentation to Congress in 1982 by the DoD called for 3994 Tomahawk missiles at sea by 1989, filling 2600 launchers. By 1984 Navy Tomahawk launcher production will already exceed missile production, prompting the Navy in 1981 to consider a second-source supplier to relieve the burden on General Dynamics.[4]

None of these options requires immediate action. Certainly no Tridents will be considered for any duty except strategic deterrence until the Navy achieves complete replacement of the current at-sea missile force. A few *Los Angeles*-class subs were already being outfitted with vertical tubes in late 1982. Other *Los Angeles* boats are already deployed with Tomahawks, which can be fired from the torpedo tubes, although vertical launchers can launch faster and fire more missiles in a shorter period of time than can tube launchers.[5]

Significant implications for the Trident program will accompany any of these options. Aside from the obvious fact a Trident carrying no less than 192 conventionally armed land-attack or antiship missiles is no longer a strategic submarine, there are several operational considerations and problems introduced by the availability of American cruise-missile submarines. First, the opportunity for establishing a survivable "strategic reserve" for existing SSBNs now exists with Tomahawk. Previously, the expense of constructing submarines—the most survivable system—meant that SLBMs represented the only cost-effective weapon for strategic submarines. But the Tomahawk's favorable size, range, and cost now make it feasible to deploy cruise missiles in a strategic role aboard submarines. The missiles' disadvantages—subsonic speed and lack of punch, at least in the anti-ship version—prevent them from being used in an offensive strategic mode or in a first retaliatory strike (too many enemy defenses would survive until reduced by ICBMs and SLBMs) and make them impractical for hitting hard targets (due to their inadequate payloads). But, after enemy defenses have been weakened by heavier strategic weapons, the Tomahawk would be effective against soft targets.[6]

Second, deployment of a number of cruise-missile submarines in forward areas would not only provide tactical and theater support for land forces and threaten sea lanes but would exert additional pressure on both Soviet ASW and air defense as well. The former would have to treat them like SSBNs, and the defenses would have to treat the missiles as bombers. Each of these threats would exert different pressures on Soviet defensive forces. Support of NATO land forces provided by cruise-missile submarines could prove invaluable in slowing an enemy armored advance, and cruise missiles can be equipped with small packet explosives to be scattered over airfields, rendering them useless, in the manner of the Vulcan bomber raids on the airfield at Port Stanley. New precision-guided munitions will only enhance the cruise missile's capability. Subs carrying cruise missiles would help offset the Warsaw Pact's huge numerical advantage in tanks and infantry and can also serve as an antiship threat. The cruise-missile submarine will also effectively expand the Trident's strategic options by posing an added strategic threat to dilute Soviet ASW efforts. This role could vary through strategic-tactical mixtures of Tomahawk aboard Trident SSBNs and 688 classes (SSGN or, perhaps, to coin a newer classification, SSCNs), allowing cruise-missile boats to attract the attention of enemy ASW units otherwise available for attacks on Tridents and, secondly, to strike at ASW surface ships and ASW air bases to reduce the number of ASW units. All of this activity could utilize the Tomahawk's ultimate land-attack range of 2000 n.m., although out-of-sight attacks on surface vessels would require targeting information supplied by satellites or aircraft.

While the assistance afforded the strategic submarine force by a new group of SSGNs will be important and, in some cases, perhaps crucial, the prospect of mixing and proliferating strategic and tactical warheads in a single missile container lacking "functionally related observable differences" between its nuclear and conventional payload concerns a number of observers who see it as a threat to arms-control agreements. In his 1982 prizewinning *Proceedings* essay, Paul Johnson urges the U.S. Navy to adopt a pattern of deployment that would clearly differentiate between platforms carrying Tomahawks armed with nuclear warheads and those bearing conventional explosives. Fearing that a proliferation of Tomahawks will blur the tactical–strategic warhead differentiation, Johnson warns that without clear deployment patterns of such weapons arms control will be impossible. Joseph Bouchard and Michael MccGwire have independently recommended different controls on cruise missiles, ranging from Bouchard's suggestion of developing separate, clearly identifiable larger missile cases for strategic Tomahawks to MccGwire's recommendation that the United States abandon deployment of cruise missiles entirely. Indeed, a number of authorities on the subject of arms control have echoed the concerns of MccGwire, Johnson, and Bouchard,[7]

Undoubtedly the Tomahawk will pose severe problems for diplomats and others who seek verifiable arms limitations. Most discussions about the impact of cruise missiles on arms control have surprisingly expressed concern only with U.S. cruise missiles, although the Soviets have had thousands in operation for over a decade. Given the cruise missile's availability even in 1982 and its ease of production, any second- or third-echelon power that covets such a weapon either now has one or will be able to obtain one in the near future from Swedish, Soviet, French, or Israeli arms producers. Nevertheless, the advantages posed by the cruise missile to be gained for the Trident and the rest of the U.S. strategic triad are too important to give up without firm guarantees of verifiability on the part of the Soviets (not to mention other powers), including on-site inspections—something to which the USSR has never been willing to submit in the past. Without such guarantees, the Tomahawk must be viewed as an important asset whose role will expand considerably in the future and thereby enhance the capabilities of the Trident; it warrants specific consideration in this role.

NAVSTAR

The second major technological development soon to be directly affecting Trident is the Air Force's satellite system known as NAVSTAR.

Referred to also as the NAVSTAR Global Positioning System, or merely GPS, the system consists of a space-based radio positioning and navigation satellite constellation providing "10 meter accuracy of three-dimensional position data, velocity information, and system time to suitably equipped military users anywhere on or near the earth." Built by Rockwell, NAVSTAR gives position fixes four to five times more accurate than current radio navigation systems. Previously the Navy relied on five lightweight satellites for similar position-fixing information. Transit, as this earlier system was called, received its fifth satellite in May 1981, but its accuracy, while good, fell short of that available from NAVSTAR. Three major components make up the Global Positioning System: space satellites, control units, and the user's Magnavox receivers. Although many different users, including civilians, can use GPS, receivers differ in receiving capabilities, with submarines coded as class F, "high accuracy" units. As a security measure against an adversary using the codes, even should one manage to modify a receiver to pick up a higher code level, pseudo-random noise variations are also generated. The constellation of satellites orbits at different levels outward from about 12,500 miles in altitude; when the final group of satellite launches brings the full complement to eighteen in 1988, the U.S. would have complete and continuous position and navigation determination for all ships, aircraft, and submarines at sea anywhere on the globe. To guard against antisatellite activities, including attacks by laser-beam weapons or particle-beam weapons, the space component of NAVSTAR is hardened and "highly survivable," with constant modifications in power to provide greater jam resistance. High orbital altitudes further ensure the survivability of GPS, as "an adversary would have to negate more than one of the 18 satellites to erode the performance capability." But the distance separating the satellites (1500+ n.m.) means even a nuclear-armed interceptor could not destroy more than one. These characteristics, along with the power-boosting modifications mentioned previously, "make jamming very difficult." NAVSTAR transmits its information to one of four monitoring stations, each of which can correct the data to allow for the difference between the satellites' clocks and the monitors' clocks. Testing conducted from 1975 to 1979 led to "never-before-achieved CEPs [circular error probability, or accuracy] for . . . [aircraft-dropped] bombs." In these tests, the Air Force used a variety of antennae as receivers, with newer antijamming antennae becoming available in 1982. For the SSBN, however, NAVSTAR represents an even more significant breakthrough. A traditional weakness of the SLBM has been its lack of accuracy. Because the launching platform itself is moving, if only slightly, a much greater probability of error exists.

NAVSTAR, however, establishes a submarine's location with pinpoint accuracy (some estimate as close as 11 feet laterally and 12 feet in altitude), thereby giving SLBMs unprecedented counterforce capability. Tied to the inertial guidance systems on the subs, NAVSTAR will provide an added service even if it is disrupted, for the user can navigate by inertial navigation from the last GPS update.[8]

NAVSTAR has had its problems, though. A key component in the satellite, the rubidium clock, developed problems aboard the second satellite in 1979. The clocks continually broadcast the time to the receiver units, which then determine how long it takes the signal to travel from sender to receiver. Program officials displayed little concern with the malfunctions because they intended the first four satellites for experimental as well as functional purposes. Moreover, by 1982 the system operated so effectively and successfully that the Air Force was "examining a $1.3-billion offer from Rockwell International for a block buy of 28 NAVSTAR spacecraft," presumably for uses apart from those of the original satellite groups.[9]

Trident-Related Satellite Programs

Submarines rely on a variety of satellites performing a number of missions to feed them data. In addition to NAVSTAR, the Navy maintains four fleet-communications satellites in orbit as well as six non-NAVSTAR navigation and four surveillance satellites. Basically, a submarine receives its weather information, navigational fixes, and general at-sea communications from satellites. In the case of hostilities, war progress reports, target changes, amended operating instructions, or, in the case of an SSBN, the missile-firing orders, would also be sent via satellite, although in some cases only as a backup, for example, to Tacamo. Although the number of satellites in orbit changes virtually by the day, well over forty U.S. military satellites circle the earth currently. Several satellites sponsored by other branches of the armed forces or by nonmilitary organizations assist the Navy by sharing their satellite information. For example, the National Oceanographic Satellite System (NOSS) was partly funded by NASA, but its ocean sensors provide valuable data to the Navy. Space and Missile Systems Organization (SAMSO), an Air Force agency, provides surveillance spacecraft that in turn produce data ultimately available to other service branches. The large Air Force KH-11 reconnaissance satellites, which transmit pictures by digital radio links, have gradually replaced the high-resolution film satellites. Still, whenever possible, the Navy has tried to maintain its own independent reconnaissance and, most important, communication links, with the latter coming primarily from Fleet Communications

Satellites (FleetSatCom), with the Hughes LEASAT worldwide four-satellite communications system becoming available in the early 1980s. An even more complex and powerful extra-high-frequency satellite system, MILSTAR, will soon replace the FleetSatCom. It will utilize a higher orbit, perhaps even higher than NAVSTAR, and will be able to signal submarines. MILSTAR will probably become available in five years. As a cruise-missile defense, the Navy has also studied radar platforms launched to altitudes of 68,000 feet, giving the fleet a line-of-sight coverage of 300 n.m. Each platform could remain aloft for up to one year, with enough launched to establish a "keepout zone" for the fleet. But NAVSTAR differs from all of these other satellite systems (except Transit) chiefly in its orbit altitude—13,000 to 30,000 miles as opposed to typical satellite orbits of 500 to 1650 miles—and in its mission of feeding positioning data to the armed forces as opposed to conducting reconnaissance.[10]

Vulnerability of the C³I Link to ASATs and Lasers

In order to assess Trident's survivability, the threat to this important and potentially vulnerable communications link bears examination, although a Trident will clearly have several other vital C³I links, each of which will be discussed later in this chapter. Enemy attacks on C³I will probably include direct strikes and ECM operations against both ground- and sea-based receivers and transmitters (Tacamo and the submarine's communications equipment) and ASAT warfare. The latter threat, discussed here first, will most likely involve several types of attacks: "killer" satellites designed to explode in proximity to the target; "minelayer" satellites which spread debris in the target's path; jamming, including nuclear jamming by means of electromagnetic pulse; and directed-energy weapons installed in space battle stations, including laser-beam weapons and charged-particle-beam weapons.

Soviet efforts in the field of ASAT technology have been well concealed, with only sketchy information leaking through to the West. While it appears the Soviet Union has concentrated on collision-type antisatellites and charged-particle-beam weapons based on satellites (a description of these weapons and their capabilities appears in the footnote), they have also experimented with explosive/proximity satellites. Few subjects have elicited such heated debate in the U.S. intelligence community as the nature and progress of Soviet beam-weapon and ASAT programs. Revelations about Soviet advances in beam research apparently shocked the U.S. scientific community in 1976, when Russian scholar Leonid Rudakov presented his research at a scientific meeting. Widespread and sometimes bitter disagreement exists over both the uncommonly casual discussion of supposedly secret developments by Rudakov and over the implications of his research. While this controversy does not immediately pertain to the Trident, its ramifications as they involve the credibility of the Soviet threat (discussed in nn. 11 and 13) warrant attention.[11]

Long regarded by writers of science fiction as the macabre "death ray," the laser (light amplification by stimulated emission of radiation) first became a reality when Theodore Maiman demonstrated a working ruby laser at Hughes Aircraft Company in California in 1959, although theoretical work on lasers had aleady been well established. Of course, lasers can literally be death beams, but their use has broadened to include communications, accurate distance measurement, and medicine.

The laser research advanced by the Soviets in weapons is of a different nature and can be used for missile defense. Laser beams burn through the shells of missiles, destroying vital navigation circuits and fusing components inside. Protection from laser beams requires additional shielding along the fuselage. For ICBMs such as the Minuteman this is a relatively simple modification, as ICBMs have few size and weight restraints relative to the solution of the threat. Sub-launched missiles are a different matter. They must fit in relatively small tubes, a factor further limiting the amount of fuel they carry or the size of rocket motor they use. Thus, a significant leap in Soviet laser technology could threaten Trident missiles more than the particle-beam advances discussed later. Should a Trident missile require booster body protection, hence extra weight, the missile's range would significantly diminish. Potentially, then, a laser advance could offset the Trident's greatest advantage, its range. Some argue any large laser-weapon satellite system could render SLBMs obsolete, for the satellite could easily blast SLBMs, which must be fired singly, instead of in a salvo like ICBMs. But SLBMs have an advantage over laser weapons that ICBMs lack. A laser beam is aimed at the booster rockets, not at the warhead, so it must hit the target before the warheads separate from the boosters. Since laser beams cannot be bent (they travel in a straight line) the laser battle station must be in line-of-sight range of the missile. In this respect, an SLBM has a significant advantage over an ICBM, for the Soviets could not possibly deploy enough satellites to cover the entire ocean within line of sight of each other. An ICBM suffers from a number of factors not affecting an SLBM. Given the fixed position of even relatively mobile ICBMs, such as the MX mobile plan, the *general* launch coordinates and restricted azimuthal trajectory make satellite ABM defense possible, and there is ample warning. An SLBM can be fired from such a limitless area as to make computation of its trajectory impossible, and a submarine launch requires of the defender far quicker reaction time.[12]

The Soviets have developed either a highly advanced laser beam program, capable of putting battle stations using laser ASAT weapons into orbit by 1983, or a moderately advanced program (deployment in 1990), depending on the source consulted. *Aviation Week*, the respected trade publication, has generally accepted earlier estimates of Soviet operations dates than has the U.S. government. Most sources agree Soviet laser ASAT capabilities are no farther away than 1990, a point made inadvertently by Representative Ken Kramer (R-Colo.), who repeated secret testimony in public, saying the Pentagon expects "a large, permanent, manned [Soviet] orbital space complex to be operational by about 1990 . . . capable of effectively attacking ground, sea and air targets." As early as 1974 "the Soviets were spending a billion dollars a year on laser-weapon research and development." By 1977 evidence mounted that Soviet advances in laser and charged-particle-beam weapons had perhaps exceeded the capability American intelligence believed it could attain, and the controversy discussed in notes 11 and 13 occurred.[13]

General Kelly Burke predicted in April 1982 that the USSR would "beat the U.S. in orbiting a satellite killing laser weapon," but the achievement would "pack more of a political than a military punch." Richard DeLauer, Undersecretary of Defense for Research and Engineering, estimated the Soviet orbiting laser weapon could be in operation by 1983, although Burke qualified his own prediction by saying the Russians would "put an effective laser weapon in space in the next five to ten years." Burke viewed these early ASAT laser weapons as being able to "blind" U.S. satellites rather than destroy them. But these types of interruptions would threaten virtually all U.S. spy and communications satellites. Further advances in the power-source capacity of such space systems would give Soviet laser stations the capability to burn satellites, especially those lacking protective shielding, thereby knocking them out. They could also pose a threat to U.S. SLBMs or ICBMs, as shown later in this chapter.[14]

Perhaps due to advances in laser weaponry taking place behind the Iron Curtain, the United States somewhat belatedly rejuvenated its own beam-weapons program, with confirmation of Soviet activities prodding the military and defense agencies to reestablish whatever experimental programs they had seen die in the previous years through lack of interest or funding. Unfortunately, the development of any charged-particle-beam and laser-beam weapon was split among a number of agencies: the Navy, Air Force, Army, Defense Advanced Research Projects Agency (DARPA), and the Department of Energy all carried out types of laser-beam or particle-beam research, often independent of each other. In 1978, the Navy requested $6 million for development of a charged-particle-beam weapon under a program known as Chair Heritage. Numerous other smaller projects involving use of collective accelerators, one of the key technologies in beam development, appeared. Among these programs, Sandia Corporation received funds from the Energy Research and Development Administration and the Air Force's Office of Scientific Research, while the University of Maryland worked under the sponsorship of the National Science Foundation. Meanwhile the Navy, working with TRW Systems under DARPA, conducted a laser test early in 1978 in which its laser destroyed a high-speed antitank missile in flight. Despite the test's success, defense officials warned that the TRW laser was "only one step removed from laboratory-type equipment." Yet soon thereafter the Air Force modified a Boeing KC-135 to carry a laser turret for testing an airborne laser-beam weapon and successfully destroyed a moving target with the mother aircraft motionless on the ground. A subsequent airborne test of the laser weapon failed, but officials remained optimistic about its eventual success. Despite these remarkable advances, many defense authorities agree the United States still trails in the laser weapons race.[15]

In addition to maintaining a significant lead in laser-beam weaponry, the USSR has accomplished striking research test results in the realm of charged-particle beams. Although "beams" and lasers have sometimes been referred to synonymously, a laser is a beam of concentrated, amplified light, while a particle-beam weapon generates a beam of charged protons or electrons which destroy a target through heat or disruption of electronics. Like the laser, a particle beam travels at light speed. In November, 1978, Clarence Robinson, Jr., reported that the Soviets had conducted eight successful particle-beam tests from manned and unmanned spacecraft, including the Soyuz craft, Salyut manned space station, and Cosmos unmanned spacecraft. Moreover, Robinson noted, evidence indicated the beam tests within the Soviet Union were coming from numerous geographic locations, confirming "a national effort to produce a strategic weapon."[16] Although eventually planned for antimissile and antisatellite use, both United States and Soviet experts examined the potential for tactical application of particle-beam and laser-beam weaponry at sea as a sort of testing ground, although early assessments were pessimistic. In their April, 1979, *Scientific American* article, John Parmentola and Kosta Tsipis analyzed the use of a charged-particle-beam weapon in a shipboard defense capacity against antiship cruise missiles. Their examination concluded such a deployment was possible but that enemy use of chaff or other countermeasures could neutralize beam defenses with little effort or at minimal expense. William Wright, a physicist who had worked at Lawrence Livermore Laboratories, disagreed in the November 1979 issue of *Proceedings*, noting several advantages to particle-beam or laser-beam weapons. "[Beam] radiation can damage or disrupt electronics in arming, fusing, guidance, and control circuits in the antiship missile, even though the beam may not score a direct hit," he explained, and the beam weapons have "an essentially unlimited ammunition supply." (Wright, ironically, is one of the new generation of physicists working at Lawrence Livermore, where many of the original "beam doubters" scoffed at reports about the progress of Soviet research.) For Wright, the primary particle-beam use would be for cruise-missile defense. The weapon's natural advantages of unlimited ammunition, a high rate of fire, "extreme lethality," "unsaturability" (the inability of the enemy to overcome it with sheer numbers), and, in contradiction to Parmentola and Tsipis, according to Wright, relative invulnerability to countermeasures, "will have a profound effect on our tactical thinking." Critics suggest that the latter "advantage" does not exist and that countermeasures can reduce the weapon's effectiveness considerably. Wright also overlooked the state of radar technology, which currently can not locate and target a spread of incoming cruise missiles rapidly enough to allow a beam weapon to destroy them. The tactical implications of beam advances as they pertain to the Trident will be further discussed in chapter 12, but it should be immediately obvious that deployment of the Tomahawk could be quickly neutralized by the successful development of a particle beam used in an anti-cruise-missile mode. Most sources believe particle-beam-weapons technology is still much farther behind laser technology and is more often considered in a ballistic-missile-defense application than it is an ASAT weapon.[16]

Particle beams and lasers may play a substantial future role in the uses and effects of Trident. Because both the Trident I and Trident II missiles are ballistic missiles, any antimissile system in space is a potential threat to them. Should the Soviets perfect a particle-beam system and deploy it aboard satellites, a Trident would have greater success delivering its missiles than land-based ICBMs or land-based bombers because the satellites' beam weapons would not only require data from other tracking satellites but also have a limited range. If the Soviets had to deploy a satellite system in relatively small numbers, the chances are they would use them in an area defense, covering certain "windows" or approaches rather than in a city-by-city defense with one satellite assigned to each city. This type of area deployment could leave some holes between satellite lanes. If, for example, a Trident approached to fire near Kamchatka and its missiles remained in a trajectory beyond the range of the particle beam, the missiles could fly through unscathed. The Trident submarine's range is of little advantage in this case, for the sub would be looking for unprotected satellite lanes (say, from the Indian Ocean) as opposed to seeking distance from the target. But even used in ballistic-missile defense modes, particle-beam and laser-beam weapons aboard satellites may be susceptible to countermeasures, such as chaff or spinning the booster rocket so that the heat from a laser beam is dissipated. Mirrors could be attached to the missile shells, deflecting the beams harmlessly away, or the beam stations themselves could be attacked directly. Yet the implications for defense are staggering: "For the first time in the atomic age, the defense could defeat the offense."[17]

Less exotic than either the laser weapons or charged-particle-beam weapons are "killer" satellites, which can use a variety of weaponry (some as harmless as plain gravel) to destroy, blind, or otherwise incapacitate enemy satellites. In its October 26, 1981, issue, *Aviation Week* reported the "Soviet Union is operating in low earth orbit an antisatellite battle station equipped with clusters of infrared-homing guided interceptors" capable of destroying "multiple U.S. spacecraft." Previously, when the USSR "killer" satellites attacked target vehicles, the United States received warning from its own radars and satellites. The battle station has given the Russians a new "capability for sneak attacks on satellites." Yet another Soviet ASAT system consists of an interceptor launched by a variant of the SS-9/Scarp, which flies near its target, then explodes, destroying the target satellite with shrapnel. Since 1968 the USSR has conducted nineteen tests of this ASAT, with the March, 1981, test actually destroying a target, and, even if test success should be measured by requiring a more stringent one-kilometer efficiency range, twelve of the tests would still have to be considered successful. All launches have lifted off from Tyuratam and have so far only reached the altitudes achievable with the SS-9 (1400 miles), which is also the range used by the U.S. space shuttle as well as by most American reconnaissance and navigational satellites. Fortunately, NAVSTAR, the fleet communications satellites, and early-warning satellites fly at higher geosynchronous orbits, out of range of the SS-9. Yet the threats posed by the Soviet ASAT capabilities are serious and will only increase, eventually placing the Trident's "eyes and ears" in a dangerous position.[18]

American Efforts to Counter the Soviet Threat

The American response to Soviet ASAT activities has involved greater protection of existing U.S. satellite systems through jamproofing, hardening, and advanced maneuverability capabilities. Jamproofing can be effected by increasing a satellite's power supply or accommodating its transmitters with multiple-beam-array antennas for more flexible transmissions. Attempting to prevent proximity-explosive ASATs from destroying their target, as described above, or trying to prevent a satellite from falling prey to "gravel sprinkler" ASATs requires the contractor to harden the satellite using a variety of methods. For the circuitry, additional radiation shielding is needed. Warning sensors have been installed in most satellites—proximity radar, for example—and the actual body casings have been hardened to withstand explosions or shrapnel. Officials hope to defend against laser weapons and particle-beam weapons in a similar fashion. Most recently, planned Air Force satellites have been equipped with additional maneuvering propellant to enable them to escape physical interception, but these will not achieve orbit until 1986. Attempts to harden satellites against radiation have been more successful, with initial test results showing electronics systems aboard operational models could survive radiation blasts and remain active. Finally, the DoD planned to launch emergency satellites to replace any destroyed by ASATs, and at least one report has suggested the Trident may carry its own communications satellite to be launched on a Trident I missile in place of arming the missile with a warhead. A submarine could thereby establish its own communications link in an emergency, should the communications satellites previously serving it be destroyed. This concept could link the sub to headquarters for the crucial war firing orders, but the satellite would be subject to ASAT warfare itself after a short operating period, although it would not have to link the sub and command systems for long.[19]

American space activites have increased recently, and the United States has continued development of its own ASAT technology. Work on lasers and particle-beam weapons for space uses variably surpasses, equals, or trails the Soviets in specific categories. While these activities are beyond the scope of this study, the struggle to gain control of the "high ground" in this context continues, and the Trident stands to gain or lose as much as, if not more than, most other weapons systems, depending on the eventual victor.[20]

Submarine Communications

Submarine communications in a crisis situation will rely on a number of different and occasionally overlapping systems besides satellites, employing UHF, VHF, and ELF transmitters and receivers. Generally, communications transmissions fall into one of two categories: intramedium (through the water) and intermedium (airborne or land-based generation directed to the marine environment). Since the advent of nuclear attack submarines and ballistic-missile submarines, new requirements have impose the necessity of reliable around-the-clock transmission and receiving capability; that is, enemy ICBM or SLBM attacks on the United States would prompt the president to issue emergency action messages authorizing a nuclear counterattack.[21]

One method of ensuring communications survivability was to make the communications platform continuously airborne, transmitting information to an SSBN on a very low frequency (VLF) to a trailing submarine's floating-wire antenna. The signal, generated by a 200-kW transmitter, is fed into the antenna of the aircraft. As the aircraft makes a tight turn, the antenna dangles vertically. Maximum penetration of the VLF signal (30 to 50 feet into the water) makes it necessary for the submarine's trailing antenna to float upward to within this depth range. At slow speeds a buoy attached to a cross-looped antenna assists in this. For higher speeds, a 1673-foot wire is trailed, with the last 200 feet capable of receiving the VLF transmissions. In 1964 the Navy selected the Lockheed C-130 Hercules to carry the transmitter (redesignated the EC-130G), and the fleet of aircraft was called the TACAMO fleet (for Take Charge and Move Out). Two improvement programs have followed, although the "force has been allowed to gradually degrade," even though "it has been known for some time that Trident Class submarines . . . would place greater demands on TACAMO." From 1964 to 1980 the costs of equipment, aircraft, and improvements totaled roughly $342 millon, but new stresses associated with the Pacific deployment of the Tridents will require higher investment in the communications link. Presently, only one TACAMO would need to survive to "maintain connectivity with National Command Authorities," but Trident operations in the Pacific will require two aircraft airborne at all times. To replace the EC-130Gs and the upgraded EC-130G/Qs, the Reagan administration plans to phase in jet aircraft (the ECX). Countermeasures against TACAMO are difficult to employ—surface-to-air missiles cannot be used against such a randomly deployed target—and jamming, while "technically feasible, would require considerable effort by the Russians," not evident in available literature. Redundancy exists both operationally and within the transmitter systems themselves, with further redundency assured by TACAMO's link to satellites. A more substantial communications problem consists of the inability of the sub to perform the antenna-trailing maneuver only once every few hours if near-surface detection is to be kept to a minimum. Better signaling capabilities are still needed for emergency situations.[22]

Attempts to improve communications with submarines led to a

twenty-year struggle by the Navy to develop an extremely-low-frequency (ELF) system. Conceptualized in 1958 by Nicholas Christofilos at the University of California, Livermore, ELF generates its frequency through a huge antenna buried in the ground. The submarine receives the signal from an antenna the boat trails behind it, not toward the surface, thus avoiding an ascent to the shallower water required to deploy the TACAMO antenna. Site-selection studies conducted in 1965, 1970, and 1975 concluded the only suitable locations in the United States were in Michigan's Upper Peninsula, Wisconsin, and Minnesota. A test site at Clam Lake, Wisconsin, proved in fifty in-depth studies that the antenna had no negative effects on wildlife or the environment whatsoever, and electromagnetic effects fell below those generated by an electric blanket or a television set. Clam Lake tests also succeeded in signaling submarines as far away as Norway. A larger version of the program, SANGUINE, would have required massive land acquisition, but fortunately advances in ELF signal reception led to a scaled-down concept called SEAFARER. Wisconsin citizens opposed the DoD's plan for establishing the program there, while attempts to place it in Texas met with similar opposition. In 1977 Michigan Governor William Milliken invited the government to consider his state for an ELF site, provided the environmental impact statement proved acceptable. Plans to build a 2400-mile ELF antenna, spread through 4000 square miles, with a transmitter at K. I. Sawyer Air Force Base, were scaled down eventually to 58 miles of antenna. Known as the Austere ELF, this limited system will be operating by 1985 and will run its cables above the surface like telephone wires, returning below ground only at the end of the cable. Its limited antenna length makes it unable to send complex messages. Rather, it acts as a "bell ringer" to "page" a submarine with a coded fifteen-minute three-letter message, which is still an improvement over pre-ELF systems. The Michigan facility will be linked to the Clam Lake test facility. Reports that the system caused health problems have been disputed by numerous studies culminating with a conclusive investigation by the National Academy of Science, which endorsed the system's general safety in 1977.[23]

For Trident, the ELF system provides an important signaling service and also provides TACAMO something of a backup. Ferdinand Brand, the project manager for special communication projects in 1972, told the Senate Armed Services Committee investigating ELF that it could continue to operate even as parts of it were being destroyed and "you still get the message delivered." He also spoke of a "back-up" system to Tacamo called Pilgrim, a shore-to-ship communication system (which could contact surfaced subs) called

Gryphon, and a ship-to-shore communication called Hydrus, but it is not evident that these systems are in operation today. Redundancies such as these further guarantee the system's survivability, and, in turn, enhance Trident's survivability.[24]

Comments to the authors by anonymous sources admit that ELF obviously cannot survive direct hits: the point is that in the event of a slow-to-moderate escalation of international tension, ELF could deliver a warning simultaneously to *all* SSBNs at sea to take precautionary measures, including descending to depths of an assuredly undetectable level. Secondly, most sources find the suggestion of environmental danger posed by ELF almost humorous. The radiation level of ELF is less than that of a normal power line. Finally, ELF costs approximately $100 million or no more than one-fourteenth the cost of a single Trident, yet the entire SSBN fleet stands to gain from its deployment.

The newest contender in the communications game is the blue-green laser. Blue-green laser beams reflected off satellite-borne mirrors have drawn the attention of DARPA as an alternative to the Seafarer. Code named OSCAR (optional submarine communications by aerospace relay), the blue-green laser program received an additional $158 million beyond the $12.9 million it had already requested from the Senate Armed Services Commitee in 1981. Basically, the blue-green laser operates at a point in the spectrum that renders water transparent, allowing the beam to pass through without diffusing. Numerous companies have blue-green laser programs underway, because "the blue-green laser itself is the cornerstone of the [defense laser] program."[25]

Under the Navy's direction, various laboratories continue conducting experiments in two fields related to laser communication. Since lasers emit different colors of light according to the type of material used to stimulate the amplified light, one cannot readily vary the type of light emitted (blue-green, red, and the like). New methods of controlling the range of radiation currently allow scientists to change the color of radiation at will but are too low-powered for use in the applications discussed here. "Tuning" a laser beam in this manner has become the goal of some laser-beam research programs, so the uses of the beam theoretically could be changed with a tuner. Its application to submarines remains limited, for only the blue-green laser functions under water; theoretically it is impossible, at least at present, to foresee any "ray gun" type of laser use underwater. Yet an equally exotic Navy communication program related to lasers offers incredible possibilities. This project involves work on particles called neutrinos, which have no charge or mass. In essence, to a neutrino all matter is highly (though not completely) transparent. Navy-funded efforts have so far stressed the testing of accelerators to produce neutrino beams. If this type of accelerator is perfected, communications would take place by simply firing the neutrino into a point on the earth—for example, if the target were the Indian Ocean, one would aim the neutrino through a point in the continental U.S.—and the beam would travel through the earth virtually without opposition to be collected in a general area of ocean water near a submarine. From there a submarine's optical sensors could detect the neutrino message sent in Morse or some similar codified language. The problem is not with sending the neutrino beam but with its modulation and detection. One expert labels this program "way out" but notes it could be worth pursuing because of its unlimited potential for submarine communication. Even with major technological and theoretical breakthroughs, neither the tunable laser nor the neutrino communicator will have any immediate impact on the Trident system, although the blue-green laser communicator may.[26]

A pulsed blue-green laser could be mounted on a satellite or based on earth and reflected off a satellite. Once again, tracking and pointing the beam in an accurate fashion require further technological advances. Nevertheless, research on the laser was proceeding at such a slow pace that Anthony Battista, a House staff member, accused the Navy of deliberately ordering researchers at the Naval Electronics Laboratory Center to hold back on the blue-green laser in order to get funds for ELF. There may have been some truth to Battista's charge, but the Navy was understandably concerned about ELF, and, when asked in April, 1980, which system he would rather have, given similar funding, Dr. Gerald Dineen, Assistant Secretary of Defense for Command, Control, Communications, and Intelligence, replied he would rather have an ELF system. Roland Starkey, in his series of articles for *Military Electronics and Countermeasures*, summarizes the problems of the blue-green laser communications system: "[It] is a high-risk program projected to cost $1–2 billion . . . [and] requisite technology . . . could delay the [inital operating capability] to the mid-1990s, although more conservative estimates have placed this closer to 2000. Serious consideration must be given to overall systems vulnerability to [radio frequency] jamming, [electromagnetic pulse] effects, and killer satellites." Even the advanced research on neutrinos just discussed makes the blue-green laser communications system for the near future merely a supplement to ELF.[27]

In the realm of less exotic communications, submarines can release their own buoys to send messages. The Sippican AN/BRC-6 buoy can rise completely to the surface to establish UHF tactical voice communications, and the company has also developed the SLOT AN/

BRT-1 one-way VHF transmitter to send messages. These frequencies can be jammed easily and are useful for sending, not receiving.

Vulnerability to Electromagnetic Pulse

Each of the communications systems, as well as the command and control land systems and the satellites, may be vulnerable to electromagnetic pulses (EMP) from nuclear explosions. First encountered in the high-altitude nuclear testing over Johnson Island in the Pacific in 1958, the electromagnetic pulse (a microsecond burst of intense, broad-frequency radio-wave energy) posed virtually no threat to the "relatively primitive vacuum tube electronics," and was simply dismissed as "interference." With the electronic revolution of the 1960s and the widespread use of solid-state electronics, the vulnerability of systems to EMP increased. A greater understanding of EMP accompanied the studies of the Safeguard ABM system in the early 1970s, and hardening of electronic systems has comprised a substantial portion of budgets for electronic systems ever since. Modern circuitry "is about a million times as easily destroyed by an EMP" in comparison to older vacuum-tube models, due to the former's sensitivity to transient charges. Glass fiber, however, can resist EMP and is being incorporated into defense communications as quickly as possible.[28]

Susceptibility to EMP effects will afflict satellites lacking hardened circuitry. Hardening in this sense means that conductors of various sorts have surge arrestors or filters attached or that equipment be protected by foil or some other shielding. Optical fibers are gradually replacing wires, and important communications installations have auxiliary generators. Still, hardening against EMP, made more difficult by the seductive gains in processing and savings in weight available from delicate solid-state electronics, proceeds at a snail's pace. Indeed, a proposed strategic satellite system designed to survive EMP "did not get off the drawing board." Each NAVSTAR satellite carries a single-channel transponder for emergency action messages, but some doubt remains as to its ability to withstand EMP. The Bell System, which has a virtual monopoly on ground communications on which the Pentagon relies, until recently has been prohibited by the Federal Communications Commission from launching its own satellites, and even though the prohibition has been lifted, Bell's first satellite will not be in orbit until 1984. Worse, a full-scale test of circuits and systems of all military-related communications did not occur until 1982, with corrections taking place thereafter.[29]

Because the communications links will play a vital role in a future war and because submarines are especially handicapped in communicating with command centers, this element must be viewed as Trident's weakest link (excepting, perhaps, the sabotage and espionage vulnerabilities mentioned in chap. 8). Fortunately, EMP effects generated in all-out nuclear strike would be dissipated within an hour after the initial explosions. With TACAMO airborne and the submarine force alerted by ELF, EMP poses no immediate threat to Trident. Most authorities agree ELF could transmit its "bell ringer" signal before an ICBM launch could destroy it, although SLBMs fired from the Atlantic Coast could eliminate the ELF transmitters. In such a case, a Soviet SLBM attack would be in and of itself an act of war and would doubtless be coordinated with other Soviet ICBM launches, which would be recognized by U.S. satellites immediately as the opening of hostilities. Thus, elmination of ELF transmitters would be of little use; TACAMO and the bomber leg of the TRIAD would be airborne upon initial warning, guaranteeing an American second strike in conjunction with SLBMs (further increasing the need for the B-1B bomber, as discussed in the next chapter). In the direst of conceivable circumstances, an operational contingency plan may include a provision whereby the *repeated* failure of submarine commanders to receive confirmation of orders, from a variety of command sources in an improbably linked sequence of a mathematically highly reassuring order, may constitute an order itself. Such a contingency might be tested by a Trident command through the use of a radiation-measuring device lifted to the surface by a buoy, which would act in the same fashion as the external buoyant thermometer. An abnormally high radiation report would be confirmation of war. But the commander might also have at his disposal his own communication satellite mounted on Trident I missile in lieu of a warhead, as one source has suggested. This could be achieved by assigning one Trident missile the task of reestablishing communications (assuming, of course, the survival of at least one base!) by placing in orbit its own communications/navigation payload. In the absence of final satellite confirmation, the reader should be aware at this point of the *incredibly* high improbability of no communications being possible, combined with radiation levels of dangerous magnitudes; a negatively confirming order to launch would automatically exist *res sic stantibus*.

Parenthetically, in terms of "the Soviet penchant for control from above," one has to wonder whether or not Soviet C³ vulnerabilities have been thought through and protected in a comparable fashion with respect to the Soviet SSBN commander's individual authority to make an equivalent decision in similar circumstances. It seems very unlikely, given the nature of the Soviet system, and therefore probably constitutes an irremediable incompetence in the USSR's warmaking capability. Indeed, in the light of the experience with the "Whiskey on the Rocks" in 1982 off the coast of Sweden, it seems likely that all capital ships, including atomic-powered or atomic-armed vessels like submarines, are subjected to the dual authority of equivalently ranked military and political or commissariat officers, so often paralytic in effect.[30]

The second broad area of space activities affecting the Trident system—specifically, the Trident missile—is ballistic-missile defense, involving both space-based and ground-based countermeasures. A submarine and its missiles are particularly vulnerable during the approach and launch stages due to ease of location by satellite, aircraft, or even surface ships. Standoff ASW weapons would be most effective in this capacity if the surface ship or aircraft could get within range to destroy the submarine before it completed its firing sequence (as discussed in chap. 8). In this case, the vulnerability span is short and response would have to be prompt, while an effective countermeasure would be for the submarine to fire only a few missiles before diving, randomly repeating the maneuver.

When the missile reaches the apex of its trajectory it will fall within the range of satellite weapons systems, including lasers and particle-beam weapons. Difficulties associated with space use of lasers and particle-beam weapons have just been discussed, and for the moment Trident missiles face no substantial threat from any type of Soviet battle station. On their descent, however, they will be subject to antiballistic-missile barrages. Most analysts agree that the Soviets have broken various sections of the ABM Treaty, including testing their radars and their SA-5 missiles (perhaps being replaced by a new interceptor designated ABM-X-3) in an ABM mode. Surface-to-air missiles, used to set up atmospheric nuclear explosions to destroy incoming missiles, much like the American Safeguard system, have also been tested.

Information on Soviet "cheating" in this regard is admittedly difficult to obtain. One can nevertheless reverse the deductive process (used to determine the extent of the American beam-weapons programs by the progress of similar Soviet programs) and examine the level of U.S. ABM technology as a means of determining Soviet capabilities. According to William Davis, writing in *National Defense*, "ballistic missile defense will work," particularly against light attacks. The basic missile-defense system consists of (1) conventional or endoatmospheric terminal defense systems, (2) exoatmospheric defenses, and, if available, (3) "exotic" defenses.[31]

The lowest-altitude defense against ballistic missiles takes the form of a high-performance interceptor using a phase-array radar and using nuclear warheads to destroy the incoming missile. It is the most advanced system, with the U.S. Safeguard and Low Altitude Defense System (LoADs) examples that have been successfully tested. Distributed data processing, necessary for an effective system, is just one of the major milestones recently passed by U.S. researchers involved in the LoADs project. Exoatmospheric ballistic-missile defense, while not as advanced technologically as conventional terminal defense systems, is the "forgotten option" of the three levels. This concept involves using any of a combination of weapons (lasers, particle beams, or nonnuclear missiles) to strike the booster launch vehicle at its apex, prior to separation of its MIRVs. In the case of the American exoatmospheric defense, called Overlay, a plan for launching would send aloft several large missiles roughly the size of Titan missiles, each carrying several "kill" vehicles homed in by infrared sensing. This system suffers from technology lags and is vulnerable to decoys. The advantage of the system lies in its ability to destroy booster rockets without detonating the nuclear warheads, but it is limited by range and trajectory angles. With LoADs, the defender is assured the attacker will come to him, while in an exoatmospheric system the defending platform has to be "in the right place at the right time." But the nuclear explosion inherent in LoADs may destroy more than one incoming RV—the MX-missile Dense Pack basing plan relies on this phenomenon, known as fratricide—in which X-rays destroy the targeting mechanisms and internal electronics of incoming RVs, and dust and debris generated by the explosion shatter the RV shell. These antiballistic missiles "can provide an 'area defense' covering thousands of square miles with relatively few installations." Still, the nuclear explosion tends to disrupt many of the other defensive systems as well, especially phased-array radars, while the explosion's electromagnetic pulse could disrupt the circuits in other defensive systems, limiting the number of defensive launches. American officials also would be highly reluctant to deploy (let alone use) a nuclear weapon near a population center, even in a defensive capacity.[32]

Undesirable side effects that would accompany any low-altitude nuclear ABM system can be avoided with nonnuclear ABMs, at both high and low altitudes. Sandia Corp. has demonstrated the feasiblity of using a number of small conventionally armed missiles to release several hundred steel cubes to destroy enemy ICBMs or RVs; the High Frontier study, conducted by the Heritage Foundation, suggested that a number of orbiting platforms armed with interceptor missiles could similarly destroy ICBMs by impact alone.[33]

Other more exotic forms of ballistic-missile defense have also been suggested, among them:

- "Dust" Also called the environmental defense, this concept calls for the detonation of "clean" nuclear weapons near the target shortly before reentry vehicles arrive. The debris and dust lofted into the air would destroy an incoming RV by direct collision or by dust erosion of the RV's "skin."
- "Swarmjet" A low-altitude nonnuclear defense, this concept consists of firing thousands of "spin-stabilized, rocket propelled projectiles" at the incoming RV.
- "Bed of Nails" Richard Garwin, a member of the DoD's special Jason panel, which studied ICBM defense, suggested putting thousands of six-foot steel-reinforced rods to the north of each U.S. missile silo in an arc. Incoming missiles striking the rods would shred themselves.

Antiballistic missiles nonetheless provide both a fascinating paradox and a practical solution. The doctrinal paradox arises because the USSR has pursued a policy of offensive expansion and yet stresses defensive weapons and civil defense, while the United States has sought a defensive status and has instead concentrated on an offensive nuclear strategy. ABM systems provide a solution, however, in the case of accidental release of a missile (by either side) or in the event of a "psychotic commander" attack, something advocates have failed to state adequately.[34]

Different ballistic-missile defense options, studied by the Office of Technology Assessment in its review of alternative basing systems to the MX missile, concluded that a combination overlay (exoatmospheric) and underlay (endoatmospheric) defense would yield a survival probability of 62 percent in defending fixed ICBM silos, grouped relatively close together, thus increasing the probable kill capacity of the overlay system. These calculations also assumed overlay efficiency of 85 percent and do not take into account decoys or other penetration aids. A decoy reduces the overlay's efficiency to 43 percent. But while this theorectical discussion by the OTA is useful in gaining a general understanding of the difficulties involved in ballistic-missile defense, it must be clear the calculations involved in the OTA study are geared toward determining the survivability of U.S. MX missiles, not population centers or numerous military targets in the USSR. Hence, these calculations will take on added importance with the availability of the Trident II missile, which may be used against hard targets, but for now at least the unimproved version of Trident I will be used primarily against soft targets and reasonably vulnerable hard targets. Important doctrinal differences exist concerning the advantages and disadvantages of ballistic-missile defense as the United States and the USSR view them. For a U.S. ballistic-missile defense system to be considered "effective" it needs only to protect *enough* ICBMs to guarantee the country's capacity for a retaliatory second strike. But a Soviet missile-defense system would have completely different objectives, assuming the USSR would launch the first strike and U.S. ICBMs would have to "ride out" the attack. In those circumstances, much of the U.S. ICBM retaliatory force would be eliminated, leaving the retaliatory burden to SLBMs, especially to Trident I missiles as they gradually replace Poseidons. In this regard it is estimated that by 1986 submarine-launched ballistic missiles will provide five out of every six warheads actually penetrating Soviet defenses. Soviet planners, therefore, would probably attempt the following defense: protect soft targets in western Russia at the expense of those in the interior, even though the latter could be hit by Trident missiles from certain locations; spread ballistic-missile defenses out and concede some "leakage" on the assumption that Tridents would not dedicate as many RVs for soft-target redundancy as ICBMs would for hard targets; deal with the "leakage" with civil defense procedures.[35]

Any ballistic-missile defense system currently in the Russian arsenal will only be enhanced by laser or particle-beam weapons mounted on satellites. Little is known about Soviet high-altitude missile defenses, although the SA-5, tested in an ABM mode in violation of the 1972 ABM treaty, is apparently an effective low-altitude defense missile, and Galosh ABMs are currently deployed for low-altitude defense. Trident Mk-4 reentry vehicles, with their W76 warheads, will doubtless also carry numerous penetration aids, to this point considered more effective than those of the USSR's SS-20. Comparatively, then, with proper penetration aids, Mk-4 RVs should penetrate at least 80 percent of the time, meaning only one in five Soviet soft targets could expect protection by a ballistic-missile defense system. This calculation could change drastically in favor of either side, depending on the numbers of RVs per target and the concentration of defenses.[36]

Civil Defense as an Aspect of Efforts to Counter SLBMs

The Soviet prospects for protecting industry and populations from an attack through civil defense, while better than in the United States, are still not bright. Since the Soviet doctrine for victory is predicated on nuclear preemption initiating a short, violent but decisive war if deterrence fails, the American task is to force them into a "prolonged nuclear/conventional war on a global scale." So seen, the "Soviet Civil Defense program is treated as a part of the general military defense effort." To quote from a Soviet publication, "Civil Defense," under modern conditions civil defense has become "*a factor of strategic importance.*" From 1966 to 1976, the USSR spent over $65 billion on civil defense, placing two-thirds of its industrial capacity outside urban areas. American civil defense experts told Congress "The Soviets' view of their civil defense organizational structure is probably a favorable one," although Russian "public attitudes about surviving a nuclear war remain skeptical." Current estimates of a hypothetical war place U.S. casualties at 60 percent of the population, with losses in the USSR at only 10 percent, due largely to the fact that only 55 percent of its population lives in large cities. "Surgical" strikes, such as those discussed in Chapter 1, have been estimated to kill 800,000 to 50 million in the United States, while a general all-out surprise attack might exterminate 100 million.[37]

Exactly how many lives might be saved with the extensive civil defense procedures now in place in the Soviet Union is difficult to estimate. Once again, a Soviet civil defense plan, assuming a first strike from the USSR, has the advantage of advance warning for its own citizens (where a comparable U.S. plan would merely be reactive). Russian citizens engage in periodic defense drills, so Soviet population areas would probably be thinned out before Trident missiles arrived with their RVs. T. K. Jones, the Deputy Undersecretary of Defense for Strategic and Nuclear Forces, has estimated the United States, with proper civil defense measures, could fully recover economically and politically from a nuclear war with the Soviet Union in two to four years. Thus Russia, with its dispersed population and advance warning, must be given an even better chance of surviving a small retaliatory attack—an attack reduced in its devastating capacity by attrition due to U.S. losses absorbed during the first strike, by countermeasures (in the case of the Trident, ASW), and by in-flight attrition (ABMs, lasers, decoys, and outright malfunction). In short, too often the argument against American civil defense is that it is not realistic in the face of actual war-related losses and subsequent disease- and radiation-related losses. However, in the case of the USSR, civil defense, particularly against the primary retaliatory force of SLBMs, attempts to minimize these related losses by placing civil defense in an overall strategy combining the advantages of geography, surprise, ballistic-missile defense, ASW, and industrial relocation.[38]

Impact of the Trident II

The introduction after 1989 of Trident II promises to invert to some extent some of both the present form of Soviet vulnerabilities and the forms their defense now takes because of Trident II's (and the various improved versions of Trident I's) nearly incomparable improvements in RV numbers, penetration aids, payload optima, and especially accuracy. These characteristics will mean that insufficient accuracy is no longer inherently a deficiency of SLBMs in comparison with ICBMs. Therefore, as disarmament groups correctly concluded, Trident II is a counterforce weapon capable of destroying hardened targets with precision. As Trident IIs are phased into the total SLBM inventory, Soviet defense specialists will face the worst of all worlds: (1) the prevailing dilemmas already generated by Trident I's capabilities as discussed; (2) the converse of those dilemmas (hard target defense versus soft target defense, for example) as Trident II deployment progressively alters the composition of the U.S. SLBM force; (3) the mixture of dilemmas of a force partly composed of each missile.

Technological advances in space may yet compose a "fail-safe" ballistic-missile defense, utilizing particle beams and lasers as a front line backed up by endoatmospheric defenses for leaks and civil defense for more complete security. But advances in these areas will also threaten communications, thereby disrupting any civil defense measures taken after the fact. Direct attacks on satellites followed by EMP bursts would make civilian relocation and emergency action more difficult because of the suspension of communications. Still, given the level of technology available in 1982, little can currently be done by the Soviets to greatly reduce the losses from a retaliatory Poseidon-Trident attack in the area of ABM systems or civil defense. Currently, the RVs delivered by a Trident, while not completely immune to chaff, decoys, or ABMs, are impervious enought to inflict unacceptable levels of damage upon the Soviets. Tests have shown the Mk-500 Evader (MaRV) an effective and compatible warhead for the Trident, further reducing its susceptibility to countermeasures and ABMs. Even without further technological advances, however, Trident still faces a threat from space surveillance.[39]

Space Surveillance as an Aspect of Trident's Vulnerability

Phil Potts, a Royal Canadian Mounted Police constable, had the unique opportunity of seeing this Soviet threat first-hand. One morning in January, 1978, while conducting his routine duties, he suddenly noted a huge fireball in the sky followed by twenty smaller fireballs. Potts had just witnessed the failure and subsequent incineration of a Soviet Cosmos 954 satellite, designed for ocean surveillance. A nuclear-powered satellite, the 954 crashed into Canada, scattering its hundred pounds of enriched uranium around the countryside. On August 25, 1981, a Cosmos 434 slammed into Australia's outback with similar results. These Cosmos satellites, only two of hundreds launched in the last twelve years, represent Soviet efforts to bolster their intelligence and surveillance capabilities. The Cosmos 954 carried a powerful radar for ocean-scanning, powered by a compact nuclear reactor, a feat thought beyond the capabilities of Russian technology. No American satellite uses a nuclear reactor.[40]

Exactly what the Soviets can detect with their satellites, now supplemented by their manned orbiters, which have Soviet space teams in orbit virtually at all times, remains an area of controversy. Whether or not they can locate shallowly submerged submarines is hardly in question, but rather the concern is with the depth beyond which they cannot "see." Some observers believe a satellite can "see" to below 200 feet of the surface. If this assumption is correct, U.S. Tridents are safe from detection until they make their launch approach or until they approach the surface to communicate. Other sources maintain that satellites can use infrared and other surveillance techniques to detect changes in the temperature or salinity of the water, biological changes in plankton caused by the passage of a submarine, or underwater wake changes. The tremendous advantage the Soviets have gained in practical experience probably surpasses comparable American programs because Soviet launches, both manned and unmanned, outnumber those of the United States substantially.[41]

At present, space surveillance appears to be the least of the three major threats to Trident, although small advances in a number of areas could alter this assessment. Even if detected by space surveillance, a Trident will still have the capability to launch a few missiles, dive, and resurface again elsewhere for another launch. Soviet ASW forces will still be constrained by the myriad difficulties described in chapter 8. And a new threat will soon be added to Soviet space capabilities: U.S. ASAT activities. Secretary of Defense Caspar Weinberger announced on June 5, 1982, plans to deploy U.S. ASAT weapons within five years, giving the country the "capability to negate, as well as disrupt, hostile space systems," including surveillance satellites.[42]

Implications of U.S. Space Activity for the Navy

The U.S. antisatellite program has proceeded along three paths, with the earliest weapon—the jet-interceptor-launched ASAT—becoming available in the next few years. A second potential instrument of antisatellite warfare could be the space shuttle or, as they become available, a fleet of them. Soviet strategists have demonstrated remarkable concern over the space shuttle, because it gives the United States a maneuverable space vehicle capable of negating hostile satellites without necessarily destroying them and because it provides an outer-space "repair service" for damaged U.S. satellites. It also has the important defense mission of hoisting aloft numerous satellites at a fraction of the cost of launching them individually. Most important, however, the space shuttle provides the capability to build a space station for a permanent U.S. orbiting base.[43]

Less likely a threat to the Soviets in the near term, U.S. laser or particle-beam satellites may nevertheless prove useful as ASAT or antimissile weapons. While many American scientists still scoff at these concepts—Kosta Tsipis calls them "Laser Weapon Fairy Tales"—apparently the Soviets have never discounted their value or dismissed their deployment as a viable defense. Experiments performed by the U.S. space shuttle will shed much light on the progress of laser ASAT and antimissile research.[44]

Thus, to restate perhaps redundantly one of the major themes of chapter 8, the Trident's effectiveness depends not just on several other systems acting independently but also on their total interaction with Trident. The survival of NAVSTAR and ELF stations, and therefore the survival of an effective SSBN force, may depend on greater attention to space. In this regard, the Navy should carefully consider its own role in supporting space systems and other programs not falling directly under its own budget lines. Perhaps, in this regard, an ASAT system or ABM system should specifically be assigned for NAVSTAR and ELF protection. Likewise, Trident missiles as deterrents will work only if communications with submarines can be made absolutely secure, if Trident missiles can defend themselves against Soviet space- and ground-based antimissile attacks, if Soviet ABMs can be negated through penetration aids and maneuverability, and if the moderating effects of Soviet civil defense can somehow be offset. To come full circle, perhaps one of the most significant additions to the U.S. arsenal, from Trident's perspective, is the deployment of the Tomahawk. By aiding in diffusing and diluting Soviet defenses—operationally, budgetarily, and organizationally—Tomahawk minimizes Soviet advantages in civil defense and ABMs. Conversely, American advantages in technology, especially as they pertain to space activities and communications, present the Navy an opportunity to enhance the survivability of its communications "weak link." At present, the greatest single technological edge the United States has in space is the shuttle. These apparently unrelated technologies are, indeed, quite related, and only a few hurdles need to be cleared before their connections become evident with crystal clarity. It will not be long before the American public is greeted by the news that the crew of the *Columbia* and the captain of the *Ohio* have mutually exchanged Christmas greetings over a space-to-sea ELF link! How ironic that the Trident should have as its two greatest potential technological allies a slow "buzz bomb," all but abandoned at one time by U.S. defense officials, and a NASA "eighteen-wheeler" belonging more to the domain of Buck Rogers than that of Captain Nemo.

10

Hydras and Half-breeds:

Trident System Alternatives, Substitutions, and Options

The American democratic process . . . virtually guarantees the possibility of technological, strategic, or political filibuster.
—Colin Gray, *The MX ICBM*

Even as the first Tridents put to sea, discussion continues about possible alternative programs, systems, and options for the sea-based deterrent force. In February, 1980, the Congressional Budget Office published a paper outlining several of the options. Others appeared during the STRAT-X study and during the initial decision period that settled on the Trident design in 1972, but they have continued to resurface throughout the funding and construction processes. While many of the suggestions, such as Hydra and SUM, were clearly intended to be alternative basing modes for the land-based MX missile, their discussion here is for the purpose of objectively evaluating them first as basing modes for MX, some of which are seaborne; second as potential competitors, at one time or another, to the Trident concept; and, third as they fit overall into the strategic TRIAD. As the debate over the MX missile and B-1 bomber gathered steam in the 1970s, the classical TRIAD concept became blurred. Thus, in addition to alternative sea-based deterrents, some sources originally suggested either a variety of land-based and air-based missile systems, a manned bomber system, or combinations thereof as an option to having a deep-sea strategic submarine force at all. As Trident's capabilities became evident, the arguments for replacing the submarine leg of TRIAD virtually disappeared, although critics still insisted that other submarine or sea-based systems would be cheaper and more effective than Trident. The advantages and disadvantages posed by each of these suggestions requires some analysis to understand better the final selection of the Trident over the sea-based alternatives and the difficulties involved in establishing a proper strategic force mixture. Moreover, the TRIAD concept, which plays a major role in deciding to accept or reject the various alternative plans, ultimately poses the single greatest argument against many of the alternative systems.[1]

Deep-diving sea-based alternatives to the Trident system have included at least five major submarine systems (plus variations), one surface system, and one combination surface/subsurface version. In the area of submarine options, this work has already dealt in detail with one of those options: the SSBN-X. Three other cruising submarines have been suggested: a new "necked-down" Trident, an elongated Poseidon, and a modernized regular-sized Poseidon. As a fifth alternative, Michael MccGwire has proposed small tethered submarines or diesel-powered submarines known as shallow underwater missile (SUM) systems, for shallow cruising only, an argument revived in the MX option study made by the Office of Technology Assessment. Others have suggested a seabed deterrent using underwater MX bases. Many of the submarine arguments already have been rendered academic by the Reagan administration's decision to develop the larger Trident II missile (which makes the use of Poseidon-sized subs impossible), but to understand that and earlier decisions, we must nonetheless examine the options. Suggestions for surface alternatives have generally centered on a freighter-type ship carrying ballistic missiles or a "cross-breed" system using surface vessels to drop containerized ballistic missiles into the water. Theoretically, these canisters could receive an order to fire by radio. Still another version of this option featured the canister anchored on the seabed, whether the seabed is in Hudson Bay, on the continental shelves, or in the Great Lakes.[2]

Early Submarine Options to Trident

Among the various submarine options, the most serious consideration has been directed to the shortened, or "necked-down," Trident. This provided the basis for the SSBN-X option, albeit with a different reactor and sonar. The necked-down Trident involves a proposal to narrow down the submarine's hull to 33 feet (from 42) aft of the missile compartment, thereby saving 3000 tons in displacement. This version could still carry twenty-four Trident II missiles but presumably would utilize a smaller reactor. Therefore any discussion of optional or alternative platforms based upon cost-effectiveness must deal with the following questions: Is a smaller reactor available, and would it have enough power to move a 15,000-ton submarine through the water with a reserve of power sufficient for high-speed evasive maneuvers? A series of smaller reactors does exist, although some sources have hinted that U.S. reactors are inferior to their Russian counterparts when power is measured as a function of weight and volume. These smaller reactors obviously can propel a Trident, but it is unclear how fast it could move even a lightened version. Money saved in this case is at the expense of speed lost. A less-costly reactor equals a slower and noisier submarine, a point Rickover has made for years. Its speed allows the Trident to move within target range sooner, adding to its total time of availability on station, and decreasing costs by taking advantage of fewer boats to generate the same total patrol time. Compare this with the four-submarine British force, which can usually keep only one sub on station while a second makes its way to the patrol area, a third sails home from there, and a fourth is in drydock. In the case of Trident submarines, three perform the job of four—one on station (when sailing to its patrol area, it is still within target range), one returning (also in target range), and one in drydock.[3]

Another factor to consider when trading reactor size for quick cost savings is noise. Smaller reactors, like small automobile engines, have to turn the turbines more rapidly to attain a speed equal to what a larger reactor can generate. This relatively greater strain increases noise. Few submariners wish to sacrifice operational quietness for any quality, including speed. The Trident system has been designed with the best combination of speed and quietness attainable. Replacing the large reactor with a smaller one would simply sacrifice the synthesis of both advantages. Finally, to remove several hundred cubic feet might greatly reduce storage areas, limiting the at-sea availability of the vessel. Each port call for the purpose of replenishment reduces the time spent on station, so much of the advantage a Trident gains over other ballistic-missile subs disappears by forcing it into more port time. Worse, from a submariner's viewpoint, the reconfiguration of the hull would also generate a hydrodynamically less acceptable sonar signature.

In short, a modification that cuts down the size of the hull in such a way as to require a smaller reactor or to displace storage area must be carefully scrutinized, for not only could many of the premises upon which the Trident concept was introduced be altered, but a reduction of the on-station time might also increase the cost beyond present levels. To decrease the on-station time of each Trident by one-tenth will eventually require another submarine to make it up since ten such reductions would require the equivalent compensation of one extra submarine. If, as proponents claim, a necked-down Trident could save 30 percent, a force of ten theoretically would save nearly $2 billion, even with the addition of an extra sub. However, these savings do not include reactor cost ($500 million at least), crew cost and training, supplies, added basing facilities, and inflation-related costs of the time added to produce the extra submarine.

With deployment of the Trident II missile in 1989 the Congressional Budget Office has estimated "a smaller SSBN that could still carry the Trident II missile might lower total costs by less than 2 percent (less than $1 billion over 30 years) at twice today's capability level [4000 warheads at sea]." This Trident II level assumes a Trident force of nine vessels but does not establish the force size of the smaller subs. If each smaller sub is 10 percent less available, then eleven subs must be built to do the same job as ten Tridents. Development costs of a new submarine are significant by themselves (80 cents out of each R&D dollar goes for development), but the cost of compensating for the off-station time would be at least equal to the cost of an additional sub (80 percent of a Trident's cost, to be generous, or still roughly a billion dollars). Not counting development costs and extra crew pay, missiles, fuel, and basing space, a smaller replacement sub could cost more to build and maintain than it would save over thirty years. In reality, such an abrupt alteration would cost far more: Electric Boat, for example, would presumably be expected to go out of the business of building the presently sized Trident, while other subsidiary factories would have to retool, more submarine crews (*of the same skill level*) would have to be provided, and supplies would have to be increased. Moreover, since the Navy generally does not include the costs of reactors when figuring prices, the actual added cost of building more submarines would probably be well beyond any possible savings. Building more new or necked-down small but less capable vessels makes little sense, if any.[4]

The Congressional Budget Office also examined two Poseidon variations: one with a hull stretched from 425 to 500 feet, with a 33-foot diameter, displacing 10,000 tons and carrying twenty-four Trident I missiles; the standard modernized version would measure 450 feet in length, have a 33-foot diameter, and displace 9000 tons. It, however, would carry only sixteen Trident I missiles.

Major problems exist in retaining the Poseidon hull design. First, the size of the hull eliminates the possibility of introducing Trident II missiles. Second, the older, smaller power plant would have to be retained, limiting the sub's speed, ensuring it will be noisier, and shortening its core life. Third, although the size of the BQQ-6 sonar in the Trident remains classified, Navy witnesses have indicated in their testimony it cannot fit in a Poseidon hull. Less-capable sonar increases the boat's vulnerability to enemy ASW attack. Fourth, the smaller Poseidon hull cannot accept some of the larger command, control, and communications systems currently available. Related to those restrictions, the older hull lacks some of the defensive capabilities and weapons made available by a larger hull. Tridents not only now have adequate space, they even have room for the next generation of software. Finally, the Poseidon hull itself simply is becoming obsolete measured by the fabrication processes at Electric Boat and by recent Soviet advances in titanium welding.

Still, a smaller hull carries with it certain apparent advantages, not the least of which is a 30-percent savings in hull construction costs, "implying a potential savings of $450 million a ship." The resulting new base cost really is a conjecture about real procurement costs at an eventual delivery date. However, adoption of the 30-percent figure rests on the provision that no new equipment other than missiles and fire controls be included. Any change in sonar, navigational equipment, power plant, or drive train translates immediately into elevated but associated cost. Surely no responsible official would suggest putting men to sea in 1960-vintage equipment to face an enemy armed with 1983-vintage equipment. If the 1960-size hull carried the 1983 equipment, then many of the savings would disappear. The potential saving is therefore a delusion. Others claim the larger Trident is more easily detected than the smaller Poseidon hull. In conjunction with this argument, opponents of the Trident have argued that a larger force of smaller submarines would stand a better chance of surviving Soviet antisubmarine warfare tactics. Colloquially, this argument says "Don't put all of your eggs in a few baskets." But the hull design of the alternative vessel, which after all is the source of most of the savings, renders it far *more* vulnerable to ASW for reasons other than size. For example, as a result of the Trident hull's unique design, the water convergence to and from the screw produces a highly undetectable trail. The hull's hydroflow pattern better obscures its power wake in the water than previous shapes. Add to these considerations the testimony of Navy officials who stated in 1977 the optimal hull size for hiding a sub from sonar is approximately 40 feet, putting the Trident at an advantage over smaller hulls. To discard these advantages for a smaller hull size is to throw Leviathan from the depths onto the sandbanks, technologically speaking.[5]

Hull size affects interior noise as well. Sound-deadening equipment, available on the larger Trident, would not be so available in a smaller hull. Smaller power plants, which must run at higher levels to maintain the same speed as larger power plants, generate more noise. Conversely, the Tridents come prepared to accept new generations of equipment that, while larger in some cases, will nevertheless be quieter.[6]

Experts disagree strongly about the disadvantage of the Trident hull compared to a Poseidon's. The minimally larger underwater wake of the larger sub might be somewhat more detectable than one of a smaller hull, but various witnesses have stated the ideal hull size more nearly matches the Trident hull than the Poseidon hull. The Congressional Budget Office report concludes "no firm conclusions about whether one type of submarine would be more prone than another to Soviet detection and destruction are clear." Given that alternatives at best could do no better than Tridents in avoiding detection and, at worst, could be extremely easier to detect, one must examine other elements of the options to determine comparative advantage.[7]

The most obvious element to examine is cost. In its report, the Congressional Budget Office presented a comparison of costs for the force alternatives at three capability levels (see table 15).

Several caveats must accompany the report. Obviously, since the *Ohio* had not yet been completed the final cost could only be estimated in this study. Second, even though one can roughly estimate the costs of the Trident II missile, it must be remembered that this also remains a future system and, as Electric Boat and the Navy have discovered with the submarine itself, unexpected costs and delays creep in at every level. Further, new developments like the stabilizer in the Trident II fuel, which has turned out to be combustible, can make significant changes in range, thus affecting the number of deliverable warheads per missile. The true measure of cost should not be the number of warheads maintained at sea but rather a much more intricate figure involving missiles, ranges, and deployments. Each missile will not invariably carry as many warheads as possible, simply, for example, because such a maximum RV loading would limit the missile (in the case of Trident I) to soft-target capabilities (such as destruction of populations) at minimum range. Neither can it be assumed that all Trident II missiles would carry their maximum RV loading, because actually with fewer RVs it might be possible to increase the range of both the missile and the submarine.[9]

One of the prime drawbacks to either the long Poseidons or the necked-down Trident would be its decreased availability at sea caused by a number of factors, such as shorter cruising range (because of less supplies), longer cruising time in the case of the Poseidon (because of reduced speed and speed/quieting tradeoffs), and longer overhauls (due to the smaller working space within the subs). Since any combination of the above problems, let alone all of them, necessitates the addition of extra boats to cover the shortage in the at-sea force, the costs of more submarines precludes either the necked-down Trident or the elongated Poseidon versions.

These considerations led the Congressional Budget Office staff to conclude that "construction of an alternative submarine and termina-

Table 15
Cost Breakdown of Five Force Options
(in billions of dollars)

Force Options	Force Levels Expressed in Numbers of Warheads Maintained at Sea			4000-Warhead Level			
	2000	**3000**	**4000**	**Research & Development†**	**Procurement**	**Operation & Maintenance**	**Total**
I. Trident SSBNs carrying 24 Trident II missiles	36	53	66	7.5	28.1	30.3	65.9
II. New "necked-down" Trident-class SSBNs carrying 24 Trident II missiles	*	53	65	8.4	26.2	30.8	65.4
III. Trident SSBNs carrying 24 Trident I missiles	35	58	80	0.0	40.8	38.8	79.6
IV. New "long" Poseidon-class SSBNs carrying 24 Trident I missiles	34	53	70	1.1	30.2	39.0	70.3
V. New Poseidon-class SSBNs carrying 16 Trident I missiles	38	63	85	1.1	39.0	45.0	85.1

*No "necked-down" Trident-class SSBNs would be procured at the 2000-warhead level.

†Includes the difference between the cost to procure the first SSBN of a new type and the average later procurement costs.[8]

tion of Trident . . . construction would probably entail changes and possible disruptions in the industrial base producing SSBNs." Introduction of another SSBN type might force the Navy to maintain two separate SSBN crew-training and logistics systems for the next thirty years. Finally, the report noted, a decision to construct a smaller-diameter submarine not capable of carrying a Trident II-sized missile "might preclude development of such a missile any time during the next 20 to 30 years." In short, no submarine option, including the SSBN-X discussed in chapter 4, provided as efficient, survivable, or economical an option as did the current Trident design.[10]

No one will know all of the proposed sea-based options presented in the STRAT-X study, at least not for a number of years. But besides the various traditional submarine designs proposed, such as those just discussed, STRAT-X introduced several radical sea-based missile platform concepts. Among these ideas, Hydra, SUM, and a seabed-launched missile aroused the most interest then and continue to have support. It should be clear that many arguments raised against these systems in the following discussion possibly could be corrected by dedicated research of the nature expended on the Trident. The point here is to show how Trident's early technological problems *comparatively* were more easily solved. Trident did not exist as the only option from its inception but, rather, evolved and was supported due to its practicality, as its design, manning, and vulnerability problems were overcome more easily than those inherent in other options. Likewise, although when carefully examined it is easy to detect serious flaws in each concept, one can also understand the original appeal of each idea.

Hydra and SUM

Hydra (for hydralaunch) is no new idea. It was an active concept between 1960 and 1965, when it was canceled. Its resurrection in 1980 seems due principally to the endorsement provided it by its former project commander, Captain John Draim, USN-ret. It has also acquired the name Containerized Ballistic Missile; early versions of this idea appeared during World War II, when the Germans toyed with ideas of towing their V-2 rockets by U-boat to areas off New York City. The Hydra concept of STRAT-X featured a ballistic missile of roughly the same size and destructive capability as the planned MX or Trident I missile but with a major new wrinkle. Each Hydra missile would hybernate in a waterproof cargo canister until it received orders through its electronic receiver to launch. Cargo ships could carry dozens of Hydras, dropping them over the side like so much bait. The missile containers could float, but in shallow areas they could sink until they received instructions to launch, at which time those still floating would flood at the bottom to put the missile in a vertical launch position. Once vertical, the rocket engines would ignite and the missile would be launched.[11]

The Office of Technology Assessment (OTA) report revived the Hydra concept, calling for a force of "30 fast merchant-like ships with movable superstructures, false hatches, and movable cranes and booms [allowing] them to change their appearance and complicate the process of radar satellite tagging of the ships." Deception, the report concluded, would be crucial, and the vessels would even have "multiple sets of navigation lights so they could be made to change appearance." With speeds of 30 knots and endurance of 20,000 n.m. (at somewhat reduced speed), at-sea availability of the force would be approximately 80 percent. Each vessel would carry eight to ten missiles, putting two hundred missiles on station at all times. The ships would also be outfitted with "Trident-like navigation," jamming devices, passive sonar, and some defensive weapons, and would have on-board security force. To stay in target range, the vessel would operate in an area of fifty to sixty million square miles.[12]

Deploying from two major bases, one on each coast, the ships would require special basing facilities. The plan called as well for 150 transponder fields to be "secretly emplaced" in the deployment area, providing accurate position and velocity information for the missiles. According to the report, "fleet deployment to these fields could be effected within 11 to 12 hours." In a complex hypothetical set of scenarios, the OTA study analyzed the various responses to Hydra ships and predicted the outcomes of such scenarios. While the study provides thorough and detailed examination of most of the problems, it has serious weaknesses, discussed in the note. Among the difficulties not discussed in the study are those relating to actual canister location, sabotage, and deployment problems.[13]

Economically, the plan appeared to have several advantages. Ships deploying the Hydras not only could carry and store more of them than any traditional submarine (although, it should be noted, each Hydra would actually carry sixteen *fewer* missiles than a Trident), but theoretically they could return to base for additional missiles after firing each load. Moreover, as one advocate suggested, "vessels used to transport the [Hydra] could be drawn . . . from redundant merchant hulls." Such a vessel might require a little refurbishing of the crew's quarters and installation of the basic storage, handling, and offloading equipment, but the ships would not need nuclear power plants, extensive defensive systems, specialized support facilities, or highly trained crews. Any standard merchant hull used to deploy the Hydras could obtain service and support functions at any base or even at sea. These ships could operate on a considerably reduced crew compared to a Trident, and the missile areas themselves could be sealed off from access to all but a few authorized crew members. However, the OTA study, recognizing the problems of these suggestions, instead used a specially built and equipped vessel for evaluation purposes. The initial acquisition costs of the system would approach $33 billion, with a ten-year life-cycle cost of $43 billion (in 1980 dollars). One should recognize that, even allowing for improvements in the procurement process, these costs might leap by 30 percent, to be conservative. In addition, there would exist the constant problems of retooling and of finding shipyards capable of handling the load. Estimated operational capability of the program, according to the report, would be 1987—although, given the delays inherent in all military programs, 1990 would be a more likely date, at which time Trident II will already have entered the deployment stage.[14]

Psychologically, there might exist subtle differences with a strategic mission between a strategic submarine crew and a Hydra crew. The "silent service" keeps quiet not only operationally in its submarines but also, relatively speaking, personally in its social interactions. This is partly due to the awareness on the part of submariners that their very survival depends completely on their stealth, no matter their mission, strategic or otherwise. Such an acute sense of secrecy probably would not inhibit the crews of Hydra surface ships. Living conditions aboard submarines facilitate a special esprit de corps not found on surface vessels, contributing to the "all for one, one for all" attitude. Chances are that the attitude of Hydra crews would be quite different, especially in port.

Even less persuasive than its transparent economic benefits are Hydra's operational advantages. If the deployment ship retained all of the missiles on board until a war actually broke out, and assuming the Soviets knew when they planned to launch an attack, they would have their aircraft, attack submarines, or surface ships locate these ships and blow them out of the water before they could unload a single missile. The location process would be made far easier than in the case of a Trident because satellites could monitor the ships' positions. Even if the Navy provided Aegis-equipped destroyers and cruisers for protection, the ballistic-missile-carrying surface ships would represent high-value targets. In fact, a Hydra ship would have most of the disadvantages of an aircraft carrier without any of its advantages. However, proponents argue the vessel would not have to wait until hostilities actually began to deploy the missiles. It could spread them all over the oceans like so many seeds, returning from time to time only to test or service a Hydra missile. "Sleeping" until activated by a radio signal, these dormant doomsday canisters theoretically would be less vulnerable than if they remained on the deployment ship. However, this procedure could prove more disastrous than the first. A variety of natural accidents could befall a lightly encased missile of this type. Rough seas, debris, passing ships, or even an occasional overly curious octopus could damage the enclosure, in which case the missile at best would not fire and at worst could sink or otherwise leak radioactive materials or propellant. Worse yet, the antennae could mistake harmless transmissions from a passing vessel for the launch order, accidentally triggering World War III. In this regard, the Soviets would not hesitate to do some experimentation of their own with the launch transmission frequencies, especially insofar as jamming is concerned.

Natural accidents aside, it would be a simple matter for a Soviet submarine to trail the deployment ship secretly and mark the location of each Hydra. No matter how ingeniously offloaded, the canisters remain subject to precise location by submarine sonar. If the Soviets were unimaginative, they would merely destroy the deployment ship as soon as it dropped its first missile into the water. An imaginative sub commander, however, might radio for one of his surface ships to pick the missile containers up, defuse the warheads, or possibly retarget them to Washington, D.C. Imagine the scenario of a Soviet freighter collecting Hydra missiles, stamping red-star decals on them, and inventorying them into the Strategic Rocket Forces in a Russian version of strategic lend-lease! The lack of security for the surface-ship Hydra concept alone makes the option ludicrous.

Allowing for all of the security problems, there could still exist numerous operational difficulties in a Hydra missile. For example, targeting could prove exasperating unless experts attached anchors to each capsule, an impossibility in most waters where deployment is otherwise preferred. Without such anchors, the tides and currents would move missiles around to an even greater degree than is characteristic of SLBMs—even though these conditions of instability are partly offset by stellar or inertial systems of guidance. Given the security and operational problems of Hydra, the surprise is not that the option was dropped but rather that, as late as August 1981, Robert Smith suggested the concept again in *Proceedings*. As with many of these "newer" options, the Navy and the Department of Defense originally considered all of the disadvantages posed by Hydra in the STRAT-X study and concluded Hydra's problems far exceeded its advantages. According to John Lehman, when questioned in 1981 about Hydra, the concept was dropped because "we did not believe it was a viable option. . . . Command and control problems with ballistic missiles bobbing around the oceans" made it unrealistic. Lehman also confirmed that "prelaunch survivability . . . is not really resolved" because the enemy could attack the cargo ship as well.[15] Despite all its shortcomings, however, the Hydra concept still holds opportunities for limited use in certain situations, as will be shown in chapter 12.

Another option, SUM, or shallow underwater missile, has received the support of Norman Polmar, Senator Mark Hatfield, Sidney Drell, and Richard Garwin. SUM would operate in small HDW (type 209) 450-ton submarines in the coastal areas of the United States under America's air and surface umbrella. (This should not be confused with the small submarine-based MX-missile option discussed by the Office of Technology Assessment, which is a substantially larger vessel.) According to Hatfield, the "Minuteman-3 force could be rapidly modified and deployed aboard these . . . submarines . . . with the entire force at sea by 1986." Moreover, according to Garwin and Hatfield, the force could cost as little as $12 billion. Various types of power for the subs have been suggested, including diesels, electric motors, small nuclear reactors, and, in one case, no power at all. The latter idea envisions boats or barges capable of holding two to four missiles, towed to their positions, tethered or anchored in place. Michael MccGwire has argued this type of submarine system would represent a positive step toward "arms control," as it would be strictly a defensive system. SUM could be manned or unmanned.[16]

Clearly, it would be a step toward "arms control" if that term means reduction of the credibility of the deterrent force. Of all the problems that could afflict SUM, one of the most ignored is that of manning them (this, of course, does not apply to the tethered sub or barges). The sketchiness of the SUM concept, possibly a deliberate move on the part of some of its original proponents, renders analysis somewhat difficult, especially with respect to the cost and security aspects of the crew. Who would man the vessels? Crews of two to five have been suggested, although the Heritage Foundation report thought twelve to fifteen crewmen would be necessary for three- to four-week voyages. Are they to be responsible for the actual firing of the missile? One would hope not. If so, they would have to double as engineers and missile gunnery experts trained in navigation, fire control operations, and missile maintenance. At present, the Navy has enough trouble attracting qualified sailors for even the smallest ships of the line. With SUM its enlistees would each have to sport a large red *S* on his chest. How would the Navy train all of these technical supermen? Assuming the Navy found the necessary number of recruits, the training time and cost for each sailor would at least be doubled to turn out a nautical version of a jack-of-all-trades, slated for assignment to the psychological equivalent of a lighthouse ship. Moreover, with each SUM carrying two missiles, it would require twelve SUMs to deploy as many missiles as one Trident. Assume that each SUM had a crew of five, ignoring the necessity to have SUM Blue and Gold crews; then a single Trident requires more than twice as many personnel as an equivalent fleet of SUMs. But if each SUM needed an officer (an indispensable requirement from the viewpoint of launching authority), twelve SUMs would need five more officers than a Trident. Moreover, because none of the jobs on a SUM would be either low-skill jobs or less specialized jobs, the SUMs would place a *heavier*, not lighter, burden on enlistment. Pay for such enlistees would jump, and when figuring budgets the Navy would have to allow for the enlarged officer load, also hiking payrolls. Obviously those are not critical disadvantages, but, rather, are typical of the problems often overlooked in proposing "ideal systems."

From the crew standpoint alone, SUM is impractical. But its proponents usually argue it would be far cheaper. Before adding crew costs back in, consider the costs and limitations of the SUM submarines. If each SUM carried four missiles (to be generous), six would be needed to carry as many missiles as one Trident. Because a SUM could not retain its small size, hence economy, with such items as defensive weapons, sonar, large storage areas, fire controls, fuel, crew space, or quieting equipment, all of those features would be eliminated. Each SUM therefore would have a noisy (and slow) diesel engine, a quiet (and slow) electric motor, or no propulsion at all, either by sail or by oar. Without sonar, speed, or defensive weapons each SUM would be a sitting duck. With a diesel engine, the SUM would have to surface repeatedly each day. No amount of surface cover could protect a fleet of these subs. Indeed, the cost of such protective forces is estimated by the Heritage Foundation to be $10 to 15 billion! An enemy might have less assurance of destroying all of them but would have more assurance of destroying a large number. The size and lack of shock-resistant features would also make this type of sub particularly vulnerable to a series of nuclear underwater blasts. Further, without the diving ability or the speed to leave the area of the Continental Shelf, the enemy could locate the entire force with little effort. To guarantee a measure of survivability equivalent (72 SUMs) to that of a dozen Tridents, the Navy would have to put at least double the number of missiles at sea—144 SUMs—since the survivability quotient used by the OTA in its studies is always double, and Michael MccGwire has estimated 160 might be needed! But this only makes their destruction easier because the more SUMs operating in a single area, the easier their destruction through open-ocean barrages. SUM presents a Catch-22: if there are not more, not enough will survive; if there are more, the ease of their destruction increases.[17]

Consider the implications for the Soviets of an American decision to substitute a SUM system for Trident, as was once suggested. Freed of their massive deep-sea ASW burden, the Russians could redirect their efforts toward this coastal missile force. Unless the "launch on warning" concept became a reality, the Soviets could station their ASW forces off U.S. shores and get a free salvo at the SUMs before a single missile could be launched. Chances are that, even with American sea and air power for protection, a large number of SUMs could be knocked out by surface ASW units. Longer-range nuclear-tipped rockets and submarine attacks would follow. Released from the toughest jobs in ASW—detection and location—the Soviets could redirect a substantial portion of their fleet to other theaters, especially the North Atlantic, where NATO forces already have their hands full. To present the Soviets the gift of reinforcing their flanks makes no sense.

Any sailor serving on a SUM submarine, whether it was used as an MX platform or a Trident substitute, would have to realize his chances of surviving an action of any type would be slight. Besides the ASW conditions facing him as described above, the sailor would know a near miss would doom his fragile vessel. Unmanned SUMs, while saving costs associated with personnel, would nevertheless be even more vulnerable to communications jamming, sabotage, or, lacking the human onboard maintenance advantage, normal adverse weather effects and mechanical breakdowns. Who would check these tethered monstrosities? A force of divers and maintenance ships, probably with a total personnel complement approaching in numbers the crews that otherwise would man the SUMs, would be needed. Finally, a maintenance check of a SUM automatically advertises its position.

Moreover, no analyst has considered effects of actually launching a 96-ton missile from a 450-ton submarine. Be it noted, indeed, that for four MX missiles 384 tons is involved! If a vertical launch system rather than an overboard system is assumed, electric motors may be necessary to run compressors to maintain a level of compression sufficient to expel the missile. Since no designs for a SUM have appeared, it is entirely speculative whether the sub could generate enough gas to launch. In a diesel sub, would there be sufficient electric power to maintain a launch level of compressed gas? Even if the missile could be launched, ballasting would prove an insuperable problem. A Trident loses only 1/586th of its weight on launch, while a SUM would lose one-fifth. No studies are available for such massive, if not convulsive, reballasting problems. Even from a theoretically generous point of view a tripling of the SUM tonnage could not appreciably alleviate such a staggering ballasting problem (1/14 of the weight). Also, unlike a Trident, which can fire a pair of missiles and then dive and move to another point, a SUM is pretty much tied to its original firing area because it lacks speed and diving capability. Since a SUM's location to the Soviets would only be a matter of recording the navigational fix, it is highly unlikely that a SUM could fire its four-missile load before its destruction. Few sailors would request duty aboard such a boat.[18]

Other features of the SUM further increase its vulnerability. Viewed technically, since it probably cannot dive beyond more than 300 feet, and since it would have to maintain a level of safety above the ocean floor (lacking the sonar of a Trident), its actual operating area would be far less than appears at first glance. The Continental Shelf area has consistently shallow depth readings. Actual operating area for a SUM would be scant indeed. Likewise, depths in the Great Lakes reach only to the 190-foot range, and then only in a few locations. Proper launch procedures demand some water above and below the subs, making attacks by frogmen a distinct possibility. Divers would not need to destroy the sub on the spot. Rather, they could attach timed or electronically controlled explosives, or devices triggered by the opening of the missile-tube hatch. Disabling a SUM at lower-than-launch level would be as effective as destroying it.[19]

In peacetime a SUM represents an environmental disaster. Any underwater earthquake, tidal upheaval, or minor storm could beach a SUM or crack its hull. The danger to the local population and the environment could be substantial, ranging from missile-propellant explosions and leakage to diesel-fuel spills in the water. Given the larger number of SUMs at sea, the chances for accident increase, and, because of sheer numbers, the safety guarantees would decrease—not increase, as MccGwire argues. Disasters of other types are possible as well. Due to its size, division of labor, logistics, and security, hijacking a Trident is virtually impossible. Not so with SUM. The tiny crew size makes it an easy target, and the sheer numbers of the vessels would tax the security systems of any base facility. Even if security forces could guarantee a boat's safety in port, the chance a psychotic Admiral Strangelove might gain control of the sub at sea greatly increases. Likewise, the opportunities for accidental or deliberate launch by crew members or a planted enemy agent increase with each added SUM.[20]

A plethora of problems arising with SUM deployment are always omitted from the discussions of proponents such as Mark Hatfield's "smaller is cheaper" school. First, the deployment schedule for a 144-boat SUM fleet entails a continuously disruptive pattern of targeting assignments, with these "low tech" boats unable to adjust automatically due to their lack of sufficient fire controls and communications systems. Second, the security of the communications systems is an even greater problem than with Trident because of the multiplicity of units involved, the increased frequency with which communications would have to be conducted, and the greater individualization of the messages that would have to be sent. Finally, controlling and commanding a fleet of 144 SUMs stationed on two coasts constitutes an administrative nightmare in comparison with the equivalent of ten Tridents.

Numerous cost factors not seen in the SUM proposal itself bear consideration. If such highly trained, high-security, multitalented, death-loving sailors can be found, their pay demands would play a major part of any budget. No SUM could stay at sea as long as a Trident—or even as long as a Poseidon, for that matter—so maintenance costs would skyrocket. Diesels, if used, gulp fuel at rates that would strike fear in the hearts of Cadillac owners, another cost to compare with the twice-a-lifetime-fueled Tridents. The Navy would have to add scores of highly trained divers to check the hulls for sabotage while in port, psychiatrists to check the "lighthouse-keeper mentality" of the crew, shipyards to build the added boats, and basing facilities to deal with a new fleet of minisubmarines. Once survivability and accident factors are considered, the SUM option is zero, just as the STRAT-X study concluded.

Other Alternatives Proposed

Arthur Markel has recommended a "submarineless" SUM derivative featuring seabed-based missile systems, each with its own miniature Atlantis. These bases, Markel suggests, could have small propulsion systems, but "because [they] would rest on the seafloor, the size and capacity of the propulsion could be minimized . . . allowing concentration on silent staying power for life support, missile systems, and other less energy-intensive needs." Using buoyancy, they could "pop up" to launch missiles or take aboard supplies, and their environmental impact "should be about zero."[21]

Unfortunately, as Markel admits, "there are only a very few precedents in deep submergence capability" and none of the type he proposes. One suspects, if such a system were priced out and expanded to include as many missiles, crews, platforms, and supplies as would be necessary to maintain a credible deterrent force, the price tag would resemble the $75 billion originally projected for the MX in its multiple protective shelter basing mode. The bases would retain most of the vulnerabilities of SUM—ease of detection and location and ease of destruction, especially in launch sequence—as well as vulnerability to communications interference while on the seabed. Markel suggests an increased use of aluminum, but it has not been shown that aluminum could stand the stress of launching pressures (if launched "dry") or that the platform could generate the energy necessary to maintain pressurized gas for "wet" launchings. A platform would suffer the same fate as a SUM in the case of storms or earthquakes, making its environmental impact somewhat more than "about zero." Like SUM, divers could easily interfere with its operations, and psychotic sailors could hold it hostage effortlessly. Unlike SUM, a seabed deterrent might be more vulnerable to operational difficulties, especially propulsion breakdowns that could condemn crews to quick watery graves. In short, neither SUM nor a seabed deterrent force could attract enough suicidal volunteers to man a small lighthouse, much less a large strategic force.[22]

Other submarine alternatives, including subs with exterior-mounted missiles, received considerable discussion in the STRAT-X study without resulting in any serious commitment at that time. Most suggestions of using external missiles begin with a reminder that the Navy had carried Regulus missiles on some of its early submarines. Proponents of the exterior mounting of missiles usually fail to note the Regulus was a midget compared to a Trident I. Nevertheless, discussion of the exterior mounting of missiles may prove useful. Until the 1981 OTA MX-missile-alternative study, only skeletal designs appeared, but one plan suggested a sub to carry two missiles alongside the hull, positioned horizontally. More radical suggestions have included as many as six missiles in an exterior, cocoonlike layer around the submarine. To launch would entail a complex sequence of ejecting the missiles, flooding their aft portions so they could assume a vertical launch position, before firing would occur. Not only would this process take more time than vertical firing (meaning that the submarine would remain vulnerable longer), but the missiles would suffer from targeting effects caused by water movement, however slight. These types of problems belie the more serious questions of cost: How many countries in the world can afford to build a submarine just to carry two missiles? Certainly not the United States when it is recollected, on the basis of OTA's previously outlined assumptions, that 240 of these two-missile "bottom huggers" are necessary to match the equivalent Trident fleet. Exterior mounting could prove at least as expensive as SUM and probably more so, because the subs presumably would be designed for deep ocean cruising, hence would require sonar, a stronger hull, long-range supplies, a larger crew, and other necessities. In attempts to make the concept nevertheless look more cost-effective, proponents have suggested increasing the number of exterior missiles carried per sub. Again, a major drawback to this modification is that only skeletal designs have been produced so far. Even so, adding missiles would increase the boat's vulnerability during launch sequence without addressing any of the survivability problems associated with a slower, noisier power train, the lack of active and passive defenses, and the disadvantages of a hull configuration that promises to be more easily identifiable than pre-World War II freighters dropping noisemakers. Last, the addition of four more missiles still makes the hull only one-fourth as cost-effective as a Trident hull, not including crew costs, maintenance expenses, greater fuel demands, and less time on station.[23]

External mounting does not deserve serious discussion because its proponents have failed to consider the impracticalities the concept entails. As with all of the other Trident alterntives rejected more than a decade ago, exterior mounting is more expensive, more dangerous (consider a careless sub captain whose vessel has exterior-mounted missiles sideswiping another ship or a dock!), less survivable, and more crew-intensive than a Trident. A similar concept rejected by STRAT-X planners consisted of a traditional sub with its firing tubes set at forward angles of 45 to 60 degrees. Launching problems afflicted this idea, as angle launching exposed the sub to considerable danger if the missile misfired and fell back upon it. Whereas ballasting also is somewhat more complicated for angled launching, a more serious consideration is the attitude of the missile at the moment its motor must fire. Second-guessers will have trouble supporting any of the alternatives, especially with a decade's evidence to examine. Yet the Office of Technology Assessment revived the SUM-type concept when reviewing alternative MX missile basing modes, unnecessarily reviewing formerly discarded options.[24]

Alternatives from Other Service Branches

Some Trident critics have supported such non-sea-based weapons systems as variants of the MX mobile missile or the B-1 bomber as alternatives to the Trident rather than as complementary elements in an overall strategic mix. This represents a paradoxical reversal of the arguments that many Trident supporters have made for the abandonment of these alternate systems in favor of a single strategic submarine "leg." The purpose here is to explain the interdependence of the three strategic legs and to advocate the retention of the TRIAD, so far and as long as possible. To do so, a discussion of the MX, the B-1, and their proposed alternatives is required.

As part of the STRAT-X study the Air Force examined various

methods of preserving ICBM survivability. Basically, the choices for the ICBMs boiled down to protecting them with hardened silos, with an antiballistic-missile screen, or with a rotation system among empty and loaded silos to make their location unknown to Soviet targeting experts. None of these three basing modes represented any novel concepts: both the U.S. and the Soviets have used hardened silos for years and the Russians have developed a sizeable antiballistic-missile system, much of it in violation of the 1972 ABM treaties. The Soviets have likewise deployed their own mobile missiles, the SS-20s, launched from mobile carriers. Although these are only intermediate-range missiles designed to hit Europe, the technology exists to move ICBMs around in the same manner. Advances in Soviet missile accuracy prompted the initial STRAT-X concerns, but further improvements in Soviet accuracy continued to accelerate in the mid-1970s, forcing a reconsideration of some of the STRAT-X thinking. New generations of Russian missiles soon achieved CEP test accuracies of 0.1 n.m., despite an earlier warning by Department of Defense officials that the U.S. missile force would be vulnerable if the Soviets achieved 0.2-nautical-mile accuracies, a goal that the Russians were not expected to reach until the mid-1980s. Consequently, mobility replaced hardening as the mode of protection for American ICBMs. As discussed in the preceding chapter, a scaled-down version of the antiballistic-missile system was also revived.[25]

The MX Missile

The Air Force developed preprototype models of the "missile experimental," or MX, in October 1976, although work had been underway since 1973. With its 192,000-pound launch weight—twice that of the Minuteman III missile—the MX not only featured greater delivery potential but also included significant accuracy improvements. One author suggests the Navy's public admission of its need for Seafarer during this period "played into the hands of the Air Force," which used the weak communications link of submarines as leverage for a ground-based MX. Gerald Ford, presented with an original deployment date of 1984, decided to try to advance the timetable by at least a year, but the Carter administration reduced the MX budget in 1977, putting it back on its original schedule. Then it reversed itself the following year by requesting more money for the MX budget.[26]

Only on September 7, 1979, when the Carter administration decided upon the multiple-shelter plan, did it receive the strategic and economic investigation it deserved from its inception. The shuttle (multiple protective shelters, or MPS) plan envisioned underground tunnels connecting a group of hardened silos. A ground transporter would carry the missile to its randomly selected silo, at which point the missile launcher could tilt vertically for launch. At the top of the silo, radiation-shielded doors could open to allow the missile to fire. Another version of this concept, called the trench concept, would have the missile "dig itself" out of a lightly covered trench. To destroy the MX missile, an enemy would have to destroy the entire trench. Combinations of both plans would have utilized covered areas and trenches, with the missile plowing itself out of the covered area into an open trench for launch.

As Congress and the public learned more about the plan, it became clear that supporters had understated the costs and environmental impacts and had overstated survivability. Consequently, an entirely new study was requested from the Office of Technology Assessment and published in 1981. It rehashed many of the original STRAT-X options, including basing the MX on small submarines, dropping the missile from large-bodied airplanes, protection by antiballistic missiles, and the multiple protective shelters favored by the Carter administration. OTA's concept of a small submarine capable of handling the MX consisted of many of the SUM and tethered-submarine ideas. The OTA used a "model" diesel-electric sub, displacing 3300 tons, 342 feet long and 25 feet in diameter. OTA hypothesized that a force of fifty-one subs armed with four missiles each would provide a suitable deterrent force. Each sub would carry the four missiles in canisters approximately 80 feet long and 10 feet in diameter outside the sub's pressure hull. When launched, the "doors" holding the canisters would open and the specially ballasted canisters would drift to the surface vertically, where the engines would ignite and propel the missiles from their capsules. OTA planned to equip the subs with inertial navigation systems, a velocity-measuring sonar, and special systems for taking fixes from NAVSTAR satellites. The subs would also include very-low-frequency radio receivers.[27]

Although OTA makes a strong case for these smaller subs, it leaves many significant problems unanswered. How would the Navy man the fifty-one submarines? How much would the training cost be? How would the Navy retain the crews? These factors play an important role in establishing a price tag that topped $32 billion, without them, in the OTA's estimate. However, when crew training and pay as well as operation and support facilities are included, the program would run at least $41 billion and probably a great deal more. None of these cost figures allows for a realistic, experiential element of constructing lead vessels—which, as the Trident's history has amply demonstrated, can account for as much as the Trident's were (30 percent, conservatively), in which case the price tag rises to nearly $55 billion.[28]

OTA's greatest concerns about the smaller subs centered on the theoretical foundations of the TRIAD. If adopted, the sub-MX concept would turn TRIAD into a "DIAD," since the former ICBM land leg would now cohabit at sea with Trident. This in turn would mean a Soviet breakthrough in antisubmarine warfare could threaten the majority of American strategic forces. The OTA report also discussed arguments about the likelihood of war if, with all missiles based at sea, an enemy assumed, because the missiles would not be on American "territory," they could be attacked without triggering a nuclear holocaust. More important, however, are some of the arguments omitted in the OTA report, for if replacing the land-based MX with another system is the only goal, a primary consideration would be to see how a sea-based alternative compares with Trident and how an air-launched MX compares with the B-1B. For example, OTA mentions nothing about a comparison of the Trident and the small submarine-based MX. Depending upon the decline in future Trident costs due to experience gains and the absence of special problems, such as the steel and welding difficulties and the trades-union strike previously discussed, six more Trident subs carrying 144 missiles with 1152 RVs could be deployed for the same cost as the fifty-one-boat MX fleet with its 2040 RVs (until the larger Trident II missiles are deployed, with a net increase of 864 *more* RVs). Estimating the crew size at forty-five per sub, as OTA did, a force of fifty-one subs would require almost 3000 officers and men. However, six Tridents, providing almost 75 percent as many Trident I missiles with 60 percent as many RVs as the proposed MX subs, would require only 45 percent of the crew. In other words, the MX subs are crew-intensive whereas Tridents are missile-intensive. These numbers improve vastly in Trident's favor when the capabilities of Trident II are considered, in which case the six Tridents would nearly equal the number of RVs of the MX-sub force while maintaining a crew advantage of 60 percent. Why build another submarine to do Trident's job? As demonstrated in the figures, Tridents would cost less by a factor of $48 billion, and even this figure seems conservative when considering lead vessel problems. For the extra $48 billion *the Navy could deploy twenty-five Tridents, with $8 billion remaining for refit and support*! The OTA report suggests no advantages of the MX sub over the Trident, and, in fact, there are severe disadvantages.[29]

Still, the report does not sufficiently discuss an even greater problem: the importance of maintaining different types of deterrents with systemically different strengths. If, for example, the Soviets suddenly made a startling breakthrough in ASW, both the "real" subs and the MX subs would be equally vulnerable. Even more important, however, is the continued improvement of *each* leg so that the Soviets are not at liberty to concentrate their research time and effort into one area. By forcing the enemy to counter several different strategic threats, the United States will better be able to guarantee that some part of this country's forces will always have a high degree of survivability against a first strike. From that perspective, even a moderately improved land-based ICBM force, especially if it is mobile, has its advantages, even if they are ultimately more distractive and economic than military and strategic.

Before discussing the two major land-based MX options—the MPS and the hardened silos, either with the possible deployment of an antiballistic-missile system—the final non-land-based option should be explored. This option is the Air Mobile concept, also called Big Bird, the brainchild of two men, Ira Kuhn, Jr., of B-K Dynamics and Abe Kerem of Leading Systems, Inc. Air Mobile proponents envisioned MX missiles of about 150,000 pounds (compared with the ground-launched 192,000-pound missile) carried inside large cargo aircraft (an aircraft indeed capable of carrying 50,000 more pounds than the C-5 transport now carries) that could deploy them in midair by use of a parachute. Once clear of the plane, the missile engines ignite. Consideration of air deployment has forced major tradeoffs among missile sizes in order to squeeze at least two missiles in each plane. Of course, because the missile would be starting its flight in midair, it would not require as powerful an engine or as much fuel. At a ratio of two missiles per plane, Air Mobile promoters anticipated needing seventy-five planes. In the most probable scenario for attacks against this type of MX, the Soviets would probably use submarine-launched ballistic missiles, which can be launched much closer to U.S. shores, hence providing far less warning time. So, reaction time is a critical factor with the Air Mobile concept.[30]

To compensate for the lack of warning time, OTA suggested three major concepts: continuously airborne planes, planes to "dash" on warning and remain airborne with some endurance, and planes to dash but without endurance. Costs promised to have a significant impact on any kind of continuously airborne force, regardless of aircraft/missile combinations, but each 900,000-pound-gross-weight aircraft in the OTA study (a hypothetical turboprop) figured to use 4000 gallons of fuel per hour. With a force of seventy-five aircraft in the air at all times for a year, the taxpayers would look at an annual estimated bill of $3 billion for fuel alone. Averaged with development costs over a thirteen-year life cycle, the planes, missiles, training for crews, bases, maintenance, and fuel costs could hit the $90+-billion figure. Since those kinds of fuel expenses would stagger a Saudi sheik, OTA moved on to the dash concepts.[31]

Assuming that the United States wanted to upgrade its tactical warning systems to a suitable level, a fleet of MX-carrying aircraft could theoretically take off upon warning. The problem is, what do the planes do once they are up? Soviet reentry vehicles targeted for current ICBM launchers now number in the thousands. If Air Mobile came on line, the Soviets would simply retarget these RVs to airstrips and/or to flyout corridors. One solution has been the "dash on warning with endurance" concept, which would furnish 4500 "austere" airbases to allow the aircraft to land after an attack. This concept has the advantage of permitting a number of missiles to be withheld after an attack, thereby preserving response flexibility. Otherwise, the Air Force would have to "use or lose" all of the missiles following an attack. With differing levels of airfield protection and with numbers of airfields varying, OTA has put the cost of the dash plus endurance plan at the rather enduring sum of $50 to $81 billion. For those taken aback by these costs, OTA provided estimates for the "use it or lose it" Air Mobile "system without endurance." This proposal would save aircraft costs, as normal-length runways would permit the use of aircraft already in production, such as the Boeing 747. Without endurance, costs could decrease to $40 billion. Another version of this plan, widely covered in the press in 1981, was a different Big Bird aircraft that would feature turboprop engines with their low fuel consumption. A fleet of these planes could remain aloft, flying at low speeds, for more than forty-eight hours. With no provision made for postattack endurance and without procurement costs for the aircraft, this version of Big Bird could cost less than $35 billion. Because these planes would be slower, however, their distance from base at the time of impact would be less than the other types of planes, making this Big Bird aircraft more vulnerable and less survivable.[32]

All Air Mobile concepts suffer from other problems. Warning systems must be flawless and reaction time perfect for large numbers of aircraft to get off the ground. The OTA report suggested that crews could be continuously stationed inside the cockpits but admitted some crews would find this duty "unattractive." If the Soviets launched a well-organized surprise SLBM attack, the aircraft's chances of becoming airborne might dwindle further, even with crews confined to their cockpits. Once again, though, besides cost, the greatest danger to the concept is theoretical. Both the ballistic-missile force and the manned-bomber force would rely on the same systems for performance of their duties: early warning, effective communications, split-second crew reactions, and undisturbed flyaway escapes. Should anything interfere with these factors, *two* TRIAD legs would be vulnerable. That conclusion alone might prompt some observers to reject air-basing of missiles; when compounded by cost, the arguments overwhelmingly demand that defense officials find other options.[33]

Multiple Protective Shelters

Since the adoption of the land-based MPS concept by the Carter administration in September 1979, the MX has received considerable media attention, much of it unfavorable. Under the Carter plan, two hundred MX transporters would each carry a 71-foot-long, 192,000-pound missile along a closed system of twenty-three shelters, one mile apart, linked by gravel roads. Hoping to hide the real missile "in a 'sea' of shelters," the Air Force planned to make the missile's characteristics while hidden identical to those of an empty shelter, forcing the Soviets to expend much of their missile force on decoys. Cost estimates for the missiles, the 4600 shelters, and maintenance ranged from official predictions of $34 billion to estimates by the special Reagan-appointed Townes Committee of $80 billion (in FY 1980 dollars). One concern present during the early discussions of the MX—arms control and verifiability—may not block new assessments, for the SALT II treaty is dead, taking with it to its grave the added expense of having to design shelters that could be opened for satellite verification.[34]

Still, the MPS idea drew heavy criticism for its cost, its impact on the environment, and its potential vulnerability. Some critics maintained that the Soviets could add warheads faster than the United States could dig shelters. Environmentally, the only suitable areas for deployment had to fit the requirements of large areas of relatively flat land to accommodate the land transporters, low population densities, and low water use. Over 83,000 square miles of land in the Great Basin of Utah and Nevada proved particularly suitable, along with sections of southern Arizona and New Mexico and the Great Plains states. When the Air Force considered all options, the Great Basin seemed to provide the most suitable sites of all. Questions of Indian land claims, oil and gas leases, mining claims, water availability, and especially community impacts due to suddenly expanded populations all extracted their toll on the concept. Utah and Nevada residents, pondering the possibility of 40,000 workers moving into the small desert communities, protested, along with the head of the Mormon church announcing his official opposition. But the bottom line remained system effectiveness, and it was becoming clear the Soviets might be willing to waste warheads on shelters if it meant there was a chance of knocking out the entire MX force.[35]

Other MX Options

This prompted the Air Force to consider utilizing a ballistic-missile defense. As discussed in the preceding chapter, the ABM systems included "exoatmospheric" (space defenses) and "endoatmospheric" (lower-atmosphere nuclear-tipped antimissiles). Suggestions also ranged from the exotic (hundreds of dart-firing guns placed near the MX) to the very exotic, exemplified by the concept of Dust. This proposal recommended burying "clean" nuclear weapons near the silos and detonating them on warning of attack, "filling the air with dust that would destroy Soviet [reentry vehicles] before they reached the ground." The OTA report concluded: "Dust defense could therefore be by far the most potent endo[atmospheric] defense system. However, it is seldom taken seriously because of concern for public reaction."[36]

President Reagan's 1981 order to produce the MX missiles themselves while exploring other basing options apparently has sounded the death knell for the MPS "racetrack" concept. Although some reporters claimed to have information showing that the administration favored the Big Bird concept, Reagan surprised the media by recommending temporary missile placement in existing hardened shelters. Actual placement of the missiles will not occur until the mid-1980s, however, and in March 1981 the Senate voted to drop initial funds for building the MX missile until a permanent basing mode was proposed by the administration. Meanwhile, other basing concepts not covered in the OTA study have surfaced. Two enjoying very recent support are the Table Mesa and the Dense Pack plans. In the process of elaborating MX basing modes on what some have quipped to be the "mode of the week" system, according to Secretary of Defense Weinberger, the only basing mode not considered was the "six-pack." According to the Table Mesa concept, utilizing the high and naturally hardened rocky mesas of Arizona and other Southwestern states, the Air Force could place the missiles deep in "mine shafts" inside the mountains. Each set of missiles would have its own digger, which would dig the missiles' firing silos from the inside out in the period after a Soviet strike. Preliminary studies show this plan to cost less than even the hardened-silo plan suggested by Reagan, and the missiles would be virtually indestructible. Environmental and social disruptions would be minimal, and security would be assured against all but Edmund Hillary imitators. Yet another concept totally reverses the original MPS idea, in which missiles were spread out to force the Soviets to use more missiles in the attacking force. This concept, which Reagan supposedly favors personally, called Dense Pack, proposed to pack a number of MX missiles tightly together in ten clumps of ten canisters each, with every canister individually capable of surviving all but a direct hit. Nine of the canisters would remain empty, and the incoming RVs would have to hit each canister in order to assure a "kill." But to fly in a formation tight enough to achieve this type of precise attack, all of the incoming RVs would be detonated by the first atomic explosion—a process called "fratricide" in military jargon—so only the first RV would actually hit its target. This plan could easily be enhanced by adding ballistic-missile defense, and the entire facility could fit in ten to fifteen square miles. If either the Table Mesa or the Dense Pack plan (or integrated basing of the two) stands up to subsequent hard study, the land-based ICBM problem will be solved. But even if it proves illusory, Reagan's decision to produce the MX was commendable in that it eliminated one more problem: lead time development. Following the Senate's action, that problem now exists once again, with another variation—the Midgetman (a smaller, portable, 1-warhead-ICBM)—recently being proposed to rival the MX. The decision to place the MX missiles in hardened silos is the only sensible option at present, if for no other reason than the fact that it replaces the Titan missiles (which are dangerous to American civilians) with MX missiles (which are dangerous to Soviet civilians). Keeping the TRIAD concept, if possible, is a position that is also to be commended for reasons discussed in the concluding chapter.[37]

Dense Pack has its weaknesses. Fratricide is not well enough understood to employ it as the only defense of MX missiles. The arrival of the warheads of one missile can be timed to within milliseconds of the others, probably eliminating or substantially diminishing any fratricide effects. Another technique is to stagger launches so as to have second strikes come in after the first explosion's harmful mushroom clouds have dissipated (half an hour later). Kosta Tsipis also argues the Soviets would counteract by targeting a huge (60-megaton) warhead to a single cluster, although it is not clear that even heavier warheads could destroy "superhardened" silos with less than a direct hit. Current plans to harden silos to 10,000 pounds per square inch would increase the protective capacity of the silo by five to ten times over the protection offered by Minuteman silos. No similar criticisms of the Table Mesa plan have appeared, although some may view its environmental effects as the same as those plaguing the MPS, even though they clearly would be significantly less. However, as the Heritage Foundation study concluded, whatever land-basing choice is eventually decided upon, "none of the three alternate basing schemes [SUM, Hydra, or Big Bird] can successfully compete with land-basing in . . . survivability, reliability, and missile accuracy."[38]

The B-1 Bomber

Rather than an actual substitute for the Trident system, as some variants of the MX were viewed, the B-1 bomber represented a competitor for funds. No one in the Air Force would have argued that the B-1 should replace the Trident, even in the early 1970s when both systems entered the initial planning phase. Instead, the Air Force might have presented a group of B-1s as an alternative to one or two Tridents.

As a proposal deriving from a series of studies begun in 1962, the original B-1 promised to be a replacement for the Boeing B-52s. Contracts for research, development, testing, and evaluation arrived at North American Rockwell's Los Angeles Division on June 5, 1970. General Electric received the contract for the F101 turbofan engine. Under the original contract and later additions in the fiscal year 1976 budget, Congress allocated funds for four flight-test aircraft and one ground-test airplane, along with twenty-seven engines. The Air Force expected to order 240 of the aircraft in addition to the prototypes, with delivery beginning in 1980. Following the 1977 cancellation by the Carter administration and revival under Reagan's October 1981 strategic program, the B-1 finally went into production, with a $2.2-billion contract for delivery of the first planes in 1985.[39]

Improvements had accompanied the interim between the original B-1 proposals and production. The variant of the B-1 under construction in 1982 consequently incorporated more advanced electronics as well as other extensive changes, thus changing its designation to the B-1B. Although the B-1B is expected to fly at slower speeds than its predecessor, it will still have supersonic capabilities, and it is intended to become airborne more quickly, operate from cruder airfields, and carry a greater payload than the B-1 despite a lower overall gross weight. Its design incorporates so-called Stealth techniques, making its radar signature conservatively given at ten times less than the early B-1 (which had a signature of at least ten times less than the B-52!). Planned procurement "covers two, seven, nine, 36, and 46 examples in the Fiscal Years 1982, 1983, 1984, 1985, and 1986 . . . with production peaking at four aircraft per month in 1986." Completed delivery is expected for 1988, with the entire complement of one hundred being available at that time. Pentagon studies anticipate Soviet air defenses will be unable to prevent penetration until the mid-1990s, at which time the aircraft will assume the role of a cruise-missile carrier. The airplane's life span of over thirty years makes it a cost-effective weapon and, once the technology is in use, the production lines will be able to produce more bombers in a time span shorter than would be possible with any other strategic weapons system. Each bomber represents a formidable weapon: armament includes twelve B-28 gravity-dropped nuclear bombs, or eight cruise missiles on a rotary launcher, or twenty-four short-range air-to-ground missiles carried in bays, as well as exterior payloads of either fourteen cruise missiles, fourteen short-range missiles, or eight nuclear bombs. It can also carry a massive payload of either thirty-eight Harpoon missiles or 126 conventional bombs, or numerous combinations thereof. This conventional payload capability gives the B-1B a weapons load of approximately 125,000 pounds. Maximum takeoff weight for the aircraft with its weapons load is 477,000 pounds.[40]

How does the B-1B relate to the Trident? Specifically, the bomber fits into a sophisticated and complex strategy, especially as it pertains to targeting. Trident missiles, assuming the availability of 80 percent of the B-1B bomber force, would be directed at "hard" targets such as missile silos, communications networks, and air defenses. Once air defenses have been reduced, the real strategic value of the bomber becomes evident. Relatively free of surface-to-air missile attack, subject to reduced fighter-interceptor interference, the bombers would be able to attack "soft" targets such as cities, remaining airfields, or other military installations. Because bombers are flexible weapons—the human pilots can change direction in flight—it is possible to attack targets other than those originally designated. This might be necessary if, upon arriving at the original target, the bomber crew finds that it has been moved, destroyed by other attacks, or perhaps is nonexistent due to inaccurate intelligence.[41]

Other relationships are more subtle and do not automatically translate into quantifiable gains or losses directly related to the Trident. As A. G. B. Metcalf has written in his editorial for *Strategic Review*, the strategic bomber force "is clearly the only leg of the triad which currently forces the Soviets to invest heavily in active defenses which pose no direct threat to the United States." Soviet air defenses alone require as much manpower as the entire U.S. Air Force. Metcalf makes another dramatic point: "The manned bomber is the only strategic delivery system that has ever successfully been employed in war." It should not be discarded lightly. Moreover, the B-1B can perform important maritime missions, including reconnaissance, antiship warfare (especially valuable when used in the context of protecting the Trident force from surface ASW ships), and minelaying. These capabilities alone make the bomber valuable to the Trident, not to mention the conventional capabilities that make the B-1B superior or equal to any other bomber in the world, including the Soviet Backfire and Blackjack. Moreover, these conventional capabilities cannot be dismissed, for two good reasons. First, the ability to influence strategic developments in a conventional mode might prevent a nuclear escalation. For example, consider the possibility of Warsaw Pact attacks in Europe, using the massive advantage in tanks and manpower. Assuming that the decision to use either theater nuclear weapons or neutron warheads is delayed, the B-1B might provide crucial air support with its conventional weapons, especially in destroying enemy airfields. Second, the United States has been involved in two major military operations since World War II (Iran rescue-type missions excluded), and in neither conflict—Korea or Vietnam—did the United States face the Soviet Union directly. While the B-1B might be obsolete as a strategic penetration bomber in a war against the Soviet Union by the year 2000 but hardly obsolete in this role against every other power, it would still be fifteen years *ahead* of any other technology in the world. Given the vulnerability of American B-52s to Vietnamese missiles in the Vietnam War, this consideration takes on added significance.[42]

It also appears that supporters of an Advanced Technology Bomber, or Stealth, may have half a loaf after all. Funding for Stealth research is to continue under the Reagan plan, with a final combination Stealth/B-1B bomber force totaling perhaps 250 aircraft. However, if Senator John Glenn's arguments as to Stealth's vulnerabilities prove accurate, it may be an obsolete bomber itself by the time its deployment date nears.[43]

Both the B-1B and some type of land-based missile must be viewed in the context of the role they play in an upgraded TRIAD, *not* independently. For the Trident to remain the most survivable element of the strategic forces, as submarines have been since the early 1960s, it cannot become the focus of the entire Soviet research and development effort. Whatever virtues alternative systems presented to those looking for a substitute to the Trident (or, more recently, the MX), they all must not be entirely ignored. Some of the systems—SUM, Hydra, and other sea-based alternatives—clearly have been rejected on grounds of impracticality. But other ideas studied, including forms of missile defenses and air-launched missiles, may incorporate some useful elements. This is particularly so in the case of the various ABM systems. Although the Trident and the B-1 did not compete for funds in the same way that the MX competed with Trident (both budgetarily and, in the example of the sea-based MX systems, conceptually), the B-1 nevertheless represented an element of the strategic force that placed an understandable demand on the budget. Most important of all, however, the TRIAD mandates continual maintenance and upgrading. Every ruble spent on achieving greater accuracy by Soviet missiles aimed at ICBMs is a ruble that will not be spent on antisubmarine warfare. No one makes this argument more effectively than Colin Gray in his book on the MX; Gray concludes that, at present, MX is needed, although he seems to conclude the available MX options are barely better than nothing.[44]

Strength of the TRIAD Concept

Aside from economics, a healthy TRIAD also forces a Soviet scientific and technological commitment in three distinct areas. Not only must the Soviets dedicate economic resources to aircraft and land-based missile defenses, they must also divide their scientific community into correspondingly specialized areas and the chances of a breakthrough in any one area shrink correspondingly. This is likewise true in terms of deployment. Air defenses, for example, must be deployed across the entire nation, along all borders, and around all major cities. Operationally, such a massive deployment creates serious coordination problems—problems magnified even more by the difficulty of fostering interservice coordination. A "psychic pressure" can be exerted by TRIAD on the Russian defense community as a whole and on individual functional branches or geographic subdivisions that might not be "pulling their weight." From the American perspective, continuance of the TRIAD allows, to some extent, subtle control over the direction of *Soviet* research and development. If the United States suddenly announces plans to introduce a B-70 bomber again, the forced reaction on the part of the Soviets is to have to build another version of the MiG-25 Foxbat. Pressure of this nature can be altered and maneuvered to introduce and establish research uncertainty in Soviet circles, an element acting in favor of the American strategic leg most secure, in this case the Trident.

Cruise missiles will enhance the TRIAD even more by expanding the flexibility and capability of each leg. As discussed in the previous chapter, the cruise missile has a direct relationship to Trident deployment. But this "half-breed" weapon will require even further reallocation of Soviet resources—which, in turn, contributes once more to the Trident's survivability and effectiveness.

Lest this view appear too elitist from the Navy's quarters, the arguments can be reversed, and circumstances can change. In 1965, American ICBMs were relatively survivable. Five years prior to that, American bombers had a high probability of penetrating Soviet air defenses.

If, as foreseen in chapter 9, beam weapons begin to play a significant role in warfare, submarine-launched missiles might become as vulnerable as land-based missiles, and yet another major shift in weapons concepts and design may evolve to replace or alter one or another of the TRIAD's legs. Thus, it is in the Navy's best interest (and, more specifically, in the best interest of the Trident program) to upgrade the other two TRIAD legs. Many of the Trident alternatives were technologically or practically unsound, but many of them also represented conceptual deviations from a true strategic TRIAD. For Trident to live up to its potential and justify its investment, continued TRIAD maintenance is essential, and, for that reason, the B-1B is conceptually complementary to the Trident, while the SUM-type MX is not. Hydra and its numerous sister alternative programs, while having some appealing characteristics, should not push TRIAD onto the back burner, for, like the Hydra canisters, much of the TRIAD's advantage lies unseen below the waterline of economic and systems debate.

11

A Common Interest:

National Deterrents, Trident, and NATO Reform

> *If the West prepares for war and no war comes, we may enjoy the freedom of criticizing ourselves for our foolishness. If war comes and the West is unprepared, not merely to fight but to win, then there can be no greater folly. Our freedom will have died, killed by our blindness. Our losses will be total and irrevocable; there will be no distant armies of liberation raised to free us as we once freed Western Europe. We must be prepared to fight; if need be, for years, if necessary, alone.*
>
> —Harold W. Rood, *Kingdoms of the Blind*

More by coincidence than by design Europeans have succeeded in making their wars at sea relatively short and decisive. Except for submarine warfare during both world wars and occasional raiding missions by such vessels employed in *guerre de course* as the *Graf Spee* or the *Bismarck*, control of the seas has largely turned on individual, monumental battles. Incinerated by fire boats and buffeted by gale winds, the Spanish Armada in 1588 became the first famous European navy to break under English superiority. Stifled by Nelson at Aboukir Bay in 1798, Napoleon abandoned hopes of marching to India, further enhancing the myth of English invincibility at sea. Nelson's renowned victory at Trafalgar constituted the high point of respect for British naval invincibility. Despite a tactical victory in 1916 at Jutland, the German High Seas Fleet retreated to the safety of its own coastlines, reaffirming again the British strategic dominance of the waves. Yet within the overall framework of its reputation England has consistently lost many moderately significant naval actions, especially in the opening phases of major conflicts. French Admiral De Grasse at Sandy Hook in 1781 dealt a crushing defeat to the English fleet during the American Revolution, allowing George Washington to seal a climactic victory in the war at Yorktown. In the War of 1812 the tiny American fleet had defeated British and Canadian forces on the Great Lakes and Lake Champlain and in other well-known but insignificant, individual high-seas actions. World War II in the Atlantic provided a glimpse of future naval warfare; there, lacking the decisive battle, navies engaged in a war of attrition emphasizing roles previously considered undignified (supply, transport, and blockade) or dull (antisubmarine warfare and invasion support). Some officers nostalgically longed for a return to the day of the decisive battle, an earlier time in which naval battles were conclusively resolved by the "decisive weapon," whether it was a 24-pounder, the 16-inch naval gun, or the carrier-borne bomber.

Nevertheless, naval planners have realized since World War II that, barring the use of ships and submarines in direct strikes against the enemy, support, transport, sea-lane protection, and ASW will be the primary jobs for the navies in a future European or global war. The European allies, especially those that are members of the North Atlantic Treaty Organization (NATO), have an important stake in the Trident program. The size of the U.S. Trident force, its impact on European ship construction, and deployment of the Trident submarines will all greatly affect how the Europeans view the U.S. role within the alliance. More importantly, it will affect how they view their own strategic needs and postures. Deployment of the Trident submarines and the sale of Trident missiles (either the Trident I or Trident II) to Great Britain could help renovate that country's strategic forces and will have the greatest immediate effect on the NATO alliance. Britain has indicated it cannot financially support a modernized SSBN strategic force, an extensive surface and SSN–ASW attack force, and an effective conventional surface fleet simultaneously. Should the British have to reduce their commitment to ASW activities and surface protection of sea lanes in the GIUK Gap, other countries, such as the United States or Britain's other European allies, would find it difficult to cover the operational void.[1]

Great Britain as a Trident Customer

Britain's decision to refurbish its nuclear arsenal holds implications for one important NATO member, France. Since their withdrawal from the integrated command structure of NATO in 1967, the French have maintained a potent and independent nuclear retaliatory force. In 1981 the government of François Mitterand announced that it plans generally to upgrade this force and to add at least one more ballistic-missile submarine to its fleet. To sort out activities by the NATO countries and France and to assess the options that Trident deployment presents to these countries, it will be helpful to examine the two major European nuclear forces—those of Great Britain and France—as well as the naval role of the non-nuclear NATO powers. A clearer understanding of the political considerations and strategic goals they entail will better illustrate the impact of the Trident program on the NATO alliance in general and on France specifically.

Since World War II Britain has had to face the reality of its declining world empire. The prospects of surrendering to the forces of nationalism many previous colonial and semicolonial territories seemed inconsistent with the postwar prestige and status otherwise conferred on Great Britain as a member of the victorious Allies. When Britain detonated its first atomic device in 1952 and its first hydrogen bomb in 1957, the country had to choose between remaining a major power in a strategic sense and falling back into the ranks of the second echelon of the world's military powers. Winston Churchill's Conservative government in 1951 took the initial step by turning "the nuclear aversion in British policy [of Clement Atlee's Labour government] . . . into a nuclear bias." Adoption of the Sandys Plan of 1957 reflected this change by calling for cuts in defense expenditures that would be offset by greater reliance on nuclear weapons. In fact, a number of considerations caused Britain to develop its own nuclear force. Conceivably, such a hostile power as the USSR might threaten Britain directly without threatening any other free Continental power or the United States. Meeting such threats as these suggested the necessity of an independent retaliatory capability. Most of all, though, the 1956 Suez crisis proved to many Britons that America "might not be a wholly reliable ally," especially when non-European British interests were involved. Patterned after the early American strategic bomber forces, the first British deterrent system consisted of Victor, Valiant, and Vulcan bombers carrying atomic bombs. However, the V-force also progressively began to suffer from the same growing inability to penetrate Soviet air defenses that now affects especially the U.S. B-52 bomber fleet.[2]

British defense advisers then chased a series of flops, such as Blue Steel, Blue Streak, and Skybolt missiles, luckily avoiding committing the nation or any long-term funds to any of them. One week after Britain dropped Skybolt, President John Kennedy offered at a Nassau summit meeting to sell Britain Polaris missiles without the warheads at an agreeable cost and further offered assistance in building the submarines, presumably meaning thereby the provision of assistance in the realm of nuclear propulsion. The British accepted, and their four submarines (built in Britain) cost 13 percent less than estimated. These four boats have provided the most survivable element of the British nuclear deterrent since that time. But in the 1970s, like the American Polaris/Poseidon force, the British ballistic-missile subs began to exhibit their age. To replace them, Her Majesty's government has had to face the decision of whether to continue its nuclear deterrent force and, if so, whether or not to modernize the submarine force particularly.[3]

At about the same time American strategists conducted the STRAT-X study, British Prime Minister Harold Wilson ordered a similar review for the purpose of making recommendations about improving England's strategic forces. The program, known as Chevaline, that emerged from the study proposed to improve the Polaris missile warheads, equip them with greater penetration aids, and replace the deteriorating propellant with more stable and powerful compounds. However, the decision to undertake the Chevaline program and to continue it at a critical point was made by a select group of five ministers (the Prime Minister, the Chancellor of the Exchequer, and the Home, Foreign, and Defense Secretaries). The "closed" nature of the decision led later to concern over the proposal to buy Trident missiles, since many feared that the country's strategic decisions might be made without sufficient debate. About the same time the government adopted the Chevaline program it started to grapple with the more substantial problem of finding a follow-on to the Polaris missile. Cabinet committees decided that a new-generation deterrent was necessary, but left the specifics up to the political winds.[4]

Soon after Margaret Thatcher became prime minister in the summer of 1979, she visited Washington to discuss American contributions to a potential Polaris replacement, although Mrs. Thatcher made it clear that Britain had not yet finalized the decision to follow Polaris with another submarine missile system. By July, 1980, though, the government had reached its decision, and the Prime Minister and the Cabinet opted for Trident missiles, to be purchased from the United States and borne in a new generation of British-built SSBNs. The United States offered to pay the development costs of the missile, and the British would get the most favorable terms of sale arrangeable. Besides building its own submarines, Britain agreed to pay a 5-percent surcharge as a contribution to the development costs and to pay for the manning of the Rapier surface-to-air missile sites protecting American air bases in England. Once again, a strategic deterrent decision had been made largely without the participation of Parliament, a form of tight decision-making that sparked numerous heated debates.[5]

Conjuring up memories of the Nassau agreement on Polaris, whereby both President John Kennedy and Prime Minister Harold Macmillan agreed that Britain needed a "non-nuclear sword" as well as a "nuclear shield," Mrs. Thatcher stated that the government intended to use anticipated "savings" generated by a reduction of obsolete surface units and by a joint sharing of production costs of the Trident I missiles to bolster the conventional forces. The White House confirmed this goal by announcing that the British "were *committed* to taking the estimated $4 billion they would 'save' and using it to improve their conventional capability." British defense officials estimated the Trident I program cost at $9.2 billion by the 1990s, with another billion needed if a fifth sub should be added. Costs of this magnitude prompted members of Parliament to hustle out their pocket calculators and realize that there would not be any savings with the Trident purchase. Quite the opposite, it would cut into the defense budget in other areas. Opponents quickly backed an alternative plan that featured nuclear-powered submarines carrying cruise missiles, while the British antinuclear forces took to the streets, replete with death's-head masks and "No Nukes" banners. Parliament erupted into a major defense policy debate, according to one source, the first of its type in fifteen years.[6]

Implications of the Proposed Trident Missile Purchase

What is at stake in the British Trident purchase? What is its impact on other forces, conventional and nuclear, submarine-related and non-submarine-related? What is Trident's political impact on its supporters and opponents? And, finally, how will the answers to these questions affect the rest of NATO?

One of the thorniest problems involved in estimating Trident's impact is that the British must replace their *Resolution*-class submarines with new subs capable of launching the Trident I missile, at the very least, if the United Kingdom shall continue to belong to the world's strategically significant big powers. As of 1983 the *Resolution*-class force consisted of four submarines, each 425 feet long with a 33-foot hull diameter. Each nuclear-powered sub is capable of making 25 knots and carries sixteen Polaris A-3 missiles, each with three nonmaneuverable reentry vehicles of 200 kilotons each. Launched in 1968, the *Revenge* represents the last boat in this class, with the age of the entire force now dictating that a successor be developed soon if the force is to avoid block obsolescence. The British government, however, continues to hesitate in producing and approving designs or in issuing the corresponding long-lead orders for submarine construction.[7]

In a startling move, John Nott, the defense secretary, suggested in 1981 that the Reagan administration's decision to accelerate development of the Trident II missile might benefit the United Kingdom as well. Nott argued that by the time the British were ready for the Trident I missiles in the 1990s, the United States might have shut its production line down in favor of the Trident II. Thus Britain would either have to buy the Trident I missiles early and store them, pay extra to reopen the Trident I production lines, or buy the Trident II with its increased capability before Britain would have an available SSBN platform. Since the Trident II will not be available until 1989, the Thatcher government could, according to Nott, also defer its heavy costs, thereby minimizing the immediate drain on the country's beleaguered finances, exacerbated by the unexpected defense expenditures (nearly $1.5 billion) occasioned by the 1982 Falklands "punitive expedition."[8]

When early designs finally appeared, at least in rough form, a concept for two different submarines capable of carrying both the Trident I and Trident II missiles was suggested. The larger Trident II sub would displace 14,700 tons, have a hull diameter of 42 feet, and have a length of 450 feet, compared to the Trident I sub with its proposed diameter of 34 feet and 10,000-ton displacement. Cost estimates put the smaller vessel at £5,125 million, with the larger sub estimated to cost £474 million to £1000 million more. Each Trident II missile would carry six more reentry vehicles than the Trident I, with a 1500-mile increase in range for a total range of 5500 miles. Expense attributable to the differential in missile cost alone is about £390 million. But the increased cost due to inflation and the declining value of the pound relative to the dollar totals almost four times *more* than the added cost of the Trident II missile. Moreover, the percentage of the defense budget allocated for strategic forces amounted to only 9 percent, even with the Trident II purchase.[9]

The debate over upgrading British nuclear forces developed a number of unusual turns. Public debate represented the first official, prolonged discussion about Britain's military policy in fifteen years. Following the appointment of a number of committees by the House of Commons, another aspect became apparent: the members did not even consider whether to continue the country's nuclear deterrent but only what form it should take. Experiences with the Skybolt and the Blue Streak missiles, combined with growing evidence of Soviet antimissile and antiaircraft improvements, led the British to consider sea-based deterrents and ballistic-missile submarines almost exclusively.[10]

Many experts, especially from Her Majesty's Loyal Opposition, believed Britain had no need for a system with the size, cost, or capability of the Trident. For these experts, a cruise-missile submarine force would provide a cheaper alternative more attuned to British goals of "credible minimum deterrent." Colonel Jonathan Alford recommended a cruise-missile submarine force to the select committee of the House of Commons in July 1980. It would not require the sophisticated onboard guidance systems of the Polaris and Trident missiles, because it would not be aimed at hard targets. Thus, according to a July 20, 1980, editorial in the Manchester *Guardian*, "Britain needs only a crude deterrent." Dependence on the Americans would not be alleviated by the use of cruise missiles, the *Guardian* admitted, and first-generation cruise missiles might not be able to penetrate Soviet air defenses. Nevertheless, most civilian critics, voicing their concerns in newspapers and magazines such as the *Guardian* and *The Economist*, viewed cruise missiles as a "cheap" alternative to the Trident force. David Fairhall called the cruise missile, mounted in Royal Air Force ground batteries, "the cheapest nuclear deterrent we could buy," and only somewhat less expensive but also less vulnerable "would be Royal Navy Submarines equipped for . . . launching long range Cruise missiles." This type of force with an equivalent number of missiles (not warheads), according to Fairhall, would leave £200 million for development costs and still save £4000 million. A March 29, 1980, issue of *The Economist* urged "Don't Forget the Cheap One" and asserted that a cruise-missile force of two hundred "would probably be less than a fifth of [the cost of] the Trident system's £5 billion." *Guardian* writer Peter Jenkins, calling for a delay in purchasing the Trident, agreed that a cruise-missile force might be cheaper. However, he resisted supporting a cruise option because it might have a detrimental impact on arms limitation talks. His position excepted, most letters to the editors supported a cruise option acquirable for £800 million. Yet others viewed the cruise missile as a "defensive" weapon, while Trident missiles represented "offensive" weapons.[11]

Despite some of the public's displeasure with the Trident over its impact on the arms race or over costs in general, Parliament demonstrated greater concern about the impact of Trident sales on conventional naval forces, particularly those forces committed to ASW or otherwise pledged to NATO. Responding to the 1980 Soviet invasion of Afghanistan, the British announced an increase in defense spending of 3.5 percent in real terms for the 1980–1981 budget. Besides the Trident and submarine programs, Britain embarked on a major effort to improve the weapons of the army, including replacement of the Chieftain battle tank with a more modern model. Also included in the budget was the establishment of the first two squadrons of Sea Harrier aircraft especially adapted to serve as submarine killers (although these aircraft demonstrated unexpected versatility in air-control and ground-support roles in the Falklands war as well). By November, 1980, however, the worsening financial situation clouded the issue of force modernization, leading the chief secretary to the Treasury, John Biffen, to suggest to defense minister Francis Pym cuts in defense of £400 million. Among the weapons potentially affected by the recommended cuts, the Harrier, a new ASW helicopter under development in conjunction with Italy, and other navy programs for surface vessels, all would have an impact on Britain's ASW capability in NATO. Originally the government had promised the Royal Navy that Trident funds would not be charged against its share of the defense budget "but would come from a special strategic section in the ministry's overall budget." But the November, 1980, review led navy officials to expect the worst.[12]

John Nott, Secretary of State for Defense, led the review with the intention of trimming the fat and yet maintaining a 3-percent-per-year rise in real terms. Nott wanted to "exploit new technology and tactics," an admittedly broad goal including purchase of new heavyweight torpedoes to take better advantage of the Royal Navy's attack subs, and to make decisions on the best course to proceed in the purchase of the Harrier force. Just under half of the 1981–1982 budget consisted of equipment expenditures, with 10 percent of that fraction dedicated to submarine expenditures alone. Inevitably, Nott concluded, Great Britain had to reduce its rate of shipbuilding. He also revealed that, in addition to planned development of the Sea Eagle missile, the ASW Harriers would carry free-fall nuclear bombs.[13]

When further details of Nott's plan became known, the Tories erupted in "shock and anger." Nott had suggested cutting $2 billion from the defense budget over a ten-year period, with 75 percent of the cuts coming from the Royal Navy. Half of the surface fleet of frigates and destroyers would have been lost under the plan through early retirement and canceled projects, although Nott wanted to increase the availability of funds for attack submarines and sea-patrol aircraft by $367 million. Leaks plagued Nott's attempts to present the package to Parliament himself, with the most severe breaches emanating from Keith Speed, Undersecretary for the Navy. In a speech warning against cuts in navy spending, Speed hinted that Nott planned to reduce the navy to a coastal defense force and disband the Royal Marines. Mrs. Thatcher quickly demanded Speed's resignation, but Speed delivered some parting shots in a speech in the House of Commons. His concerns were echoed in Europe, and especially in West Germany, where one defense analyst said "We don't consider it wise for Britain to consider weakening the alliance's conventional defense in order to finance an independent nuclear deterrent." But Nott responded that England "can no longer afford to defend itself against its enemies and be sentimental on the way." Britain's contribution of ships to NATO would be cut by nine vessels, a reduction to a total of fifty ships, consigning most of the older vessels to mothballs. Another eight non-NATO-assigned surface ships would also face early retirement.[14]

Whether the British eventually move to the Trident II system or not underscores the more important conclusion at which the British government has arrived: Britain continues to feel it needs an independent nuclear deterrent force. This conclusion rejects calls for unilateral disarmament and singularly rejects calls to reduce British forces to a purely conventional role. Serious questions about the nature and composition of the British armed forces nevertheless remain. R. N. Rosecrance in *The Defense of the Realm* has shown that the United States has not always seen its interests as compatible with those of the United Kingdom, as evidenced in the 1956 Suez crisis, for example. Paradoxically, the "ban-the-bomb" movements have increased rather than reduced Britain's reliance on the United States for nuclear technology. Admiral Peter Hill-Norton has divined yet another important factor in favor of a separate British deterrent: "The value of Britain's missile subs to the alliance lies not in their numbers but in that they are a nuclear force committed to the alliance . . . with the center of decision about their use elsewhere than in the hands of an American president." In short, the goal of both American and British deterrence has always been individually and jointly to make the threat of a retaliatory strike against an enemy so costly that it would not dare undertake overt aggression. This duality of capability increases the uncertainty that any hostile leader would face in deciding whether and how to employ nuclear weapons. David Fairhall, in one of his more mature discussions, explains that "a Russian military commander, let alone his political superior, would be mad to stake the survival of his major cities on the ability to destroy two [*sic*] British submarines simultaneously somewhere in the open Atlantic."[15]

One cannot underplay a number of subtleties absent from the standard anti-Trident arguments. If Chevaline was considered a necessity for penetrating the Soviet defenses of the 1970s, it will be nearing the obsolete stage soon. Improvements in Soviet air defenses may have already rendered many of the British Polaris reentry vehicles ineffective through Soviet deployment of reentry-vehicle decoying techniques and through more sophisticated ABM capability. By the end of the 1980s a Polaris force—even fully improved by the Chevaline program—might pose only a modest threat to the Soviets. Likewise, as an alternative, cruise missiles have great capabilities but also great weaknesses. They are slow enough to be destroyed by aircraft with look-down-shoot-down capability as well as by missiles, and, due to the long subsonic flight time from England to Russia, virtually every aircraft in

Eastern Europe would have a chance to attack cruise missiles. Given an expected extremely high attrition rate, very few land-based cruise missiles would penetrate Soviet defenses in the event Britain acted independently. In awareness of these limitations, and realizing the Soviets would have thousands of strategic missiles survivable against a cruise-missile attack, it would be madness for British military leaders to expect a handful of surviving cruise missiles to deter a Soviet attack. Moreover, the suggestions to base cruise missiles on land as the sole British deterrent overlook the potential of the Soviets to use SLBMs in a surprise attack to eliminate the cruise-missile bases before they can launch. The United States has extensive plans to use cruise missiles, but only in a TRIAD context as a follow-on saturation weapon to be used *after* ICBMs have destroyed air defenses. Use in a theater context is also planned, but no American plans exist for primary strategic reliance on the cruise missile.

Total British nuclear disarmament would probably also generate ripples substantially affecting the French strategic modernization programs. Recollection of eight Anglo-French wars between 1689 and 1815 may no longer stir emotions on either side of the Channel, but a fifteen-year span of history turned postwar Germany from foe to friend, and a similar dramatic shift in the present European balance-of-power system could witness other less amicable changes in roles; these, while clearly not anticipated, always remain in the realm of the possible. Since Germany is banned from possession of nuclear weapons by the 1955 agreements bringing the Federal Republic into NATO, France would thus be the sole nuclear power on the Continent except Russia. Imagine, for example, the scenarios sometimes suggested by European disarmament advocates. The United States and the Soviet Union, out of a misunderstanding, embark upon a long-range war that leaves Europe, for whatever motives, temporarily untouched. Neither superpower remains a viable national entity, and Europe is transformed overnight (barring extensive side effects from the nuclear strikes, a hypothetical point that is disputed) roughly back to her pre-1914 status, except that the dominant power on the Continent would suddenly have the only nuclear force left. One could also imagine a more likely situation in which a coup or revolution in France could replace that stable democracy with a Qaddafi-type megalomaniac. Under such circumstances a separate British deterrent would be critical and an independent German nuclear force would even be desirable. Perhaps less frivolously, it should be pointed out that the presence of two European powers with strategic forces also softens intra-European NATO political bargaining since they tend to countervail each other, thereby enabling European non-nuclear powers within

NATO to feel less threatened by a monopoly, not to mention the fact that even an unintegrated European nuclear club also modestly adulterates the political attitude of NATO's transatlantic superpower as well.[16]

A successor to Polaris thus seems a necessity, one incapable of fulfillment by cruise-missile submarines. Either Trident I or Trident II will take a bite out of the budget—of that there can be no doubt. Where, then, should this impact be felt? Britain must maintain its ASW capability for NATO to have any hope of reinforcing the Continent in the event of a war with the Soviet Union. Consequently, the fifteen attack submarines in operation and under construction for the Royal Navy must receive funds. But for the British to speed up their attack submarine construction, other things being equal, would be unwise. Some semblance of a balanced fleet must be maintained for, among other reasons, proper defense of the GIUK Gap. It is important that the British surface-mounted ASW capability continue to receive funds along with attack subs. Fleet aircraft cariers and "through-deck carriers" ought to continue to play a significant role in ASW operations alongside the SSNs and smaller surface-borne ASW platforms, and these should not be abandoned. Less important for the British is their continued retention of the Vulcan bomber force, short of its resale, for example, after the Falklands episode, to such unpredictable powers as Argentina! Soviet surface vessels or Oscar submarines firing cruise missiles today could put the British V-bomber air bases out of action in short order. Without an effective surface force to clear the marginal nonterritorial waters of surface and submarine threats, the bomber force faces problems. Wherever the British eventually plan to place the burden of their cuts, the process will be painful, and it may require a thorough review of the British presence in Germany as a part of NATO. Two areas must remain intact, however, in some form: the British strategic deterrent and the British ASW contribution. Protection of these areas seemed to be assured in April 1982 when Nott, in announcing the decision to purchase the Trident II, also stated that ASW would receive 20 percent of defense procurement funds over the next fifteen years.[17]

The Role of France

Like Great Britain, France has had to undergo a substantial image reassessment since World War II. Under Charles de Gaulle, France withdrew from the integrated command structure of NATO in 1967 and suddenly faced the challenge of providing for its own strategic defense (although the French continue to send observers to NATO maneuvers, maintain at least two divisions inside Germany, and depend upon NATO early-warning systems for launch-time notification for their bomber and IRBM force). France has maintained separate targeting independent of the NATO forces and, unlike Britain, which relies only on SSBN submarines and manned bombers, has developed a TRIAD system of its own. In 1982 France had five nuclear-powered ballistic-missile submarines, each carrying sixteen M-20 missiles. Each missile carries only one warhead of one megaton (with penetration aids) and has a range of 1850 nautical miles. Two squadrons of intermediate-range ballistic missiles add eighteen more warheads to the defensive forces. The land-based missiles have approximately the same range as their submarine-launched counterparts. France also has a force of thirty-seven Mirage IV-A strategic bombers, of which most will be phased out by 1985.[18]

Also called the *force de frappe* and the *force de dissuasion*, the French strategic triad (officially entitled the Force Nucléaire Stratégique, or FNS) uses weapons systems built and developed in France. The bomber force, the oldest of the triad elements, dating as a strategic system back to 1964, consists of Dassault Mirage IV-A bombers complete with electronic jamming devices to enhance low-altitude penetrations. Of the forty-seven Mirage bombers still in service, ten have been assigned to reconnaissance and training roles. Thirty-seven remain as strategic bombers, their 2000+-mile range supplemented by twelve Boeing KC-135F tankers to perform in-flight refuelings. Each Mirage carries one 60-kiloton bomb. Based at nine dispersed airfields, the bomber force faces a greater warning-time reaction challenge than its American counterpart since it is susceptible to Soviet intermediate-range mobile missiles as well as a threat common to the American land-based forces, submarine-launched missiles. Concerns over increasing Soviet arms buildups have led France to extend the retirement deadlines, once scheduled for 1975, by a decade. In 1980, a "lively debate" over the French defense budget produced evidence that, in addition to extending the lives of these aircraft further, they probably will be armed with air-to-surface missiles with warheads five times more powerful than those on the gravity bombs currently in use.[19]

Intermediate-range ballistic missiles form the second leg of the French nuclear triad. Operational in 1972, the missile system is located on the Albion Plateau in southeastern France and consists of two groups of nine missiles placed in individually hardened shelters. Initially, S-2 missiles, each carrying a 150-kiloton warhead and capable of achieving ranges of approximately 1700 miles, made up the entire force. Newer S-3 missiles with range improvements of 300 miles and one-megaton warheads replaced half of the force in 1980. In 1982

France replaced the remainder of the force and has also begun development of a new series of missiles "capable of carrying nuclear warheads . . . designed for both strategic and tactical warfare." New M-4 sea- and land-launched missiles have been developed, improving the range over that of the S-3 by 400 miles. These missiles also increase the payload by carrying six MRVs of 150 kilotons each. In November 1981 French Defense Minister Charles Hernu announced plans for the addition of two new missiles with ranges of approximately 200 miles, each capable of carrying standard nuclear and neutron warheads. One of these new missiles, the Hades, will replace the Pluton missile, while the other is to be truck-mounted. Although these missiles most likely would be used in a theater and subtheater capacity, their addition will nevertheless further upgrade the French nuclear capability.[20]

Improvements such as these help strengthen two of the legs of the French triad. Still, most French defense officials agree that the ballistic-missile submarine force "is undoubtedly the most important component of the triad in terms of . . . its relative invulnerability, . . . its throwweight and . . . its penetrability against ABM defences." *Le Redoubtable*, the first French ballistic-missile submarine, made its maiden cruise as a deterrent in 1971, with three sister ships following between 1973 and 1976 and with a fifth submarine joining the fleet in 1980. Each SSBN carries sixteen M-20 missiles, each with a range of 1800 miles and delivering a one-megaton warhead. By 1980 the M-4 missile, which France intends to use in a dual role as both IRBM and SLBM, was being tested. French ballistic-missile subs also have four torpedo tubes forward, with an 18-torpedo inventory. Due to the extra SSBN submarine in force, with a sixth given approval for construction in 1981, France will have three submarines on station at all times. Thus France can maintain more SLBMs at sea than England can, although the British Polaris missiles far outperform the M-20s, both in range (2500 miles against 1600 miles) and in number of reentry vehicles (3 RVs × 200 kt vs. 1 × MT) carried. However, this, too, will change when the sixth submarine enters the force, as *L'Inflexible* will carry the new M-4 missile with its increased range (2500 nm) and its increased number (seven) of reentry vehicles. France will also retrofit the other submarines with the M-4.[21]

A New European Strategic Arrangement and Trident

Apparently, then, in light of the tremendous budgetary drag the Trident missile purchase will place on Britain and given the French commitment to a modernized TRIAD of strategic systems, both nations inevitably will feel the budgetary pinch. France cannot much longer maintain a penetrating bomber force at a technological level sufficient to ensure numerically adequate penetration, let alone the ability to inflict vital damage at any significant level. Neither can the British, and even the American B-1B, although now in production, will require constant upgrading to perform its duties. Both the British and the French, of course, could totally scrap their strategic concept of nuclear bomber forces (they should *not* abandon them entirely, especially in terms of subtheater missions or against other potential adversaries, as the British learned about the utility of the Vulcan bomber in its "last" year of deployment during the Falklands crisis). Furthermore, a major partner in the Western alliance is ignored in the entire discussion—Germany. Nearly forty years have elapsed since the end of the Second World War. The Nazis no longer are in power, a real neo-Nazi revival is improbable, and the Nazi past should not be politically paid for eternally, so it is time the Germans share in their own strategic defense as well as in continuing to provide quite substantially for their own conventional defenses. Russia has, despite wailing and gnashing of teeth, accepted the principle of nuclear missiles in Germany under NATO command in the form of the "two keys" control concept. Increasing costs must eventually lead the British, French, and Germans to the consideration of a combined European strategic force along the general lines of the earlier but ill-fated European Defense Community (EDC) scheme of 1954. It is simply in the better interests of these three major allies to effect a truly fair readjustment of their present unequal strategic statuses among themselves and thereby also to effect a more mature, more autonomous and coherent European theater strategic capability vis-a-vis the American nuclear umbrella. By putting the ten-submarine combined Anglo-French force into the hands of an EDC-type joint command, with expenses split three ways or perhaps shared on a pro rata basis between the three nuclear "seniors" and the other European nonnuclear "juniors" (especially Italy), the advantages would more than offset the loss of the strategic bomber forces. For example, with the Trident II missile's greater payload, the ratio of boats on patrol would not be as critical as it now is, especially for the British alone, while the modestly larger total force at a given time under one command would strengthen the overall deterrent. With Germany sharing the costs of the joint seaborne deterrent, Great Britain would be better able to support its existing surface fleet and its ASW capability as well. Roughly, the "neo-EDC" concept would distribute duties and burdens as follows: Germany would continue to provide the bulk of NATO's land forces and pay for one-third of the strategic force (leaving aside, for a moment, the variables of the American cruise missiles). France would progressively phase out its strategic bomber force in the manner outlined above and continue to maintain both its land-based missiles and its expanding submarine force. Both of these would be funded out of the pooled funds. Britain would phase out its bomber force in the above sense and, using pooled funds, while stretching out its present Resolution class SSBNs, also effect the transition to the eventual Trident II class. Germany, for its part, would gain direct access to the joint command of a NATO-coordinated, European-theater, independently controlled nuclear weapons strategic force for its one-third contribution. France would gain assistance in paying for its DIAD, and Britain would gain assistance in funding its MONAD. Also, unlike the personnel complications involved with the culturally and operationally complicated McNamara-era multilateral force scheme, which entailed multiethnic "mixed" crews, the EDC-like sea deterrent system might lend itself much more easily to crew changeovers of a consistently national basis, so that at any time at least one EDC ballistic-missile submarine would be manned by one crew from each of the three major joint participants.[22]

Besides the "middle-range" option of consigning to an EDC-like strategic command structure either or both (the maximal objective) the British and French existing SSBN fleets, later followed by the consignment of either or both the British Trident II and French *L'Inflexible* classes (again, the maximal objective, naturally), a "lower" and a "higher" option are also conceivable within the overall framework of the EDC concept. The lower option would be, as more Tridents become available to the United States Navy, perhaps at the point when the seventh SSBN has been operationally deployed, to lease on a *rotational* basis a *Lafayette*-class SSBN now retrofitted with the Trident I missile. This option would spare the British defense budget the necessity of buying the Trident II missile and the associated home-built vessels while nevertheless equipping the EDC with a constantly available deterrent with greater operational range and capability, greater missile range, greater warhead reentry vehicle numbers, and greater megatonnage than either or both of their respective strategic forces could furnish. The higher option would be, perhaps at the point when the tenth or twelfth Trident has been operationally deployed by the United States, to lease on a rotational basis an *Ohio*-class SSBN equipped either with the Trident I or Trident II missile. This option would further spare the British and French defense budgets, allowing them to freeze their own SSBN commitments and slowly phase them out while nevertheless equipping the EDC with maximum SSBN–SLBM capabilities in all categories of performance on a thoroughly

EDC budgetary basis. From the viewpoint of the military security of United States submarine technology, the risks of compromise generally scale up the higher the option chosen, but this risk ought to be substantially offset by Allied budgetary savings, stronger conventional forces (assuming the "savings" between the separate pursuit of two independent SSBN systems and the commitment to an EDC Trident system of some sort are really dedicated to this purpose), more tightly coordinated targeting, greater survivability, and increased EDC–NATO–USA strategic commonality. In the longest possible perspective of the EDC concept, indeed, a total integrated progression of all of these options can be envisaged in which each naturally follows the other in policy, systems, and cost terms rather than in viewing each as an alternative choice to the others. Finally, again, no option of lower, middle, or higher range is incompatible with the multilateral concept of crew-manning on a scheduled revolving basis by nationality, with the Lion team being British, the Fleur-de-Lis team being French, and the Bier-und-Brot team being German!

Clearly this is a novel and provocative suggestion, and admittedly it entails the necessity to resolve some thorny political, security, and institutional problems. Moscow, for example, would vehemently object to Germans having possession of "the bomb." France would have to confront the reality of the problems associated with abandoning an absolutely independent force, while the United Kingdom would have to buy still another "continental ticket" of admission to another European community when it is still not sure of the price-worthiness of its original admission to the European Community itself. While it is not predicted here that this incomparable arrangement might develop, at least its proposal illustrates more clearly a number of European strategic problems and simultaneously points out that certain European political elites have ignored earlier European ideas of the "classical" era of the 1950s unification movement while continuing somewhat hypothetically to castigate United States leadership for its "overbearing," "untrustworthy," or "indifferent" superpower attitude toward Europe's "real" needs. In short, whereas European constituent nation-state members institutionally devised an answer to place effectively every member's "finger on the trigger" of the European Atomic Agency, the Coal and Steel Community, the European Common Market (now called the EC, or European Community), and the European Parliamentary Assembly, comparable political and institutional ingenuity in the realm of strategic defense has consistently not been manifested—though the opportunities, needs, and solutions seem readily evident. Hopefully, then, this analysis presumes simply to suggest that a Europewide setting is a solution far superior to a purely British force plan for a seaborne missile with the accuracy, payload, range, and cost of the Trident II.

The U.S. Trident and European Forces in Strategic Interaction

Hypotheticals aside, how, then, does the U.S. Navy's Trident force fit into the picture for the French, or even the British, exclusive of the budgetary problems involved in the purchase of the missile? The situation must be viewed in two ways. First, its contribution to the existing European strategic forces will enable those forces to develop greater flexibility. On the other hand, the capabilities of the U.S. Navy's Trident might well signal the obsolescence of the less capable SSBNs in the French and British submarine fleets. Trident will automatically force the Soviets to intensify and broaden their ASW capability, possibly to the extent that Soviet ASW improvements will seriously threaten Allied subs lacking Trident's defensive weapons, range, speed, and quietness.

With its increased patrol range, the United States Trident force will permit the deployment of French and British strategic submersible fleets farther out to sea in a more expansive arc, subsequently drawing Soviet ASW capability also correspondingly farther out. Since Trident missiles could, theoretically, cover Soviet targets farthest away, the French and British subs need move only somewhat farther out to sea and target only the closer Soviet targets. To be operationally even more effective than now, the British and French submarines could cruise somewhat *outside* their actual range, relying on their speed to take them quickly back within firing range shortly after warning or after attack itself. This additional band of operational flexibility could extend the range of these forces by an additional 30 to 40 miles or more—which means, for example, an effective surface operating area increase of 20,000 square miles. The option provided by the presence of an American Trident submarine is a gift of greater range to the Allied subs with no proportional decrease in the Alliance's ability to cover any and all targets. Furthermore, U.S. Tridents could temporarily "cover" the British forces by compensating variations in their own targeting commitments so that no British target set would be uncovered simply because a British SSBN was unexpectedly unable to maintain the minimum desirable force on station or because of a breakdown in the relief schedule affecting the turnaround time of a vessel in port. This would effectively double the British forces at sea. Deploying the British and/or French forces farther away from the Continent (and Soviet land-based ASW aircraft) also enhances their individual and joint survivability.

Implications of the Falklands War

In the wake of mounting its military response to the Argentine seizure of the Falkland Islands, British naval authorities necessarily have had to mull over in an incipient form a number of lessons—operationally, structurally, and architecturally—about the Royal Navy today. The first stark lesson is that it is extremely hazardous to make blanket assumptions about the convenience of war to the British Isles. Probably no defense ministry in the world had in its inventory of battle scenarios one suited to the Falklands situation, certainly not the British ministry. The second stark lesson is that it is hazardous in the extreme to mount punitive expeditions or any other fleet operations, especially some 7000 miles from appropriate land-based power, without conventional fleet carrier air cover or some equivalent in nearby land-based capability. Indeed, would the Argentines, assuming all other conditions for the invasion prevailing in 1982, have invaded the Falklands five years ago, when the Royal Navy still possessed five traditional fleet carriers? The last such carrier, the *Ark Royal*, was decommissioned in 1978. Through-deck V/STOL commando attack and ASW carriers appear marginally (and luckily) to be survivable only in exceptional circumstances without fleet air cover of sufficient scope to destroy airborne platforms armed with tactical missiles before they come within their own range. The third lesson is that, even allowing for British good fortune in the combined use of Sea Harriers equipped with the latest antiaircraft AIM-9L Sidewinder missiles and with the selectively available shipboard medium-range Sea Dart and short-range Sea Slug and Sea Wolf missiles for air defense, insufficient numbers of these weapons plagued the forces in the South Atlantic. These systems needed to be further enhanced by airborne early-warning aircraft, either like the United States AWACS system or the upcoming modified Nimrod system. The fourth lesson is that the reduction of even a tradition-rich force like the Royal Navy down to "very little bare metal" enjoys little margin of flexibility in undertaking unexpected and very distant assignments, even if no ships should be lost (the British lost seven ships of various categories, ranging from destroyers to requisitioned naval auxiliaries). This lesson applies not only to the operation specifically at hand but also to other ongoing NATO and non-NATO operations such as backing up the garrison in Belize, protecting North Sea oil rigs, and conducting GIUP surface and submerged ASW duties.

To ignore the size and kind of force that will hereafter have to be maintained in the Falklands itself will also tax the Royal Navy. So seen, the next great debate in Parliament over the mission, structure, and cost of the Royal Navy will doubtless see a more complex and realistic evaluation of all options, including again the Trident II commitment, perhaps with policy conclusions this time more agreeable to Admiral of the Fleet Lord Hill-Norton's rejected propositions of July 1981. However, with the advantages of a post-Falklands perspective, if it perhaps appears that Great Britain might be better off spending the $13-billion Trident II money on replacing losses, modernizing existing equipment, solving the fleet air cover problem, expanding her existing surface fleet, further extending the life of the Resolution-class strategic submarines, building more Trafalgar-class nuclear attack subs, and building up its conventional forces, it does not necessarily follow that European theater defense is better off without an alternative European seaborne basing mode for the Trident II as discussed earlier in this chapter.[23]

The recent growth within the United States of economically nationalistic attitudes, foreign policy neoisolationism, and military antinuclearism confronts a similar set of provincial attitudes among West European states. These provincial views are evidenced partly by the policy fluctuations of the smaller NATO allies regarding the stationing of cruise missiles or Pershing II missiles on their territory, partly by persistent German Federal Republic attitudes toward the Soviet natural gas pipeline and toward undiminished trade with the Soviet Union and its satellite bloc irrespective of Afghan and Polish developments, and partly by West European sympathies for arms "freezes" or "reductions" irrespective of the politico-military necessity of interim rearmament to redress the existing Warsaw Pact–NATO strategic asymmetries. At the Versailles economic conference of June 1982, President Reagan may have partly and temporarily arrested these twin parochial attitudinal dynamics on both sides of the Atlantic. "[O]ld-world nationalism and cultural anti-Americanism," reinforced by European resentment of continued high United States interest rates and correspondingly adverse European and Japanese exchange ratios, nevertheless seriously continue to undermine transatlantic community feelings of economic, military, and political interdependence. The resulting revival of a sentimental search for a solution to Soviet–United States bipolar superpower rivalry in the form of a "third force" is further bolstered by the disarmament movement on both sides of the Atlantic, carefully nurtured by the Soviet Union and its various satellite organizations through propaganda as well as financial and diplomatic assistance of an experienced and sophisticated sort.[24]

Some cynics dedicated to the NATO community have quipped at moments of transatlantic crisis that NATO has more or less always been a "basket case never quite ready for burial," but the Atlantic alliance in 1983 truly appeared in some ways to be closer to progressive abandonment or disintegration than could ever have been conceivable ten years earlier. In a spirit highly reminiscent of the era when Senate Majority Leader Mike Mansfield from Montana annually submitted his call for nonnegotiated and uncompensated U.S. armed forces reductions in Europe, congressmen of diverse political persuasions in 1982 similarly issued superficially sensible calls for troop withdrawals. Liberals hoped thereby to reduce the Pentagon's budget in order to preserve favorite social programs, while the more conservative leaders sought to force the West Europeans and the Japanese, especially, to shoulder a share of the Free World's defense more proportionate to the continuing and unrelieved American burden. A 1982 study published by the Institute of Foreign Policy Analysis in Washington echoed these calls for a pullout in Europe, as well as from Japan and South Korea, based on "two seminal events." One, the "steady and apparently irreversible disintegration" of NATO, the major subtheme of this chapter as it involves the Trident, has been discussed. Also included was the "emergence of a host of new threats . . . in Southwest Asia and in other areas outside Europe." U.S. forces are threatened "as much by what our allies are not doing as by what our adversary might do."[25]

An actual unilateral United States force reduction at this time, ignoring its politico-military impact upon Warsaw Pact intentions, would probably intensify subliminal as well as overt West European fascination with a penultimate posture of "Finlandicized repose"—although be it noted that the Mitterand government constitutes a resolute strategic force exception, since French governments rather consistently, beginning with President De Gaulle, have refused to be bound by U.S.–Soviet bilateral disarmament agreements. Nevertheless, given the political instability that characterizes a number of European governmental attitudes about cruise missiles, the Pershing II, and force reductions in general, the exacerbated post-Falklands British budgetary and strategic dilemma over Trident II, and given the mounting electoral and coalition pressure on the governments in Bonn, France's *force de dissuasion* could turn out to be a monopoly situation from a European viewpoint. Such a reduction out of budgetary elimination (Britain), historical and legal disqualification (West Germany), underdeveloped community sense of common defense (Western Europe), and uninnovative Free World superpower leadership (USA) is really not in anyone's ultimate interest at any level between Bonn and Washington, D.C.

Contrariwise, some version of the EDC concept, if implemented over the next three or four years, not only could avail itself of cruise missile, Pershing II, and Trident technology on an integrated European community theater basis, but it could also rather thoroughly reverse the lively danger of outworn *Ostpolitik*–detente policies degenerating into Finlandicization by the back door of abandoning promised NATO increased expenditures because START negotiations are making them "premature" if not ultimately "unnecessary." The EDC concept would allow considerable cost reductions at the strategic level for all participating European powers and would simultaneously becalm the moral sails of many advocates of unilateral or unequal and unverifiable disarmament by compelling them to choose a feasible policy alternative not in the utopian world of global government (Jonathan Schell in his book *The Fate of the Earth,* for example). The political obstacles to the adoption of such a scheme of regional cooperation, if not integration, are probably greater than the military difficulties, to ignore certain problems for the United States in reconciling some patterns of NATO practices with an emergent EDC pattern. But the Trident SSBN–SLBN system in all of its variations delineated here has much real security, savings, and opportunities to offer the European allies of the United States. It remains to be seen, even with the United States leadership in advocation of such an approach (so far not evident under the Reagan–Weinberger team), whether the Europeans can progress politically and institutionally beyond the incomplete structure of the European Community of 1983 and whether for the first time since July, 1962, U.S. foreign policy has progressed in alliance sophistication beyond the stillborn Kennedy slogan of Atlantic Partnership. The one feature of American foreign policy that consistently ought to generate historical concern is that newer weapons systems, by themselves, are pragmatically regarded as the primary answers to military problems. Hence the United States consistently fails to extract from its advanced military technology the reservoir of political influence its weapons systems inherently contain. The United States has failed to receive maximum benefit from previous weapons arrangements, not only monetarily but also geographically and politically. For once, a colossally significant strategic system like the Trident deservedly ought to be used by the United States to provide the free world not only with greater military prowess but with greater political security as well. The Trident is not a computer chip to be charitably given away for no political advantage; nor is it, to mix metaphors, a provincial virgin which unilaterally should be closeted forever for fear that she won't make a perfect alliance!

12
Knots and Splices

The price of freedom is resolute vigilance; the cost of blindness, defeat. It is far cheaper to win an arms race than to lose a war.

—Harold W. Rood,
Kingdoms of the Blind

While this work has attempted to discuss as thoroughly as possible the Trident program, including the submarines, missiles, and bases, a few related areas have been so far omitted largely because to do otherwise would have involved digressions more involved than should have been undertaken earlier. However, a nucleus of topics deserves some attention even though none warrants a separate chapter. Before a final assessment of the Trident program and a conclusive allocation of praise or blame, the following subtopics will be examined as they relate to Trident:

1. Personnel, organization, and administration
2. The Law of the Sea Treaty and implications for the environment
3. SALT I, II, START, and arms control in general
4. Alternative designs and future uses of the Trident hull system, especially
5. Targeting.

As in the case of technological advances, many of these topics may relate to Trident far more than is readily discernible.

Personnel

In FY 1981 the U.S. Navy exceeded its total enlisted goal, recruiting 106,322 personnel. For twenty-six straight months the Navy made over 100 percent of its quota, and the quality, according to Secretary of the Navy John Lehman, "has been steadily increasing." High-school-graduate enlistees comprised over 80 percent of the total, while trained career personnel retention improved by 21 percent over 1979 figures. Overall, the Navy is returning into the service these highly skilled people at a rate above 1000 per month. Improvements in nuclear officer retention had increased by 23 percent since 1980, with the Navy striving to reduce the time these officers spend at sea, eventually, to eleven years out of the first twenty. Largely due to the recession of 1981–1982 and the pay increases voted by Congress in 1980 and 1982, enlistments continue to rise, accompanied by "a growing awareness on the part of the American public in favor of personnel serving their nation in uniform." Attrition through desertion declined more than 30 percent since 1981, and sea duty extensions increased 58 percent, signs Admiral Thomas Hayward called "healthy indicators." Petty officers remained in short supply (the Navy was 22,000 petty officers short at one point) but the shortage has declined in the past few years.[1]

Submarine personnel forces in the past had experienced severe shortages, but Vice Admiral N. R. Thunman, the U.S. Navy Deputy Chief of Naval Operations for Submarine Warfare, told the House Seapower Subcommittee on March 21, 1982, that the Navy had made "recent gains." In addition to both officer and enlisted-personnel retention, recent trends showed increases in enlistments. Thus, "the overall shortage of nuclear submarine officers which was nearly 1500 five years ago has been reduced to about 1000 [in 1982]." However, for the nuclear field, recruiters had met their goals every month since June 1980. Retention was similarly on an upswing. In 1981 the Navy "had only 70% of the supervisory billets in submarines manned by the required senior petty officers and chief petty officers," while a year later the number had increased to 84%. Shortages of midgrade officers continued, despite the overall improvement in retention.[2]

The average submarine officer currently spends fourteen of his first twenty years of service on submarine sea duty. Nuclear-trained personnel have "sea to shore duty ratios of 5 years to 2 years," a ratio Thunman categorized as a "tough burden." It is the at-sea time, according to many sailors, that is the most difficult in submarine work. In a strategic submarine, two months out of three are normally spent on patrol. A Trident will be at sea seventy days, but its in-port time will be reduced from thirty days to twenty-five. Even with its two crews (Blue and Gold) alternating, a Trident's complement will spend more time at sea than its Poseidon counterparts previously did. Submariners are all volunteers who attend a seven-week sub school in New London, Connecticut, where "more than 1 in 5 washes out."[3]

Besides the expected hazards associated with staying cooped up with more than 150 other men for seventy days, the *Ohio*'s crew, like the crew aboard other nuclear subs, must be wary of radiation. Each sailor and officer wears a thermal-luminescent dosimeter at all times to measure his exposure to radiation, but, said one crew member aboard the *Tecumseh,* "I'll pick up less radiation over two-and-a-half months at sea . . . than I will from one day at the beach." Still, other pressures on submariners make for a less-than-easy tour of duty. Frequent relocation strains family life, a factor that caused the Navy to give attention to its personnel's geographic and social stability when the Bangor base was designed. Captain A. K. Loposer, the first commanding officer of the Trident training facility at Bangor, summarized the advantage of the base for its personnel: "For the first time, if a man really wants to, he can put in almost an entire Navy career here."[4]

On board the Trident, submariners live by an eighteen-, not a twenty-four-hour, day: six hours on duty, twelve off. Without "day or night," sleeping schedules are rearranged, with the average sailor sleeping three to four hours out of eighteen. They spend three to four hours of their off time either training or on preventative maintenance, while six hours are available to them. This schedule may in part contribute to higher turnover rates among submarine personnel. According to the latest research on human circadian clocks—the biological timepieces that run people's schedules—individuals operate at less than full efficiency when pulled off a twenty-four-hour schedule, despite individual choice of sleep time. Martin Moore-Ede in an article argues that the submarine crews' eighteen-hour schedules cause "considerable problems with insomnia, emotional disturbance, and impaired coordination, and their sleep is highly fragmented compared with that of personnel on shore-based installations." Moore-Ede claims there would be "considerable advantage to adopting a 24-hour work-rest schedule for the whole crew, not just for officers, as is the current practice." But if the sleep schedule on Tridents has remained the same as on the Polaris/Poseidon boats, other parts of the shipboard routine have improved. Recreational time can be spent in the gymnasium, reading, or watching a movie. Sixty different films are carried on board, with an individual film shown twice a day. The movies are screened and selected in advance by review panels picked by the crews. Trident subs also have television sets with a full complement of videotapes (and, perhaps by now, video games). To break the monotony, special celebrations mark Hump Day, the midpoint in the patrol. Food, while better than on surface ships, is still "Navy food." Each mess steward must plan meals costing no more than $4.05 per man per day. One Poseidon mess steward said his goal was to serve steak once a week and a specialty dish, such as veal Cordon Bleu, once a patrol. Menus, however, are planned in advance by a crew-member review board, as a consequence of which hamburger appears to be a crew favorite. Subs keep lots of dehydrated milk on board because they run out of fresh milk after two weeks, but crews drink less coffee than is depicted in movies—three to four cups per man per day. Although the *Ohio* at one time had quarters for a medical officer, it and its sister ships no longer have doctors aboard; medical corpsmen now attend to health problems and even to fairly serious emergencies. If an illness becomes serious enough, the submarine will surface for a medical evacuation.[5]

At the Trident's Bangor home, each sub's Blue and Gold crews share in getting the boat into its refit and resupply cycle (see figure 12-1). Immediately upon returning from patrol, the Trident's off crew (say Gold in this instance) immediately goes on a four-day liberty while the Blue crew takes over. At the end of four days, the Gold crew returns to assist the on crew with the refit but is not assigned any watches, working only a normal weekday schedule. The workload is therefore cut all the way around, and work is facilitated by having the training site at the same base as the refit facility, thus eliminating the previously heavy workload for a single refit crew. In fact, one of the yet-uncalculated savings of the Trident program is its fiscal cost gains associated with the availabilities of these two functions at a single base, economizing on fuel and supplies normally used in sailing from one facility to another, entailing wasted time of on-duty personnel who would otherwise have to wait for the submarine. Following rest and recreation, the off crew returns to begin a seven-week training period. Trident crews can be trained at the Bangor facilities nearly 20 percent faster than was previously possible due to new automated monitoring systems, new visual aids, simulators, and teaching techniques. On base, the proximity of quarters to the training facility makes the latter easily accessible by foot.[6]

Until the retirement of Admiral Rickover, high standards for submarine officers were particularly demanding and somewhat unpredictable due to the requirement that potential nuclear submarine officers endure a personal interview by the admiral. Using essentially subjective criteria, Rickover more or less personally "built" the nuclear submarine officer corps, which has proved to be excellent. Rickover, however, also drove off many potentially fine officers. Recruiting and retention of nuclear submarine officers has also been difficult because of low pay, a problem corrected in part by the military pay bills passed in the last five years. In 1979 and 1980 the Navy lacked sufficient numbers of candidates for nuclear training, so it initiated a "draft" of nonvolunteers, but the Navy found the higher attrition rates of the draftees made the program unprofitable, so it returned to pay as its basic inducement.[7]

For Trident, however, the single greatest personnel-related problem

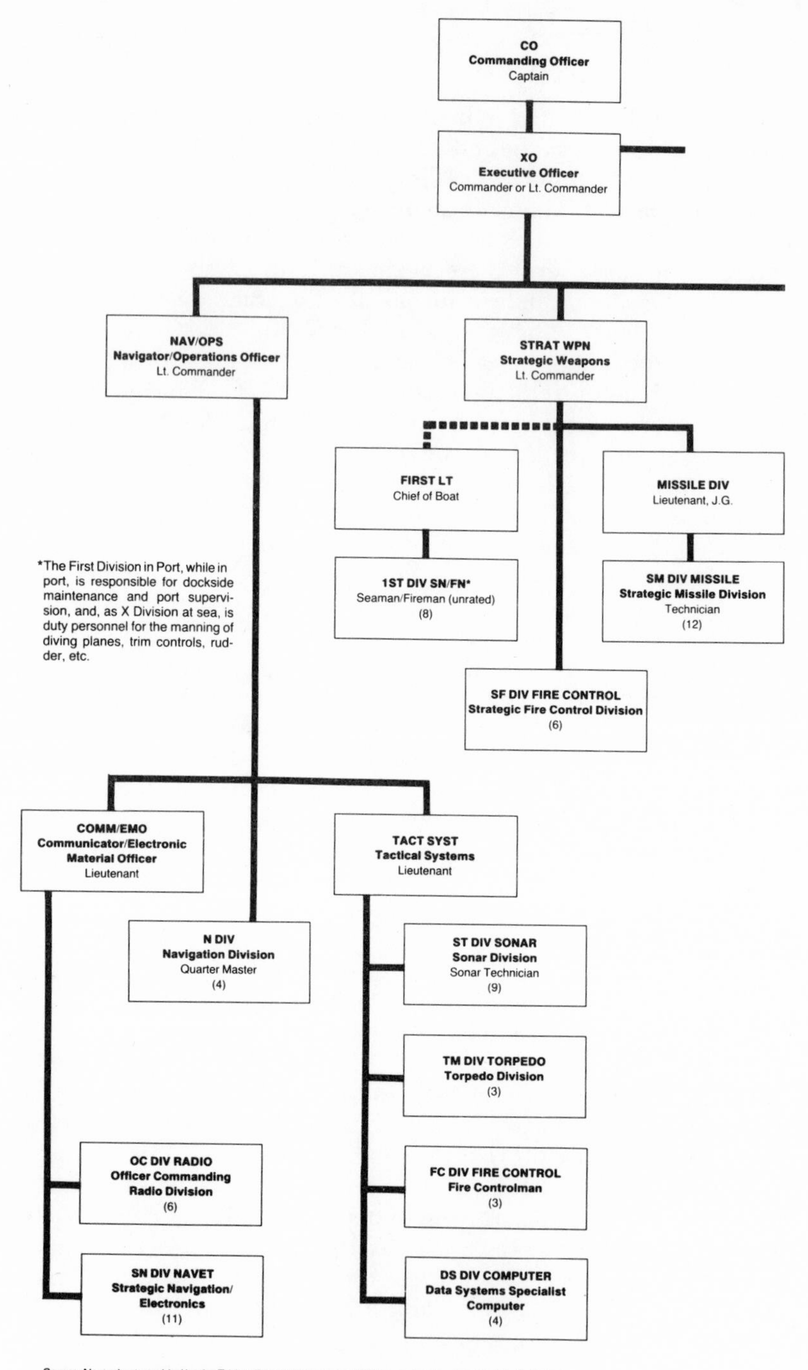

Source: Navy chart provided by the Trident Project Management Office, revised and clarified April, 1983.

Fig. 12-1. Trident organization chart.

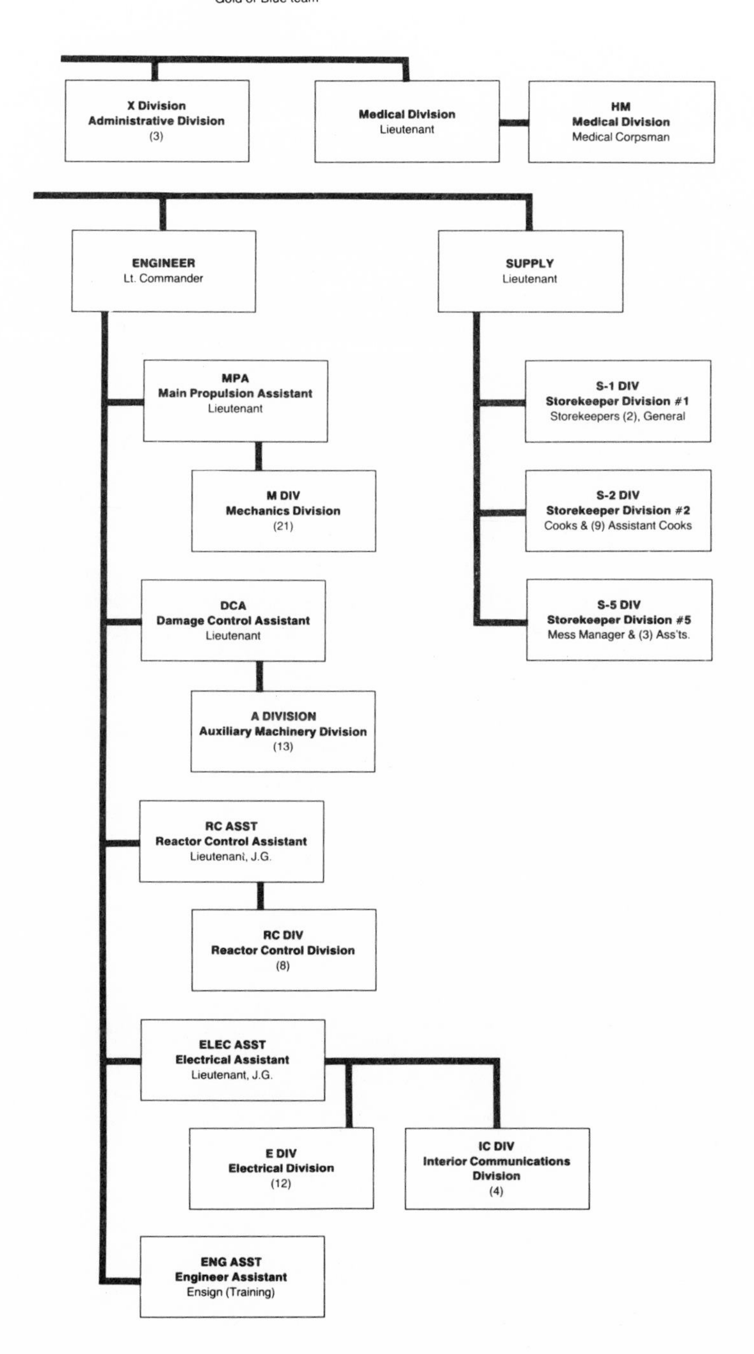

15 officers
142 enlisted men
157 total crew per
Gold or Blue team
X Division
Administrative Division
(3)
Medical Division
Lieutenant
HM
Medical Division
Medical Corpsman
ENGINEER
Lt. Commander
SUPPLY
Lieutenant
MPA
Main Propulsion Assistant
Lieutenant
M DIV
Mechanics Division
(21)
DCA
Damage Control Assistant
Lieutenant
A DIVISION
Auxiliary Machinery Division
(13)
RC ASST
Reactor Control Assistant
Lieutenant, J.G.
RC DIV
Reactor Control Division
(8)
ELEC ASST
Electrical Assistant
Lieutenant, J.G.
E DIV
Electrical Division
(12)
IC DIV
Interior Communications
Division
(4)
ENG ASST
Engineer Assistant
Ensign (Training)
S-1 DIV
Storekeeper Division #1
Storekeepers (2), General
S-2 DIV
Storekeeper Division #2
Cooks & (9) Assistant Cooks
S-5 DIV
Storekeeper Division #5
Mess Manager & (3) Ass'ts.

exists in the organizational structure associated with the construction and quality-control aspects of the program.

The Trident Program in Its Organizational Setting

Whereas Trident, as a weapons system dedicated to deterrence first and retaliation second, will dwell beneath the watery depth for most of its life, its original conception took place on land in a bureaucratic womb. It will continue to produce offspring in the same generative way and to receive sustenance, purpose, communication, and preventive and restorative care by shore-born organizational activity of a complicated nature.

This ever-present cradle of functional-institutional attention therefore needs to be examined somewhat briefly for Leviathan's paradoxical existence to be better appreciated, commencing basically as of the *Ohio*'s keel-laying ceremony on April 10, 1976. While any such chronological point of departure is artificial at least in part, it nevertheless provides a sensible and controllable way to correlate the progress of the strategic system with those perhaps less exciting but inherently indispensable media of "man-in-function." Here the constructive and nutritious processes are programmatically sustained on a systemic basis. This occurs despite the professional and individual alterations, expirations, and successions that take place in order to assure that individual cell units in the life of the military organism are rewarded, tested, fulfilled, advanced, discarded, and replaced.

After acknowledging that cell units are never completely irreplaceable, although occasionally they may become nearly indispensable, a few organizational questions should be posed about the Trident program:

1. What is the position of the Trident program specifically in the bureaucratic web of the Department of Defense and in the Department of the Navy?
2. What are various bureaucratic lodgments in the course of the movement of a Trident from its construction phase to its operational phase?
3. What different structures service, maintain, and husband it and train its crews when it seeks its base for respite and asylum at the end of each deployment cycle?
4. What, selectively, are some other bureaucratic functions that provide contributory support to Trident continuously, without which it could not really perform optimally?
5. What rough observations can be made about extremes of personnel stability and instability that may have benefited or hampered

the Trident program's progress and may therefore have made separate contributions of a different sort to Trident's (*Ohio*'s) program delay?

6. What new bureaucratic appendages may be elaborated in the future and which, if any, may atrophy over the near and intermediate future of the program?

The answers to some of these questions will turn out to be suggestive rather than conclusive, but nevertheless valuable. A more thorough discussion is presented in note 8, and will necessarily involve the use of acronyms, which have been correlated to figures 12-2 and 12-3.[8]

Viewed overall, in the absence of a very precise analysis conducted on the basis of months rather than years served, confident judgements about relative personnel stability/instability operating within those various commands, divisions, and offices as they might influence the progress of the Trident project overall seems very difficult. The roles of Rickover and Smith, however, stand out as very conspicuous exceptions, as they both occurred at the crucial point of transforming a concept into a real construction program. The suspicion must be firmly entertained that Trident would not have made it without them at that time, regardless of their subsequent roles.

Otherwise, the tentative conclusion seems to be that the Trident program is organized somewhat complexly but along fairly rational lines of division of labor. The real worry is not that there is a great deal of instability in any one functional authority but that there may be a very extensively destabilizing cumulative effect as personalities in every constituent bureaucracy routinely change. They arrive at different times, coming from different operational, staff, or professional backgrounds, and sometimes barely succeed in getting all the lines of the Trident network clear in their minds to the point of reasonable mastery before the next era of career development occurs at a subsequent echelon before retirement. Whereas fairly regular rotation of assignment is indispensable for command and operational growth, it may not necessarily be the most productive expectation for a long-term, complex, and highly expensive project like Trident, involving bewildering relationships with the world of civilian contracting as well. The Navy's technique for major project acquisition, at least, probably deserves some rethinking and quiet reform.

The Law of the Sea

United Nations Conferences on the Law of the Sea have met several times since 1958, leading in 1982, after eight years of negotiations, to a draft Law of the Sea Treaty. Provisions of the treaty included controls

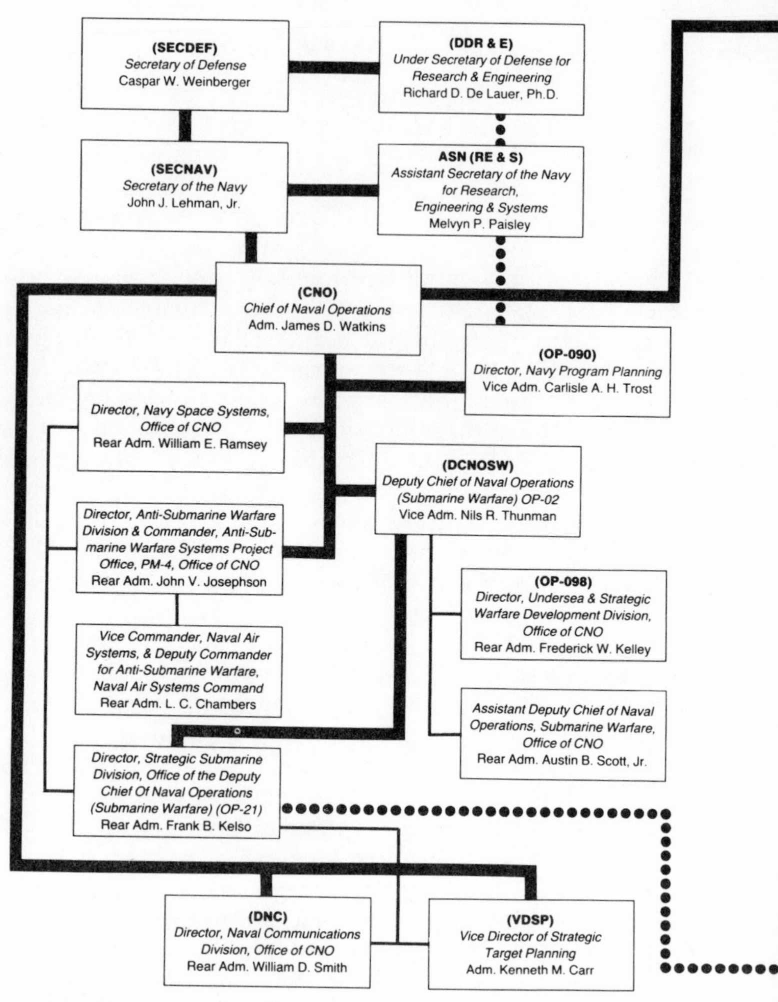

Fig. 12-2. Trident project structure, June 1, 1983.

This organizational chart is intended to clarify three dimensions of organization related to the Trident system: (1) the relationship of Trident as a system to the Department of Defense, the Secretary of the Navy, the Chief of Naval Operations, and to those commands involved in submarine warfare; (2) the agencies which must interact in terms of directing the ongoing fulfillment of the Trident construction project; (3) the relationship of the Bangor base, now complete and being occupied by SSBN-726 (*Ohio*), and the developing Kings Bay facility, awaiting the second Trident squadron. Clearly a number of other command functions are more or less of vital interest to Trident as well, such as Vice Adm. Landow W. Zeck, Jr., Chief of Naval Personnel; Rear Adms. Fred H. Baughman and Edwin Barrineau, Pacific Missile Test Center; Rear Adm. John V. Josephson, Director of Anti-Submarine Warfare Division; Rear Adm. John B. Mooney, Jr., Director, Oceanography Division; Rear Adm. William C. Wyatt III, Fleet Maintenance Officer; Rear Adm. Ronald M. Eytchison, Director, Submarine and Nuclear Power Distribution Control Division of Naval Military Personnel. Also of operational significance are NOSC (Naval Ocean Systems Center), NSOC (Naval Satellite Operations Center) and OSIS (Ocean Surveillance Information System) and others too numerous to be cited. The Trident missile (T-I and T-II) programs have not been shown.

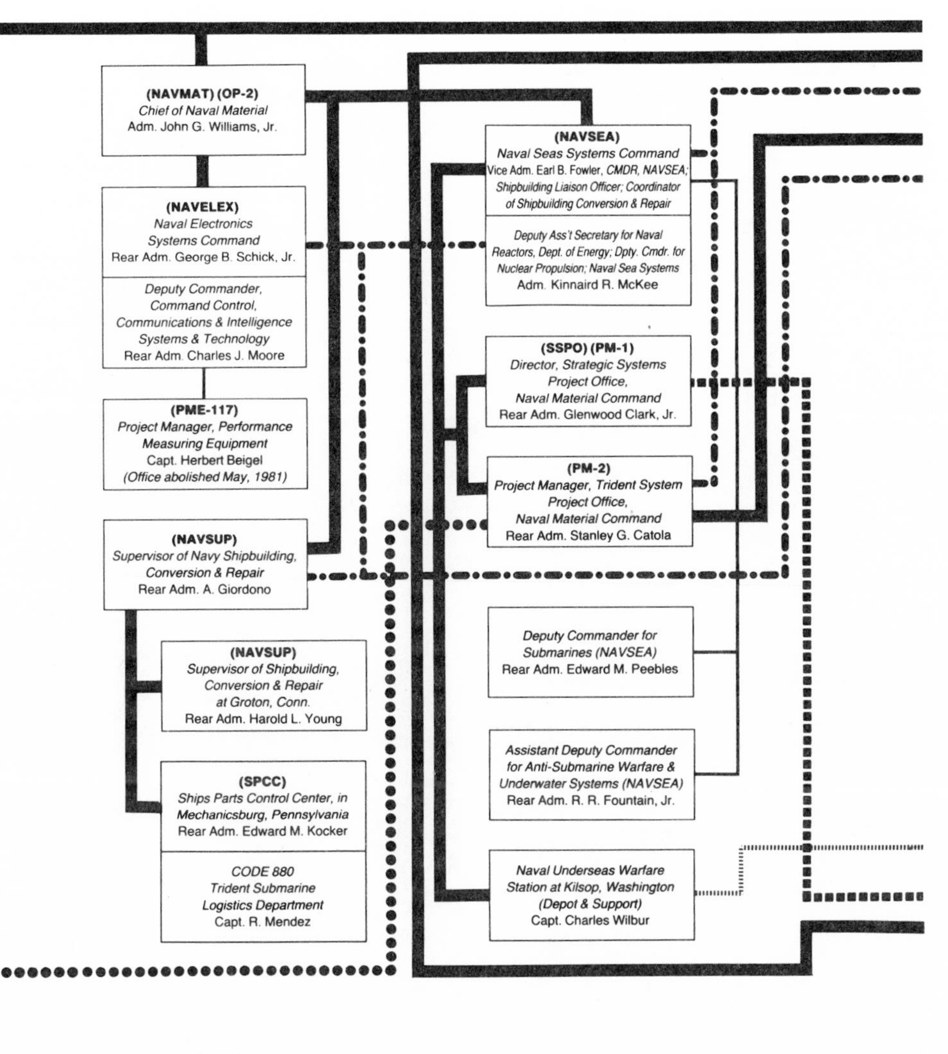

Sources: *Naval Review* for the years 1977, 1978, 1979, 1981, and 1982, *Proceedings; Trident Project Structure*, obtained from Commander Scott Sears, Trident Project Office; information obtained from Chief of Naval Information; additional information and confirmation obtained from the respective command headquarters.

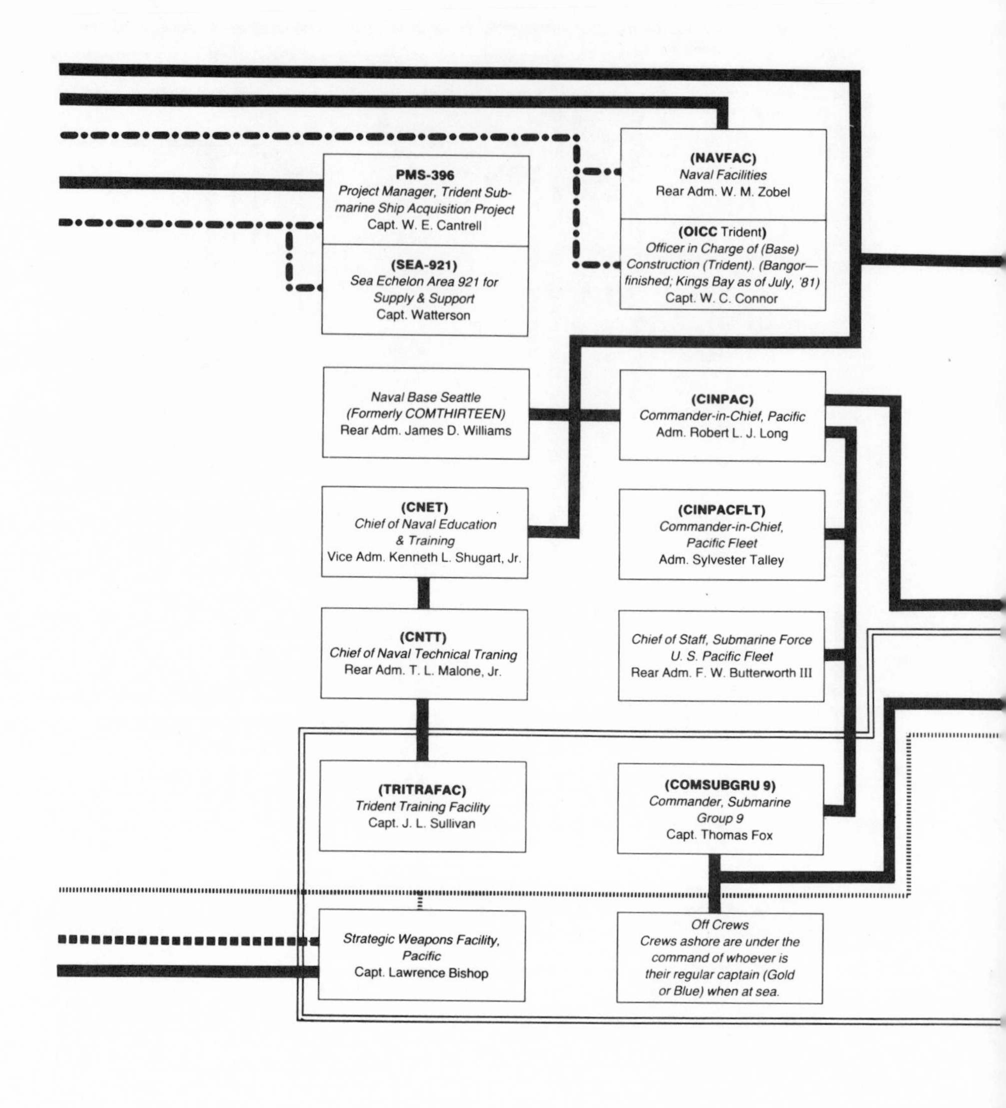

(NAVFAC)
Naval Facilities
Rear Adm. W. M. Zobel
PMS-396
Project Manager, Trident Submarine Ship Acquisition Project
Capt. W. E. Cantrell
(OICC Trident)
Officer in Charge of (Base) Construction (Trident). (Bangor—finished; Kings Bay as of July, '81)
Capt. W. C. Connor
(SEA-921)
Sea Echelon Area 921 for Supply & Support
Capt. Watterson
Naval Base Seattle
(Formerly COMTHIRTEEN)
Rear Adm. James D. Williams
(CINPAC)
Commander-in-Chief, Pacific
Adm. Robert L. J. Long
(CNET)
Chief of Naval Education & Training
Vice Adm. Kenneth L. Shugart, Jr.
(CINPACFLT)
Commander-in-Chief, Pacific Fleet
Adm. Sylvester Talley
(CNTT)
Chief of Naval Technical Traning
Rear Adm. T. L. Malone, Jr.
Chief of Staff, Submarine Force U. S. Pacific Fleet
Rear Adm. F. W. Butterworth III
(TRITRAFAC)
Trident Training Facility
Capt. J. L. Sullivan
(COMSUBGRU 9)
Commander, Submarine Group 9
Capt. Thomas Fox
Strategic Weapons Facility, Pacific
Capt. Lawrence Bishop
Off Crews
Crews ashore are under the command of whoever is their regular captain (Gold or Blue) when at sea.

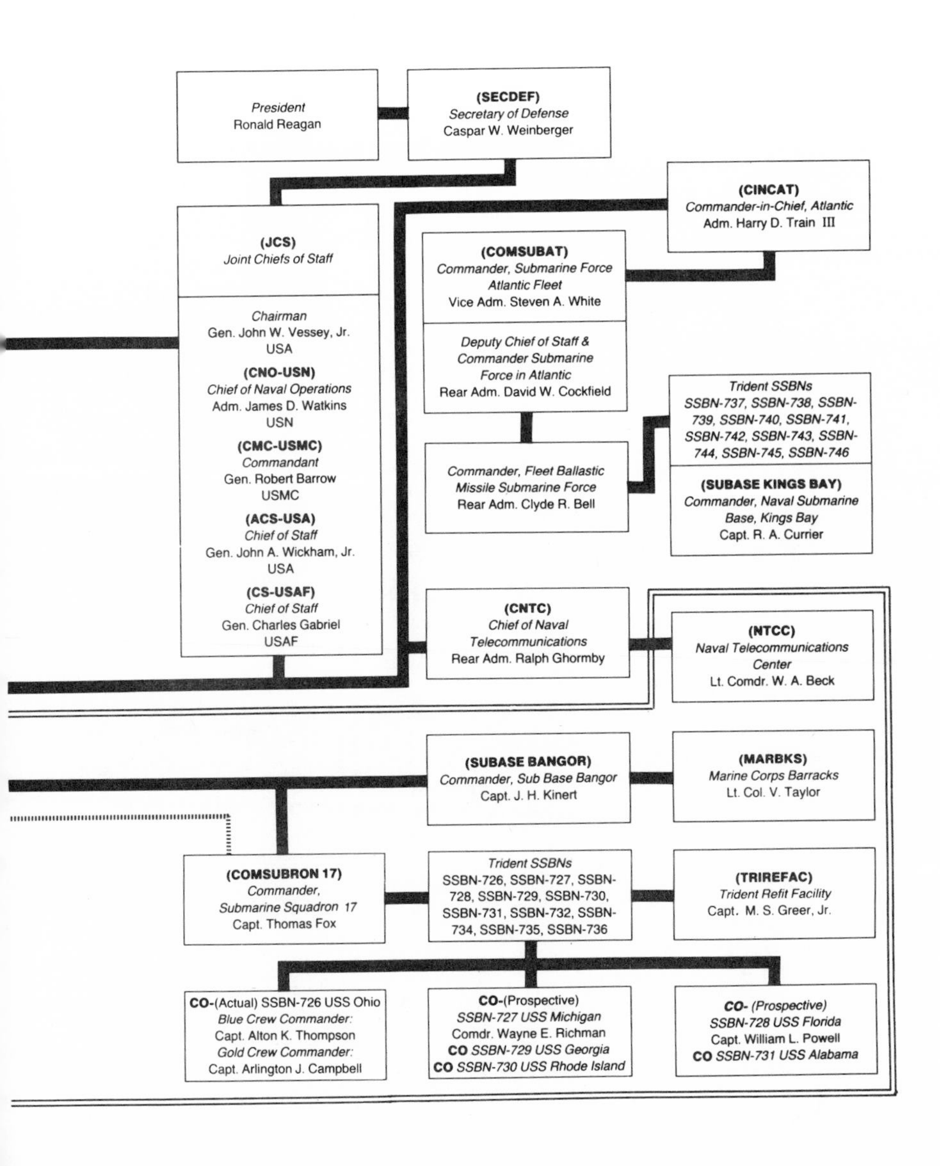
President
Ronald Reagan
(SECDEF)
Secretary of Defense
Caspar W. Weinberger
(CINCAT)
Commander-in-Chief, Atlantic
Adm. Harry D. Train III
(JCS)
Joint Chiefs of Staff
Chairman
Gen. John W. Vessey, Jr.
USA
(CNO-USN)
Chief of Naval Operations
Adm. James D. Watkins
USN
(CMC-USMC)
Commandant
Gen. Robert Barrow
USMC
(ACS-USA)
Chief of Staff
Gen. John A. Wickham, Jr.
USA
(CS-USAF)
Chief of Staff
Gen. Charles Gabriel
USAF
(COMSUBAT)
Commander, Submarine Force
Atlantic Fleet
Vice Adm. Steven A. White
Deputy Chief of Staff &
Commander Submarine
Force in Atlantic
Rear Adm. David W. Cockfield
Commander, Fleet Ballastic
Missile Submarine Force
Rear Adm. Clyde R. Bell
Trident SSBNs
SSBN-737, SSBN-738, SSBN-739, SSBN-740, SSBN-741, SSBN-742, SSBN-743, SSBN-744, SSBN-745, SSBN-746
(SUBASE KINGS BAY)
Commander, Naval Submarine
Base, Kings Bay
Capt. R. A. Currier
(CNTC)
Chief of Naval
Telecommunications
Rear Adm. Ralph Ghormby
(NTCC)
Naval Telecommunications
Center
Lt. Comdr. W. A. Beck
(SUBASE BANGOR)
Commander, Sub Base Bangor
Capt. J. H. Kinert
(MARBKS)
Marine Corps Barracks
Lt. Col. V. Taylor
(COMSUBRON 17)
Commander,
Submarine Squadron 17
Capt. Thomas Fox
Trident SSBNs
SSBN-726, SSBN-727, SSBN-728, SSBN-729, SSBN-730, SSBN-731, SSBN-732, SSBN-734, SSBN-735, SSBN-736
(TRIREFAC)
Trident Refit Facility
Capt. M. S. Greer, Jr.
CO-(Actual) SSBN-726 USS Ohio
Blue Crew Commander:
Capt. Alton K. Thompson
Gold Crew Commander:
Capt. Arlington J. Campbell
CO-(Prospective)
SSBN-727 USS Michigan
Comdr. Wayne E. Richman
CO SSBN-729 USS Georgia
CO SSBN-730 USS Rhode Island
CO- (Prospective)
SSBN-728 USS Florida
Capt. William L. Powell
CO SSBN-731 USS Alabama

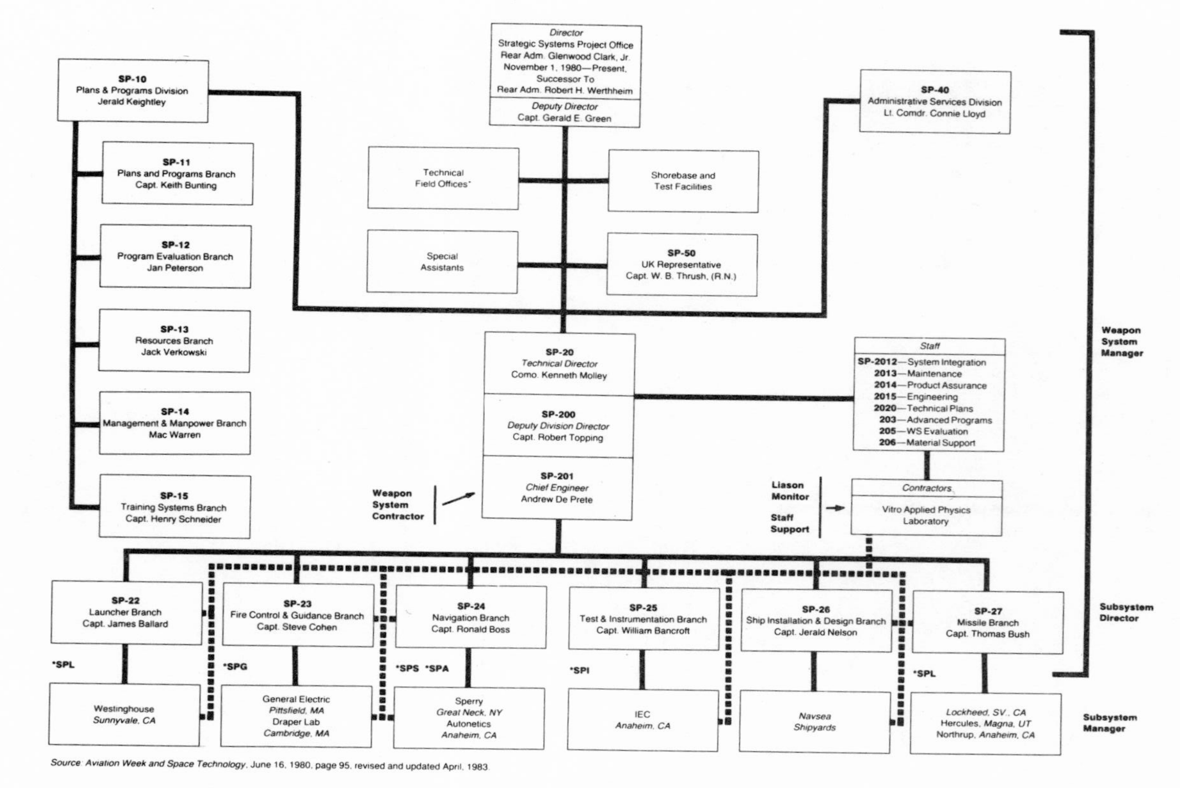

Source: *Aviation Week and Space Technology*, June 16, 1980, page 95, revised and updated April, 1983.

Fig. 12-3. Special Strategic Projects Office (SSPO) organizational chart.

on seabed mining, passageway navigation, and overflight rights. But significant among the provisions from the viewpoint of submariners was an "international straits" clause by which there was no recognized right of submerged transit for submarines, explicit authorization being necessary for the passage of all warships (including surfaced submarines). When the conferees as a whole rejected these provisions, the nations near international straits armed themselves "to a level where they could unilaterally, or in concert, inhibit the use of 'their' straits." Among these nations purchasing antiship missiles, Spain, Morocco, Libya, Malaysia, Indonesia, and Algeria control vital passages through which, in the case of the Mediterranean, U.S. antisubmarine-warfare forces with the Sixth Fleet could experience difficulties, and, in the case of numerous South Pacific straits, the Trident itself would be affected. Spain's recent entry into NATO and British control of Gibraltar do not remove the threat to the Strait of Gibraltar immediately posed by Libya or Algeria should either decide to enforce its own version of straits-traffic sovereignty. Fortunately for the United States, the Reagan administration voted against the final treaty in 1982, joined by Israel, Venezuela, and Turkey, with another seventeen nations, including Italy, West Germany, and Britain, abstaining.[9]

While the Reagan administration rejected the treaty primarily because of its seabed mining provisions, the Navy and, especially, the submarine forces may eventually be the true beneficiaries. Of course, even nations with the capability to wage war against surface craft will usually possess much more limited ASW capability in the near future. While the United States generally respects territorial limits and international law, the same cannot be said for the Soviets. The provisions regarding submarine passage would thus provide a "legal" net for the Soviets politically and indirectly to constrict passageways crucial for submarine operations. For the Trident, passage to the Indian Ocean from the Pacific could be inhibited, and closing vital operating areas to the Trident SSBN force could be adversely effected at little economic, technological, or military expense to the USSR.

Under the guise of concern for the environment, the Law of the Sea Treaty attempts to sublimate the greed of developing nations, which obviously lack the equipment and skills to extract resources from their own waters. Serious environmental questions related to warships and submarines should eventually be addressed, however. The fate that befell the *Thresher* and the *Scorpion* could have resulted in environmental damage more noticeable than was actually the case. While the United States has made these disasters public, the number of similar Soviet submarine problems remains known essentially only to the Politburo. In this regard, should the worse occur—a sinking accident involving a Trident at sea—its effects would be equivalent to a nuclear aircraft carrier going down. Twenty-four missiles, a reactor, and probably some highly explosive Mk-48 atomic warheads would litter the ocean floor. No other U.S. sea disaster could approximate what would be the submarine equivalent of the *Titanic* tragedy.

SALT I, II, and START

Henry Kissinger, the U.S. Secretary of State, and Anatoly Dobrynin, the Soviet ambassador, were the chief architects of the 1972 agreement limiting strategic offensive arms, called the Strategic Arms Limitation Talks, or SALT. Three protocols signed on May 26, 1972, included two agreements on strategic arms, specifically ICBMs and SLBMs, and the ABM Treaty. Under the first agreement, known as the Interim Agreement, the total number of ICBMs a country could have could not exceed the number in existence or under construction before July 1, 1972. A second document, called a Protocol to the Interim Agreement, set numerical ceilings on the number of submarines and SLBMs the USSR and the United States could have (62 strategic submarines and 950 SLBMs for the Soviets, 44 submarines and 710 SLBMs for the United States). Although neither country had that number of SLBMs at the time of the signing, increases in SLBMs could be effected by retiring ICBMs. This replacement alternative was called the freedom to mix. The ABM Treaty limited the signatories to two fields of 100 ABMs each, with the number again reduced, in 1974, by agreement. One field could be anywhere, but each party agreed to deploy one ABM field around its capital, while the other field had to be at least 1300 km away.[10]

Negotiations on a more permanent agreement providing numerical equality of strategic systems, as stipulated by the Jackson Resolution, began in November 1972. These negotiations produced the basic agreement known as SALT II, which limited each side to 2400 strategic nuclear delivery vehicles of all sorts (bombers, ICBMs, SLBMs), with the ceiling lowered in 1981 to 2250. Additionally, an aggregate limit of 1320 was placed on the total number of launchers of MRVed ballistic missiles and on heavy bombers equipped for long-range cruise missiles, with the MRV launcher ceiling limited to 1200. Lieutenant James George, in his article "SALT and the Navy," explained the limits of SALT II that would have affected the Navy were primarily those related to the MRV sublimits. The U.S. advantage "is in warheads," specifically achieved through MRVing. However, the hiatus in deploying a Minuteman follow-on meant that, out of a possible 9000 warheads deployed in the 1980s (assuming a force of ten Tridents),

"Well over 7,000 of them will be on Navy submarines. . . . When people talk of MRV advantage, they are talking about warhead advantage," George concluded. "In short," he noted, "the Navy *is* MRV."[11]

Current Reagan administration plans to rescue the MX have not substantially altered the important role George saw the Navy playing. Given the death of SALT II, many problems associated with the treaty have become academic, such as the problem of Trident II deployment possibly causing the Trident to bump up against the MRV limits. Assuming eight *Ohio*-class subs are on patrol by early 1986, the United States will have exceeded the SALT-I ceiling on SLBM launchers (also assuming that some combinations of Poseidon subs with Poseidon and Trident missiles are at sea). The continued Trident construction toward a fleet of twenty to twenty-seven therefore implies one of several logical conclusions: (1) The Reagan administration is implicitly escaping from SALT-I limitations without a unilateral denunciation to that effect, *res sic stantibus*; (2) Despite its strong advocacy of the MX system in a virtual merry-go-round of basing modes, the administration plans ultimately to trade in MX launchers for SLBM launchers, as allowed in the treaty; (3) The Navy could, upon meeting the limit, begin a more rapid retirement of those nineteen Poseidon subs that cannot be modernized by backfitting with the Trident I; or (4) The administration could remain trapped in the categories of the TRIAD "legs" by acquiescing in the continued vulnerability of the Minuteman II and III missile force. Ratification of SALT I depended upon one American condition—the continued modernization of all three of the U.S. strategic "legs," discussed in Chapter 3—and *absolute* Soviet compliance with three applicable conditions: (1) the Soviets would not replace light ICBMs with heavy ICBMs; (2) they would not produce mobile ICBMs; and (3) they would not construct more than sixty-two strategic submarines. Not only have all conditions for both sides been abrogated, but the United States has deactivated "26 percent of [its] total megatonnage" or more, in compliance with SALT I and without congressional approval. In some cases, the Navy has used appropriations for operations and maintenance to dismantle two Polaris submarines and to deactivate three other Polaris subs, to comply with SALT I.[12]

Proliferation of nuclear-tipped cruise missiles, combined with advances in accuracy, are eroding even further the base on which both SALTs were negotiated. Strategic weapons on both sides no longer consist of ballistic missiles. The trend in the U.S. Navy toward greater deployment of cruise missiles, especially aboard subs and potentially aboard Tridents in the 1990s, will further deteriorate the concept of "launchers" used in the SALT agreements. Moreover, this trend is already near the point of irreversibility, and there is no indication that the Soviets even wish to consider cruise missiles as strategic weapons, except for the land-based cruise missiles scheduled for European deployment in 1983. For Trident, with its 240 launchers and 1920 MIRVs for a ten-Trident force, the theoretical death of SALT I merely means that U.S. options to mix its launchers in the most optimal manner will be secured. This could prove extremely important if none of the various MX basing modes manages to please Congress and the public. Moreover, the actual death of SALT II, which has not been ratified (and probably never will be), nevertheless has laid the foundation for a true and unmuddled arms-reduction dialogue. As the *Wall Street Journal* editorialized, "No longer would the Soviets be permitted to use strategic arms talks as a screen for buildups in other areas." Under the Reagan SALT substitute, START (Strategic Arms Reductions Talks), the goal is to reduce the numbers of warheads and megatonnage, not merely launchers. Should the START proposal eventually bear fruit, the Soviets would be limited to a certain number of warheads, totaling a megatonnage limit. If they wished to build 500 SLBMs instead of, say, 300 SS-19s, then they could make that choice. Such an arrangement would allow the United States to shift to more survivable systems, such as Trident, from more vulnerable ICBMs. While SALT could have ultimately posed a threat to Trident, it is highly unlikely U.S. negotiators will again make such disadvantageous concessions. Meanwhile, continued production of Trident ensures future arms-control agreements will not be dictated by Moscow to a strategically emasculated United States.[13]

Implications of Yellow Rain on Arms Control

Neutralist and pacifist movements in Europe, touched upon previously, have pressured the United States to enter into further arms-control agreements. Yet, as the *Wall Street Journal* has noted, "the 'arms race' metaphor has little relation to reality." In fact, the sheer explosive power of the U.S. nuclear arsenal today is less than half what it was in 1960. On the other hand, the USSR, known for traditionally breaking agreements and treaties of all types without resulting moral hangovers, has most recently demonstrated its contempt for international arms control by engaging in genocide against Hmong villagers in Laos through the use of chemical and biological warfare, known as Yellow Rain by the villagers. Similar reports soon came from Afghan refugees in Pakistan and Cambodian refugees in Thailand who had fled, respectively, the Soviet invasion of Afghanistan and the Soviet-backed Vietnamese invasion of Cambodia. As best as can now be determined, perhaps 400,000 Hmong tribesmen have been exterminated by Yellow Rain. This notably occurred without a single protest march on the part of 'arms-control' groups in the United States. Ultimately, the Yellow Rain story is typical of the traditional weaknesses of international agreements to limit weapons and demonstrates the absolute powerlessness of the international community to enforce them. Yellow Rain serves as a grim visual reminder of the contractual and behavioral limitations of arms-control agreements themselves.[14]

A variety of factors controls arms races in no way relating to international agreements. First, to the extent people must man weapons, the size of a population to a large degree numerically limits the construction and deployment of weapons numbers. In this regard, a more productive society, such as the United States, cannot and will not dedicate a great deal of its manpower to manning weapons, essentially a nonproductive task. Thus are more productive nations correspondingly forced to rely less on men and more on technology. Second, to the extent ships and other weapons age, obsolescence plays an irresistible role in weapons levels. Weapons simply must be replaced as obsolescence approaches, despite international agreements; hence, evasions are induced in one form or another. Third, economics and technology combine to determine how much any nation can afford. A nation such as the USSR, which has defense-spending levels approaching 15 to 17 percent of its GNP, will always outproduce a nation with less resources committed to defense. Technology only complicates the choices by making the cost decisions tougher. Ideology, as a fourth factor, may direct a nation (such as Hitler's Germany) toward an arms race irrespective of the politico-military dispositions of its neighbors. Fifth, interservice rivalries do much to determine what weapons are developed, a point just as true of Hitler's Germany as it is of the United States or the USSR. In the competition for resources, no one service branch can completely predominate over any other. The evolution of the Soviet Navy since 1955 is rivaling the Strategic Rocket Forces, Air Defense Forces, the Red Army, the Rear (Tyl) Forces, and the Red Air Force. Even within the single force of the Soviet Navy, rivalry occurs between surface and subsurface interests. This type of ongoing rivalry means no one weapons system will ever totally control the procurement process or dictate it, thus generating several countervailing "arms races" within the larger national system. To keep service branches happy, even within the framework of international arms-control agreements, interservice institutional rivalry with multiple foci is built in and beyond the total control of any state, the exception being an absolute abolition of all armed forces, including police forces, in an Ayn Randian–type futuristic Eden.

Sixth, one's strategic situation dictates certain arms requirements. New Zealand, for example, can survive easily without a large land army, relying instead on its navy and air force, because no large enemy land forces are juxtaposed. Conversely, the USSR must always concern itself with land invasions, perhaps to the detriment of its air and sea forces, given the Chinese threat on its southeastern border, which is at least as serious objectively and historically as the threat posed by NATO. Russia's shape, in this regard, also influences its force composition: while a NATO land invasion is in reality hardly a serious threat, the Chinese can sever the entire eastern third of the USSR from the rest, cutting off the maritime provinces. However, the USSR has always had a "safe" border to its Arctic north. All of these considerations only underscore the fact that there is usually a multiplicity of participants in an arms race, and a nation must accordingly tailor its own defenses to a variety of kinds and directions of threats, not to just one "imperialist reactionary power." Seventh, a nation's political nature shapes its arms needs. In the case of the USSR, large and loyal standing forces are needed, supplemented by separate political police forces (the KGB and the MVD, with their very substantial and well-equipped armed forces), to prevent a "man on horseback" from seizing control of the system. In addition, arms are an effective diversion to public attention from an otherwise obvious decay of the nation's rotting economic system. As long as a non-Communist nation exists, the Soviets can use it as a potential "threat" to the perfect collectivist society—a threat requiring extensive actual preparations for a possible armed response.[15]

There is also the historical fact of an "arms race" existing since the dawn of man, partly due to the violence (or sin) involved in human nature and partly due to the continuous advance of science in all areas, some of which will always have combat uses. The former point is well delineated by Michael Novak, who accurately observes "A system built on sin is built on very solid foundations indeed," to which Thomas Sowell poignantly adds "This is true of both economic and political systems." The latter point is well documented by Bernard Brodie in his book *From Crossbow to H-Bomb*. In the intermediate future, given the state of laser-beam and particle-beam technology, ICBM–SLBM-type warfare could conceivably become obsolete without ever having been employed, a point most antinuclear disarmament protesters seem unable to grasp. In contrast, mountain tribesmen in Pakistan and warring groups in the jungles of Indonesia have been quite effective at killing relatively extensive portions of their populations (for them, virtually "all life on earth") without a single atomic bomb. Some Indian tribes in North America suffered virtual annihilation at the hands of enemy Indian tribes, none of which had firearms, let alone atomic weapons.

Yet, for them, all life on earth was destroyed, just as surely as if a nuclear holocaust had truly ended "all life on earth." In either case, the strength provided by a defense that absolutely deterred any attack would be preferable. In a similar vein, noted economist Sowell again explains the illogic of the "overkill" theory: "It may well be that when France surrendered to Nazi Gemany in 1940 it had enough bullets to kill every German soldier twice over. . . . Would anyone say that a lone policeman confronting three criminals had 'overkill' because his revolver contained enough bullets to kill them twice over?"[16]

Can an international agreement, therefore, really control an arms race? The history of arms agreements is that they never succeed for very long in controlling all parties possessing equivalent weapons. For example, the French, with their complete suit of atomic weaponry, are not a party to SALT I, and the People's Republic of China, with its atomic capability, is not a signatory to either SALT or the nonproliferation treaty, just as the Weimar Republic was not a party to the Washington Conference of 1922 that limited the size of navies or the London Naval Conference of 1930. To the extent certain powers are not included in a formal agreement, an arms race of some sort is occurring between the unregulated powers and the contractual parties. Indeed, parties to an arms agreement frequently end up proportionately disarming themselves in the presence of other nations which subsequently become more serious military threats than the contracting parties previously were to one another. Disarmament agreements also tend to divert the evolution of military technology into other technologies not restrained by the agreement. In SALT I, concern with launcher levels led to emphasis on multiple warheads per launcher and upon enhanced destructive capability. Because arms agreements are symmetrical, having equal effects on the same types of weapons, they create asymmetries in each contracting party's total balance of forces. Each side attempts to compensate itself for the treaty's uncomfortable and dysfunctional restraints by overemphasizing other compensating arms systems. In the case of the USSR, the heavy commitment to tanks and mass artillery technologically offsets its disadvantage in tactical nuclear weapons, while in NATO's case the commitment to tactical atomic weapons is needed to compensate for reduced tank and manpower levels.[17]

Another effect of an agreement is that each party almost immediately begins to hedge against the effects of the agreement by finding technically acceptable ways to evade it; for example, in 1922, to escape 35,000-ton limits on battleships the Royal Navy built the HMS *Rodney* and HMS *Nelson* with secret but empty water compartments, holding 2870 tons of water in wartime, to compensate for the otherwise unallowable but necessary weight of side armor desired. The USSR has engaged in an equivalent evasion by deploying the SS-20, whose existence does not violate SALT I since the Soviets include it in the category of theater (rather than strategic) weapons, although it really constitutes the two stages of the Soviet SS-16 ICBM.

Arms agreements, entered into for widely different motives and purposes, frequently tend to protect one party against further exposure to a technological disadvantage and restrain the other party from exploiting one. If you can't keep up with the Joneses, so to speak, then keep them from getting ahead. This tactic is classically designated "poverty pacifism." For the United States, in view of the difficulty in settling upon an MX basing mode, it could develop that the SALT I limitations on SLBM launchers could constitute a serious overhead problem. Also, since agreements of this type tend to deal with tangible things—ships, tonnage, gun caliber, missiles—they neglect intangible warmaking capability such as morale, preparation, staff efficiency, strategic audacity, espionage efficiency, and desperation or tradition.[18]

Since the United States is a contract-minded nation, evidenced by its constitutional history, there is a tendency for America to become a captive of national commitments after they no longer serve national interests. Whereas international law emphasizes equally the interpretive criteria that "pacts should be honored" (*pacta sunt servanda*) and "things so standing" (*res sic stantibus*), meaning they should not, the Anglo-Saxon constitutional tradition in these matters tends to prefer the former over the latter in the twentieth century. As an illustration, the American commitment to the ABM Treaty, limiting the USSR and the United States (in the original agreement) to two sites only, now appears to be a severe and inconvenient restriction with respect to desirable defense measures able to protect the nation's vulnerable Minuteman III missile sites. Yet Americans have historically found absolute, public, and unilateral repudiation of agreements difficult.

Finally, arms control of the type discussed by Jonathan Schell in *The Fate of the Earth* presents problems far exceeding the utopian pining for "peace" on the part of "all people," which Schell and others would enforce through a single monolithic world government. To say the least, world government is institutionally impractical, and poses religious questions for some. In any case, as Inis Claude long ago made clear and as the American Civil War attests, government, regardless of scale, continental or global, does not make at least civil war inherently impossible. Consequently, if for no reason other than to illustrate the philosophical pitfalls of arms-control agreements, the above discussion has shown that more is involved here than merely counting missiles, warheads, and megatonnage. Thus, when the question "What is the 'arms control' impact of Trident?" is asked, it might be useful to clarify which of the above points the questioner has in mind. For Trident, the versatility of the hull might ultimately mean that limitations on ICBMs or SLMBs would push development of laser beams and particle beams, resulting in their second-stage deployment aboard Tridents. As discussed in this chapter's final subsection, arms control could enhance alternative uses of the Trident hull, and it could easily be one of the first weapons of the nuclear age to make the technological leap to the laser age.[19]

Alternative Hull Uses

Trident's size makes it potentially "the Boeing 747 of the seas," capable of performing a variety of diversified tasks both inside and outside military roles. Once a force level is reached whereby the "window of vulnerability" is closed, more attention will probably be given to Trident's nonstrategic and unorthodox uses. For example, the power-generation requirements of laser-beam and particle-beam weapons necessitate, at present, a large capacity for power storage or accelerator space. The Trident hull can uniquely offer space usable for either purpose. Ultimately, a Trident-type design could prove the most optimal for picket duty in a cruise-missile defense around carriers. Pointing and tracking operations, as well as the actual beam or laser firing operation itself, would occur mounted in a sail area possibly of reduced size or (at least) height, with the bulky generating equipment stored below. With its low profile in a partly submerged state, only the pointing, tracking, and firing mechanisms would be above the surface, in line of sight to cruise missiles. Incoming weapons would have little chance to strike such a picket, and the rapid rates of fire combined with "an unlimited ammunition supply," as Wright pointed out (chap. 9), make such a vessel a potent and survivable defender. Depending on range limitations, it could find a similar use against aircraft.

Lasers and submarines can combine in a different, more feasible fashion, however. One system receiving considerable research effort since 1980, and meeting with some success, has been a laser-beam device powered by a nuclear explosion. The available energy pulse from such a device is so powerful that hardening becomes practically unfeasible. Several "small cylinders of lasing material . . . could be made a part of a nuclear bomb, fixed to its exterior and gimbaled so that each would be aimed independently at a single enemy missile. A tracking system could aim the lasers just prior to the explosion, and they would spread out less than other lasers." Most analysts see submarine-launched missiles carrying such devices as the first line of a defense. Actually, such SSBNs in an antimissile mode could be deployed in a net across the ocean with their firepower directed at the approach slit. A Trident's hull and magazine capacity make it the logical choice for such a defense. Trident missiles, upon warning, could be fired to several points between the attacker and the U.S., with each lasing explosion cutting down the number of approaching missiles. Under such conditions, communication would be even more critical than now, but subs on such missions could sail nearer the surface with fleet cover, since they would be strictly defensive weapons, and since the general area of approach would require some proximity to the attacking missiles to cut down reaction time. Hull applications of this type remain in the future, with their advance possibly speeded by arms-control limitations on nuclear weapons, funding dedicated to R&D, or espionage activities. Limitations on nuclear weapons development, for example, would encourage greater activity in the field of lasers.[20]

Several other prospects for Trident hull use may be feasible in the intermediate term. Among them, use as (1) a mine layer, (2) a containerized ballistic-missile launcher, (3) a cruise-missile launcher, and (4) a mixed-force launcher, all present interesting possibilities. Incorporating intensive minelaying capabilities into a Trident hull should not require extensive engineering changes. A Trident could carry either Captors or IWD mines in substantial numbers. According to weights listed for the Trident II, the magazine can hold 1368 tons; therefore, given certain loading restrictions, the same magazine should nevertheless hold some 1200 tons worth of conventional mines or, for the Captor, a Trident could carry 1200 mines, in theory. It could carry at least 1000 IWD mines but, of course, at the practical level the laying and buffering equipment would doubtless somewhat alter these figures, included here only for the purpose of illustration. Whereas a Trident hull engaged in minelaying activities is too valuable to risk in "close" straits such as the Dardanelles, it would be quite effective in the Sea of Japan or the North Sea. Still, its potential as a minelayer is enormous. Perhaps with comparatively slight engineering modifications mines could be dispensed from "inverted missile tubes" loaded at the top and later released through the bottom of the hull by the weight of the mine itself.

A second use of the hull, which may be investigated in the not-too-distant future, is as a deployment vehicle for containerized ballistic missiles, although certainly not in a Hydra- or SUM-like fashion. Other than communications and espionage, Trident's only real weakness is its detectability from space during the firing sequence. One remedy for this involves releasing the missiles in automatically self-ballasting containers at deep levels; they would "set" below the surface depth invisible to space satellites until fired by a radio order or by a timer inside the container. Each canister would have its own buoyancy control and timer, so the missiles could all ascend together to launch level. In this manner the entire magazine could be deployed like a necklace prior to a salvo firing. Unlike the weaknesses of Hydra, however, the deployment vessel—Trident—would be far less detectable and, unlike SUM, far safer. The missiles could be safe in this type of deployment as well, because their release into the water would not be made under observation from a trailing sub. Moreover, because the sub would generally deploy all of the missiles as quickly as possible, they would remain relatively free of interference by marine life, divers, or rough seas. If, however, the deployment ship suspected it was being trailed, it could deploy a pair, then move on to another spot before deploying more. Or a combination of containerized and normally launched missiles might exist. SUM and Hydra proponents applied an intriguing concept to what were otherwise ludicrous and impractical deployment vehicles. Of course, this tactic could not bear actual deployment except in a war situation.

Third, the Trident hull, as discussed in chapter 9, provides the space and potential launching capacity for a large number of Tomahawk cruise missiles. Under current launcher configuration, one observer suggested that a Westinghouse rotary launcher might accommodate five to eight cruise missiles. Yet eight seems a low estimate, with at least nine cruise missiles able to fit in a Trident II-sized tube. The height of a cruise missile, though, might allow a single launcher, with the proper buffer, to hold two submagazines superimposed vertically, meaning effective numbers could be doubled, perhaps to 432 to 528 per vessel! A payload of this size surpasses the bomb load of a B-1B by almost four times, exceeds a B-1B's cruise-missile load by fourteen to seventeen times, and exceeds a B-52's air-launched cruise-missile load by twenty-six times. While each B-1B costs $200 million, each Trident, at seven times the bomber's cost, carries fourteen times more missiles. Thus seven B-1B's would still carry fewer cruise missiles than a single Trident. Put another way, a Trident is more cost-effective! No one could scoff at the potential capability of this hull to deliver theater-level support to ground troops, in which role it could represent a major redressing of U.S. conventional inadequacies.

Still, the most fascinating of Trident hull uses might involve the individual use of various mixtures of Trident I and II SLBMs, both in regular and containerized firing modes, Tomahawk cruise missiles, and mines, with perhaps a navigation satellite mounted on a Trident missile for good measure. Thus, each and every scenario and weakness could be accounted for by at least one set of Tridents, from soft-target and hard-target kill capabilities to ground support and immediate navigation and communication reestablishment, not to mention anti-ship capabilities. Indeed, a highly specialized Trident vessel can be imagined, designed in such a manner as to exhibit typical but camouflaged strategic capabilities but devoid of a real "Sherwood Forest" launching compartment in deference to a space devoted to the sequestration of more or less a battalion of special raiding forces, à la the British Falklands campaign. Or, equally feasible might be a *passive* version of an SSBN-726 hull, specially designed for troop convoy for an anti-Andropov-doctrine preventative landing in Yugoslavia, towed by an SSN-688-class underwater "tug." The details of these proposals we leave to Navy planners, naval engineers (who frequently need to be reminded of daring, imagination, and so-called non-cost-effective but audacious operations), and to executive-level managers of operational crises. After all, even in terms of total losses, how cost-effective is a commando raid on a Norweigan heavy-water plant to prevent the Third Reich from developing the atom bomb in comparison with the incredible but futile efforts from 1940 to 1944 to defeat Nazi Germany by "strategic" bombing? Costs may be rationally analyzed in these matters, but successful audacity of an effective sort is inherently priceless!

Outside the realm of military uses, the Trident hull construction process makes it a potential liquefied natural gas submarine supertanker. Since there is virtually no limit to the number of hull sections Electric Boat workers can join together, a Trident-type hull could extend past 560 feet, although the docks at the Groton Land Level facility might easily run out of space to hold a vessel of much greater length. A better construction might be to link several carrier hulls together around one hull containing the propulsion system. Electric Boat has already done basic research work on these types of submarine tanker, estimating that one tanker could displace 950,000 tons and stretch over 1470 feet long, or almost three times as long as the *Ohio*. Since the Marine Division of General Dynamics builds both LNG tankers and the Tridents, mating the two technologies should be less difficult for it than for competing companies. Such a nuclear-powered vessel could make the 3200-mile voyage under the Artic ice cap from the oil fields of Prudhoe Bay, Alaska, to Europe; it would be cheaper to operate than a conventional LNG tanker, with each submarine carrying 37 million gallons of gas. Technology in the area of sonars will also aid in transiting Arctic regions and in providing overall safety.[21]

Yet another potential hull application might see a Trident-size vessel as a giant underwater research laboratory. Its combination of deep-diving ability and size would make it a perfect mother ship for smaller submersibles. A Trident hull fitted with optical sensors, imaging sonars, and other research tools could provide basic area-search facilities, and its size could accommodate a variety of computers for signal processing and navigation data. It could also serve as a launching platform for a variety of robot submarines, such as the RCV-225 or the MUT bottom crawler. Possibilites for quick data processing, immediate repair, and extended range via electronic cable emanating from the larger hull could revolutionize seabed research.[22]

Targeting

One almost universally overlooked aspect of ballistic-missile submarine strategy has been the impact of variations of warhead loadings as they affect changes in combinations of decoys and reentry vehicles. An interaction will necessarily occur that can either enhance the survivability and deliverability of individual warheads on a target or detract from it. These variations range in minimum and maximum possibilities for a single missile type, from a combination of ten to fourteen decoys and RVs for Poseidon C-3, six to eight for Trident I, and seven to fourteen for Trident II, respectively. (No mathematical allowance has been made for a zero/zero combination, which, although hypothetically possible, is completely impractical.) The combination of RVs and decoys will be determined partially by the missile type. Variations in relative emphasis on the percentage of decoys versus RVs per missile will also be substantially determined by the type of target against which the missile is directed; the greater the degree of ABM/defense capability, in most cases, the higher the mixture of decoys to RVs is likely to be to assure the survivability of an adequate number of RVs. Conversely, with less ABM capability around a target, the Navy can increase the proportion of RVs to decoys. Very soft targets with absolutely no ABM defense would probably receive the optimum of RVs undiluted by any decoys.

These considerations have a special impact on a per-magazine basis for each individual vessel. This impact will then vary by type of vessel, from 160 to 224 RVs or decoys per Poseidon submarine equipped with C-3 missiles, 96 to 128 RVs to decoys for Poseidon vessels equipped with Trident I missiles, 144 to 192 RVs or decoys for an *Ohio*-class vessel with Trident I missiles, and 168 to 336 RVs or decoys for a Trident equipped with Trident II missiles. These variations for flotillas (defined by the total number of ships therein) turns out to give, in the nineteen-ship Poseidon group equipped with C-3 missiles, a variation of 3040 to 4256 RVs or decoys, 1152 to 1536 RVs or decoys for the twelve Poseidons equipped with Trident I missiles, and 1152 to 1536 RVs or decoys for the eight *Ohio*-class vessels equipped with Trident I missiles. For calculation purposes, three kinds of unit forces can be used:

1. A five-vessel multiplier unit, of convenience for the reader, to facilitate calculation of subcomponents of Trident forces scheduled to receive Trident II missiles as original outfitting (beyond the first eight vessels already committed to receiving Trident I)
2. A second unit of calculation of twelve vessels (see note)
3. A homogeneous fleet of twenty Tridents with Trident II, with all C-3 missiles phased out.

With some qualifications, the variations for such unit compositions would be as follows: For the five vessels, 840 to 1680 RVs or decoys; 2016 to 4032 RVs or decoys for the twelve vessels; and, for the mixed fleet of eight Tridents (with Trident I) and twelve Tridents (with Trident II), a variation between 3168 and 5568 RVs or decoys. For a twenty-ship homogeneous force equipped with Trident IIs, a minimum of 3360 to a maximum of 6720 RVs or decoys would be combined.[23]

Once these combinations are in place, viewed on a fleet basis of nineteen Poseidons with C-3, twelve Poseidons with Trident I, eight Tridents with Trident I, and twelve Tridents with Trident II, a variation between 7360 RVs or decoys and 11,360 RVs or decoys would exist. Again, assuming an exclusively Trident-missile-equipped force of the near future, including twelve Poseidons with Trident I missiles and twenty Tridents with Trident II, a variation of 4512 to 8256 RVs and decoys would be established.

The next consideration is a megatonnage overview, composed of seven factors: missile type, magazine capacity, flotilla capability, fleet capability, fleet operational availability, fleet operational capability as affected by missile reliability, and a calculation for equivalent megatonnage (that is, accuracy). Three other factors have been identified, which have as a set been ignored by authors in the past, although no calculation of performance can be included here: functional reliability of the RV, the survivability of the RV against defended targets, and the accuracy of the RV itself as enhanced by Terminal Fixed Source target guidance or as diminished more or less by homing in a MRV versus a MaRV mode. While acknowledging these factors, a general calculation of megatonnage can be made.

First, using missile type, minimum and maximum variations in kilotons from C-3 to Trident I to Trident II are, respectively, 500–700 kt, 600–800 kt, and 2100 kt (with seven 300-kt RVs or fourteen 150-kt RVs). Two other variations of Trident II RVs have been discussed, including possibly seven or fewer RVs of 335 kt, for a missile total of 2345 kt and an unknown maximum, and seven 475-kt RVs for a total of 3325 kt, again with the maximum unknown.

By magazine type, the Poseidons, with sixteen launchers firing C-3 missiles, would embrace a variation of 5300 to 11,200 kt. If backfitted with the Trident I, the same vessels would have a 9600-to-12,800-kt variation. In contrast, a twenty-four-launcher Trident I outfit would have a variation between 14,400 and 19,800 kt, while a twenty-four-launcher Trident II outfit would pack a 50,400-kt wallop. Assuming either the 335-kt warhead or the 475-kt proposal, these numbers could change to 56,280 up to 79,800 kt. No maximum on these warheads is known.

Flotilla capability again expands these numbers. To use the nineteen Poseidons, minimum and maximum, the explosive force available varies from 100,700 kt to 212,800 kt. Backfitted vessels would carry a variation of 115,200 to 153,600 kt. The eight Tridents originally outfitted with Trident I missiles vary in kilotons from 115,200 to 158,400. Finally, a Trident II–equipped flotilla could generate, for the five-unit force, 252,000 kt; for the twelve-unit force, 675,360 kt, up to an unknown maximum; and for the twenty-vessel force, 1,596,000 kt.

Fleet capabilities (combining all of the above vessels for a total force estimation of forty-four) total a minimum and maximum of 583.1 megatons (mt) to 676.8 mt. But one cannot assume this entire force would be available all the time. Rather, an estimation of 55 percent operational availability for Poseidon vessels, regardless of missile type, is assumed. Trident's availability—regardless of type of missile—is estimated here at 70 percent, engendering a range of megatonnage availability from a minimum of 375.7 to 488.8 mt.

However, even if the available vessels could fire all available missiles, some missiles evidently will misfire in such a way as to affect one or more of their stages. Thus a reliability factor of 85 percent is assumed (even though current Trident I tests are running at an 82 percent reliability rate, some natural improvement is expected). Given this reliability factor, the variable range declines to 319.4 to 415.5 mt.

A final calculation is a rather general one of equivalent megatonnage (EMT) whereby raw megatonnage is divided by two-thirds to allow for accuracy—that is, all of the explosive force cannot be assumed to drop exactly where it is intended. But two-thirds is a generous allowance when taking RV failure, attrition, blast effect, or target accuracy into account. A better calculation is perhaps an exponent of half. This would yield an EMT of 159.2 to 207.7. However, this, too, must be modified for missile and RV type because, as noted earlier, EMT is a measurement of *in*accuracy. A more accurate Trident II could carry precisely the same megatonnage as a Trident I and yet have greater deliverable destructive force. Since a Trident II is currently estimated to be about two and one-half to seven times more accurate than a Trident I, the essential EMT of the twenty-ship Trident II force, when compared to the mixed forty-four-ship force, could be anywhere from 542.3 to 589.8 real EMTs better. Moreover, if TFS Trident target guidance is assumed, the difference is a staggering 1891.2 to 1938.9 EMTs. Or, to put this in final perspective, Trident II deployment will easily overcome, in accuracy improvements, even substantial functional unreliability. When EMTs are considered in this fashion, the improvements to be gained by Trident II deployment will mean that Poseidon vessels can be retired even earlier without any significant on-patrol loss in megatonnage. Only a new threat to the Trident sub itself from Soviet ASW would significantly alter this conclusion.

Also, the actual combinations of real warheads to decoys, with twenty-four missiles available, yields the mind-boggling possibility of nine to the twenty-fourth power, or 79,766,443,060,000,000,000,000 combinations on a single Trident! In view of the fact that ABM defensive management faces this range of possibilities deliverable from a single SSBN on a 360-degree plane, Soviet computer countermeasure reckoning must take account of each of these possibilities from an infinite number of threat angles and from an entire fleet of SSBNs with similar capabilities.

Complicating both the targeting for U.S. forces and defense for Soviet forces, TRIAD assignments stagger the launch times of surviving forces for maximum impact. A decrease in Minuteman II and III survivability and the irresolution of the MX production and deployment increasingly has shifted some of the counterforce responsibilities onto the SSBN force. Consequently, as counterforce assignments increase, traditional SSBN assignments will decrease, including antidefense (ABM) strikes, countervalue strikes, a theater "cleanup function," or second reserve strikes. In all probability, given all the hypothetical variations previously discussed, each SSBN will have to manage target assignment with these five variations in mind. Perhaps ten missiles would be assigned to anti-ICBM counterforce, four to ABM destruction, two to four for cleanup, and six to eight for a second strike. In the event of some sort of intraflotilla targeting coordination and C^3I interchange, additional forms of division of targeting become possible, including individual-vessel exclusive targeting assignments, relative flotilla and fleet mutual specialization, and timed absolute progressive destruction.

13
Conclusion

"Time is on our side." A quiet voice answered: "Time is an unfriendly neutral on the side of the strongest."

—Martin Gilbert and Richard Gott, *The Appeasers*

Implications and Conclusions

Certainly by now it should be evident the Trident is not just another submarine. Sophisticated equipment, a comparatively huge hull, advanced design in both interior and exterior applications all combine to make Trident one of the most unusual submersible ships in the world. Given the diversified applications to which the hull may eventually be put, Trident could easily become the most valuable ship in the world as well. Its revolutionary construction process allows certain hull changes to be made with a minimum of cost or engineering difficulty. In their primary—and, for the present, only—role of strategic deterrence, the Trident-class boats should prove the most effective weapon any service has ever deployed for that purpose. With striking power relatively surpassing the Minuteman ICBM force in the period prior to its vulnerability; with survivability relatively exceeding the B-52s in their heyday; and with range, speed, and crew comfort far beyond those of its predecessors, the Trident has no equal, absolutely, in the case of the *Typhoon*, or in a relative historical setting.

Still, to argue "things turned out all right" begs the questions of cost overruns, delivery delays, and quality control. These items have each been treated separately in previous chapters and will now be summarized in a more general fashion.

"Cost overruns," while an effective media slogan, are meaningless in historical perspective. The Trident program experienced growing costs for a variety of unrelated and often uncontrollable reasons.

Almost a billion dollars' worth of increased cost due to inflation is attributable to the Navy's failure to procure long-lead items for the three extra submarines it would eventually need when force level numbers were first discussed from 1972 to 1974. But this is, for the most part, *not* the Navy's fault. The budget "game" requires the service get what it can when it can. If the U.S. Navy had presented a complete and thorough estimate of program costs from 1972 through 1982 to Congress in the early years of funding, including realistic or even pessimistic inflation figures, the *Ohio* would still be a preliminary design, buried in a file cabinet with thousands of similar designs. Congress must assume overall responsibility for any added costs in this respect—or, perhaps, the blame might even be better placed on "the democratic process." Admiral Rickover once compared defense procurement in the United States to the Soviet process in these terms: "The head of their defense establishment is a member of the Politburo. . . . They have a group of people who assemble every year and listen . . . and everybody says 'Da.' That is the end of it." Unfortunately for the Trident but fortunately for the democratic process as a whole, many American lawmakers say "Nyet" on occasion. Chalk some added and inevitable costs up to the price of a representative government.[1]

As an example of how confusing and politically sensitive the budget process is, in early 1983 the Reagan administration, using DoD cost data, announced substantial savings in many programs. Later, during hearings, it appeared as though savings in the Trident II program were contrived and that the Navy had deliberately created a "new" submarine to mislead the lawmakers. However, the witness had actually only presented a poorly worded statement: accounting procedures required a new budget line to be opened beginning with SSBN 734, which was the first Trident to be fitted with Trident II launching cradles from the outset. The cost effect of not fitting the subs with Trident I cradles was not a "savings" in a literal sense, but the cost of refitting the subs at a later date ($680 million) was avoided. Hence the Navy lost a golden opportunity to enhance its image and actually received bad publicity about its initially ambiguous statement.[2]

Of course, some very specific cost overruns did occur. But who in 1972, or 1974, could budget for a five-month draftsman's strike? Who at that time could predict that *negotiations alone* over the Trident claims and the indirectly related 688 claims would eat up eight months of working time? It is highly unlikely that even the Navy suspected the number of design changes it would later submit, so who could account for those in the budget?

No one at Electric Boat would deny that startup deficiencies existed in the shipyard. Any attempt to increase a skilled workforce in such great numbers as occurred in 1974 at Electric Boat will always require a training and, unavoidably, an on-the-job learning period. The adverse effects of this early manpower buildup became evident in the welding and steel problems. Available evidence suggests, contrary to the GAO report of 1982, that those difficulties were one-time problems and have since been corrected to normal levels.

Nor should the Navy deny its own responsibility for defective government-furnished equipment or for a myriad of design changes. Once again, the former problem appears to have been corrected subsequently, and design changes for follow-on ships after the *Ohio* will be drastically reduced by the nature of the serial shipbuilding process.

The fact that inflation is seldom subtracted from cost overruns makes the term all the more meaningless. Cost overrun reports have, in reality, become a semantic distraction to real, actual, objective analysis regarding the progress of this system, with the distractive effects constituting a political mythology with which the Congress, the Navy, Electric Boat, and DoD have had to deal. While "defense programs over budget" makes compelling nightly television news stories, the problem of inflation is generally ignored in defense reports brought out by the media. Indeed, virtually no report has dealt with the costs and delays caused by the mandates of the Occupational Safety and Health Administration or the Environmental Protection Agency, for example, yet the effects of their regulations on Trident costs are substantial.

More important than any single problem area are the unknowns associated with lead-ship construction. These were magnified and exacerbated in the Trident's case by the so-called fixed-price contract. Among the unknowns of a practical sort from the outset are: (1) an incomplete engineering design; (2) practical engineering difficulties; (3) adaptation of design to real building problems; (4) lead-time delays, unknowns, deficiencies, and gaps; (5) recognition, resolution, and solution of construction problems *not* originally fathomed, which manifest themselves throughout the entire building process the first time around; (6) the tension in the interaction of the engineering and building process of developing *one-time-only* solutions for problems with the lead vessel versus the necessity to engineer by design and system the long-term serial solution of a feasible, reliable, and repeatable answer; (7) the necessity in time for an engineer, shop foreman, or whoever to generate mentally or practically a solution of uniqueness or complexity for a practical difficulty (problems do not solve themselves instantaneously but require thought and practical application); the experienced judgment that nearly all (95 percent) of the piping, for example, can be carried by identical hanger straps but of the remaining

5 percent, say, nearly every other strap has to be individualized because the piping is perhaps not running through the even-sized portion of the hull diameter but through convergences in the bow and stern cones.

The Trident system (and the *Ohio* as a lead vessel, particularly) involves an incredibly technologically intensive system for which as a program there are comparatively few copies relative to other systems like the B-52 (A-H), the FB-111, the *Spruance*-class destroyer (one contract for thirty vessels awarded June 23, 1970, to Ingalls Shipbuilding Division of Litton Industries at Pascagoula, Mississippi, under which delays nevertheless occurred for labor and technical problems), the HC-60 helicopter, the M-1 tank, and the F-15. Therefore, the overruns for these many other systems with a high level of production repeats, which ought to be lower in cost estimates (using the same standards employed critically against the *Ohio*), have actually turned out to be multifold factors (2x–6x) of overrun for systems or platforms also produced in a shorter span of production run where the exposure to inflation and strikes is shorter, not longer, as in Trident's case.[3]

Most military weapons systems, no matter what procurement process is used, result in cost overruns. Compare, for example, the cost increase of the TFX aircraft (now called the FB-111), which exceeded its budget by 220 percent. This might be compared to the *Ohio*'s over-budget excess of less than 100 percent in 1982 inflation-escalated dollars, and yet the TFX development took place in an era lacking the inflation of the 1970s. Other comparisons of the Trident should include such escalations in currently pending weapons systems as have occurred, selectively, for the following in the period merely from January, 1980, to March, 1981, (per weapon, in millions of dollars): the UH-60 helicopter, $5.54 versus $3.71, or an overrun of 49 percent; the Hellfire missile, from $.04 to $.12, or a 300-percent overrun; the F-18 jet fighter, $32.01 versus $22.38, or an overrun of 43 percent; or the ground-launched cruise missile, $5.80 versus $4.20, an overrun of 38 percent. Once again, these escalations are given only for a one-year-plus period, compared with the Trident's figures, which are usually computed for eight to ten years.[4]

Attempts to blame cost overruns on this agency or that contractor tend to ignore a crucial, overriding fact: the normal acquisitions process is inherently unsuited to procuring a system so vast and technologically intensive as the *Ohio*. The ship is incomparable to other systems of far less complexity, which have themselves gone over budget. Moreover, the herky-jerky funding and appropriations process in Congress makes a construction schedule a nightmare from the shipbuilder's viewpoint. Alfred D. Chandler's prize-winning book *The Visible Hand* stresses the improvement in efficiency and savings generated by private corporate planning, yet the procurement process makes gains of the type achieved by Chandler's managerial hierarchy impossible for a company like General Dynamics. As in the companies discussed by Chandler, Electric Boat's management knew, before a marked decrease in per-unit costs can occur, regular scheduling must first take place. The Groton–Quonset Point joint facility is designed to fabricate Tridents steadily, but congressional authorizations and appropriations are erratic from one session to another, while there are also compound effects generated by changes in administrations. There has also been a steady deterioration of the Navy's own shipbuilding capacity, with the resulting unrelieved dependence, especially for sub construction, upon Electric Boat solely for Trident and upon Electric Boat and Newport News for 688s, further complicated by McNamara-era cost-effective reforms, compounded by a shrinking in the size of the community of naval architects, intensified by bad attitudes prevailing mutually between the Navy and many of its suppliers and by the more recent impact of Rickover upon the defense community. Thus Chandler's model, which might otherwise apply to the defense industry, cannot be used in context with Electric Boat.[5]

A significant conclusion also must be reached about the role of a "private" government contractor holding monopolistic control over its products: market forces do not pertain. Moreover, to try to force a company such as Electric Boat into an artificial free-market situation probably is worse than admitting to its monopolistic status and proceeding accordingly. As is eminently clear, competition for high-cost, limited-production items such as the Trident has been virtually nonexistent.

Monopolistic control alone fails to account for the cost-overruns, however. Rickover's impact on the Trident program contributed to built-in cost overruns and delays in a number of ways. First, the "father of the nuclear navy" came to predominate temperamentally and institutionally over a vaster province than his own specialty. The systemic and long-term effects of this complex should not be underestimated even in the wake of his retirement.

Ultimately, Rickover's personality became institutionalized, and his formulas eventually passed the point of diminishing returns because of their critical predictability and monotony of theme. Rickover's impact on the naval-oriented defense contractor, at least, is a legacy of Navy–contractor antagonism—originally unnecessary, artificial, and dysfunctional. Furthermore, not only should it be possible for the Naval Sea Systems Command to design vessels in a more innovative and uninhibited fashion now that it is relieved of Rickover's increasingly conservative designs, but hopefully the Nuclear Reactors Branch will also be able to forge ahead with newer reactor designs radically more effective than even the S8G reactor aboard the Trident. Hopefully too, relative improvements here can be made in time for the second flotilla of Tridents, so they can more easily outrun as well as outwit the *Alpha*. Rickover, in short, did not make a personal contribution to Trident equivalent to that made by Veliotis. Navy investments of a different sort are nevertheless now more necessary than ever.

While assessing Rickover's impact on the program and placing the responsibility for the force-level confusions on the Navy are fairly clear-cut propositions, the assignment of responsibility for block obsolescence in the strategic submarine force is somewhat more difficult to fix. The Navy commissioned the *Will Rogers* (SSBN-659) on April 1, 1967, and the *Ohio* was delivered on October 28, 1981—a gap of almost fourteen and a half years. Vietnam provides a partial answer, as does the *Ohio*'s own delay, but planning a follow-on class should have occurred earlier than STRAT-X in 1967. A similar scenario has developed with the B-1 bomber, which will appear in time to replace aging B-52s that should have been retired in the mid-1970s. Once again, a democratic government seems able to procrastinate, debate, and delay to the extent, as historical evidence suggests, that its very existence is at stake. Proponents of the future Stealth as an alternative to the present B-1B illustrate only one of the temptations that too easily encourage lawmakers to slight real defense needs in favor of future "wonder weapons." It has already been demonstrated that an early commitment to ten Tridents could have saved tremendous sums of money. How much did the delay of the B-1 bomber add to its final cost? The most recent figures indicate roughly 100 percent, from $24 billion to produce 244 to a FY 1981 cost of $20 billion for 100. The block obsolescence of U.S. ICBM forces is also approaching, yet the MX missile is no closer to deployment now than it was in 1977. In 1979, the Air Force spent $22 million to repair one single Titan II ICBM silo and missile, which is *half* as much as it would cost to replace all of the Minuteman II missiles now deployed with updated Minuteman III missiles (not counting the cost of the missiles). But when the Minuteman force begins to deteriorate, it will then quickly surpass in repair costs the deployment expense of MX. What happened to the strategic submarine force will be replayed, but probably at higher costs, with attendant increased national security risks.[6]

Because defense contractors perform their services for the government, it is sometimes forgotten they must operate within the structure of the economy as a whole. They are sensitive to high interest rates, union demands, the declining productivity of U.S. manufacturers such as steel, and to massive government-caused inflation. Their performance requires a consideration of these factors, and they have corporate obligations to report a profit as well. John Newell, whose masterful article "The Breakdown in Naval Shipbuilding" explains a number of causes for cost overruns and delays, notes "the Congress and the Navy have been preoccupied with control of *profit* to the neglect, unfortunately, of costs." Newell also cites the detrimental system of shipbuilding instituted "by two men with little or no shipyard experience." However, the shipbuilder cannot be faulted for seeking any legitimate contractual means to ensure a profit. For example, Senator Howard Metzenbaum denounced the Navy for allegedly agreeing to pay the financial losses of shipbuilders who lost their cases against the Internal Revenue Service. If the shipbuilders won, the Navy would cover the legal fees. The Navy has frequently used shipbuilders that employed dummy corporations for the purpose of simplifying the contract transactions and limiting investor liabilities from unrelated activities. Again, measures such as these are often necessary to guarantee the shipbuilder a profit.[7]

Officially the U.S. Navy (or any other branch of military service) has no direct and ultimate responsibility to see that a defense contractor makes a real profit. However, why should it naturally occur that a defense contractor all too often go profitless at best and bankrupt at worst on behalf of the Army or the Navy? Why should a defense contractor, contrary to the interests of the stockholders or the future of his company, not make a profit because of the fact his particular kind of production provides the military means of defending the national-economic system by which all other corporations and businesses profit? Why is the United States corporately, nationally, politically, or economically more secure when defense contractors are prejudicially harassed by the media, by certain interest groups, or by attacks like Rickover's, to the point of becoming less profitable than other comparably scaled industries? Why is this contractor's profit inherently more immoral, atypical, or deliberately and enthusiastically self-corruptive than other normal, traditionally profitable enterprises? National security is the rootstock of all other social services. The Trident is now already making its particular contribution to this maintenance, and Electric Boat Company's ± $450-million investment in the appropriate facilities at Groton and Quonset Point came from the resources and good credit of a profitable corporation.

Moreover, it is important to realize the $450-million investment was no pearl plucked from an oyster. It was achieved by entrepreneurial risk—the nature of which is well illustrated by Veliotis' role in the investment, more particularly the Quonset Point facility. While it was based on analogous experience with the automated construction of gas domes for the LNG ships of General Dynamics, a more complicated undertaking than the automated frame and cylinder facility, it nevertheless was not the good old-fashioned way submarines had heretofore been built. It was therefore a highly risky step and apparently provocative. Indeed, in initial and manifest confirmation of pessimistic Navy suspicions, the facility at first exhibited nothing but losses because of the incomplete record of learning-curve effects. However, as if to confirm Veliotis' faith and determination, the facility is now performing in an incomparably more advanced fashion than even Electric Boat imagined possible. Having made his point, as a matter of style, self-confidence, and insight as well as a matter of responsibility, Veliotis effectively restructured Electric Boat–Navy relationships by emphasizing that the *Navy* contracted with *Electric Boat* to build the Tridents and the attack-class 688s and that, within the conditions of the contract, Veliotis was in charge of the building process on Electric Boat's grounds. This was true even to the point where Electric Boat regarded an acceptable profit as being relevant. Veliotis' comments regarding the developments at Electric Boat since his departure further underscore the fact that the struggle for control of the yard is not yet over.

Criticisms of the Trident schedule have been dealt with throughout this work. It seems obvious, when the drafting strike (five months) is accounted for, combined with the negotiations over Navy changes (eight months cumulative), a substantial portion of the *Ohio*'s delay is accounted for in a manner no one could have originally suspected. Strikes ignore schedules, the Navy's or anyone else's. But even granting this as a thirteen-month "grace period" to the Navy and Electric Boat, original schedules on the part of all involved simply failed to reflect an understanding of the magnitude and complexity of the undertaking. In a sense, the Trident became "too good"—imbued with more and better technology, constructed by a shipbuilding process of a revolutionary nature, and involving higher levels of skill and managerial expertise than either the Navy or the shipbuilder had previously encountered. If American technology had remained static, it might be argued, the *Ohio* would have sailed down the Thames sooner. Once again, however, given the erratic nature of the appropriations process, the Navy found itself trying to squeeze out an additional 10 percent of performance. In this the Navy appears justified.

Often overlooked in the sometimes sterile analysis of service-contractor relationships, and a point touched upon throughout this work, is the comprehensive nature of the interaction between the Navy and various contractors as well as various programs in different stages of development. The 688 program became thoroughly interrelated to the Trident program and, in turn, this meant that Navy decisions in one program not only reached across other programs but also across competing contractors. To assure contractor harmony, tradeoffs were necessary throughout the entire process, and an award of submarine contracts to Newport News might require a "balancing" award of destroyers to Litton-Ingalls. Complicating this process even more is the cumulative effect of decision-making: each decision becomes a consequence of a previous decision. All of these pressures make the contractual-appropriations game even more difficult.

Finally, Trident's overall place in the TRIAD presents another dilemma by exerting continued pressure on systems competing for funds, especially the MX missile and the B-1B bomber. At present, the latter seems safe. But the MX may yet force a rethinking of the type of TRIAD the Unitd States pursues.

The MX program has become a political soccer ball, reflecting indecisive systems dalliance, kicked from one basing mode to another. It has ultimately arrived at the point of logical argumentative inversion—from scattered multiple pack (MPS) to Dense Pack—if not to the point of exhaustion. Thus, if only to provide the devil's-advocate argument, regardless of the possibility of finally discovering a viable basing mode, why not spend the MX program's ±$37.26 billion for an acceleration of the Trident system both in terms of hulls and Trident II missile production?

The sea constitutes a natural form of silo "hardening" by reason of its vastness, its opaqueness, its depth, its penetrability by the SSBN while in navigation, and by reason of its provision of a protective cover not only for the missile carrier, so to speak, but for a whole magazine of twenty-four launchers rather than for each launcher separately. Conversely, even superhardening for land-based missiles up to 10,000 pounds per square inch does not work very well in terms either of shock resistance, general survivability, costs of construction, or other economic trade-offs against the detonation of a heavy Soviet RV upon any *one* single land-based silo. Furthermore, except insofar as real silos are numerically or statistically protected by a disproportionate number of equally expensive alternate or diversionary silos, a land-based silo is finitely located basically in a two-dimensional fashion (unless, like the Soviet SS-20 theatre weapon it is mobile in a tracked version), while an SSBN's whole magazine is constantly mobile on an erratic pattern of tridimensional maneuver. A land-based missile system increasingly needs apparently to be defended by an ABM system, as is argued by many MX advocates with a LoADs system, while a sea-based system does not so far need an ABM equivalent. Land-based systems, as Dense Pack does virtually and deliberately, draw and concentrate the enemy's

ICBM force toward the homeland one is strategically trying to defend, while SSBNs draw counter-SSBN and counter-SLBM enemy activities away from one's homeland.

The converse side of the effectively critical arguments about the vulnerability of Dense Pack, especially with an ABM complementary system, is the unpersuasive argument made in support of a Soviet open-ocean barrage system (see chap. 8) against the U.S. Navy's SSBN force. Viewing this issue from a doctrinal and historical perspective, in its third (Polaris–Poseidon–Trident) generation of existence, the SSBN–SLBM system's survivability has not met as specific and serious a challenge as have the Minuteman and MX land-based systems. Moreover, SLBMs are progressively becoming nearly as accurate as ICBMs, a trend likely to continue with forthcoming modifications of the Trident I before the 1989 initial deployment of the Trident II can incorporate its accumulation of Trident I accuracy-improvment modifications—before going on to its *own* generation of modifications. Also, while admitting the significance of the MX's heavy payload in megatonnage versus the Trident I, the availability of the Trident II's fourteen-to-16-RV payload relatively diminishes this temporary spurt of advantage between 1982 and 1989.

Yet, even as its proponents await a resolution to the nondecisive process of finding some sort of a basing mode, the MX's history of going through so many already indicates, in comparison with SSBNs as *the* basing mode for SLBMs, no basing mode for MX so far seems survivable technically, statistically, or systemically. Even allowing for the conceptual, strategic, and professional dedication of defenders of the MX as a land-based system and acknowledging that the rejuvenation the B-52 and FB-111 bomber leg will soon begin with the influx of B-1B bombers, decisions must be made for the right reasons. A presidential- and Pentagon-level desire to satisfy the Air Force MX pressure group, simply in order not to transform it (and its associated contractors) into a prospectively negative constituency, does not, ipso facto, constitute a positive case for the MX. Given the history of the MX basing-mode decision process, a "be-done-with-it" attitude may do more to resolve the matter than rational decision and careful thought. Thus, many are beginning to suspect the best possible land-based ICBM force is probably no longer operationally, politically, psychologically, or strategically as good as the best sea-based system. In terms of the impact of time, cost, engineering, inflation, technical paradox, treaty limitations (ABM particularly), environmental, and regional political considerations, their suspicions have solid foundations. Given the thrust of the above observations about the direction in which the land-based ICBM system seems to be going and given the fact that, in

1981, U.S. SLBMs constituted 32 percent of its launchers, 50 percent of its total warheads, and 25 percent of its throw-weight while SLBMs constituted for the Soviets only 38 percent, 20 percent, and 15 percent respectively, and that, conversely, ICBMs were 51 percent of U.S. launchers, 24 percent of its warheads, and 33 percent of its throw-weight while they were for the Soviets 56 percent, 75 percent, and 70 percent respectively, the Soviets turn out to be disproportionately dependent upon the increasingly *more* vulnerable land missile force while the United States proportionately is not. At the same time, the United States is upgrading its apparently two best systems with Trident and the B-1B.[8]

If this strategic version of the "scissors crisis" continues, the Soviets should become substantially less secure and the United States more secure if this country does not waste money, time, attention, concept, and devotion on land-based follow-on systems like MX. Viewing the trends, dependencies, and apparently inherently different systems vulnerabilities, an intensification of America's relative advantage qualitatively and/or quantitatively in SSBNs and bombers would whipsaw the Soviets strategically. Penultimately, perhaps, the *old* TRIAD strategic system lamentably must eventually be recognized as obsolete fiscally, strategically, operationally, and systemically. Perhaps, then, it can be admitted that a reconstituted TRIAD, for the United States at least, does and should consist principally of the bomber for the Air Force, the SLBM and carrierborne capability of the Navy, the theatre-weapon capability (Pershing II) for the Army, and the cruise missile in its various versions for each service. What is wrong with TRIAD being "born again" differently?

Finally, it should be recalled that the economic rationale behind the dispersing effects of the original version of the TRIAD was that its maintenance tends to prevent a single scientific breakthrough from simultaneously endangering all three legs of the TRIAD. But this almost religiously held belief may no longer necessarily be collectively true for each, all, or any combination of legs. This is especially true if alternately available funds (for MX) are shifted to the systemically superior sea leg of the TRIAD so that the current relative systems advantage is maintained or, preferably, accelerated and intensified. The structure of the TRIAD should not be any more systemically or conceptually sacrosanct than the original distinction between the Field and the Coast Artillery or between the old Army Air (heavy bombardment) Force and the Army's tactical air force today. In short, what strategic gains would be made by the United Sates if the MX budget of $37.5 to $80 billion was substantially transformed into an acceleration of the *whole* Trident program? This shift would include the provision of the second set of Trident boats with more efficient hydrodynamics, reactors, communications, and sail design. Complementary shifts with other portions of the MX programs' total funds might suggest an exhilarating advance of the country's defensive and offensive ASW capability, the adoption of a publicly visible and reassuring program of civil defense, and a more rapid deployment of the cruise missile program, a cosmopolitan advantage, be it noted, to every branch of the armed forces. One suspects the Soviets really could not compete under such a newfound economic, strategic, and systemic challenge if the parochial competition between Trident and other weapons programs did not always require having subordinate or constituent losers. Unlike the *Ohio* overrun as a single and lead vessel of a limited-copy class, the present wonder might be in what direction an MX appropriation, equivalent in FY 1981 dollars of between twenty-seven and fifty-seven Tridents already, will eventually run? In other words, for the amount spent on MX, the nation might have purchased twenty-four to twenty-seven Tridents! What would have been the fate of the Trident program if its original sponsors had asked in 1972–1974 for the FY 1980 equivalent of $5.6 billion for the first four boats then contracted?

If the MX can be defended literally, it is with an ABM system, and if it can be defended theoretically, it is on the grounds suggested in chapter 10. Requiring continued Soviet spending on its own defenses against ICBMs is a factor that, for the present, continues to justify a land-based leg of the TRIAD. But developments in cruise-missile technology, assuming satisfactory U.S. overseas bases, may require a drastic shift in the nature of the TRIAD unless an abrogation of the ABM Treaty is considered. Improvements in cruise missiles and Pershing IIs may herald the use of a truly mobile land-based missile. Whatever decision is eventually made, it is clear that each service branch will continue to play a role in strategic defense. The ultimate life, death, or other career of the MX should not become a stumbling block to an improved and integrated strategic defense procurement process. While the Trident is no longer in competition with the MX, both serve as reminders of the numerous twists and turns a strategic weapons system makes on the path from inception to deployment.

How ironic it is that the growing awareness of ICBM vulnerability has turned many early critics of Trident into supporters of the sea-based leg. Even more paradoxical, however, is the fact that development of the Trident II makes it possible to consider doing away with the MX *at all*—ironic because had the early proponents of a smaller, "austere" Trident succeeded, the larger missile could not be carried in the alternative hull. Thus, by taking advantage of existing and forthcoming technology, by being farsighted enough to see the impact of the Trident II (at the time almost twenty years away), by sticking to its guns about the question of the larger hull, and by allowing for the unpredictable, the Navy overcame its numerous political errors and managerial deficiencies to the degree that it has grasped preeminence in the strategic defense of the United States for at least a decade.

The MX basing dilemma also reveals that no preferable criterion for determining cost effectiveness has evolved since the tenure of Defense Secretary McNamara. Thus, when the concept of cost overruns is discarded and when a TRIAD redesign is employed, the question of Trident's cost effectiveness takes on new implications. It is both costly and effective. If "effective" means meeting or attaining all its design objectives, the *Ohio* has far surpassed its original goals.

But cost-effectiveness implies more than merely meeting or surpassing design goals: it is a concept of value, overlooked with regularity in American military history. For example, in 1794, in order to deal with the Barbary pirates, Congress authorized six frigates, three of which were rated at forty-four guns, although actually only the *United States* and the *Constitution* carried such a number, while the *America* and the *Congress* carried thirty-eight guns each, and the *Constellation* thirty-six guns. The *Constellation* cost $302,718, a figure that broke down to just about $7000 of ship for each gun carried and portended for the incoming administration of President Thomas Jefferson a "cost-ineffective" program. So, Congress next authorized, between 1805 and 1807, 263 gunboats, of which 176 actually were built. Most of these were one-gun, fifty-foot craft requiring a crew of twenty-five and costing $14,000 each. The real "savings" meant that, for the price of one *Constellation*, the Navy got twenty-one gunboats but also only twenty-one guns rather than forty-four guns. Figured differently, to get forty-four guns deployed at sea, 1100 crew members would be necessary and $616,000 would have to be appropriated—the equivalent of nearly two *Constellations*! In the War of 1812 most of these gunboats were swamped, beached, scuttled, burned, hidden, or otherwise abandoned in the face of British men-of-war blockading Chesapeake Bay, while the *Constitution* went out to deep water to defeat the *Guerrière* and the *Java*. Fittingly enough, the Smithsonian Institution houses one such Jeffersonian gunboat indoors, while the *Constitution* is still afloat in Boston Harbor. Certainly the Trident in this regard resembles the multigun frigate in terms of cost effectiveness more than it does the Jeffersonian gunboat—"too small a boy for a man-sized job."[9]

Moreover, as discussed in this chapter, the current use of the hull as an SSBN platform represents only a fraction of the potential uses to which the hull eventually may be put, including civilian uses. As they exist now, Trident subs, appropriately modified, have even more capabilities than most observers involved in the early stages of design ever contemplated. Trident's speed, diving ability, and quietness have met or exceeded expectations. Yet current judgments about cost effectiveness may be meaningless in light of the future applications of the hull. Its ability to serve as a laser-beam or particle-beam platform may make Trident a member of the next generation of weapons as well as a member of the current one. Mobility, another quality Trident has, is not a quality of land-based or necessarily of space-based laser-beam weapons. How, then, does one assess cost effectiveness with those possibilities considered? For the sums appropriated for Trident, the nation simply has the finest, most effective, and most survivable submarine in the world. At a price tag of about $1.4 billion per copy, the United States has begun to upgrade its deterrent force in a significant way, possibly in time to deter the USSR from a surgical preemptive strike against U.S. ICBMs. For the ±$30-billion cost of the Trident program to date, the United States has probably gained at least thirty more years of security. Is a year of freedom worth $1 billion, or should yet another formula for cost effectiveness be invoked? The birth pains needed to see the Trident to fruition seem symptomatic of weapons procurement in a democratic government, with the ominous postcript being that they seem to get worse with each new delivery. Yet no democratic government can delay procurement of needed weapons in the atomic age, where no margin of error is possible, where no massive national effort, such as that exhibited in World War II, can possibly redress a strategic imbalance in the nick of time. Consequently, Trident's arrival offers hope for the process, while at the same time its legislative and shipbuilding history must continue to generate genuine concern for future trends. Leviathan's presence under the seas should serve as a constant reminder that the use of force usually ensues after policy fails. Conversely, the continued deterrence of nuclear war, in a way the most paradoxical, extravagant, and passive combat in history, should prove well worth whatever treasure this nation sensibly has to offer, since the costs of World War III are infinite.

Meanwhile, Trident for the foreseeable future will restrain time's otherwise unfriendly disposition toward a nation that has sometimes even enthusiastically frittered away its earlier strategic advantages in the golden days of the traditional Triad. Defense analysts in and out of government must nevertheless succeed in thinking more profoundly and sensibly than they did during the era of détente, with its self-delusory vocabulary. Strategic parity, essential equivalence, graduated response, mutual assured destruction, SALT I and II, first-strike capability, START, and mutual assured vulnerability never can serve as alternatives to the ability to conduct war, when necessary, in the national defense. Fortunately, Trident can fight as well as deter.

Appendixes
Notes
Bibliography
Acknowledgments
Index

Appendix A

Trident Submarine Contractors to 1972

(Amounts in $ thousands)

(Strategic Weapon System)

Agency or Contractor	Task	FY 1970 & Prior	Fiscal Year 1971	Date All Costs Incurred
AEC (Sandia)	Reentry body design			
APL/JHU	System integration	500		
BUPERS	Training studies	2	148	6/71
Control Data Corp. Current contract no.: N00030-72-C-008; coverage dates: 4/72–7/72	Training studies & development		23	6/71
Challenger Research. Current contract no.: N00030-72-C-0103; coverge dates: 11/71–7/72	Fire control studies		75	6/71
Consultech	System integration	107	7	8/71
Eng. physics lab	System integration	38		
General Dynamics, Electric Boat. Current contract no.: N0024-71-C-0311; coverage dates: 4/27/71–6/30/73	Ship installation, design studies, & system integration	300		

Agency or Contractor	Task	FY 1970 & Prior	Fiscal Year 1971	Date All Costs Incurred
GE, Ordnance Systems Division. Current contract no.: N00030-72-C-0100; coverage dates: 1/72–7/72; type: cost. Current contract no. N00030-72-C-0124; coverage dates: 10/71–7/72	Guidance and fire control development & training studies	475	415	9/71
HUMRO	Personnel & training	48		
Hydronautics	System integration	210		
Hydrosystems	Training studies		23	8/71
Interstate Electronic Corp. Current contract no.: N00030-72-C-0097; coverage dates: 9/71–8/72; type: cost. Current contract no.: N00030-72-C-0153; coverage dates: 9/72–8/72	Test instrumentation	60	93	6/71
International Research Inc.	System engineering—logistic study		98	9/71
Kaman Nuclear	Reentry-body vulnerability studies			
NUWC	Launcher-test facilities	50		

Trident Contractors to 1972

Agency or Contractor	Task	FY 1970 & Prior	Fiscal Year 1971	Date All Costs Incurred
Lockheed. Current contract no.: N00030-72-C-0102; coverage dates: 8/71–9/72; type: cost. Current contract no.: N00030-72-C-0133; coverage dates: 1/72–8/72; type: cost. Current contract no.: N00030-72-C-0108; coverage dates: 11/71–8/72	Missile and reentry body development, test instrumentation development and training studies and development	3300	3664	8/71
MIT/Draper Lab. Current contract no.: N00030-72-C-0085; coverage dates: 7/71–7/72	Guidance development	250	3500	6/71
NAFI	Fire control—circuit	33	50	6/71
NAVSEC	System integration	9	63	8/71
NAVRAADIODF-FLAB	System integration		5	8/71
NOL	Reentry-body studies	122	75	9/71
NWL	Fire-control & effectiveness studies & system integration	17	100	6/71
Operation Research Inc.	System integration	78	109	6/71
Raytheon	Guidance development			
Singer Co.	Guidance development			

Agency or Contractor	Task	FY 1970 & Prior	Fiscal Year 1971	Date All Costs Incurred
SPCC	System integration		30	7/71
Sperry Systems management division. Current contract no.: N00030-72-C-0131; coverage dates: 10/71–7/72; type: cost. Current contract no.: N00030-72-C-009; coverage dates: 1/72–7/72	Navigation development, training studies & development	375	330	9/71
VITRO. Current contract no.: N00030-72-C-0011; coverage dates: 7/71–7/72	System integration	717	452	6/72
Westinghouse. Current contract no.: N00030-71-C-0123; coverage dates: 12/71–7/72	Training studies, launcher development	890	672	7/71
Puget Sound NSY	Ship design studies			
TOTAL		7581	9952	
Air Force/Lincoln Labs	System engineering			
Bolt, Beramek & Newman. Current contract no.: in process	Acoustics, sonar	30		
Booz-Allen	Technical support		26	12/71
Bradford. Current contract no.: N00024-72-C-0271; coverage dates: 4/1/72–6/30/73	Integrated logistics, support/reliability, maintainability & availability (RMA)			
Challenger. Current contract no.: in process	Sonar			

Trident Contractors to 1972

Agency or Contractor	Task	FY 1970 & Prior	Fiscal Year 1971	Date All Costs Incurred
Charleston NSY	Machinery systems, support facility	5	10	9/71
CONSULTECH	Management support	100		
Computer Systems Corp. Current contract no.: in process	Technical support			
Ehrenpreis	Hull structure	175		
Electric Battery. Current contract no.: in process	Electric plant			
General Dynamics, Electric Boat. Current contract no.: N00024-71-C-0311; contract dates: 4/2/71–6/30/73	Ship design & systems integration TECHEVAL, auxiliary systems, subsystem design tradeoffs, project management, ILS, acoustics, shock & vibration, support facilities, command & surveillance	2890	14,921	3/72
General Electric	Sonar		30	12/71

Agency or Contractor	Task	FY 1970 & Prior	Fiscal Year 1971	Date All Costs Incurred
Knolls Atomic power Lab. Current contract no.: N00024-70-C-5027; contract dates: 7/1/69–6/30/72 Nuclear reactor development	Nuclear reactor development	2000	7000	8/71
Gould Battery. Current contract no.: in process	Electric plant			
Hamilton Standard. Current contract no.: in process	Acoustics			
Hobbs Association. Current contract no.: in process	Command & surveillance			
Honeywell. Current contract no.: in process	Command & surveillance			
IBM	Sonar			
ITT. Current contract no.: in process	Command & surveillance			
LMSC	Support facilities & logistics		477	8/71
Long Beach NSY	Support facilities			
Mare Island NSY	Materials development	73	550	3/72
Martin-Marietta	Command & surveillance		94	9/71
MPL	Sonar		50	8/71
NAVFAC	Industrial facilities		10	1/72
NAVSEC Washington	Ship design & technical management	1480	1855	2/72

Agency or Contractor	Task	FY 1970 & Prior	Fiscal Year 1971	Date All Costs Incurred
NAVSEC Mech	ILS			
NAVSEC Phil	Auxiliary systems		111	4/72
NAVSUP	Integrated logistics	5	25	2/72
NCEL	Hull structure	60		
NELC	Systems engineering/integration design, model fabrication & testing	67	65	12/71
NOL	Magnet concealment & sonar		375	1/72
Northrop. Current contract no.: N00024-72-C-0263; contract dates: 12/6/71–12/31/72	Management support		93	12/71
NPRDL	Integrated logistics support		5	12/71
NRL	Damage control & life support		30	12/71
NSRDC	Acoustics, structures & ship control	856	2452	3/72
NSRDC/UERD	Shock & vibration, nonnuclear propulsion			
NSSF	Facilities & ILS		214	10/71

Agency or Contractor	Task	FY 1970 & Prior	Fiscal Year 1971	Date All Costs Incurred
NURDC, San Diego	Acoustics, sonar	497	206	1/72
NURDC, Pasadena	Survivability		123	12/71
NUSC	Sonar, command & surveillance, information display	25	880	1/72
NWESA	Integrated logistic support			
Operational Research Inc.	Threat assessment	8		
Pearl Harbor	Hull structure/coating		74	1/72
Portsmouth NSY	Hull structure		5	12/71
RCA	Command & surveillance		97	9/71
San Francisco	Submarine design	194		
SPCC	Integrated logistics support			
Teledyne. Current contract no.: in process	Auxiliary systems			
Tetra Tech	Acoustics		467	3/72
Tracor	Sonar	30		
UCLA	Effectiveness assessment		75	12/72
University of Pennsylvania. Current contract no.: in process	Command & surveillance			

383
Trident Contractors to 1972

Agency or Contractor	Task	FY 1970 & Prior	Fiscal Year 1971	Date All Costs Incurred
VITRO. Current contract no.: N00024-72-C-0228; contract dates: 9/13/71–9/30/72	Project management, coordination & integration		560	7/71
Washington Associates	Sonar		12	5/71
Westinghouse. Current contract no.: in process	Machinery development	165	45	2/71
U.S. Time-sharing	Project management		13	6/71
Undetermined	Magnetic concealment, sonar support facilities, hull structure, non-nuclear propulsion plant, electric plant, command & surveillance, auxiliary systems, project management, advance development model fabrication	——	——	
TOTAL		8979	33,698	

Source: *Senate Hearings*, Armed Services Committee, Ad Hoc Committee on Research and Development, 92d Cong., 2d sess., March 22, 1972, pp. 3200–3203.

Appendix B

Interview with P. Takis Veliotis, June, 1982

QUESTION: Mr. Veliotis, the newspapers and publicity surrounding your arrival in 1977 seemed to indicate you were taking over a shipyard in serious trouble. Can you describe the situation as you found it in 1977 and tell us what steps you took to correct it?

ANSWER: When I came down from Quincy Shipbuilding to EB there were a number of very apparent problems. In a nutshell, they centered around manpower, morale, material, methods and money. The financial situation at the yard was desperate. Because of the many drawing revisions for the 688 class, the company was losing millions of dollars a month and was bogged down in a complicated claim litigation which did not offer any near term relief. The Corporation was spending millions to keep the place open but had just about reached the end of the line. The situation finally reached a point where we were forced to advise the Navy that unless the situation was resolved we would be compelled to stop work in the SSN 688 program. Few people know this but we had actually printed the lay-off notices for many of our people. Fortunately, we were able to work with then Secretary of the Navy Hidalgo and reach an agreement before the lay-off slips were distributed. Public Law 85-804 resulted in a $359 million loss to General Dynamics but did allow us to go on with our building programs.

Another major problem we found was manpower. It was very clear that we simply had too many people. The company had undertaken a massive shipyard build-up in an attempt to meet delivery schedules which were not achievable. One of our first acts was to devise challenging but attainable schedules and budgets, and bring the manpower situation in line.

We also found that the overhead and support situation was overstaffed. I undertook one of the most difficult actions in my career. It was absolutely essential that these costs come under control, and that required the lay-off of 3,000 people. I judged that it was best all around to effect these reductions in one swoop. Accordingly, we accomplished the lay-offs in one week. There was severe and widespread criticism of our action, but the survival of the company and the thousands of remaining jobs demanded action.

Electric Boat's material situation was another immediate focus. We found that no one knew how much material the yard had, versus how much was required or had already been used. Accordingly, we first created a Bill of Material for SSN 688's. That is, we precisely defined the material required to build the ship. With that in hand, and the existing TRIDENT Bill of Material, we shut the shipyard down for one week, and conducted a "hands-on" wall to wall inventory of every piece of material in the yard—over 90 million separate items.

In addition, we found that the methods and business systems in use at Electric Boat were sorely lacking in efficiency. There was a prevalent attitude which went along the lines of: "We've always done it this way before". We forced people to look at the way things were done and come up with better methods. For instance, for management and control, we devised the Submarine Computer-Oriented Management System (SUBCOM). SUBCOM is able to provide cost and schedule status to an infinitesimal level of detail thereby flagging production problems at their source for timely corrective action.

We also looked closely at the construction techniques themselves. The production of submarine frames and cylinders was an area where drastic improvements could be achieved. At the time, most of this work was done at Quonset, using largely manual techniques that had not varied in twenty years. The process was labor intensive, expensive and slow. Our response has been the $100 million Automated Cylinder Manufacturing Facility at Quonset Point. In this ultra-modern facility we use highly automated machinery which, with massive jigs and fixtures, produces extremely high quality cylinders at a fraction of the cost and time. Most important though, is that these cylinders are produced to exact, repeatable dimensions. In the later stages of construction such as hull joining and installation there is a big payoff in knowing the exact dimensions and tolerances of framing.

Finally, we found morale to be a major problem. There was an obvious lack of discipline and unusually high levels of absenteeism and attrition. Also, the physical conditions of the yard were dirty and disorganized. We moved quickly to step up disciplinary measures and enforcement of labor contract language. Absenteeism control became a high priority. We instituted daily, random productivity checks. We organized a major, general clean-up of the yard. We moved and consolidated manufacturing and support functions closer to actual work areas and we took steps to sharply upgrade the caliber of our first line supervisors through training, retraining and the recruitment of engineers and other high caliber individuals for foremen slots.

We saw improvements in morale almost immediately as we improved work environment, improved supervision and communicated work requirements and objectives to our people.

QUESTION: What were the overall results of this program of improvements?

ANSWER: I have always believed that the best proof is performance. At Electric Boat we began to get that performance. During 1978 and into 1979 we delivered two submarines in overhaul, as well as three LOS ANGELES Class submarines. These ships were all delivered under budget and ahead of schedule, measured against the goals we set on my arrival. On SSN's 692–696 we realized a savings of almost $7 million against our budgets. On the TRIDENT program, the OHIO was on track to delivery in November 1980, and the MICHIGAN was on schedule to deliver a year later. The reduction we made in overhead and support areas were yielding annual savings averaging over $150 million. These savings were significant enough that the Navy was able to go to the Congress and reprogram almost $80 million from the FY 1981 TRIDENT account—on the basis of our demonstrated savings. These savings, as well as the benefits accrued from our new facility at Quonset made the Company a competitive entity again. Prior to 1977 we had lost eight ships to our competitor Newport News in head-to-head competitions. In early 1979, we went head-to-head with Newport News again, for two SSN's, and came away with the award.

I regard that performance record as an endorsement of the program we undertook in 1977. We had turned Electric Boat around and were getting the performance we needed.

QUESTION: What was the status of the Trident program when you arrived in October 1977?

ANSWER: The design of the ship was clearly not advanced to the point that would permit the ship to be delivered on the scheduled date. There had been an unrealistic optimism on building the first ship and in thinking that it was similar to the earlier FBM submarines. The Trident submarine is not only an order of magnitude larger than any previous submarine, but many of her design features advanced the state of the art technology to new horizons. You must remember that when the construction contract for OHIO was signed the design was perhaps only 10% complete. We made a complete analysis of both status of design and construction back in the fall of 1977. In light of the design status and all the changes that were taking place, we recommended to the Navy a new contract date of November 1980 and the Navy concurred.

QUESTION: It is widely maintained that the OHIO was delivered 2½ years late. I know that you take exception to that statement. Can you explain why?

ANSWER: First of all, it is true that the original delivery of the OHIO was April 1979. It is also true that the ship [was] delivered in October 1981. Considering only those two facts, you can say we were 2½ years late. However there are more facts that bear on the matter and cannot be ignored. One overlooked fact is that the present contract delivery date for

OHIO is October 31, 1981, and the ship was delivered on October 28. It is more correct to say that the ship was delivered three days early than 2½ years late. But that is also an oversimplification.

The construction of a ship as sophisticated as the TRIDENT is an enormously complicated task which spans six years and involved millions of manhours of labor. Remember that the contract was signed with the Navy which set April 1979 as the delivery was signed in July of 1974. On the basis of what we and the Navy knew at the time, April 1979 was targeted for delivery. As must be expected, events arise which could not have been foreseen over seven years in advance of the delivery. When we signed that contract the design of the ship was only 10% complete, not to mention the fact that the facilities to build OHIO at Groton and Quonset didn't exist.

In recognition of the uncertainties which surround naval ship construction (any Naval ship—not just OHIO) there is a contractual mechanism for taking into account emergent problems or developments. Simply put, the contract date is formally extended as a result of change orders. Government-responsible causes of delay and other circumstances allowable under the contract entitle the shipbuilder to additional time for delivery.

In the case of OHIO, the contract has been modified by the Government on several occasions, primarily to reflect the impact of design changes which required rework or expanded the scope of work. This is a common occurrence in the construction of a lead ship of a class.

To illustrate the point, the lead ship of *every* recent class of surface ships and submarines has actually been delivered later than its original contract delivery date. As might be expected, the extent of delay increases with the complexity of the ship. CVN-68 was delivered 19 months "late", whereas FFG-7 was delivered 8 months "late". It is a simple fact of life in naval shipbuilding that these delays will occur, it is not a reflection on the quality of the shipbuilder.

The simplistic statement that OHIO was 2½ years "late" is not a fair or accurate assessment of the situation.

QUESTION: What was the basic cause of the problems wherein everyone seemed to believe these early optimistic schedules?

ANSWER: I wasn't at Electric Boat at the time those contracts were signed so I do not have any first hand information. From discussions I have had with people the conclusion I would draw would be basically the same as described by Morton Mintz in the Washington Post article last September. The Navy issued the request for proposal for a fixed price contract.

Initially Electric Boat refused to go on a fixed price basis and insisted on a cost plus proposal because of the tremendous risks that were involved. Remember this ship was hardly designed and was to be built on an entirely new facility not yet constructed, so we could not accurately give the Government a realistic fixed price proposal. The Navy rejected our cost plus proposal and insisted that it must be done on a fixed price basis. Electric Boat finally responded with a fixed price but again reiterated the unusual risks associated with the contracting. However, EB insisted on having full and complete coverage of the effects of inflation, a very high selling price, and a very flat share line to minimize the financial risk to Electric Boat.

QUESTION: Doesn't this type of contract, i.e. fixed price on undesigned lead ship, conflict with Navy policy?

ANSWER: You are quite right. Frequently, the Navy has stated that as a matter of policy the first ship of a class should be cost plus fixed fee. In fact, I believe the Assistant Secretary of the Navy George Sawyer, in an interview in SEAPOWER Magazine reiterated this policy and noted that until the first ship is built and the design stabilized, fixed price contracts are very, very risky.

QUESTION: As you mentioned in the beginning, the schedules you found in 1977 were overly optimistic and at that time you recommended to the Navy a November 30, 1980 delivery date which the Navy approved. Now with the advantage of 20/20 hindsight, was the November 1980 a realistic date?

ANSWER: With the information available to us at the time we made the recommendation, that was a good schedule. In fact up until November of 1979 we were doing a little better than expected against that delivery date. Then a series of major unforeseen events hit us. First was the replacement of the main rotors in the government furnished main propulsion turbines. This had to be accomplished after the engine room was essentially built and tested. A long string of design changes continued by the hundreds which we clearly had not allowed schedule contingency for, nor could they have been foreseen.

QUESTION: Aside from the main turbine problems, when did you see that the magnitude of the design changes was becoming a significant impediment?

ANSWER: Early in 1980 some drastic action had to be taken to both minimize the number of changes and to streamline the authorization procedure to perform those which must be accomplished. In February and March of that year we wrote the Navy on four different occasions advising them of the absolute necessity to initiate a system for the daily review of changes and to prioritize the work. In fact, we even forwarded to the Navy a procedure that the Navy had previously used with Electric Boat on earlier designs which did utilize daily meetings between the Supervisor of Shipbuilding and the Electric Boat, and a streamlined method for handling paper flow which would drastically cut down the time and eliminate the red tape complication that we were faced with on the Trident program.

QUESTION: Did the Navy promptly adopt such a streamline procedure?

ANSWER: No. They not only refused to adopt it but they refused to participate in daily discussions. Finally, the Secretary of the Navy, Mr. Hidalgo, got into the act and through his direction, positive steps were taken to start meaningful daily meetings, but that did not occur until 8 months after the urgent requests had been made to the Navy.

QUESTION: Wasn't there a special provision in your contract noting the priority of the Trident program?

ANSWER: Yes. At the time the contract for OHIO was signed, Electric Boat recognized the need for something more than a business-as-usual approach on the part of the Navy if there were to be any chances in meeting an accelerated delivery.

There was a special provision in the contract that recognized the urgency and that the Navy would have to take extraordinary steps to support Electic Boat.

QUESTION: It appears from what you say that the Navy followed a course of action that was not only inconsistent with the intent of the contract, but was also inconsistent with previous precedent established for assisting the contractor in expediting changes. Is that so?

ANSWER: Yes, and in fact it is even worse than that, because in April we were directed by the contracting officer not to proceed with any work until it had been fully priced; a complete analysis as to any possible impact on the delivery schedule and changes must be fully negotiated with the Navy.

To put this into perspective, you must realize that we were receiving changes at the rate of 20 per day, in excess of 100 per week. Every single one had to be evaluated in house for entitlement, for schedule impact, for cost and for domino effect, since so many of these changes are interrelated to others. This in itself became a new requirement and a monumental task to staff up and manage.

QUESTION: Why couldn't you refuse this course of action by the Navy when it clearly would further compound the scheduling problems?

ANSWER: By our contract requirements we *must* follow directives of the contracting officer. However, we strongly objected to this new procedure. In fact in a letter that we sent to the Supervisor of Shipbuilding, Captain Yurso, on April 28, 1980, I stated ". . . such a procedure would undoubtedly prove more costly to the Navy than retaining the present system . . . The Government should be prepared to assume responsibility for the additional cost of schedule delay which may result from this procedure". I had hoped and expected that this letter which was very strong would cause the Navy to reconsider their position or at least discuss it with us. However, they remained adamant.

QUESTION: What was the impact then to the program following this new system?

ANSWER: Terrible, terrible. In the course of the final testing of the ship, unpredictable problems would arise that would require designing modifications. These modifications could not be made in a timely fashion due to the imposition of these procedures. Many of these modifications, both in their own right and in just the sheer numbers, were causing delays that were irrecoverable. The Navy refused to accept the fact that potential delays existed and insisted that we do the work but with a statement that no delays in delivery would result. Clearly it would be fraudulent on our part if we misrepresented these problems to the Navy and agreed that certain items did not cause a delay when in our best judgment they did in fact cause a delay.

QUESTION: Did the Navy authorize these changes or how did the Navy handle them?

ANSWER: A major percentage of these changes were held in limbo by the Navy for 5, 6 or 7 months even though many of them had to be performed for the ship to operate satisfactorily. I finally became so frustrated that in October I wrote the Navy a letter stating I could no longer give them any schedule until the design problems stabilized. Needless to say, that letter infuriated the Navy but it did begin to finally get some action but even then had it not been for Secretary Hidalgo's personal intervention we would probably still be fighting this battle today.

QUESTION: I just can't believe that no one in the Navy understood what was happening.

ANSWER: I think many in the Navy understood what was happening. My sources clearly indicated that it all boiled down to one admiral, and nobody was in a position to argue or overrule him.

QUESTION: Is this Admiral Rickover you refer to?

ANSWER: That's what our Navy sources told us.

QUESTION: Was the ship itself delayed by this administrative nightmare?

ANSWER: Absolutely.

QUESTION: Speaking of Admiral Rickover, it has been stated that you accused Admiral Rickover of failing to give proper orders during a sea trial of a 688 attack submarine, and the lack of untimeliness of that order caused the ship to go out of control. Do you care to comment on that?

ANSWER: First let me say that we did not accuse Rickover of anything. I forwarded to the Chief of Naval Operations two reports that were a factual account as to what happened on two separate sea trials. In my forwarding letter I asked for an investigation and specifically requested that if any Electric Boat personnel were found at fault that I be notified promptly in order to take proper action. I would also like to add one of the reasons we forwarded these reports to Washington was that the local Supervisor of Shipbuilding Admiral Young requested Electric Boat's factual account be transmitted to Washington.

QUESTION: Were you satisfied with the response you received from the Chief of Naval Operations?

ANSWER: The response was very bland in that it said the test was not unsafe, which we agree with, but it did not indicate any specific corrective action nor did it recognize the fact that the ship did in fact go out of control for reasons beyond the requirements of the test procedure.

QUESTION: You have been quoted on several occasions stating Rickover had basically been running Electric Boat. Just how was he running Electric Boat before you arrived?

ANSWER: Within a few days after I took over in 1977, I visited Rickover in Washington, more as a courtesy visit. At that time he presented me a letter addressed to Rickover for me to sign. Basically the letter stated that I would abide by all the previous agreements made by former general managers of Electric Boat with Rickover. I asked if he had a list of these previous agreements or how was I to know what these previous agreements were. The reply was basically he'll tell me when they come up. Basically he wanted a blank check and I would have no idea as to what I was agreeing to in signing such a letter. Naturally, I refused. If he could have been definitive as to what those agreements were and given me an opportunity to research and discuss them, I might well have agreed with many of these previous agreements. But that was not the situation. He advised me that all previous general managers had signed such a letter.

In addition, virtually all senior management appointments were cleared through Rickover's office, prior to announcement. Similarly, many management policies were cleared through his office.

I have been advised former general managers were instructed to call him every day, sometimes three times a day so he knew everything that was going on. Clearly he was the type of man that gave considerable free advice and beware to the man that did not follow it.

QUESTION: You say beware of the man who did not follow it. What types of pressure could Rickover bring?

ANSWER: You may recall in 1978 Rickover frequently testified before Congress about fraud allegations at Electric Boat, and through his insistence the Justice Department spent almost 4 years investigating all the facts. In January of 1982 the Justice Department announced that they had completed their study and closed their books, and no charges were to be preferred. Both the Government and Electric Boat spent hundreds of thousands of dollars on this case. But clearly it put tremendous pressure on the company. There is also a history of contracts being suddenly given to the other parties as was the case in March of 1981. Rickover had the ability to make your life very difficult.

QUESTION: Now that Rickover has departed what advice would you give to Admiral McKee who has replaced him?

ANSWER: Clearly the most important thing is to regain the technological advances that we once held over the Soviets. To do this, free enterprise should be permitted to function. Private industry with its enormous capabilities for technology should be challenged to come up with innovative submarine designs without undue Government interference.

QUESTION: Do you know now of significant advances that could be made?

ANSWER: Absolutely. We have suggested several to the Navy in recent years but apparently pride of authorship is so strong within certain factions of the Navy that our suggestions have not gotten any serious attention. It is my firm belief, however, that with the cooperation of the Navy which I feel confident will come to pass with Admiral McKee, we could again see a major breakthrough in submarine design, perhaps even equivalent to what was achieved when we went from diesel to nuclear power.

QUESTION: Having now turned over day-to-day control of Electric Boat, what is your assessment of the Company's current situation?

ANSWER: I believe Electric Boat today is once again the free world's premier submarine designer and builder. Our recent problems are behind us, as we conclusively demonstrated in 1981 by delivering a record seven submarines, including the OHIO. There is now a seasoned and highly skilled workforce in place. General Dynamics' $300 million in private investment has provided unique and modern shipbuilding facilities which have proven their worth and versatility.

In short, the yard has all the tools to build submarines at a rate significantly higher than the Navy is budgeting.

QUESTION: What is Electric Boat's building capacity?

ANSWER: The physical plant between Groton and Quonset is fully capable of accommodating 3 SSN 688's and 2 TRIDENT's per year. The other critical half of the equation is, of course, manpower. Present manpower levels are adequate to support a building rate of 3 SSN's and 1½ TRIDENT's per year. It would require a manageable, phased buildup of the workforce to reach the higher rate. It would not be a difficult increase.

Unfortunately, the Navy is not buying either TRIDENT's or SSN 688's in significant numbers to test our capacity.

QUESTION: In your judgment what should the annual procurement rate be for SSN 688's and TRIDENT's?

ANSWER: I have a natural bias towards submarines on the basis of my experiences both as a submariner and a submarine builder. I am quite convinced that the submarine is the most effective weapons platform available to the Navy today. As a tactical naval weapon it has no peer. Its ability to operate undetected gives it a clear margin of superiority over surface vessels which have become increasingly vulnerable to Soviet missile and aviation threats. In my judgment the Navy should be buying as many attack submarines as it can get built. That number is now about 5 a year; 2 per year at Newport News and 3 per year at Electric Boat.

Notes

Because these notes contain a substantial amount of explanatory material, we have made efforts to reduce the size and complexity of the citations whenever possible. We have used a short form after each original citation. In addition to the first full citation in the note, the entire citation reference appears in the bibliography. Generally speaking, the sequence of each note follows the evolution of the analysis in the text unless an interjectory comment was required.

For House and Senate hearings, in most cases the page numbers refer to the pagination in the *Congressional Record* or in the appropriate committee hearings. However, in some cases the authors have used actual hearings statements supplied by Electric Boat and the Navy, both for convenience and to avoid the inaccuracy of editing for publication by the Government Printing Office. In these cases, the pagination supplied correlates only with the actual pages of those statements. The hearings are cited as House or Senate hearings before the appropriate committee or subcommittee. The actual titles of the hearings have been omitted, but the dates and the names of the witnesses have been included. The citations for hearings do not give parts (e.g., "Defense Hearings, pt. 5."). If there is intervening material and use of an ibid is precluded but the citation is the same as the hearing previously cited, only the date and name of witness will be given.

U.S. Naval Institute Proceedings is referred to as *Proceedings*, and *Aviation Week and Space Technology* is shortened to *Aviation Week*. Newspaper sections and pages have been omitted, although headlines have been retained, and, when possible, authors' names given. Occasionally, long newspaper and article titles are shortened.

We feel the material in the notes, while often too detailed to be contained in the text, is relevant and important enough to be included here.

Introduction

[1]Norman Polmar and Thomas Allen, *Rickover: Controversy and Genius* (New York: Simon, 1982), pp. 576–77; "Cheers, Jeers, and Soviets Accompany Trident Send-off," *Arizona Republic*, June 18, 1982; Martin Heerwald, "Protestors Prepare a Special Welcome for N-Submarine," *Los Angeles Times*, July 25, 1983.

1. The Ultimate Weapon? Development of the American Strategic Submarine and Strategic Planning

[1]W. Scott Thompson, ed., *National Security in the 1980s: From Weakness to Strength* (San Francisco; The Institute for Contemporary Studies, 1980), pp. 191, 382; Richard Pipes, "Why the Soviet Union Thinks It Could Fight and Win a Nuclear War," *Air Force Magazine*, Sept., 1977, pp. 55–66. For specific advances in particular weapons, see *Aviation Week and Space Technology*'s monthly notes. See, for example, "Washington Round-up," Sept. 6, 1976, p. 27; Herbert Coleman, "Soviets Push Huge Arms Buildup," Apr. 12, 1976, pp. 12–15; Eugene Kozicharow, "Panel Disputes U.S.–Soviet Arms Parity," June 28, 1976, pp. 19–20; Clarence Robinson, Jr., "Soviets Grasping Strategic Lead," Aug. 30, 1976, pp. 14–18; Cecil Brownlow, "Soviet Strategic Lead Seen by 1980s," Feb. 14, 1977, pp. 18–19; "U.S.S.R. Arms Build-up Seen Threat to U.S.," Dec. 18, 1978, p. 18; "Soviet Defense Spending Expected to Sustain Rise," July 24, 1978, p. 60; "Soviets Outspend U.S. by 25% a Year," Jan. 29, 1979, p. 56; "The Soviet Global Threat," Apr. 16, 1976, p. 9; "Soviet Global Military Capability Gains," May 29, 1978, pp. 60–61; "Significance of SS-18 Role Questioned," July 16, 1979, pp. 23–25; Clarence Robinson, Jr., "Soviets Developing Two Bombers," Feb. 19, 1979, pp. 14–18.

[2]For comparisons of strategic levels of the United States and the Soviet Union (usually excluding allies), see Richard Rosecrance, "Detente or Entente," *Foreign Affairs*, Apr., 1975, pp. 464–81; Elliot R. Goodman, "Reflections on the Shifting East-West Balance of Forces," *Survey*, Summer and Fall, 1976, pp. 58–62; Donald S. Marshall, reviews of *American and Soviet Trends Since the Cuban Missle Crisis* by John Collins and Douglas Mitchell and *World Power Assessment 1977: A Calculus of Strategic Drift* by Ray Cline, *Strategic Review*, Summer, 1978, pp. 77–80; William Lee, "Soviet Defense Spending, Planned Growth 1976–1980," *Strategic Review*, Winter, 1977, pp. 74–79. Of course, this subject has been the focus of national debate since the Vietnam War, and continued arguments appear in a variety of forums, including "Soviet Strength and U.S. Purpose" (a debate between Amos Jordan, R. W. Komer, Les Aspin, and Earl Ravenal), *Foreign Policy*, Summer, 1976, pp. 32–50; Les Aspin, "What Are the Russians Up To?" *International Security Review*, Summer, 1978, pp. 30–54 (in which Aspin tries to compare Russia in the 1970s with Nazi Germany's military buildup in the 1930s and concludes that it "isn't even 'reminiscent of Nazi Germany's rearmament' . . . [and that] rhetoric about 'Nazi-like' buildups only hinders our efforts to devise a measured response [p. 50]"). Jake Garn, "Soviet Superiority: A Question for National Debate," *International Security Review*, Spring, 1979, pp. 1–25, provides a capable rebuttal to Aspin's arguments, although Aspin himself is not mentioned, and R. J. Rummel, "Preparing for War? The Third Reich Versus the Soviet Union Today," *International Security Review*, Fall, 1979, pp. 207–30, shows the important methodological errors Aspin made, concluding "the Soviet arms drive appears to parallel in trend and exceed in absolute and relative magnitude what Hitler saw as necessary for rearmament and war" (p. 227). Garn presents an even more effective argument that the Soviets have gained an exploitable strategic nuclear advantage in "Exploitable Strategic Nuclear Superiority," *International Security Review*, Summer,

1980, pp. 173–92. In general terms of the results of nuclear war and its probability, see Jiri Weiss, "Nuclear War," *Stanford Magazine*, Fall, 1980, pp. 10–21. For comparisons of strategic and tactical naval forces, see William Manthorpe, "The Soviet Navy in 1975," *United States Naval Institute Proceedings* (henceforth referred to as *Proceedings*), May, 1976, pp. 205–12; William Manthorpe, "The Soviet Navy in 1976," *Proceedings*, May, 1977, pp. 203–14. Also see Robert Leggett, "Letter to the Editor," *Sea Power*, Sept., 1976, pp. 5–6 (see especially the editor's response); Sayre Swartztrauber, review of *Soviet Naval Policy* by Michael MccGwire, *Proceedings*, Feb., 1976, pp. 85–87; Peter Vigor, "Soviet Military Developments—1976," *Strategic Review*, Spring, 1977, pp. 74–82; James Eberle, "The Naval Balance: Quality vs. Quantity," *Rusi*, Dec., 1978, pp. 56–59; Joseph Hopkins and William Warren, "Countering Soviet Imperialism," *Proceedings*, June, 1979, pp. 59–65; "Fears of Declining U.S. Seapower Told," *Los Angeles Times*, Apr. 7, 1978; Harry Train, "The Growing Soviet Naval Menace," *Atlantic Community Quarterly*, Spring, 1981, pp. 50–62. Many label a recitation of these statistics "alarmist" (Boston Study Group, *The Price of Defense* [New York: New York Times Books, 1979]) without actually denying the numbers.

[3]*Los Angeles Times*, Nov. 2, 1981; Colin Gray, "Strategic Forces: The Reagan Story," *International Security Review*, Winter, 1981–82, pp. 437–47. Trident's problems are the central subject for subsequent chapters. However, for a brief review of some of the problems, see "Inside Story of the Trident Debacle," *U.S. News & World Report*, Mar. 30, 1980, pp. 21–22., "Navy's Trident Sub: One More Massive Miscalculation," ibid., Dec. 12, 1977; Benjamin Schemmer, "A Blunted Trident," *Armed Forces Journal*, June, 1979, p. 42 (and the retraction, Apr. 1980, pp. 36–37, 61–62); *U.S. Defense Industrial Preparedness: Issue for the 97th Congress, Issue Brief* (Washington, D.C.: Congressional Research Service, June 8, 1982), p. 5; and Norman Polmar, "The U.S. Navy: Strategic Missile Submarines," *Proceedings*, Mar., 1980, pp. 141–42.

[4]Drew Middleton, *Submarine: The Ultimate Naval Weapon* (Chicago: Playboy Pr., 1976).

[5]Middleton, *Submarine*, p. 116. Part of the reason for the slow pace of guided missile programs was that authorities were awaiting a smaller-sized warhead, eventually developed as the H-bomb. See James Baar and William Howard, *Polaris!* (New York: Harcourt, 1960), p. 16.

[6]Polmar and Allen, *Rickover*, pp. 113–79 passim; Middleton, *Submarine*, pp. 117–30. Although Rickover was the moving force behind the nuclear-powered ship, William Raborn contributed greatly to the marriage of missile and boat (Barr and Howard, *Polaris!*, pp. 36–51). Compare the roles of Rickover and Sergei Gorshkov, the "Father of the Soviet Navy," in Norman Polmar's "Soviet Nuclear Submarines," *Proceedings*, July, 1981, pp. 31–39.

[7]Middleton, *Submarine*, pp. 132–36. One of the most thorough and detailed studies of the Polaris system appears in Harvey M. Sapolsky, *The Polaris System Development: Bureaucratic and Programmatic Success in Government* (Cambridge, Mass.: Harvard Univ. Pr., 1972). Sapolsky's work viewed the Polaris program as a successful model for future programs. For further information on the Polaris program in general, see Sapolsky's n.1, p. 3. Also see Richard Boyle, "1960: A Vintage Year for Submarines," *Proceedings*, Oct., 1970, pp. 36–41.

[8]Middleton, *Submarine*, pp. 131–58; Norman Polmar, ed., *Ships and Aircraft of the U.S. Fleet*, 12th ed. (Annapolis: Naval Institute Pr., 1981), pp. 15–57. Another fine summary of the ballistic-missile submarine force can be found in Joseph S. Knowles, "America's Nuclear-Powered Submarines," *Sea Classics*, May, 1973, pp. 27–63.

[9]Middleton, *Submarine*, p. 136. See also "Polaris: Fleet Ballistic Missile Weapon System Fact Sheet," United States Navy, June 1, 1966, and "Polaris Chronology: History of the Fleet Ballistic Missile Weapon System Development Program," July, 1966.

[10]Jake Garn explains the throw-weight problem in "Soviet Superiority," pp. 8–13. One warhead does not equal one destroyed target: "There are presently over 1,400 hardened silos for ICBMs in the Soviet Union. . . . Poseidon would have little capability against such hard targets, and Trident [I] warheads only marginally more" (p. 11).

[11]*Arizona Republic*, Sept., 19, 1977; *Sea Classics*, Mar., 1979, p. 37; *New York Times*, Dec. 4, 1977. See Garn's comment that "the Carter Administration [is] the only Administration to deliberately plan our forces on a basis that would create two strategic force crisis situations—one in the early to mid-1980's and another in the late 1980's to early 1990's. . . ." Garn, "Exploitable Superiority," p. 182; "U.S. Nuclear Strategy May Well Remain Three Legged," *Los Angeles Times*, Dec. 4, 1977; "Defense Triad with Two Bad Legs," *Arizona Republic*, Sept. 19, 1977; Schemmer, "Blunted Trident," p. 42.

[12]William Schneider and Francis P. Hoeber, eds., *Arms, Men, and Military Budgets* (New York: Crane, Russak & Co., 1976), pp. 9, 294. During his term Carter reduced spending for the strategic forces by $396 million (−3.6%) and for research and development by $251 million (−2.3%) (ibid., 1979, p. 6). Robert Ellsworth, "Quick Fixes in Intelligence," in *National Security in the 1980s*, p. 175. CIA estimates proved about 50 percent below actual Soviet spending.

[13]"Launch Under Attack" is possibly the ace in the hole that has deterred attack since the late 1970s. Enemy land-based missiles, even under optimum conditions, take 30 minutes to reach targets in the United States. Secretary of Defense Harold Brown "has quietly reminded the Soviet High Command of this possibility at least four times in his fiscal year 1980 annual report" (Edwin Black, "Presidential Directive 59: The Beginning of a New Nuclear Strategy," *Proceedings*, Jan., 1981, pp. 93–94. Also see the criticisms of the "Launch Under Attack" policy in "U.S. Nuclear Strategy May Well Remain Three Legged." Surprisingly, the same groups that developed MAD refused to protect the ICBMs with an antimissile force. See Garn, "Soviet Superiority," pp. 15–20.

[14]The Soviet targeting plan, apparently long known to U.S. advisers, has been made public only recently. An anonymous article entitled "The Danger Is Defeat, Not Destruction" published in *Remnant Review*, Aug., 1979, explains the problem well. Also see Garn, "Exploitable Superiority"; Lewis Frank, "Soviet Power After Salt I: A Strategic-Coercive Capability," *Strategic Review*, Spring, 1974, pp. 59–61. For Soviet responses see R. Simonyan, "The Concept of 'Strategic Sufficiency,' " *Strategic Review*, Spring, 1977, pp. 102–4, and "The Concept of 'Selective Targeting,' " ibid., pp. 105–7. When American defense experts became aware of the seriousness of the targeting

problem, President Carter issued Presidential Directive 59, changing ICBM's targets from population centers to military targets and missile bases. Secretary of the Navy John Lehman said Carter's hasty decision caught "his entire arms control community . . . flatfooted" ("The Soviet Strategic Nuclear Advantage," *International Security Review*, Fall, 1980, pp. 271–85. Arguments for such a strategy had appeared already: "A Shift in U.S. Nuclear Strategy," *Strategic Review*, Winter, 1979, pp. 8–9. Reactions by the Soviets appear in "The Soviet Strategic View," *Strategic Review*, Fall, 1980, pp. 79–84, and ibid., Winter, 1981, pp. 70–71. The major problem in American strategic planning appears to be that the Soviets *believe* they can *win* a nuclear exchange. See "Soviets Planning to Win," *Scottsdale Daily Progress*, Jan. 24, 1981; George Keegan, "An Editorial in the Form of a Letter," *Strategic Review*, Spring, 1977, pp. 6–11; Clare Boothe Luce, "Two Doctrines of War," *Strategic Review*, Spring, 1977, pp. 12–13. Some of the Soviets' civil defense procedures are explained in their own material: A. Zaytsev, "A Double Advantage," *Strategic Review*, Summer, 1974, pp. 97–100; A. Altunin, "The Main Direction," *Strategic Review*, Summer, 1974, pp. 91–96. Altunin makes it clear that there is a solid, structured civil defense organization in which training facilities are established even on the local level. A more thorough examination of Soviet nuclear strategy appears in Joseph Douglas and Amoretta Hoeber, *Soviet Strategy for Nuclear War* (Stanford, Calif.: Hoover Institution Pr., 1979). Clearly, much of the failure to appreciate the Soviets' powerful position can be blamed on poor media emphasis—especially by national televised news. For example, as reported in a letter to *National Review*, Daniel Sobieski notes: "In a minute-by-minute analysis of all CBS Evening News programs, broadcast in 1972 and 1973, a total of 196 hours, Dr. Ernest Lefever of Georgetown University found CBS to have devoted all of one minute to the most significant fact of our time—a direct comparison of the military strength of the United States and the Soviet Union. . . . In 1972 and 1973, CBS Evening News carried almost no information on growing Soviet military might. . . . There was no direct reference to a new 4,500-mile submarine missile, the annual production of five to nine missile subs, a new generation of ICBM's carrying multiple warheads and capable of destroying Minuteman missiles in their silos, a system to destroy U.S. satellites, a new supersonic strategic bomber, etc." (*National Review*, Apr. 17, 1981, p. 390). Likewise, CBS ran a five-part series on national defense in the summer of 1981 that was highly biased. See, for example, F. A. McAulliffe's comment in the *Armed Forces Journal*, Sept., 1981, p. 6. As for American apathy and acquiescence, see Albert Wohlstetter, "Racing Forward or Ambling Back?" *Survey*, Summer and Fall, 1976, pp. 163–217. Wohlstetter's comments on political language vis-à-vis the arms race are typical of the lack of critical attention paid the Soviet buildup.

[15]"A Submarine That Can Destroy Russia," *U.S. News & World Report*, Feb. 12, 1979, pp. 30–31; *House Hearings*, Armed Services Committee, Subcommittee on Research and Development, 96th Cong., 2d sess., Feb. 7, 1980, p. 33, statement of William J. Perry. Certainly not all have given up on the mixed-force concept ("Senate Supports Bomber Mixture, Using Missiles," *Arizona Republic*, Oct. 8, 1977). Also see "Nuclear Subs: Defenders of the Deep," *Los Angeles Times*, Apr. 3, 1977.

[16]Stansfield Turner, "The Naval Balance: Not Just a Numbers Game," *Foreign Affairs*, Jan., 1977, pp. 339–54. Previously the carrier forces were the focal point in planning, and in a majority of situations carriers still can perform more varied tasks than a submarine. In this context—strategic deterrence only—the submarine has superseded all other naval forces. See also Gary Hart, "Against Reducing America's Naval Strength," *New York Times*, Apr. 9, 1978. Hart notes a "shift from a sea-power to a European land-power strategy," but argues for numerous "low-cost . . . diesel submarines." His implication, like those in the *Counterbudget* group, hinges on cost rather than effectiveness.

[17]William Schneider et al., eds., *Arms, Men, and Military Budgets, 1980* (New York: Crane, Russak & Co., 1980), p. 120.

[18]*Congressional Quarterly*, Mar. 31, 1973, pp. 711–18.

[19]Ibid.; Russell Warren Howe, *Weapons: The International Game of Arms, Money and Diplomacy* (Garden City, N.Y.: Doubleday, 1980), p. 39.

[20]News coverage of the Trident has leaned toward sensationalism: "Inside Story of the Trident Debacle," *U.S. News & World Report*, Mar. 30, 1981, pp. 21–22; "Navy's Trident Sub: One More Massive Miscalculation," *U.S. News & World Report*, Dec. 12, 1977, p. 37. Even sympathetic journals harped on Trident's woes (erroneously in this case): Schemmer, "A Blunted Trident," p. 42, and retraction, Benjamin Schemmer, "All Wet About a 'Blunted Trident,' " Apr. 1980, pp. 36–37, 61–62.

[21]*House Hearings*, Appropriations Committee, Subcommittee on Defense, 97th Cong., 1st sess., May 5, 1981, pp. 1–359, statement of Admiral Hyman Rickover.

2. The Look of Leviathan: A Description of Trident

[1]*Trident System Issue Brief* (Washington. D.C.: Congressional Research Service, 1981), pp. 1–21 (henceforth referred to as *Trident Issue Brief*). Material for this chapter has been acquired through Electric Boat sources, Navy sources, and authors' visits to Groton, 1981–82. Also see Gerard Burke, "The Need for Trident," *Proceedings*, November 1978, pp. 32–41, and Norman Polmar, "The U.S. Navy: Strategic Missile Submarines," *Proceedings*, Mar., 1980, pp. 141–42.

[2]For a picture of the Trident with its telemetry mast extended, see "The War Beneath the Seas," *Newsweek*, Feb. 8, 1982. For a picture of one in place on a submerged submarine, see Polmar, *Ships and Aircraft of the U.S. Fleet*, p. 337. For information on the total array of sonar and ECM equipment other than the BQQ-6 bow sonar aboard Trident, see the "U.S. Navy: Electronic Warfare (Part 1)," by Norman Polmar in *Proceedings*, Oct., 1979, pp. 137–38, and his treatment thereof on p. 17 and pp. 352–55 in *Ships and Aircraft of the U.S. Fleet*, 12th ed.

[3]Information on television cameras in periscopes was obtained by an interview in July with submarine personnel of Submarine Group 6, stationed in San Diego.

[4]Interview with O. B. Nelson, Groton, June, 1981; *House Hearings*, Armed Services Committee, 94th Cong., 2d sess., Feb. 18, 1976, pp. 2–3, statement of J. C. Metzel.

[5]For information on MOSS, see Norman Polmar, "The U.S. Navy: Sonars," pts. 1 and 2, *Proceedings*, July–Sept., 1981, pp. 119–20, 135–37, and Polmar, *The Ships and Aircraft of the U.S. Fleet,* 12th ed., pp. 353, 414.

[6]Interview with O. B. Nelson, at Groton, June, 1981.

[7]Polmar, "Sonars," pp. 119–20; Polmar, "The U.S. Navy: Electronic Warfare (Part 1)," *Proceedings*, Oct., 1979.

[8]Ibid.

[9]Tom Nugent, "The Trident Story," *All Hands*, Feb., 1975, pp. 2–7. Also see Rear Admiral Albert L. Kelln's statement before the Research and Development Subcommittee of the Senate Armed Forces Committee, 94th Cong., 2d sess., p. 12, Mar. 23, 1976.

[10]Interview with P. Takis Veliotis at Groton, June, 1981.

[11]"USS *Michigan*: World's Most Dangerous Weapon," *Detroit News* Jan. 9, 1983.

[12]Polmar and Allen, *Rickover*, p. 577.

[13]"Trident Missile Capabilities Advance," *Aviation Week*, June 16, 1980, pp. 91–117; Edgar Ulsamer, "In Focus," *Air Force Magazine*, Oct., 1981, pp. 16–17. For a report of early launch tests, see "Weather Chief Problem in Trident Tests," *Aviation Week*, Oct. 31, 1977, pp. 46–47.

[14]"Trident Missile Capabilities Advance," pp. 97–99. For a picture of the aerospike, see p. 92; *House Hearings*, Feb. 18, 1976, Viewgraph 16, statement of J. C. Metzel. Whereas all early Navy Fact Sheets, including the comparative schematic publicity being distributed as late as 1981, specified Trident I as being 65,000 pounds, in "Trident Missile Capabilities Advance," the weight is now given as 73,000 pounds and the Poseidon C-3 weight as 64,000 pounds. Some variation in missile weight is due to variations in warhead configurations but the 8000-pound difference for Trident II figures is probably accountable by design maturation.

[15]Polmar and Allen, *Rickover*, app. F; "USS *Michigan," Detroit News.*

[16]"A Submarine that Can Destroy Russia," *U.S. News & World Report*, Feb. 12, 1979, pp. 30–31; "Trident Missile Capabilities Advance," p. 106; "USS *Michigan," Detroit News.*

[17]*House Hearings*, Feb. 18, 1976, pp. 7–8, statement of J. C. Metzel; *Chief of Naval Operations Report, Fiscal 1981*, Department of the Navy.

[18]*Chief of Naval Operations Report, Fiscal 1981*, Department of the Navy.

[19]"Trident Story," *All Hands*, pp. 2–7; "USS *Michigan," Detroit News.*

[20]"Trident Story," *All Hands*, pp. 2–7.

[21]"FBM Facts," (Washington, D.C.: Strategic Systems Project Office, 1978), pp. 1, 6–13; Clarence Robinson, Jr., "Trident Post-Boost Control Tests Planned," *Aviation Week*, Oct. 27, 1975, pp. 63–73.

[22]"Trident Missile Capabilities Advance," pp. 91–92; "FBM Facts," pp. 6–13; "Navy to Develop New Trident Warhead," *Aviation Week*, Jan. 17, 1983, p. 26.

[23]"Trident Missile Capabilities Advance," pp. 91–117; "FBM Facts," pp. 6–13; Ulsamer, "In Focus," pp. 16–17; Clarence Robinson, Jr., "New Propellant Evaluated for Trident Second Stage," *Aviation Week*, Oct. 13, 1975, pp. 15–19; "Navy to Develop New Trident Warhead," p. 26.

[24]"Trident Missile Capabilities Advance," pp. 91–117; "FBM Facts," pp. 6–13.

[25]"Trident Missile Capabilities Advance," pp. 99–100; Ulsamer, "In Focus," pp. 16–17.

3. Trident's Budgetary Birth: Planning, Programming, and Funding, 1968–1974

[1]"How to Spend a Trillion: Arming for the '80s," *Time*, July 27, 1981, pp. 6–21. See *U.S. News & World Report* articles, *Armed Forces Journal*, "Blunted Trident," etc.

[2]Robert Art, *The TFX Decision: McNamara and the Military* (Boston: Little, 1968), pp. 40, 86, 98; Robert Coulam, *Illusions of Choice: The F–111 and the Problem of Weapons Acquisition Reform* (Princeton: Princeton Univ. Pr., 1977).

[3]Ingemar Dörfer, *System 37 Viggen: Arms Technology and the Domestication of Glory* (Oslo: Universitetsforlaget, 1973). Also see Jacques Gansler, *The Defense Industry* (Cambridge, Mass.: MIT Pr., 1980), pp. 97, 201; Ted Greenwood, *Making the MIRV: A Study of Defense Decision Making* (Cambridge, Mass.: Ballinger, 1975); and Robert Kaufman, *The War Profiteers* (New York: Bobbs-Merrill, 1970).

[4]Sapolsky, *Polaris System*, pp. 230–54; Baar and Howard, *Polaris!*, passim. Sapolsky warns that it would "be a mistake to attribute the success of the program simply to the structural independence and product orientation of the development agency." There are, he adds, "no magical management system cures" and "no magical structural cures." One factor aiding the adoption of the Polaris system was a national commitment "to a rapid expansion of its ballistic missile programs" (Sapolsky, *Polaris System*, p. 240). A fine short review of the Polaris development appears in William Whitmore, "The Origin of Polaris," *Proceedings*, Mar., 1980, pp. 56–59.

[5]*The Trident System* (Washington: Navy Department, Trident System Project Office, 1977), p. 2. Look, for example, at the Trident program's organizational chart (figs. 12–2, 12–3).

[6]Polmar and Allen, *Rickover*, pp. 564–65; James Canan, *The Superwarriors: The Fantastic World of Pentagon Superweapons* (New York: Weybright & Talley, 1975), pp. 174–77. The IDA is a consortium of twelve universities created in 1956 to assist the Department of Defense. See Canan, "Lending a Hand to the Pentagon," *Electronics*, June 12, 1967, pp. 155–58.

[7]Morton Mintz, "Depth Charge," *Washington Post*, Oct. 4, 1981; Polmar and Allen, *Rickover*, p. 566 and app. F.

[8]Polmar and Allen, *Rickover*, pp. 566–67; Mintz, "Depth Charge."

[9]Mintz, "Depth Charge"; *Senate Hearings*, Armed Services Committee, Subcommittee on Research and Development, 95th Cong., 1st sess., Apr., 5, 1977, p. 6660, statements of Admirals Don Harvey, Albert Kelln, and J. C. Metzel.

[10]*Congressional Quarterly*, Mar. 31, 1973, pp. 711–18; *Department of Defense Annual Report* (Washington: Government Printing Office, various years; henceforth referred to as *Department of Defense Annual Report*), fiscal year 1968, p. 20; *Senate Hearings*, Armed Services Committee, 91st Cong., 2d sess., Mar. 17, 1970, p. 1360; *House Hearings*, Armed Services Committee, Subcommittee on Research and Development, 92d Cong., 2d sess., Mar. 1, 1972, statements of Admirals H. E. Lyon and Robert Kaufman. All dollar figures given in that year's dollars: $21 million in 1968 is expressed in 1968 dollars throughout unless otherwise specified.

[11]Sapolsky, *Polaris System*, pp. 11, 41–48; Richard Hewlett and Francis Duncan, *Nuclear Navy* (Chicago: Univ. of Chicago Pr., 1974).

[12] *Congressional Quarterly*, Mar. 31, 1973, pp. 711–18. *Department of Defense Annual Report*, fiscal year 1968, p. 20; *Senate Hearings*, Armed Services Committee, 91st Cong., 2d sess., Mar. 17, 1970, p. 1360; *House Hearings*, Armed Services Committee, Subcommittee on Research and Development, 92d Cong., 2d sess., Mar. 1, 1972, statements of Admirals H. E. Lyon and Robert Kaufman; *Department of Defense Annual Report and Defense Progress*, 1970–74, p. 62; Canan, *Superwarriors*, p. 180. Surprisingly, Secretary of Defense Clark Clifford, in a 1968 statement for the *Defense Industry Bulletin*, did not mention the ULMS as being a part of the study. He noted only "on the basis of [STRAT–X] we have included $56 million in the fiscal year 1969 budget for advanced technology in ICBMs" (Mar., 1968, p. 17). In 1980 Dr. David Mann, the Navy Department's Assistant Secretary for Research, Engineering, and Systems, told the House Research and Development Subcommittee that the good programs one always cites (Polaris, Poseidon, and, he included, Trident) are different from regular R&D programs. One difference, he noted, "is above all a sense of urgency, which is widely held and widely shared. The reason Polaris went to sea so quickly was because everybody in the country wanted it, and because they were willing to put up the money [to get it]" (*House Hearings*, Armed Services Committee, Subcommittee on Research and Development, 96th Cong., 2d sess., Feb. 27, 1980, p. 1061).

[13] *Congressional Quarterly*, Mar. 31, 1973, p. 712; *House Hearings*, Armed Services Committee, Subcommittee on Research and Development, 92d Cong., 2d sess., Mar. 22, 1982, pp. 3145–46, 3207; statement of Admiral Lyon, *Department of Defense Annual Report*, fiscal year 1971, p. 115; *Senate Hearings*, Armed Services Committee, 91st Cong., 2d sess., Mar. 17, 1970, p. 1360; *House Hearings*, 1972, "Development Concept Paper Decision," pp. 2636, 2639. According to a 1973 Congressional Research Service Issue Brief, the rounded-off totals for R&D for the ULMS from fiscal year 1968 to fiscal year 1972 are as follows:

FY-68	FY-69	FY-70	FY-71	FY-72
0.6	5.9	10.0	43.7	104.8

Source: *Issue Brief*, 1973, p. 5

[14] Mintz, "Depth Charge"; *Congressional Quarterly*, Mar. 31, 1973, p. 712; interview with O. B. Nelson, June, 1981.

[15] *House Hearings*, 1972, p. 2636; *Senate Hearings*, Armed Services Committee, Ad Hoc Committee on Research and Development, 92d Cong., 2d sess., Mar. 22, 1972, pp. 2651–60, statements of Admirals Beshany and Kaufman.

[16] *House Hearings*, 1972, p. 2636; *Senate Hearings*, Armed Services Committee, Ad Hoc Committee on Research and Development, 92d Cong., 2d sess., Mar. 22, 1972, pp. 2651–60, statements of Admirals Beshany and Kaufman.

[17] *House Hearings*, 1972, pp. 2636–40, 3156, statements of Admirals Lyon and Kaufman.

[18] Polmar and Allen, *Rickover*, pp. 564–68.

[19] *House Hearings*, 1972, pp. 2635–45, statements of Admirals Lyon and Kaufman; *Senate Hearings*, Armed Services Committee, Ad Hoc Committee on Research and Development, p. 2681; Mintz, "Depth Charge."

[20]*House Hearings* 1972, pp. 2639, 3135; *Department of Defense Annual Report*, fiscal year 1973, pp. 69–70. Laird made available an additional $3.5 million from FY 1972 money, which possibly made up the difference in the Navy's request and the actual allocation. Proxmire's question was partially answered by Admiral Levering Smith in 1976: "The Trident I . . . missile program is most certainly not a 'fly-before-buy' program and . . . has never been presented to the Congress as 'fly-before-buy' program." Without direct reference to the ULMS program, he clearly implied the same went for the Trident (*House Hearings*, Armed Services Committee, Subcommittee on Research and Development, 94th Cong., 2d sess., Feb. 26, 1976, p. 887). Paul Warnke, the Assistant Secretary for Internal Security Affairs under Ford, suggested liberals were as guilty as the hard-line promilitary members: "If you called for an end to the Trident Submarine, you'd see some liberal senators rise in opposition, because it involves too many jobs in Connecticut and Rhode Island" (Elizabeth Drew, *American Journal* [New York: Random, 1976]). The following paragraph in text is from the sources listed above.

[21]*Department of Defense Report*, fiscal years 1972–76, 1972 budget, p. 65; *House Hearings*, 1972, pp. 2642–47; *Congressional Quarterly*, p. 712; *House Hearings*, 1972, 92d Cong., 2d sess., Fiscal Year 1973 R.D.T.&E., N Program Data—Submarine System, n.p.; *Senate Hearings*, Armed Services Committee, 92d Cong., 2d sess., 1972, p. 101, statement of Admiral Elmo T. Zumwalt; *Senate Hearings*, Armed Services Committee, Ad Hoc Committee on Research and Development, 92d Cong., 2d sess., Mar. 22, 1972, statements of Philip Beshany (p. 3157) and Admiral Lyon (p. 2667). A list of contractors identified as such in congressional hearings appears in app. A. Congress and subsequent administrations did not fully honor the reciprocal relationship between SALT and force modernization, since only in the Reagan administration was the B-1 bomber revived, while the MX continues to flutter from one basing-mode option to another. Even while knowing that the policy decisions of one administration are not legally binding on the next, the entire 1972 package deal was unexpectedly "ambushed" by the administration elected in 1976.

[22]*House Hearings*, 1972, Fiscal Year 1973 R.D.T.&E., N Program Data—Submarine System; *Senate Hearings*, 1972, statement of Admiral Zumwalt.

[23]*House Hearings*, 1972, p. 2645; *Congressional Quarterly*, Mar. 31, 1973, p. 712; Mintz, "Depth Charge"; Polmar and Allen, *Rickover*, pp. 566–68.

[24]*Senate Hearings*, Armed Services Committee, 92d Cong., 2d sess., Feb. 16, 1972, p. 724, statement of Melvin Laird, Secretary of Defense; ibid., Ad Hoc Committee on Research and Development, Feb. 5, 1972, Dr. M. Halpern, "Sea Power Comes Back Into Its Own" (quoted in *Senate Hearings*, p. 2649); *Senate Hearings*, Ad Hoc Subcommittee on Research and Development, Mar. 22, 1972, p. 3192, statement of Admiral Kaufman.

[25]*Senate Hearings*, Armed Services Committee, 92d Cong., 2d sess., Feb. 16, 1972, p. 2633; *House Hearings*, 1972, pp. 2642–47; *Congressional Quarterly*, Aug. 5, 1972, p. 1964.

[26]Polmar and Allen, *Rickover*, pp. 568–70.

[27]*Senate Hearings*, Armed Services Committee, Ad Hoc Research and Development Subcommittee, 92d Cong., 2d sess., Mar. 1, 1972, pp. 2645–3145, statements of H. E. Lyon and Robert Kaufman; *Congressional Quarterly*, Mar.

31, 1973, p. 712; Canan, *Superwarriors*, p. 184. Henry Kissinger cited the one-vote margin as an example of the antimilitary attitude in Congress, recalling that the ABM had passed by a single vote in 1969 (Henry Kissinger, *For the Record: Selected Statements, 1977–80* [Boston: Little, 1977–78], p. 281).

[28]*Congressional Quarterly*, Mar. 31, 1973, pp. 712–13; *Senate Hearings*, Armed Services Committee, 92d Cong., 2d sess., Mar. 9, 1972, pp. 1735–45, statement of Dr. Herbert Scoville; "A Conversation with Admiral Kidd," *Sea Power*, May, 1981, pp. 31–41.

[29]*Congressional Quarterly*, Mar. 31, 1973, pp. 6–7. Kissinger remarked five years later that, "given the . . . slow pace of the Trident production, there is almost no chance that the United States can reach the permitted total of 2,250 [launchers] except perhaps by keeping in service ten older Polaris submarines. . . ." (Kissinger, *For the Record*, p. 211).

[30]*Congressional Quarterly*, Mar. 31, 1973, pp. 716–17; *Senate Hearings*, Armed Services Committee, Subcommittee on Research and Development, 92d Cong., 2d sess., Mar. 22, 1972, p. 3160.

[31]*Congressional Record*, Senate, 93d Cong., 1st Sess., Sept. 22, 1973, pp. 30981–82; *Congressional Quarterly*, Mar. 31, 1973, pp. 716–17.

[32]*Senate Hearings*, Armed Services Committee, Ad Hoc Committee on Research and Development, 92d Cong., 2d sess., Mar. 22, 1972, pp. 3141–42, 3151, 3171, statement of Vice Admiral Philip Beshany.

[33]Canan, *Superwarriors*, p. 177; *Trident System*, p. 2.

[34]Polmar and Allen, *Rickover*, p. 243.

[35]*House Hearings*, Armed Services Committee, Subcommittee on Seapower, 94th Cong., 1st sess., Mar. 17, 1975, p. 848, statement of Admiral Hyman Rickover; *Trident System*, p. 2; *Senate Hearings*, Armed Services Committee, Ad Hoc Subcommittee on Research and Development, 92d Cong., 2d sess., Mar. 22, 1972, p. 3207, statement of Admiral Lyon; letter to authors from National Forge, Aug. 10, 1981. Rickover was a master of playing these types of funding games. Part of Electric Boat's contract for the Trident includes a provision that Electric Boat train the crew in the new technology, thereby defraying naval budget considerations while inflating the costs ascribed to Electric Boat's production record.

[36]*Joint Hearings*, Subcommittees on Military Construction, House Armed Services Committee and Senate Committee on Appropriations, 92d Cong., 2d sess., May 25, 1972, p. 284, statement of W. M. Enger, Naval Facilities Engineering Command; Howe, *Weapons*, p. 50.

[37]*Congressional Quarterly*, Mar. 31, 1973, p. 713; *Trident System*, p. 7. *Time*, Feb. 17, 1975, pp. 12, 17. Ironically, the same charges were leveled against former President Jimmy Carter when the construction of a second Trident base to be located in King's Bay, Georgia was announced.

[38]*Congressional Quarterly*, Mar. 31, 1973, p. 718; *Senate Hearings*, Armed Services Committee, 92d Cong., 2d sess., Mar. 9, 1972, statement of Joseph S. Clark.

[39]*Senate Hearings*, May 5, 1972, p. 108. Henry Kissinger, Secretary of State under Nixon, viewed the 1972 SALT agreement as "an opportunity to catch up—which we sought to do by pushing the development of . . . the Trident submarine." The catch was, he added, "every one of these programs [the B-1 bomber, the Trident, the MX missile, and cruise missiles] has been cancelled, delayed, or stretched out by the [Carter] Administration, so that we are at a

point where only the Trident (with only the most limited counterforce capability) can be operational during the period of the projected SALT treaty" (Kissinger, *For the Record*, pp. 200–206).

[40]*Department of Defense Report*, fiscal year 1974, p. 57.

[41]*Congressional Quarterly*, Sept. 1, 1973, p. 2357; Sept. 15, p. 2474; Sept. 22, pp. 2554–55; Sept. 29, 1973, p. 2619; Oct. 20, 1973, p. 2824; Dec. 1, 1973, p. 3143; Dec. 29, 1973, pp. 3329, 3353, 3460; Canan, *Superwarriors*, pp. 184–86; *Senate Hearings*, Armed Services Committee, Ad Hoc Committee on Research and Development, 92d Cong., 2d sess., Mar. 22, 1972, p. 3172, statement of Vice Admiral Philip Beshany; Polmar and Allen, *Rickover*, p. 569; Mintz, "Depth Charge." Zumwalt's position was surprising, considering his recent attacks on naval brass for continuing to build big carriers. Also see *Trident Fact Sheet Weekly Report* (Washington: Congressional Quarterly, 1973), p. 711.

[42]Mintz, "Depth Charge"; Gansler, *Defense Industry*, pp. 84, 138–39; J. R. Hiller and R. D. Tollison, "Incentive vs. Cost-Plus Contracts in Defense Procurement," *Journal of Industrial Economics* 26 (1978):239–48.

[43]Mintz, "Depth Charge."

[44]Ibid.

[45]Ibid.; interview with Veliotis, 1981.

[46]Mintz, "Depth Charge."

[47]Ibid.

[48]Ibid.

[49]Ibid.

[50]Ibid.

[51]Ibid.

[52]Ibid. Also see Polmar and Allen, *Rickover*, pp. 570–71.

[53]Mintz, "Depth Charge."

[54]Ibid.

[55]Ibid.

[56]Ibid.

[57]Ibid.

[58]*Senate Hearings*, Armed Services Committee, Ad Hoc Subcommittee on Research and Development, 92d Cong., 2d sess., Mar. 22, 1972, pp. 3192–95, statements of Admirals Lyon, Beshany, and Kaufman. The distribution for the entire 41-ship Polaris/Poseidon program was divided among the major shipbuilders as follows:

Construction Dates for Total Program	**SSBN No.**	**Electric Boat**	**Newport News**	**Mare Island**	**Ports-mouth**	**Total**
1/11/57 to 11/31/61	598	2	1	1	1	
14/9/59 to 4/1/63	608	2	3	–	–	
1/17/61 to 19/12/64	616	7	6	4	2	
25/5/63 to 1/4/67	640	6	4	2	–	
Total (keel-laying to commissioning):		17	14	7	3	41

Therefore, of the 41 SSBN boats built before the onset of the Trident program, 31 were built by two private contractors and only 10 were built by the two qualified naval yards. Indeed, the record points out that the Navy's competitive ability to participate at all in SSBN construction fell off dramatically after its six-ship rate in the construction of the 616 class. The Navy was not even a mute competitor in the 726 contract negotiations.

[59]Senate Hearings, Armed Services Committee, Ad Hoc Subcommittee on Research and Development, 92d Cong., 2d sess., March 22, 1972, statements of Admirals Lyon, Beshany, Smith, and Kaufman.

[60]*House Hearings*, 94th Cong., 1st sess., 1975–1976, p. 4567, statement of Admiral Nicholson; *Congressional Quarterly*, p. 712; letter from FMC/NOD Corp. to authors, June 30, 1981. The Poseidons were also backfitted with ULMS integrated radio rooms (*Senate Hearings*, Armed Services Committee, Ad Hoc Subcommittee on Research and Development, 92d cong., 2d sess., Mar. 9, 1972, pp. 2841–42, statement of Ferdinand L. Brand, project manager of special communications). Recently some have criticized Electric Boat for taking on more than it could handle. Congressman David Emery of Maine said of Electric Boat: "I think they're overtasked there. A lot of questions arise when one of the best yards in the world has so many problems" ("How to Spend a Trillion," p. 12).

[61]Electric Boat Company statement in authors' possession. See, for example, the *Trident Issue Brief*, pp. 3–4, and 1976 statement of Admiral J. C. Metzel before Senate Armed Services Committee, Subcommittee on Research and Development, 94th Cong., 2d sess., Mar. 23, 1976, p. 6; *House Hearings*, 1974, 93d Cong., 2d sess., pp. 857–58 statement of Rear Admiral Albert Kelln.

[62]*House Hearings*, House Armed Services Committee, Subcommittee on Seapower, 94th Cong., 1st sess., Mar. 17, 1975, p. 3649, statement of Admiral Rickover; *House Hearings*, Armed Services Committee, Subcommittee on Military Construction, 95th Cong., 2d sess., 1978, pp. 811–14, statement of Admiral Kelln. The chances are that Rickover had the question planted in the hearings to introduce the figure of ten ships as a predetermined fact.

[63]One of the problems at Electric Boat has been that the first workers were not sufficiently trained to cope with the new system, especially with a ship as large as the Trident.

[64]Statement of Vice Admiral Earl B. Fowler, Mar. 12, 1981, before the Seapower and Strategic and Critical Materials Subcommittee, House Armed Services Committee, 97th Cong., 1st sess., pp. 1–25; *Trident Issue Brief*, p. 6.

[65]The components for this figure were obtained from the text material preceding n.41. This figure can be determined in a number of ways. One way is to use a formula for compound inflation (8.85) for the cost of raw materials for the 3 additional boats purchased. Thus, (3 × $343.8 million)(.0885) = $91.2 million times 10 years = $912 million. Of course, the inflation figures are totally subjective, and the argument over what is a true inflation rate rages on. A more accurate estimate could be gained by using the exact inflation figures on the materials involved, but since the relative amounts of each metal, for example, are unknown, it becomes an impossible task.

[66]*House Hearings*, Armed Services Committee, Subcommittee on Research and Development, 94th Cong., 2d sess., Feb. 26, 1976, pp. 857–58, statement of Rear Admiral Kelln; *Department of Defense Annual Report*, 1975, Table 1; *House Hearings*, Armed Services Committee, Subcommittee on Research and

Development, 94th Cong., 1st sess., Mar. 13, 1975, p. 4570, statement of H. Tyler Marcy, Assistant Secretary of Navy, Research and Development.

[67]*House Hearings*, House Armed Services Committee, Subcommittee on Research and Development, 94th Cong., 2d sess., Feb. 26, 1976, pp. 857–58, statement of Rear Admiral Kelln. One can never be sure how much material has been purchased under long-range contracts that do not include inflation and cannot be negotiable.

[68]*Department of Defense Annual Report*, 1974, p. 57; *Department of Defense Annual Report*, 1973, p. 57; Statement of Admiral Metzel, 1976, pp. 6, 14; *House Hearings*, statement of Rear Admiral Nicholson, (p. 3315) statement of Vice Admiral Fowler (Issue Brief, p. 6).

[69]A scan of the newspapers during the funding fights reveals that President Nixon had more to worry about than a submarine. Although Ford, and later Carter, supported a larger fleet, they both referred only to surface vessels and, on occasion, attack submarines. Neither supported an acceleration of SSBN production. Also see Philip Odeen, "In Defense of the Defense Budget," *Foreign Policy*, Fall, 1974, pp. 93–108. Odeen notes that lack of prototype development "in many weapon developments—Army tanks, the B-1 bomber, the Trident submarine" leaves an alternative of "no new system at all—usually an unacceptable answer" (p. 107). Defense expenditure trends have been down. This makes the Navy's success in getting the Trident through even more impressive. Department of Defense expenditure trends from 1964 to 1977 are given below (in billions of constant 1977 dollars):

Fiscal Year	Total Obligational Authority (TOA)	Baseline TOA	Percent Change from Baseline
1964	115.4	110.4	0
1965	112.6	105.8	−4.2
1966	140.3	102.7	−7.0
1967	149.0	108.2	−2.0
1968	150.2	106.5	−3.5
1969	148.0	104.3	−5.5
1970	132.7	100.7	−8.8
1971	121.2	97.2	−12.0
1972	116.5	98.3	−10.9
1973	111.6	95.8	−13.2
1974	107.3	94.9	−14.0
1975	100.7	92.3	−16.4
1976	105.3	94.2	−14.7
1977	112.7	101.5	−8.1
1978*	120.6	109.6	−0.7
1979*	129.9	118.1	+6.9
1980*	139.8	127.1	+15.1
1981*	149.7	136.4	+23.6

Source: William Schneider and Frances P. Hoeber, eds., *Arms, Men, and Military Budgets* (New York: Crane, Russak & Co., 1978), p. 3.
*DOD projections.

One can also see the relatively slow growth of the R&D budgets from 1958 to 1977:

DOD Obligations for RDT&E
(in billions of FY 78 dollars)

Year	Amount	Year	Amount
1958	4.347	1968	7.460
1959	5.144	1969	7.491
1961	5.479	1970	7.082
1962	6.165	1971	7.259
1963	6.346	1972	8.063
1964	6.887	1973	8.109
1965	6.873	1974	8.150
1966	6.575	1975	8.661
1967	7.608	1976	9.543
		1977	10.863

Source: William Schneider and Frances P. Hoeber, eds., *Arms, Men, and Military Budgets* (New York: Crane, Russak & Co., 1978), p. 193.

4. Adolescence and Maturity: Planning Programming, and Budgeting the Trident, 1974–1982

[1]*House Hearings*, Armed Services Committee, Subcommittee on Military Installations and Facilities, 94th Cong., 1st sess., May 12, 1975, pp. 410–16, statement of Admiral H. E. Lyon; *Senate Hearings*, Armed Services Committee, 95th Cong., 1st Sess., Mar. 22, 1977, p. 687, statements of Admirals J. C. Metzel, A. L. Kelln, and A. R. Marschall; *House Hearings*, Armed Services Committee, Subcommittee on Military Installations and Facilities, 94th Cong., 2d sess., Feb. 25, 1976, pp. 309–33, 856, statements of Rear Admiral A. R. Marschall and Admiral J. C. Metzel.

[2]*House Hearings*, Armed Services Committee, Subcommittee on Military Installations and Facilities, 94th Cong., 2d sess., Feb. 25, 1976, pp. 309–33, 856, statements of Admirals Marschall and Metzel; *House Hearings*, House Armed Services Committee, Subcommittee on Military Installations and Facilities, 94th Cong., 1st sess., May 12, 1975, statement of H. E. Lyon.

[3]*House Hearings*, Armed Services Committee, Subcommittee on Military Installations and Facilities, 94th Cong., 2d sess., Feb. 25, 1976, pp. 309–27. Little mention was made during these hearings of the Cape Canaveral missile test center, funded separately but also a part of the Trident program.

[4]*Joint Hearings*, Armed Services Committees, Subcommittees on Military Construction, and Senate Appropriations Committee, 92d Cong., 2d sess., May 25, 1972, p. 284, statement of Admiral W. M. Enger, Naval Facilities Engineering Committee; *House Hearings*, House Armed Services Committee, Subcommittee on Military Installations and Facilities, 94th Cong., 2d sess., Feb. 25, 1976, p. 333; *Trident System*, p. 4.

[5]Ibid., p. 329. It is not clear from testimony exactly which buildings these were, but clearly they were of minor importance.

[6]*House Hearings*, Armed Services Committee, Subcommittee on Seapower, 94th Cong., lst sess., Mar. 17, 1975, pp. 3832, 4460–70, statement of Dr. Malcolm R. Currie; James Canan, *War in Space* (New York: Harper, 1982), p. 78.

[7]*Trident Issue Brief*, p. 12; *Department of Defense Annual Report*, fiscal year 1975, p. 59.

[8]Ibid., pp. 4462, 4555–56; *House Hearings*, Armed Services Committee, Subcommittee on Research and Development, 95th Cong., 2d sess., Mar. 9, 1978, pp. 952–74, statement of David Mann, Assistant Secretary of Defense, Research Engineering and Systems; Canan, *Superwarriors*, pp. 187–88; Gansler, *The Defense Industry* p. 98.

[9]*House Hearings*, Armed Services Committee, Subcommittee on Seapower, 94th Cong., 1st sess., Mar. 17, 1975, pp. 4553, 4569, statement of Dr. Malcolm R. Currie.

[10]*House Hearings*, Armed Services Committee, Subcommittee on Research and Development, 94th Cong., 2d sess., Feb. 26, 1976, pp. 856–57, statement of Admiral Kelln.

[11]*Department of Defense Annual Report*, fiscal year 1975, pp. 59–61; Canan, *Superwarriors*, p. 147.

[12]*Department of Defense Annual Report*, fiscal year 1975, p. 59; *Issue Brief*, p. 9. A Poseidon carried sixteen of the modified Trident I missiles.

[13]*Department of Defense Annual Report*, fiscal year 1975, p. 58. One can imagine the military acronyms a re-retrofitted sub might require.

[14]*House Hearings*, Armed Services Committee, Subcommittee on Seapower, 94th Cong., 1st sess., Mar. 17, 1975, pp. 3832, 4560–61, statement of Dr. Malcolm R. Currie.

[15]*House Hearings*, Armed Services Committee, Subcommittee on Research and Development, 94th Cong., 2d sess., Feb. 26, 1976, p. 849, statement of Admiral Kelln; *House Hearings*, Armed Services Committee, Subcommittee on Research and Development, 95th Cong., 2d sess., Mar. 9, 1978, p. 953, statement of David Mann, Assistant Secretary of Defense, Research Engineering, and Systems; *Department of Defense Annual Report*, fiscal year 1976–77, p. II–31.

[16]*Department of Defense Annual Report*, fiscal year 1976–77, p. II-33.

[17]Ibid., table 1 and app. C, p. II–31.

[18]Gansler, *The Defense Industry*, p. 66.

[19]*Department of Defense Annual Report*, fiscal year 1976–77, p. II–31; *House Hearings*, Armed Services Committee, Subcommittee on Military Installations and Facilities, 94th Cong., 2d sess., Feb. 25, 1976, p. 321.

[20]*House Hearings*, Armed Services Committee, Subcommittee on Research and Development, 94th Cong., 2d sess., Feb. 26, 1976, p. 3338, statement of Rear Admiral John Nicholson; *Senate Hearings*, Armed Services Committee, Subcommittee on Research and Development, 94th Cong., 2d sess., Mar. 23, 1976, p. 6540, statement of John Walsh; *Congressional Quarterly*, Feb. 7, 1981, p. 251. The consideration behind Walsh's assertion has already been explained in the preceding chapter.

[21]*House Hearings*, Armed Services Committee, Subcommittee on Military Installations and Facilities, 94th Cong., 2d sess., Feb. 25, 1976, p. 321, statement of Rear Admiral A. R. Marschall; "Negotiators Reach Tentative EB Pact," *Hartford Courant*, Nov. 21, 1975.

[22]*Congressional Quarterly*, Mar. 20, 1976, p. 626; *Senate Hearings*, Armed Services Committee, 94th Cong., 1st sess., Mar. 7, 1975, pp. 874–947 statements of Richard Garwin, Sidney Drell, and Henry Niles. A Trident contract for submarine guidance equipment went to General Electric in September 1976 (*Wall Street Journal*, Sept. 15, 1976).

[23]*Congressional Quarterly*, Feb. 15, 1975, pp. 336–37; ibid., May 17, 1975, pp. 1011–12; ibid., May 25, 1975, p. 1078; "Sugar Daddy to the Navy," *Wall Street Journal*, Mar. 14, 1981.

[24]*House Hearings*, Armed Services Committee, Subcommittee on Research and Development, 94th Cong., 2d sess., Feb. 26, 1976, p. 891, statement of Admiral Levering Smith; *Congressional Quarterly*, Mar. 15, 1975, p. 533; ibid., June 14, 1975, p. 1213; Aug. 2, 1975, p. 1738; Oct. 4, 1975, p. 2102; Nov. 15, 1975, p. 2493. Ironically, the amounts authorized by the House committee, despite the vocal opposition of Aspin and others, averaged 1.5 percent less than the request. The Senate, by comparison, authorized an average of 6.1 percent less than the request, while the entire Congress averaged 9.2 percent less than requested (*Congressional Quarterly*, Feb. 15, 1975, p. 337).

[25]George Wilson, "Defense Spending Up Whoever Wins," *Manchester Guardian*, Oct. 24, 1976, n.p.; William Gregory, "Continued Defense Spending Rise Seen," *Aviation Week*, Apr. 19, 1976, p. 43 (also see May 17, 1976, for defense approvals and cuts); Clarence Robinson, Jr., "Defense Budget to Spur Clash," *Aviation Week*, Nov. 15, 1976, pp. 14–16; James Hessman and Vicki Smithson, "Controversy and Politics Mark Start of FY '77 Defense Debate," *Sea Power*, Feb. 1976, pp. 21–29; James Hessman, "Next Year $7.8 Billion for Shipbuilding," *Sea Power*, Nov., 1976, pp. 33–36; *Congressional Quarterly*, Mar. 20, 1976, p. 626; Mar. 27, 1976, pp. 691–96. The requests and recommendations are as follows (in billions of dollars):

Year	Administration Request	Committee Recommendation	Percent Change
1966	16.9469	17.8581	+5.38
1967	21.0664	21.4350	+1.75
1968	22.3851	21.6370	−3.34
1969	21.9637	21.6370	−2.80
1970	20.2715	21.3479	+0.17
1971	21.8938	20.2375	−0.08
1972	22.8820	21.8752	−6.38
1973	21.9591	21.3188	−2.57
1974	23.1301	21.3950	−2.11
1975	28.2624*	22.6430	−6.07
1976	32.7278	26.5450	+2.13
		33.4240	

*Does not include $1.3 billion to South Vietnam or $300 million for a special weapons sale.

In reference to Seiberling's comment, Robert C. Herold and Shane E. Mohoney presented a case study of Soviet and U.S. military procurement, which concluded the "American system, with its greater resources . . . can usually obtain what it wants; but it seems to have great difficulty in avoiding what it does not want. . . . The USSR, because it lacks technical resources, has relatively more difficulty in getting what it wants . . . but less difficulty in preventing what it does not want" ("Military Hardware Procurement: Some Comparative Observations on Soviet and American Policy Processes," *Comparative Politics*, July 1974, pp. 571–99).

[26] *Congressional Quarterly*, May 8, 1976, pp. 1138–39; Apr. 17, 1976, p. 931. When it became apparent that Ford would win the nomination, defense again was downplayed. It appeared near the end of the Republican platform. Aso see Barry Blechman, "The Future of the Navy," *Proceedings*, Jan., 1977, pp. 28–34.

[27] *Congressional Quarterly*, May 8, 1976, pp. 1128–39; Apr. 17, 1976, p. 931. For Lockheed's contract, see *Wall Street Journal*, Mar. 1, 1977, and Nov. 11, 1977. For related contract work, Automation Industries, Sperry Rand, Singer, Control Data Corp., and Analytic Sciences Corporation all received contracts in Oct., 1977 (*Wall Street Journal*, Oct. 10, 1977), and General Telephone and Electronics received a $3.1-million contract to work on radio communications (*Wall Street Journal*, Dec. 20, 1977). In October, numerous other Trident contracts went out to Martin Marietta, General Dynamics, Raytheon, Mech-Con Corp., Heller Electric, Avco Corp., Numax Electronics, and IBM, in Trident-related industrial work (*Wall Street Journal*, Oct. 3, 1977).

[28] *Congressional Quarterly*, June 12, 1976, pp. 1498–99, and June 26, 1976, p. 1651. See also commentary on *Arms, Men, and Military Budgets* by James Hessman in *Sea Power*, May, 1976, pp. 14–16.

[29] *Congressional Quarterly*, May 22, 1976, pp. 1267–68; June 5, 1976, p. 1453; June 19, 1976, p. 1574; May 20, 1978, p. 1261. There was growing discussion about the capabilities of foreign shipyards, perhaps as alternate builders (*Christian Science Monitor*, Mar. 18, 1977, p. 26). Some blamed the increased Navy section of the budget on the Trident ("Cost of Pentagon Weapon Projects Climbs," *Wall Street Journal*, Sept. 9, 1976; and "First Trident Sub's Delivery to be Late and Its Cost to Leap," ibid., Nov. 30, 1977); "Navy Awards $699 Million Job for Two Tridents," ibid., Feb. 28, 1978.

[30] *Senate Hearings*, Armed Services Committee, Subcommittee on Research and Development, 94th Cong., 2d sess., Mar. 23, 1976, pp. 6535–36, statements of Admirals Kelln and Harvey; ibid., 95th Cong., 1st sess., Apr. 5, 1977, pp. 6621–24.

[31] Ibid., Apr. 5, 1977, pp. 6651, 6670; *Senate Hearings*, 95th Cong., 1st sess., Mar. 22, 1977, pp. 687, 691, 700, statements of Admiral A. R. Marschall and Mr. M. J. Moynihan of NAVFACECOM. For related submarine contract work, see *Wall Street Journal*, Mar. 16, 1977, and Aug. 9, 1977. Among those given contracts were Gould (sonars) and Thiokol (general FBM work).

[32] *Senate Hearings*, Armed Services Committee, Subcommittee on Research and Development, 95th Cong., 1st sess., Mar. 22, 1977, pp. 694–710, statement of Admiral A. R. Marschall.

[33] *Congressional Quarterly*, June 25, 1977, p. 1308; Aug. 20, 1977, p. 1781.

[34] "Military's 'Wish List' for New Weapons Up by $18.5 Billion," *Christian Science Monitor*, Feb. 22, 1977; "Pentagon's Weapons-Cost Estimate Rises $18.5 Billion in Biggest Spurt Since 1970," *Wall Street Journal*, Feb. 16, 1977; "U.S. Weapons Bill Soars," *Denver Post*, Feb. 16, 1977; Canan, *War in Space*, p. 21;

Cecil Brownlow, "Defense Cut Proposals Draw Opposition," *Aviation Week*, Jan. 24, 1977, and Feb. 7, 1977; "Military Leaders Clash on Soviet Threat," *Aviation Week*, Feb. 7, 1977; "Compromise $36.1 Billion Weapons Bill Seen Set for Approval by Congress," *Wall Street Journal*, June 20, 1977; "Pentagon Estimate of Weapons Cost Declines $19 Billion," *Wall Street Journal*, Nov. 16, 1977. Also see "Stabilizing Defense Budgets," *Aviation Week*, Jan. 3, 1977, p. 9; "Major Weapon System Spending Detailed," ibid., Jan. 24, 1977; Cecil Brownlow, "Carter to Consider Defense Cuts," ibid., Jan. 31, 1977; "Fund Curb Hits Pentagon Plans," ibid., Aug. 29, 1977. Carter, a Naval Academy graduate and former submariner, took a cruise on the *Los Angeles* to inspect firsthand "the capabilities and limitations of our strategic force" [the *Los Angeles* is not a strategic sub (*Phoenix Gazette*, May 27, 1977)].

[35]*Department of Defense Annual Report*, fiscal year 1978, pp. 130–31; "General Dynamics Has Navy Sub Order for $354.4 Million," *Wall Street Journal*, June 7, 1977. General Dynamics also received engineering contracts totaling $65.3 million (*Wall Street Journal*, Oct. 28, 1977).

[36]*Congressional Quarterly*, Jan. 28, 1978, p. 170; June 9, 1979, p. 1114; *House Hearings*, Armed Services Committee, Subcommittee on Research and Development, 95th Cong., 2d sess., Mar. 9, 1978, p. 957, statement of David Mann, Assistant Secretary of Defense, Research Engineering and Systems.

[37]"Ruling Reversed on Navy Dispute with Shipbuilder," *Wall Street Journal*, Mar. 2, 1978; "General Dynamics Rejects Navy's Offer to Settle Claims, Will Halt Work on Subs," ibid., Mar. 14, 1978; "Deadline Is Eased by Electric Boat in Sub Dispute," ibid., Mar. 24, 1978.

[38]"Battle Between Navy and Submarine Maker Is Stirring Big Waves," ibid., Apr. 7, 1978; "Sub Cost Overruns Blamed on Drugs, Sex, and Booze," *Boston Globe*, May 20, 1978; interview with William Bennett, June 1982.

[39]"Navy Settlement with Contractor Is Major Victory," *Wall Street Journal*, June 12, 1978; "Battle Between Navy," ibid., Apr. 7, 1978; "Litton and Navy Settle Dispute over Ship Orders," ibid., June 21, 1978; "$931 Million Navy Payout Is Questioned," *Arizona Republic*, July 7, 1978. See also, "Battle Rages over Shipyard Costs," *New York Times*, June 11, 1978.

[40]*Congressional Quarterly*, Aug. 5, 1978, p. 2020; Jan. 27, 1979, pp. 135–39; *Senate Hearings*, Armed Services Committee, Subcommittee on Research and Development, 95th Cong., 1st sess., Apr. 5, 1977, pp. 6657–59, statements of Admirals Harvey, Kelln, and Metzel.

[41]*Senate Hearings*, Armed Services Committee, Subcommittee on Research and Development, 95th Cong., 1st sess., Apr. 5, 1977, p. 6660, statements of Admirals Harvey, Kelln, Wertheim, and Metzel; *Wall Street Journal*, Mar. 14, 1977.

[42]*Senate Hearings*, Armed Services Committee, Subcommittee on Research and Development, 95th Cong., 1st sess., Apr. 5, 1977, pp. 6639–54, statements of Admirals Harvey, Kelln, and Metzel. Contracts went out in June to Goodyear Aerospace Corporation for torpedo warheads (*Wall Street Journal*, June 5, 1978), and Lockheed was given $5.1 million for the fleet ballistic missile program (*Wall Street Journal*, June 16, 1978). Sperry Rand also received $3 million for unnamed "submarine work" (*Wall Street Journal*, Aug. 25, 1978). Other companies to get 1978 sub-related contracts included Automation Industries, General Electric, Raytheon, and General Dynamics

(*Wall Street Journal*, Apr. 19, 24, June 26, July 3, and Oct. 17, 1978). In addition to its smaller contract, Lockheed landed the 1978 Trident missile contract worth $343.4 million (*Wall Street Journal*, Mar. 19, 1978). In the case of General Dynamics, the 1978 contracts were not part of the nearly $1 billion deleted in general Trident funds.

[43]*Senate Hearings*, Armed Services Committee, Subcommittee on Research and Development, 95th Cong., 1st sess., Apr. 5, 1977, p. 6640; *Congressional Quarterly*, June 9, 1979, p. 1114; *Trident Issue Brief*, pp. 9–11; *Fiscal Year 1982 Arms Control Impact Statements* (Washington, D.C.: Government Printing Office, 1981), Joint Hearings, Foreign Affairs and Foreign Relations Committees, 97th Cong., 1st sess., pp. 72–84; Howe, *Weapons*, pp. 50–51. For a discussion of casualties involved in a nuclear war, see Henry S. Rosen, "The Need for a New Analytical Framework," *International Security Review*, Fall, 1976, pp. 130–146, fn. 8. Also see "Analysis of Effects of Limited Nuclear Warfare," *Senate Hearings*, Committee on Foreign Relations, Subcommittee on Arms Control, International Organizations and Security Agreements, 94th Cong., 1st sess., Sept. 1975, p. 113. The Trident I production was slowed by a strike at Lockheed during October of 1977 ("Lockheed Strike Slows Missile, Jet Production," *New York Times*, Oct. 11, 1977). Also see the full-page ad in the *Wall Street Journal* entitled "Total Success—The First Five Trident Launches" (July 28, 1977).

[44]*Trident Issue Brief*, pp. 11–12; *New York Times*, Apr. 10, 1977 ("Budget Office Offers Options on Defense").

[45]*Department of Defense Annual Report*, fiscal year 1980, pp. 120–21; Letter of Harold Brown to Melvin Price, *House Hearings*, Armed Services Committee, Subcommittee on Research and Development, 96th Cong., 2d sess., pp. 505–7. Brown projected that for 650 SLBMs, either the force could be built with 27 Tridents having 24 missiles each (smaller warheads) or the larger missile deployed in 16–18 subs. The former system would cost $34 billion and the latter $28–39 billion, depending on development costs. However, the reduced number of subs would save $500 million a year in operating costs (p. 506). Dickenson's question appears on page 525. *Trident Issue Brief*, pp. 9–10.

[46]*Department of Defense Annual Report*, fiscal year 1980, p. 21; *Aviation Week*, Jan. 30, 1978, pp. 22–23.

[47]"Budget Cuts Navy Plans," *Aviation Week*, Jan. 2, 1978; Jan. 30, 1978; Richard Cross, "The United States Naval Shipbuilding Programmes—1979," *Rusi*, September 1980, pp. 78–82; Canan, *War in Space*, pp. 43, 46, and ch. 2, passim.

[48]*Department of Defense Annual Report*, fiscal year 1980, pp. 11–18, 122. With the ELF system, the combinations of Trident I, Trident II, and Harpoon, and the Bangor/Kings Bay basing, the answers to the SLBM column would all be "yes." Also see Francis West, "Planning for the Navy's Future," *Proceedings*, Oct., 1979, pp. 26–33, and Cross, "Naval Programmes," pp. 78–82. Trident-related contracts concluded in 1979 included work on radar sets to Texas Instruments, electronic equipment work to Loral Corporation, "countermeasure set" work to Westinghouse Electric, sonar systems contracts to EDO Corporation, general submarine work to General Electric, and missile contracts to Raytheon. Other companies receiving awards included Honeywell

and McDonnell Douglas (torpedoes), Sperry (computers and periscopes), Cubic Corporation (display subsystems), E-Systems Inc. (for communications equipment), IBM (sonar and software), Tracor (engineering and sonar), Rockwell International (electronic parts), Lockheed (Trident missiles), RCA (radio room changes), American Telephone & Telegraph (sonar), General Electric (sonar improvements), and Computer Sciences Corporation (maintenance and data retrieval) (*Wall Street Journal*, Jan. 11, 24, Mar. 6, 22, Apr. 2, 6, 11, 23, 30, May 7, 22, July 5, 31, Aug. 1, 7, Sept. 14, 17, 27, Oct. 3, 5, 10, 29, Dec. 6, 1979).

[49]*Department of Defense Annual Report*, fiscal year 1980, p. 122.

[50]*Congressional Quarterly*, May 31, 1980, p. 1522; Feb. 2, 1980, pp. 250–52; Nov. 22, 1980, p. 3400; Nov. 29, 1980, p. 3440; *House Hearings*, Armed Services Committee, Subcommittee on Military Construction, 95th Cong., 2d sess., 1978, p. 816, statement of Admiral Kelln; Canan, *War in Space*, ch. 2, passim. Former Secretary of Defense Donald Rumsfeld labeled Carter's shipbuilding plan "unacceptable" as early as 1977 (*Proceedings*, Feb. 1977, pp. 17–25). For Carter's decision on the B-1, see *Christian Science Monitor*, "The President and the Bomber" (June 16, 1977), "Why the Shift on the B-1 Bomber" (June 30, 1977), and "Carter Stirs Guns-Butter Debate with B -1 Decision" (July 5, 1977). "Air Force Plans to Revive F-111 as Manned Bomber," *New York Times*, Aug. 28, 1977. Carter and Defense Secretary Brown tried to stress the positive aspects of the budget—military spending was up—but with little success. Senator John Tower of Texas said of the B-1 decision, "They are breaking open the vodka bottles in Moscow" (*Christian Science Monitor*, July 5, 1977). Brown held that the "strategic nuclear weapons [issue] is taking away from the more important conventional forces buildup" (*Aviation Week*, Jan. 17, 1977, p. 25), and Carter vowed to match the Soviets in arms (*Phoenix Gazette*, Aug. 26, 1977).

[51]*Congressional Quarterly*, Feb. 2, 1980, pp. 250–52; Nov. 29, 1980, p. 3440; Dec. 13, 1980, p. 3567.

[52]Ibid., Apr. 4, 1981, p. 590; May 9, 1981, p. 813; May 16, 1981, p. 854; *House Hearings*, Armed Services Committee, Subcommittee on Seapower and Strategic and Critical Materials, 97th Cong., 1st sess., Mar. 12, 1981 pp. 1–25, statement of Vice Admiral Earl B. Fowler, Commander, Naval Sea Systems Command; *Senate Hearings*, Armed Services Committee, Subcommittee on Research and Development, 95th Cong., 1st sess., Apr. 5, 1977, p. 6674, statement of Admiral J. C. Metzel.

[53]*House Hearings*, Armed Services Committee, Subcommittee on Research and Development, 96th Cong., 2d sess., Feb. 7, 1980, p. 157, statement of William J. Perry, Secretary of Defense for Research and Development (discussion about *Alpha* with congressional staff member Anthony Battista, pp. 525–46, Feb. 12, 13, 1980); *Balance Sheet 1980*, p. 172; "Negotiators," *Hartford Courant*, Nov. 1, 1975; "EB Unions Gain Contact," ibid., July 1, 1979, and "Draftsman Negotiators Sign Agreement with EB, " ibid., May 24, 1980; *House Hearings*, Armed Services Committee, Subcommittee on Seapower and Strategic and Critical Materials, 97th Cong., 1st sess., Mar. 12, 1981, pp. 1–25, statement of Vice Admiral Earl B. Fowler, Commander, Naval Sea Systems Command (*Telegraph*, statements cited from hearing).

[54]*House Hearings*, Armed Services Committee, Subcommittee on Research and

Development, 96th Cong., 2d sess., pp. 24–25, 381, statement of William Perry. In nonacoustic ASW, Perry reported, "the effort to characterize the signature of submarines in the presence of the background noise field has resulted in a highly successful experiment" (Perry statement, p. 146). He also reported that a submarine simulator was "continuously tracked" during another experiment.

[55]*Trident Issue Brief*, p. 7; *House Hearings*, Armed Services Committee, Subcommittee on Procurement and Military Nuclear Systems, 97th Cong., 1st sess., Mar. 9, 1981, p. 6, statement of Vice Admiral Hyman Rickover, Deputy Assistant Secretary for Naval Reactors. For discussions on attack submarines, see Polmar, "U.S. Navy: Attack Submarines," pp. 121–22; Van Saun, "Attack Submarine," pp. 100–103; Milton Jones, "Toward Smaller, Simpler Submarines," *Proceedings*, June 1981, pp. 110–13; Ruthven Libby, "The Role of the Submarine . . . ," *Strategic Review*, Sept. 1973, pp. 29–32.

[56]*House Hearings* Armed Services Committee, Subcommittee on Procurement and Military Nuclear Systems, 97th Cong., 1st sess., Mar. 9, 1981, p. 6, statement of Vice Admiral Hyman Rickover, Deputy Assistant Secretary for Naval Reactors.

[57]*Trident Issue Brief*, pp. 3–4. *Department of Defense Annual Report*, Fiscal Year 1982, p. 112. Even the *Trident Issue Brief* is unclear about Trident force levels, for on page 4 it states "Had the original schedule been implemented, 18 ships would have been authorized between FY74 and FY85, *instead of the 14 currently planned* [emphasis added]." On page 1, the *Brief* reports fifteen "projected to be authorized." Moreover, the original schedule would have seen twenty or twenty-one ships authorized between FY74 and FY85, not eighteen. According to early Navy testimony, the Navy may have expected even a few more. Earl Fowler's 1981 statement refers to a fifteen-submarine program.

[58]*Department of Defense Annual Report*, Fiscal Year 1982, pp. 113, 124; *Defense Budget—FY82 Issue Brief* (Washington, D.C.: Congressional Research Service, 1982), pp. 10, 25; "California Vote Keeps Lockheed Trident Work," *Aviation Week*, June 9, 1980, p. 21.

[59]*Defense Budget—FY82 Issue Brief*, p. 10; Benjamin Schemmer, "Strategic Initiatives to Bridge a Budget Chasm Too Big for Dollars Alone to Cure," *Armed Forces Journal*, Mar. 1981, pp. 42–53; "House Unit Votes Defense Budget of $135.6 Billion," *Wall Street Journal*, May 13, 1981. Total Trident funding dropped by $1.8 billion (*Wall Street Journal*, May 22, 1981).

[60]"Skepticism Rises on Bigger Fund for Military," *New York Times*, June 7, 1981; "Reagan Takes a Flyer on Foreign Affairs," *Los Angeles Times*, June 7, 1981; "How to Spend a Trillion," pp. 6–21; James Fallows, "America's High-Tech Weaponry," *Atlantic Monthly*, May, 1981, pp. 21–33; "Reagan's Defense Buildup," *Newsweek*, Mar. 16, 1981, pp. 22–24; James Fallows, *National Defense* (New York: Random, 1981); Donald Holt, "What We Need for Defense," *Fortune*, Nov. 3, 1980, pp. 60–66. CBS News also sponsored a five-part critique of the new defense budget called "The Defense of the United States" during July, 1981. The general conclusion of this report closely resembled that of Fallows. For Seesholtz's critique of this general line of thinking, see "Is Technology the Culprit," *Proceedings*, June, 1982, pp. 47–50.

[61]Lawrence J. Korb, "The FY 1981–85 Defense Program: Is a Trillion Dollars Enough?" *Naval War College Review*, Mar.–Apr., 1980, pp. 3–16; *House Hearings*, Armed Services Committee, Subcommittee on Research and Development, 96th Cong., 2d sess., Feb. 12, 1980, p. 463, statement of William J. Perry.

[62]"Hard Choices on Defense Spending Begin Now," *Wall Street Journal*, Jan. 21, 1981; Albert Wohlstetter, "His Defense Spending Will Help Address a Perilous Imbalance," *Los Angleles Times*, Jan. 22, 1981; "Reagan Budget Request Is Likely to Seek Added $20 Billion in Fiscal 1980," *Wall Street Journal*, Feb. 5, 1981. See also Feb. 19, 1981. As might be expected, Navy contractors opposed the reactivated ships because they preferred new ones to be built (*Wall Street Journal*, Apr. 4, 1981). As a result of outlays trailing authority, the money appropriated by Congress tends to "pile up in the U.S. Treasury" (Canan, *War in Space*, p. 53). This fund had a number of observers concerned, reported Canan, many of whom considered the money a "slush fund" (p. 53).

[63]"Pentagon Budget Would Hit $368 Billion by Fiscal 1986 Under Reagan's Proposal," *Wall Street Journal*, Mar. 5, 1981; "Larger Naval Expansion than Disclosed with Rise in U.S. Shipbuilding Is Mulled," ibid., Mar. 27, 1981.

[64]"House Gives Reagan Budget Victory," *Wall Street Journal*, May 8, 1981; "U.S. Says NATO Agrees to Spend More," ibid., May 13, 1981; "Weinberger Says Military Spending Rise Won't Spur Inflation or Disrupt Economy," *Wall Street Journal*, July 29, 1981; Arthur Laffer, "Politicians Are Conspiring to Block the Public's Will," *Los Angeles Times*, Apr. 25, 1982; George Gilder, *Wealth and Poverty* (New York: Basic Books, 1981), p. 226. For a good discussion of the impact of defense spending on inflation, see Gansler, *Defense Industry*, p. 13. Gansler concludes that there is no simple answer and that the impact on inflation depends on a number of things, such as national economic conditions. He points out that defense spending creates a greater multiplier "than expenditures in other areas of government, because defense is more capital intensive."

[65]*Trident Issue Brief*, May 3, 1982, pp. 14–15; "Defense Program Sails Through Senate . . . ," *Wall Street Journal*, Dec. 7, 1981.

[66]"Cheers, Jeers and Soviets Accompany Trident Send-off," *Arizona Republic*, June 18, 1982; *House Hearings*, Armed Services Committee, Subcommittee on Seapower and Strategic and Critical Materials, 97th Cong., 2d sess., Mar. 11, 1982, p. 10, statement of Vice Admiral N. R. Thunman; "Washington Roundup," *Aviation Week*, Jan. 25, 1982, p. 17.

[67]*Trident Issue Brief*, May 3, 1982, pp. 14–15; "FY83 Budget Compromise Disrupts Process; DoD Budget Far from Finished," *Armed Forces Journal*, June 1982; Caspar Weinberger to Mark Hatfield, Melvin Price, John Tower, and Jamie Whitten, June 1, 1982 (in authors' possession). Also see "Congressional Unit Criticizes Report," *Aviation Week*, July 12, 1982, p. 62.

[68]Gilder, *Wealth and Poverty*, p. 188. For further discussion of "supply-side" economics, which have been pitted against defense spending, rather than more properly against domestic spending and tax increases, see Jude Wanniski, *The Way the World Works* (New York; Basic Books, 1978); Bruce Bartlett, *A Walk on the Supply Side* (New Rochelle, N.Y.: Arlington House, 1981); Arthur Laffer and Jan Seymour, eds., *The Economics of the Tax Revolt*

(New York: Harcourt, 1979); "Inflation to be Cut by Proposition 13," *Wall Street Journal,* July 7, 1978. For the CBO's predictions, see The Congressional Budget Office, *Proposition 13: Its Impact on the Nation's Economy, Federal Revenues, and Federal Expenditures,* reprinted in Laffer and Seymour, *Economics,* pp. 110–13.

[69]*Trident Issue Brief,* pp. 12–13.

[70]Statement of Electric Boat Company in authors' possession, reproduced in chap. 3. "Profit at General Dynamics Fell for 4th Quarter," *Wall Street Journal,* Feb. 6, 1981.

[71]John Newwell, "The Breakdown in Naval Shipbuilding," *Proceedings,* Jan. 1978, pp. 25–31.

[72]"How to Spend a Trillion," p. 12. Finally it should be noted that some programs increase in cost despite the best efforts of everyone involved to "hold the lid on." David Mann complained the Lamps III costs have grown despite "almost Draconian measures" to hold it down (*House Hearings,* Armed Services Committee, Subcommittee on Research and Development, 96th Cong., 2d sess., Feb. 27, 1980).

5. A Hangar Strap Here, a Continuous Weld There: The Trident Construction Process

[1]"Nuclear Submarines," pamphlet by General Dynamics, Electric Boat Division, n.d., p. 1; Gerard Burke, "To Build Trident," *Proceedings,* Oct. 1979, pp. 117–20.

[2]Joseph S. Knowles, "America's Nuclear-Powered Submarines," *Sea Classics,* May, 1973, p. 29.

[3]"Quonset Point Facility," pamphlet by General Dynamics, Electric Boat Division, n.d., pp. 1–2; Burke, "To Build Trident," p. 118; interview with P. Takis Veliotis, spring 1981; *House Hearings,* Armed Services Committee, Seapower and Strategic and Critical Material Subcommittee, 97th Cong., 1st sess., Mar. 25, 1981, p. 22, statement of P. Takis Veliotis.

[4]"Nuclear Submarines," pp. 1–3; Burke, "To Build Trident," p. 118.

[5]"Quonset Point Facility," pp. 1–3.

[6]Ibid.; interview with Veliotis; interview with William Bennet, Vice President of the Quonset Point facility, June, 1982.

[7]Burke, "To Build Trident," p. 118; *House Hearings,* p. 22; interview with Bennett.

[8]Interview with Bennett.

[9]Ibid.

[10]Ibid.

[11]"Quonset Point Facility," pp. 1–3; interview with Bennett.

[12]"Quonset Point Facility," pp. 1–3; Burke, "To Build Trident," p. 118.

[13]"Nuclear Submarines," p. 2.

[14]Ibid.; *House Hearings,* p. 23 (see hearing transcript fig. 19).

[15]See fig. 18 in *House Hearings,* p. 22.

[16]One can best see the process in Veliotis' fig. 17, *House Hearings,* p. 21. In this picture the *Ohio* is in the water, the *Michigan* is on the left dock for final construction, and the *Florida* is emerging from the building.

[17]Burke, "To Build Trident, p. 119.
[18]*House Hearings*, p. 31.
[19]Interview with Veliotis.
[20]Burke, "To Build Trident," p. 119; *House Hearings*, p. 2.
[21]Burke, "To Build Trident," p. 120; *House Hearings*, p. 2; "EB, Union Gain Contract," *Hartford Courant*, July 1, 1979.
[22]*House Hearings*, passim.
[23]Ibid.
[24]Ibid., pp. 17, 30.
[25]Ibid.
[26]Ibid., p. 26; Burke, "To Build Trident," p. 119.

6. Claim-as-you-go?: Trident and Quality Control

[1]*House Hearings*, Appropriations Committee, 97th Cong., 1st sess., May 5, 1981, statement of Vice Admiral Hyman Rickover, p. 2. Parts of this chapter have appeared in "The Final Salvo: Rickover, Electric Boat, the Navy, and the Trident Submarine Program," *Weapons and Warfare Quarterly*, Apr., 1983, and "The Trident Submarine Program in Bureaucratic Perspective," *Naval War College Review*, Jan.–Feb., 1984.
[2]*House Hearings*, Armed Services Committee, Subcommittee on Seapower and Strategic and Critical Material, 97th Cong., 1st sess., Mar. 12, 1981, pp. 1–25, statement of Vice Admiral Earl Fowler.
[3]See chaps. 3 and 4 for claims battles with other shipbuilders; *House Hearings*, Appropriations Committee, 97th Cong., 1st sess., May 5, 1981, pp. 2–169, statement of Hyman Rickover.
[4]*House Hearings*, ibid., p. 46.
[5]*House Hearings*, Appropriations Committee, 97th Cong., 1st sess., May 5, 1981, pp. 1–169, statement of Hyman Rickover.
[6]Once again, for procurement comparisons with other programs, see sources cited in chap. 3, nn. 2 and 3.
[7]*House Hearings*, Appropriations Committee, 97th Cong., 1st sess., May 5, 1981, p. 46.
[8]*House Hearings*, Appropriations Committee, 97th Cong., 1st sess., Mar. 24, 1981, p. 576, statement of John Lehman; *House Hearings*, Appropriations Committee, 97th Cong., 1st sess., May 5, 1981, pp. 5–6, statement of Hyman Rickover. One questioner explained that "historically, the Navy's insurance was interpreted to cover only unforeseen or unexpected events such as fires" (p. 576). Rickover has a reputation of keeping intentionally dilapidated offices—"every penny goes for nuclear power."
[9]*House Hearings*, Appropriations Committee, 97th Cong., 1st sess., May 5, 1981, pp. 5–6, statement of Hyman Rickover; "General Dynamics' Sub Cost Overruns Draw U.S. Inquiry," *Wall Street Journal*, Apr. 27, 1981.
[10]*House Hearings*, Armed Services Committee, Subcommittee on Seapower and Strategic and Critical Material, 97th Cong., 1st sess., Mar. 12, 1981, pp. 2–4, statement of Vice Admiral Earl Fowler.
[11]Ibid., pp. 4–5.
[12]Ibid., pp. 5–8. There is discrepancy over the number of bad welds, with numbers ranging from 6000 to 10,000.

[13]Ibid., p. 9.
[14]Ibid., pp. 10–13.
[15]Ibid., pp. 13–14.
[16]*Senate Hearings*, Armed Services Committee, 97th Cong., 1st sess., Feb. 5, 1981, p. 905, statement of Admiral Thomas Hayward; interview with Electric Boat officials, June 1981.
[17]*House Hearings*, Appropriations Committee, 97th Cong., 1st sess., Mar. 24, 1981, pp. 573–78, and May 5, 1981, pp. 2–169.
[18]*House Hearings*, Armed Services Committee, Subcommittee on Seapower and Strategic and Critical Material, 97th Cong., 1st sess., Mar. 12, 1981, pp. 14–16, statement of Earl Fowler.
[19]*Ibid.*, pp. 16–17.
[20]"Delays May Force Navy to Scrap Trident Sub," *Arizona Republic*, Mar. 18, 1981; "U.S. Seeks Builder for Some Trident Subs, Again Attacks General Dynamics' Work," *Wall Street Journal*, Mar. 30, 1981; Deborah Meyer, "More Political Rhetoric than Fact Behind Navy Blast at General Dynamics," *Armed Forces Journal*, June, 1981, p. 16; "Navy Drops Option for Ninth Trident Sub," *Wall Street Journal*, Apr. 2, 1981; "Navy Caused Submarine Program Delays Bitter General Dynamics Tells Congress," ibid., Mar. 26, 1981.
[21]*House Hearings*, Armed Services Committee, Subcommittee on Seapower and Strategic and Critical Material, 97th Cong., 1st sess., Mar. 25, 1981, pp. 1–35, statement of P. Takis Veliotis. Also see the interview with Veliotis (app. B).
[22]*House Hearings*, Armed Services Committee, Subcommittee on Seapower and Strategic and Critical Material, 97th Cong., 1st sess., Mar. 25, 1981, pp. 1–5, statement of P. Takis Veliotis. According to Veliotis, savings gained were:

Overhead and Support Savings
($ millions)

	1978	1979	1980	1981	Avg.
Indirect headcount	26	27	29	31	28
Overhead cost reduction	20	21	23	26	23
Fringes (direct personnel)	30	32	34	36	33
Support personnel	38	41	44	47	42
Total	114	121	130	140	
Total average annual savings					126

Source for all figures: Ibid., pp. 3–35.

[23]Ibid., pp. 6–7.
[24]Ibid., p. 8.
[25]Ibid., p. 9. Veliotis submitted the following chart:

	SSN 698 Bremerton	SSBN 726 Ohio
1. Total Welds Requiring MT* Inspection	74,100	117,400
a. Reactor Plant	8,400	9,250
b. Shop Fabrication	38,100	67,800
c. Ship Installation	27,600	40,350
2. Total MT Welds Requiring Repair	2,502	2,772
3. Percentage Requiring Repair	3.4	2.4

*Magnetic particle testing

[26]Ibid., pp. 9–10. Veliotis compared welding problems in both the SSN 698 and the *Ohio*:

	SSN 698	SSBN 726
Total Length of Weld per Ship (requiring MT inspection)	2,240,000 in.	4,132,000 in.
Length of Defective Welds	16,000 in.	18,700 in.
Percentage of Defective Welds	0.7	0.5

[27]Ibid., p. 11.
[28]Ibid.
[29]Ibid., pp. 12–13.
[30]Ibid., p. 13.
[31]Ibid., pp. 13–16.
[32]Ibid., p. 18.
[33]Ibid., p. 19; interview with Veliotis (app. B).
[34]*House Hearings*, Armed Services Committee, Subcommittee on Seapower and Strategic and Critical Material, 97th Cong., 1st sess., Mar. 25, 1981, pp. 28–32, statement of P. Takis Veliotis.
[35]Ibid., p. 32. For an example of representative delivery delays in other ship classes, see figs. 6–7. Also see the statement to the same House subcommittee, Oct., 1980, by Rear Adm. J. A. Webber, Vice Commander of NAVSEA.
[36]"U.S. Seeks Builder for Some Trident Subs," *Wall Street Journal*, Mar. 30, 1981.
[37]"Navy Drops Option," ibid., Apr. 2, 1981; *Senate Hearings*, Appropriations Committee, Subcommittee on Defense, 97th Cong., 1st sess., Apr. 9, 1981, pp. 1–12, statement of P. Takis Veliotis; *House Hearings*, Appropriations Committee, 97th Cong., 1st sess., May 5, 1981, p. 93, statement of Hyman Rickover.
[38]Canan, *Superwarriors*, pp. 192–93; *House Hearings*, Appropriations Committee, 97th Cong., 1st sess., May 5, 1981, pp. 9–22, 90, 130, 133, 153, 169, statement of Hyman Rickover.
[39]Ibid., pp. 90–130.
[40]*House Hearings*, Appropriations Committee, 97th Cong., 1st sess., May 5, 1981, pp. 81–83, 93, 104.
[41]Ibid., pp. 82, 153; letter from Hyman Rickover to Chief of Naval Operations, Aug. 14, 1978.
[42]Ibid., pp. 44–46, 90. See Rickover's memo to the Chief of Naval Material, Jan. 7, 1981 (pp. 45–46).

[43]Ibid., p. 120 (letter dated Mar. 4, 1980); "Navy Should Build Its Own Submarines," *Wall Street Journal,* May 6, 1981. Other shipbuilding companies, including Bath and Lockheed, pointed out in their advertisements that they had turned out products *ahead* of schedule (an apparent slam against Electric Boat).

[44]Interview with Veliotis (app. B).

[45]*House Hearings,* Appropriations Committee, 97th Cong., 1st sess., Mar. 24, 1981, pp. 573–78, statement of John Lehman, Secretary of the Navy; *Senate Hearings,* Armed Services Committee, 97th Cong., 1st sess., Feb. 5, 1981, p. 905, statement of John Lehman, Secretary of the Navy; letter from Hyman Rickover to the Secretary of the Navy, June 24, 1980 (*House Hearings,* Appropriations Committee, 97th Cong., 1st sess., May 5, 1981, p. 255).

[46]Ibid., pp. 573–74, 655–56.

[47]Ibid., Meyer, "More Political Rhetoric," p. 16.

[48]"Report of the Special Committee to the Honorable John F. Lehman, Jr., Secretary of the Navy, Apr. 20, 1981 (in authors' files); *House Hearings,* Appropriations Committee, 97th Cong., 1st sess., May 5, 1981, p. 90, statement of Hyman Rickover.

[49]"Report of the Special Committee," pp. 2–10; Meyer, "More Political Rhetoric," p. 16. The schedules of the *Ohio* and *Michigan* were listed as follows:

Event	(Ohio)	(Michigan)
First sea trials	06/21/81	06/20/82
Delivery	10/31/81	10/31/82

[50]"Electric Boat (Mr. Veliotis)—Naval Sea Systems Command (VADM Fowler), Side by Side," U.S. Navy, Office of Legislative Affairs, May 5, 1981, in author' files, pp. 1–6; letter from Representative Charles Bennett, Chairman, House Subcommittee on Seapower, to Milton J. Socolar, Acting Comptroller General of the United States, Apr. 6, 1981 (in authors' files).

[51]Ibid., pp 7–10.

[52]Ibid., p. 11.

[53]Ibid., pp. 12–14.

[54]Ibid., pp. 15–22. In addition, the Navy agreed to contract modifications, according to the statement, in "the reality of the Contractors' lack of progress" and because Electric Boat "released the Government from any and all causes for ship delivery and associated costs" (p. 19).

[55]Ibid., p. 31; *House Hearings,* Appropriations Committee, 97th Cong., 1st sess., Mar. 24, 1981, pp. 573, 655–56, statement of John Lehman; May 5, 1981, pp. 44–46, statement of Hyman Rickover. See, especially, Rickover's memo to the Chief of Naval Material, Jan. 7, 1981, (pp. 45–46), and letter dated Mar. 4, 1980.

[56]*House Hearings,* Appropriations Committee, 97th Cong., 1st sess., May 5, 1981, pp. 44–46, statement of Hyman Rickover. Again, see Rickover's memos as dated above.

[57]"Navy Says General Dynamics Must Settle Its Claims to Get More Trident Contracts," *Wall Street Journal,* Sept. 16, 1981; "General Dynamics Won't Ask Navy to Pay Costs on Flawed Subs, Wins Chance at Bid," *Wall Street Journal,* Sept. 17, 1981; "Navy, General Dynamics Reconcile Feud," *Wall Street Jour-*

nal, Oct. 23, 1981. Gansler had also pointed out the advantage a large firm, such as Electric Boat, has over a smaller firm in negotiating, an advantage that doubtless was used in this case (*Defense Industry*, pp. 138–39).

[58]Meyer, "More Political Rhetoric," p. 16.

[59]Ibid.; "How to Spend a Trillion: Arming for the '80s," p. 12; interview with Veliotis, June, 1981; "Firm Says Adm. Rickover Endangered Two Subs at Sea," *Los Angeles Times*, Aug. 21, 1981; interview with Veliotis (app. B). Also see R. James Woolsey, "Rickover's Lengthening Shadow," *Armed Forces Journal*, Oct., 1981, p. 16.

[60]"General Dynamics Hints Aide Will Leave Electric Boat Post, in Gesture to Navy" *Wall Street Journal*, Oct. 6, 1981; interview with Veliotis, Nov., 1981; executive memorandum concerning Veliotis' retirement, June 3, 1982, provided by Electric Boat Company. "General Dynamics Ex-officials, Others Alleged to Have Taken $4.5 Million Bribes," *Wall Street Journal*, May 20, 1983.

[61]Polmar and Allen, *Rickover*, passim., esp. chap. 31; Woolsey, "Rickover's Lengthening Shadow," p. 16; *Los Angeles Times*, Nov. 10, 1981; Howe, *Weapons*, pp. 194–95; "An Old Admiral Is Cast Adrift," *Newsweek*, Nov. 23, 1981, p. 43.

[62]Gansler, *Defense Industry*, pp. 188, 191; *House Hearings*, Armed Services Committee, Subcommittee on Seapower and Strategic and Critical Materials, 97th Cong., 1st sess., Mar. 25, 1981, pp. 1–4, statement of P. Takis Veliotis.

[63]Compare Veliotis' testimony (pp. 6–8) with the Navy's side-by-side of May 5, pp. 3–7.

[64]Ibid., Veliotis (pp. 9–11) with Navy (pp. 8–10).

[65]Ibid., Veliotis (p. 11) with Navy (p. 11).

[66]Ibid., Veliotis (pp. 12–13) with Navy (p. 13).

[67]"Cost Growth and Delivery Delays in Submarine Construction at Electric Boat Are Likely to Continue," Comptroller General of the United States, Apr. 19, 1982 (in authors' files), pp. 15, 4–8, 10–14, ii.

[68]A. M. Barton to W. H. Sheley, Feb. 24, 1982 (in authors' files), pp. 1–3.

[69]Ibid., p. 3.

[70]"GAO Notes" on copy of letter from Richard DeLauer to W. H. Sheley, Feb. 26, 1982.

[71]Richard DeLauer to W. H. Sheley, Feb. 26, 1982.

[72]Milton Socolar to Charles Bennett and Joseph Addabbo, Apr. 19, 1982.

[73]John Lehman to Charles Bennett, June 3, 1982.

[74]*House Hearings*, Appropriations Committee, Subcommittee on Defense, 97th Cong., 2d sess., Mar. 31, 1982, pp. 8–9, 12, 14–15, statement of Earl Fowler.

[75]Ibid., pp. 14–15.

[76]Ibid., p. 9; Gilder, *Wealth and Poverty*, pp. 180, 242, 262, and chap. 20, passim. Of course, surprises can be both positive and negative, which was the essential point of chap. 3's discussion of the original design's novelty.

[77]Gansler, *Defense Industry*, p. 200; *House Hearings*, Appropriations Committee, 97th Cong., 1st sess., May 5, 1981, p. 75, statement of Hyman Rickover.

[78]Loren Thompson, "The Defense Industrial Base: Going, Going . . . ," *International Security Review*, Summer, 1981, pp. 237–72; *Senate Hearings*, Armed Services Committee, 96th Cong., 2d sess., 1980, p. 980. Also see *U.S. Defense Industrial Preparedness Issue Brief*, June 8, 1982; "Strategic-material Supply Vulnerable," *Arizona Republic*, June 13, 1982.

[79]*The Economist,* Sept. 1, 1979; Thompson, "Defense Industrial Base," p. 238; Gansler, *Defense Industry,* p. 99, n. 7.

[80]Thompson, "Defense Industrial Base," p. 250; James Hansen, "High Strategic Stakes in Southern Africa," *National Defense,* May–June, 1982, pp. 42–46. Apparently, the Soviets, once considered self-sufficent in titanium, have imported the metal in great quantities and have ceased to be self-sufficient in titanium (an unsurprising fact when it is understood that the USSR uses 65 percent of its titanium for military purposes). Also see "America's Gap in Strategic Minerals," *U.S. News & World Report,* Feb. 8, 1982, p. 59, for an illustrated view of this dependence as it applies to a jet engine.

[81]*House Hearings,* Appropriations Committee, 97th Cong., 1st sess., May 5, 1981, p. 93, statement of Hyman Rickover; "General Dynamics Hints Aide Will Leave," *Wall Street Journal,* Oct. 6, 1981. Regarding Rickover's constant calls for reopening government shipyards, Clinton Whitehurst has written in *Proceedings* that "the day of the naval shipyard is probably over," and that "the Navy has larger fish to fry." Whitehurst instead urges "complete reliance on the private sector" ("Is There a Future for Naval Shipyards," Apr., 1978, pp. 31–40). Nevertheless, criticism of private contractors has continued. See "Lawmaker Says Navy Is Botching Ships' Overhauls," *Arizona Republic,* Feb. 6, 1981; "Pentagon Management Pacts Awarded Without Competition, Probe Finds," ibid., Apr. 8, 1981; John Correll, "The Industrial Substructure: Trouble at the Bottom," *Air Force Magazine,* July, 1982, pp. 48–51.

[82]Gansler, *Defense Industry,* pp. 27–28.

[83]Kaufman, *War Profiteers,* p. 109.

[84]Whitmore, "Origin of Polaris, p. 59.

7. Not Your Basic Bases: Bangor, Kings Bay, and Support Facilities

[1]*Trident Issue Brief,* p. 12; *Senate Hearings,* Armed Services Committee, Subcommittee on Research and Development, 94th Cong., 2d sess., Mar. 23, 1976, pp. 13–20, statement of Admiral Kelln. ibid., Mar. 22, 1972, p. 3144, statement of Admiral Philip Beshany.

[2]Jim Davis, "Building the Trident's Home," *Proceedings,* Mar., 1979, pp. 62–73.

[3]*House Hearings,* Appropriations Committee, Subcommittee on Military Construction, 95th Cong., 1st sess., Mar. 22, 1977, pp. 714–15, statement of Admiral Marschall.

[4]Ibid., statement of Representative Norman O. Dicks, pp. 761–62. Also see *Senate Hearings,* Armed Services Committee, Subcommittee on Military Construction, 95th Cong., 2d sess., Apr. 19, 1978, p. 486, statement of Perry Fliakas, Deputy Assistant Secretary of Defense (Installations and Housing). See especially the February 1977 letter from the Assistant Secretary of Defense summarizing military base economic adjustment projects in which he discusses the types of jobs provided by the military in civilian areas.

[5]House Hearings, Appropriations Committee, Subcommittee on Military Construction, 95th Cong., 1st sess., Mar. 22, 1977, pp. 763–64. Dicks supported Jackson's claim that nobody had lobbied for the base. When asked if Kitsap,

Mason, and Jefferson counties had not petitioned to have the Bangor base, Dicks replied, "No, sir, nobody asked for it. In fact, we were never consulted out there about this base in advance, and the former Governor of the State of Washington was a constant—I wouldn't say critic, but close to it, about the fact that the State had never been consulted . . ." (p. 765). People generally supported the base construction, he said, because they "really did get a commitment, almost in blood . . . that we were going to get this [federal] help."

[6]Ibid., pp. 764–66, 718–22.

[7]Ibid., pp. 765, 770–71.

[8]Ibid., pp. 710–11; *Senate Hearings*, Armed Services Committee, Subcommittee on Research and Development, 94th Cong., 2d sess., Mar. 23, 1976, pp. 13–20, statement of Admiral Kelln; Davis, "Building the Trident's Home," pp. 64–65. Because the lawsuit was filed in Washington, D.C., it may not have been filed by local Bangor residents but by professional environmental lobbyists.

[9]*House Hearings*, Appropriations Committee, Subcommittee on Military Construction, 95th Cong., 1st sess., Mar. 22, 1977, pp. 714–15.

[10]Ibid.

	Scheduled Start	Actual Start
Items that fell behind in the construction schedule		
Refit pier 1	10/1975	12/1975
Bachelor enlisted quarters	7/1975	8/1975
Refit industrial facility	1/1976	4/1976
Drydock phase 1	9/1976	11/1976
Delta support facility	8/1976	4/1977
POL tank farm	1/1976	5/1976
Missile motor magazines	12/1975	2/1976
Dispensary dental clinic	1/1976	5/1976
Trident DASO/data processing support facility	4/1976	12/1976
Dockside handling building	12/1976	1/1977
Vertical missile packaging building 3	11/1976	12/1976
Container storage area	1/1977	3/1977
Fire station	12/1976	3/1977
Trident support facility administration building	2/1977	12/1978
Dockside handling building	12/1976	1/1977
Guardhouse	8/1976	2/1977
Transfer facility	7/1976	6/1977
Bachelor officers quarters	12/1976	4/1977
Post office	12/1976	6/1977
Trident missile tracking facility	11/1976	5/1977
Items that ran ahead of schedule		
Servmart	2/1977	11/1976
Trident test equipment installation	1/1977	12/1976

[11]Ibid., pp. 771–74.

[12]Ibid., pp. 774–81; Norman Dicks to Gunn McKay, Apr. 26, 1977. To be eligible for federal funds, the access roads had to provide "new connections between either old or new military installations and main highways," or had to be excluded from primary federal aid, or required "urgent improvements to avoid intolerable congestion of any highway [due to] defense generated traffic." (p. 778).

[13]*House Hearings*, Armed Services Committee, Subcommittee on Military Construction, 95th Cong., 1st sess., Mar. 22, 1977, p. 711, statement of Admiral Marschall. *Senate Hearings*, Armed Services Committee, Subcommittee on Seapower, 94th Cong., 2d sess., Feb. 18, 1976, p. 15.

[14]*House Hearings*, Armed Services Committee, Subcommittee on Military Construction, 95th Cong., 1st sess., Mar. 22, 1977, pp. 711–30, statement of Admiral Marschall.

[15]Ibid.

[16]*Senate Hearings*, Appropriations Committee, Subcommittee on Military Construction, 95th Cong., 2d sess., Apr. 19, 1978, pp. 159–74, statement of Rear Admiral Donald Iselin; Martin Heerwald, "Protestors Prepare a Special 'Welcome' for N-Submarine," *Los Angeles Times*, July 25, 1982.

[17]*House Hearings*, Armed Services Committee, Subcommittee on Military Construction, 95th Cong., 1st sess., Mar. 22, 1977, pp. 710–77, statement of Admiral Marschall; *Senate Hearings*, Appropriations Committee, Subcommittee on Military Construction, 95th Cong., 2d sess., Apr. 19, 1978, pp. 159–74, statement of Rear Admiral Donald Iselin. The wharf increased in cost by 52 percent (*House Hearings*, Armed Services Committee, Subcommittee on Research and Development, 96th Cong., 2d sess., Feb. 7, 1980, p. 45, statement of William Perry, Secretary of Defense for Research and Engineering.

[18]*House Hearings*, Armed Services Committee, Subcommittee on Military Construction, 95th Cong., 2d sess., Mar. 22, 1978, pp. 778–99, statements of Admirals Kelln, Metzel, and Marschall.

[19]Ibid., pp. 786–89.

[20]Ibid., pp. 798–802; Davis, "Building the Trident's Home," p. 65; Tritten, "Trident System," pp. 61–63.

[21]*House Hearings*, Armed Services Committee, Subcommittee on Military Construction, 95th Cong., 2d sess., Mar. 22, 1978, p. 808, statements of Admirals Kelln, Metzel, and Marschall.

[22]Davis, "Building the Trident's Home," p. 65; G. Brian Estes, "Trident Base East," *Military Engineer*, Sept.-Oct., 1981, pp. 322–27.

[23]*House Hearings*, Armed Services Committee, Subcommittee on Military Installations and Facilities, 97th Cong., 1st sess., Mar. 27, 1981, pp. 452–61, statement of Admiral Zobel; *Senate Hearings*, Armed Services Committee, Subcommittee on Military Construction, 95th Cong., 2d sess., Apr. 19, 1978, pp. 70–89, statements of Edward Hidalgo and Admiral Donald Iselin.

[24]Davis, "Building the Trident's Home," pp. 65–65.

[25]"Protestors Prepare 'Welcome' "; "Antinuclear Activists' Ships Awaiting Trident Submarine," *Arizona Republic*, Aug. 8, 1982; "Sub Reaches Port; Antinuclear Blockade 'Sunk,' " *Arizona Republic*, Aug. 13, 1982; Paul Scotti, "Guarding the Navy: Coast Guard Style," *Armed Forces Journal*, Oct., 1982,

pp. 92–97. As for charges of "brutality," Admiral Clifford Dewolf said the actions of the Coast Guard were characterized by "tremendous responsibility, restraint, and professionalism" (Scotti, "Guarding," p. 97). The constant use of Auschwitz in antinuclear propaganda (see chap. 8) is in itself a revealing practice. Robert J. Loewenberg ("The Trivialization of the Holocaust as an Aspect of Modern Idolatry," *St. Johns Review*, Winter, 1982, pp. 33–43) divines the true dangers of this theme, while at the same time revealing the philosophical relativism, and ultimately nihilism, as Leo Strauss warns, inherent in the approach of the "peace protestors." Loewenberg concludes that members of the American Left who must often invoke this theme in theoretical thought, if not in actual practice, more closely adhere to the tenets of Nazi doctrine than do those groups they protest against. For a fine treatment of the historicist approach, which has been rejected here, see Leo Strauss, *Natural Right and History* (Chicago: Univ. of Chicago Pr., 1952). Loewenberg condenses the argument in " 'Value-Free' versus 'Value-Laden' History: A Distinction Without a Difference," *Historian*, May, 1976, pp. 439–54.

[26]*House Hearings*, Armed Services Committee, Subcommittee on Military Construction, 95th Cong., 2d sess., Mar. 22, 1978, p. 821, statements of Admirals Kelln, Metzel, and Marschall; *Senate Hearings*, Armed Services Committee, Subcommittee on Military Construction, 95th Cong., 2d sess., 1978, pp. 438, 575, 580, statement of Perry Fliakas, Deputy Assistant Secretary of Defense (Installations and Housing).

[27]*House Hearings*, Armed Services Committee, Subcommittee on Military Construction, 95th Cong., 2d sess., Mar. 22, 1978, pp. 821–24, statements of Admirals Kelln, Metzel, and Marschall; *Senate Hearings*, Appropriations Committee, Subcommittee on Military Construction, 95th Cong., 2d sess., Apr. 19, 1978, p. 224, statement of Admiral Kelln; *Trident Issue Brief*, p. 12. See, for example, Admiral Kelln's statement that the "operational characteristics of having a Trident submarine . . . some 560 feet long, navigating the Cooper River with high currents, deep draft, frequent siltation, and dredging required [figured in the vote for Kings Bay]. Maneuvering that ship in and out of a highly dense traffic river. . . . Those factors were all pointed out and considered" (p. 821).

[28]*House Hearings*, Armed Services Committee, Subcommittee on Military Construction, 95th Cong., 2d sess., Mar. 22, 1978, pp. 825–48, statements of Admirals Kelln, Metzel, and Marschall. *Senate Hearings*, Appropriations Committee, Subcommittee on Military Construction, 95th Cong., 2d sess., Apr. 19, 1978, pp. 204–33, statement of Admiral Kelln.

[29]*Senate Hearings*, Appropriations Committee, Subcommittee on Military Construction, 95th Cong., 2d sess., Apr. 19, 1978, pp. 204–33, statement of Admiral Kelln.

[30]*House Hearings*, Armed Services Committee, Subcommittee on Military Construction, 95th Cong., 2d sess., Mar. 22, 1978, pp. 445–61, statements of Admirals Kelln, Metzel, and Marschall; Estes, "Trident Base East," p. 327.

[31]J. Paul Wyatt, " 'Invasion' by Navy Hits Rural Georgia" *Los Angeles Times*, Sept. 2, 1979.

[32]Ibid.

[33]*Senate Hearings*, Appropriations Committee, Subcommittee on Military Con-

struction, 95th Cong., 2d sess., Apr. 19, 1978, pp. 121, 224, statement of Admiral Kelln.

[34]Ibid., pp. 106, 115, 211.

[35]*House Hearings*, Armed Services Committee, Subcommittee on Military Installations and Facilities, 97th Cong., 1st sess., Mar. 27, 1981, pp. 449–56, statement of Rear Admiral William Zobel, Naval Facilities Engineering Command; Estes, "Trident Base East," p. 327; Department of Defense News Release, Oct. 23, 1980. David Boren cites a delay in the opening of the Kings Bay base, changing the original completion date from 1990 to 1992, although the *Ohio* did put into Kings Bay on its way to Cape Canaveral tests. See "U.S. Strategic Buildup Can Deter Soviet Supremacy," *International Security Review*, Winter, 1981–82, pp. 411–36.

[36]*Senate Hearings*, Armed Services Committee, Subcommittee on Military Construction, 95th Cong., 2d sess., Apr. 19, 1978, pp. 431, 434, statement of Perry Fliakas, Deputy Assistant Secretary of Defense (Installations and Housing). Total construction costs for the Trident facilities appear below (in millions of dollars):

Fiscal Years	Construction	Support	Total
1968–1977	530.0	496.7	1,026.7
1978	96.0	162.9	258.9
1979	19.7	125.6	145.3
1980	38.8	170.9	209.7
1981	35.6	227.7	263.3
1982*	123.9	365.2	489.1

*Requested.
Source: *Trident Issue Brief*, p. 14.

[37]See chap. 4, passim.

8. Bearing Down: Soviet ASW Capability and Trident Operational Survivability

[1]Sergei Gorshkov, *The Sea Power of the State* (Annapolis: Naval Institute Pr., 1979), p. 276. Office of the Chief of Naval Operations, *Understanding Soviet Naval Developments*, 4th ed. (Washington, D.C.: Department of the Navy, 1981), p. 7; Donald Mitchell, *A History of Russian and Soviet Sea Power* (New York: Macmillan, 1974), p. 512; A. A. Sidorenko, "The Offensive," *Strategic Review*, Spring, 1974, pp. 93–99; Peter Vigor, "Strategy and Policy in Soviet Naval Warfare," *Strategic Review*, Spring, 1974, pp. 68-75. The Soviets' infatuation with the surprise factor cannot be overstated. See A. Krasnov, "The Surprise Factor," *Strategic Review*, Spring, 1974, pp. 105–7 (reprinted from *Krasnaya Zvezda*, Feb. 3, 1974, p. 2), who offers this bit of military advice: "Strike a surprise blow and victory is assured." Once again, the elements of surprise are clear in Douglas and Hoeber, *Soviet Strategy*, p. 18: "The first [of *five* conditions for total victory] is surprise. The objective is . . . the prevention of surprise *by* the West . . . [and] the accomplishment of surprise *of* the West." See also K. Moskalenko, "Constant Combat Readiness

Is a Strategic Category," *Voyennaya mysl'*, Jan., 1969 (trans. 1969), p. 14, and A. Zheltove, *Methodological Problems of Military Theory and Practice*, trans. by U.S. Air Force, Foreign Technology Division, Wright-Patterson Air Force Base (Dayton, Ohio: U.S. Air Force, Dec. 18, 1971), p. 355. Americans insist on misinterpreting or ignoring this Soviet doctrinal aspect, as seen in William Scott, "Soviet Military Doctrine and Strategy: Realities and Misunderstandings," *Strategic Review*, Summer, 1975, pp. 57–66. Scott notes a "strange reluctance in the West to examine these Soviet writings in their totality" (p. 65). Sergei Gorshkov's writings appear in *Morskoi Sbornik*, 1972 and 1973, collected and reprinted in *Red Star Rising at Sea*, trans. Theodore Neely, Jr., ed. Herbert Preston (Annapolis: Naval Institute Pr., 1974). Various analysts have examined this work in detail. For a verification of the "operations vs. the land" and the priority of the submarine, see Bruce Watson, "Comments on Gorshkov's 'Sea Power of the State,' " *Proceedings*, Apr., 1977, pp. 42–47, and Edgar Prina, "The Gorshkov Doctrine: Seapower and the World Ocean," *Sea Power*, Oct., 1976, pp. 33–37. Also see David Cox, "Sea Power and Soviet Foreign Policy," *Proceedings*, June, 1969, pp. 32–44; J. Oswald, "The Great Bear Hug,"*Rusi*, June, 1978, pp. 36–41; Jack Bauer, "What Are You Up To, Sergei?" *Proceedings*, Dec., 1974, pp. 34–37; Julien LeBourgeois, "What Is the Soviet Navy Up To?" *NATO Review*, Apr., 1977, pp. 14–19; Michael MccGwire, "Naval Power and Soviet Global Strategy," *International Security Review*, Spring, 1979, pp. 134–89; Max Beloff et al., "The Peacetime Strategy of the Soviet Union," *Strategic Review*, Summer, 1973, pp. 61–69. For the role and development of the Soviet Navy specifically, see John E. Moore, *The Soviet Navy Today* (Briarcliff Manor, N.Y.: Stein & Day, 1976), and his *Warships of the Soviet Navy* (London: Janes, 1981); Norman Polmar, ed., *Soviet Naval Developments* (Annapolis: Nautical and Aviation Publishing Company of America, 1979); Norman Polmar, *Soviet Naval Power: Challenge for the 1970s*, rev. ed. (New York: Crane, Russak and Co., Inc., 1974); Eric Morris, *The Russian Navy: Myth and Reality* (Briarcliff Manor, N.Y.: Stein & Day, 1977); Michael MccGwire et al., eds., *Soviet Naval Policy: Objectives and Constraints* (New York: Praeger, 1975); Michael MccGwire, ed., *Soviet Naval Developments: Capability and Context* (New York: Praeger, 1973); David Fairhall, *Russian Sea Power* (Boston: Gambit, 1971); George Quester, ed., *Sea Power in the 1970s* (New York: Dunellen, 1975). A history of Russian maritime affairs appears in David Woodward, *The Russians at Sea: A History of the Russian Navy* (New York: Praeger, 1965).

[2]Mitchell, *History*, p. 566; Norman Polmar, "Thinking About Soviet ASW," *Proceedings*, May, 1976, pp. 109–28. Some observers have questioned the zone concept, especially the forward deployment zone. Gary Charbonneau suggests that the longer-range Soviet missiles now appearing make this type of deployment unnecessary ("The Soviet Navy and Forward Deployment," *Proceedings*, Mar., 1979, pp. 35–40).

[3]Chap. 9 discusses differences between American and foreign (French and British) SSBN systems. For an imaginative, but probably realistic, view of the procedure aboard a Trident in combat, see Howe, *Weapons*, pp. 18–22.

[4]Polmar, *Soviet Naval Developments*, p. 8; Canan, *Superwarriors*, p. 212. Some analysts add a fifth category to the ASW components—localizing the submarine—but this is included here as identification. An illustrated view of

ocean surveillance appears in "The Techniques of Surveillance, 1945–80," pp. 156–65, especially the diagram on pp. 158–59. Polmar suggests that, while American sonars are better than Soviet sonars, "there are other methods of submarine detection, ranging from wake detection to psychic" ("Soviet Nuclear Submarines," pp. 1–36). Also see John Byron, "The Victim's View of ASW," *Proceedings*, Apr., 1982, pp. 39–43.

[5]Information on Soviet ships, submarines, aircraft, and various sonar, radar, and weapons systems appears in Siegfried Breyer and Norman Polmar, *Guide to the Soviet Navy*, 2d ed. (Annapolis: Naval Institute Pr., 1977), *Jane's Fighting Ships, 1977–78* (New York: Franklin Watts, 1977), and *Jane's Weapons Systems, 1977* (henceforth referred to as *Jane's*); Jean Labayle Couhat, *Combat Fleets of the World, 1980/81: Their Ships, Aircraft and Armament* (henceforth referred to as *Combat Fleets*), trans. by A. D. Baker III (Annapolis: Naval Institute Pr., 1980). Deployments appear in Morris, *Russian Navy*, pp. 135–36. Obviously these vary, but they provide a concept of Soviet priorities. One must also project that no long-range ASW scout force will be allowed to fly about untouched. The chances that any Allied power—the Japanese in the Pacific, for example—will close off air lanes as well as sea lanes is high. The question of Soviet mechanical and equipment reliability and durability is especially important to this discussion but is difficult to assess, for Soviet mishaps are seldom publicized. Apparently, the nuclear-powered Soviet icebreaker *Lenin* "was laid up and abandoned for several years," too hot "after an apparent reactor accident." Polmar also reports "special submarine pay . . . referred to as 'childlessness' pay in recognition of the dangers involved" ("Soviet Nuclear Submarines," pp. 36–37). On Mar. 17, 1982, Secretary Lehman revealed information indicating that "a number of Soviet crewmen have been killed by accidents aboard nuclear submarines" because of inadequate safeguards in the power plant leading to radiation leaks ("A-Sub Accidents Plague Soviets, U.S. Claims," *Santa Barbara News Press*, Mar., 17, 1982). According to Lehman, the Soviet Navy squeezes "more performance out of their [*sic*] submarines" by taking safety risks, and has had to evacuate subs on occasion. Moreover, in 1968, a Soviet *Golf*-class submarine exploded and sank in the Pacific. Recovered, apparently successfully (following an initial Navy report that the project failed), the sub yielded "a technical mother lode of stuff." Not until *Time* reported the recovery project's success (*Time*, Dec. 6, 1976, p. 23) was the affair made public. Trying to peg Soviet technology levels is always difficult, even for the CIA. Nevertheless, some evidence exists. Jim Bussert summarized the technological levels in "Soviet Naval Electronic Technology" (*Proceedings*, Feb., 1978, pp. 105–8). Among the items that Bussert points out, the arrangement of the radar room "suggests a redundancy of units and repair problems. . . . " When the Hughes *Glomar Explorer* raised the previously mentioned *Golf*-class Soviet submarine in 1974, investigators revealed the hull to be uneven and pitted . . . not uniform in thickness. Hatch covers and valves were also crudely constructed." The sub even "used wooden two-by-fours in the building of some compartments." In the 1975 Apollo–Soyuz space mission, astronauts reported that the technology of the Soyuz space ship was 5–10 years behind current American technology. Although most Soviet systems contain heaters, few carry coolers or air conditioners, which has prevented

Indian Ocean deployments of some ships because they would perform poorly in the hot climates. Bussert concludes that a "40% larger-and-heavier thumb rule" for Soviet technology can be applied, and he adds that it should be multiplied by two "for redundancy." Yet another report labels the quality of Russian shipbuilding "suspect" and notes that, in addition to a great deal of warship repair done by East German yards, "many Soviet vessels are also built in Finnish and West European yards" (Mitchell, *History*, p. 488). Despite Polmar's implication that the American and Soviet submarine services are nearly equal in their maintenance and operational records, a "relatively low percentage of the Soviet SSBN force . . . is deployed," counters Clinton Harris. He suggests that this is due to the "poor maintenance and [lack of] operational reliability" in their subs (*Proceedings*, Sept., 1978, p. 21). Information coming out of Russia is highly restricted, but some observers think the flash detected in 1979 off the South African coast was the result of an explosion aboard a Soviet submarine ("Soviets Deny Reports of Explosion on Sub," *Arizona Republic*, Oct. 30, 1979). Finally, one cannot dismiss the nationalistic and ethnic tensions in the Soviet Navy, where officers must give orders in several languages and where strong feelings of separatism still live in the more than a hundred nationalities (W. J. Manthorpe, "The Influence of Being Russian on the Officers and Men of the Soviet Navy," *Proceedings*, May, 1978, pp. 129–43).

[6]Morris, *Russian Navy*, pp. 135–36. Also, consult Joel S. Wit, "Are Our Boomers Vulnerable?" *Proceedings*, Nov., 1981, pp. 62–69, for an excellent multifaceted analysis of U.S. SSBN survivability in general and of Trident survivability in specific.

[7]Paul H. Nitze et al., *Securing the Seas: The Soviet Naval Challenge and Western Alliance Options* (Boulder, Colo.: Westview Pr., 1979), p. 98; Jurgen Rohwer, "The Role of the Kiev and Her VTOL Fighter Group," *International Defense Review*, Dec., 1976, p. 912; Andrew Hull, "Potential Soviet Responses to the U.S. Submarine Threat in the 1980s," *Proceedings*, July, 1978, pp. 25–30. Present indications are that most of the *Kiev* class is intended for the Mediterranean. The *Kiev* has had its own problems. In its first year of operations, it put in only two weeks at sea before it was forced to anchor off Murmansk. NATO has "been aware of the problem for some time." Further, reported the *Daily Telegraph* in London, the Yak 36 vertical-takeoff fighters apparently could not operate in combat conditions from the deck. Observers "speculated that the downward thrust of heat from their jets may have damaged the takeoff facilities" (*Daily Telegraph*, cited in *Phoenix Gazette*, Nov. 25, 1977). Other problems, including desertion and mutiny, have plagued Soviet surface vessels. On Nov. 9, 1975, part of the crew of the destroyer *Storozhevoy* sailed out of Riga. Caught within four hours, the ringleaders of the mutinous crew were executed. However, the effort to corral the destroyer without sinking her resulted in a trailing Krivak destroyer suffering rocket hits from Soviet planes. There is also evidence that the Soviets are building a new large-deck carrier (*Proceedings*, 1979, p. 126; and *Aviation Week*, June 30, 1980. p. 14). Some observers have reported a drydock for the *Minsk* already built in Vladivostok weighing in at 80,000 tons, and a second built in Japan of the same capacity also available (Mitchell, *History*, p. 132).

[8]J. W. Kehoe and K. S. Brower, "One of Their New Destroyers: Sov-

remennyy." *Proceedings*, June, 1981, pp. 121–25; William Clark, "Kirov," *Sea Classics*, May, 1981, pp. 56–61. Once again, apply the maintenance factor for an estimate of actual *at sea* availability.

[9]Gerard Burke, "The Trident Missile: America's Future Deterrent," *Proceedings*, Mar., 1980, pp. 131–34; George Quester, ed., *Navies and Arms Control* (New York: Praeger, 1980), p. 77. Arctic deployment is even more effective due to inability of surface craft and planes to track in that area. The Soviet Pacific fleet as of May 1980 totaled 758 vessels, including 130 submarines (60 nuclear-powered) and the carrier *Minsk* ("Industry Observer," *Aviation Week*, May 19, 1980, p. 15). Also see John Tritten, "The Trident System; Submarines, Missiles and Strategic Doctrine," *Naval War College Review*, Jan.—Feb., 1983, pp. 61–76. Tritten's useful chart (p. 66) uses the *stated* availability of 66 percent for Trident. But, in fact, Trident missiles are available at a much higher rate because they are actually in range *before* they are on patrol. Hence, most of Tritten's analysis severely understates availability. Trident II will be, in essence, an ICBM while in port. Furthermore, Tritten's reliance on "equivalent megatonnage" (EMT) misleads insofar as it is a measurement of *inaccuracy*. A force of Tridents on patrol with 400 EMT in Trident I missiles would be far superior in terms of sheer destructive power to a force of Poseidons with the same EMTs in Poseidon missiles, simply because the Trident I is a more accurate missile. Trident II promises to be even more accurate, rendering EMT an even less useful measurement of capability.

[10]Couhat, *Combat Fleets, 1980–81*, pp. 545–52; *Stern*, May 3, 1979, p. 38; Wit, "Boomer," p. 68. The justification of this speed estimate on the *Ohio* is derived from a computation of the reactor's horsepower (given in chap. 2), the vessel's displacement, and the hydrodynamic friction created by its hull size in diameter and length.

[11]Polmar, "Soviet Nuclear Submarines," p. 37; *Time*, Dec. 6, 1976, p. 23. Information about the *Alpha* is limited. See Michael MccGwire, "The Rationale for the Development of Soviet Seapower," *Proceedings*, May, 1980, pp. 155–83. Some comments on maintenance problems facing the Soviets appear in "The Wartime Role of Soviet SSBNs," *Proceedings*, Sept., 1978, p. 21. Torpedo speeds are classified, but one source puts the improved Mk-48's speed at 50 knots, with a range of 30 miles. In essence, then, an *Alpha* would have to be at top speed with enough distance between itself and the torpedo to "outrun" it through relatively greater endurance and range (Richard Humble, *Undersea Warfare* [Birmingham, England: Basing Hall, 1981], p. 174). The U.S. Navy's ADCAP (Advanced Capability) torpedo program is designed to offset the *Alpha*'s speed, while the new REGAL (remotely guided autonomous lightweight) torpedo incorporates its own acoustic array and signal processing (*House Hearings*, Armed Services Committee, Subcommittee on Research and Development, 97th Cong. 1st sess. Mar. 11, 1981, p. 111, statement of staff member Anthony Battista). Discussion concerning the effectiveness of torpedoes appears in Norman Polmar's "The U.S. Navy: Torpedoes," *Proceedings*, Nov., 1978, pp. 159–60; Frank Andrews, "Torpedoes: Our Wonder Weapon! (We Wonder if They'll Work)," *Proceedings*, Mar., 1979, pp. 94–97; Guy Reynolds, "Comment," *Proceedings*, July, 1979, pp. 92–93. A. Winslow ("Comment," *Proceedings*, Sept. 1980, pp. 119–20)

disputes the claim that the torpedoes are ineffective. It would be erroneous to assume that even if an *Alpha* can reach 45 knots it could outrun a torpedo dropped from a helicopter or airplane. No submarine routinely cruises at top speed. In most cases a submarine would not be aware of an incoming air-dropped weapon until it was too late. Polmar makes a detailed analysis of Soviet vs. American submarines, including speed and durability ("Soviet Nuclear Submarines").

[12]Quester, *Navies*, p. 56. Michael MccGwire contends that the *Alpha* may only be the first in a series of technological advances that may or may not be continued in this class of sub (*Naval Review*, 1980, p. 180). Like the Foxbat, however, the *Alpha* may have only a few high-technology features and some fairly primitive ones. For other explanations of the *Alpha*'s speeds, see Norman Stone, "Dolphins, Submarines, Speed and Surprises," *Military Electronics & Countermeasures*, Aug. 1980, pp. 46–51.

[13]*Senate Hearings*, Armed Services Committee, Subcommittee on Research and Development, 94th Cong., 2d sess., Mar. 23, 1976, pp. 6536, 6667, statement of Admiral Albert Kelln; Michell, *History*, p. 533; Burke, "Need for Trident," p. 55. During the Cuban missile crisis, the five or six Soviet subs sent to the waters off Cuba were all trailed and could have been destroyed "with little difficulty" (ibid., p. 519); Wit, "Boomers," pp. 67–68. For the role of trailing trawlers, see Jack Anderson, "Many Soviet Fishing Trawlers . . . ," Denver *Rocky Mountain News*, May 19, 1978. This is true of foreign ports as well, although in Trident's case it is inapplicable. For Cuba's role in ASW, see Edward Kolcum, "Cuban Military Forces Being Upgraded," *Aviation Week*, May 3, 1982, pp. 62–63; Jiri Valenta, "Soviet Strategy in the Caribbean Basin," *Naval Review*, 1982, pp. 169–81. An excellent pictorial view of strategic mineral dependence and its relationship to SLOC, see Frank Barrett, "A New Strategy For the West," *Optima*, vol. 30, no. 2. Implications of satellite tracking are discussed in chap. 9. Robert Fossum of DARPA reported in 1980 the first successful firing of a SIAM, which destroyed a drone aircraft without an explosive warhead (*House Hearings*, Armed Services Committee, Subcommittee on Research and Development, 96th Cong., 2d sess., Feb. 13, 1980, pp. 571–72), statement of Robert Fossum of the Defense Advanced Research Projects Agency (DARPA). Fossum warned "it is a short-range missile" and the doctrine associated with it is to "be sure you are under attack" before you fire.

[14]Ranges of various weapons appear in *Jane's Weapons Systems, Jane's, 1977–78,* Couhat, *Combat Fleets*; Royal United Services Institute and Brassey's *Defense Yearbook 1980* (London: Brassey's Publishers, 1979), pp. 182–91; Thomas Burns, *The Secret War for the Ocean Depths: Soviet American Rivalry for Mastery of the Seas* (New York: Rawson Associates Pub., 1978), pp. 32–77. For an interpretation of weapons' effects on submarines, see Charles Jones, "Weapon Effects Primer," *Proceedings*, Jan., 1978, pp. 50–55. He notes that "acoustic shock energy from any underwater explosion . . . leads to somewhat unexpected damage results to various targets. Ships that are *farthest* away from the explosion *may* receive the *most* damage" (p. 54). A major debate has erupted over the purpose of the SS-N-14 and a sudden change in its classification to an ASW weapon in July 1977 (Norman Polmar, "Soviet Navy Surface-to-Surface Missiles," *Proceedings*, July, 1977, pp. 90–91). Nor-

man Polmar suggests the Soviet surface fleet may be primarily an ASW fleet and that the role of Soviet surface ships in an anticarrier mode has been overplayed. Others have either disagreed (Enzio Bonsignore, "SS-N-14: Another Look," *Proceedings*, August 1979, pp. 102–6) or modified Polmar's position (Norman Friedman, "SS-N-14: A Third Round," *Proceedings*, June, 1979, pp. 110–14). Under any circumstances, the missile probably is limited to a range of about thirty miles.

[15]At one time there was even the suggestion that the Soviets were creating a polar base on an iceberg ("Soviet Base Near Canada?" *Christian Science Monitor*, June 29, 1977); Wit, "Boomers," p. 68.

[16]This type of curtain can be found in David Easter's "ASW Strategy: Issues for the 1980s," *Proceedings*, Mar., 1980, pp. 35–41. Once again, deception multiplies the effectiveness of such a strategy. Not all Australians are happy about current United States presence in their country. See Peter Elliott, "U.S. Bases a Threat to Australians," *Manchester Guardian*, June 28, 1981.

[17]Others in this line of ships are expected, including one named the *Kursk* (J. W. Kehoe et al., "U.S. Observations of the *Kiev*," *Proceedings*, July, 1977, pp. 105–11; and Ulrich Schulz-Torge, "The Kiev: A German View," ibid., pp. 111–15). John Barron, *MiG Pilot* (New York: Avon, 1980), pp. 169–86. The supposedly advanced MiG-25 showed several rust spots. If a land-based plane accumulates rust in this manner, think of the problems the Yaks must be experiencing at sea. See the review of *MiG Pilot* in the *Arizona Republic*, Mar. 22, 1981. Worse, the MiGs must maintain positive ground control or return to base (*Aviation Week*, Oct. 25, 1976). In 1981, American-made Israeli warplanes shot down two Syrian MiG-25's '*Arizona Republic*, July 30, 1981) and in 1982 racked up an incredible kill ratio in the Lebanese war.

[18]Bruce Watson and Margurite Walton, "Okean 75," *Proceedings*, Aug., 1976, pp. 93–97. See also "Kiev Carries New Forger," *Aviation Week*, Jan. 22, 1979, p. 19; "Soviet Build-up Worries Danes," *The Guardian*, May 9, 1976; Joel Larus, "Diego Garcia: Political Clouds Over Vital U.S. Base," *Strategic Review*, Winter, 1982, pp. 44–54; Wit, "Boomers," pp. 62–69. For Japanese, New Zealand, and Far Eastern contributions to ASW, see Horace Feldman, "The U.S., Japan & The Tricky Terrain of Defense," *Strategic Review*, Fall, 1981, pp. 31–38; David Davies, "The Royal New Zealand Navy: Life Begins at 40," *Proceedings*, Mar., 1982, pp. 139–41; J. V. P. Goldrich and P. D. Jones, "Four Eastern Navies," ibid, pp. 60–65. The Soviets, despite their massive shift of operations to the Kola Peninsula, cannot duplicate their repair and support facilities that exist on the Baltic. Danish mining of the Kattigat and Skagerrat would render those bases useless for some time. A similar limitation on Soviet forces in the Mediterranean puts them at a disadvantage in that area; The Soviets "have to anchor on sand bars conserving fuel while support ships bring them supplies from Black Sea ports" (*Proceedings*, Nov., 1976, p. 116). These support ships must traverse the Dardenelles, also (hopefully) in NATO hands. Finally, the great debate over the vulnerability of so-called high-value targets such as aircraft carriers is ironically magnified when considering the Soviet position: if just one of their helicopter carriers is sunk they have lost anywhere from one-fourth to one-half of their ASW carrier force. This is the equivalent of the United States losing four main battle carriers!

[19]Office of Technology Assessment, *MX Missile Basing* (Washington, D.C.: Government Printing Office, 1981), p. 179 (henceforth referred to as OTA); Wit, "Boomers," pp. 68–69.

[20]Nitze, *Securing the Seas*, p. 366; Jones, "Weapon Effects Primer," pp. 54–55; Samuel Glasstone and Phillip Dolan, compilers, *The Effects of Nuclear Weapons*, 3d ed. (Washington, D.C.: Department of Defense and Department of Energy, 1977), p. 245. The Soviets apparently are developing a version of SUBROC and ASROC (Nitze, *Securing the Seas*, pp. 269–70), and the United States is developing a new "anti-submarine standoff weapon to replace SUBROC" (*House Hearings*, House Armed Services Committee, Subcommittee on Research and Development, 96th Congress, 2d session, Feb. 27, 1980, p. 1133, statement of David Mann, assistant Secretary for Research, Engineering, and Systems, Department of the Navy); Wit, "Boomers," pp. 65–66. A standard Soviet problem—no reloads—is compounded by fire controls that can direct only *one* missile to a target at a time. Moreover, Soviet ASW ships appear able to sustain little battle damage, a problem that could raise its head during a nuclear attack on an American sub.

[21]Joseph Alexander, "Comment," *Proceedings*, Feb., 1982, p. 112; "Appeal Delaying Trial in Theft of Navy Arms," *Santa Barbara News Press*, Feb. 24, 1982; "Gunmen Flee with $200,000," *Los Angeles Times*, Oct. 27, 1978; "Stolen Tank Blitzes City, Lands in River," *Arizona Republic*, July 11, 1982; "Soviet Sabotage of Starfighter?" *Manchester Guardian*, Sept. 5, 1976; "Secret NATO Papers Found in Street," *Scottsdale Daily Progress*, May 2, 1983; "9 Charged for Defacing Submarine," *Scottsdale Daily Progress*, July 6, 1982; *Senate Hearings*, Armed Services Committee, Subcommittee on Research and Development, 95th Cong., 1st sess. Apr. 5, 1977, p. 6628, Statement of Admiral Kelln; John McLaughlin, "The Russians Are Here," *National Review*, Nov. 12, 1982, p. 1396. The ultimate irony—and most plausible of all potential nuclear "threats"—is that a "peace" group, which claimed to have stolen four unarmed warheads from a General Electric plant in Philadelphia, may decide in a Weathermanish fashion to arm and use them in a demonstration of Strangelovian proportions. See "Peace Group Has 'Warheads'; GE Denies It," *Arizona Republic*, Aug. 26, 1982.

[22]"Former CIA Officer Arrested in Secret Satellite Manual Sale," *Aviation Week*, Aug. 28, 1978, p. 22; James Ott, "Espionage Trial Highlights CIA Problems," *Aviation Week*, Nov. 27, 1978, pp. 21–23; "LA Pair Sold 'Killer' Lasers to Russ," *Las Vegas Sun*, Dec. 14, 1980.

[23]"Russians Publish Secrets," *Phoenix Gazette*, Dec. 7, 1979; "Airman Gave Soviets Titan Secrets," *Phoenix Gazette*, June 1, 1981; "CIA Says Stealth, B-1 Secrets Lost," *Santa Barbara News Press*, Apr. 28, 1982; "Convicted Spy Gave Polish Agent Details of Stealth . . . ," *Wall Street Journal*, Apr. 29, 1982; "U.S. Tries to Cut Trade in Items that Russians Might Use for Military," *Wall Street Journal*, Feb. 11, 1982; "A Clever Fibre-Optical Illusion," *MacLeans*, Apr. 12, 1982; "CIA Denies 'Mole' Counterspy Charge," *Phoenix Gazette*, Feb. 28, 1979; David Martin, *Wilderness of Mirrors* (New York: Harper, 1980); Sally Jacobsen, "Soviet Bloc Stealing U.S. High Technology," *Santa Barbara News Press*, Feb. 25, 1982; "The High-Tech Secrets Russia Seeks in West," *U.S. News & World Report*, May 3, 1982; "Disinformation: War with Words," *Air*

Force Magazine, Mar., 1982; "Washington Roundup," *Aviation Week*, May 10, 1982, p. 13; "Soviets Raiding Western Technology: Weinberger," *Los Angeles Times*, May 23, 1982; "Seething About Trade Sanctions," *Time*, Jan. 18, 1982; Gareth Parry, "Claim that MI5 Chief a Soviet Spy Suspect," *Manchester Guardian*, Mar. 29, 1981; Bob Woodward, "Top Soviet Spy Ending Stay in U.S.," *Los Angeles Times*, Jan. 10, 1982; Stephen Rosenfeld, "On Being Used by the KGB," *Manchester Guardian*, Mar. 22, 1981; "High-Tech Burglary" *Wall Street Journal*, Jan. 21, 1982; Caspar Weinberger, "Technology Transfers to the Soviet Union," ibid., Jan. 12, 1982; "Defense Secrets Book Still on Sale," *Manchester Guardian*, Nov. 16, 1980; "They Bagged an Eagle," *Newsweek*, Feb. 15, 1982; "Moscow Forging U.S. Documents," *Wall Street Journal*, July 9, 1982. U.S. officials, when possible, have turned the tables on their KGB counterparts and sabotaged equipment, especially computers, bound for Eastern-bloc countries. Said one U.S. agent, "It could be six to twelve months before they discover what a screwed-up mess they really have" ("Espionage Boom," *Newsweek*, July 5, 1982, p. 54).

[24]James Hansen, "High Strategic Stakes in Southern Africa." *National Defense*, May-June 1982, pp. 42–45; Wit, "Boomers," p. 68. Hansen's reference to the *Typhoon* appears on p. 44.

[25]Breyer and Polmar, *Guide to the Soviet Navy*, pp. 118–61; Robert Trimble, "Ships of the New Soviet Navy," *Sea Combat*, Oct., 1978, pp. 39–59; "Soviets Amassing Missiles in Stormy, Northern Waters," *Christian Science Monitor*, Mar. 14, 1979; "Invulnerable Soviet Submarines," *Manchester Guardian*, Dec. 19, 1976; "Russian Missile Subs Edge Nearer U.S., "*Manchester Guardian*, Mar. 6, 1977; *Der Spiegel*, Nov. 24, 1980: "Giant Soviet Sub Imperils Carriers," *Arizona Republic*, Jan. 9, 1981; Joel S. Wit, "Advances in Antisubmarine Warfare," *Scientific American*, Feb., 1981, pp. 31–41; Wit, "Boomers," p. 68. An excellent refutation of some of Wit's points appears in "Comment," *Proceedings*, Feb., 1982, p. 17, in which Richard Guida points out that the Soviet submarine fleet of 300 ships makes up 50 percent of its major combatants, while the United States dedicates only 16 to 20 percent of the Navy's R&D budget to ASW. There is some indication that the Soviets are planning to shift building emphasis, perhaps to these new classes (*Proceedings*, Nov., 1979, p. 23), which can fire multiple-warhead missiles (*New York Times*, Dec. 6, 1976).

[26]Easter, "ASW Strategy," p. 36; Burns, *Secret War*, pp. 37, 97; Wit, "Boomers," pp. 63–67. NATO has developed nuclear sea bombs in depth-charge form (*Proceedings*, Aug., 1976, p. 104). Also see Gerald Synhorst regarding Soviet cover for SSBNs in the Barents Sea ("Soviet Strategic Interest in the Maritime Arctic," *Proceedings*, May, 1973, pp. 90–111) and "Soviets Unveil New Missile," *Arizona Republic*, Mar. 23, 1977.

[27]Polmar, "Torpedoes," pp. 159–60. Polmar's comment on the Tomahawk appears in *Arms, Men and Military Budgets, 1980*, p. 122. *Proceedings*, Aug., 1976, pp. 104–5; *House Hearings* (see n. 16, statement of William Perry, Secretary of Defense for Research and Engineering, Feb. 7, 1980, p. 381); Quester, *Navies*, p. 58; James Eberle, "Strategic Choice and Maritime Capabilities," *Proceedings*, April 1982, pp. 65–72. For the Tomahawk's range, see ibid., p. 229. According to David Mann in the same hearings, the Tomahawk "meets or exceeds" the range capability of all similar Soviet missiles. One or two Poseidons might be targeted for White Sea/SLBM duty. Michael

McGwire, although suggesting the use of tactical nuclear weapons at sea is possible, argues against deployment of the Tomahawk ("The Rationale for the Development of Soviet Seapower," *Proceedings*, p. 182), but it appears to be the cheapest and fastest way of expanding the deterrent force. It should not be surprising to find that, because of the distance from the launcher that nuclear ASW requires, it favors American forces. See Linton Brooks, "Tactical Nuclear Weapons: The Forgotten Facet of Naval Warfare," *Proceedings*, Jan., 1980, pp. 28–33.

[28]"Russian Missile Subs Edge Nearer U.S.," *Manchester Guardian*, Mar. 6, 1977. This report notes that the "Russian submarine captains have found a passage under the polar ice" into the channel between Greenland and Ellsmere Island. Soviet activities in the Arctic have increased recently ("The Soviet Arctic May Yet Become a New Mediterranean," *New York Times*, July 2, 1978). Also see "Russia Breaks the Ice," *Los Angeles Times*, Aug. 21, 1977; Synhorst, "Soviet Interest in the Arctic," pp. 90–111. A large-scale American-Canadian venture, Operation AIDJEX, established a series of long-term bases in the Beaufort Sea area. Besides the Soviet *Arktika*, the U.S. Coast Guard is building an icebreaker capable of reaching the North Pole on the surface. See N. Venzke, "The Polar Icebreakers; In a Class by Themselves," *Proceedings*, Jan., 1976, pp. 91–94, and Brian Shoemaker, "Ships of Ice," *Proceedings*, Feb., 1976, pp. 103–6. Synhorst's article is of particular value in presenting general doctrinal arguments not necessarily related to the frozen North. The Soviet buildup in Murmansk, held by many to be defensive, gives the Soviet Union the ability to overwhelm Norway and Denmark. Also, forty-one icebreakers are working to keep the sea routes open longer. But Synhorst's direct insight—that Soviet subs are now traversing the Davis Strait area—portends Russian submarines occasionally even in Hudson Bay!

[29]Burns, *Secret War*, pp. 153–58; Norman Friedman, "SOSUS and U.S. ASW Tactics," *Proceedings*, Mar., 1980, pp. 120–22; Norman Polmar, "SURTASS and T-AGOS," *Proceedings*, Mar., 1980, pp. 122–24; Franklin Buckley, "MATASS: A Moored Airship Towed Array Sonar System," *Proceedings*, Mar., 1980, pp. 124–27; Wit, "Boomers," pp. 67–69. "Soviets Detail U.S. Submarine Loss," *Christian Science Monitor*, Feb. 25, 1977. Also see Robert Largess, "The Rigid Airship in the Sea Control Mission," *Proceedings*, Oct., 1977, pp. 74–75. *Senate Hearings*, Subcommittee on Research and Development, 95th Cong., 2d sess., Mar. 9, 1978, pp. 6108–11, statement of Robert Fossum, Director of Defense Advanced Projects Research Agency. To "determine the fundamental physical and technological limitations on undersea acoustic surveillance," DARPA set up an acoustic research center at Moffett Field, California, under project SEAGUARD in 1975. For information on TACTAS, see the FY 1980 *Department of Defense Annual Report*, p. 165. For a report of a Soviet sub trying to get through the detection lines, see "023 Victor (NH) Runs the Gauntlet," in "The Navy vs. Soviet Subs," *U.S. News & World Report*, Nov. 13, 1978, pp. 28–81. Even newer technological advances have been reported. Robert Fossum of DARPA told the House Research and Development Subcommittee in 1980 of a successful "undersea sound experiment" called AUSEX involving aircraft-towed arrays (*House Hearings*, House Armed Service Committee, Subcommittee on Research and Development, 96th Cong., 2d sess., Feb. 13, 1980, p. 595, statement of Robert Fossum). House staff member Anthony Battista remained unconvinced

about the survivability of SOSUS: "When the balloon goes up I think SOSUS is going to be the first thing to go down" (ibid., Feb. 13, 1980, p. 546).

[30]"U.S. Chases Crazy Ivan," *Arizona Republic*, Dec. 9, 1979; "The Navy vs. Soviet Subs," pp. 78–81; Wit, "Advances," pp. 31–41. DARPA currently is concentrating on new and expanded submarine-detection methods, especially focusing on wake-effects studies, infrared scanning, "over-the-horizon" radar, and plankton detection (which reveals changes in the number of plankton brought about by the passage of a sub through the water). See Wit, "Advances in Antisubmarine Warfare," pp. 31–41. Two conversations between the authors and U.S. SSN captains confirm the conclusion that Soviet submarine commanders are not as operationally qualified to maneuver their vessels with individual flair and expertise as are their Western counterparts. This conclusion would seem to be confirmed by the 1982 episode of a Soviet *Whiskey* class submarine foundering on rocks within Swedish territorial waters, apparently with the Soviet Baltic Sea submarine flotilla commander himself aboard. The Swedes seemed to have handled the situation with an excess of "neutral" generosity, since the *Whiskey* was also within a highly secret Swedish naval security zone (Deam Given and William Cashman, "Whiskey on the Rocks," *Proceedings*, Apr., 1982, pp. 112–15). Also see Donald Fields, "The Fears that Whiskey Brought to the Surface," *Manchester Guardian*, Nov. 15, 1981.

[31]Wit, "Boomers," p. 64.

[32]Roy Hoffmann, "Offensive Mine Warfare: A Forgotten Strategy?" *Proceedings*, Nov., 1977, pp. 144–55; Jeremy Taylor, "Mining: 'A Well Reasoned and Circumspect Defense,'" *Proceedings*, Nov., 1977, pp. 40–45; Robert Smith, "Mine Warfare: Promise Deferred," *Proceedings*, Apr., 1980, pp. 27–33; Daniel Powell, "Comment," *Proceedings*, June, 1980, p. 79; *Senate Hearings*, Senate Subcommittee on Research and Development, April 5, 1977, p. 618, statement of Rear Admiral Donald Harvey; Mathew Whelan, "Soviet Mine Warfare: Intent and Capability," *Proceedings*, Sept., 1980, pp. 109–14; James Layton II, "Soviet Mine Barrier Warfare Capabilities in a Central Nuclear War," *Naval War College Review*, July-Aug., 1980, pp. 42–52; Wit, "Boomers," p. 64. A complete examination of mines and mining appears in Gregory Hartman, *Weapons That Wait* (Annapolis: Naval Institute Pr., 1979).

[33]*Senate Hearings*, Armed Services Committee, Subcommittee on Research and Development, Apr. 5, 1977, p. 618, statement of Rear Admiral Donald Harvey. Actual, requested, and proposed mine-related funds appear below (in millions of dollars):

	Actual FY 1978	**Planned FY 1979**	**Proposed FY 1980**	**Proposed FY 1981**
Mine countermeasures ship	3.5	4.7	5.8	140.7
CAPTOR mine	77.6	17.7	64.4	155.3
Quickstrike	8.5	11.0	14.9	5.1
Intermediate water depth mine (IWD)	2.4	13.7	3.0	22.4
Sub-launched mobile mine	.4	–	–	–
(included above in Quickstrike)	(2.5)	(4.3)	(3.8)	(2.2)

Source: Department of Defense Report, FY 1980, p. 171.

David Mann, the Navy Department's Assistant Secretary for Research, Engineering, and Systems, told a House subcommittee in 1980 that the CAPTOR needs more testing (*House Hearings*, Armed Services Committee, Subcommittee on Research and Development, 96th Cong., 2d sess., Feb. 27, 1980, p. 1134. As early as 1978 the Navy began to bolster its minesweeper-building program, but in 1981 the General Accounting Office reported the Navy's mine warfare capability was "inadequate" (*Arizona Republic*, June 16, 1981); Norman Polmar, "The U.S. Navy: Ships That Wait," *Proceedings*, Apr., 1982, pp. 125–27.

[34]Michael Cairl, "Through-Deck Cruiser: The New Capital Ship," *Proceedings*, Dec., 1978, pp. 35–42; Wayne Meyer, "Comment," *Proceedings*, June, 1979, p. 93; "Sea Harrier Tested on Aircraft Carrier," *Aviation Week*, Jan. 19, 1981; James Holloway, "The Transition to V/STOL," *Proceedings*, Sept., 1977, pp. 19–24; James George, "The V/STOL Catch 22s," *Proceedings*, Apr., 1978, pp. 23–29; Harold Pulver, "A Sea-Based Interdiction System for Power Projection," *Proceedings*, July, 1980, pp. 86–87; "New Navy Wings," *Aviation Week*, Jan. 31, 1977, p. 9; Clarence Robinson, Jr., "Industry Proposes Supersonic V/STOL Development," *Aviation Week*, Jan. 12, 1981, pp. 36–42. For information on ASW aircraft, see Couhat, *Combat Fleets*, p. 43; William Scott, "S-3A Weapons Improvement Under Way," *Aviation Week*, Sept. 21, 1981, p. 86; "Navy Seeks to Reengine P-3C," *Aviation Week*, Sept. 21, 1981, p. 60; Robert Lawson, "The Viking at Sea," *Proceedings*, July, 1979, pp. 70–79; Frederick Glaeser, "E-3A (AWACS): An Untapped Maritime Support Resource," *Proceedings*, Aug., 1979, pp. 108–11; Ted Mouton, "The Right Aircraft at the Wrong Time?" *Proceedings*, Sept., 1980, pp. 106–9; Robert Ropelewski, "Lockheed Plans to Update P-3 Orion," *Aviation Week*, Dec. 8, 1980, pp. 41–46; Michael Murray, "Sea King: ASW Workhorse," *Proceedings*, June, 1981, pp. 99–100; *Aviation Week*, Nov. 21, 1977, p. 9; and "Future Antisubmarine Weapons," *Proceedings*, July, 1981, p. 126. General antisubmarine warfare tactics are discussed in Glenn Peters, "ASW—the Deterrent," *Electronic Warfare, Global Edition*, July-Aug., 1976, pp. 49–54; Andrew Jampoler, "ASW for the 1980s," *Proceedings*, Mar., 1980, pp. 118–19; "Advanced Sensors Major Anti-Submarine Warfare Goal," *Aviation Week*, Jan. 31, 1977, pp. 134–45; William Taylor, "Surface Warships Against Submarines," *Naval Review*, 1979, pp. 168–81; Sherman Wright, "ASW and the Modern Submarine," *Proceedings*, Apr., 1973, pp. 63–68; "No Penny-Pinching on ASW," *Proceedings*, Aug., 1977, p. 109; A. M. Harms, "Comment," *Proceedings*, Mar., 1980, pp. 93–95, 99; A. Van Saun, "Tactical ASW: Let's Fight Fire with Fire," *Proceedings*, Dec., 1976, pp. 99–101, and "Comments," *Proceedings*, Mar., June, Oct., Dec., 1977, pp. 80–81, 82, 68, 81, respectively; W. Bramlett, "ASW: Some Surface Views," *Proceedings*, Apr., 1976, pp. 99–101. Other ASW discussions appear in "Sonobuoy-Aircraft Combination Nullifies Submarines' Advantages," *Sea Technology*, Feb., 1976, pp. 16–19; "Navy Currents," *Sea Technology*, Oct., 1976, pp. 22–30; Deborah Meyer and Benjamin Schemmer, "Interview with Adm. John B. Hayes, USCG," *Armed Forces Journal*, Mar., 1981, pp. 33–40. Spending trends in American ASW are as follows:

Research and Development, Down:		Procurement for ASW Forces, Up:
1970	$423 million	$1.7 billion
1971	$551 million	$1.8 billion
1972	$549 million	$2.9 billion
1973	$368 million	$3.0 billion
1974	$314 million	$2.8 billion

Source: William Schneider and Frances Hoeber, *Arms, Men, and Military Budgets* (New York: Crane, Russak & Co., 1976), pp. 88–90.

NATO has also been standardizing frigates, thereby saving on expenses (Anthony Preston, "Standard NATO Frigates," *Sea Classics*, May, 1981, pp. 15–19). For Canadian developments, see Roy MacGregor, "Not Enough Bangs for Our Bucks," *Maclean's*, Aug. 31, 1981, pp. 23–27; "Canada's Defense Is Labeled 'Bluff,' Building Is Urged," *Arizona Republic*, Feb. 13, 1982. The effectiveness of Nordic ASW defenses still remains in question after a rash of spottings of Soviet subs in Swedish and Norwegian waters in the 1980s. Efforts to destroy the subs have failed so far ("Nordic Leaders See Mystery Subs as Part of Soviet War Planning," *Christian Science Monitor*, May 5, 1983).

[35]For information on LAMPs, see "LAMPs Mk. 3 Prototype Rolled Out," *Aviation Week*, Sept. 3, 1979, p. 21, and "LAMPs Equipped for Multiple Missions," *Aviation Week*, Apr. 3, 1978, pp. 40–44; R. E. Hammond, "The LAMPShip Team," *Proceedings*, Mar., 1978, pp. 154–61.

[36]The Air Force probably would aid in ASW efforts. See Hamlin Caldwell, "Air Force Maritime Missions," *Proceedings*, Oct., 1978, pp. 29–36. Currently a great debate is raging over active versus passive sonar. See P. Taylor Lonsdale, "ASW's Passive Trap," *Proceedings*, July, 1979, pp. 35–40. Lonsdale maintains that "passive sensors . . . usually require elaborate methods, multiple contacts, and considerable time to convert a detection into a fix accurate enough for weapon employment" (p. 35). William O'Neil ("Naval Technology: Passive Sonar Has the Edge," *Proceedings*, Apr., 1978, pp. 105–7) argues for passive sonars. For information on traditional or *Virginia*-class ships, see George Davis, "USS *Virginia* (CGN-38)," *Proceedings*, Aug., 1977, pp. 85–106; Norman Polmar, "The U.S. Navy: Frigates," *Proceedings*, July, 1980, pp. 118–19; Todd Blades, "DDG-47: Aegis on Its Way to Sea," *Proceedings*, Jan., 1979, pp. 101–5. New platforms may be developed as mini-ASW carriers, especially several ideas involving the modified battleships *Iowa* and *Missouri*. See Charles Myers, "A Sea-Based Interdiction System for Power Projection," *Proceedings*, Nov., 1979, pp. 103–6, and "Comments,", *Proceedings*, June, 1980, p. 85, and Feb., 1980, pp. 74–75. Also see Todd Blades, "Needed: Heavy Firepower," *Proceedings*, July 1979, pp. 51–54, and "Navy Wants to Overhaul Old Ships," *Arizona Republic*, Nov. 20, 1977. Also see chap. 9, n. 4. The new V-STOL battleship report appears in *Aviation Week*, Mar. 2, 1981, p. 15. Other traditional ships that could aid in ASW include traditional cruisers (see Thomas Hoback, "The Very Traditional Cruiser: A Ship Killer," *Proceedings*, Dec., 1979, pp. 111–14), destroyers (see David Clark, "Destroyers for the 21st Century," *Proceedings*, Mar.,

1979, pp. 25–33), corvettes (see Robert Shade, "The Corvette Makes a Comeback," *Proceedings*, Nov., 1978, pp. 135–39), and Coast Guard cutters (see Bruce Stubbs and Richard Kelly, "Technology, ASW and the Coast Guard," *Proceedings*, Oct., 1980, pp. 29–35). Attempts to use smaller, more exotic craft are discussed in John Kelly, "Requiem for the PHM Program," *Proceedings*, Aub., 1977, pp. 79–81, Ronald Adler, "In the Navy's Future: The Small, Fast Surface Ship," *Proceedings*, Mar., 1978, pp. 102–11, Arthur Horn, "SES: A Revolution in Naval Warfare," *Sea Combat*, Winter 1979, pp. 24–33, and George Halvorson, "The Role of High-Speed Ships in the U.S. Navy," *Proceedings*, Jan., 1979, pp. 33–41.

[37]General information on antisubmarine weapons appears in Brassey, *Defense Yearbook*, pp. 182–90, and *Jane's Weapons Systems, 1977–78*, pp. 805–18. A more detailed analysis of each weapon appears in *Jane's*, pp. 126–36. Also see Couhat, *Combat Fleets*, pp. 531–32, for a comparison with Soviet weapons, and Nitze, *Securing the Seas*, pp. 92–101, for a general analysis. New weapons may soon have an impact on ASW, such as missiles (see William Ruhe, "Missiles Make ASW a New Game," *Proceedings*, Mar., 1980, pp. 72–75). The latest missile to be considered in an ASW mode is a medium-range air-to-surface missile similar to the Tomahawk (the Navy's cruise missile). See David Griffiths, "Proposal Set on Air-to-Surface Missile," *Aviation Week*, Dec. 29, 1980, pp. 23–25.

[38]Linton Brooks, "Pricing Ourselves Out of the Market: The Attack Submarine Program," *Naval War College Review*, Sept.-Oct., 1979, pp. 2–17. Costs of *Los Angeles*-class subs vary as much as do those of the Trident, but Norman Polmar in the June, 1982, *Proceedings* ("The U.S. Navy: Attack Submarines—Pro and Pro," pp. 121–22, and A. Van Saun's "Attack Submarine, The Hidden Persuader," ibid, pp. 100–103) puts the cost at $866 million, or $11 million higher than the figure given in our text, probably due to inflation. Once again, in his effective arguments for smaller boats, Polmar nevertheless ignores the start-up costs incurred by shifting to a different class.

[39]For contributions of Spain and Greece, see Shannon Keenan, "Spain and NATO," *Proceedings*, Apr., 1982, pp. 117–20; Don Cook, "Spain Racing to Join NATO . . ." *Los Angeles Times*, Nov. 22, 1981; "Greek Leader Advocates Stronger Anti-NATO Stand," *Aviation Week*, Nov. 30, 1981, p. 27. The multifleet problem eventually means that the Soviets must gain friendly bases in foreign countries. One particular area of interest—the Indian Ocean—has led to the recent invasion of Afghanistan and opens up the potential for a Soviet base in the Indian Ocean. See Alvin Cottrell and R. Burrell, "The Soviet Navy and the Indian Ocean," *Strategic Review*, Fall, 1974, pp. 25–35. For an analysis of Soviet moves in other areas, see Phillip Luce, "Major Soviet Aims in the Early 1980s," *Westwatch*, May, 1980, pp. 1–12; Robert Scheina, "African Navies South of the Sahara," *Proceedings*, Mar., 1982, pp. 56–59; William Dowdy, "Middle Eastern, North African and South Asian Navies," ibid., pp. 48–55; Raphael Danziger, "The Naval Race in the Persian Gulf," ibid., pp. 93–98; A. T. Culwick, "Southern Africa: A Strategic View," *Strategic Review*, Summer, 1974, pp. 30–38; Patrick Garrity, "South African Strategy: The Strategy of an International Pariah," *Naval War College Review*, Sept.-Oct., 1980, pp. 23–30; "Soviet Weapons Being

Stockpiled at Strategic Points in Africa," *Los Angeles Times*, May 31, 1977. A broader examination of the problem is presented by Paul Lendvai, "How to Combine Detente with Soviet Hegemony?" *Survey*, Autumn, 1970, pp. 75–92, and by J. B. Brown, "Detente and Soviet Policy in Eastern Europe," *Survey*, Nov. 20, 1974, pp. 46–58. Also see Donald Zapria, "Into the Breach: New Soviet Alliances in the Third World," *Foreign Affairs*, Spring, 1979, pp. 733–54 (particularly noticeable is the growing relationship with Syria), and Ulrich Weisser, "Soviet Naval Policy and Atlantic Strategy," *Rusi*, Dec., 1977, pp. 60–65. The need for available bases underscores the importance of Russia's current ports (see *Los Angeles Times*, "Odessa Fills Vital Role as Busy Port," Feb. 26, 1978) and the maintenance of its Pacific fleet (*Los Angeles Times*, "Growing Soviet Fleet Raises Pacific Alarms," Apr. 9, 1978, and "Soviet Pacific Fleet Growing," *Vancouver Sentinel*, May 31, 1978). For analysis of the strategic significance to Balkans, Adriatic, and Mediterranean security interests of NATO as they would be affected by a Soviet invasion of Yugoslavia, see *Yugoslavia After Tito: Scenarios and Implications* by Gabriel D. Ra'anan (Boulder, Colo.: Westview Pr., 1977), especially pp. 55–107, and *The End of the Tito Era: Yugoslavia's Dilemmas*, by Slobodan Stankovic (Stanford, Calif.: Hoover Institution Pr., 1981), especially pp. 34–52.

[40]Albert Romaneski, "Nordic Balance in the 1970s," *Proceedings*, Aug., 1973, pp. 33–41; Steven Canby, "Swedish Defense," *Survival*, May/June, 1981, pp. 116–23; Milan Vego, "The Royal Swedish Navy," *Proceedings*, Mar., 1982, p. 128; Anthony Hockley, "Defense in the Higher Latitudes" *Atlantic Community Quarterly*, Winter, 1981/82, pp. 449–54. Note Canby's point concerning the importance of mine warfare. Conversely, the United States must also be aware of renegade nations such as Libya, and potential terrorism at the hands of the PLO and Puerto Ricans seeking independence.

[41]Again, for information on Cuba, see n. 13. One example of another South American navy capable of upsetting any Soviet plans at sea in the South Atlantic is Brazil. See Eduardo Pesce, "The Brazilian Naval Modernization Program," *Proceedings*, Mar., 1982, pp. 145–48. After the Falklands War, however, fleet units not accompanied by aircraft carriers must be considered even more vulnerable.

[42]*Senate Hearings*, Armed Services Committee, Subcommittee on Research and Development, 95th Cong., 1st sess., Apr. 5, 1977, p. 6666, statement of Admiral Kelln; Quester, *Navies*, p. 56. MccGwire has suggested that withholding Polaris/Poseidons may be useful in denying the Soviet Union the use of western Europe as an alternative economic base for rebuilding the Socialist system (i.e., a scorched-earth policy—a rather ironic position from a man who favors renouncing the Tomahawk as a strategic system because it contributes to the arms race).

[43]Gansler, *Defense Industry*, p. 276.

[44]Wit, "Boomers," p. 69.

9. Buck Rogers Meets Captain Nemo: Technological Changes and Trident

[1]Walter Hendrickson, "The Cruise Missile Returns," *National Defense*, Sept., 1981, pp. 36–39; James Mullen, "The Cruise Missile Comes of Age," *Defense*,

Nov., 1981, pp. 1–7; Paul Johnson, "Tomahawk: The Implications of a Strategic/Tactical Mix," *Proceedings*, Apr., 1982, pp. 26–33; Alexander Vershbow, "The Cruise Missile: The End of Arms Control?" *Foreign Affairs*, Oct., 1976, pp. 133–46; Rodney Rempt, "Vertical Missile Launchers: Part I," *Proceedings*, Oct., 1977, pp. 86–89; Andrew Hull, "Potential Soviet Responses to the U.S. Submarine Threat in the 1980s," *Proceedings*, July, 1978, pp. 25–30; Deborah Meyer, "Harpoon: 'Smart,' Successful, and Amazingly Reliable," *Armed Forces Journal*, Feb., 1982, p. 55. General strategic themes of the chapter were presented in a paper to the Western Social Science Convention, Apr., 1982 ("Trident and the TRIAD: Systems Flexibility and Durability"), by the authors. Also see reports about progress on cruise missile development in *Aviation Week*, Sept., 17, 1979, pp. 68–71; June 16, 1980, pp. 119–21; Mar. 2, 1981, pp. 49–50; May 4, 1981, p. 19; Aug. 31, 1981, pp. 61–63; Feb. 22, 1982, p. 15; Mar. 1, 1982, pp. 63–64; May 17, 1982, p. 147. Also see Ned Temko, "Moscow Developing New Cruise Missiles," *Christian Science Monitor*, Apr. 13, 1982.

[2]Mullen, "Cruise Missile," p. 4.

[3]Meyer, "Harpoon," p. 55; "Science/Scope," *Aviation Week*, Aug., 1979, n.p.; "Decoding the Secret Soviet Radar Beams," *Christian Science Monitor*, Apr. 13, 1977; Bernard Nossiter, "Riddle of Soviet Radio Beams," *Manchester Guardian*, Feb. 27, 1977; "Washington Roundup," *Aviation Week*, June 28, 1982, p. 19; Herbert Coleman, "Subsonic Cruise Missile Engine Needed," ibid., pp. 201–3. In the Falklands War, the HMS *Sheffield* did not have its radar switched on during the attack, so it could not have had advance warning of the missile, nor was it protected by long-range fleet air power or by an airborne early warning system, such as Nimrod.

[4]"Submarine Cruise Missile Plan Mulled," *Aviation Week*, June 16, 1980, pp. 119–20; James Perry, "The Cruise Missile and an Old Romance Revive the Battleship," *Wall Street Journal*, Dec. 22, 1981; Howard Serig, "The Iowa Class: Needed Once Again," *Proceedings*, May, 1982, pp. 134–49; William Honan, "Return of the Battleship," pt. 1, *New York Times Magazine*, Apr. 4, 1982, pp. 27–29, 72–89; William Honan, "Return of the Battleship," pt. 2, *New York Times Magazine*, Apr. 11, 1982, pp. 24–25, 38–43, 45, 66; Robin Nelson, "The Born-Again Battlewagon," *Popular Mechanics*, June, 1982, pp. 73–75, 141–43; Joseph Antoniotti, "The BB(V)," *Proceedings*, Feb., 1982, pp. 99–100; *Cruise Missile Issue Brief*, Apr. 1, 1982, pp. 11–12; "Second-Source Contract Expected on Tomahawk," *Aviation Week*, Aug. 31, 1981, pp. 61–63; "Industry Observer," ibid., Feb. 22, 1982, p. 15; "GE Tests Supersonic Cruise Engine Design," ibid., May 31, 1982, p. 15.

[5]"Submarine Cruise Missile Plan Mulled," pp. 119–20.

[6]Johnson, "Tomahawk," pp. 26–33.

[7]See the "Comment" on Johnson's article by Joseph Bouchard, *Naval Review*, 1982, pp. 22–26. A good review of the cruise missile and its relation to SALT II appears in Robert Moffit, "The Cruise Missile and SALT II," *International Security Review*, Fall, 1979, pp. 271–93.

[8]Leonard Jacobson and Michael Bittner, "NAVSTAR GPS," *The Navigator*, Spring, 1981, pp. 24–26; Howe, *Weapons*, p. 200; David Holmes, "NAVSTAR Global Positioning System: Navigation for the Future," *Proceedings*, Apr., 1977, pp. 101–4; James Austin, "GPS: Global Positioning System, an 18-STAR Navigation Constellation," *Military Electronics and*

Countermeasures, June 1980, pp. 63–70; J. A. Strada, "Navstar Goes to Sea," *Proceedings*, July, 1979, pp. 106–8; "Navigation Satellites . . . ," *Wall Street Journal*, July 9, 1981. Of course numerous surveillance satellites play an important role in all aspects of defense. See "Ocean Surveillance System Launched," *Aviation Week*, Mar. 10, 1980, p. 18; "Industry Observer," ibid., June 28, 1976, p. 11; "Industry Observer," ibid., Aug., 1979, n.p.; "TRW to Develop $33-million USAF Space Surveillance Net," ibid., May 22, 1978, pp. 24–25. To go along with the Air Force system, the National Oceanic Satellite System (NOSS) took over work on satellites using ocean sensors ("Industry Observer," *Aviation Week*, Oct. 16, 1978, p. 13).

[9]"Rubidium Clock Failures Plague Navstar," *Aviation Week*, Oct. 8, 1979, p. 45; "Industry Observer," *Aviation Week*, May 17, 1982, p. 15.

[10]"Science/Scope," *Aviation Week*, Mar., 1979, n.p.; "Cut in Fleet SatCom Questioned," ibid., Nov. 14, 1977, p. 21; "Filter Center," ibid., Sept. 28, 1981, p. 75; "Space Reconnaissance Dwindles," ibid., Oct. 6, 1980, pp. 18–20; "KH-11 Recon Satellite . . .," ibid., Feb. 18, 1980, p. 23; "Navy Studies New Surveillance Capability," ibid., May 21, 1979, p. 59: Barry Miller, "Advances in Missile Surveillance Pushed," ibid., July 12, 1976, pp. 17–18; "Better and Better U.S. Spies in the Skies," *U.S. News & World Report*, June 1, 1981, p. 37; Howe, *Weapons*, pp. 198–207; E. M. Fitzgerald, "The Command of Space," *Rusi*, Mar., 1981, pp. 34–38. According to *Washington Post*, Aug. 23, 1978, a former CIA officer sold the Soviets the technical manual on the Big Bird, but both it and the Samos satellites continue to fly missions uninterrupted (see Cecil Jones, "Photographic Satellite Reconnaissance," *Proceedings*, June, 1980, pp. 41–51; Jay Lowndes, "Communications Satellite Users Seek Broader Role," *Aviation Week*, Mar. 9, 1981, pp. 95–98). Other space surveillance can be provided by GEODSS (Ground-based Electro-optical Deep Space Surveillance) or by high-flying spy planes to cover gaps in satellites' vision. See "5 Earth Stations Will Watch Skies with 'Smart' Eyes," *Arizona Republic*, Nov. 16, 1980; Bruce Smith, "Ground-Based Electro-Optical Deep Space Surveillance System Passes Reviews," *Aviation Week*, Aug. 27, 1979, pp. 48–53; Donald Fink, "Role of U-2 High-Altitude Surveillance," *Aviation Week*, June 16, 1980, pp. 200–211. Despite these devices, military space officials still feel that America's space surveillance may be inadequate. See "Space Surveillance Deemed Inadequate," *Aviation Week*, June 16, 1980, pp. 249–54.

[11]The controversy created by Soviet space activities and American assessments of them involves a digression, but it bears recounting here. In an article published in the 1974 issue of *Strategic Review*, General Jacob Smart initiated a flood of literature about the strategic implications of space, reporting that the Soviets had developed "maneuvering satellites . . . designed to intercept, inspect and destroy or otherwise neutralize orbiting satellites." The U.S. had not developed a comparable system ("The Strategic Implications of Space Activities," *Strategic Review*, Fall, 1974, pp. 19–24). For further evidence of the activities Smart reported, see, for example, "Another Soviet Space Intercept Test Conducted," *Aviation Week*, Apr. 26, 1976, p. 21. The first Soviet test occurred in Feb., 1976. A complete summation of space and its strategic implications appears in Thomas Karas, "Implications of Space

Technology for Strategic Nuclear Competition" (The Stanley Foundation, Muscatine, Iowa, July, 1981).

In July, 1976, Soviet physicist Leonid Rudakov presented his recent discoveries in electron-beam fusion to his American counterparts during a visit to Lawrence Livermore Laboratory. His revelations confirmed the predictions of General George Keegan, who in 1975 discovered that the Soviets had neared development of a weapon to neutralize U.S. ICBMs (Clarence Robinson, Jr., "Soviets Push for Beam Weapon," *Aviation Week*, May 2, 1977, pp. 16–23). The basic properties of the Soviet weapon consisted, theoretically at least, of a device that "focuses" and "shoots" a beam of electrons or protons at an object. As the particles are being forced through the air or space at nearly the speed of light, they virtually dissolve whatever they hit through impact and heat. The beams more or less disrupt their target. Laser beams, often referred to in connection with, or mistakenly in place of, particle beams, actually are unidirectional concentrated beams of light encompassing only a single color of the spectrum. They also travel at light speed—186,000 miles per second—and their concentration of focus can cause intense, destructive heat. The fact that Rudakov revealed considerable Russian testing of these weapons did not mean a great deal in itself: particle-beam weapons particularly suffer from a number of deficiencies. Particle-beam weapons require substantial energy to "fire," and the beam itself tends to degrade as the earth's magnetic field works on it and as the charged particles repel each other. Also, the interaction of the charged particles with the atmosphere (due to the particles ionizing the atmosphere) acts to degrade the beam. Laser beams have greater range capabilities but require great amounts of energy. Each "color" and type of laser beam may require a different light-emitting device, such as a hydrogen fluoride chemical laser or a helium-neon laser, which emits a visible red light, and a carbon dioxide laser, which emits invisible infrared light. Until recently, shifting from one color to another was impossible without changing devices. Lasers suffer from some of the weather disadvantages of the particle-beam weapons, and some question their ability to devastate a target. For information on these weapons see *Aviation Week*, which describes both the laser and the particle beam as "directed energy weapons" (July 18, 1980, pp. 32–66; Aug. 4, 1980, pp. 44–67). Also see *Aviation Week*, Jan., 26, 1981, p. 61; "G.A.O. Warns of Lag in Space Research," *New York Times*, Feb. 16, 1981. For the Soviet reaction to the space shuttle, see James Oberg, "The Space Shuttle and Soviet Propaganda," *National Review*, July 24, 1981, pp. 828–30.

[12]David Andelman, "Space Wars," *Foreign Policy*, Fall, 1981, pp. 94–106. Andelman also argues that because a laser beam hits the booster rocket and not the warhead, it renders ICBMs with MIRVs obsolete (p. 103). Some argue that hardening would be a cheap laser defense, and incorporation of other defensive techniques discussed in this chapter could similarly negate beam-weapon efforts. There is considerable MAD opposition to laser weapons on principle, as explained astutely by Walter McDougall: "Why [MAD] held sway for so long will be an interesting problem for historians. The ascendancy of liberalism was certainly a factor, since MAD permitted the U.S. to freeze nuclear delivery systems for 15 years, cut arms spending sharply . . .

and relegate military history, strategy and leadership to the category of the disreputable." Nuclear weapons, according to the MAD theology, had "changed the world": "since war was now unthinkable . . . strategy was obsolete." Indeed, this view logically presupposes that history is linear, or that we have arrived at the "end of history," or both. See McDougall's "How Not to Think About Space Lasers," *National Review*, May 13, 1983, pp. 550–56, 580–81.

[13]"Pentagón Sees Soviet Space Threat by '90," *Santa Barbara News Press*, Mar. 3, 1982; William Beane, "The High-Energy Laser: Strategic Policy Implications," *Strategic Review*, Winter, 1977, pp. 100–106.

Once again, the story has been so confused by conflicting claims that its inclusion is important. Rudakov discussed only particle-beam weapons, but his revelations, according to unnamed observers, startled the U.S. physics community because he so casually discussed the material, considered highly secret in the United States, with the result that American scientists "had to sit there with their mouths open." The reaction by U.S. scientists is a matter of disagreement. One anonymous physicist claimed the reported surprise of the U.S. scientific community simply was "not true." This physicist also suggested that Keegan is, to paraphrase, a "crackpot." Yet, perhaps because of Keegan's access to information, little public criticism of the general or rebuttal of his evidence has been forthcoming. In fact, just the opposite has happened: most supposedly informed writers accept Clarence Robinson's articles reporting Keegan's findings. Physicists who write for journals with nonscientific audiences, including Kosta Tsipis, who has authored articles appearing in *Scientific American*, have criticized the theoretical application of Keegan's conclusions but have not denied his (or Robinson's) facts. *Aviation Week*, which in its editorials blasted the Carter administration (Secretary of Defense Harold Brown in particular and the U.S. scientific community in general) for intellectual smugness, may have a case, as evidenced by a recent report that Israeli precision-guided antiarmor weapons deployed in the Lebanese invasion have worked effectively. A similar American weapon, the Sadar, still remains in the experimental stages. Thus, either Israeli technology has surpassed that of the United States in this area (a sobering thought, given that nation's limited resources) or the Israelis received basic technology from the United States in violation of treaty provisions, possibly through espionage. At any rate, if the Israelis have actually perfected the weapon, American defense officials said they would consider it a "stunning achievement" ("Israelis Used Superweapon . . . ," *Arizona Republic*, July 1, 1982).

Keegan's reputation as a loner has not endeared him to the main-line intelligence community. Keegan had disclosed his 1975 findings to William Colby, then director of the Central Intelligence Agency, and Colby in turn convened the CIA's Nuclear Intelligence Panel to consider the information. In a three-day session, Keegan's group presented its findings (Robinson, "Soviets Push for Beam Weapon," pp. 16–23).

What information had Keegan uncovered? The center of his attention, a research facility 35 miles south of Semipalatinsk in Russia, was being developed for nuclear-power generation related to particle-beam weapon work. Keegan reported that the Russians were conducting beam-weapons research: the ground testing of a small hydrogen-fluoride high-energy laser, preparations to test it aboard a spacecraft, and testing of a "new, far more powerful, fusion-pulsed magnetohydrodynamic generator." The magnetohydrodynamic generator can provide more power than electric generators (Robinson, "Soviets Push for Beam Weapon," pp. 16–19, and Howe, *Weapons*, pp. 210–16).

Although Colby mentioned the discovery to Secretary of State Henry Kissinger, no one informed either the White House or the National Security Council. Evidence mounted that Keegan was correct, but no one except Keegan had any clear idea for what the facility was being used. Theories ranged from a "ramjet test site" to a commercial nuclear reactor. Gradually, intelligence verified the Soviets had "achieved a level of success in each of seven areas of high-energy physics." The Air Force convened a special panel of its Scientific Advisory Board to study Keegan's data, but this panel of experts rejected the Keegan group's hypothesis, "denigrated all suggestions of nuclear explosion generation, power storage, power transmission and collective acceleration." Keegan then recruited physicists to try to solve some of the panel's "theoretical roadblocks." Within a few months they succeeded. Skeptics remained, and, as one official commented on the American physics community, "this is pure Buck Rogers to [them]." One of the central problems the American scientists had in accepting the Air Force conclusions was that the United States had tried and failed to develop a charged-particle-beam device earlier in a project named Seesaw. Therefore, many reasoned, if the U.S. could not produce such a device, neither could the Russians. Another explanation for the scientific reluctance to admit the existence of a weapon that would make nuclear weapons obsolete appeared in a July 28, 1980, subarticle of *Aviation Week*. According to a "senior career official," the " 'technology monopoly of weapons created in World War 2 [sic] for offensive strategy' " was upset by the arrival of a " 'new technology of lasers and particle beams.' " The new energy technology upsets the power and prestige accrued by those " 'whose background is in nuclear weapons design . . . and it poses severe problems for the nuclear warhead design community' " (p. 55). It also poses a substantial threat to the disarmament movements around the world by presenting a viable defense against nuclear weapons, making "world holocaust," to use the jargon of Ground Zero Week supporters, less imminent and making defense less "dirty" and costly than preparation for surviving a first strike.

Clarence Robinson, Jr., broke the full story behind Keegan's efforts in the May 2, 1977, issue of *Aviation Week and Space Technology*. According to Robinson, the successful Soviet experiment occurred in 1976, monitored by an American satellite over the Indian Ocean. The test was significant because Marshal P. F. Batitsky controlled it, and Batitsky's simultaneous command of PVO–Strany (the Soviet national air defense force) indicated a "near-term weapons application for these experiments." According to one official, the Soviets needed only long-range precision radars now deployed in violation of the ABM agreement to detect avenues or windows for reentry-vehicle trajectories against targets in the USSR. By aiming rapidly pulsed proton beams into these windows, "ICBMs and SLBMs could be quickly saturated and destroyed." Locating the windows 1000 to 2000 miles in space, and scattering the beam over a wide area with the window concept, gave the

USSR the potential to protect itself from a U.S. strike with only a few of these devices. Moreover, there is a more simple deployment scheme possibly in operation: some special accelerators can be placed in vertical silos—silos that currently number 150 and are defined as "command and control centers."

More evidence that the Soviets had tested the weapon appeared throughout 1977, prompting Senator William Proxmire to ask Admiral B. R. Inman, the director of the Defense Intelligence Agency, if Moscow was developing a beam for antimissile purposes, if the Russians were preparing to test a laser as a satellite killer, and if Russia could have a prototype beam weapon operational by 1980. Admiral Inman found all three propositions "doubtful." Pressed on the "laser gap," Defense Secretary Harold Brown likewise rejected the reports of a Soviet lead, saying "the evidence does not support the view that the Russians have made such a breakthrough or indeed that they are very far along in [the development of a beam]. I'm convinced that we and they can't expect to have such a weapons system in the foreseeable future" (*Aviation Week*, Mar. 20, 1978, pp. 13–16; Howe, *Weapons*, pp. 213–14). After a year, the Carter administration apparently had accepted the Soviet weapon as a serious threat—Brown found Soviet advances "somewhat troubling"—and along with these tests construction on a High-Energy Laser Systems Test Facility began in 1978 (*Aviation Week*, Mar. 20, 1978, pp. 14–16).

Criticisms about the feasibility of such weapons came from John Parmentola and Kosta Tsipis in a 1979 issue of *Scientific American*. They argued that "the performance characteristics of a [particle-beam antimissile system] would not overcome the vulnerabilities and weaknesses of earlier ABM schemes. . . . It is therefore highly questionable that such a system could function at all, let alone be operationally effective." In 1980, another study under Tsipis' direction at the Massachusetts Institute of Technology concluded that laser weapons were militarily impractical and would create "profound strategic instabilities" (something that has not concerned the Soviets). The study states, since an "ideal system cannot be built," it is not worth trying to build one (John Parmentola and Kosta Tsipis, "Particle Beam Weapons," *Scientific American*, Apr., 1979, pp. 54–65). Also see "Soviets Have Built Anti-satellite Laser, U.S. Report Says," *Arizona Republic*, May 2, 1980; "Laser Arms in Space Termed Impractical and a Potential Trigger to Nuclear War," *Wall Street Journal*, Dec. 22, 1980. Also see the *New York Times*, Feb. 10, 1980, for a reference to U.S. intelligence knowing of the Soviet laser. Garwin did tell Harry Reasoner in an interview for the television show *60 Minutes* that the $24 million in research money for particle-beam weapons is money well spent, even if it shows us that there is no promise there. Because very often, you spend money not to build something but to find out that it can't be done, that the other side can't do it either" (interview, Nov. 17, 1978, broadcast Dec. 17, 1978, full interview reprinted in "60 Minutes on Particle Beam Weapons," *Bulletin of Atomic Scientists*, Feb., 1979, pp. 50–52). Clarence Robinson, Jr., "Beam Weapons Effort to Grow," *Aviation Week*, Apr. 2, 1979, pp. 12–16. Also see David Griffiths, "Beam Weapon Impact Called Uncertain," *Aviation Week*, Apr. 30, 1979, p. 28; Robert Hotz, "Beam Policy Reversal," ibid., May 7, 1979, p. 7; and William Gregory, "Exotic Weapons Challenge," ibid., July 28, 1980, p. 7, who noted that "technology demonstrations so far have been encouraging, not discouraging." Also see *Aviation Week*, Jan. 5, 1981, p. 9; William Wright, "Charged Particle Beam Weapons: Should We? Could We?" *Proceedings*, Nov., 1979, pp. 28–35; Clarence Robinson, Jr., "Soviets Test Beam Technologies," *Aviation Week*, Nov. 13, 1978, pp. 14–20; "Soviets Developing Laser Antisatellite Weapon," *Aviation Week*, June 16, 1980, pp. 60–61; *House Hearings*, Armed Services Committee, Subcommittee on Research and Development, 96th Cong. 2d sess. Feb. 7, 1980, p. 426, statement of Arden L. Bement, Deputy Undersecretary of Defense for Research and Advanced Technology. Also see *Aviation Week*, Nov. 6 (pp. 50, 59), Oct. 30 (p. 42), Oct. 16 (p. 42), Oct. 9 (p. 42), Oct. 2 (p. 14).

Robinson's second crucial report is in "Beam Weapons Race," *Aviation Week*, Oct. 2, 1978, p. 9; *Aviation Week*, Nov. 13, 1978, p. 20. Publicly, however, the Carter administration refused to accept the prospect of the tests tying in with the development of a weapon. One source said, the "party line in the [Carter] administration is that there is no direct correlation between Soviet work on high-current acceleration and beam weapons application" ("Soviets Developing Laser Antisatellite Weapon," *Aviation Week*, June 16, 1980). The U.S. physics community had generally accepted the potential for particle-beam and laser weapons, for a group of 36 physicists, selected for their technical competence, outlined a five-year program for the development of particle-beam technology under the sponsorship of the Los Alamos National Laboratory and the Defense Department. Nevertheless, the United States remained behind in most areas, as evidenced by data provided to *Aviation Week* by intelligence agencies:

	U.S.	**USSR**	**Comment**
SPACE (neutral particle)	1990	1986–1989	Soviet previous experience in putting electron beam in space gives definite edge. Soviet lack pulse-power technology, otherwise could be sooner. U.S. in infancy on everything except pulse-power technology [the ability to generate a beam in a pulse]. Only some testing involving neutral beams is being pursued.
AIRCRAFT (proton)	1990	1983–1986	Aircraft testing will not occur until proton stability and dispersion is known, which undoubtedly will be ground tested first. Pulse-power technology will still be major problem for the Soviets.
GROUND (proton)	1986–1989	1980–1983	Soviets appear to lack only efficient accelerator technique. Possibly started on relevant accelerator techniques in 1974. Could be sooner if accelerator creates no problems. U.S. lacks everything except for steering magnets—Chair Heritage electron beam tactical weapon technology transfer keeps 1986 viable.

Source: *Aviation Week*, Nov. 13, 1978, p. 20.

[14]Burke's statement appears in *Wall Street Journal*, Feb. 11, 1981 ("Soviets Could Build Laser Weapon to Kill Satellites in 5 Years, Pentagon Aide Says"); "Pentagon Sees Soviet Space Threat . . . " *Santa Barbara News Press*, Mar. 3, 1982.

[15]Walter Mossberg, "Pentagon Aide Believes Soviets Are Ahead of U.S. in Efforts to Orbit a Laser Weapon," *Wall Street Journal*, Apr. 23, 1982; "Orbiting Lasers Ready in a Year, Official Claims," *Scottsdale Daily Progress*, Mar. 3, 1982; "Nuclear Star Wars: Yesterday's Fiction Is Today's Fact," *New York Times*, Mar. 21, 1982; Howe, *Weapons*, pp. 213–14; Robinson, "Beam Weapons Race," p. 9, and Nov. 13, 1978, p. 20; *Aviation Week*, Mar. 20, 1978, p. 13; "Laser Destroys Missile in Test," ibid., Aug. 7, 1978, pp. 14–16.

Some American scientists still discounted the Soviet advances. In 1978 Richard Garwin, who had opposed Trident submarine funding in 1975, derided the *Aviation Week* article as "irrelevant" because the problems involved in creating an ABM system using charged-particle-beam (CPB) weapons make its effectiveness "highly questionable." The "CPB threat," as Garwin calls it, is "brought to us by some of those same maverick Air Force intelligence officers" who brought the "1960 'missile gap' experience" (Richard Garwin, "Charged Particle Beam Weapons?" *Bulletin of Atomic Scientists*, Oct., 1978, pp. 24–27). "Washington Roundup," *Aviation Week*, Jan. 2, 1978. In that same issue, *Aviation Week* reported another killer-satellite test (pp. 13–23); Barry Miller, "USAF Pushes Satellite Survivability," *Aviation Week*, Mar. 28, 1977, pp. 52–54; "Washington Roundup," *Aviation Week*, Nov. 28, 1977, p. 13.

[16]Robinson, "Soviets Test Beam Technologies," pp. 14–20; *Aviation Week*, July 28, 1980, pp. 32–66, Aug. 4, 1980, pp. 44–67; *Antisatellites Issue Brief* (Washington, D.C.: Congressional Research Service, May 17, 1982), p. 2. Parmentola, "Particle-Beam Weapons," pp. 60–63; Wright, "Charged Particle Beam Weapons," pp. 30, 32–33.

[17]*Antiballistic Missiles Issue Brief* (Washington, D.C.: Congressional Research Service, May 3, 1982), p. 9. See Wright's chart on this page for a comparison of the advantages and disadvantages of each weapon for air defense suggesting charged particle beam weapons are best for antiaircraft work. Joel Wit, in "Advances in Antisubmarine Warfare" (*Scientific American*, Feb., 1981, pp. 31–41), claims that "lasers mounted on satellites might also be useful someday in an antisubmarine role" but does not give any specifics.

[18]*Antisatellites*, pp. 3–4; *Aviation Week*, Oct. 26, 1981.

[19]Howe, *Weapons*, pp. 213–214; "Defense Satcoms Stress Jam-Resistance, Flexibility," *Aviation Week*, Oct. 17, 1977, pp. 116–21; Barry Miller, "USAF Pushes Satellite Survivability," pp. 52–54; William Scott, "Radiation Hardening Found Effective," *Aviation Week*, Mar. 15, 1982, pp. 71–74; "Spacecraft Survivability Boost Sought," ibid., June 16, 1980, pp. 260–61; James Dunnigan, *How to Make War: A Comprehensive Guide to Modern Warfare* (New York: Morrow, 1982), pp. 257–65.

[20]Frances Kane, "Anti-Satellite Systems and U.S. Options," *Strategic Review*, Winter, 1982, pp. 56–64. The Navy has been in the forefront of U.S. laser work. Under a program known as Sea Lite, the Navy planned to modify a combination laser-tracking system that downed four practice missiles in 1978 and a target helicopter in 1980. Primary program goals were antiair-

craft and antimissile defense for aircraft carriers, but soon officials discussed using aircraft-mounted lasers to counter submarine-launched ballistic missiles, a role some officials believed represented the use of lasers most quickly obtainable. See Paul Nahin, "Laser BMD and Other Radiant Energy Weapons: Some Thoughts," *IEEE Transactions on Aerospace and Electronic Systems*, AES-13, Mar., 1977, pp. 96–107; Bruce Smith, "High-Energy Laser System Designed," *Aviation Week*, Sept. 24, 1979, p. 182; "ABM Promise Seen in Space-Based Lasers," *Aviation Week*, Oct. 8, 1979, p. 15; *Proceedings*, Oct., 1979, p. 140, and Dec., 1979, pp. 21–22; *Aviation Week*, Feb. 4, 1980, p. 25; *Los Angeles Times*, Mar. 16, 1980; *Arizona Republic*, Mar. 9, 1980.

Navy participation in the laser development work underscored one of the problems of high-energy weapons research and development in that it falls into no single, clean-cut category, and no single branch of the service has claim to airborne laser weapons. Development costs remain extremely high, so no branch wants the burden of developing a beam weapon—a process extending over many years—during which time beam development funds may seriously affect funding for other operating systems. Since ultimate development probably will be shared among all branches, the service arm that provides the development would receive little more than a pat on the back.

A 1981 DoD report urged an increased effort to put a U.S. space-based laser into orbit. Malcolm Currie had told the Senate Research and Development Subcommittee that technology in lasers had outstripped funds. Critics of laser systems had suggested the Soviets could easily counter such a system by hardening their ICBM casings or satellite shells. With this in mind, the defense report requested a powerful laser capable of penetrating hard casings. The proposed 25-megawatt/15-meter-diameter system, which would require 20 years to build and cost $100 billion to complete, represented the "perfect laser system." By February, scientists from Lawrence Livermore Laboratory tested a small, compact laser device powered by X-rays from a small nuclear detonation (of the type Richard Garwin said could *not* be used to power beam weapons). Clarence Robinson, Jr., "Laser Technology Demonstration Proposed," *Aviation Week*, Feb. 16, 1981, pp. 16–20; Clarence Robinson, Jr., "Advance Made on High-Energy Laser," *Aviation Week*, Feb. 23, 1981, pp. 25–27; Edgar Ulsamer, "The Long Leap Toward Space Laser Weapons," *Air Force Magazine*, Aug. 1981, pp. 58–64; "Free-Electron Laser Technology Gains," *Aviation Week*, Sept. 28, 1981, pp. 60–61; Clarence Robinson, Jr., "Beam Weapons Technology Expanding," *Aviation Week*, May 25, 1981, pp. 40–71.

In May, 1981, the National Security Council reassessed the U.S. program of space defense based on several developments. First, the Senate added $50 million to the FY1982 Defense Authorization Bill for space-based laser weapons development, and the Senate specifically directed the Air Force to establish a space-based weapons office. Then, to handle the service-jealousy dilemma, Congress paid serious attention to establishment of a new branch of the armed forces called, futuristically enough, Space Command. Third, various companies have submitted proposals for demonstrator models of laser weapons stations and manned utility cruisers to maintain such stations. The space shuttle will assist in testing a "space laser triad" that will develop three key laser technologies; precise tracking and pointing (Project Talon Gold, scheduled for 1985), high-efficiency infrared chemical laser devices (Project Alpha), and mirror and beam control optics (Project LODE). In 1983 the shuttle carried a sensor, code-named Teal Ruby, into orbit to test its detection capabilities. The Pentagon also plans to test a 12-by-13-inch hunter-killer satellite described as a "flying tomato can" ("A Space Age Arms Race," *Newsweek*, Apr. 28, 1981, p. 39). Also see "New Weapons Could Blind Spy Satellites," *New York Times*, May 18, 1980; Craig Covault, "Planners Set Long-Term Goals," *Aviation Week*, Mar. 9, 1981, pp. 75–78; *Fiscal Year 1983 Research and Development Program* Department of Defense, III, 37, 43, 50; *Fiscal Year 1983 Department of Defense Program for Research, Development, and Acquisition*, statement by Richard DeLauer to 97th Cong., 2d sess., passim; Dino Lorenzini and Charles Fox, "2001: A U.S. Space Force," *Naval War College Review*, Mar.– Apr., 1981, pp. 48–67; Howe, *Weapons*, p. 20.

[21]R. J. Starkey, Jr., "The Renaissance in Submarine Communications, Pt. I," *Military Electronics and Countermeasures*, Nov., 1980, pp. 38–47.

[22]Ibid., "Pt. II," Dec., 1980, pp. 52–57.

[23]Ibid., "Pt. III," Jan., 1981, pp. 26–39, and "Pt. IV," Feb., 1981, pp. 29–34; William Rempel, "Radio Project in the North Causing Waves of Unrest," *Los Angeles Times*, Oct. 11, 1981; "President's Intervention Saves Endangered ELF Project," *Sea Power*, May, 1981, pp. 18–19; "Pentagon to Build Scaled-Back System for ELF Sub Signals," *Wall Street Journal*, Oct. 9, 1981; "Navy Critic Changes Mind After Test of Radio System," *Santa Barbara News Press*, May 27, 1982; Robert Carlin, "Communicating with the Silent Service," *Proceedings*, December 1981, pp. 76–78; Henry Beam, "Resurrection of ELF," ibid, Apr., 1983, pp. 115–17. *Los Angeles Times*, despite the tone of its article, endorsed the ELF (October 18, 1981). The anti-ELF position appears in *The ELF Odyssey: National Security vs. Environmental Protection*, by Lowell Klessig and Victor Strite (Boulder, Colo.: Westview Pr., 1981), which fails to explain how much of an "environment" is left after a Soviet nuclear strike, preventable by ELF, among other deterrent enhancements.

[24]*Senate Hearings*, Armed Services Committee, Ad Hoc Subcommittee on Research & Development, 92d Cong., 2d sess., Mar. 9, 1972, pp. 2845–50, 2904, statement of Ferdinand Brand, Project Manager, Special Communications Project.

[25]"Laser Applications in Space Emphasized," *Aviation Week*, July 28, 1980, pp. 62–63.

[26]R. J. Starkey, Jr. "The Renaissance in Submarine Communications: Pt. V", *Military Electronics and Countermeasures*, Mar., 1981, pp. 48–54; interview with Roger A. Freedman, Theoretical Physics, University of California, Santa Barbara; Steven Thompson, "Lasercom: The Green Dragon Awakens," *Air Force Magazine*, July, 1981, pp. 49–52.

[27]Starkey, "Renaissance in Submarine Communications: Pt. V (continued)," pp. 48–54, Apr., 1981, pp. 44–69, and May, 1981, pp. 55–66; "Brown: Blue-Green Laser No Substitute for ELF," *Armed Forces Journal*, Mar., 1979, pp. 9–10. The Russians apparently have their own ELF operational. See "Brown," p. 10.

[28]*Nuclear Explosions in Space: The Threat of EMP (Electromagnetic Pulse) Issue Brief* (Washington, D.C.: Congressional Research Service, May 4, 1982); Robert

Marsh, "Electronics Trends and Challenges," *Air Force Magazine*, July, 1981, pp. 38–46; William Broad, "Nuclear Pulse (I): Awakening to the Chaos Factor," *Science*, May, 1981, pp. 1009–12; "Nuclear Pulse (II): Ensuring Delivery of the Doomsday Signal," ibid., June, 1981, pp. 1116–20.

[29]"Nuclear Pulse (III): Playing a Wild Card," ibid., June, 1981, pp. 1248–51; "Communications Systems Vulnerable to One 'Pulse Bomb,'" *Los Angeles Times*, June 21, 1981.

[30]Dunnigan, *How to Make War*, pp. 262–63; Theodore Neely, Jr., "A Soviet View of Soviet Naval Doctrine and Perceptions," *Proceedings*, Dec., 1981, pp. 120–22. Admiral Gorshkov reminds us that "today's [commander] has a new weapon in his arsenal: special computer software embodying the 'artificial collective intellect' of the Soviet naval thinkers to aid him in decision making and the control process" (p. 121).

[31]William Davis, "Ballistic Missile Defense Will Work," *National Defense*, Dec., 1981, pp. 16–22, 42; William Schneider, Jr., "Survivable ICBMs," *Strategic Review*, Fall, 1978, pp. 13–28; Clarence Robinson, Jr., "New Ballistic Missile Defense Proposed," *Aviation Week*, Mar. 8, 1982, pp. 269–71; Philip Klass, "Missile Defense Keyed to Technology," ibid., Apr. 19, 1982, pp. 79–82. For discussions of ABM proposals, see Eugene Rabinowitch and Ruth Adams, eds., *Debate the Antiballistic Missile* (Chicago: Educational Foundation for Nuclear Science, 1967). For Soviet advances, see "Soviets Developing Laser Antisatellite Weapon," *Aviation Week*, June 16, 1980, pp. 60–61. As early as 1972 interceptors, which destroyed by impact alone, were considered (*Senate Hearings*, Armed Services Committee, Ad Hoc Subcommittee on Research and Development, Mar. 22, 1972).

[32]Davis, "Ballistic Missile Defense," pp. 20–22.

[33]"Low-Cost ABM Radar Given Emphasis," *Aviation Week*, Mar. 1, 1982, pp. 74–75; Klass, "Missile Defense," pp. 79–80.

[34]OTA, *MX Missile Basing*, pp. 126–29; Howe, *Weapons*, p. 57; "Sensor Key in Missile Warning System," *Aviation Week*, Sept. 29, 1980, pp. 23–25.

[35]OTA, *MX Missile Basing*, pp. 131–39;

[36]Desmond Ball, "Can Nuclear War Be Controlled?" *Adelphi Papers* 169; OTA, *MX Missile Basing*, pp. 131–39.

[37]Richard Foster, "On Prolonged Nuclear War," *International Security Review*, Winter, 1981–82, pp. 497–518; Peter Osnos, "Kremlin Priority to Civil Defense," *Manchester Guardian*, Nov. 21, 1976; Ball, "Can Nuclear War Be Controlled?" p. 27; Edgar Ulsamer, "Civil Defense in a Nuclear War," *Air Force Magazine*, June, 1981, pp. 70–73; P. T. Yegorov, et al., *Civil Defense*, 2d ed., trans. by U.S. Air Force, Moscow, 1970, pp. 6–7, 71.

[38]Robert Scheer, "U.S. Could Survive War in Administration's View," *Los Angeles Times*, Jan. 16, 1982; "Views Diverge on Strong Civil Defense," *Aviation Week*, May 3, 1976; Ed Zuckerman, "How Would the U.S. Survive a Nuclear War?" *Esquire*, Mar., 1982, pp. 37–46. For the approach that nuclear war is unwinnable and, hence, civil defense is useless, see Robert Scheer, *With Enough Shovels: Reagan, Bush, and Nuclear War* (New York: Random, 1982), and compare with Yegorov, *Civil Defense*, passim.

[39]*Fiscal Year 1983 Arms Control Impact Statements* (Washington, D.C.: Government Printing Office, 1982), p. 39.

[40]"Soviet Spy Satellite Burns Up," *Phoenix Gazette*, Jan. 24, 1978: "Soviets

Confirm Crash of Satellite," ibid., Aug. 25, 1981; "Satellites Assist Ships in Oceanographic Research," *Arizona Republic*, October 18, 1979; "Soviet Launches in 1980 Seven Times U.S. Figure," *Aviation Week*, Jan. 26, 1981, p. 61; Jeffrey Levoritz, "Soviets Study Long-Duration Missions," ibid., Sept. 28, 1981, pp. 41–43; Cecil Jones, Jr., "Photographic Satellite Reconnaissance," *Proceedings*, June, 1980, pp. 41–51; "Cosmos No. 1,000: New Secret in Orbit," *Los Angeles Times*, Apr. 16, 1978; "Soviet Satellite Has Reactor Characteristics," *Aviation Week*, Mar. 16, 1981. Following the Canadian incident, the Soviets apparently put their nonnuclear spacecraft on ocean surveillance missions ("Soviets Change Ocean Missions," *Aviation Week*, Apr. 30, 1979, p. 33). Also see Craig Covault, "New Soviet Antisatellite Mission Boosts Backing for U.S. Tests," *Aviation Week*, Apr. 28, 1980, p. 20; "Bigger Space Stations are Soviet Goal," *New Uork Times*, Apr. 12, 1981).

[41]Soviets Continue Aggressive Space Drive," *Aviation Week*, Mar. 9, 1981, pp. 88–89. The Soviets, of course, have their own space shuttle program. See Carl Forbrich, "The Soviet Space Shuttle Program," *Air University Review*, May–June, 1980, pp. 55–62; Craig Covault, "Soviets Developing Fly-back Launcher," *Aviation Week*, Mar. 20, 1978, p. 20, and "Soviets Confirm Shuttle Vehicle Effort," *Aviation Week*, Oct. 16, 1978, p. 25.

[42]Richard Halloran, "Pentagon Plans System to Fight Soviet Satellites," *Wall Street Journal*, June 6, 1982; "Weinberger Backs Use of Outer Space . . . ," *Wall Street Journal*, July 8. 1982. For this purpose, many have called for the creation of a "U.S. Outer Space Force." See Bruce Smith, "USAF Officer Cites Need to Plan Orbital Strategy," *Aviation Week*, June 22, 1981, pp. 104–5; "AF Orders Feasibility Study of Separate Space Command," *Santa Barbara News Press*, Jan. 27, 1982; Craig Covault, "Space Defense Organization Advances," *Aviation Week*, Feb. 8, 1982, pp. 21–22. Equally exotically Pentagon thinkers have examined atmospheric alteration through space devices. This alternative was considered for affecting ground forces, but its implications for sea-based forces is tremendous. Consider, for example, a fleet of ASW vessels that suddenly find themselves pitched about by way of an unexpected violent storm!

[43]Edgar Ulsamer, "Space Shuttle Mired in Bureaucratic Feud," *Air Force Magazine*, Sept. 1980, p. 72; "Day and Night 1,100 Workers Fight Shuttle's Problems," *New York Times*, July 22, 1980; "A Space Age Arms Race," *Newsweek*, Apr. 27, 1981, p. 39; Howe, *Weapons*, p. 201. American killer satellites were tested in 1980, shot from under the wings of an F-15 ("New Weapons Could Blind Spy Satellites," *New York Times*, May 18, 1980); "Military to Shroud Future Shuttle Use," *Scottsdale Daily Progress*, Apr. 1, 1982; Bruce Smith, "Greater Defense Shuttle Role Urged," *Aviation Week*, Feb. 1, 1982, pp. 22–23; Deborah Meyer, "U.S./Soviet Space Race Spurs New Strategy, Weapons," *Armed Forces Journal*, Apr., 1982, p. 24; Edward Kokum, "Defense Moving to Exploit Space Shuttle," *Aviation Week*, May 10, 1982, pp. 40–41; Thomas O'Toole, "The 'Militarization' of the Space Agency," *Washington Post*, May 8, 1982; Tad Szulc, "Nuclear Star Wars: Yesterday's Fiction Is Today's Fact," *Los Angeles Times*, Mar. 21, 1982; *Space Policy and Funding: NASA and DoD Issue Brief* (Washington, D.C.: Congressional Research Service, June 4, 1982).

[44]Kosta Tsipis, "Laser Weapon Fairy Tales," *Christian Science Monitor*, Apr. 7, 1982. Tsipis contends five tons of fuel and one ton of consumables would be needed to "crack the skin" of an ICBM and "burn a hole in it." To attack 1000 missiles, 50,000 tons of fuel would be needed, costing $100 billion for transport expenses. In a final "it-can't-be-done" coup de grâce, he explains, "If the U.S. had four space shuttles and each made four trips a year . . . loaded just with fuel for the lasers, it would take a hundred years" to get the necessary fuel in orbit. Of course, this reasoning ignores the effects of, say, a breakthrough in fuel by which the same power could be generated with a minute fraction of current fuel requirements. Similar advances might come from improvement in the laser device or from a myriad of other sources. Other advances might be made in the area of propulsion. For example, the electromagnetic "rail gun," or "mass driver," as envisioned by Dr. Gerard O'Neill, could eventually be used, which could put objects in orbit for a dollar a pound, or fifty times less than estimates for the cost of space-shuttle use. See "Electromagnetic Guns and Launchers," *Physics Today*, Dec., 1980, pp. 19–21. Such a device would solve Tsipis' theoretical problems with laser weapons in a hurry. Moreover, an effective ICBM defense would require only the destruction of *some* enemy missiles if combined with an ABM system, and this argument avoids the important use of lasers as ASAT weapons. See *Antisatellites Issue Brief*, pp. 5–9, especially the High Frontier study, which challenges Tsipis' conclusions.

10. Hydras and Half-breeds: Trident System Alternatives, Substitutions, and Options

[1]"The U.S. Sea-Based Strategic Force: Costs of the Trident Submarine and Missile Programs and Alternatives" (Washington, D.C.: Congressional Budget Office, 1980).

[2]Ibid. Also see chap. 4, passim.

[3]"U.S. Sea-Based Force," p. xii; material on the English submarine force is found in "FBM Facts," p. 5, and in chap. 9 herein.

[4]"U.S. Sea-Based Force," p. xv. Since Electric Boat is the only manufacturer at this time capable of building a necked-down Trident and since the company is operating at near-capacity levels, the result would be to delay putting a satisfactory number of missiles to sea by as much time as it would take to build the necessary compensatory boats. If Electric Boat could build the subs at a rate of three years per sub and if the force needed two extra subs to compensate for the replaced missile capacity, it would take six years longer to put an equivalent number of missiles to sea than it would to keep the Trident program intact.

[5]"Savings Seen in Smaller A-Subs," *Washington Post*, May 16, 1979.

[6]"U.S. Sea-Based Force," p. 50.

[7]Ibid., p. 52.

[8]Ibid., pp. 32–33.

[9]Even if there appears to be a full complement of warheads on a missile, some

of them (or conceivably all of them) could be decoys equipped to draw off defensive systems.

[10]"U.S. Sea-Based Force," p. 60. For a slightly different approach, again using EMT as a significant variable, see Tritten, "Trident System," pp. 68–69. As pointed out earlier, EMT is a measurement of *in*accuracy, so it is misleading to conclude, as Tritten does from the CBO report, that to increase EMT levels to higher amounts, "Trident II-equipped *Ohio* submarines were about as expensive as other alternatives" (p. 68). Destructive force actually delivered on a target will increase with Trident II, not remain constant in terms of EMT, making an *Ohio* equipped with Trident II even *more* effective. Tritten also failed to challenge the CBO's assumption that "7 new-design Poseidon ships with 24 tubes armed with Trident I missiles would be $2 billion cheaper [than Trident II-equipped *Ohio* subs]." This assumption ignores the entire experience of Trident, start-up costs, retooling, and lost Trident construction time.

[11]Robert Smith, "Containerized Ballistic Missiles," *Proceedings*, Aug. 1981, pp. 64, 68, 71; Clarence Robinson, Jr., "Ballistic Missile Defense Emphasis Urged by Teller," *Aviation Week*, Oct. 13, 1980, pp. 18–21; Jeffrey Barlow, "Backgrounder: MX Deployment—Inadequacy of the Air and Sea Based Options," Heritage Foundation, Aug. 31, 1981. The latter publication argued that "either an extensive new shipbuilding program or major refitting of mothballed victory ships" would be necessary for Hydra. Either, of course, is time-consuming and expensive (p. 6).

[12]*MX Missile Basing*, pp. 235–54.

[13]Ibid., pp. 236, 240–44. The manpower problem, ignored throughout the OTA study, becomes especially acute with Hydra. A trained security force for each vessel, plus replacements on shore, would be a recruiting problem in and of itself. To man the 30-vessel force used in the OTA calculations would require 2310 men at least, assuming highly automated shipboard systems, or the rough equivalent of a 15-Trident-force Blue crew.

A ship as large as the Trident, which the OTA Hydra model is, would be severely susceptible to antiship weapons and terrorism. To achieve the cost reductions in the vessel itself, no armor-plating would be added, and one has only to examine the fate of the *Sheffield* when hit by an Exocet in the Falklands war to imagine what would happen to one-tenth of the U.S. sea-based strategic force if an "unaligned" terrorist decided to strike a blow for "freedom and liberation." These ships would also be more susceptible to surface storms, much like tankers. In this regard, the ships would be more exposed to storms than Tridents (with their relative invulnerability to surface storms) and even more vulnerable than other warships, which can leave station and return to a port during a storm. Hydras would not have that option. Moreover, their strength is based on a two-dimensional deceptive basing while a Trident's is three-dimensional. The Hydra's location would be secret only insofar as it can maintain its deception, but the Trident's *location* is secret.

Finally, the full fleet of 50 ships, operating at 20 knots cruising speed, covering a 20,000-mile patrol tour, would require 42 days. Since each vessel uses at least 159 tons of fuel a day at this speed, 200,340 tons of fuel would be used by the fleet per patrol period, or 1,741,050 tons per year per fleet. Compare this with the *Ohio*'s one refueling every nine years.

[14]Smith, "Containerized Ballistic Missiles," p. 68; *MX Missile Basing*, p. 254.

[15]*Senate Hearings*, Armed Services Committee, 97th Cong., 2d sess., Feb. 5, 1981, p. 908, statement of John Lehman. For information on comparative fuel economies between nuclear and oil, see *House Hearings*, Armed Services Committee, Subcommittee on Procurement and Military Nuclear Systems, 97th Cong., 1st sess., Mar. 9, 1981, statement of Hyman Rickover. Paradoxically, the Soviets may be experimenting with a Hydra-type idea. Recently, a Soviet freighter sank near Nova Scotia but the crew refused to abandon ship, leaving one to wonder what cargo could be so valuable as to require the crew to go down with the vessel ("Why Did Soviets Refuse to Abandon Freighter?" *Santa Barbara News Press*, Feb. 17, 1982).

[16]Mark Hatfield, "Alternative to MX: The SUM," *Manchester Guardian*, Oct. 7, 1979. Also see Fallows, *National Defense*, p. 166.

[17]Quester, *Navies and Arms Control*, pp. 73–77; *MX Missile Basing*, pp. 178–184; Barlow, "Backgrounder," p. 18.

[18]Quester, *Navies and Arms Control*, pp. 73–77.

[19]For depth ranges see Melville Grosvener, ed., *National Geographic Atlas of the World*, 4th ed. (Washington, D.C.: National Geographic Society, 1975), pp. 170–75.

[20]Quester, *Navies and Arms Control*, p. 77.

[21]Arthur Markel, "Comment, The U.S. Navy: Strategic Problems and Options," *Proceedings*, July, 1981, p. 125. Yet another option would have put ballistic missiles on surface ships, a prospect that contains all the disadvantages of all options previously discussed. See *Senate Hearings*, Armed Services Committee, 97th Cong., 2d sess., Feb. 5, 1981, p. 969, statement of John Lehman.

[22]Ibid.

[23]Polmar and Allen, *Rickover*, p. 566.

[24]Polmar and Allen imply that they favor a type of launch *other* than vertical (*Rickover*, p. 567).

[25]See chap. 9, passim.

[26]Thomas Etzold, *Defense of Delusion? America's Military in the 1980s* (New York: Harper, 1982), pp. 169–70; Canan, *Superwarriors*, p. 173.

[27]*MX Missile Basing*, pp. 167–214.

[28]Ibid., p. 211. Assume that one Trident vessel costs $1.2 billion and allow $0.4 billion for reactor and missiles, although no crew costs are included. This figure overstates the cost of most Tridents, since the bugs accounted for a great deal of the *Ohio*'s cost, as did Navy changes, two factors that would not apply to this model.

[29]Ibid.

[30]Ibid., pp. 217–32.

[31]Ibid., pp. 230–31. The Heritage Foundation study put the cost of the program at $75 billion (Barlow, "Backgrounder," pp. 23–24).

[32]*MX Missile Basing*, pp. 221–22, 230–31.

[33]Ibid., pp. 220–22, 230–31.

[34]Ibid., p. 221.

[35]Ibid., pp. 33–107.

[36]Ibid., pp. 111–43. The Dust concept appears on pp. 113, 126–27. Also see chap. 9.

[37]"U.S. Considers Mesas as 'Superhard' Sites for MX," *Arizona Republic*, Jan. 26, 1982; "MX Missile-Basing Methods under Study," *Santa Barbara News Press*, Apr. 13, 1982; Clarence Robinson, Jr., "USAF Presses Survivable MX Basing," *Aviation Week*, Mar. 29, 1982; Clarence Robinson, Jr., "U.S. to Press MX Deployment During START Talks," ibid., June 14, 1982; Brad Knickerbocker, "MX Missile: Why 'Dense Pack' Idea Rockets Ahead," *Christian Science Monitor*, May 20, 1981; *MX Basing Debate: The Reagan Plan and Alternatives Issue Brief* (Washington, D.C.: Congressional Research Service, May 3, 1982); Jonathan Medalia, "Assessing the Options for Preserving ICBM Survivability" (Washington, D.C.: Congressional Research Service, Sept. 28, 1981).

[38]"Dense Pack or Dunce Pack?" *Newsweek*, July 19, 1982, pp. 24–25; Barlow, "Backgrounder," p. 27; "Harder MX Silos Called More Likely to Survive Attack," *Arizona Republic*, Jan. 25, 1982.

[39]Information on the B-1 bomber appears in *Jane's All the World's Aircraft Supplement*, reprinted in *Air Force Magazine*, Feb., 1982, pp. 97–99; "Rockwell Wins B1 Bomber Work of $2.2 Billion," *Wall Street Journal*, Jan. 21, 1982. Also see "Rockwell Signs $2.2-Billion B-1 Contract," *Aviation Week*, Jan. 25, 1982, p. 19; "Rockwell Awarded $2.2-billion to Begin B-1B Production," *Armed Forces Journal*, Mar., 1982, p. 26; "In Focus," *Air Force Magazine*, Mar., 1982, pp. 22–25; "SAC General Defends Worth of B-1 Despite Price Tag," *Santa Barbara News Press*, Feb. 25, 1982; "Study Group Backs B-1 Bomber," *Arizona Republic*, Apr. 23, 1981; A. G. B. Metcalf, "The B-1: A Strategic Imperative," *Strategic Review*, Winter, 1982, pp. 9–12.

[40]*Air Force Magazine*, pp. 97–99. For advances in technology expected to be contained in the B-1B, see "Defense Contract Puts Focus on Devices to 'Hide' Aircraft," *Wall Street Journal*, Apr. 24, 1981; "Pentagon Hails Breakthrough in Jet Radar," *Phoenix Gazette*, Feb. 24, 1982. Among the B-1B's other capabilities are "radar absorptive" materials ("Pentagon Hails Breakthrough"); "very low" flying levels (one source indicated "if you were looking out the window of a high rise [apartment building], you'd be looking down at it," ibid.); terrain-following radar, allowing the aircraft to fly at 700 miles per hour at low levels in bad weather or at night (ibid.); and an extremely advanced inertial navigation system (*Aviation Week*, Feb. 8, 1982).

[41]Metcalf, "The B-1," pp. 9–12. Also see "Soviets Surpass U.S. in Aircraft Researchers," in which the editor of *Jane's All the World's Aircraft*, John Taylor, called the bomber a "sharp spearhead of the U.S. deterrence" and lauded its "greater flexibility compared with a missile force," *Arizona Republic*, Dec. 25, 1981. Furthermore, those in the Congress who have been holding out for the Stealth bomber instead of the B-1 have been engaged in a "technological filibuster," according to Senator John Glenn ("Stealth: A Technological Filibuster," *Strategic Review*, Winter, 1982, pp. 5–7). He notes that support for Stealth has come from those "not usually known for backing a strong U.S. defense posture." This strategy, used by Hitler in the last days of the Third Reich, reveals a "brief tantalizing glimpse of an ankle" while the whole Stealth remains hidden. Thus, under claims of security, supporters of

Stealth can praise a "wonder weapon" in order to avoid buying a weapon now ready for production. Even more germane to the debate, a Stealth bomber as now envisioned would have many of the disadvantages of the B-1 and almost no other advantages. Glenn maintains that it would not make a good conventional bomber, nor could it carry cruise missiles. In other words, it is being designed for a role that might not exist by the time it is ready to be deployed. Finally, in an ironic case of reverse obsolescence, the Stealth, designed to be less visible on radar using radio-frequency energy, may have to contend with the new optical radar that uses amplified light waves.

[42]Metcalf, "The B-1," pp. 9–12.

[43]*Bomber Options for Replacing the B-52s Issue Brief* (Washington, D.C.: Congressional Research Service, May 3, 1982), p. 12.

[44]Colin Gray, *The MX ICBM and National Security* (New York: Praeger, 1981). As Gray points out, the invulnerable weapon is unattainable, and constant attempts to use technological advances to make the MX invulnerable threaten to delay it permanently. One such example is Thomas Clancy's "The Floating Shell Game" (Proceedings, July, 1982, pp. 115–18). Although Clancy's arguments are well-reasoned, questions about the platform remain and the delay factor is again injected. For a more thorough discussion of the pressures on the current TRIAD, and the trends it is taking, see D. Douglas Dalgleish and Larry Schweikart, "Trident and the TRIAD: Systems Flexibility and Durability," unpublished paper presented to the Western Social Science Association's 1983 meeting.

11. A Common Interest: National Deterrents, Trident, and NATO Reform

[1]Bruce George and Karl Pieragostini, "British Defence in the 1980s: What Price Trident?" *International Security Review*, Winter, 1980–81, pp. 425–54; John Nott, "Decisions to Modernize UK's Nuclear Contribution to NATO Strengthen Deterrence," *NATO Review*, Apr., 1981, pp 1–5; Stewart Menaul, "Great Britain and NATO Theater Nuclear Forces," *Strategic Review*, Spring, 1981, pp. 61–66; Peter Nailor and Jonathan Alford, "The Future of Britain's Deterrent Force," *Adelphi Papers*, 156 (Spring, 1980); Ian Smart, "The Future of the British Nuclear Deterrent," *Survival*, Jan.-Feb., 1978, pp. 21–24; Stewart Menual, "The Future of Britain's Strategic Nuclear Force," *Strategic Review*, Spring, 1979, pp. 25–41; Martin Edmonds, "British Security Concerns in the 1980s," *International Security Review*, Summer, 1980, pp. 209–30; "Britain Is Studying New Nuclear Force," *New York Times*, Nov. 11, 1979. Also see Admiral of the Fleet Lord Hill-Norton and John Dekker, *Sea Power: A Story of Warships and Navies from Dreadnaughts to Nuclear Submarines* (London: Faber & Faber, 1982). See especially the epilogue containing Lord Hill-Norton's speech to Parliament in July, 1981; *U.S. Air and Ground Conventional Forces for NATO: Fire Power Issues* (Washington, D.C.: Congressional Budget Office, 1978).

[2]Lawrence Freedman, *Britain and Nuclear Weapons* (London: Macmillan, 1980), p. 3; George and Pieragostini, "British Defence," pp. 429–30, 437–41;

Richard Rosecrance, *Defense of the Realm: British Strategy in the Nuclear Epoch* (New York: Columbia Univ. Pr., 1968), pp. 162–68, 192, 263–79, 290–91; Other histories detailing British policy decisions up to 1981 include John Baylis, ed., *British Defense Policy in a Changing World* (London: Croom Helm, 1977); C. J. Bartlett, *The Long Retreat* (London: Macmillan, 1972); F. S. Northedge, *Descent from Power* (London: George Allen & Unwin, 1974); A. J. R. Groom, *British Thinking About Nuclear Weapons* (Lindon: Frances Pinter, 1974); Andrew Pierre, *Nuclear Politics* (London: Oxford Univ. Pr., 1972); and Richard Neustadt, *Alliance Politics* (New York: Columbia Univ. Pr., 1970). It is important to note that considerable disagreement exists over the nature and timing of the British decision to employ nuclear weapons. See, for example, Laurence Martin, *Arms and Strategy: The World Power Structure Today* (New York: David McKay, 1973), p. 35.

[3]George and Pieragostini, "British Defence," pp. 429–30, 437–41.

[4]Ibid., pp. 438–42. For more on the Chevaline program, see David Brown, "British Seeking Stronger Nuclear Force Capability," *Aviation Week*, June 16, 1980, pp. 263–64.

[5]Edmonds, "British Security Concerns," p. 218; George and Pieragostini, "British Defence," pp. 439–42; "Britain's Submarine Debate Surfaces," *Christian Science Monitor*, Jan. 21, 1982; David Fairhall, "Trident Deal on the Lines of Polaris," *Manchester Guardian*, July 27, 1980; "Britain to Replace Its Polaris Submarines with U.S.-Made Trident Missile System," July 16, 1980; David Brown, "British Affirm Decision to Buy Trident SLBMs," *Aviation Week*, July 21, 1980, pp. 23–25. The deal also included fire-control equipment.

[6]George and Pieragostini, "British Defence," pp. 442–47; David Brown, "Cuts Imperil British Force Planning," *Aviation Week*, Nov. 10, 1980, p. 57; "Britain, Revamping Defense Policy, Deals Sharp Blow to Conventional Naval Forces," *Wall Street Journal*, June 26, 1981; David Fairhall, "Government Wants Better Value for Defence Spending," *Manchester Guardian*, May 26, 1981.

[7]*Jane's Fighting Ships, 1980–8l*, p. 549.

[8]"Britain Nears Trident II Countdown," *Wall Street Journal*, Feb. 25, 1982; "The Cost of Nuclear Supremacy," *Manchester Guardian*, Dec. 13, 1981; David Brown, "Britain, U.S. to Discuss Roles in Trident Program," *Aviation Week*, Mar. 22, 1982, pp. 20–21.

[9]"Britain to Buy Dearer Trident," *Manchester Guardian*, Mar. 21, 1982; "Britain Projects Trident D5 Cost Overrun," *Aviation Week*, June 21, 1982, p. 53; David Brown, "British Stress Antisubmarine Warfare," ibid., Apr. 26, 1982, pp. 149–51.

[10]George and Piergostini, "British Defence," pp. 442–47.

[11]"Which New Deterrent—If Any?" *Manchester Guardian*, July 20, 1980; "Doubts About Cruise," ibid.; David Fairhall, "A Deterrent that Is Both Cheap and Flexible," ibid., Mar. 16, 1980; Peter Jenkins, "Wrong Choice, Wrong Time, and the Wrong Reasons," ibid., July 27, 1980; "Don't Forget the Cheap One," *The Economist*, Mar. 29, 1980; "Dumb Defence," ibid., Feb. 2, 1980. Among the misguided arguments used in support of the cruise, S. C. McFarlane's characterization of it as a "defensive" weapon (*Guardian*, July 27, 1980) is the most exotic. The Soviets have made it clear that they intend

to use their cruise missiles in an offensive mode, particularly at sea. Another fantastic suggestion proposed that "should diplomacy fail . . . we have a country that can defend itself by conventional/guerilla means" (David Karlzberg of the Survival Action Movement, ibid.). Just how many guerrillas would remain after a successful nuclear strike by the Russians is unclear. Rodney Vail (*Guardian*, Apr. 13, 1980) established the £800-million figure. Also see James Goldsborough, *Rebel Europe* (New York: Macmillan, 1982), p. 79.

[12]Brown, "Cuts Imperil British Force Planning," p. 57.

[13]David Fairhall, "Government Wants Better Value for Defence Spending," *Manchester Guardian*, Apr. 26, 1981.

[14]"Britain Denies Plans to Slash Defense Funds," *Phoenix Gazette*, May 19, 1981; "Defense Debate Stirs U.K. Worry Over Tory Plans," *Wall Street Journal*, May 21, 1981; "Britain Revamping Defense Policy, Deals Sharp Blow to Conventional Naval Forces," *Wall Street Journal*, June 26, 1981.

[15]Michael Carver, "The Case for Conventional Defence," *Manchester Guardian*, Dec. 27, 1981; Rosecrance, *Defense of the Realm*, pp. 168, 290–91; David Fairhall, "Polaris Could Pre-Empt Trident," *Manchester Guardian*, Jan. 24, 1982; Brown, "Britain, U.S. to Discuss Roles," p. 21.

[16]Walter Schwarz, "The Trouble with the French—and British," *Manchester Guardian*, Oct. 5, 1980.

[17]"British Stress ASW," *Aviation Week*, p. 149.

[18]Paul Stares, "The Future of the French Strategic Nuclear Force," *International Security Review*, Summer, 1980, pp. 231–57; Alan Sabrosky, "The Defense Policy of France," in *The Defense Policy of Nations: A Comparative Study*, ed. Douglas Murray and Paul Viotti (Baltimore: Johns Hopkins Univ. Pr., 1982), pp. 230–67; Paul Stares, "The Modernisation of the French Strategic Nuclear Force," *Rusi*, Dec., 1980, pp. 34–41; Jean Klein, "France's Military Policy for the 1980's," *International Security Review*, Winter, 1980, pp. 455–76; James Bellini, *French Defence Policy* (London: Royal United Services Institute for Defence Studies, 1974); David Yost, "The French Defence Debate," *Survival*, Jan.-Feb., 1981, pp. 19–28; Pierre Gallois, "The Future of France's Force de Disuasion," *Strategic Review*, Summer, 1979, pp. 34–41; Paul Chadwell, "Foreign Military Developments," *National Defense*, May-June, 1981, pp. 193–94; D. Bruce Marshall, "Mitterand's Defense Policies," *Strategic Review*, Fall, 1981, pp. 39–50; *Strategic Survey, 1981–82* (London: IISS, 1982), pp. 61–64.

[19]Stares, "The Future of the French Force," p. 232. For developments in the French bomber force, see Justin Galen, "The Changing Missions and Structure of the French Air Force in the 1980s," *Armed Forces Journal*, Nov., 1979, pp. 18–20, 66. For further details on the configuration of the strategic bomber force, see *Jane's Weapons Systems 1979–80*.

[20]Bassett, "French Push Strategic Missile Plan," p. 15; D. Bruce Marshall, "Mitterand's Defense Policies: The Early Signals," *Strategic Reveiw*, Fall, 1981, pp. 39–50.

[21]Stares, "Future of the French Nuclear Force," pp. 246–48.

[22]For discussions of the EDC, see Hans Schmitt, *The Path to European Union: From the Marshall Plan to the Common Market* (Baton Rouge: Louisiana State Univ. Pr., 1962), pp. 206–41; and Roy Willis, *France, Germany and the New*

Europe, 1945–63 (Stanford, Calif.; Stanford Univ. Pr., 1965). Also see Ronald C. Nairn's comment on the NATO concept in "Why NATO Doesn't Work," *Wall Street Journal*, Mar. 26, 1982. Nairn urges withdrawal from NATO, but from an anti-Atlanticist, Eurocentristic, isolationist view. Other observers, particularly in the press, have picked up the "NATO-is-dead" theme. See "U.S., Europe: Patching the Fabric of the Atlantic Alliance," *Christian Science Monitor*, Mar. 16, 1982; Irving Kristol, "Exorcising the Nuclear Nightmare," *Wall Street Journal*, Mar. 12, 1982; Hodding Carter, "A 'Great Debate' on the Atlantic Alliance," *Wall Street Journal*, Mar. 11, 1982; Robert Rudney, "France, History, and the Atlantic Alliance," *Armed Forces Journal*, June, 1981, pp. 26–33. Urging a repudiation of first use of nuclear theater weapons are McGeorge Bundy et al., "Nuclear Weapons and the Atlantic Alliance," *Foreign Affairs*, Spring, 1982, pp. 753–68. A more appropriate treatment appears in Graeme Auton, "Nuclear Deterrence and the Medium Power: A Proposal . . . ," *Orbis: A Journal of World Affairs*, Summer 1976, pp. 367–99; Michael Gelter, "Will France Reenlist?" *Manchester Guardian*, Aug. 26, 1979. For a general survey of defense burden, see *Defense Burden Sharing Issue Brief* (Washington, D.C.: Congressional Research Service, May 27, 1982).

[23]David Brown, "Britons, Argentines Weigh Falkland Islands Losses," *Aviation Week*, May 31, 1982. The controversy pitting proponents of big ships (large nuclear-powered carriers and cruise-missile-armed battleships) against proponents of small ships (a larger number of smaller ships, with aircraft carriers along the lines of British "through-deck cruisers") took on renewed intensity during the Falklands war. A running discussion in the *Wall Street Journal* summarized the major arguments of each side. See the June 2, 4, 16, and 23 issues of the *Journal*. Basically, the arguments against large ships boil down to two criticisms: (a) larger ships entail a greater capital expense, but they are as vulnerable to missile attack as smaller, less expensive ships; and (b) a greater number of cheaper ships would disperse the fleet, making it less vulnerable, with less chance of a single attack putting a substantial portion of the fleet out of action.

Surface forces are designed mostly for transport, combat, support, and ASW, yet they represent the weakest part in the ASW forces and require air protection to perform this mission. Air power is therefore indispensable to fleet unit activity.

The answer drawn by some observers (Admirals Elmo Zumwalt and Stansfield Turner) that the sinking of the *Sheffield* illustrates the stark vulnerability of surface ships to missiles is an erroneous conclusion. Badly deployed beyond flotilla protection and lacking defensive missiles, the *Sheffield*'s sinking showed only that a helpless ship can be sunk.

In contrast to the conclusions drawn by Zumwalt and Turner, the *Sheffield* episode actually rendered other lessons. For example, in the realm of passive defense of classical utility, the following measures need to be reviewed: (a) Vessels need greater beam and a correspondingly greater length to absorb the impact of missiles. (b) More compartmentalization is needed for watertight precautionary measures, (c) There is a need for greater side armor (a *New Jersey*-class battleship with 12-inch armor plate would have shrugged off the Exocet that sank the *Sheffield*). (d) Aluminum superstructures should be avoided because of the metal's low melting point and tendency to fracture. (e) Electronic wiring needs better shielding. (f) Ships need decentralized and autonomous fire-fighting units.

These points add up to larger platforms if the ships are to be more survivable. Finally, there appears to have been an overemphasis on ships with a single-mission capability, which has reduced deployment of active defensive shipboard systems. Historically, World War II testifies to this fact, as U.S. and British ships at the onset of the war were undergunned from an antiaircraft viewpoint. Thus the United States is only partly right in redressing antiaircraft deficiencies by introducing Aegis antimissile ships. Antiship-missile countermeasures can be effective. In the 1973 Yom Kippur War 54 antiship missiles fired at Israeli vessels failed to score a hit, largely due to electronic countermeasures (Abraham Rabinovich, "British Antimissile Defense Scores Low Points in Israel," *Christian Science Monitor*, May 28, 1982).

Admiral Thomas Hayward in his *Proceedings* article "Thank God for the Sitting Ducks!" (June 1982, pp. 22–25) notes that in World War II more than 70 of the 90 U.S. carriers operating were considered "small" compared to the larger fleet carriers. Only one large carrier (1/20) was lost, compared to ten (1/7) of the smaller carriers, and the large carriers usually were the primary targets. Moreover, a large carrier like the *Enterprise* (CVN-65) operates over a lifetime of 46 years, making its average amortized cost $10 million per year. In dollars per ton, the modern *Oliver Hazard Perry*-class frigates cost eighteen times more than the *Enterprise*. Also see William Hawkins' letter in *Armed Forces Journal*, June 1982.

A similar argument can be applied to attack subs, where the big-versus-small battle rages. For a view opposite Hayward's on this topic, see Polmar, "The U.S. Navy: Attack Submarines," pp. 121–22. However, one lesson seldom mentioned is that perhaps naval architects need to consider using quasi-submersible, low-profile ships for certain sea-battle conditions as picket outposts against low-level "skimming" antiship missiles. As applied to a true surface ship, see Robert Powers, "The Offensive-Passive Ship," *Proceedings*, Jan., 1982, pp. 46–49.

For discussions of the Falklands war, see "Painful Lessons for All," *U.S. News & World Report*, May 17, 1982, pp. 24–27; David Brown, "Missiles Used in Falklands Conflict," *Aviation Week*, May 10, 1982, p. 25; "Exocet Missile Sinks Ship," ibid., p. 25; "British Prove Capability of New Missile," ibid., May 17, 1982, p. 25; David Fairhall, "Task Force Spearheaded by Doublethink," *Manchester Guardian*, Apr. 11, 1982. For an expanded discussion of these points, see Damien Housman, "Lessons of Naval Warfare," *National Review*, July 23, 1982, pp. 894–96. The first book-length treatment is by the London Insight Team, *War in the Falklands: The Full Story*, 1982, especially chaps. 8, 13, 17, 18, and 20.

[24]Michael Feazel, "NATO Withdrawal Threatened," *Aviation Week*, May 10, 1982, pp. 15–18; Debbie Tennison, "Study Group Warns That Provincialism Is Major Threat to the Atlantic Alliance," *Wall Street Journal*, May 12, 1982. For Soviet activities in peace movements, see Rael Jean Issac and Erich Issac, "The Counterfeit Peacemakers: Atomic Freeze," *American Spectator*, June, 1982, pp. 8–17.

[25]William F. Buckley, Jr., "Can It Be True?" *National Review*, Aug. 7, 1981, p.

920; Justin Galen, "Theater Nuclear Weapons and the Crisis in Europe's Leadership," *Armed Forces Journal*, Nov., 1981, pp. 42–48; Alex Gliksman, "The Problem of Modernizing NATO's Theater Nuclear Force," *National Defense*, Mar., 1982, pp. 34–38; Michael Getler, "Why Pershing Alarms the Russians," *Manchester Guardian*, Apr. 4, 1982; "U.S. Ground Forces Pullout in Europe, South Korea Urged," *Arizona Republic*, June 12, 1982; Manfred Wörner, "The 'Peace Movement' and NATO: An Alternative View from Bonn," *Strategic Review*, Winter, 1982, pp. 15–26. Of course, these groups are anything but "peaceful," as noted in chap. 8, n. 21, and as shown by Robert Loewenberg, "The Violent Quakers," *Commentary*, Mar., 1982, pp. 15–18, and certainly in the United States not all student groups support the so-called peace movement. See *Dartmouth Review*, Apr. 26, 1982, for a list of Ivy League student groups opposed to a nuclear freeze.

The 1979 NATO rankings by percentage of Gross National Product expended on defense would be: United States (5.2%), Britain (4.9%), France (3.9%), Netherlands (3.4%), Germany and Belgium (3.3%), Norway (3.1%), Italy (2.4%), Denmark (2%), and Canada (1.7%); the 1980 NATO rankings by per capita expenditures would be: United States ($644), Britain ($437), Germany ($4l0), Norway ($383), Belgium ($378), France and Netherlands ($374), Denmark ($274), Canada ($177), and Luxembourg ($134). Some powers have been omitted in this ranking because of a noncomparable status (Portugal) or because the data are not easily categorized from a NATO perspective (Greece and Turkey). (Source: *The Military Balance 1980–1981* [London: International Institute for Strategic Studies, 1980], p. 96).

For opposing assessments of the strength of the NATO alliance, see Benjamin Schemmer, "We Can Count on *Our* Allies . . . ," *Armed Forces Journal*, Jan., 1982, pp. 25–28, 32–39, and "A Growing Anti-Alliance Attitude Threatens Free World Defense," ibid., Feb., 1982, pp. 66–77. Also see Jean-François Revel, "The Alliance Is Working All Too Well," *Wall Street Journal*, Feb. 3, 1982; Bernard Rogers, "The Atlantic Alliance: Prescriptions for a Difficult Decade," *Foreign Affairs*, Summer, 1982, pp. 1145–56; Robert Komer, "Maritime Strategy vs. Coalition Defense," ibid., pp. 1124–44. As discussed in chap. 8, n. 23, Western sales of technology to the Soviet block comprise a major obstacle to better U.S.–European relations. See Gerald Seib, "Reagan Move Widening Soviet Sanctions Is Generating New Friction Among Aides," *Wall Street Journal*, July 12, 1982.

12. Knots and Splices

[1]*Senate Hearings*, Armed Services Committee, 97th Cong., 2d sess., Feb. 25, 1982, pp. 29–31, statement of John Lehman; ibid., statement of Thomas Hayward, pp. 38–44.

[2]*House Hearings*, Armed Services Committee, Subcommittee on Seapower and Strategic and Critical Materials, 97th Cong., 2d sess., Mar. 11, 1982, pp. 15–17, statement of N. R. Thunman. See also Donald Pilling, "The Dwindling Muster," *Proceedings*, June, 1982, pp. 35–39.

[3]*House Hearings*, Armed Services Committee, Subcommittee on Seapower and Strategic and Critical Materials, 97th Cong., 2d sess., Mar. 11, 1982, p. 17,

statement of N. R. Thunman; Michael Tollefson, "Solving the Submarine People Problem," *Proceedings*, Dec., 1980, p. 86; Richard Petrow, "PM Dives with Our Deadliest Missile Sub," *Popular Mechanics*, Mar., 1978, pp. 94–95, 212–14, 216. One potential problem involves the manning of the IST–AKX Maritime Positioning Ships with civilians paid at double Navy pay scales ("Same Navy, Different Dress—and Very Different Pay Checks," *Armed Forces Journal*, Apr., 1980, p. 38).

[4]Petrow, "PM Dives," p. 214; Joi Atchison, "Trident: Building a Better Base," *All Hands*, May, 1978, pp. 20–29.

[5]Judy Jaicks and Benjamin Schemmer, "New Navy Dilemma: Too Few Officers to Man New Sub Buildup," *Armed Forces Journal*, Sept., 1981, pp. 41–43; Petro, "PM Dives," p. 214; Martin Moore-Ede, "Sleeping as the World Turns," *Natural History*, Oct., 1982, pp. 28–36.

[6]Nugent, "Trident Story," pp. 56; "Trident," *All Hands*, p. 28.

[7]Polmar and Allen, *Rickover*, pp. 269–93. Also see Zumwalt, *On Watch*, p. 85; Jaicks and Schemmer, "New Navy Dilemma," p. 41; Robert Pohtos, "A Crisis in Manning," *Proceedings*, Apr., 1982, pp. 110–12. Also see Barnard Collier, "The Navy Shapes Up," *Parade*, Sept. 27, 1981; Joseph Rehyansky, "Admiral Antinuke," *American Spectator*, Sept. 1982, pp. 21–24.

[8]All data in the composition of these organizational charts were generated from an original format provided the authors in June 1981 by Commander Scott Sears of the Trident Project Office, revised and updated by personnel data from "Flag and General Officers of the Naval Services," as this section appeared in the Naval Institute *Proceedings* in its annual Naval Review for the years 1976–1983. Supplementary data were obtained from *National Defense*, Jan., 1982, pp. 35–45; *Aviation Week*, June 16, 1980, pp. 93–97, 111–13; "FBM Fact Sheet," passim; *Ships and Aircraft of the U.S. Fleet*, 12th ed., pp. 6–7; and from *Aviation Week*, June 16, 1980, p. 95, for the scheme of organization in fig. 12-3 depicting the Strategic Systems Project Office.

First, in terms of its position in the Defense Department's hierarchy, the Trident System Project Office (PM-2), currently under the command of Rear Admiral Stanley G. Catola, is located under Naval Seas System Command (NAVSEA) within the Naval Material Command (NAVMAT), under the command of Admiral John G. Williams, Jr., a direct subordinate to today's Chief of Naval Operations (CNO), Admiral James O. Watkins. For all of these positions and their corresponding official occupants, as well as for all subsequent exposition, consult the organizational charts (figs. 12-2 and 12-3). Progressing upward, the CNO is in turn subordinate to the Secretary of the Navy, currently John F. Lehman, Jr., who, in turn, is one of the principal service secretaries to Secretary of Defense Caspar W. Weinberger, the cabinet-level appointee of President Reagan. Such, in simplified terms, is the chain of command so much beloved of chartists who attempt to portray complicated, overlapping, and informally exceptional patterns of influence and real command authority in organizational corrals. At this point only the locus of the Trident System Project Office has been placed in partial perspective.

Within NAVMAT, PM-2 can be seen on a plane of subordination roughly equal to the authority of Strategic Systems Project Office (SSPO) under its Director, Rear Admiral Glenwood Clark, Jr. In some ways, in terms of

Trident project management, PM-2 perhaps can also be viewed as very modestly inferior from the viewpoint of its organizational prospects of long-term survival, however. Further lines of management activity exist between PM-2 and: (1) Naval Electronics System Command (NAVELEX), under Rear Admiral George B. Schick, Jr., including Performance Measuring Equipment (PME-117) under Captain Herbert Beigel; (2) Naval Shipbuilding, Conversion and Repair (NAVSUP), under Rear Admiral A. Giordono, including NAVSUP local supervisor at Groton, under Rear Admiral Harold L. Young, Ship's Parts Control Center (SPCC) under Rear Admiral Edward M. Koker, and Code 880 (Trident Submarine Logistics Dept.) under Captain R. Mendez; (3) Naval Sea Systems Command (NAVSEA), under Vice Admiral Earl B. Fowler, Trident Submarine Ship Acquisition Project (PMS-396) Manager Captain W. E. Cantrell, Sea Echelon Area 921 (SEA 921) commanded by Captain Watterson, and Naval Underseas Warfare Station Kitsap (NTS Kitsap) providing, through its commander Captain Charles Wilbur, off-base depot and support services in the state of Washington to the Commander of (Trident) Submarine Squadron 17 (COMSUBRON 17), Captain Thomas Fox. The latter relation is a duty function provided by NAVSEA to operationally deployed Tridents at the Bangor base rather than to PM-2 in NAVMAT. Admiral Kinnaird R. McKee, the first successor to the position of recently retired Admiral Hyman Rickover, directs the process of supplying through NAVSEA the S8G reactors, turbines, shaft, and related drive equipment PM-2 needs for each Trident being built and supervises the sea-trial testing and certification of the final installation. Finally, Naval Facilities (NAVFAC) under Rear Admiral W. M. Zobel with its Officer-in-Charge of [Base] Construction [Trident], or OICC Trident, Captain W. C. Connor, engages in the construction of the second Trident squadron's future base at Kings Bay, Georgia, following the first squadron's Bangor base completion in June, 1981. Such is the Trident System Project Office apparatus and its command, management, and collaborative relationships (with one exception discussed next) as NAVMAT directs the base, vessel, and missile acquisitions processes on behalf of the CNO.

On the Trident operational deployment and command side, the lines of authority out of the CNO's office follow somewhat parallel paths at the outset, before resolving themselves essentially in a singular fashion. Overall, submarine warfare on behalf of the CNO is formulated and directed by Vice Admiral Nils R. Thunman as Deputy Chief of Naval Operations (Submarine Warfare) at OP-02. His subordinate, Rear Admiral Frank B. Kelso in OP-21, is responsible for SSBN warfare in his role as Director, Strategic Submarine Division, Office of the Deputy CNO for Submarine Warfare, in which capacity Kelso provides PM-2 with various forms of coordination and support prior to any particular Trident's actual deployment and operational direction.

Besides the command, planning, and operational input generated at the CNO level by Admirals Thunman and Kelso, the chain of command next simplifies at the point of the Commander-in-Chief, Pacific Fleet (CINPACFLT), under Admiral Robert L. J. Long, under whom Rear Admiral Frank W. Butterworth III receives his orders as Commander,

Submarine Force Pacific (COMSUBPAC), from Admiral Sylvester Talley, Commander-in-Chief of the Pacific Fleet (CINPACFLT). He, in turn, issues orders to Captain Fox, simultaneously commander of Submarine Group 9 (COMSUBGRU 9) and Trident Submarine Group 17 (COMSUBGRU 17). He, as fig. 12-2 reveals, is in charge of: (1) off crews; (2) all Tridents at sea or in base; (3) the Trident Refit Facility (TRIREFAC), under Captain M. S. Greer, Jr.; and (4) the Bangor Sub Base, through Captain J. H. Kinert, with (MARBKS) Marine Lieutenant Colonel V. Taylor responsible for installation and personnel security. The chart has been broken down to clarify the number of the Trident vessels that in all likelihood will be assigned there ultimately, with as much specific information as is available about the names and commands of at least SSBN-726 through SSBN-731.

Outside the direct chain of operational command, but located on the premises of the Bangor base (with the exception of the NTS Kitsap facility mentioned above), are three functional commands of correlative importance to Trident operations. The first is the Strategic Weapons Facility Pacific (SWFPAC), under the command of Captain Lawrence Bishop, in charge of the weapons payloads and missiles provided Tridents at the Explosive Handling Wharf. Coordinated management is provided by Rear Admiral Glenwood Clark, Jr., in NAVMAT's Strategic Systems Project Office (SSPO). The Trident Training Facility (TRITRAFAC) under Captain J. L. Sullivan represents the second command. His facility is responsible for training prospective and actual Trident crews and for retraining assigned crews in order to maintain ongoing technical proficiency and acquaint them with technical changes in torpedo warfare, communications, navigation, missile maintenance, oceanographic sensing observations, acoustic detection and warfare, and electronic warfare and counterwarfare (not to mention counter-counterwarfare). Third, the Naval Telecommunications Center (NTCC), under Lieutenant Commander W. A. Beck, working for Chief of Naval Telecommunications (CNTC) Rear Admiral Ralph Ghormley, completes the Trident-related command organization.

Another vertical line of future Trident command authority is encountered on the Atlantic side of things, so to speak, beginning with the Atlantic Commander-in-Chief, Admiral Harry D. Train II, and ending with the Kings Bay facility. Obviously, in 1983 it was not possible to elaborate a command and organizational structure comparable to the one given for the Bangor base and for COMSUBRON 17's sister squadron of Tridents. However, what is organizationally intriguing but unclear now (and prospectively as a command authority) is the position of Rear Admiral Clyde R. Bell as Commander, Fleet Ballistic Missile Submarine Forces, which presumably empowers him to command all SSBN units fleetwise. This would include at least the SSBNs of FBM Submarine Force TF-64 with the Sixth Fleet, the three SSBNs of SUBGRU 2 at Groton (apparently under repair at the Portsmouth Naval Shipyard), the seven SSBNs of SUBGRU 6 and the four SSBNs of SUBGRU 18 based at Charleston, South Carolina, and the five SSBNs of SUBGRU 16 based at Kings Bay, Georgia. Bell is also commander of SUBGRU 8, with a submarine tender stationed at Naples, Italy. Besides the complexity of the overlapping titles and responsibilities, Bell is presumably responsible for at least all Poseidon SSBNs assigned to the Atlantic,

Arctic, and Mediterranean. But the word *Forces* also suggests he is responsible, probably under Kelso and Thunman, for all SSBN forces everywhere, Atlantic or Pacific.

Finally, so far as command lines of authority are concerned, the relationships of the respective Atlantic and Pacific SSBN forces to the Joint Chiefs of Staff (JCS), the Secretary of Defense, and the President have been shown in the upper right-hand corner of Figure 12-2 so that the reader can start with the President's "red button" and trace its precipitate effects downward to the individual Trident commander's finger on the strategic fire control system aboard any SSBN-726-class vessel.

Mention must next be made of a number of bureaucratic functions that provide contributary support to Trident continuously so that the whole strategic submarine fleet can operate at optimal level. No effort will be made here to provide an exhaustive matrix of functions, since the input of some services, such as the Office of Naval Intelligence (ONI) may be crucial at certain points (for example, espionage material might show that the *Alpha* suffers from overheating after restricted bursts of maximum power in the tactical pursuit of U.S. SSBNs). However, information of this nature may be only erratically influential. The input of some other services, such as the Division of Electronic Warfare and Cryptology, may be routinely influential, so as to be taken for granted, or the input of some services, such as the Division of Undersea and Strategic Warfare Development, the Division of Oceanography ("SSBNs have to swim like whales and sound like porpoises"), or the Naval Telecommunications Command may be so prospective or esoteric as to be incomprehensible to all but career Navy bureaucrats. But, as will be noted on fig. 12-2, a number of CNO–level functions have been selected whose relevance to SSBN warfare should be more or less directly and consistently obvious, such as Naval Electronics Systems Command, Naval Space Systems, Navy Program Planning, Strategic Target Planning, and Naval Communications Division, not to mention the Director of Naval Warfare or the Antisubmarine Warfare Division, and so on. The point to be emphasized, of course, is that SSBN warfare in general (and Trident's role therein specifically) takes place within a whole matrix of contributory, correlative, and informational activities without which it would be a blind and futile endeavor. A development of the full panoply of these activities and functions as they relate to SSBN warfare would be a research project in its own right.

The issue of personnel stability and instability remains to be analyzed within the time frame of Apr., 1976, to Sept., 1982 (see fig 12-3). Since the specific months of actual service per position are not calculated, the conclusions admittedly will be rough but suggestive enough to allow drawing some broad conclusions. Analysis will commence with the Office of Naval Operations and therefore civilian-level patterns overhead, beginning with the lowest level of Assistant Secretary of the Navy, through the Secretary of the Navy, through the Assistant Secretaries of Defense, to the Defense Secretary's office itself. Some of these positions will be ignored, though they have already been determined to be quite illuminating.

There have been only three CNOs for the period chosen, beginning with Admiral James L. Holloway III in the years 1976–1978 and Admiral Thomas B. Hayward for the years 1979–1982, ending with the fresh career of Admiral J. D. Watkins, launched in the spring of 1982. The pattern for the office of the CNO, hence, appears stable enough. The next position, for Submarine Warfare, was first created in 1971 by CNO Admiral Elmo Zumwalt's appointment of Vice Admiral Philip A. Beshany as Deputy CNO for Submarine Warfare (OP-02). He was succeeded in 1972 by Vice Admiral Wilkinson. For the period of interest here four figures have served, beginning with Rear Admiral Robert L. J. Long (1976–1977), Rear Admiral Charles H. Griffiths (1978–1980), Vice Admiral John G. Williams, Jr. (1981), with Vice Admiral Nils R. Thunman inaugurating his term in 1982. Reasonable stability also seems evident in this position. Exceptional stability, despite semantic variations in titles, is evident with respect to the simultaneous occupancy of the positions of Director of the Division of Naval Reactors in the Department of Energy and Deputy Director for Nuclear Propulsion in Sea Systems Command, since Hyman Rickover had held this joint appointment not only for nearly all of the period here under discussion but, indeed, following Aug. 4, 1948, when he became Head of Nuclear Power Branch in the Bureau of Ships, and after Feb., 1949, when he became Director of Reactor Development in the Atomic Energy Commission. Therefore, perfect continuity was obtained here until Admiral Kinnaird R. McKee assumed the mantle in the spring of 1982. As has already been argued elsewhere, both by the authors and by Norman Polmar and Thomas Allen, stability has prevailed to the point of ossification. Hopefully, beginning with McKee, a modern, lighter-weight, more powerful, less voluminous, and even quieter reactor than S8G will be available for at least the second squadron of Tridents.

Three other bureaucratic structures crucial to the progress of Trident in the construction phase are next examined. For the years 1976–1978, Admiral Frederick Michaelis served as Chief of Navy Material (NAVMAT), followed by Admiral Alfred Whittle, Jr., for the period 1979–1981, with Admiral J. G. Williams, Jr., assuming the post for 1982. Allowing again, as is clear in the above cases—where a command in 1982 is probably but the first of two or three assignments—the NAVMAT record is typically stable. Rear Admiral Robert Gooding was commander of Naval Sea Systems (NAVSEA) in 1976, followed by Rear Admiral Clarence R. Bryan for the period 1977–1980, with Vice Admiral Earl B. Fowler, Jr., filling the position for 1981–1982. Finally, the position of Commander of Naval Electronics Systems Command (NAVELEX) for the period under consideration was filled by Rear Admiral Julian S. Luke in 1976, succeeded by Rear Admiral Earl B. Fowler, Jr., for the period 1977–1979, winding up for the period 1981–1982 with Rear Admiral Henry D. Arnold. Again, for these constituent elements of NAVMAT there are three figures for the seven years involved.

The concluding focus will also alternately shine on three organizational beehives more directly related to the Trident project's progress than any others, commencing with the office of Director of the Strategic Submarine Division and Trident Program Coordinator. Rear Admiral Albert L. Kelln filled the position between 1976 and 1978, followed by Rear Admiral James D. Murray, Jr., for the year 1979 and presumably for 1980 as well (the Naval Review for 1980 omits the position, probably in error), and ending with Rear

Admiral Frank B. Kelso II for the period 1981–82. Again, apparently three authorities served during the seven years surveyed. Next, for directors of the Strategic Systems Project Office in NAVMAT, a distinctive pattern is launched with the succession to Rear Admiral Ignatius J. Galantin of Rear Admiral Levering Smith on February 16, 1965, in which position Smith presided over the STRAT-X study period of 1966–1967, the ULMS phase of 1968–1972, and the Trident phase of 1972 and thereafter. Rear Admiral Robert H. Wertheim replaced him as director on Nov. 14, 1977. He served the period thereafter until replaced by Rear Admiral Glenwood Clark, Jr., for the year 1981. Clark still was serving in the position in the spring of 1982, having become Technical Director under Wertheim in 1980. Exceptional stability has characterized this office, with Smith enjoying a term of twelve and a half years, Wertheim one of at least five years, and Clark a fresher term of two years so far. Finally, as Manager of the Trident Project Office, with Rear Admiral Jeffrey C. Metzel, Jr., replacing Rear Admiral Francis L. Wadsworth in 1976, a two-year minimum term for him is followed by Rear Admiral Donald P. Hall's service in 1978–1979, the 1980–1981 term of Rear Admiral James D. Murray, Jr., with Rear Admiral Stanley G. Catola commencing his managerial career in 1982. Thus, for the history of the project, five managers are cited—four for the period under consideration. Reasonable but not exceptional stability seems evident here.

[9]James Hazlett, "Strait Shooting," *Proceedings*, June, 1982, pp. 70–73; "U.S. Firms Won't Be Harmed by Rejection of Law of Sea Treaty, Reagan Aides Say," *Wall Street Journal*, July 12, 1982. Also see Leigh Ratiner, "The Law of the Sea: A Crossroads for American Foreign Policy," *Foreign Affairs*, Summer, 1982, pp. 1006–21; Dennis Neutze, "Whose Law of the Sea?" *Proceedings*, Jan., 1983, pp. 44–48.

[10]Amos Jordan and William Taylor, Jr, *American National Security Policy and Process* (Baltimore: Johns Hopkins Univ. Pr., 1981), pp. 522–23.

[11]James George, "SALT and the Navy," *Proceedings*, June, 1979, pp. 28–37; Gerard Smith, *Doubletalk* (New York: Doubleday, 1980); Strobe Talbott, *Endgame* (New York: Harper, 1979).

[12]Boren, "U.S. Strategic Buildup," pp. 411–36.

[13]"A New Start," *Wall Street Journal*, Nov. 19, 1981. Also see David Sullivan, "Lessons Learned from SALT I and II: New Objectives for SALT III," *International Security Review*, Fall, 1981, pp. 355–86.

[14]James Phillips, "Backgrounder: Moscow's Poison War" (N.p.: Heritage Foundation, Feb. 5, 1982), pp. 1–14; "Denial," *Wall Street Journal*, Dec. 30, 1981; "Whitewashing Yellow Rain," ibid., Nov. 23, 1981; "ABC's Deadly Evidence," ibid., Dec. 18, 1981; "Yellow Rain: The U.N.'s Pitiful Farce," ibid., Dec. 30, 1981; "Yellow Rain: Gaining Speed," ibid., Mar. 11, 1982; "Flight from Grim Reality," ibid., May 14, 1982; "Dangerous Addiction," ibid., May 28, 1982. Sterling Seagrave (*Yellow Rain* [New York: M. Evans & Company, 1981]) reports that chemical-related deaths in Laos as of 1979 were "more on the order of 15,000 to 20,000" than Pentagon estimates of 1000 (p. 29). Despite this valuable insight and the astute observation that Sweden and Switzerland are the only European countries to face the threat of Soviet chemical weapons "squarely" (p. 215), Seagrave drifts into the arms-control approach as a solution. However, his note on Sweden—which

serves as the perennial voice of disarmament—is revealing: "Diplomatically, Sweden did not know that chemical warfare existed. Realistically it was preparing for chemical and biological warfare at a rate surpassing any other country on earth" (p. 200).

[15]Pipes, "Why the Soviet Union Thinks It Could Fight and Win a Nuclear War," pp. 134–153; Edward Warner III, "The Defense Policy of the Soviet Union," in *The Defense of Nations*, eds. Douglas Murray and Paul Viotti (Baltimore: Johns Hopkins Univ. Pr., 1982), pp. 81–111.

[16]Michael Novak, "A Closet Capitalist Confesses," *Wall Street Journal*, Apr. 20, 1976; Bernard and Fawn Brodie, *From Crossbow to H-Bomb* (Bloomington: Indiana Univ. Pr., 1973); Thomas Sowell, *Knowledge and Decisions* (New York: Basic Books, 1980), pp. 372, 381.

[17]For weaknesses in U.S. arms negotiations, see John Ballantine, "Arms Negotiations: Soviet Path to Power," *International Security Review*, Winter, 1981–82, pp. 519–32; Colin Gray, "SALT: Time to Quit," *Strategic Review*, Fall, 1976, pp. 14–22; Francis Hoeber, "The SALT II Treaty and the Security of the United States," *International Security Review*, Summer 1979, pp. 105–31.

[18]See, for example, John Prados, *The Soviet Estimate* (New York: Dial Pr., 1982).

[19]For examples of disarmament arguments, see Barbara Tuchman, "The Alternative to Arms Control," *New York Times Magainze*, Apr. 18, 1982, pp. 44–45, 90–98; Ron Rosenbaum, "The Subterranean World of the Bomb," *Harper's*, Mar., 1978, pp. 85–105. Tuchman's plea for a "stuffed goose" approach, whereby the United States somehow supplies (sells?) the USSR so much grain and consumer goods that it would not dare undertake war, is remarkable, especially for a historian. The Confederacy relied upon somewhat similar logic in the Civil War, reasoning that England would be so dependent upon King Cotton that the North would not dare sever the British cotton-trade link for fear of inviting intervention by the British. For the "scare-headline" approach, see Peter Newman, "Is World War III Inevitable?" *Macleans*, Feb. 15, 1982. For a review of the "nuclear holocaust" rhetoric, see Michael Kinsey, "Nuclear Holocaust in Perspective," *Harper's*, Mar., 1982, pp. 8–12.

Likewise, former Soviet Premier Brezhnev moved to gain control of Western disarmament movements ("Brezhnev Offers to Cut Missiles in West USSR," *Wall Street Journal*, Nov. 24, 1981) while Reagan tried to pin the Russians down to actual reductions in ICBMs, not just obsolete SS-4s and SS-5s ("Reagan Expected to Urge U.S. and Russia Forego Medium-Range Missiles in Europe," ibid., Nov. 18, 1982; "U.S. Welcomes Soviet Proposal for Arms Freeze," ibid., Nov. 5, 1981). The Soviets have also found an effective wedge to drive between the United States and its European allies in the "no-first-use" pledge, which entails a pledge by the Soviets not to use nuclear weapons first in Europe. Brezhnev's pledge against first use followed the article in *Foreign Affairs* (cited in chap. 11, n. 22). Four German officials, upset by the article, responded in the following issue (Karl Kaiser, Georg Leber, Alois Mertes, and Franz-Josef Schulze, "Nuclear Weapons and the Preservation of Peace," ibid., Summer, 1982, pp. 1157–70). Their response laid the "no-first-use" option bare and convincingly showed it would encourage war and destruction rather than the opposite. Schell's treatment appears in *The Fate of the Earth* (New York: Knopf, 1982). At its root, the world government concept poses a number of attacks upon religious doctrines, especially those relying on revelation, and suggests a strain of philosophical anti-Semitism. While Schell and others probably do not consider themselves anti-Semitic in the least, the very concept of world government (for whatever reason) is grounded on a relativism of nationalities, in that no one people can be "better" or "worse" than another in whatever sense. Clearly, this type of relativism rejects any concept of "chosenness," for a chosen people prefer to be obedient ultimately to laws higher than those of the world government. Furthermore, and more pertinent, the experience of divine revelation might lead them among other things to build weapons, even possibly nuclear weapons.

A marvelous moral argument against the freeze is presented in Michael Novak's "Moral Clarity in the Nuclear Age," *National Review*, April 1982 (entire issue).

[20]Malcolm Browne, "Stopping Missiles with Energy Beams," *Discover*, June 1983, pp. 28–32 (quotation on p. 31). Currently the Soviets are deploying their own laser antimissile defense aboard their *Kirov* battle cruisers ("Washington Roundup," *Aviation Week*, June 7, 1982, p. 13).

[21]"Submarine Supertanker," *Newsweek*, Nov. 30, 1981, p. 88.

[22]William Kumm, "What's Going On Down There?" *Proceedings*, Apr. 1973, pp. 37–45; "Mobile Lab for Undersea Probes?" *Christian Science Monitor*, Aug. 5, 1977; Peter Britton, "Robot Subs Trouble-Shoot in the Deep," *Popular Science*, Dec., 1981, pp. 70–72; Robert Delaney and Patrick Townsend, "Defense of the Depths," *Proceedings*, Nov., 1979, pp. 37–41; William Siuru, Jr., "Deep Submergence Rescue Vehicles," *Proceedings*, Jan., 1980, pp. 104–7; Scott Day, "Spacecraft Under the Sea," *Sea Classics*, July, 1978, pp. 28–33.

[23]Minima and maxima variations are employed as ranges in each category because different combinations of warhead loadings exist in terms of variable factors of payload, target type, RV megatonnage, desired range, and MIRV package complexity as affected by MaRVing or not. Five vessels are employed here as a multiplier unit of convenience to facilitate calculation of subcomponents of those Trident flotilla forces that will receive T-II missiles as original outfitting, beyond the first eight units officially dedicated to T-I equipment. Twelve units are assumed here as two flotillas each assigned to Bangor and Kings Bay bases, respectively, complementing the first eight boats loaded with T-I missiles. Whereas it is likely a flotilla of ten Tridents exclusively equipped with T-II eventually would be assigned to Bangor because of the T-II's greater range advantage when deployed in the Pacific, the first eight T-I Tridents probably will be assigned at the outset to Bangor and reassigned to the Atlantic on a substitute basis beginning with SSBN-736 (vessel 11) or following backfitting of SSBN-726 through SSBN-733 during their successive overhauls eight or so years following initial deployment. Regardless of the eventual pattern of base distribution, the *mixed* elements of two such ten-vessel flotillas generate the following results: (a) a minimum for twelve vessels with 2016 T-II RVs or decoys, plus (b) a minimum for eight vessels with 1152 T-I RVs or decoys, equals (c) a total for twenty vessels of 3168 *mixed* T-I and T-II RVs or decoys. As an alternative, (d) a maximum for twelve vessels with 4032 T-II RVs or decoys, plus (e) a maximum for eight vessels with 1536 T-I RVs or decoys, equals (f) a total for twenty vessels

of 5568 *mixed* T-I and T-II Rvs or decoys. These totals for two tenship flotillas assume a *homogeneous* fleet equipped exclusively with T-II missiles and assume the retirement of the nineteen vessel Poseidon fleet. Since open literature has infrequently discussed a possible twenty-seven-vessel fleet, the corresponding minimum and maximum decoy-RV ranges for it would be 4536 and 9072 units, respectively. All figures were taken from Figure 22 and from Joel Wit, "American SLBM: Counterforce Options and Strategic Implications," *Survival*, July/Aug., 1982, pp. 163–74; "Navy to Develop New Trident Warhead," *Aviation Week*, Jan. 17, 1983, p. 26; and Tritten, "Trident System," pp. 63, 66, 68–69, 71. Estimates of decoy/RV possibilities were enhanced by an informal paper prepared by George Watson for the authors. Also see Robert Kuenne, *The Polaris Missile Strike* (Columbus: Ohio State Univ. Pr., 1966), for a similar treatment of the subject as applied to the Polaris submarine.

13. Conclusion

[1]*House Hearings*, Armed Services Committee, Subcommittee on Procurement and Military Nuclear Systems, 97th Cong., 1st sess., Mar. 9, 1981, p. 16, statement of Admiral Hyman Rickover.

[2]"Enlargement of Trident Programs Reportedly Is on Drawing Board," *Arizona Republic*, February 6, 1983.

[3]Polmar, *Ships of U.S. Fleet*, p. 103.

[4]Art, *TFX Decision*, p. 86; "Trident System Fact Sheet" (N.p.: U.S. Navy, June, 1982), p. 67; "Projected Cost Overruns for Defense," *Chicago Tribune*, reprinted in *The State* (Columbia, S.C.), July 31, 1982.

[5]Alfred D. Chandler, *The Visible Hand: The Managerial Revolution in American Business* (Cambridge, Mass.: Belknap Pr., 1977). Some of Chandler's students and supporters have nevertheless argued that defense spending overall has been one of the leading causes of economic instability in the United States. Yet Chandler seems to draw just the opposite conclusion: "Only during and after the Second World War did the government become a major market for industrial goods. . . . That market has been substantial, but it has been concentrated in a small number of industries" (p. 495). Businessmen and professional managers "*supported the efforts* . . . to provide *stability* through fiscal policies involving the building of highways and *shifting defense contracts*" (p. 497 [italics added]).

[6]Boren, "U.S. Strategic Buildup," pp. 432–33.

[7]Newell, "Breakdown," pp. 25, 27; "Navy Denounced in $2.73 Billion 'Sweetheart Deal,'" *Arizona Republic*, Feb. 25, 1983.

[8]D. M. O. Miller, et al., *The Balance of Military Power* (New York: St. Martin's Pr., 1981), p. 16.

[9]Theodore Roscoe and Fred Freeman, *Picture History of the U.S. Navy* (New York; Bonanza Books, 1956), p. 125 (fig. 257); Russell Weigly, *The American Way of War: A History of United States Military Strategy and Policy* (New York; Macmillan, 1973), pp. 42–45; Bradford Perkins, *Prologue to War, 1805–1812* (Berkeley: Univ. of California Pr., 1968), p. 51.

Selected Bibliography

Much information for this work was obtained through personal interviews. Many, but not all, of those named in the acknowledgments granted us interviews, for which we are grateful. Although we used many newspaper sources, those have been cited in the notes and will not be reproduced here. Finally, our use of U.S. Senate and House hearings has been extensive and is reflected in the notes. Those hearings, on a variety of subjects related specifically to the Trident and to the defense in general, dated from 1970 to 1982. In many cases, we have used the original hearing testimony supplied by the Navy or Electric Boat Company, and those have been numbered according to the original pagination. Therefore the reproductions in the published versions of the House and Senate hearings will not correspond by page to our citations. Likewise, we have made use of several unpublished documents furnished by the U.S. government, the Navy, Electric Boat Company, the General Accounting Office, or other sources, including individuals. What follows, then, is a selected list of some of the more important sources used. For all other sources, consult the notes.

Government Publications—Issue Briefs

Antiballistic Missiles Issue Brief. Washington; D.C.: Congressional Research Service, May 3, 1982. Issue Brief IB81003.

Anti-satellites (Killer Satellites) Issue Brief. Washington, D.C.: Congressional Research Service, May 17, 1982. Issue Brief IB81123.

Bomber Options for Replacing the B-52s Issue Brief, Washington, D.C.: Congressional Research Service, May 3, 1982. Issue Brief IB81107.

Cruise Missile Issue Brief. Washington, D.C.: Congressional Research Service, April 1, 1982. Issue Brief IB81080.

Defense Budget—FY82 Issue Brief. Washington, D.C.: Congressional Research Service, 1982. Issue Brief IB81002.

Defense Budget—FY83 Issue Brief. Washington, D.C.: Congressional Research Service, 1983. Issue Brief IB82030.

Defense Burden Sharing Issue Brief: U.S. Relations with NATO Allies and Japan. Washington, D.C.: Congressional Research Service, May 29, 1982. Issue Brief IB81067.

MX Basing Debate: The Reagan Plan and Alternatives Issue Brief. Washington, D.C.: Congressional Research Service, May 3, 1982. Issue Brief IB81165.
MX Intercontinental Ballistic Missile Program Issue Brief. Washington, D.C.: Congressional Research Service, Sept. 15, 1982. Issue Brief IB77080.
Nuclear Explosions in Space: The Threat of EMP (Electromagnetic Pulse) Mini Brief. Washington, D.C.: Congressional Research Service, May 4, 1982. Issue Brief MB82221.
Space Policy and Funding: NASA and DoD Issue Brief. Washington, D.C. Congressional Research Service, June 4, 1982. Issue Brief IB78093.
Space Shuttle Issue Brief. Washington, D.C.: Congressional Research Service, June 4, 1982. Issue Brief IB81175.
Trident System Issue Brief. Washington, D.C.: Congressional Research Service, 1982. Issue Brief IB73001.
U.S. Defense. Industrial Preparedness: Issue for the 97th Congress. Washington, D.C.: Congressional Research Service, June 8, 1982. Issue Brief IB81109.
U.S. Strategic Nuclear Force Options Issue Brief. Washington, D.C.: Congressional Research Service, May 27, 1981. Issue Brief IB72046.

Navy Publications

Chief of Naval Operations Report, Fiscal 1981. Department of the Navy, n.d.
"FBM Facts." Washington, D.C.: Strategic Systems Project Office, 1978.
"Polaris Chronology: History of the Fleet Ballistic Missile Weapon System Development Program." United States Navy, July, 1966.
"Polaris: Fleet Ballistic Missile Weapon System Fact Sheet." United States Navy, June 1, 1966.
"Trident Fact Sheet Weekly Report." Washington, D.C.: Congressional Quarterly, 1973.
The Trident System. Washington: Navy Department, Trident System Project Office, 1977.
"Trident System Fact Sheet." United States Navy, June, 1982.

Department of Defense Publications

Department of Defense. *Annual Report and Defense Progress, 1970–1974.* Washington, D.C.: Government Printing Office.
Department of Defense. *Annual Report, Fiscal Year 1976–1977.* Washington, D.C.: Government Printing Office.
Department of Defense. *Annual Reports, Fiscal Years 1968–1982.* Washington, D.C.: Government Printing Office.
Fiscal Year 1983 Department of Defense Program for Research, Development, and Acquisition. Statement by Richard DeLauer to 97th Cong., 2d sess.
Fiscal Year 1983 Research and Development Program. Department of Defense, pt. 3.

Other Government Publications

Congressional Quarterly. Washington, D.C.: Government Printing Office, 1968–1982.
Fiscal Year 1982 Arms Control Impact Statements. Washington, D.C.: Government Printing Office, 1981.
Fiscal Year 1983 Arms Control Impact Statements. Washington, D.C.: Government Printing Office, 1982.
Office of Technology Assessment. *MX Missile Basing*. Washington, D.C.: Government Printing Office, 1981.
"The U.S. Sea-Based Strategic Force: Costs of the Trident Submarine and Missile Programs and Alternatives." Washington, D.C.: Congressional Budget Office, 1980.

Electric Boat Company Pamphlets

"Launching Ceremony for U.S.S. Georgia," n.d.
"Nuclear Submarines," n.d.
"Quonset Point Facility," n.d.

Books

Art, Robert. *The TFX Decision: McNamara and the Military*. Boston: Little, 1968.
Baar, James, and Howard, William. *Polaris!* New York: Harcourt, 1960.
Baker, David. *The Shape of Wars to Come*. Briarcliff Manor, N.Y.: Stein & Day, 1982.
Barlett, C. J. *The Long Retreat*. London: Macmillan, 1972.
Baylis, John, ed. *British Defense Policy in a Changing World*. London: Croom Helm, 1977.
Bellini, James. *French Defence Policy*. London: Royal United Services Institute for Defense Studies, 1974.
Bidwell, Shelford, ed. *Word War 3*. Englewood Cliffs, N.J.: Prentice-Hall, 1978.
Breyer, Siegfried, and Polmar, Norman. *Guide to the Soviet Navy*. 2d ed. Annapolis: Naval Institute Pr., 1977.
Burns, Thomas. *The Secret War for the Ocean Depths: Soviet-American Rivalry for Mastery of the Seas*. New York: Rawson Associates, 1978.
Canan, James. *The Superwarriors: The Fantastic World of Pentagon Superweapons*. New York: Weybright and Talley, 1975.
Canan, James. *War in Space*. New York: Harper, 1982.
Chandler, Alfred D. *The Visible Hand: The Managerial Revolution in American Business*. Cambridge, Mass.: Belknap Pr., 1977.
Couhat, Jean Labayle, ed. *Combat Fleets of the World, 1980/81: Their Ships, Aircraft and Armament*. Translated by A. D. Baker III. Annapolis: Naval Institute Pr., 1980.
Coulam, Robert. *Illusions of Choice: The F-111 and the Problems of Weapons Acquistion Reform*. Princeton, N.J.: Princeton Univ. Pr., 1977.

DiCerto, J. J. *Missile Base Beneath the Sea: The Story of Polaris*. New York: St. Martin's, 1967.

Dörfer, Ingemar. *System 37 Viggen: Arms Technology and the Domestication of Glory*. Oslo: Universitetsforlaget, 1973.

Douglas, Joseph, and Hoeber, Amoretta. *Soviet Strategy for Nuclear War*. Stanford, Calif.; Hoover Institution Pr., 1979.

Dunigan, James. *How to Make War: Comprehensive Guide to Modern Warfare*. New York: William Morrow, 1982.

Edwards, John. *Superweapon: The Making of MX*. New York: Norton, 1982.

Etzold, Thomas. *Defense or Delusion? America's Military in the 1980s*. New York: Harper, 1982.

Fairhall, David, *Russian Sea Power*. Boston: Gambit, 1971.

Fallows, James. *National Defense*. New York: Random, 1981.

Fessler, E. Anthony. *Directed-Energy Weapons: A Juridical Analysis*. New York: Praeger, 1979.

Freedman, Lawrence. *Britain and Nuclear Weapons*. London: Macmillan, 1980.

Gansler, Jaques. *The Defense Industry*. Cambridge, Mass.: MIT Pr., 1980.

Gilder, George, *Wealth and Poverty*. New York: Basic Books, 1981.

Glasstone, Samuel, and Dolan, Phillip, comps. *The Effects of Nuclear Weapons*, 3d ed. Washington, D.C.: Department of Defense and Department of Energy, 1977.

Goldsborough, James. *Rebel Europe*. New York: Macmillan, 1982.

Gorskov, Sergei. *Red Star Rising at Sea*. Translated by Theodore Neely, Jr., and edited by Herbert Preston. Annapolis: Naval Institute Pr., 1974.

Gorskov, Sergei. *The Sea Power of the State*. Annapolis: Naval Institute Pr., 1979.

Gray, Colin. *The MX ICBM and National Security*. New York: Praeger, 1981.

Greenwood, Ted. *Making the MIRV: A Study of Defense Decision Making*. Cambridge, Mass.: Ballinger, 1975.

Groom, A. J. R. *British Thinking About Nuclear Weapons*. London; Frances Pinter, 1974.

Harkavy, Robert, and Kolodzeij, Edward. *American Security Policy and Policy-Making*, Lexington, Mass.: Lexington Books, 1980.

Hartman, Gregory. *Weapons that Wait*. Annapolis: Naval Institute Pr., 1979.

Hewlitt, Richard, and Duncan, Francis. *Nuclear Navy*. Chicago: Univ. of Chicago Pr. 1974.

Hill-Norton, Lord, and Dekker, John. *Sea Power: A Story of Warships and Navies from Dreadnaughts to Nuclear Submarines*. London: Faber & Faber, 1982.

Hoeber, Frances, et al., eds. *Arms, Men and Military Budgets*. New Brunswick, N.J.: Transaction Books, 1980.

Howe, Russell Warren. *Weapons: The International Game of Arms, Money and Diplomacy*. Garden City, N.Y.: Doubleday, 1980.

Humble, Richard. *Undersea Warfare*. Birmingham, England: Basing Hall, 1981.

Jordan, Amos, and Taylor, William, Jr. *American National Security Policy and Process*. Baltimore: Johns Hopkins Univ. Pr., 1981.

Kaufman, Robert. *The War Profiteers*. New York: Bobbs-Merrill, 1970.

Klessig, Lowell, and Strite, Victor. *The ELF Odyssey: National Security vs. Environmental Protection*. Boulder, Colo.; Westview Pr., 1981.

Kuenne, Robert. *The Polaris Missile Strike*. Columbus: Ohio State Univ. Pr., 1966.
Langford, David. *War in 2080: The Future of Military Technology*. New York: Morrow, 1979.
Luns, J. M. A. H. *The Balance of Military Power*. New York: St. Martin's, 1981.
Martin, David. *Wilderness of Mirrors*. New York: Harper, 1980.
Martin, Laurence. *Arms and Strategy: The World Power Structure Today*. New York: David McKay, 1973.
MccGwire, Michael, ed. *Soviet Naval Developments: Capability and Context*. New York: Praeger, 1973.
Miller, D. M. O. *The Balance of Military Power*. New York: St. Martin's, 1981.
Moore, John E. *The Soviet Navy Today* . Briarcliff Manor, N.Y.: Stein & Day, 1976.
Moore, John E. *Warships of the Soviet Navy*. London: James, 1981.
Morris, Eric. *The Russian Navy: Myth and Reality*. Briarcliff Manor, N.Y.: Stein & Day, 1977.
Murray, Douglas, and Viotti, Paul, eds. *The Defense Policy of Nations: A Comparative Study*. Baltimore: Johns Hopkins Univ. Pr., 1982.
Neustadt, Richard. *Alliance Politics*, New York: Columbia Univ. Pr., 1970.
Nitze, Paul; Sullivan, Leonard, Jr.; and the Atlantic Council Working Group on Securing the Seas. *Securing the Seas: The Soviet Naval Challenge and Western Alliance Options*. Boulder, Colo.: Westview Pr., 1979.
Northedge, F. A. *Descent from Power*. London: George Allen & Unwin, 1974.
Pierre, Andrew. *Nuclear Politics*. London: Oxford Univ. Pr., 1972.
Polmar, Norman, ed. *Ships and Aircraft of the U.S. Fleet*, 12th ed. Annapolis: Naval Institute Pr., 1981.
Polmar, Norman, ed. *Soviet Naval Developments*. Annapolis: Nautical and Aviation Publishing Company of America, 1979.
Polmar, Norman, ed. *Soviet Naval Power: Challenge for the 1970s*, rev. ed. New York: Crane, Russak & Co., 1974.
Polmar, Norman, and Allen, Thomas. *Rickover: Controversy and Genius*. New York: Simon & Schuster, 1982.
Prados. John. *The Soviet Estimate*. New York: Dial Pr., 1982.
Quester, George, ed. *Navies and Arms Control*. New York: Praeger, 1980.
Quester, George, ed. *Sea Power in the 1970s*. New York: Dunellen, 1975.
Rabinowitch, Eugene, and Adams, Ruth, eds. *Debate the Antiballistic Missile*. Chicago: Educational Foundation for Nuclear Science, 1967.
Ritchie, David. *Space War*. New York: Atheneum, 1982.
Rosecrance, Richard. *Defense of the Realm: British Strategy in the Nuclear Epoch*. New York: Columbia Univ. Pr., 1968.
Sapolsky, Harvey M. *The Polaris System Development: Bureaucratic and Programmatic Success in Government*. Cambridge, Mass.: Harvard Univ. Pr., 1972.
Schmitt, Hans. *The Path to European Union: From the Marshall Plan to the Common Market*. Baton Rouge: Louisiana State Univ. Pr., 1962.
Schneider, William, and Hoeber, Frances, eds. *Arms, Men and Military Budgets*. New York: Crane, Russak & Co., 1976.
Smith, Gerard. *Doubletalk*. Garden City, N.Y.: Doubleday, 1980.
Sowell, Thomas. *Knowledge and Decisions*. New York: Basic Books, 1980.

Stine, G. Harry. *Confrontation in Space*. Englewood Cliffs, N.J.: Prentice-Hall, 1981.

Strategic Survey, 1981–82. London: International Institute for Strategic Studies, 1982.

Strauss, Leo. *Natural Right and History*. Chicago: Univ. of Chicago Pr., 1973.

Talbott, Strobe. *Endgame*. New York: Harper, 1979.

Thompson, W. Scott, ed. *National Security in the 1980s: From Weakness to Strength*. San Francisco; The Institute for Contemporary Studies, 1980.

U.S.–U.S.S.R. Relations and Strategic Balance. Washington, D.C.: Government Printing Office, 1976.

Willis, Roy. *France, Germany and the New Europe, 1945–63*. Stanford, Calif.; Stanford Univ. Pr., 1965.

Woodward, David. *The Russians at Sea: A History of the Russian Navy*. New York: Praeger, 1965.

Yegorov, P. T., and Shlyakov, I. A.. *Civil Defense Handbook*, 2d ed. Translated by U.S. Air Force. Moscow, 1970.

Zheltove, A. *Methodological Problems of Military Theory and Practice*. Translated by U.S. Air Force, Foreign Technology Division, Wright-Patterson Air Force Base. Dayton, Ohio: U.S. Air Force, Dec. 18, 1971.

Zumwalt, Elmo. *On Watch*. New York: Quadrangle, 1976.

Articles

"ABM Promise Seen in Space-Based Lasers." *Aviation Week and Space Technology*, Oct. 8, 1979, p. 15.

Adler, Ronald. "In the Navy's Future: The Small, Fast Surface Ship." *U.S. Naval Institute Proceedings*, Mar., 1978, pp. 102–11.

"Advanced Sensors Major AntiSubmarine Warfare Goal." *Aviation Week and Space Technology*, Jan. 31, 1977, pp. 134–45.

Altunin, A. "The Main Direction." *Strategic Review*, Summer, 1974, pp. 91–96.

"America's Gap in Strategic Minerals." *U.S. News & World Report*, Feb. 8, 1982, p. 59.

Andleman, David. "Space Wars." *Foreign Policy*, Fall, 1981, pp. 94–106.

Andrews, Frank. "Torpedoes: Our Wonder Weapon (We Wonder If They'll Work)." *U.S. Naval Institute Proceedings*, Mar., 1979, pp. 94–97.

"Another Soviet Space Intercept Test Conducted." *Aviation Week and Space Technology*, Apr. 26, 1976, p. 21.

Antoniotti, Joseph. "The BB(V)." *U.S. Naval Institute Proceedings*, Feb., 1982, pp. 99–100.

Aspin, Les. "What Are the Russians Up To?" *International Security Review*, Summer, 1978, pp. 30–54.

Atchison, Joi. "Trident: Building a Better Base." *All Hands*, May, 1978, pp. 20–29.

Austin, James. "GPS: Global Positioning Systems, an 18–STAR Navigation Constellation." *Military Electronics and Countermeasures*, June, 1980, pp. 63–70.

Auton, Graeme. "Nuclear Deterrence and the Medium Power: A Proposal. . . ." *Orbis: A Journal of World Affairs*, Summer, 1976, pp. 367–399.

Ball, Desmond. "Can Nuclear War Be Controlled?" *Adelphi Papers* 169.
Barlow, Jeffrey. "Backgrounder: MX Deployment—Inadequacy of the Air and Sea Based Options." *Heritage Foundation Report*, Aug. 31, 1981.
Barrett, Frank. "A New Strategy for the West." *Optima*, vol. 30, no. 2.
Bauer, Jack. "What Are You Up to Sergei?" *U.S. Naval Institute Proceedings*, Dec., 1974, pp. 34–37.
Beane, William. "The High-Energy Laser: Strategic Policy Implications." *Strategic Review*, Winter, 1977, pp. 100–106.
Beloff, Max. "The Peacetime Strategy of the Soviet Union." *Strategic Review*, Summer, 1973, pp. 61–69.
Blades, Todd. "Needed: Heavy Firepower." *U.S. Naval Institute Proceedings*, July, 1979, pp. 51–54.
Blechman, Barry. "The Future of the Navy." *U.S. Naval Institute Proceedings*, Jan., 1977, pp. 28–34.
Bonsignore, Enzio. "SS-N-14: Another Look." *U.S. Naval Institute Proceedings*, Aug., 1979, pp. 102–6.
Boren, David. "U.S. Strategic Buildup Can Deter Soviet Supremacy." *International Secutiry Review*, Winter, 1981–82, pp. 411–36.
Bouchard, Joseph. "Comment." *U.S. Naval Institute Proceedings*, May, 1982, pp. 22–26.
Bowman, Richard. "NATO Command and Control." *Armed Forces Journal*, Feb., 1982, pp. 58–65.
Boyle, Richard. "1960: A Vintage Year for Submarines." *U.S. Naval Institute Proceedings*, Oct., 1970, pp. 36–41.
Bramlett, W. "ASW: Some Surface Views." *U.S. Naval Institute Proceedings*, Apr., 1976, pp. 99–101.
"Britain Projects Trident D5 Cost Overrun." *Aviation Week and Space Technology*, June 21, 1982, p. 53.
Broad, William. "Nuclear Pulse (I): Awakening to the Chaos Factor." *Science*, May, 1981, pp. 1009–12.
———. "Nuclear Pulse (II): Ensuring Delivery of the Doomsday Signal." *Science*, June, 1981, pp. 1116–20.
———. "Nuclear Pulse (III): Playing a Wild Card." *Science*, June, 1981, pp. 1248–51.
Brooks, Linton. "Pricing Ourselves Out of the Market: The Attack Submarine Program." *Naval War College Review*, Sept. Oct., 1979, pp. 2–17.
———. "Tactical Nuclear Weapons: The Forgotten Facet of Naval Warfare." *U.S. Naval Institute Proceedings*, Jan., 1980, pp. 28–33.
Brown, David. "Britain, U.S. to Discuss Roles in Trident Program." *Aviation Week and Space Technology*, Mar. 22, 1982, pp. 20–21.
———. "British Affirm Decision to Buy Trident SLBMs." *Aviation Week and Space Technology*, July 21, 1980, pp. 23–25.
———. "British Seeking Stronger Nuclear Force Capability." *Aviation Week and Space Technology*, June 16, 1980, pp. 263–64.
———. "Britons, Argentines Weigh Falkland Islands Losses." *Aviation Week and Space Technology*, May 31, 1982.
———. "Cuts Imperil British Force Planning." *Aviation Week and Space Technology*, Nov. 10, 1980, p. 57.

Brown, J. B. "Detente and Soviet Policy in Eastern Europe." *Survey*, Nov. 20, 1974, pp. 46–58.

Brownlow, Cecil. "Soviet Strategic Lead Seen by 1980s." *Aviation Week and Space Technology*, Feb. 14, 1977, pp. 18–19.

Buckley, Franklin. "MATASS: A Moored Airship Towed Array Sonar System." *U.S. Naval Institute Proceedings*, Mar., 1980, pp. 124–27.

Bundy, MGeorge; Kennan, George; McNamara, Robert; and Smith, Gerard. "Nuclear Weapons and the Atlantic Alliance." *Foreign Affairs*, Spring, 1982, pp. 753–68.

Burke, Gerard. "The Need for Trident." *U.S. Naval Institute Proceedings*, Nov., 1978, pp. 32–41.

———. "The Trident Missile: America's Future Deterrent." *U.S. Naval Institute Proceedings*, Mar., 1980, pp. 131–34.

Bussert, Jim. "Soviet Naval Electronic Technology," *U.S. Naval Institute Proceedings*, Feb., 1978, pp. 105–8.

Byron, John. "The Victim's View of ASW." *U.S. Naval Institute Proceedings*, Apr., 1982, pp. 39–43.

Canan, James. "Lending a Hand to the Pentagon." *Electronics*, June 12, 1967, pp. 155–58.

Carlin, Robert. "Communicating with the Silent Service." *U.S. Naval Institute Proceedings*, Dec., 1981, pp. 76–78.

Chadwell, Paul. "Foreign Military Developments." *National Defense*, May-June, 1981, pp. 193–94.

Charbonneau, Gary. "The Soviet Navy and Forward Deployment." *U.S. Naval Institute Proceedings*, Mar., 1979, pp. 35–40.

Clancy, Thomas. "The Floating Shell Game." *U.S. Naval Institute Proceedings*, July, 1982, pp. 115–18.

Coleman, Herbert. "Soviets Push Huge Arms Buildup." *Aviation Week and Space Technology*, Apr. 12, 1976, pp. 12–15.

"Comment." *U.S. Naval Institute Proceedings*, Mar., 1977, pp. 80-81; June, 1977, p. 82; Oct., 1977, p. 68; Dec., 1977, p. 81; Oct., 1978, pp. 23–24; Oct., 1979, pp. 97–98; Feb., 1980, pp. 74–75; Apr., 1980, pp. 21–22; June, 1980, p. 85.

"Congressional Unit Criticizes Report." *Aviation Week and Space Technology*, July 12, 1982, p. 62.

Covault, Craig. "New Soviet Antisatellite Mission Boosts Backing for U.S. Tests." *Aviation Week and Space Technology*, Apr. 28, 1980, p. 20.

———. "Planners Set Long-Term Goals." *Aviation Week and Space Technology*, Mar. 9, 1981, pp. 75–78.

———. "Soviets Developing Fly-back Launcher." *Aviation Week and Space Technology*, Mar. 20, 1978, p. 20.

———. "Soviets Developing 12-Man Space Station." *Aviation Week and Space Technology*, June 16, 1980, pp. 26–29.

———. "Space Defense Organization Advances." *Aviation Week and Space Technology*, Feb., 1982, pp. 21–22.

Cox, David. "Sea Power and Soviet Foreign Policy." *U.S. Naval Institute Proceedings*, June, 1969, pp. 32–44.

Culwick, A. T. "Southern Africa: A Strategic View." *Strategic Review*, Summer, 1974, pp. 30–38.

"Cut in Fleet Sat Com Questioned." *Aviation Week and Space Technology*, Nov. 14, 1977, p. 21.

Dalgleish, D. D., and Schweikart, Larry. "The Final Salvo: Rickover, Veliotis, and the Trident Submarine." *Weapons and Warfare Quarterly*, Dec., 1982.

"The Danger Is Defeat, Not Destruction." *Remnant Review*, Aug., 1979, n.p.

Davis, Jim. "Building the Trident's Home." *U.S. Naval Institute Proceedings*, Mar., 1979, pp. 62–73.

Davis, William. "Ballistic Missile Defense Will Work." *National Defense*, Dec., 1981, pp. 16–22, 42.

"Defense Stations Stress Jam Resistance, Flexibility." *Aviation Week and Space Technology*, Oct. 17, 1977, pp. 116–21.

Delaney, Robert, and Townsend, Patrick. "Defense of the Depths." *U.S. Naval Institute Proceedings*, Nov., 1979, pp. 37–41.

Earls, J. H. "Human Adjustment to an Exotic Environment: The Nuclear Submarine." *Archives of General Psychiatry*, Jan., 1969, pp. 117–23.

Easter, David. "ASW Strategy: Issues for the 1980s." *U.S. Naval Institute Proceedings*, Mar., 1980, pp. 35–41.

Eberle, James. "The Royal Navy." *U.S. Naval Institute Proceedings*, Aug., 1980, pp. 26–31.

———. "Strategic Choice and Maritime Capabilities." *U.S. Naval Institute Proceedings*, Apr., 1982, pp. 65–72.

Edmonds, Martin. "British Security Concerns in the 1980s." *International Security Review*, Summer, 1980, pp. 209–30.

"Electromagnetic Guns and Launchers." *Physics Today*, Dec., 1980, pp. 19–21.

Estes, G. Brian. "Trident Base East." *Military Engineer*, Sept.-Oct., 1981, pp. 322–27.

Fallows, James. "America's High-Tech Weaponry." *Atlantic Monthly*, May, 1981, pp. 21–23.

Feazel, Michael. "NATO Withdrawal Threatened." *Aviation Week and Space Technology*, May 10, 1982, pp. 15–18.

Feldman, Horace. "The U.S., Japan and the Tricky Terrain of Defense." *Strategic Review*, Fall, 1981, pp. 31–38.

Fitzgerald, E. M. "The Command of Space." *Rusi*, Mar., 1981, pp. 34–38.

Foster, Richard. "On Prolonged Nuclear War." *International Security Review*, Winter, 1981–82, pp. 497–518.

"Free-Electron Laser Technology Gains." *Aviation Week and Space Technology*, Sept. 28, 1982, pp. 60–61.

Friedman, Norman. "SOSUS and U.S. ASW Tactics." *U.S. Naval Institute Proceedings*, Mar., 1980, pp. 120–22.

———. "Speed in Modern Warships." *U.S. Naval Institute Proceedings*, May, 1979, pp. 151–67.

———. "SS-N-14: A Third Round." *U.S. Naval Institute Proceedings*, June, 1979, pp. 110–14.

Gallois, Pierre. "The Future of France's Force de Disuasion." *Strategic Review*, Summer, 1979, pp. 34–41.

Garn, Jake. "Soviet Superiority: A Question for National Debate." *International Security Review*, Spring, 1979, pp. 1–25.

Garwin, Richard. "Charged Particle Beam Weapons?" *Bulletin of Atomic Scientists*, Oct., 1978, pp. 24–27.

George, Bruce, and Pieragostini, Karl. "British Defence in the 1980's: What Price Trident?" *International Security Review*, Winter, 1980–81, pp. 425–54.

George, James. "SALT and the Navy." *U.S. Naval Institute Proceedings*, June, 1979, pp. 28–37.

———. "The V/STOL Catch 22s." *U.S. Naval Institute Proceedings*, Apr., 1978, pp. 23–29.

Gregory, William. "Exotic Weapons Challenge." *Aviation Week and Space Technology*, July 28, 1980, p. 7.

Griffiths, David. "Beam Weapon Impact Called Uncertain." *Aviation Week and Space Technology*, Apr. 30, 1979, p. 28.

Hazlett, James. "Strait Shooting." *U.S. Naval Institute Proceedings*, June, 1982, pp. 70–73.

Herold, Robert, and Mahoney, Shane. "Military Hardware Procurement: Some Comparative Observations on Soviet and American Policy Processes." *Comparative Politics*, July, 1974, pp. 571–99.

Hiller, J. R., and Tollison, R. D. "Incentive vs. Cost-Plus Contracts in Defense Procurement." *Journal of Industrial Economics* 26 (1978):239–48.

Hoeber, Frances. "The SALT II Treaty and the Security of the United States." *International Security Review*, Summer, 1979, pp. 105–31.

Hoffmann, Roy. "Offensive Mine Warfare: A Forgotten Strategy?" *U.S. Naval Institute Proceedings*, Nov., 1977, pp. 144–55.

Holloway, James. "The Transition to V/STOL." *U.S. Naval Institute Proceedings*, Sept., 1977, pp. 19–25.

Holmes, David. "NAVSTAR Global Positioning System: Navigation for the Future." *U.S. Naval Institute Proceedings*, Apr., 1977, pp. 101–104.

Housman, Damien. "Lessons of Naval Warfare." *National Review*, July 23, 1982, pp. 894–96.

Hull, Andrew. "Potential Soviet Responses to the U.S. Submarine Threat in the 1980s." *U.S. Naval Institute Proceedings*, July, 1978, pp. 25–30.

"Inside Story of the Trident Debacle." *U.S. News & World Report*, Mar. 30, 1980, pp. 21–22.

Issac, Rael Jean, and Issac, Erich. "The Counterfeit Peacemakers: Atomic Freeze," *American Spectator*, June, 1982, pp. 8–17.

Jacobson, Leonard, and Bittner, Michael. "NAVSTAR GPS." *The Navigator*, Spring, 1981, pp. 24–26.

Jaicks, Judy, and Schemmer, Benjamin. "New Navy Dilemma: Too Few Officers to Man New Sub Buildup." *Armed Forces Journal*, Sept., 1981, pp. 41–43.

Jampoler, Andrew. "ASW for the 1980s." *U.S. Naval Institute Proceedings*, Mar., 1980, pp. 118–19.

Johnson, Paul. "Tomahawk: The Implications of a Strategic/Tactical Mix." *U.S. Naval Institute Proceedings*, Apr., 1982, pp. 26–33.

Jones, Charles. "Weapons Effects Primer," *U.S. Naval Institute Proceedings*, Jan., 1978, pp. 50–55.

Jones, Milton. "Toward Smaller, Simpler Submarines." *U.S. Naval Institute Proceedings*, June, 1981, pp. 110–13.

Kaiser, Karl; Leber, Georg; Mertes, Alois; and Schulze, Franz-Josef. "Nuclear Weapons and the Preservation of Peace." *Foreign Affairs*, Summer, 1982, pp. 1157–70.

Kane, Frances. "Anti-Satellite Systems and U.S. Options." *Strategic Review*, Winter, 1982, pp. 56–64.
Karas, Thomas. "Implications of Space Technology for Strategic Nuclear Competition." The Stanley Foundation, Muscatine, Iowa, July, 1981.
"Kiev Carries New Forager." *Aviation Week and Space Technology*, Jan. 22, 1979, p. 19.
Kinsey, Michael. "Nuclear Holocaust in Perspective." *Harper's*, Mar., 1982, pp. 8–12.
Klass, Philip. "Missile Defense Keyed to Technology." *Aviation Week and Space Technology*, Apr. 19, 1982, pp. 79–82.
Knowles, Joseph. "America's Nuclear-Powered Submarines." *Sea Classics*, May, 1973, pp. 27–63.
Korb, Lawrence. "The FY 1981–85 Defense Program: Is a Trillion Dollars Enough?" *Naval War College Review*, Mar.-Apr., 1980, pp. 3–16.
Kozicharow, Eugene. "Panel Disputes U.S.–Soviet Arms Parity." *Aviation Week and Space Technology*, June 28, 1976, pp. 19–20.
———. "Soviets Exhibit Technologies." *Aviation Week and Space Technology*, June 22, 1981, pp. 42–45.
Kumm, William. "What's Going On Down There?" *U.S. Naval Institute Proceedings*, Apr., 1973, pp. 37–45.
Lawson, Robert. "The Viking at Sea." *U.S. Naval Institute Proceedings*, July, 1979, pp. 70–79.
Layton, James. "Soviet Mine Barrier Warfare Capabilities in a Central Nuclear War." *Naval War College Review*, July-Aug., 1980, pp. 42–52.
Le Bourgeois, Julian. "What Is the Soviet Navy Up To?" *NATO Review*, Apr., 1977, pp. 14–19.
Lee, William. "Soviet Defense Spending, Planned Growth 1976–1980." *Strategic Review*, Winter, 1977, pp. 74–79.
Levoritz, Jeffrey. "Soviets Study Long-Duration Missions." *Aviation Week and Space Technology*, Sept. 28, 1981, pp. 41–43.
Libby, Ruthven. "The Role of the Submarine. . . ." *Strategic Review*, Sept., 1973, pp. 29–32.
Loewenberg, Robert. "The Violent Quakers." *Commentary*, Mar., 1982, pp. 15–18.
Lonsdale, P. Taylor. "ASW's Passive Trap." *U.S. Naval Institute Proceedings*, July, 1979, pp. 35–40.
Lorenzini, Dino, and Fox, Charles. "2001: A U.S. Space Force." *Naval War College Review*, Mar.-Apr., 1981, pp. 48–67.
MacGregor, Roy. "Not Enough Bangs for Our Bucks." *Maclean's*, Aug. 31, 1981, pp. 23–27.
Manthorpe, W. J. "The Influence of Being Russian on the Officers and Men of the Soviet Navy." *U.S. Naval Institute Proceedings*, May, 1978, pp. 129–43.
MccGwire, Michael. "Naval Power and Soviet Global Strategy." *International Security Review*, Spring, 1979, pp. 134–89.
———. "The Rationale for the Development of Soviet Seapower." *U.S. Naval Institute Proceedings*, May, 1980, pp. 155–83.
McKeoch, Ian. "Submarine Warfare." *NATO's Fifteen Nations*, Dec., 1980–Jan., 1981, pp. 56–66.

McLaughlin, John. "The Russians Are Here." *National Review*, Nov. 12, 1982, p. 1396.

Menaul, Stewart. "The Future of Britain's Strategic Nuclear Force." *Strategic Review*, Spring, 1979, pp. 25–41.

———. "Great Britain and NATO Theater Nuclear Forces." *Strategic Review*, Spring, 1981, pp. 61–66.

Meyer, Deborah. "More Political Rhetoric than Fact Behind Navy Blast at General Dynamics." *Armed Forces Journal*, June, 1981, p. 16.

Meyers, Charles. "A Sea-based Interdiction System for Power Projection." *U.S. Naval Institute Proceedings*, Nov., 1979, pp. 103–6.

Moore-Ede, Martin. "Sleeping as the World Turns." *Natural History*, Oct., 1982, pp. 28–36.

Murray, Michael. "Sea King: ASW Workhorse." *U.S. Naval Institute Proceedings*, June, 1981, pp. 99–100.

Nahin, Paul. "Laser BMD and Other Radiant Energy Weapons: Some Thoughts." *IEEE Transactions on Aerospace and Electronic Systems* AES-13 (Mar., 1977), pp. 96–107.

Nailor, Peter, and Alford, Jonathan. "The Future of Britain's Deterrent Force." *Adelphi Papers* 156.

"Navy's Trident Sub: One More Massive Miscalculation." *U.S. News & World Report*, Dec. 12, 1977, p. 37.

"The Navy vs. Soviet Subs." *U.S. News & World Report*, Nov. 13, 1978, pp. 28–81.

Neely, Theodore, Jr. "A Soviet View of Soviet Naval Doctrine and Perceptions." *U.S. Naval Institute Proceedings*, Dec., 1981, pp. 120–22.

Newell, John. "The Breakdown in Naval Shipbuilding." *U.S. Naval Institute Proceedings*, Jan., 1978, pp. 25–31.

Newman, Peter. "Is World War III Inevitable?" *Macleans*, Feb. 15, 1982, pp. 30–40.

Nugent, Tom. "The Trident Story." *All Hands*, Feb., 1975, pp. 2–7.

Oberg, James. "The Space Shuttle and Soviet Propaganda." *National Review*, July 24, 1981, pp. 828–30.

"An Old Admiral Is Cast Adrift." *Newsweek*, Nov. 23, 1981, p. 43.

O'Neil, William. "Naval Technology: Passive Sonar Has the Edge." *U.S. Naval Institute Proceedings*, Apr., 1978, pp. 105–7.

Parmentola, John, and Tsipis, Kosta. "Particle Beam Weapons." *Scientific American*, Apr., 1979, pp. 54–65.

Peters, Glenn. "ASW—The Deterrent." *Electronic Warfare, Global Edition*, July-Aug., 1976, pp. 49–54.

Petrow, Richard. "PM Dives with Our Deadliest Missile Sub." *Popular Mechanics*, Mar., 1978, pp. 94–95, 212–14, 216.

Phillips, James. "Backgrounder: Moscow's Poison War." *Heritage Foundation Report*, Feb. 5, 1982, pp. 1–14.

Pilling, Donald. "The Dwindling Muster." *U.S. Naval Institute Proceedings*, June, 1982, pp. 35–39.

Pipes, Richard. "Why the Soviet Union Thinks It Could Fight and Win a Nuclear War." *Air Force Magazine*, Sept., 1977, pp. 55–66. Reprinted from *Commentary*, July, 1977.

Pohtos, Robert. "A Crisis in Manning." *U.S. Naval Institute Proceedings*, Apr., 1982, pp. 110–12.
Polmar, Norman. "Soviet Navy Surface-to-Surface Missiles." *U.S. Naval Institute Proceedings*, July, 1977, pp. 90–91.
———. "Soviet Nuclear Submarines." *U.S. Naval Institute Proceedings*, July, 1981, pp. 31–39.
———. "SURTASS and T-AGOS." *U.S. Naval Institute Proceedings*, Mar., 1980, pp. 122–24.
———. "Thinking About Soviet ASW." *U.S. Naval Institute Proceedings*, May, 1976, pp. 109–28.
———. "The U.S. Navy: Attack Submarines—Pro and Pro." *U.S. Naval Institute Proceedings*, June, 1982, pp. 121–22.
———. "The U.S. Navy: Electronic Warfare (Part 1)." *U.S. Naval Institute Proceedings*, Oct., 1979, pp. 137–38.
———. "The U.S. Navy: Ships That Wait." *U.S. Naval Institute Proceedings*, Apr., 1982, pp. 125–27.
———. "The U.S. Navy: Sonars (Part 1)." *U.S. Naval Institute Proceedings*, July, 1981, pp. 119–20.
———. "The U.S. Navy: Sonars (Part 2)." *U.S. Naval Institute Proceedings*, Sept., 1981, pp. 119–20.
———. "The U.S. Navy: Strategic Missile Submarines." *U.S. Naval Institute Proceedings*, Mar., 1980, pp. 141–42.
———. "The U.S. Navy: Torpedoes." *U.S. Naval Institute Proceedings*, Nov., 1978, pp. 159–60.
Rempt, Rodney. "Vertical Missile Launchers: Part I." *U.S. Naval Institute Proceedings*, Oct., 1977, pp. 86–89.
Robinson, Clarence, Jr. "Advance Made on High-Energy Laser." *Aviation Week and Space Technology*, Feb. 23, 1981, pp. 25–27.
———. "Ballistic Missile Defense Emphasis Urged." *Aviation Week and Space Technology*, Oct. 13, 1980, pp. 18–21.
———. "Beam Weapons Effort to Grow." *Aviation Week and Space Technology*, Apr. 2, 1979, pp. 12–16.
———. "Beam Weapons Race." *Aviation Week and Space Technology*, Oct. 2, 1978, p. 9.
———. "Beam Weapons Race." *Aviation Week and Space Technology*, Nov. 13, 1978, p. 20.
———. "Beam Weapons Technology Expanding." *Aviation Week and Space Technology*, May 25, 1981, pp. 40–71.
———. "Laser Technology Demonstration Proposed." *Aviation Week and Space Technology*, Feb. 16, 1981, pp. 16–20.
———. "New Ballistic Missile Defense Proposed." *Aviation Week and Space Technology*, Mar. 8, 1982, pp. 269–71.
———. "New Propellant Evaluated for Trident Second Stage." *Aviation Week and Space Technology*, Oct. 13, 1975, pp. 15–19.
———. "Soviets Developing Two Bombers." *Aviation Week and Space Technology*, Feb. 19, 1979, pp. 14–18.
———. "Soviets Grasping Strategic Lead." *Aviation Week and Space Technology*, Aug. 30, 1976, pp. 14–18.

———. "Soviets Push for Beam Weapon." *Aviation Week and Space Technology*, May 2, 1977, pp. 16–23.

———. 'Soviets Test Beam Technologies." *Aviation Week and Space Technology*, Nov. 13, 1978, pp. 14–20.

———. "Trident Post-Boost Control Tests Planned." *Aviation Week and Space Technology*, Oct. 27, 1975, pp. 63–73.

Acknowledgments

With a research effort spanning six years, embracing such a range of technical complexity, exposed to the relentless erosion of its topicality by technological modification and political vagary, and requiring a variety of photographic and statistical rendition, the authors obviously carry on their joint ledger book a vast debt of gratitude they realize can never be fully discharged. Our specific expressions of heartfelt appreciation for the time, effort, money, and expertise to so many persons who have contributed to our undertaking would be inadequate even if possible. Our best effort to do so nevertheless follows in the warmest and most decorative fashion we can muster.

A primary and original debt of gratitude is owed to Bruce B. Mason and Elijah Ben-Zion Kaminsky, fellow colleagues at Arizona State University, for recognizing that the senior author's courses in national defense policy could benefit greatly from his participation in the 1974 session of the National Security Education Seminar, under the direction of Frank Trager of New York University, held at Colorado Springs where he acquired greater conceptual breadth and analytical substance in the analysis of defense policy at the very time the *Ohio*'s keel-laying was taking place, an event repeatedly discussed among the seminar participants that summer, and therein lies the seminal origin of this work.

Besides the debt of gratitude due Professor Trager, a collective debt of gratitude is owed to the formative and provocative skills and personal dedication bestowed upon NSES student participants by the seminar staff, the late and much-respected Fred A. Sonderman, especially. This gracious host proved an inspiring example to all during those many seminars held over the years, so fittingly conducted "between" Fort Carson and Cheyenne Mountain. No less enthusiastic appreciation is also owed to Laurence W. Martin, Robert Bowie, Charles Moskos, Donald G. Brennan, Klaus E. Knorr, the late Bernard

Brodie, dean of American post-1945 strategists, and Paul Wolfowitz (to name the stalwarts), for the diversity, vigor, and richness of their conceptual and analytical contributions to the intellectual edification of so many NSES participants. Professors Mason and Kaminsky would join in a final bow of respect, again, for Professors Sonderman and Brodie.

Through the 1974 NSES discovery of the Trident program, and because of Professor Martin's confident, direct, and eminently sensible lectures on sea power, another debt of gratitude is due the 1976 sabbatical visit to the Naval War College so thoughtfully and effectively rendered productive by Professor Frederick A. Hartmann, the erudite and charming occupant of the Alfred T. Mahan Chair of Strategic Studies. His authority and interest in the analysis of the Trident program opened a number of vital doors, behind which were discovered such incomparable repositories of expert knowledge about strategic submarines as those shared by Professor James E. King, Captain Herbert Cherrier, Chief of War Gaming, and Captain Robert Connelly, Chief of Submarine Warfare. Had they all not imparted their knowledge of the basic technology, strategy, and operations underlying submarine warfare in general and SSBN warfare in particular, this work would still be wallowing about, conceptually "down by the head." Also, if the early winter storms made the west wall of the library basement so cold that gathering research material was an arctic exercise, the library staff at the Naval War College library must be extolled for the warmth, knowledge, efficiency, and convenience with which they greeted every outlandish request for obscure sources on SSBN operations. They also facilitated access to copying machines at odd hours, almost literally in the dead of night. No one who is engaged in research on naval matters can ever, of course, ignore the inspirational effect of either the halls of the Naval War College itself or the environs of Newport.

Indispensable to the overall conduct of this research, and especially for the authors' comprehension of the Trident construction process, the origin and nature of the claims controversy, the controversy over quality control, and the causation of the program's cost overruns, was the contribution made by P. Takis Veliotis, former general manager of Electric Boat Company at Groton, Connecticut. He and his staff dedicated a full day of their time to answering questions, generating analyses, ordering materials, assigning follow-up requests, and conducting a personal tour of SSBN-726 and SSN-688 construction facilities. Complementary roles were also significantly played by R. E. Holt, assistant general manager for public affairs; Arthur Barton, assistant general manager for business affairs; William Gourvine, legal counsel; and O.

B. Nelson, chief engineer, who dedicated an afternoon to an exposition on the implications of the STRAT-X study, on the design possibilities of the Trident hull, and on the matrix of capabilities built into the existing vessel. What Hartmann, King, Cherrier, and Connelly began, O. B. Nelson completed. Honorary recognition must also be rendered to "Specs" Seitz and Anne Cremmins, both of the Groton office, and William Bennett of the Quonset Point facility. While "Specs" provided technical insights, Anne facilitated the social and administrative dimensions of the 1981 visit; William graciously tolerated an hour's delay getting lost on the way to a special presentation by him of the role of the Quonset Point facility in the production of hull frames and cylinders, on their fitting out and unit wedding, and on the process of their barge shipment to Groton.

While Mr. Veliotis was general manager at Electric Boat, a forthright and productive relationship with the authors prevailed in every respect; however, most regrettably this relationship changed in the spring of 1982, making it impossible thereafter to verify many issues of fact, interpretation, and description.

The Office of Information, Department of the Navy, has provided inestimable assistance throughout the entire history of this endeavor, and therefore special appreciation is hereby noted to Captain Larry D. Hamilton and his successor, Captain L. B. Patterson, for their sensitizing of their staffs to the most prompt and complete fulfillment of our unending requests for statements, data, explanations, and photos. Captain Hamilton, especially, must be thanked for organizing a staff conference of all relevant Navy personnel in June, 1982, as a result of L. E. Holt's recommendation to that effect as a way to resolve our central dilemma, mentioned above. Whereas the results were not those expected or planned, through the agencies of Lt. John Carmen, head of media services, and his successor, Lt. Keith Arthurburn, a whole range of specific requests was most satisfactorily fulfilled. Unbounded appreciation goes to Anna C. Urband, assistant head of media services, who walked many a mile of the Pentagon's corridors with and for us, traced down droves of obscure documents, statements, and photos, and who always clarified and complied with every request by timely telephone calls and replete cover letters. If ever a faithful servant of the Pentagon deserved a civilian medal of merit, we would be the very first to order its casting on her behalf. Additional thanks to the Office of Information are also owed to Robert A. Carlisle for his assistance in January, 1983, in the identification and selection of a whole set of Trident photographs, to facilitate the comprehension of the text. Similar appreciation is owed Susan E. Weidner, Public Affairs Office, Naval Sea Systems Command, and Lieutenant T. C. Campbell, Strategic

Systems Project Office, Department of the Navy, for tending an earlier rough draft of the manuscript and for safeguarding our conceptual vulnerabilities in those early phases of this endeavor.

The authors wish to express their appreciation to John Medalia, responsible for the conduct of many defense and budgetary research projects in the Congressional Research Service of the Library of Congress. John opened up the full range of his files not only on the Trident program but constantly kept the authors updated with each and every Trident Issue Brief immediately upon its appearance.

Three authoritative personalities made invaluable contributions to the tone, balance, concept, analysis, and descriptions contained in our second-stage version, only one of whom, David Allison, historian for Naval Research Laboratories, can be acknowledged formally for having read the entire manuscript in a spirit of constructive criticism. The other two Navy readers, who also expended comparable efforts, *ex officio,* on our behalf, must remain anonymous, although the first of these stalwarts knows he is owed much more than a bottle of Highland malt whiskey a Marine once delivered to him as a valuable "canister," while the second blue "ghost" will recognize himself as the bright young officer who not too long ago sacrificed a good share of a Saturday to convey to us corrections and comments generated by twice reading the manuscript, once, as he confessed "in bits and batches" and, the second time, with a clearer appreciation of the work's central purpose. Both the authors and the book's readers are much the better off for his sacrifice of time in an incredibly busy schedule. A glass of beer and a sandwich at the Twin Bridges Marriott Hotel is not even a penny's down payment on this debt.

The following colleagues must be recognized and appreciated for their various services in reading and commenting upon those specific chapters for which they disposed of highly relevant insight, expertise, and experience: Professor W. Elliot Brownlee and Joachim Remak, both of the University of California at Santa Barbara, and Robert J. Loewenberg and George Watson, in the History and Political Science departments, respectively, at Arizona State University. Roger A. Freedman, Theoretical Physics, University of California at Santa Barbara, read and commented on those chapters dealing with the frontiers of high technology as it affects strategic submarine warfare of the future. He was always available to discuss and explain these highly eccentric and baffling phenomena. We also profited from the comments of defense analyst Tom Hone, who read a portion of the manuscript as it appeared in article form.

No *dramatis personae* can ignore the genuineness and significance to a total presentation by a number of offstage contributors. Their indispensable contributions were necessary to production. Bettie Spriggs, Public Affairs, Office of the Secretary of Defense, for example, dug out still another photographic component without which the manuscript would be substantially less illuminating, not to ignore the similar contributions made for the Navy by Petty Officer Judy Jutte, and for the Air Force Office of Information by Lieutenant Pete Meltzer. Finally, with respect to advice, clarification, and supplementary explanation, the roles of Captain R. Wigley, Lieutenant (J.G.) J. J. Collins, and Lieutenant Commander John H. Woodhouse—all stationed at the Bangor Base, Washington, are gratefully acknowledged.

In June 1982 the authors were graciously received for a visit aboard SSN-662, the *Gunard*, by Captain Nathan A. Huberger, Chief of Staff to Rear Admiral Frederick W. Kelley, Commander of Sub Group 15, in San Diego. Here they were treated to a salty view of the attack perspective with which the SSBN must contend for survival. The trip not only invested them with an introductory appreciation of the problems of underwater warfare but also instilled an appreciation of why this service is so "silent" when it must be.

The authors also wish to express their gratitude to Alexander McCleod, city editor of the *Seattle Times*, for having dug up the excellent clips about the Bangor base and the Trident fleet written by staff correspondents Warren King, Lee Moriwaki, Carol Ostrom, Julie Emery, and Tomas Gullen. They did much to provide insight into the local impact of the Trident program and to convey a sense of the flavor of the Trident protest movement. Equally important was a series of articles written by Jim Rothgeb, staff writer for the *Bremerton Sun*. Kristi Vaughan contributed a most useful series of articles from the *Hartford Courant*. The editorial staff of *Pacific Northwest Magazine* graciously forwarded an especially useful article on the Trident's impact on Washington, as did the editor of the *Detroit News* in dispatching Jerry Lipman's January 9, 1983 article on the USS *Michigan*.

Portions of the manuscript were presented at the Phi Alpha Theta regional meeting, California State University, Los Angeles, 1982; at the Pacific Coast Branch meeting of the American Historical Association, San Francisco, 1982; at the Southwest Social Science Association meeting, Houston, 1983; and at the Western Social Science Association meeting, Albuquerque, 1983. To the readers, discussants, and critics who participated in these meetings we also owe thanks. Special thanks to the University of California, Santa Barbara, and its history department for a travel grant to the San Francisco meeting, and to the Phi Alpha Theta chapter at UCSB for assistance in travel to the regional meeting.

Also, some material taken from the manuscript has been published in article form in *Weapons and Warfare Quarterly* March, 1983. Reviews of other works in the *Public Historian* and *History, Numbers, and War* have also included some of this material.

Research staffs and the interlibrary loan staffs at Arizona State University and the University of California, Santa Barbara, contributed to this project by tracking down and ordering obscure documents, for which we are deeply grateful. Heidi Osselor and David Crowe both assisted in gathering or checking research material, and Dan Bolyn allowed us the use of his paper on French strategic force modernization. Each of these individuals deserves our deepest heartfelt thanks.

Perhaps no individual spent more time with this project than our typist, Jack C. Steinhoff. He saved us from many errors of syntax, interpretation, and style, and always met our deadlines. Perry Steinhoff artistically and professionally supplied many of the graphics and charts, sometimes reconstructing them from congressional documents and other times creating them from scratch. We could not have completed this book without the help of each of these professionals. For the numerous other friends who have rendered us assistance, but whom we may have forgotten, both our apologies and our thanks.

Finally, our editor, Herbert L. Kirk, efficiently aided in paring the material down and putting it in more appealing form. The staff at Southern Illinois University Press graciously tolerated our constant reworking of the manuscript, and Joyce Atwood, Gordon Lester-Massman, James Simmons, Dan Gunter, Tammy Campbell, and Kenney Withers all gave us their unflinching support and encouragement throughout the project. But no tolerance or support exceeded that extended by our wives and families. Their distractions were welcomed because we were reminded of our ultimate purpose in undertaking such a task.

Index